AN ANSWER

TO

JOHN MARTIALL'S

TREATISE OF THE CROSS.

AN ANSWER

TO

JOHN MARTIALL'S

TREATISE OF THE CROSS.

BY

JAMES CALFHILL, D.D.,

DEAN OF BOCKING, ARCHDEACON OF COLCHESTER,
AND BISHOP-ELECT OF WORCESTER.

EDITED FOR

The Parker Society,

BY THE

REV. RICHARD GIBBINGS, M.A.,

RECTOR AND VICAR OF RAYMUNTERDONEY, IN THE DIOCESE OF RAPHOE.

PUBLISHERS
Eugene, Oregon

Wipf and Stock Publishers
199 W 8th Ave, Suite 3
Eugene, OR 97401

An Answer to John Martiall's Treatise of the Cross
By Calfhill, James
ISBN 13: 978-1-55635-059-7
ISBN 10: 1-55635-059-7
Publication date 11/8/2006
Previously published by Cambridge, 1846

AN AVNSWERE
TO THE TREATISE
OF THE CROSSE:
wherin ye shal fee by the plaine and vndoubted word of God, the va-nities of men disproued: by the true and Godly Fathers of the Church, the dreames and dotages of other controlled: and by lavvfull Counsels, conspiracies ouerthrowen.

Reade and Regarde.

Si quis diuersam sequitur doctrinam, & non acquiescit sanis sermonibus Iesu Christi, et ei quæ secundum pietatem est doctrinæ, is inflatus est, & nihil scit. Paul⁹. 1. ad Tim. 6.

If any man teach otherwyse, and agreeth not to the holesome wordes of Jesus Christ, & to the doctrine which is according to Godlinesse, he is puft vp & knoweth nothing.

IMPRINTED AT LONdon, by Henry Denham, for
Lucas Harryson.
Anno. 1565.

[CALFHILL.]

BIOGRAPHICAL NOTICES

OF

CALFHILL AND MARTIALL.

"JAMES CALFHILL, or CALFIELD, a Shropshire man born[1], made his first entry into the University, an. 1545, or thereabouts; and after the last foundation of Ch. Ch. had been finished by K. Hen. VIII., he was soon after made a Student thereof, an. 1548, aged 18: where going through the usual classes of Logic and Philosophy, proceeded M. of Arts, and was junior of the act celebrated in St Mary's church, 18 July, 1552. From the time that he was first made Student of Ch. Ch. he always gave great hopes that he would prove a considerable person in his time; being composed from his youth to gravity, and endowed with an acute genie, and a quick vigour of mind. In 1560 he was made the second Canon of the second Prebendship of the said church; was admitted to the reading of the Sentences the year following; and afterwards became Doctor of D., Dean or Rector of Bocking in Essex, Archdeacon of Colchester, (in the place, as it seems, of Joh. Pullayne deceased;) and at length, upon the translation of Dr Edwyn Sandys from Worcester to London, in 1570, he was nominated by the Queen to succeed him; but before consecration thereunto he died. He was in his younger days a noted Poet and Comedian; and in his elder an exact Disputant; and had an excellent faculty in speaking and preaching."

"May 16, 1562, Calfhill was instituted to the Rectory

[1] [Strype states that he was a native of Edinburgh.]

of St Andrew Wardrobe, London; and in the same year was appointed Proctor for the Clergy of London, and the Chapter of Oxford, in the Convocation that determined on the Thirty-nine Articles; as well as to the Prebend of St Pancras, in the Cath. church of St Paul, October 4. He was also Sub-Dean of Christ Church, and Vicar of West Horsley in Surrey. In the year 1569, he made application to Secretary Cecil, Chancellor of Cambridge, for the Provostship of King's College, but without success."

"This ingenious person died at Bocking before-mentioned, (having a little before resigned his Canonship of Ch. Ch.) and was buried in the chancel of the church there, 22 Aug. in fifteen hundred and seventy, saith the register belonging to that church; which, I suspect, is false, because there was a commission issued out from the Prerogative court of Canterbury at Lond. to Margaret his Widow, dated 21 Aug. 1570, to administer the goods, debts, and chattels of him the said Dr Jam. Calfhill, lately Archd. of Essex, (as there he is styled,) deceased. So I presume he died about the beginning of that month."

"Calfhill must have died before the 20th of August, 1570; for Thomas Watts was presented to the Rectory of Bocking on that day." (Wood's *Athenæ Oxonienses*: ed. Bliss. Vol. i. coll. 377—80. Lond. 1813.)

"The business, first agitated by the exchange of friendly Letters betwixt the said reverend Prelate" [Bp Jewel,] "and Dr Henry Cole, the late Dean of St Paul's, more violently followed in a book of Rastal's, who first appeared in the lists against the Challenger; followed therein by Dorman and Marshal," [Martiall,] "who severally took up the cudgels to as little purpose: the first being well beaten by Nowel, and the last by Calfhil, in their discourses writ against them." (Heylin's *Hist. of Queen Eliz.*, p. 130. Lond. 1660.)

"JOHN MARTIAL, Bachelor of Law, sometime Usher of Winchester School, and now a Student in Divinity at Louvain, had published a Treatise of the Cross; and had the confidence to dedicate his book to Queen Elizabeth: emboldened upon her aforesaid retaining the Image of the Cross in her chapel; terming it her good *affection* to it. But this year, 1565, a learned Answer came forth against that Treatise, by Scripture, Fathers, and Councils; written by James Calfhil, B.D. of Christ's-Church, Oxon, as I conjecture, though his name be not to it." (Strype's *Annals*, Vol. i. Part ii. p. 200. Oxford, 1824.)

"He published some things against one Mr Calfhill, in defence of the Cross: and, in memory of this engagement and conquest, he left a ring, with a valuable stone, to adorn a piece of our Saviour's Cross, religiously preserved in the collegiate church in Lisle." (Dodd's *Church History of England*, Vol. ii. p. 113. Brussels, 1739.)

"I write nothing about Marshal, [Martiall,] for fear of defiling my paper." (Bp Jewel. *Zurich Letters;* first Series, p. 12. Camb. 1842.)

The editor has a few remarks to make. He wishes to express his obligations to the Council of the Parker Society for the readiness with which they permitted him to be guided by his own judgment, or fancy, with respect to the typographical arrangement of this work, and the addition of notes where they seemed desirable. He is conscious of having suffered from the disadvantage of residence at a great distance from Dublin; but nevertheless he has aimed at all possible accuracy both in the verification and correction of references:—*expertus discet quam gravis iste labor:*—and it is scarcely necessary to say, that he is responsible for every thing inserted within [ ] crotchets.

SUPPLEMENTAL OBSERVATIONS.

Since the notes in page 44 were written, the editor obtained a copy of the edition of Josephus, (a Latin version ascribed to Rufinus; folio, apud Jo. Froben. Basil. 1524.) which Calfhill appears to have used; or perhaps we might, with more preciseness, speak of it as the edition which Bp Ridley used: for our author evidently was acquainted with the *Treatise against worshipping of Images*, first published by Fox. Compare *Acts and Mon.* iii. 833. Lond. 1684.

With regard to one of the "tracts of Penance" attributed to S. Chrysostom, p. 64, the reader may consult the observations made by Mr Ayre in page 77 of the *Early Works* of Becon: and as to the charge advanced by Calfhill against the author of the questioned treatise, it would seem likely to be greatly mitigated, (and there is here an instance of the injudiciousness exhibited in passing a hasty censure upon any of the Fathers;) if we remember, that whatever defect may be conceived to be in S. Chrysostom's supposed language concerning penitence and humiliation, the same will be found to occur in the prayer of our Commination-Service in which we make mention of "*weeping, fasting*, and praying," as well as in the following passage taken from a writer who is not generally suspected of unsoundness : " We must *repent, fast*, pray, *give alms*, forsake ourselves, condemn ourselves, with bitter *tears* and trembling work our salvation," &c. (Bp Pilkington's *Works*, p. 448. ed. Parker Soc.)

Page 75, note. Erase the comma after Heroldt's surname.

It may be presumed that Ptolemæus, or Bartholomæus Lucensis is the "Ptolome" referred to in page 128: but the position of Scythia, "far distant from Grecia," is defined in the *Cosmographia* of Claudius Ptolemy; Lib. vi. sigg. D 3, 4. Vicenciæ, 1475.

To complete what has been said in note 5, p. 137, concerning the pictorial representations of our Saviour sanctioned by the Quinisext Council, and to correct and elucidate the text, it may be added, that the seventy-third Canon of the same Synod commanded that figures of the Cross, made on any pavement, should be entirely effaced. The object of this injunction was similar to that of the Decree which had been previously issued by the Emperors Theodosius II. and Valentinian III.: (p. 190.) namely, to prevent the sign of The victory obtained for Christians from being slighted and trodden under foot:—" ne forte, pedibus conculcatum, vilescat salutare victoriæ nostræ trophæum." (Matth. Blastaris *Syntagma Alphabet.* apud Bevereg. *Pandectt.* ii. ii. 228.) Martiall may have found the Trullan Ordinances, (the greater part having been " recens Latinitate donata,") in the collections of Joverius, Carranza, Hervetus, or Du Tillet; and he was probably deceived by the heading, " *Can. Constantinop. Con. sex. Univer.*" The place "in the Pope's law," which Calfhill does not more fully than thus describe, is *Dist.* xvi. C. *Habeo librum;* and it is to be seen in Ivo likewise. Par. iv. Cap. 121.

As the conjecture in note 12, p. 193, with reference to the "Bishop of Orleance," cannot be considered satisfactory, except upon the supposition of the existence of more than one mistake, it is apparently preferable to decide that Jonas Aurelianensis was intended. See his first book against Claudius, Bishop of Turin, and his " nævos " enumerated by the Magdeburg Centuriators. (ix. x. 526. Basil. 1565.)

The editor is indebted to his kind friend and fellow-labourer Mr Ayre for having suggested to him the propriety of adding to note 1, p. 212, this remark; that possibly Calfhill may have followed, and therefore should only share the blame with, other writers, relative to the account he has given of the origin of Sponsors.

By the phrase "*ut Collectam facerem,*" "to perform the Collect," which our author (p. 253.) erroneously translates "to make a gathering," we are to understand, that the object of S. Epiphanius was to celebrate the holy Communion, anciently called "*Collecta,*" or "Σύναξις." See Du Cange, *Glossar.* and Fleury, xix. xliv. 231. Oxf. 1842.

Page 276. The words "M. Hide, late," at the commencement of the first marginal note, have been accidentally obliterated after the final revision of the sheet.

In the "Table," pp. 395, 399, it is inaccurately stated that the Council of Constantinople, an. 754, was held "under Leo Isauricus." Constantine Copronymus should have been mentioned; for Leo the Isaurian died in the year 741. Vid. *L'Art de vérifier les Dates,* p. 424. A Paris, 1750.

MYRAGH GLEBE, DUNFANAGHY,
Dec. 29, 1846.

TO JOHN MARTIALL,

STUDENT IN DIVINITY,

JAMES CALFHILL, BACHELOR OF THE SAME, WISHETH THE SPIRIT OF TRUTH AND MODESTY, WITH INCREASE OF KNOWLEDGE IN THE FEAR OF GOD.

IT is not very long ago since the famous report of your (Martial) affairs came unto mine ears, and treatise of defence unto my hands. Indeed, as a young scholar, (for so ye say ye are, and I by your workmanship may well conjecture,) ye have said for the Cross so far as your skill doth serve you, or as the honesty of the cause deserveth. I suppose it had been more honesty for you, and would have furthered your purpose better, if either your weakness had wrestled at the first on a better ground, or so weak a cause had got some sturdier champion to defend it. Now that you fight more eagerly than wisely in a Cross quarrel, ye lie so open to be cross-bitten[1], that the cause itself and your poor credit go to the ground together. For, though ye use to face men with all such terms and titles of estimation, as rather of some be gotten by continuance, than given by desert; as Bachelor of law, and Student in divinity: yet, if ye had joined more logic with your law, your reasons should not have run so lawless (as they do:) or, if you had remembered your old humanity, you would not have stained your new divinity with such slanders and lies, such vain supposals and idle tales, as I am ashamed to hear of any that challengeth to himself the name of learning. But man's law striketh so great a stroke with you, that God's rule and conscience is excluded from you: and, being so deep in your popish divinity, you have forgotten all christian humanity. Wherefore, the censure of S. Paul, which, in the beginning, I used as my word, may justly be applied to you: that, inasmuch as ye give no ear to the sound doctrine, nor content yourself with that religion which accordeth to piety, ye are but puffed up with vain glory: ye seek for praise of men; which, of

1 Tim. vi.

---

[1] [thwarted, or deceived.]

the wiser sort ye shall never purchase. How well your poesy serveth against us whom you would seem to touch, when the Apostle inveighed against the enemies of the Cross of Christ, (which you are, and not we,) shall afterward be seen in the discourse. But among you, the wilful wanderers, of one affection, of one bringing up, the saying is verified which Horace hath[1]: *Scribimus indocti doctique poemata passim.*

<small>Horatius in Arte Poetica.</small>

First came into our stage a gay disguised guest, a sudden convert, (and I fear me greatly lest an Apostata,) M. Doctor Harding. He, because he is right worshipful M. Doctor, and hath otherwise some opinion of learning, (words indeed at will;) he must needs be thought to say something. But how this something in effect is nothing, the Bishop of Salisbury abundantly doth prove. Next to the master came the worthy scholar: and yet, worthy *Man*, he gave but a *Dor*[2]. We do easily see in whose forge he was framed: he savours of the fire that flew out before: and yet, neither of them both, for all their heat of railing, hath any warmth of religion. His proofs I pass to the Reproof published abroad already. Only I am sorry M. Nowell had not a more learned adversary. Then comes in M. Rastall, and puts in his rejoinder. All against M. Jewell. Alas! I pity the poor soul; he maketh his match so far amiss. *Dares Entellum*[3]. Nay, *Hinnulus Leonem*[4]. Yet he saith that he will but fight with a penknife; he will overthrow with a breath, if he can. O noble courage! He leaveth the bloody lances and terrible halberds, for hardy Harding and doughty Dorman: he himself will come after, and blow his enemies afore him. If I should deal with this dangerous bug[5], I would, for all that, provide myself of a longer sword; for belike he hath a very strong breath; and yet with a bodkin he may be borne over. I will not touch this proud peacock's tail: I will leave it at leisure to be pulled of an-

---

[1] [Horat. *Epist.* ii. i. 117.]

[2] [A drone, or a beetle: so that *Dor-man* is made to signify *a dronish man*. The phrase "He gave but a dor" means that he buzzed like a beetle; making sound without sense.]

[3] [Vid. Erasmi *Adagia*, fol. lv, b. Argent. 1510. (Tit. *Malum accersitum.*)]

[4] [Ibid. Tit. *Excellentiæ.*]   [5] [bugbear.]

other. To make up the mess, steps out M. Stapleton. He will not stand by, and be but a looker on. Having therefore never a weapon of his own, he runs to a ruffian, and borrows his sword. He hath put on a new scabbard on it: he hath varnished the hilts. The blade itself is all to behacked[6]. It hath been already in so many frays, and borne away so many blows, that it is now scarcely able to scratch. This young man, therefore, will fight with the scabbard. But if a man give him a dry blow or two, (as, for his wilfulness, he well deserveth,) we shall see hereafter what fence he hath for it.

There is none of all these but may with more ease make fifteen such books as they cumber the printers of Antwerp withal, than answer fifteen leaves of sound doctrine. The parties be known: their skill, their qualities we are, (God wot,) too well acquainted with, to be now abused by dog's eloquence. If your causes were better, (as worse they cannot be,) forsooth you should find of your old acquaintance enow to match you; and, unless ye were sounder, to shame you too. This advantage ye have, (God be thanked for it,) that ye have nothing else to do but commit to writing your peevish fancies, and send them into England to set us a work withal. We ourselves are occupied otherwise, (as friends to the flock of Christ which we have in charge,) than that we can or will attemper our doings to the lewd desert of our contemned enemies; or mispend our time in answering of that, which, in the ears of all indifferent, carrieth a sufficient confutation with it. Notwithstanding, lest some more simple than other may be deceived by you; and you yourselves be fooded in your folly, through too much forbearing and silence of ours; we have humbled ourselves beneath the honesty of our cause: we have, for charity's sake, vouchsafed to say more than the cause requireth, or all the college of your conspiracy can, with good reason, answer.

As for you, (good Sir,) which only come to make up a number, and seem to do something; choosing to entreat of a plausible matter, (as your discretion doth take it;) if ye had held your tongue, I might have esteemed you somewhat, and reputed you wise. Ye remember the proverb: *Stultus si tacuerit.* Thus ye write, all: some more, some less; Prov. xvii.

[6] [altogether hacked.]

learned, unlearned, wilful, and witless; but *mera poemata*, stale jests or fables: and especially you, whom, among the rest, I may pity rather than envy. For learning have ye little, discretion less, good manners least of all. Your friends that most embrace your opinion are ashamed of your proofs when ye speak of yourself: so fond they are, so senseless and unsound. Nor I do derogate so much from myself, but I would be ashamed to answer such a book; unless I thought good, upon this occasion of unseasonable sowing of your rotten seed, to plant again, in the Lord's field, the seed of salvation and certain truth; to the comfort of the weak, and confusion of the wicked. Wherein I marvel not if the doctrine be higher than your skill can reach unto. For I know what Doctor presented you: I know who made you start up a writer. *Magister artis ingeniique largitor venter*[1]. Your exhibition belike failed you, and therefore ye thought to pick a quarrel to the alms-basket. But more alms it were, with stripes enow to send you to school again, than to reward you as a schoolmaster to other. For this must I needs say; that either ye have not well learned your sophistry, or else you think you have to do with fools. For three kinds of paralogisms of false arguments, or fond cavils, are most familiar with you. First, by inserting oft into your writing *Non causam pro causa*: taking that for a buttress and defence of your cause, which maketh nought to purpose. Then, by arguing *Ab eo quod est secundum quid, ad simpliciter*: making a general consequent of that which in part is true; an absolute rule of that which was done or spoken only in some respect: and, most of all, *A consequenti*: when ye rashly gather that doth not truly follow. Ye may peradventure bring us into hatred, by these sinister means, with them that by prejudice have a pleasure in your fancies: but your proofs, for all that, shall be nothing the sounder; nor our substantial truth the weaker. As for the whole drift and conclusion of your tale, whereby ye heap all mischiefs on us; derive the cause of the plagues of God, and our sinful lives, from the spring of doctrine, which in Christ we profess; therein ye bewray your wilfulness, and your ignorance: wilfulness, in speaking against a known truth; ignorance, in reasoning to overthrow yourself.

[1] [Persius, *Prolog.* 10, 11.]

For though we deserve most evil at God's hands; being still better learned[2], and not better lived; yet, if ye remember yourself, (M. Martiall,) there was never age so free from miseries, specially in England, as, since the preaching of the Gospel, this of ours hath been: and sure a pitiful piece of work it is, when Papists in honesty shall contend with them whom ye call Protestants. A slender point of defence it is, when you give such a prick as makes yourselves to bleed.

But ye may not be touched, ye think: you have dedicate your book to the Queen's highness: ye craftily come with a fair view, commending her Majesty in appearance; but, in effect, with a false proffer, (to your shame and confusion be it spoken,) ye condemn her. Thus traitorously ye seek for defence at her hands, whose person ye flee, whose doings ye impugn. You have received from your Jove of the Capitol a Pandora's box, to present, (and God will,) to our Prometheus. But she, (God be thanked,) is too wise to credit you. Ye may seek for some other popish Epimetheus, that, accepting your offer, may set abroad your mischiefs. I doubt not but the lewdness of such her enemies shall work great advantage both to her Highness, and to us her true subjects. Ye call her "gracious and clement Princess Elizabeth; by the grace of God, Queen of England, France, and Ireland." The rest of her style ye wittingly omit. That which is the chief praise in a christian Prince, to be *Defender of the faith,* ye abridge her of: belike ye repute her not to be such a one. That which your great god[3], much like to Caiphas' prophecy, was

^{Folio 1.}

---

[2] [Boys's *Exposit. of Dominical Epistles and Gospels:* Spring Part, p. 183. Lond. 1610.]

[3] [A question has been raised as to the justness of the charge very frequently brought by our writers against Romanists, with respect to the assumption of divine power by their pontifical Dictator. Independently of the assertion in the Canon Law, (Dist. xcvi. C. *Satis evidenter.* fol. cvii. Parrhis. 1518.) that the Bishop of Rome was called a God by Constantine, and that accordingly he could not be judged by men, it appears from the Gloss upon the Extravagant *Cum inter,* that the Pope has received the title of "OUR LORD GOD." (*Extr.* Joan. xxii. De verb. sig. Tit. xiv. Cap. iv. §. Declaramus, prope finem.) Father Parsons, in his *Warn-word,* assures us that he could never find the expression; and his brother Jesuit Eudæmon-Joannes maintains that the word "God" is a typographical error. (*Apol. pro Hen. Garneto,* p. 138. Colon. Agripp. 1610.) Mr Butler's repetition of the

contented to give to her predecessor, you, "loving subject and true beadsman[1]," be loth to grant her, the true successor. That which is the only proof of king-like authority, within her own realms and dominions to be the supreme governor under God of all persons and causes, ye deny to her; and yet ye grant her to be the Queen. She to be Queen, and yet a subject to other: you to be Englishmen, and yet no subjects to her. Indeed, good cause you have, with all the rabble of your perverse confederates and outlaws, to call her

statement, (*Book of R. C. Church*, p. 130. Lond. 1825.) that the term "*Deum*" is not to be found in the Vatican MS. of Zenzelinus, is not of any greater importance than the argument of Allatius, and of Alban Butler, (*Lives of Saints*, Vol. ii. p. 89. Dubl. 1833.) against the existence of Pope Joan, founded on the "true" copy of the Chronicle of Martinus Polonus, "kept in the Vatican Library;"—for we must remember the confession of Possevinus about Manuscripts: "Ad istos enim quoque purgatio pertinet." (*Bibl. Sel.* Lib. i. Cap. xii. p. 58. Romæ, 1593.)

The state of the case seems to be this: "Pope Gregory the thirteenth employed and enjoined certain of the Cardinals to revise and correct the Gloss of the Canonists: when, as many editions thereof had this word *Deum*, God, and yet some had it not, they set forth a new copy; and, by the authority of Pope Gregory, they restored that word *Deum*, which before had been wanting in some few of their editions. Neither in the Censures of the Gloss, set out by the command of Pope Pius the fifth, nor yet in the Index Expurgatorius, is the least mention made of any mutation or alteration of the word *Deum*, for which we challenge them." (Squire's *Lectures* on 2 Thess. ii. p. 271. Lond. 1630. Conf. Dounami *Papa Antichristus*, pp. 310—11. Lond. 1620. Abbotti *Antilogia*, Cap. v. foll. 78, seqq. Lond. 1613. Mayeri *Theorem. Theol. de vulneribus Eccles. Rom. necdum curatis*, Par. i. Vulnus i. §. ii. Basil. 1612. Foulis's *Romish Treasons*, pp. 29, 30. Lond. 1681. Roscoe's *Leo X.*, i. 121. Liverp. 1805. Morton's *Grand Imposture*, p. 252. Lond. 1628. Gieseler's *Text-book of Eccles. Hist.* iii. 46—7. Philadel. 1836.)

It is said that Domitian had previously styled himself "Dominus et Deus noster;" (Selden's *Titles of Honor*, p. 47. Lond. 1614.) and the papal adoption of the blasphemous title may be seen in the following editions of the Canon Law: Lugduni, 1526, 1556, 1559, 1572, 1584. Lutet. Paris. 1522, 1561, 1585, 1601, 1612.—If it be pretended that the Roman Pontiff cannot be held responsible for the adulation bestowed by his creatures, the same excuse might have been made for Herod, when "the people gave a shout, saying, It is the voice of a god, and not of a man."]

[1] [One who says prayers for his patron.]

gracious and clement Princess; if grace and clemency it may be called, which, suffering you to your self-will, taketh not the sword of vengeance in her hand, but lets you run headlong on your own destruction. Her Grace might punish, where she forbeareth: she might justly pronounce the sentence of death, where she remitteth an easy prisonment. Therefore clement she is. Ye say right well. But whether her Majesty (gracious otherwise to all,) be gracious unto you, I doubt. For if it had pleased her royal Grace to have bridled you ere this with shorter reins, ye had not been at this day so headstrong as ye are. Many hundreths of you, (repenting your rebellious hearts,) had been converted to Christ; and by severity learned that which clemency shall never teach you. Now is your insolence grown to such excess, that ye abuse all other and yourselves too: that ye think men dare not for fear do that, which for tender heart and pity they do not: that ye think with hypocrisy to deceive God, and with flattery the world. Ye threaten kindness on the Queen's Majesty; saying "that her noble personage in all princely prowess," (for so ye term it,) "and her good affection to the Cross," (which is the matter ye treat of,) moved you so presumptuously to adventure; so adventurously to presume, (I should say;) as to recommend your treatise to her Highness. Indeed we have a most noble Princess; (God for His mercy prosper her, long to reign over us, in despite of your malice, and increase of our joy;) such a one as is beautified with rare gifts of nature, in wisdom marvellous, in virtue singular. Prowess she leaveth to the other sex. Subjects she hath enow to practise it. As for her private doings, neither are they to be drawn as a precedent for all; nor any ought to creep into the Prince's bosom, of every fact to judge an affection. This can the world well witness with me, that neither her Grace and Wisdom hath such affiance in the Cross as you do fondly teach; neither takes it expedient her subjects should have that which she herself, (she thinketh,) may keep without offence[2]. For the multitude is easily, through ignorance, abused: her Majesty too well instructed for her own person to fall into popish error and idolatry.

Now, for that which followeth: if ye were so good a sub-

Folio 1, b.

[2] [Strype's *Annals*, Vol. i. Part i. p. 262. Oxford, 1824. *Life of Parker*, ii. 35. Ib. 1821.]

ject as you ought, and framed yourself to live according to the laws, ye should see and consider how good order is taken "by public authority, not privy suggestions," that Roods and Images should be removed, according to God's law, out of churches, chapels, and oratories; and not so despitefully thrown down in highways, as you most constantly do affirm : the contrary whereof, as by our law is established, so in effect is proved. For we do see them in many places stand, nor are at all offended therewith. And do not you give us a good cause to credit you in the rest, who, in the first entrance of your matter, make so loud a lie?

But, that your impudence may be the more apparent, ye stay not so : ye stick not to father of the ancient Fathers' faith such falsehoods and absurdities as they never thought; good man never gathered. For where ye say, by their authority, "that, ever since Christ's death, christian men have had the sign of the Cross in churches, chapels, oratories, private houses, highways, and other places meet for the same," it shall be evident by their own writings, (such as none shall againsay,) that, four hundred year after Christ, there was not in the place of God's service any such sign erected. By the way I report me to that which Erasmus[1], a great stickler in the Cross quarrel, writeth : *Usque ad ætatem Hieronymi, erant probatæ Religionis viri, qui in templis nullam ferebant Imaginem, nec pictam, nec sculptam, nec textam ; ac ne Christi quidem, (ut opinor,) propter Anthropomorphitas :* "Until Hierom's time, there were men of good Religion," (which is to be noted, lest ye say they were heretics,) "that suffered not in churches any Picture at all, either painted, or graved, or woven ; yea, not so much as the Picture of Christ, because of the Anthropomorphites, (as I suppose.)" Now this was above four hundred year after Christ : for, by Hierom's own computation[2], it must be after the sixth year of Arcadius' Consulship, which falls out anno four hundred and eight; and Prosper Aquitanicus maketh it to be four hundred and twenty-two year after Christ[3]. But

---

[1] In Catechesi sua, Cap. 6. [*Symboli Catechesis* vi. p. 163. Basil. 1533. ed. princ. 4to : vel sig. i 5. Ib. 1551. 8vo.]

[2] In Prooemio 3. Comment. super Amos. [S. Hieron. *Præfatio in lib. tert. Proph. Amos*, sig. h iii. Venet. 1497.]

[3] [There must be some error here; for S. Jerom died in the year

as much as this the Fathers themselves shall be witnesses of, to disprove your vanity. "Then that they worshipped the sign of the Cross, or counselled other to do the same," is as true as the other: yea, a thing it was, when use of such signs was received indeed, most abhorred of them. I appeal to your Pope, Gregory the Great[4], the first that ever defended Images. He found fault with Serenus, Bishop of Massilia[5], for breaking the Images that he found in his church: yet he condemneth your doctrine for worshipping them; saying in one place: *Et quidem zelum vos, ne quid manu factum adorari possit, habuisse laudavimus:* "And truly we commended you, in that ye had a zeal, that nothing made with hand should be worshipped." *Tua ergo fraternitas et illas servare, et ab earum adoratione populum prohibere debuit:* "Therefore your brotherhead should have preserved them, and forbidden the people that they should not worship them." And this Gregory was six hundred year after Christ. Where then was the reverence done to the sign? Where gave they the counsel to creep to the Cross[6]? See you not how shamefully ye abuse the Prince with slanders and untruths?

As for the third substantial ground, whereupon ye build the buttress of your cause; "that no fear or mistrust of idolatry can be where the Cross is worshipped;" that position and more than paradox is as true as the rest: as true as the Jews could commit no idolatry in worshipping the brazen Serpent[7]: and yet that sign was commanded once[8]; this sign to us-ward was commanded never. Wherefore, since your ware

---

420. Vid. Petavii *Rationar. Temp.* p. 316. Franeq. 1694. Pagi *Crit. in Annall. Baron.* Tom. ii. p. 176. Colon. Allob. 1705. Besides, in the "editio Consularis," or "vulgata," of Prosper's *Chronicon*, which is annexed to the Eusebian and Hieronymian Chronicles, published by Joseph Scaliger, it is distinctly stated that the sixth Consulship of Arcadius, and the first of Probus, occurred in the year 407. See page 191. Amstel. 1658; and compare Baronius, ad an. 406. Tom. v. p. 259. Antverp. 1658.]

[4] Ep. Li. vii. Indict. ii. Cap. 109. [*Opp.* Tom. ii. fol. 234, b. Antverp. 1572.]

[5] [Marseilles.]

[6] [See Bp. Latimer's *Sermons*, p. 132. ed. Parker Soc.]

[7] 2 Reg. [Kings] xviii. [4.]

[8] Num. xxi. [8.] Joan. ix. [S. John iii. 14.]

is no more worth, (M. Martiall,) you, like a pelting[1] pedlar, putting the best in your pack uppermost, I see not where ye may have utterance for it, unless it be to serve to sluttish uses. And that ye should rest in any hope that the Queen's Majesty, amidst her great affairs, should have so much vacant time as to take a view of your vain devices, is a miracle to me; and makes your folly to appear the more, the more ye conceive a liking of yourself. The story that ye bring of Socrates' report[2], not truly quoted, (for I think ye never read it,) maketh small for your purpose. What though Sisinnius, an heretic, a Novatian, did give advice, for appeasing of the Arrians' heresy, that the ancient Fathers should be called to witness; will you take example of one not well instructed, nor wise, in this case as it appeared? Were the ancient Fathers sufficient to appease the cause? Were they not enforced, (that notwithstanding,) each man to bring his opinion in writing, and stand to a further judgment and determination? Read ye the place. They neither could, nor can, for imperfections that remain amongst them, content the conscience in doubtful cases; nor ought at any time to be judges of our faith. S. Augustin, *Contra Maximinum Arrian. Epis.*, hath a goodly rule, better to be followed and observed than yours. For when, in the like controversy with the Arrians, the Council of Ariminum, where many Fathers were assembled, made for the one part, and the Council of Nice confirmed the other; Augustin, to declare that we ought not to depend upon man's judgment, but wholly and solely upon the truth of God's word, said[3]: *Nec ego Nicænum, nec tu debes Ariminense, tanquam præjudicaturus, proferre Concilium. Nec ego hujus authoritate, nec tu illius detineris. Scripturarum authoritatibus, non quorumque propriis, sed utrisque com-*

---

[1] [paltry, petty, pitiful. See Shakspeare's *King Richard II.* Act ii. Scene i. line 60. *Measure for Measure,* Act ii. Scene ii. *Midsummer Night's Dream,* Act ii. Scene ii.—Becon speaks of "pedlar-like Papists." (*Catech.* &c. p. 451. Camb. 1844. ed. Parker Soc.)]

[2] It is Socratis Lib. v. Cap. x. [*Eccles. Hist.* fol. 245, b. Lut. Paris. 1544: or English translation, p. 335. Lond. 1709.]

[3] Epist. Lib. iii. Cap. xiv. [This reference is incorrect. The passage may be found in S. August. Lib. ii. contra Maximin. Arian. *Opp.* Tom. viii. col. 499. Cf. col. 460. Antwerp. (Amstel.) 1700. ed. Bened. a J. Cler.]

munibus testibus, res cum re, causa cum causa, ratio cum ratione concertet: which words, in English, be these: "Neither I must bring forth the Council of Nice, nor thou the Council of Ariminum, as one to prejudice the other. Neither I am bound to the authority of the one, nor thou restrained to the determination of the other. But by the authorities of the Scriptures, (not peculiar witnesses unto either of us, but common and indifferent unto us both,) let one matter with another, cause with cause, and reason contend with reason." Then is it no outrage, (as it pleaseth your wisdom to term it,) to refuse your order; since most of the Fathers, yea, every one of them, have had their errors, as afterward more clearly shall appear. Yet for all your dotages, whereof peradventure ye dreamed in some drunken phrensy, for all your absurdities, I dare and will join issue with you. Let the doctrine of the received Fathers (for you make Fathers of Friars, and legend lies laws,) decise the controversy that is betwixt us. If I bring not more sound antiquity to confirm my truth, than you can avouch for maintenance of your error: if the selfsame Fathers direct me not in the right way, which you misconstrue for the cross way: let our Theodosia deal as she lusteth with me; the shame to be mine. Otherwise, (if it be God's will,) the amendment to be yours. Amen.

Folio 3.

THE PREFACE TO THE READERS.

If neither experience of elder age, nor present authority of Scripture were to put us in mind of the sleights of Satan, how he continually doth bend his force against the fort of our afflicted souls; yet the subtle conspiracies of these younger days, the practice of the Papist, that Martials now the Devil's host, and marcheth forward with a forged ensign, appearing outwardly to be the friend of Christ, whose faith and religion he utterly subverteth, may serve as a warning piece out of the watch-tower, to make us run to the walls of faith, betaking ourselves each man to his defence in the certain truth of God's eternal Testament. For if the groundwork be shaken once, whereupon we build our health and salvation, (which is the affiance in Christ our God, and credit to His word,) then enters our enemy with banner displayed, and beateth us down to the pit of damnation. Wherefore, he, seeking to supplant Christ, and pull our hearts from service of Him, compasseth by all means to win himself some credit with us; and the knowledge of God, revealed in His word, by a little and a little to be taken from us. But he hath of himself too ill a name to be esteemed so: and therefore, under visor of that that he is not, he wins men to yield to that that they should not. He becometh therefore in all his works an ape of God; to imitate and resemble, after his hellish manner, to the utter overthrow and destruction of our souls, that which our heavenly Father hath provided for our health, salvation, and bliss. Herein hath he handled himself so workmanly, that he looks very narrowly that can discern the difference. Yea, the eyes of his heart must be better cleared than by the light of reason, or else he shall be blinded in the mist. We see that, even from the beginning, after God's Spirit had moved Abel and the holy Patriarchs to offer sacrifice unto Him, that should be figures all of that one Sacrifice, which Christ, according to the prefixed pleasure of the eterne Deity, should, at His time, on the Cross perform; the Devil, in worshipping of his Idols, did come so near the same, that the self-same did seem to be done in both. Yea, generally, in all the superstitions and detestable rites of the heathen folk, he took his pattern out of the ordinance of the Hebrews, and manners of the Christians. Which thing Tertullian, among the Latin writers the most ancient and chief, right well declareth[1]: *Ipsas quoque res Sacramentorum divinorum in Idolorum mysteriis æmulatur*, &c. : "Yea, the very matter and substance of the divine Sacraments he counterfeits in his Idol-service." He hath his Baptism[2], whereby such as do believe in him have forgiveness promised them: he marketh his men with signs in the forehead: he hath his offerings, his sacrificers, his virgins, and his votaries. That, if we look on the superstitions of Numa Pompilius; the badges, the privileges, the offices of his Priests; the vessels, the ceremonies, the furniture of his sacrifices; we shall see how the Devil *morositatem illam*, as Tertullian termeth it, *Judeæ gentis imitatus est:* "did imitate the fancies and self-willness of the Jews." As Moses went up into the mount Sina, and there received the Law tables, whereof the author God Himself should be; so Minos, afterward, among the Grecians[3], hiding himself awhile

---

[1] De Præscriptionibus advers. Hæret. [*De Præscript. Hæreticor.* Cap. xl. Opp. p. 216. Lut. Paris. 1675. Cf. *De exhort. Cast.* Cap. xiii. p. 524: "Dei Sacramenta Satanas adfectat."]

[2] ["Tingit et ipse quosdam, utique credentes et fideles suos: expositionem delictorum de lavacro repromittit; et, si adhuc memini, Mithra signat illic in frontibus milites suos: celebrat et panis oblationem...; habet et virgines, habet et continentes. Ceterum si Numæ Pompilii superstitiones revolvamus; si sacerdotalia officia, insignia, et privilegia; si sacrificalia ministeria, et instrumenta, et vasa ipsorum sacrificiorum, ac piaculorum et votorum curiositates consideremus; nonne manifeste Diabolus morositatem illam Judaicæ legis imitatus est?" (Tertull. loc. sup. cit. pp. 216-17.)]

[3] ["Quænam est ergo Græcorum incredulitas? Num nolle credere veritati, quæ dicit Legem per Mosen datam esse divinitus? cum ipsi ex iis quæ apud se scripta sunt Mosen honorent, et Minoëm referant ad Jovis antrum venientem, novem annorum spatio leges a Jove accepisse." (Clem. Alex. *Strom.* Lib. i. *Opp.* p. 351. Conf. L. ii. p. 367. ed. Sylburg. Lut. Paris. 1641.) "Sabinus Rex...astutiam Minois voluit imitari, qui se in antrum Jovis recondebat; et ibi diu moratus, leges tanquam sibi a Jove traditas afferebat: ut homines ad parendum non modo imperio, sed etiam Religione constringeret." (Lactant. *De falsa Relig.* Lib. i. Cap. xxii. Cf. Betuleii *Comment.* p. 78. Basil. 1563. Homeri *Od.* Lib. xix. 178, 179. Mitford's *Greece*, Vol. i. Chap. i. Sect. ii. Dionysii Halicarnass. *Antiq. Rom.* Lib. ii. Cap. lxi.)]

in Jupiter's cave, came forth at length, and gave them laws, from mighty Jove, as he pretended. And, to the end the people might the more be bound in obedience, the like practice had the Roman King[1], of whom I spake before: saying that, in the night time, he had secret conference with Ægeria; and she delivered him such wholesome laws as the mighty Gods had decreed on. Whereby what other thing was attempted of the Devil, but that all credit should be denied to Moses; inasmuch as Minos and Numa too did allege the like authority for themselves, and yet it was evident they were but fables?

Will ye go to the circumstances of place and persons? Then, as God ordained His service to be had first in the tabernacle, then in the temple at Hierusalem; so would the Devil have his hills and groves. As God did raise up His holy men and Prophets, that, being inspired with the Holy Ghost, might declare His will, and by force of miracles win the more credit; so hath the Devil his conjurors, his witches, his figure-flingers, and his sorcerers, with the spirit of illusion to work strange effects. As we have a place of eternal rest, so have they their heaven: *Elysios campos, et amœna vireta fortunatorum nemorum*[2]*:* "the sweet pleasant paradise, and places of good hap." As we have hell, even so have they: that, if we preach the blessedness of the faithful[3], by the merits and mercies of Christ our Saviour, then step the godless out, and take it as a tale of the Poets' paradise: if we threaten vengeance to the misbelievers[4], and extreme torment of hell-fire,

[1] ["Numa Pompilius, ut populum Romanum sacris obligaret, volebat videri sibi cum Dea Ægeria congressus esse nocturnos, ejusque monitu accepta Diis immortalibus sacra instituere." (Valer. Max. Lib. i. Cap. ii. Conf. Liv. Lib. i. Cap. xix. Juven. *Sat.* iii. 12. Plutarch. in *Vit. Numœ*, §. δ. Cic. *De Legib.* Lib. i. Cap. i. ad calc. Ovid. *Fast.* Lib. iii. 275—6.)]

[2] [" Devenere locos lætos, et amœna vireta
      Fortunatorum nemorum, sedesque beatas."
                                    (Virg. *Æn.* vi. 638—9.)]

[3] ["Si Paradisum nominemus, locum divinæ amœnitatis recipiendis Sanctorum spiritibus destinatum,...Elysii campi fidem occupaverunt." (Tertull. *Apologet.* Cap. xlvii.)]

[4] ["Gehennam si comminemur, quæ est ignis arcani sub terra ad pœnam thesaurus, proinde decachinnamur; sic enim et Pyriphlegeton apud mortuos amnis est." (Tertull. *Apol.* ib. Conf. *Ad Nat.* Lib. i. C. xix. Dan. vii. 10. Euseb. *Prœpar. Evangel.* Lib. xi. Cap. xxxviii. p. 567. Colon. 1688.)]

the Devil's limbs laugh us to scorn again; and do resemble it to Plato his Purgatory; or to the scalding of Pyriphlegeton, a river so devised by the heathen folk, to burn in hell with flames unquenchable.

Such sleights hath Satan, to put us in security of any further pain: to pull us from the hope of perfecter estate, that here we may live as the Devil would have us; in the end to receive as the Devil can reward us. And he hath not wanted his instruments of old. He hath made himself ministers from time to time, that, in the world's eye, were most worthy reverence, and likelier than the rest to compass his desire. Among them all, to the Devil's behoof never so faithful servants; to the destruction of the people never so pestilent instruments, as the Papists are. For what have they not done, to the utter subversion of all true Religion? As Christ commanded the believers in His name to be baptized, so they, in the Devil's name, have baptized Bells, with the same ceremonies and solemnities that they would use in Infants' christening: save that the Devil would have in his Sacrament a certain more majesty than God in His. Therefore the Papists, by the spirit of the Devil, ordained that a Bishop must needs christen a Bell; whereas every poor Priest may christen a Child[5]. And because that, through water, consecrated by

---

[5] [Bellarmin asserts that all this is a slanderous device of heretics; and wonders that it has not been stated that provision has been made for the catechizing of a Bell as well as for baptizing it. (*De Rom. Pont.* Lib. iv. Cap. xii. *Disp.* Tom. i. col. 1009. Ingolst. 1601.) The accusation of profaneness cannot, however, be so easily dispelled; as will appear from an examination of the Pontifical, *De benedictione Signi vel Campanæ*, either in an old edition, as that Lugd. 1511, fol. cl., or in an impression revised by the authority of Pope Urban VIII., p. 371, sq. Antverp. 1663. Bishop Bale (*Acta Rom. Pontt.* Lib. iv. p. 133. Francof. 1567.) and the Centuriators (*Cent.* x. col. 294. Basil. 1567.) inform us, that Pope John XIV., about the year 973, was the first who gave names to baptized Bells: and Crashawe, in his valuable *Sermon at the Crosse*, (pp. 115—20. Lond. 1608.) has discussed the matter; and drawn a parallel, from which it is evident that, with respect to ceremonies, sponsors, prayers, and the minister employed, a Bell* has

* [The duties of a Bell are thus described on a MS. leaf in a Sarum Manual, Duaci, 1610:

"En ego Campana nunquam denuncio vana:
Laudo Deum verum, Plebem voco, congrego Clerum:
Funera plango, fulgura frango, Sabbatha pango:
Excito lentos, dissipo ventos, paco cruentos."]

the word of God, sins are remitted; not by the force of water, but power of the Spirit; therefore the Devil would have his consecration of water. and of salt, *qua cuncti sanctificentur ac purificentur aspersi:* as it is written in the Pope's Decrees[1]: that whosoever are sprinkled therewith are by and by sanctified, purified, made clean and holy. Go no further than to their Portesses[2]; and you shall see how they approve greatly the advantage of a Child.—Bellarmin and others insist on *Benediction* being the word that should be used in this case, and not *Baptism:* but it might suffice to say, that the latter term is so far from being an invention of Protestants, that it is as old as the days of Charlemagne; who, in a Capitular, bearing date anno 789, issued an injunction, "ut Clocas" [or "Gloggas," in Irish *Cloch,* in French *Cloches,* German *Glocken,* or *Gloggen,*] "non *baptizent.*" (Baluzii *Capitularia Regum Francor.* Tom. i. col. 244. Paris. 1677.) The papistical derivation of the word can be inferred, likewise, from the title of the fifty-first of the *Centum Gravamina* in Orthuinus Gratius; viz: "De superstitione inani, *in baptizandis Campanis,* ne scilicet animæ perdantur earum." (*Fascic. Rer. expet. ac fugiend.* fol. clxxvi., b. Colon. 1535.) These Hundred Grievances of the German nation have, by some Romanists, been absurdly "stigmatized as a Lutheran production:" (see Mendham's *Council of Trent,* Introd. p. 8. Lond. 1834.) but the editor is in possession of an original copy of them, printed at Nuremberg, in 1523, (when the assembly which formed them was dissolved,) as well as of the reprint, with Luther's preface, Vittemberg. 1538.]

[1] De Consecr. Dist. iii. [Cap. xx. "Aquam sale conspersam populis benedicimus, ut ea cuncti aspersi sanctificentur et purificentur." This is an extract from the first spurious Epistle of Pope Alexander I., who is commemorated in the Canon of the Mass, and to whom is falsely attributed the introduction of the use of Holy Water, about the year 115. The argument upon which the ordinance is founded, in this Decree, is derived from an impious citation of the verses, Heb. ix. 13, 14: "Nam si cinis vitulæ," &c.: "For if the ashes of an heifer, sprinkling the unclean, sanctifieth to the purifying of the flesh; how much more shall"—*not* "the blood of Christ," but "aqua sale aspersa,"— *water sprinkled with salt* sanctify and cleanse the people?! This fictitious Epistle is adduced not only in the Canon Law, but in the *Sacerdotale,* fol. 191. Venet. 1579; and also by Bellarmin, (*De cultu Sanctt.* Lib. iii. Cap. vii.) and Collin. (*Traité de l'Eau Bénite,* pp. 132, 143, 173. A Paris, 1776.) Conf. Gretser. *De Benedictt.* L. ii. Cap. vi. Ingolst. 1615.]

[2 Breviaries.—The Latin name *Portiforium,* derived from *portare foras,* gave rise to the French *porté-hors:* (the *s* was anciently pronounced.) The word "Porthors" was corrupted to "Porthose"; and thence came Portuse, Portass, Portess.]

it³. *Aqua Benedicta deleantur tua delicta. Aqua Benedicta sit tibi salus et vita*⁴.

"By the Holy Water so,
Be thy offences put thee fro.
Let the Holy Water be
Salvation and life to thee."

These words were in their daily service. But O blasphemous mouths, to attribute that to their inventions which is the work of God alone, the price of the blood of Christ our Saviour. Yet will they have, as their father had, when he came forth with *Scriptum est*⁵, the Scripture for them: applied, I promise you, to as good a purpose as when the witch, by her *Pater noster*, made her pail go a milking. For why should I not compare the Priests, (that consecrate Crosses and ashes, water and salt, oil and cream, boughs and bones, stocks and stones; that christen bells that hang in the steeple; that conjure worms that creep in the field⁶; that give S. John's Gospels to hang about men's necks;) to the vilest witches and sorcerers of the earth? Each Prince hath his people; and delivereth his laws to be observed of them: which if they keep, they shew they are his. And God, (that His servants might be known to the world, by walking according to His will,) ordained some works, wherein He would have us to exercise ourselves; as the fear, the faith, the love to God-ward, the repentance of our evils, the profession of the Gospel, the furtherance of the same, prayer, thanksgiving, and praise of God, patience, perseverance, justice, charity, and such other like. What doth the Devil now? To seal his servants into league with him, he deviseth ordinances to make them to be known by:

³ [The form for consecrating salt and water, together with a declaration of the benefits they confer when exorcised, may be seen in the *Portiforium ad usum Eccles. Sarisb.* Par. Hiem. fol. 191, b, sqq. Rothom. 1556. *Manuale Sarisbur.* pp. 265—271. Duaci, 1610. *Rituale Roman.* pp. 186—9. Colon. Agripp. 1628. *Missale Rom.* pp. cvii—ix. Antverp. 1765.]

⁴ [Conf. Siberi *Hircus Aquam Bened. bibens*, pp. 31, 40. Lips. 1712.]

⁵ [S. Matth. iv. 6.]

⁶ [The "Benedictio contra Aves, Vermes, Mures, vel Locustas," is to be found in the *Sacerdotale*, fol. 225. Venet. 1579: and in the Sarum Manual appears the "Benedictio ad omnia quæcunque volueris."]

[CALFHILL.]

as, strange attire, difference of meats, refusal of marriage,
rising at midnight, shutting up in a cloister, erecting of
Images, worshipping of Saints, service in Latin, gadding on
pilgrimage, making of vows, most wilful beggary, most vile
hypocrisy. Hereby the simple have been so deluded, that
they thought God's service to consist herein; and so the
Devil for God was honoured. Hereby the Devil's children
have so magnified themselves, that, (God's law neglected,) their
beastly fancies have been had in reverence. For proof
whereof, go no further than to this. Sole life is not by
God commanded[1]: the Devil doth exact it in his ministers.
Adultery is by God condemned[2]: the Devil in his ministers
makes a trifle of it. That filthy vice, which, by the testimony of the Apostle Paul[3], doth quite exclude us from the
kingdom of heaven, they make but a game of, or a sin
venial. If ye credit me not, read the Decree of Alexander,
the third of that name[4]. There he affirmeth, that as for
adultery and such other faults, which he accompteth, by express word, *crimina leviora*, "trifling offences," the Bishop may
dispense with. And yet some good fellows will say that we
preach liberty. We, or the Papists? Judge ye. Pelagius the
Pope, as we read in a certain Decretal of his[5]; (and when I
speak of Decrees and Decretals, think that I speak of no
other matter than that which the Papists have in as sovereign a price as the Bible;) gives a worthy censure in the like
case. A man that had been married would needs, after the

[1] Genes. xxvi. [3, 4, 24.]   [2] Exod. xx. [14.]
[3] 1 Cor. vi. [9, 10.] Heb. xiii. [4.]
[4] Cap. At si Clerici. paragra. de Adult. [*Decretall. Greg. IX.*
Lib. ii. Tit. i. Cap. iv. coll. 524—5. Paris. 1585.—"De Adulteriis vero
et aliis criminibus, quæ sunt minora, potest Episcopus cum Clericis
post peractam pœnitentiam dispensare."]
[5] Dist. xxiv. Cap. Fraternitatis. [*Dist.* xxxiv. Cap. vii.—"Fraternitatis tuæ relatione suscepta, ejus latorem secundas quidem nuptias
expertum non fuisse didicimus; castitatem tamen cum priori non ser-
vasse conjugio designasti. Et quamvis multa sint, quæ in hujusmodi
casibus observari canonice jubeat sublimitatis autoritas; tamen quia
defectus nostrorum temporum, quibus non solum merita, sed corpora
ipsa hominum defecerunt, districtionis illius non patitur in omnibus
manere censuram; et ætas istius, de quo agitur, futuræ incontinentiæ
suspicionem auferre dignoscitur; ut ad Diaconatum possit provehi,
temporum, ut dictum est, condescendentes defectui, concessisse nos
noveris."]

decease of his wife, become a Priest; and sued for his orders. The Prelates fell of examining the matter, whether he were *Bigamus* or no: that is to say, whether his wife was not a maid when he married her; or whether he himself had married a second wife. For if either of these had been found in him, he had been unmeet to enter into orders. But found he was to be an adulterer; who, after his wife's death, had a child by another woman. Now what saith the holy father? "Inasmuch as he is not found to be *Bigamus*, but yet proved incontinent, we hope well of him: let him have his orders. As for his lechery, we bear with him, in respect of the weakness of this our age." See the Religion of Popery. If it had been his hap to have married a widow, or the second time to have entered into the holy state of matrimony, this man should have had no orders: now that he is become a whoremaster, he hath them. Here comes in place the famous judgment of him that makes the gloze, not in mockery, but in good earnest: *Ecce casus, ubi plus valet luxuria quam castitas*[6]: "Behold a case, where incontinence hath a more privilege than chastity." Thus, I suppose, ye see how the Devil doth advance his works; and, by the ministry of the Papists, set up himself in place of God.

Now that his Religion should in all points, to the world's eye, be as perfect as God's, and that men should not want helps enow to hell: as God appointed the prayers unto Him to be made through Christ our mediator; so, when the Devil will be served best, he deputeth Saints to be intercessors, and every one of them hath his charge limited[7]. One to deliver us from the fever quartan; another to preserve us from the danger of the sea. One to restore the goods that we have lost; another to defend our folds from the fox. One for the plague; another for the purse. One for ourselves; another for our swine. And is not this mere Gentility[8]? Yet is it

---

[6] ["Ecce casus, ubi plus juris habet luxuria quam castitas: quia castus repelleretur, si contraxisset cum secunda; sed fornicator non." (Gloss. in verb. Non patitur. *Dist.* xxxiv. fol. xxxviii, b. Paris. 1518.)]

[7] [Vid. Tilemani Heshusii *Sexcenti Errores*, fol. 126. Witeb. 1612. Fulke on 1 Tim. ii. *New Test.* p. 676. Lond. 1617. Brevint's *Saul and Samuel at Endor*, pp. 72—4. Oxf. 1674. *Early Works* of Becon, pp. 138—9. ed. Parker Soc. Bp. Cosin's *Works*, i. 146—7. Oxf. 1843.]

[8] [Gentilism, heathenism.—The following remarkable passage, to

right Popery. As they had Juno for women in childbed, so we the blessed Virgin in her place with us. As they had Æsculapius to save them from diseases, so had we S. Roke to supply that room. As they had Mars to help them in warfare, so had we S. George to make us win the field. Finally, lest there should want any thing to please the wanton world; as God, of His mercy, did make man after the image and likeness of Himself, so the Devil hath put in the mind of man to make Images after the likeness of God, and so to transfer His honour unto creatures. The blockish Images, the dead Crosses, have been crept to, been worshipped. The lively images of Christ Himself have been brought to the Cross, and burned cruelly. May I not therefore, with Clement, the Apostles' successor, say[1]: *Quis est iste honor Dei; per*

the same effect, occurs in an uncorrupted edition of the Commentary of Ludovicus Vives upon S. Augustin's *City of God:* (Lib. viii. Cap. xxvii. Paris. 1541.) "Multi Christiani in re bona plerumque peccant, quod Divos Divasque non aliter venerantur quam Deum. Nec video in multis, quod sit discrimen inter eorum opinionem de Sanctis, et id quod *Gentiles* putabant de suis Diis." These words have been omitted by the Louvain Divines; (Vid. p. 372. edit. Paris. 1585.) and we must not expect to discover them in the *Appendix Augustiniana* by Le Clerc. (p. 581. Antwerp. 1703.) It is very observable, that sentence of expurgation was not passed upon them by the Indexes, Antverp. 1571; Madriti, 1584; Romæ, 1607; Ulyssip. 1624; Hispali, 1632; Madriti, 1640, and 1707; all of which review the Commentary of Vives, and annihilate the succeeding note. The *Indice Ultimo* of Madrid, 1790, informs us, p. 19, "que muchas Ediciones de las Obras de S. Agustin hechas por Hereges, especialmente las que salieron antes del año 1576, han sido manchadas con Indices, Notas marginales, ó Escolios viciados": and the single instance of secret depravation, just pointed out, is sufficient to prove, that we have reason for being on our guard against private as well as printed, arbitrary as well as formal, processes of false dealing in Romanistic publications.]

[1] Recog. Li. v. [p. 94. Basil. 1526.—" Quis ergo iste honor Dei est; per lapideas et ligneas formas discurrere, et inanes atque exanimes figuras tanquam Numina venerari; et hominem, in quo vere imago Dei est, spernere"?—Calfhill is grievously mistaken in ascribing the books of the Recognitions, or the Itinerary of S. Peter, to S. Clement of Rome: but he speaks in accordance with a notion predominant in his time; and he may have been misled by the title-page of the first edition by Sichardus, just referred to; or by the assertion of Rufinus, (*Lib. de adult. Lib. Origen.*) that the author was "Apostolicus vir, immo pæne Apostolus." We have only a Latin version of these books,

lapideas et ligneas formas discurrere, atque exanimes figuras venerari; et hominem, in quo vera Dei imago est, spernere? "What honour of God is this; to run about the counterfeits of timber and of stone, and to worship the shapes that are without soul; and despise man, in whom the true shape of God is?" Yet have we often heard, and sometime to our grief have seen, that, for the quarrel of stocks and stones, many learned men have lost their lives: and where the learned and godly books, containing God's undoubted word, have been torn in pieces and despitefully burned, these Laymen's books[2] have, with no grief at all, been suffered to stand; but, for the pulling down, have procured the death and destruction of many. Thus, for the Idol sake, the true image of Christ hath been defaced, and painted Images been suffered to the abuse; the thing taken from us that should teach us the right use. It is not unknown to all the world, with what cruelty and rage Satan hath upholden and maintained his device, by executing of thousands for contempt of an Image: but, for the contempt of God, and

by Rufinus; and this not quite complete, as some parts were by him purposely "reserved for others." It appears certain that the author could not have lived until about the year 180: and Le Nourry (*Appar. ad Bibl. max. Patt.* col. 222. Paris. 1703.) and Ittigius (*Dissert. de Patrib. Apost.* p. 223. Lips. 1699. *Hist. Eccles. Sæc. i.* pp. 56—7. Ib. 1709.) suppose him to have been an Ebionite heretic. This, however, is denied by Grabe; who thinks it "altogether likely" that he was orthodox; but that his writings have been wretchedly distracted and interpolated. (*Spicileg.* Tom. i. p. 279. Oxon. 1714.) The Roman Council, held under Pope Gelasius, in the year 496, denounced the work as "apocryphal"; (*Dist.* xv. Cap. iii.) and this censure has been adopted in the Catalogue of heretical books, issued by the Tribunal of the Inquisition at Venice, in 1554, and reprinted by the learned Mr Mendham, in 1840.]

[2] [The name "Idiotarum libri." has been frequently assigned to Images from the days of Pope Gregory the Great; who declares that "quod legentibus scriptura, hoc idiotis præstat pictura cernentibus." (*Epistt.* Lib. ix. Cap. ix.) The passage is cited in the Canon Law; (*De Consec.* Dist. iii. Cap. xxvii.) and has been a staple authority with Romish controvertists, from Eckius to Dr Milner. (Vid. Eck. *De non tollend. Imagin.* Cap. v. Ingolst. 1522. *End of Controv.* p. 259. Lond. 1824.) It will not add much to the strength of the argument, if we remember that the Heathen made use of the same pretence: for S. Athanasius tells us, that they affirmed that their Images served "ὡς γράμματα τῆς ἐπὶ Θεὸν θεωρίας," "instar literarum ad Deum contemplandum". (*Orat. contra Gentes,* §. xxi.)]

murdering of His Saints, what conscience was there ever in Papist?

When the people of Antioch[1] had, in despite, pulled down the brazen Image of Theodosius his wife, (who then was Emperor;) for this their outrage and disobedience, they were threatened, (as they well deserved,) to lose their liberties, and be committed to the sword. But when the men of war approached, a silly man whose name was Macedonius[2], devoid of learning and great skill, but virtuous otherwise, did stay their rage with this kind of oration: "Tell the Emperor, (my friends,) that he is not only an Emperor, but a man too: therefore he ought not only to respect his empire and rule, but also his own condition and nature. For whereas he is a man, he hath subjects of the like estate with himself; and the nature of man is made after the image and likeness of God. Wherefore he ought not so cruelly and outrageously to slay the image of God, lest the Maker of that image should be incensed thereby to wrath. He should rather consider that this extremity is used only for an Image of brass; and none there is, unless he be mad, but can tell the difference between a dead and senseless thing, and that which hath both life and soul. Let him also remember this, that it is easy for us, for one Image of brass to restore many: but he, for all his power, is not able to make one hair of them that shall be destroyed for it." With report hereof the good Emperor was quieted; and, instead of cruelty, extended courtesy. But, since Idolatry hath taken root, how many thousand Christians have, without redemption, been burned and hanged, only for disproving the abuse of Imagery? And with them that be wedded to their own wills, yet to this day a greater fault it is, to speak against an Image of any kind of metal, than doing of a trespass against the majesty of God. And therefore we see that Pictures and Images,

---

[1] Theodoret. Lib. v. Cap. xix, & xx. [*Eccles. Hist. Auctores:* edit. Græc. ex off. Rob. Steph. fol. 343, b. Lut. Paris, 1544: vel edit. Lat. Joachimo Camerario interp. p. 508. Basil. 1549. The narrative is in the twentieth chapter in the edition by Valesius, Paris. 1673.]

[2] [An account of this Monk is given in Theodoret's *Historia Religiosa*, n. xiii. Opp. Tom. ii. pp. 447—9. Colon. Agripp. 1573. He is spoken of also in the seventeenth of S. Chrysostom's *Homilies on the Statues*, §. 3; and is named in Damascen's *Apolog. pro venerat. sanctar, Imag.* Lib. iii. fol. 82, b. Paris. 1555.]

which, partly of Gentility, partly of a blind and foolish zeal, were received, at the first, to be signs of good-will, and provocations to virtue, have been, in process, the destruction of Religion, and maintenance of gross Idolatry. I omit the offence and cause of stumbling unto the weak; which, in the Scripture, is oft accursed[3].

Justinus, in his book *De Monarchia*[4], sheweth how man's nature had understanding at the first granted, to the end that the truth might be learned of them, and the true worship of the one God, the only Maker and Lord of all. But the Devil's malice craftily came in place; and caused men to forget their own estate, and the majesty of God, for their own imaginations. Which thing experience itself hath taught us; that the flesh, delighting in her own devices, hath made us prone, above all other faults, to superstition and wicked worshippings. Esay saith[5]: "Their land was full of Idols; and they worshipped the work of their own hands." Wherein the order of words is to be noted: how first the Prophet doth name the matter, be it silver or gold; then afterward he comes to the use, which consequently always doth follow. For it cannot be chosen, but with the Idol must go the abuse; as of the fire, if ye lay on wood, ariseth flame. Nor only in our days this vile corruption hath had the upper hand; but by the same deceitful train, ever from the beginning, Satan hath inveigled the hearts of the simple. Ezechiel affirmeth[6], that when the Israelites were yet in Egypt, they had rebelled against the Lord; they had not cast away the abominations of their eyes, nor yet forsaken the Idols of the country: wherefore God, intending to wean them from the breast of fornication, to leave the sucking of such dregs of Idolatry, for this only respect delivered unto them most part of His ceremonies. Yet all they were not able to keep them within the compass of God's true service, but that they would fall to their own inventions. We see how they forced Aaron[7], afore his brother Moses could descend from the mount, to make them a golden calf, to fall down and do worship to it. We see how, when they were in the land of promise, under their Judges and their Kings, they went a madding after their Idols. We see that, after the

---

[3] Deut. xx. [18.] Levit. xix. [14.] Matth. xviii. [6.]
[4] [S. Just. Mart. *De Monarchia Dei Liber.* Opp. p. 103. Lut. Paris. 1615. Cf. Euseb. *Hist. Eccles.* Lib. iv. Cap. xviii.]
[5] Cap. ii. [8.]   [6] Cap. xx. [8—12.]   [7] Exod. xxxii. [1.]

zealous Kings Ezechias and Josias had reformed Religion, the people were so prone to the contrary, that, immediately upon their decease[1], they returned again to their old vomit. Yea, when the ten tribes were brought to captivity, for serving God otherwise than He would[2], the tribe of Judah was not, by this their brethren's plague, amended[3]; nor, when they were brought under yoke themselves[4], they considered any whit the cause of their distress[5], which was the forsaking of their Lord and God. For, being in Babylon, they went as near as they could to the rites of Gentility[6]; and, restored again unto the land of promise[7], under Antiochus they fell again[8]. Such is the violent persuasion of error; such is the force of superstition; that, as soon as ever occasion is ministered, our corrupt nature inclineth to it. Whereof we need to fetch no further proof than our own days. That idol of Winchester, Stephen Gardyner, subscribed, in King Edward's reign, against the use of Images; comparing them to a child's book, that ought to be taken from him, if he only delighted in the golden cover: yet, in Queen Mary's days, he forgat himself, and commanded them every where to be erected. For fourteen year together, as by good depositions it is to be seen, he preached against the Pope's supremacy, vehemently, pithily, earnestly, very earnestly, forwardly: but, as soon as ever opportunity served him, he brought, (in the Devil's name,) the idol in again[9]. What shall I speak of men's private doings? Generally we heard, in our Josias' reign, when he had pulled down the high places, that our affections had been laid too low; that we had been deceived. And as for pilgrimages, pardons, and such idle toys, who would defend them? who would not confess that they had been abused by them? Yet, in that terrible interreign of Antichrist, a pilgrimage in Wales was straight erected. Fair fruit followed. Much resort unto it; and never any of the learned fathers opened once his mouth against it. Such is the trust to men:

---

[1] 2 Reg. xxi, & xxiii. [2 Kings xxi. 3. xxiii. 32.]
[2] [1 Kings xiv. 16. 2 Kings xvii. 20—23.]
[3] [2 Kings xvii. 19. Jer. iii. 8.]
[4] [2 Chron. xxxvi. 20. Ezra v. 12.]
[5] [Jer. xliv. 23. Lam. i. 8. Baruch vi. 2.]
[6] [Hosea iii. 4. *Song of the three Children*, v. 14. Willet's *Synopsis Papismi*, p. 461. Lond. 1634.]
[7] [Ezra ix. 8, 9.]   [8] [1 Macc. i. 10—15. 41—52.]
[9] [Bp. Pilkington's *Works*, p. 587. ed. Parker Soc.]

so ready and apt we are to follow, (as the Prophet saith, and as I did allege before,) the abominations of our own eyes; attempering God's service unto our outward senses. Whereby it comes to pass, as Lactantius doth say[10]: *Ut Religio nulla sit, ubi Simulachrum est:* " That no Religion is there, where an Image is."

And since, (to come near to our present purpose,) Crosses in market-places, and not in churches, are, (as by good proof we find,) great stumbling stones, not only to the simple, but also to such as will seem to be wiser; impossible methink it is, a Cross to be erected in place of God's service, and Him that hanged on the Cross to be honoured as He ought. For the mind is rapt from heavenly consideration to the earthly creature; from the soul to the substance; from the heart to the eye. Cause we can assign none other but, as the same Lactantius doth say[11]: *Esse aliquam perversam potestatem, quæ veritatis sit semper inimica: quæ humanis erroribus gaudeat: cui unicum* [al. *unum*] *ac perpetuum sit opus offundere tenebras, et hominum cæcare mentes, ne lucem videant; ne denique in cœlum aspiciant, ac naturam corporis sui servent:* " There is a certain perverse power, which always is enemy unto the truth: which taketh pleasure in man's error: whose only and continual work it is to overcast clouds and mists of darkness, to blind the minds of men that they see not the light; that they look not up into heaven, and keep the nature of their own body." For whereas other living creatures[12], in that they have not re-

---

[10] De fal. Rel. Li. ii. Cap. xix. ["Quare non est dubium, quin Religio nulla sit, ubicunque Simulacrum est." (*De origine Erroris,* Lib. ii. Cap. xix.)]

[11] De fal. Rel. Li. ii. Cap. i. [*De orig. Error.* Lib. ii. C. i.]

[12] ["Nam cum cæteræ" (al. cæteri) "animantes pronis corporibus in humum spectent, quia rationem ac sapientiam non acceperunt; nobis autem status rectus, sublimis vultus ab artifice Deo datus sit; apparet istas Religiones Deorum non esse rationis humanæ, quia curvant cœleste animal ad veneranda terrena." (Lactant. ubi supra.) This passage may naturally remind us of the derivation of Ἄνθρωπος, as given in Plato's *Cratylus;* and of the well-known lines of Ovid: (*Metamorph.* Lib. i. 84-5-6.)

"Pronaque cum spectent animalia cætera terram,
Os homini sublime dedit, cœlumque tueri
Jussit, et erectos ad sidera tollere vultus."

See Boys's *Sermon* for the third Sunday in Lent: *Exposit.* p. 83. Lond. 1610. Bp. Andrewes's *Sermons,* p. 465. Lond. 1635. Cicero, *De*

ceived wit and reason, bend grovelling to the ground; but we have an upright state, a countenance aloft, from God our Maker given us; it appeareth that that Religion and service of God accordeth not unto men's reason, which bends and bows the heavenly creature to worship, to kneel, to knock to the earthly. God would have us to look upon the heavens[1]; to seek for our Religion there, in that place which is the seat of His glory; to behold Him in heart, whom with our eye we can never see. And is not this an extreme folly, yea, a mere madness, to advance the metal which is but corruptible, to abase the mind which is eterne: whereas the shape and proportion of our bodies do teach us no less, but that our minds should be lifted thither, whitherward ye see our heads erected? Yet hath our enemy so enchanted us, that we have, for his sake, forsaken our friend; forgotten God, and ourselves too.

But he hath not done this at once and altogether: by a little and a little he hath crept in upon us; till at the length he hath wholly possessed us. At the first, Images, among christian men, were only kept in private houses, painted or graven in story-wise; which had some meaning and signification in them. Afterward they crept into the church, by a zeal not according to knowledge, as by Paulinus at Nola; yet nothing less was meant than worship of them. So that, at the first, they seemed in some respect to be tolerable, as means to excite men to thankfulness and devotion; until the Devil shewed himself in His likeness, and turned the glory of the immortal God to the service of a vile and earthly creature. Yet, if we had not seen that effect follow, which indeed we have, too lamentably, to the desperate destruction of many christian souls; we might, notwithstanding, justly condemn the whole faithless and fond invention. For it was but a willworship, a naughty service, having no ground of the word of

---

Legib. Lib. i. Cap. ix. Prudentius, *Cont. Sym.* L. ii. Opp. p. 403. Lugd. 1553. S. Cyprian, *Ad Demetr.* Opp. pp. 191-2. ed. Ox. Lactantius, *De Vita beata,* Lib. vii. Cap. v. *De Opificio Dei,* Cap. viii. ad init.]

[1] ["Spectare nos cœlum Deus voluit... ut Religionem ibi quæramus; ut Deum, cujus sedes illa est, quem oculis non possumus, animo contemplemur. Quod profecto non facit, qui æs, aut lapidem, quæ sunt terrena, veneratur. Est autem pravissimum, cum ratio corporis recta sit, quod est temporale, ipsum vero animum, qui est æternus, humilem fieri: cum figura et status nihil aliud significent, nisi mentem hominis eo spectare oportere quo vultum." (Lactantius, ut sup.)]

God, and only spring of error and Gentility. For, according to the commandment of the Almighty[2], "Every man must not do whatsoever seemeth good in his own eyes. Whatsoever God hath commanded us, we must take heed to it; neither adding any thing unto it, nor taking any thing away from it." Likewise the Prophet Jeremy doth advise us[3], "not to hearken to them that speak the vision of their own heart, and not out of the mouth of the Lord. For what is chaff to wheat?" And the Apostle, to the same effect[4]: "Whatsoever is not of faith is sin: faith is by hearing, and hearing by the word of God." Wherefore Tertullian doth well affirm[5]: *Quod nobis nihil licet de nostro arbitrio indulgere;* [al. *inducere;*] *sed nec eligere quod aliquis de arbitrio suo induxerit. Apostolos Domini habemus authores: qui nec ipsi quidquam de suo arbitrio quod inducerent elegerunt; sed acceptam a Christo disciplinam fideliter nationibus assignarunt:* "That it is not lawful for us to flatter ourselves with any thing of our own judgment and discretion; nor to choose that which any man hath brought in of his own head. We have the pattern of the Apostles for us: which took nothing to bring in after their own pleasure; but faithfully assigned to the nations the doctrine that they had received of Christ." Cyprian also[6]: *Non hominis consuetudinem sequi oportet, sed Dei veritatem; cum per Esaiam Prophetam Deus loquatur et dicat: Sine causa autem colunt Me, mandata et doctrinas hominum docentes. Et iterum Dominus in Evangelio hoc idem repeat, dicens: Rejicitis mandatum Dei, ut traditionem vestram statuatis:* "We must not follow the custom of man, but the truth of God; inasmuch as He speaketh by His Prophet Esay, and saith: 'They honour Me in vain, teaching the doctrines and precepts of men.' And again, in the Gospel, Christ Himself repeateth the same, saying: 'Ye refuse the commandment of God, to establish your own tradition.'" And learned Austin doth teach us no less, writing on this sort[7]: *Extat authoritas divinarum Scripturarum,*

[2] Deut. xii. [8, 32.]
[3] Jerem. xxiii. [16, 28.]   [4] Rom. xiv. [23. x. 17.]
[5] De præs. advers. Hæret. [*De præscript. Hæreticor.* Cap. vi.]
[6] Cæcilio fratri. Epis. 68. [Ad Pamelii et Episc. Oxon. numeros, *Ep.* lxiii.: Ad Erasm. Lib. ii. *Epist.* iii. Lugd. 1550.]
[7] De Trinita. Lib. iii. Cap. xi. [§. 22. col. 570. *Opp.* Tom. viii. Antw. 1700.]

unde mens nostra deviare non debet : nec, relicto solidamento divini eloquii, per suspicionum suarum abrupta præcipitari; ubi nec sensus corporis regit, nec perspicua ratio veritatis elucet: "There is extant with us the authority of holy Scripture, from the which our mind ought not to swerve: nor, leaving the substantial ground of God's word, run headlong on the perils of our own surmises; where we neither have sense of body to rule us, nor apparent reason of truth to direct us." Wherefore, sith the Scripture hath taught, and Fathers confirmed, that only God is sufficient schoolmaster; and His word prescribeth us one certain order, each man by preaching to be instructed in the truth[1]; what should we run to dumb doctors, which take out nothing else but lessons of lies? For, as Hieremy saith[2]: *Eruditio vanitatum lignum:* "The stock is a doctrine of vanity;" and Abakuk[3]: "An Image is the teacher of lies." Shall we then discredit the counsel of our God, saying[4]: *Scrutamini Scripturas:* "Search ye the Scriptures;" and follow the device of the Devil, teaching: *Contemplamini Picturas:* "Look upon Pictures?"

Let men bring in what pretence they lust, that Images do serve for men's instruction: yet evident it is, that they came from Gentility; and that doth Eusebius prove[5]. For he reporteth that he saw in the city of Cæsarea a certain Image. But where? *Ante domus illius fores:* "Before the door," in the street, not in the church; which old men said was made as like to Jesus as it could. Another Image there was, made like a woman kneeling afore Christ, holding up her hands; containing the history of her that was diseased with the issue of blood[6]. Now come to the judgment of the ecclesiastical writer on it. *Nec mirum videri debet, eos, qui ex Gentibus olim a Servatore nostro curati sunt, ista fecisse; quando et Apostolorum Illius Imagines, Pauli videlicet et Petri, denique et Ipsius Christi, in tabulis coloribus depictas asservari vidimus: quod veteres, ex Gentili consuetudine, eos, quos servatores putarunt, ad hunc modum honorare soliti fuerint:* that is to say: "Nor it ought to seem any marvel, that they, which

---

[1] [Rom. x. 14.]
[2] Cap. x. [Jer. x. 8.]
[3] Cap. ii. [Hab. ii. 18.]
[4] Joan. v. [S. John v. 39.]
[5] Eccl. Hist. Li. vii. Cap. xviii. [Calfhill quotes from the Latin version by Wolfgangus Musculus, p. 113. Basil. 1549.]
[6] Matth. ix. [20-22.]

from among the Gentiles were cured of our Saviour, did
these things; whereas we have seen the Pictures of His
Apostles, of Paul and Peter, of Christ Himself, reserved in
tables set forth with colours: because men of old time, (by
custom that came from the Gentiles,) were wont to honour, on
this sort, them that they thought to be the helpers and pre-
servers of them." In which words two things are especially
to be observed. First, that erecting of Images came from
Paganism[7]: when such as were newly converted to the Christianity could not clearly be weaned from all their Gentility;
no more than we, returning from Popery, can willingly leave
the rags of Rome. And surely many things might be borne
withal in them, which, being far stept in years, came at length
to the truth; and hardly forsook that, that all their lives they
had been inured to. And therefore, as, in Paganism, they
made Images of them that had well deserved; so, in Christianity, they did the like observance to Christ and His Apostles.
Furthermore, by the testimony of Eusebius it appeareth, that
in his time, (which was three hundred and twenty-five year
after Christ,) neither Images, nor Pictures, nor any such Counterfeits were brought into the churches, nor yet received of
all Christians; (for he made a wonder and strange sight of
that that he there saw;) but only privately some took it up:
not for Religion, not for God's service, but for a witness of
their own good-wills; as we, in our houses, have the Pictures
of them whom we hold dearest, and do love best.

The first that ever we do read of, to have brought in
Imagery into the church, was Pontius Paulinus, a Bishop of
Nola; which lived in the reign of Theodosius and Martian,
Emperors, four hundred and three score year after Christ. The
occasion of his inconsiderate zeal was this[8]. The people were
accustomed, every year once, to celebrate the feast of Felix the
Martyr; and in the church to banquet and make good cheer.
The Bishop, seeing some abuse therein, to the end he might
keep them from surfeiting and riot, caused the walls of the
temple to be painted with stories taken out of the Old Testament; that they, beholding and considering the Pictures,
might give themselves the more to temperance and sobriety.
About the same time, Prudentius reporteth, how he saw

[7] [" ἐθνικῇ συνηθείᾳ."]
[8] [Compare Bingham's *Antiquities*, ii. 508—9. Lond. 1840.]

painted and pourtrayed, in the church, the history of S. Cassian[1]. Thus Imagery came from private houses to public places; from painting also to embossing; yet neither privately nor openly, painted or embossed, we read that they were honoured, until it was about six hundreth year after Christ: when, through barbarity of Goths and Vandals, (which burst into Italy, spoiled all places, and burned libraries,) virtue decayed, learning went to wreck, Religion was little seen unto: then, by common ignorance of God's word, negligence of the Bishops, and unruly reign of barbarous aliens, Images were not only set up, but began to be worshipped. Therefore Serenus, Bishop of Massile, the head town of Gallia Narbonensis, now called the Province, seeing the people, by occasion of Images, fall to Idolatry, brake all that were in that city to pieces, were they either of Christ or of His Saints; and was therefore complained upon to Gregory, the first of that name, then Bishop of Rome. And as this was the first learned Bishop that did allow the open having of Images in churches, so upon him do all Image-worshippers at this day ground their defence. He reproved Serenus for breaking down of them[2]: he commended the having of them; but the worshipping of them he utterly condemned. He would not have had it to be abolished, which was set up not to be worshipped, but only to instruct the minds of the ignorant. He would have had the sight of the story; but the service and honour to the thing that was seen, he willed by all means to be avoided. How well this doctrine took place afterward; how soon the thing wherein he minded best came to wickedest end; the horrible mischiefs, that in the east and west Churches ensued, are a lamentable example to us. For although the Images taught not the people, but blinded them indeed; though, contrary to Gregory's determination, they were abused to most damnable Idolatry; yet have they had, and yet have their defenders: yea, with such zeal, such earnest affection, this quarrel of Images hath been maintained, that it bred a schism between the east and the west Churches; that it engendered hatred between one Christian and another; set Council against

Fruits of Images.

---

[1] [*Peristeph.* Passio Cassiani. *Opp.* p. 204. Lugd. 1553.
"Erexi ad cœlum faciem: stetit obvia contra
Fucis colorum picta Imago Martyris."]

[2] Epist. Libr. vii. Indict. ii. Cap. cix.

Council, Church against Church, Prince against Prince. Hence rose rebellions, treasons, unnatural and cruel murders; the daughter digging up and burning her father, the Emperor, his bones; the mother murdering her own son, being an Emperor[3]. At the last, the tearing in sunder of Christendom and the empire into two pieces: till the infidels, the Turks, (the common enemies to both parts,) have most cruelly vanquished, destroyed, and subdued the one whole part, all the empire of Greece; and have won a great piece of the other empire; and put all Christendom in most dreadful fear and horrible danger. All which matters are, in the discourse, more at large opened. Gregory, therefore, if he had lived but awhile longer; and seen the least part of all the miseries which all the world hath felt since, only for maintenance of those Mammots[4]; he would, and well might have cursed himself, for leaving behind him so lewd a precedent.

But, by the way, to prosecute a little the two points of Gregory's determination. First, that they teach not according to his will; then, that they be worshipped contrary to his will: if any instruction might be taken of them, and there were no peril annexed to them, God, that omitted nothing necessary for our salvation and comfort, would not so earnestly, in Scripture, have forbidden them. I refer you to the places themselves, most manifest in that behalf, too many to be rehearsed. But I have quoted the book, the chapter, and the sentence, that you may easily find them; and I exhort you to reading of them. Exod. xx. 4; Levit. xix. 4; Numer. xxiii. 23; Deut. iv.: from the first sentence to the 48; [40?] Psal. cxv. 4, and so forth; Psal. cxxxv. 15; Sap. [Wisdom] xiii, xiv, xv.; Esay xl. 18, and forward; Esay xlii. 8; Esay xliv. 9; Ezechiel vi.; Baruch vi.; Act. vii. 48; Act. xv. 28; Rom. i.; 1 Cor. v. 10; 1 Cor. x. 14; 2 Cor. vi. 14; [16?] Gal. v. 20; 1 John v. 21. And although there be none that think the gold and silver, the stock or the stone, to be God Himself; yet is it great prejudice, great derogation from the glory of God, to seek so great a God after so base a sort. Yet seeking it is not, but rather forsaking; whatsoever pretext or good intent go with it. Michah, when he had stolen the xi. c. sicles

---

[3] [Vid. Spanhemii *Rest. Hist. Imagg.* Sect. v. *Opp.* Tom. ii. Lugd. Bat. 1703.]

[4] [Mammets, puppets.]

[eleven hundred shekels] of silver from his mother[1], being somewhat religious otherwise, and fearing the curse that she laid upon the thief, confessed the fact, and brought the goods home again. His mother was glad; and, as the story witnesseth, did dedicate straight the silver for her son: not to any Idol, but to God Himself; and made an Image of it. When this was done, Michah set it up in his own house; builded a chapel; made an altar; prepared furniture; appointed service for it: the ephod, the teraphin, the alb, and the vestment; the Levite of Bethlehem, the Priest deputed for it. And say not here that I think Ephod to be Latin for an Alb, and Teraphin for a Vestment: but I know that by the names of Ephod and Teraphin all superstitious attire is signified[2]. Thus they pretended to serve God with an Image. Thus theft gave occasion of superstitions. Thus Idols brought in oratories, chapels and altars, sacrifices, vestments, and such like; which all be utterly condemned of the Lord. For it followeth in the history: "In those days there was no King in Israel; but every man did that which was good in his own eyes." But, in the Law, we read commanded the direct contrary: "No man shall do that which seemeth good in his own eyes[3]." Wherefore, in the same chapter, a certain place is prescribed, where God's service should be. And afterward, to the same intent, first the tabernacle and the one only altar; then the temple itself was builded by Salomon. Nor the temple was sooner reared, than a certain and due form of God's service was appointed: from which if the people any deal swerved, it was holden fornication; and the Prophets cried out[4]: *Dereliquistis Dominum, et serviistis Diis alienis:* "Ye have forsaken the Lord, and served strange Gods." This, as Michah did for devotion, Jeroboam afterward did for policy. For when the kingdom of Israel was pitifully divided, by the work of God, for Idolatry sake; and that only the tribe of Judah, with a few of the Benjamites, cleaved to the house of David; the rest of the ten tribes followed this wicked tyrant: he, fearing greatly lest, by the doctrine of the Levites, the kingdom might grow again into one body, if the people, ac-

---

[1] Jud. xvii.
[2] ["*Teraphim* were small Images,.. much like to Puppets." (Mede's *Works*, Book i. p. 183. Lond. 1672.)]
[3] Deut. xii. [8.]   [4] Jere. ii. [13.] v. [7.] xi. [10.] xiii. [10.]

cording to their ancient order, went up to Hierusalem to serve God; to the end he might estrange the people both from the temple and discipline of the Law, partly for fear, partly for ambition, instituted a new Religion: different from that which they had received; another than that which God appointed. Wherefore he made them two golden calves[5], not to be Idols, but to represent the true God unto them; and this in effect he said: "Ye have long taken pains to travel to Hierusalem. I pity your weary journeys: I have compassion of your great expenses. I have provided, therefore, that ye may serve God nearer home; that, at your own doors, ye may have the Religion, which is as acceptable unto God as that." Well did the wise worldling foresee, that without Religion no Policy could stand; and therefore he would have a cloke of that to cover his shame withal. He bringeth forth Images. He doth not use any new sacrifice or solemnities unto them. But, as the Israelites, in the wilderness, cried to their one calf[6], "These are thy Gods, O Israel, that brought thee out of the land of Egypt;" so do they now cry out to their two calves, "These are thy Gods, O Israel, that brought thee out of the land of Egypt." But, as they before were not so devilish and beastly, to think that Aaron's calf delivered them from Pharao his bondage; (for Aaron himself, at that time, said: *Festum Domini cras est:* "To-morrow is the feast of the Lord," not the feast of the calf or of the ox;) so now Jeroboam taught not, the people believed not, that those molten things were Gods indeed; but attributed to the sign the name peculiar to the thing that was signified: and although they directed their words to the Images, yet they erected their hearts unto God. Notwithstanding, Abiah[7] the Prophet said thus to Jeroboam[8]: "Thou hast done evil, above all that were before thee: for thou hast gone and made thee other Gods, and molten Images, to provoke Me; and hast cast Me behind thy back." For Augustin saith[9]: *Quisquis talem cogitat Deum, qualis non est Deus, alienum deum utique et falsum in cogitatione portat:* "Whosoever imagineth God to be such a one as He is

---

[5] 1 Regum [Kings] xii. [28.]   [6] Exod. xxxii. [8.]
[7] [Ahijah. Abijah was the son of Jeroboam.]
[8] 1 Regum [Kings] xiv. [9.]
[9] Quæst. sup. Jos. Lib. vi. Cap. xxix. [*Opp.* Tom. iii. col. 442. Antw. 1700.]

[CALFHILL.]

not, carrieth in his thought a strange and a false god." True
godliness telleth us, that we ought not otherwise to deem of
Him, than in His word He hath set forth unto us. Socrates
was wont to say[1], *Unumquemque deum sic coli oportere,
quomodo seipsum colendum esse præcepisset:* "Every god
was so to be honoured, as he himself had given in commandment." Wherefore, as Michah and Jeroboam grievously offended; so whosoever brings into God's service any thing of his
own device, he sinneth deadly. But Images, Crosses, and
Crucifixes are men's devices, whereby they flatter themselves
in pleasing God. They ought therefore to be abhorred.

Erasmus.

Erasmus saith, *in Cathechesi*[2]: *Ut Imagines in templis sint,
nulla præcipit vel humana constitutio.* He maketh an argument from the less to the more: saying, that not so much as
man's constitution doth bind that Images should be in churches;
therefore much less the law of God. For God, seeing the
inconvenience that should by them arise unto us, utterly forbade them; as the places above rehearsed prove. Let not
therefore the disguising cloke of a good intent make us shake
off the true garment of God, to transgress His commandment,
and derogate from His glory. Whosoever lead us but a little
awry from the path that Christ hath willed us to tread in,
lead us the right way to the Devil of hell. Beware ye therefore of these Syrene tunes, these enchanting charms, that wise
men of the world are wont to use, saying: "Bear for a time.
Use discretion. Be not too rash in reformation." We ought
rather to hearken to Christ Himself, which wills us "to walk
whilst we have the light[3]." If we suffer mists to be overcast
the clear shining sun, darkness shall sooner overtake us than
we would. There is but one gate whereby we must enter
into eternal life. There is but one way to bring us to our
journey's end. The least straying in the world shall make
us come never thither. And yet, not only for our own
sakes, but also for Christ's cause, we must take a wise way
herein. For they that go about to bereave us of our life,
(which is hidden in Christ,) would as well that God should be

[1] August. De con. Evan. Li. i. Cap. xviii. [*Opp.* Tom. iii. Par. ii. col. 8.—"Socratis enim sententia est, unumquemque deum sic coli oportere, quomodo se ipse colendum esse præceperit."]

[2] [*Explan. Symbol.* Catech. vi. p. 165. Basil. 1533.]

[3] Jean xii. [S. John xii. 35.]

disgraced in us. Wherefore, in controversies of our Religion, we should not only have respect to this, how dear our own salvation is to us, but also how far we further and advance the glory of our God. Then, if it were so, that Images were commanded, (as they are not;) and had their end to teach, (as they do not;) both our own profit, and honour of our God, might make us the willinger to embrace them. But, as they are not commanded, but accursed, so bring they no knowledge, but blind in ignorance. For if they do teach, it is for the shape, and not for the substance. Otherwise, the trees in the wood, and silver in the shop, might teach as well as they. If the shape do work an understanding in us, because it is made as the Image of a man or of a woman, then why not one Image teach as well as another? Shall the gayer coat, which maketh us peradventure more covetously disposed, or more wantonly affected, strike a more zeal of devotion into us?

We have seen Images in every church; specially of Ladies and of the Cross[4]: then why did they gad from London to Wilsdon, from Wilsdon to Walsingham, to seek for other Ladies? Could not the one teach as much as the other? Their eloquence, their voice, and diligence, was all alike. Why did my countrymen, from their own parishes, where they had Crosses enow, come on pilgrimage so oft to the very Cross of Ludlow? Why did they run from every corner of their own country to the Rood[5] of Chester? Unless ye will say, (as many thought indeed,) that the iron chain of that sturdy Champion, put about the neck, might save them from the hempen halter; which other could not do. Then must it needs be somewhat else than teaching, that maketh this people to give unequal honour to signs of equal Saints. Alexander the coppersmith will come in with his band; and there will be a stir, which shall be the dearest Diana to them[6].

[4] [Vid. Lewis's *Hist. of Eng. transl. of Bible*, p. 199. Lond. 1739.]
[5] [A Cross.—"Certe Saxones nostri Crucem ꞃob appellârunt. Etiam locum eminentiorem, quo in Ecclesiis sistebatur, posteri the Rodeloft." (Spelmanni *Glossar.* p. 494. Lond. 1687.) Calfhill seems to allude to an Image of S. George, the Patron Saint of England, who was represented "with a long spear, upon a jolly hackney, that gave the Dragon his death-wound, as the painters say, in the throat." (Bp. Hooper's *Early Writings*, p. 320. Cambr. 1843. ed. Parker Soc. Conf. Selden's *Titles of Honor*, p. 364. Lond. 1614.)]
[6] [Acts xix. 33, 34. 2 Tim. iv. 14, 15.]

Otherwise they would no more crouch to this Image or that, than they do the Bible[1]; which teacheth, (methink,) as much as they. Again, if they teach, let me ask them, whom? Learned, or unlearned? If they teach the unlearned, how can they know the Picture of Christ from the Picture of Peter? Because of the Cross. Why, both were crucified. But not after one sort. How know they that? They have learned it of other. But here they have lost the state that they were in; for they are now become to be learned. Of other also they might have learned moe lessons than that, and of more certainty. But the crown of thorn, the wound in the side, do make the matter plain. Alas, how shall the simple know that Christ was crowned, was wounded for us? They have heard it of M. Parson. Let M. Parson then preach it to them. If he preach not a truth with his tongue, the Picture by and by will teach a lie.

Stephen Gardiner.

I remember how Stephen Gardiner, (whose authority I use in answering of him who was Usher of the school where he was Bishop of the see,) was foully once abused by an Image. Whereas the King, in his great seal, was set on both sides; on the one side, as in war, the chief Captain; on the other side, as in peace, the liege Sovereign; that famous Bishop had found out there S. George on horseback: which the graver never made in it, nor the sealer never sealed with it. Yet, in his letters to M. Vaughan, of Portsmouth, answered afterward by the Council, concerning the same matter which we have now in hand, he useth these words: "He that cannot read the scripture about the King's broad seal, either because he cannot read it at all, or because the way doth not express it, yet he can read S. George on horseback on the one side." If his learned Lordship could not read aright such a common Image; if the inscription could escape his eyes; no marvel if the lay people were deceived in the like. I will tell you what these books do teach them. Carnal and gross imaginations of God: and give further occasion to feed their own wicked humour.

Amadys.

When Amadys, a goldsmith of London, lay at the point of death, his Parson presented him with the Cross; to put him, at the least, in remembrance of his Maker. But what his remembrance was helped thereby, his answer declares. For he raised himself in his bed, and said: "What is the price of an ounce?" Such is the fruit that the unlearned

[1] [Wicliffe's *Apology*, p. 90. Lond. 1842. ed. Camden Soc.]

receive by Images; yea, though they be of the best sort. As for the learned, they have better books: they need not to be warned with such idle workmanship. A lively Image is more to purpose than a dead. And if the proportion and shape of a man may move us, then why not of the living rather than the dead? If I see a poor man stretched on the Cross indeed; enemies scorning him, power oppressing him, and death afflicting him; he may for the remembrance do me more good, and for peril less harm: for I need not to doubt idolatry to him. But if I nail a dead Picture on the material Cross, and set it up in the church, my memory is little mended. I may peradventure, and not like to the contrary but I shall, be misled by it. Now suppose it were so, that a Crucifix in the church did tell me indeed, in most significant and plain letters, that Christ on the Cross died; what am I the better for that, unless I know that He died for me, and the mean how His death may be applied to me? But this by no Picture can be expressed. The promises in the word must declare me that; without the which, nothing is the Image, yea, worse than nothing. Will ye then have us to be put in mind of our estate and condition, of our redemption in Christ? No Picture can represent it; no piece of metal can set out that, which all the preaching, all the writing in the world, is not able sufficiently to beat into our dull and forgetful heads.

But oft we see that, by the Image or story, our memory is holpen. Hereto I answer, first, that it is an extraordinary, and therefore an unlawful mean: condemning the negligence of them that should be perfecter and lively remembrancers; and excluding, (as it were,) the word of God from his proper function. Then, also, there ought not any such forgetfulness to rest in us. Christ hath willed us thereof to be mindful ever. We should not stand in need of more outward helps, than He, (expert of our infirmities,) hath, of His mercy, provided for us. Consider this with yourselves; that, if an Image be put, it is an Image of God, or an Image of man. God is invisible, and hath no body: how can He then be pourtrayed? Shall we give a shape to Him, that hath no shape? "The Lord spake unto you," (saith Moses[2],) "out of the middle of fire. You heard the voice or sound of His words, but you did see no form or shape at all." And by and by followeth: "Take heed, there- Objection.

[2] Deut. iv. [12, 15, 16, 23, 24.]

fore, diligently unto your souls. You saw no manner of Image, in the day in the which the Lord spake unto you in Horeb, out of the midst of the fire: lest peradventure you, being deceived, should make to yourselves any graven Image, or likeness of man or woman." And again, in the same chapter: "Beware that thou forget not the covenant of the Lord thy God, which He made with them; and so make to thyself any carved Image, which the Lord hath forbidden to be made. For the Lord thy God is a consuming fire, and a jealous God." Thus God doth earnestly and oft call upon us to mark and take heed, and that upon the peril of our souls, to the charge that He giveth us. Then, by a solemn and long rehearsal of all things in heaven, in earth, and in the water, He forbiddeth any Image or likeness of any thing to be made. There followeth also the penalty; the horrible destruction, with a solemn invocation of heaven and earth to record, denounced and threatened to all transgressors of this commandment. Therefore, in the old Law, the middle of the Propitiatory, (which represented God's seat,) was empty; lest any should take occasion to make any similitude or likeness of Him. Esay, after he hath set forth the incomprehensible majesty of God, he asketh[1]: "To whom, then, will ye make God like; or what similitude will ye set up unto Him? Shall the carver make him a carved Image; and shall the goldsmith cover it with gold, or cast him into a form of silver plates? And, for the poor man, shall the Image-maker frame an Image of timber, that he may have somewhat to set up also?" And, after this, he crieth out: "O wretches, heard ye never of this? hath it not been preached to you sith the beginning; how, by the creation of the world, and the greatness of the work, they might understand the majesty of God, the Maker and Creator of all, to be greater than that it could be expressed or set forth in any Image or bodily similitude?" Thus far the Prophet Esay; who, from the forty-fourth chapter to the forty-fifth, entreateth, in a manner, of no other thing. And S. Paul evidently teacheth the same[2]; that no similitude can be made unto God, in gold, silver, stone, or any other matter.

By these, and many other places of Scripture, it is evident that no Image either ought, or can be, made unto God. For how can God, a most pure Spirit, whom man never saw[3], be

[1] Esay xl. [18—26.]   [2] Act. xvii. [29.]   [3] Joan. i. [S. John i. 18.]

expressed by a gross, bodily, and visible similitude? How can the infinite majesty and greatness of God, incomprehensible to man's mind, much more not able to be compassed with the sense, be expressed in a finite and little Image? How can a dead and a dumb Image express the living God? What can an Image, which, when it is fallen, cannot rise up again; which can neither help his friends, nor hurt his enemies; express of the most puissant and mighty God, who alone is able to reward His friends, and destroy His enemies everlastingly? S. Paul saith[4], that such as have framed any similitude of God, like a mortal man, or any other Image of Him in timber, stone, or other matter, have changed His truth into a lie. Wherefore, they that make any Image of God are plainly convict to be godless persons. I may reason with them as Arnobius doth with the Gentiles[5]: *Si certum est, apud vos Deos esse quos remini, atque in summis cœli regionibus degere; quæ causa, quæ ratio est, ut Simulachra ista fingantur a vobis; cum habeatis res certas, quibus preces possitis effundere, et auxilium rebus in exigentibus postulare?* " If you be assured," (saith he,) " that they which you think be Gods indeed, and dwell in the high regions of heaven; what cause, what reason is there that you make these Images; whereas ye have sure and certain things, whereto ye may pour out your prayers, and crave help when your need requireth?" So, if we have a God indeed, what do we with His Image? Forsooth, because we cannot see God any otherwise, we must both see Him and serve Him on this sort. So said the Heathen and idolaters[6]: *Quia Deos videre datum non est, eos per Simulachra colimus, et munia officiosa præstamus:* " Because it is not granted us to see the Gods," (quoth they,) "therefore we honour them by their Images, and do our duties towards them." But what doth this ancient Father answer them? The same that I do to all our Image-mongers: *Hoc qui dicit et asserit, Deos esse non credit; nec habere convincitur suis Religionibus fidem: cui opus est videre quod teneat; ne inane forte sit, quod obscurum*

Objection.

---

[4] Rom. i. [25.]
[5] Lib. vi. paulo post princip. [p. 195. Lugd. Bat. 1651.]
[6] Arnobius, Lib. vi. [p. 195.—"An numquid dicitis forte præsentiam vobis quandam his Numinum sub exhiberi Simulacris; et quia Deos videre non datum est, eos sic coli, iis et munia officiosa præstari?"]

non videtur: "He that saith and affirmeth this, believeth that there is no God at all; and is convinced that he giveth no credit to his own Religion: inasmuch as he must needs see that that he must hold; lest happily [haply] it fall out to be nothing, which is not apparent to the eye to be something."

And lest peradventure ye say, that these words of Arnobius cannot be applied unto our age, because he speaketh of Gods, and we acknowledge but one God; (although I might answer that we, having for the Image of our one God, in specialty, the same excuse which they, in generalty, had for all their Gods, are proved to be in the same fault with them; and, being in the same fault, must be partakers of the like shame; yet,) let us see whether his own scholar, which knew his master's meaning best, did not apply the pretensed reason to our one God, and Image of Him. Lactantius, *de falsa Religione*[1]: *Verentur ne omnis illorum Religio inanis sit et vacua,* [al. *vana,*] *si nihil in præsenti videant quod adorent: et ideo Simulachra constituunt; quæ, quia mortuorum sunt Imagines, similia mortuis sunt, omni enim sensu carent. Dei autem, in æternum viventis, vivum et sensibile debet esse Simulachrum.* That is to say: "They are afraid lest their Religion be void and to no purpose, if they see nothing presently that they may worship: and therefore they make Counterfeits; which, because they are Images of the dead, are like to the dead, for they be without sense. But the Image of God, who liveth for ever, must be lively and sensible." So far Lactantius. Wherefore, since God is not like unto these; for He is living, but these are dead: He hath neither hand nor foot, but these have both; though they neither strike, nor stand of themselves: He is neither old nor young, but these are painted, some gracious, some grisly, some lusty, some rusty; it followeth that they are not the Images of God, which are made by the hand of man: for, as Lactantius saith[2]: *Simulachrum a similitudine nomen accepit:* "An Image hath taken his name of likeness."

But some of the adversaries will not, in this, contend with me. They may, perhaps, grant an abuse in the Image of the Father; (whom, notwithstanding, they have suffered to stand in every church and chapel, like an old man, with a grey beard, and a furred gown, even as the painter's conceit did serve him;)

---

[1] Li. ii. Cap. ii. [*De origine Erroris*, L. ii. C. ii.]   [2] [Loc. sup. cit.]

but the Image of the Son, because He is made man for our sakes, may, (as a man,) be set forth unto us. And, therefore, they write how Christ did send His Picture to Abgar, King of Edissenes[3]. But, as it is not like that any such matter should be, and Eusebius, writing the history at the full[4], omit it; so, that we neither may, nor ought, make any Image of Christ Himself, shall by good reason appear. And, first, imagine that it were possible to have the true Counterfeit of Christ; it followeth not, therefore, that we ought to have it. For, in all cases that concern Religion, it is not only to be enquired, whether a thing may be done or no; but whether it be lawful, and agreeable to God's word, to be done or no. For all wickedness may be, and is, daily done; which yet ought not to be done. Wherefore Augustin[5] counsels us, "that we love not those sights that be subject to the eye; lest, swerving from the truth, and loving shadows, we be cast into darkness. Let not our Religion consist in our own fancies: for any truth, whatsoever it be, is better than any thing that can, of our own head, be devised of us."

But some will say, What truth have ye for you, that Images are utterly forbidden? I might refer them to that which is said and proved before: but, because they are contentious, I will add somewhat else; yet nothing beside the Commandment itself[6]: "Thou shalt not make any likeness of any thing in heaven above, in earth beneath, or in the water under the earth." Could any more be forbidden and said than this: either of the kinds of Images, which be either carved, molten, or otherwise similitudes; or of things whereof Images are forbidden to be

Objection.

---

[3] [".. Abagaro autem Christus Deus, quoniam eum videre gestiebat, transmisit." (Synod. Nicæn. II. Act. v.—*Concilia Generalia*, iii. 561. Romæ, 1612.)]

[4] [*Eccles. Hist.* Lib. i. Cap. xiii. Conf. Evagr. L. iv. C. xxvii. Nicephor. Lib. ii. Cap. vii. The earliest witness, in support of the fable of the Edessan Image, is Evagrius Epiphaniensis; who concluded his History in the year 594. Vid. Lib. vi. Cap. ult. Cavei *Hist. Lit.* Baronii *Annall.* Tom. viii. ad an. 594. n. xxx.]

[5] De vera Reli. To. i. Cap. ultimo. [*Opp.* Tom. i. col. 587. §§. 107, 108. Antw. 1700.—"Non diligamus visibilia spectacula; ne, ab ipsa veritate aberrando, et amando umbras, in tenebras projiciamur. Non sit nobis Religio in phantasmatis nostris. Melius est enim qualecumque verum quam omne quidquid pro arbitrio fingi potest."]

[6] Exod. xx. [4.]

made? Are not all things either in heaven, earth, or water under the earth? Be not our Images of Christ, and His Cross, likenesses of things in heaven, earth, or under the earth? If they say, that this Commandment concerneth the Jews only, to whom the Law was given; I answer, with all the Fathers of the Church, that it was moral, and not ceremonial: therefore it bindeth as well us as them. If they say, that these and such other prohibitions concern the Idols of the Gentiles, and not our Images; Epiphanius[1] shall answer them: who did rent a painted cloth, wherein was the Picture of Christ, or of some Saint; affirming it "to be against our Religion, that any such Image should be had in the temple[2]." Irenæus[3] also shall answer them: who reproved the heretics

Objection.

Objection.

[1] In Epist. ad Ioan. Patriar. Ierosoli. ["Deinceps præcipere, in Ecclesia Christi ejusmodi [al. istiusmodi] vela, quæ contra Religionem nostram veniunt, non appendi."—This Epistle is extant in Latin, among the works of S. Jerom, who has translated it. (Vid. *Æpistt. S. Hieron.* Par. i. Tract. iii. Ep. xix. sig. m ii. Lugd. 1508. Conf. *Apol. adv. Rufin.*) It appears as an addition to the Latin version of the works of S. Epiphanius, by the prohibited writer Janus Cornarius, Basil. 1578; and was not contained in the first impression, Ib. 1543. As to the date of the latter, Possevinus, Du Pin and Cave are greatly mistaken: for there could not have been any edition published by Cornarius in 1533, or 1540, as his Dedication was written on the Calends of November, 1542. Baronius, Bellarmin, Spondanus, Duræus, and many other Romanists find it convenient to deny the integrity of this Epistle: but it is distinctly adduced as genuine evidence in the *Caroline Books*, (iv. xxv.) composed about the year 790; and in the Acts of the Synod of Paris, held A. D. 825. (Goldasti *Imperialia Decreta*, p. 665. Francof. 1608.) Alphonsus a Castro candidly reproaches S. Epiphanius for having been an Iconoclast. (*Cont. Hæres.* de Imagg.) Waldensis, "cum magistro Roberto," supposes that he was "seized with zeal, but not according to knowledge;" (*Sacramentalia*, Tit. xix. Cap. clvii. fol. cccxxv. Paris. 1523.) and John Damascen decides the point by saying that "One swallow makes no summer." (*Apol. pro ven. S. Imagin.* Lib. i. fol. 15, b. Paris. 1555. Conf. Baxter's *Key for Catholicks*, p. 167. Lond. 1659. Natal. Alexand. *Hist. Eccles.* Sæc. iv. C. vi. Art. xxviii. Paris. 1699. Hospinian. *De Templis*, fol. 49, b. Tiguri, 1587. Stillingfleet's *Defence of Discourse*, p. 501. Lond. 1676.)]

[2] ["Tale enim Simulacrum Deo nefas est Christiano in templo collocare." (S. August. *Lib. de Fide et Symb.* Cap. vii. §. 14. Opp. Tom. vi. col. 116.)]

[3] Li. i. Cap. xxiv. [*Adv. Hæres.* p. 61. Paris. 1575.—" Gnosticos se autem vocant: etiam Imagines quasdam quidem depictas, quasdam

called *Gnostici*, for that they carried about the Image of Christ, made truly after His own proportion, in Pilate's time, (as they said;) and therefore more to be esteemed than these lying Images of Him which we now have. Augustin[4] also shall answer: who greatly alloweth M. Varro, affirming "that Religion is most pure without Images;" and saith himself[5]: "Images be of more force to crook an unhappy soul, than to teach and instruct it." And he saith further: "Every child, yea, every beast, knoweth that it is not God that they see. Wherefore, then, doth the Holy Ghost so often warn us of that which all men know?" He answereth thus: "For when Images are placed in temples, and set in honourable sublimity[6], and begin once to be worshipped, forthwith breedeth the most vile affection of error." Thus all the Doctors have thought the Commandment to extend to us; and that our Images are forbidden by it.

Now, if they will yet reply and say, that Images are in- Objection.

autem et de reliqua materia fabricatas habent; dicentes formam Christi factam a Pilato, illo in tempore quo fuit Jesus cum hominibus." Conf. S. Epiphan. cont. Carpocr. *Hæres*. xxvii.]

[4] De Civitate Dei, Libr. iv. Cap. iii. [Cap. xxxi.—"Quapropter cum solos dicit animadvertisse quid esset Deus, qui Eum crederent animam mundum gubernantem; castiusque existimat sine Simulacris observari Religionem; quis non videat quantum propinquaverit veritati?"]

[5] In Psal. xxxvi. & Psal. cxiii. [*Enarr. in Psal.* cxiii. Serm. ii. §. vi.—"Plus enim valent Simulacra ad curvandam infelicem animam ... quam ad corrigendam."—Item §. iii. (Conf. §. ii. et *Enarr. in Psal.* xxxvi. Serm. ii. §. xiii.) "Quis puer interrogatus non hoc certum esse respondeat, quod 'Simulacra Gentium os habent, et non loquentur; oculos habent, et non videbunt;' et cætera quæ divinus sermo contexuit? Cur ergo tantopere Spiritus Sanctus curat Scripturarum plurimis locis hæc insinuare, atque inculcare velut inscientibus, quasi non omnibus apertissima atque notissima; nisi quia species membrorum, quam naturaliter in animantibus viventem videre, atque in nobismetipsis sentire consuevimus, quamquam, ut illi asserunt, in signum aliquod fabrefacta, atque eminenti collocata suggestu, cum adorari atque honorari a multitudine cœperit, parit in unoquoque sordidissimum erroris affectum?"]

[6] [Calfhill here, as on an occasion previously noted, seems to have had other words of S. Augustin likewise in his mind: for elsewhere we find the expressions, "Verumtamen cum his *locantur* sedibus, *honorabili sublimitate*," &c. (*Epist.* cii. Quæst. iii. §. 18. Opp. Tom. ii. col. 212.)]

deed forbidden; not to be had, but to be worshipped: for, otherwise, the works in cloths of arras, the Images in Princes' coins, the art of painting, and carving, &c., were wicked: I answer to this, that Images, for no superstition; Images of none worshipped, nor in danger to be worshipped, are indeed tolerable: but Images, placed in public temples, cannot be possibly without danger of worshipping; and therefore are not there to be suffered. The Jews, to whom this law was first given, (who should, of congruence, have the true sense and meaning of it,) thought that it was so generally to be taken, that neither, in the beginning, they had any Images publicly in their temples, as Josephus writeth; neither, after the restitution of the temple, would, by any means, consent to Herod[1], Pilate[2], or Petronius[3], that Images in the temple at Hierusalem should be placed only; although no worship was required at their hands: but rather offered themselves to the death, than to assent that Images should once be placed in the temple of God. Neither would they suffer any Image-maker to dwell among them[4]. Origen addeth this cause: "Lest their minds should be plucked from God, to the contemplation of earthly things." The Turks, taking some part of their Religion, observe, to this day, the same. For he that writeth their story, annexed to the Alchoran, saith[5]: *Picturas seu sculpturas omnium Imaginum sic abhorrent et*

---

[1] Anti. Jud. Li. xvii. Cap. viii. [*Antiqq.* xvii. Cap. vi. §. ii. Vol. i. pp. 842—3. ed. Havercamp.—Lib. ιζ'. Κεφ. ή. p. 529. edit. princ. Basil. 1544.—Lib. xvii. C. viii. p. 596. Colon. 1691. Conf. *Bell. Jud.* Lib. i. Cap. xxxiii. §. ii.]

[2] Lib. xviii. Ca. v. [*Antiqq.* xviii. Cap. iii. §. i. ed. Haverc. Vol. i. p. 875.—Lib. ιή. Κεφ. δ'. p. 551. ed. Basil.—L. xviii. Cap. iv. p. 621. ed. Colon. Cf. *Bell. Jud.* ii. ix. §§. ii, iii.]

[3] Lib. xviii. Ca. xv. [*Ant.* Lib. xviii. Cap. viii. Vol. i. p. 899. ed. Hav.—Lib. ιή. Κεφ. ιά. p. 568. ed. Basil.—L. xviii. Cap. xi. p. 639. ed. Colon. Conf. *Bell. Jud.* ii. x.]

[4] ["Nam in civitatem eorum nullus Pictor admittebatur; nullus Statuarius; legibus totum hoc genus arcentibus: ne qua occasio præberetur hominibus crassis; neve animi eorum a Dei cultu avocarentur ad res terrenas, per hujusmodi illecebras." (Origenes, *Contra Celsum*, Lib. iv. pp. 181—2. ed. Spencer. Cantab. 1658.)]

[5] Cap. x. ["Unde, ex hoc Alcorano edocti Turci, hunc hodie observant vivendi morem; ut frater ille, qui duos et viginti annos illic servierat captivus, prodidit. Inprimis Imagines omnes, seu pictas, seu sculptas, abhorrent ac detestantur; usque adeo ut Christianos, quoniam his oblectantur, Idolatras, Dæmonumque cultores, et vocitent

detestantur, ut Christianos qui in hiis tantum delectantur, Idololatras et cultores Dæmonum vocent, et in veritate esse credant. Unde, dum essem in Chio, et ambasiatoribus Turcorum pro recipiendo tributo illuc venientibus, introductis in ecclesiam nostram, vellem persuadere de Imaginibus; nequaquam acquiescentes, sed omnibus rationibus refutatis, hoc solum affirmabant, Vos Idola colitis. Which words may thus be turned into English: "They so abhor and detest all painting and graving of any Images, that they call, and verily believe, the Christians that only delight in them, to be idolaters and worshippers of Devils. Wherefore, when I was in Chio, and would have persuaded the ambassadors of the Turks, which came thither to receive tribute, (after I had brought them into our church,) as touching Images; they would not agree, but, refuting all reason, this only they affirmed, 'You worship Idols.'" And surely Jews and Turks will never come to our Religion, while these stumbling-blocks of Images remain amongst us, and lie in their way.

Now that I have proved, as well by the words of Scripture, as by the true sense and meaning of it, so understood of all the faithful, that it is a piece of infidelity, to have an Image in place of God's service, it might suffice to decise the controversy that is in hand. But an Image cannot be made of Christ, unless it be a lying Image; as the Scripture peculiarly calleth Images lies, as I proved before. For Christ is God and man. And since, of the Godhead, which is the most excellent part, no Image can be made, it is falsely called the Image of Christ; and they that do apply any honour to it are mere idolaters: making Christ thereby inferior to the Father; cleaving only to His humanity; whereas we are, by Christ's own words, commanded, "that all should so honour the Son as they honour the Father[6]." But, against this, a crafty Papist may reply and say, that, by the same reason, it is not lawful to paint a man; for he consisteth of soul and body; and the soul, which is the chief part of him, no art or cunning is able to express. But I answer to this, that the reason is nothing like. For the soul may be severed from the body; as daily, by death, we see experience: nor it is impiety to think upon or behold

et firmiter credant." (Jo. Cuspiniani *Turcorum Religio,* fol. 65, b. Antverp. 1541. Cf. Leunclavii *Pand. Hist. Turc.* p. 139. Francof. 1596.)]'
[6] Jo. v. [23.]

the shape of a man without a soul. But the divinity of Christ cannot be separate from His humanity: neither is it lawful to imagine an humanity without a divinity, lest we fall into the heresy of Nestorius; as, in the third article, where I shall have occasion to speak of the Council, assembled by commandment of Constantine the fifth, at more large is opened.

2. And, whereas Christ hath carried His flesh up into heaven with Him, no more to be known according to the flesh[1]; we, fleshly creatures, do fall from His will, and make a counterfeit of a mortal flesh; whereas His is glorified. Furthermore, unknown

3. it is, what was the form and countenance of Christ[2]. So many places, so many Images[3]; and every one of them, (as they affirm,) the true and lively Image of Christ; and yet never a one of them like to another. Wherefore, as soon as an Image of Christ is made, by and by a lie is made, which is forbidden by God's word. Wherefore, since our Religion ought to be grounded upon truth, Images, which cannot be without lies, ought not to be made; or put to any use of Religion.

Thus have I declared the unlawfulness of Images, in which respect they are intolerable. Now a word for the folly of them, which, among us, is nothing sufferable. Athanasius[4] appointeth two ways to come to the knowledge of God; *Animam, et Opera;* "the soul of man;" which, by the Word, may behold the Word, and so enter into the privy chamber of the Almighty: and, if that suffice not, "the works of God;" whereby the invisible things of His eterne virtue and divinity may be seen of us[5]. Then, us to seek any new ways, since these are ordained ever since the beginning and creation of the world, is too much foolishness. If we seek for comparisons, and will have one thing set forth by another, why should we not rather follow Christ's institution, than be addicted to our own devices? Christ, in the Scripture, hath resembled Himself to many of His creatures, which daily and hourly are before our

---

[1] [2 Cor. v. 16.]

[2] [The Epistle of Lentulus, alleged by Molanus and others, in defence of representations of the Saviour, is, of course, spurious.]

[3] [Videantur Reiskii *Exercitationes Historicæ de Imaginibus Jesu Christi,* Jenæ, 1685.]

[4] Oratione contra Idol. [*Contra Gentes,* §§. 34, 35. Opp. Tom. i. ed. Bened.]

[5] Rom. i. [20.]

eyes: and can we not be contented with them; but make new creatures, of our own heads, to put us in mind of our bounden duties? We see the light and shining sun; and see we not the power of Christ in it? We see the ways and doors to our houses; and see we not Christ, the ready path to heaven? We see the hens, clocking of their chickens; and see we not Christ, continually calling us? We see poor shepherds, feeding of their sheep; and see we not Christ, the true feeder of our souls? We see ourselves, the lively images and perfect counterfeits of Christ Himself; and shall Christ be forgotten, unless we have a Crucifix? There is nothing, I promise you, but madness in this meaning. There is nothing that can so lively express the affects, (as I may term them,) and qualities of Christ, as those things which He thought good to serve our understanding. Shall we then refuse the more evident argument, and fall to the darker signification? Shall we contemn Christ and His order, and set so much store by a blind Picture? Nero, I remember, was sometime so wanton, *ut gladiatorum pugnas spectaret in smaragdo*[6]. He had an emerald in his ring, that would give to the eye the resemblances of things that were before it. Wherefore, when the masters of defence came to play their prises[7], he would behold them in his ring. I wis[8] he might have discerned them better, if he had looked on their own selves, and not have tooted[9] in a stone to see them. But nothing can content the curious; and the flesh delighteth in her own devices.

Thus is it proved that Images do not, according to Gregory's mind, teach; but, in all respects, be vain and foolish: and, if they did teach, yet, by the Scripture and word of God, such schoolmasters are forbidden to us. Now, that they are honoured, contrary to his mind, experience of long time hath proved, and the popish doctrine hath confirmed. For order is taken how they shall be hallowed[10]: first, with exorcism of water and of salt; then with hypo-

[6] [C. Plinii Sec. *Natur. Hist.* Lib. xxxvii. Cap. v.]
[7] [Prizes, trials of skill.]   [8] [Pret. and Part. pass. *Wist.*]
[9] [looked pryingly. See Spenser's *Shepheard's Calender*: March; l. 66. Pierce the Ploughman's *Crede*, sign. B. i, B. iii. 1553. Fairfax, *Tasso*, x. 56. xiv. 66. Latimer's *Sermons*, pp. 283, 287. Cranmer's *Works*, p. 229. l. 3. Cambr. 1844. ed. Parker Soc.]
[10] In Pontificali.

critical and blasphemous prayer; afterward with censing, anointing, kissing, erecting, and an hundreth other most vile observances. Privileges and pardons be granted to them; candles and tapers be lighted afore them; much gold and jewels are bestowed on them: and, lest authority should want to error, in all their sayings, in all their writings, and in their general Councils, they have confirmed the worshipping of them; as in the second at Nice [1], and that which was assembled at Rome by Gregory the third [2]. But, of these idolatrous deeds and doctrines, I shall have occasion hereafter to entreat. Sufficeth now that I have shewed, how the Devil abuseth the works of God, to his own purpose: how Images have crept into the church: how necessarily they are naught: both by the word of God, and authority of good men condemned. And, sith they teach not otherwise than lies; and are, notwithstanding, honoured, to the shame of us, and derogation of God's glory; they ought, in general, to be removed from the place of peril; the place of God's service. We must not give place to our own reason: we must not measure God with the line of our fancies; but build according to the plat [3] laid before us, and shew our thankfulness by obedience. If we once give place to our enemy, which daily doth assault us, I confess, (with Martiall,) that we give occasion of our own fall. ' If we be not circumspect, and wise in Christ, we shall unwares be set upon and betrayed. We see how he suborneth his ministers, by all crafty means to seduce us, if he can. They were wont to say: "There is small store of Saints, when the Devil carrieth the Cross:" but we may justly suspect, that there is small goodness in the Cross, when it is carried by the Devil and his Saints. Martiall, much like to Virgil's Sinon, (of whom he took a precedent, to make an artificial lie,) for three leaves together, in his preface, telleth undoubted trothes [4]; to the end that the falsehoods, which, foolishly, (God wot,) he doth infer, may have the more credit. And whensoever I bring any of Martiall's allegations, I note, in the margent, the leaf of his book, where ye shall find it; after this sort: Fol. with *a* or *b*, for the first or second page: because it were vain to recite more of his idle

Note.

---

[1] [An. 787.]
[2] ["Romanum V. & VI. ann. 731, 732. habita. In utroque de cultu Imaginum actum est." (Cavei *Hist. Lit.* i. 645. Oxon. 1740.)]
[3] [Plot, design: contracted from the French *complot.*]
[4] [truths.]

words; which might well increase the volume, but cumber too much and loathe the reader.

He beginneth, then, with a long process; and hath couched Fol. 3, b. all his eloquence together, to tell a good tale of his master the Devil. He labours busily about that, which no man contends with him of. There he forgat the rule of logic, *de Reciprocatione*. That is an ill argument which serveth both parts. I grant that Satan hath gone about, first by persecution and fear, afterward by fair promises, to make the moe to hang upon him. We have had experience of this in some of his own sect; whom D. Harding. these two Doctors, fear of death, and hope of promotion, within the space of a month instructed more than in seven years he could learn before. We see the trial of this in every one of the new colligioners of Lovain, who could be contented with all their hearts to reform themselves; unless, in their M. the Devil's service, they feared, on the one side, a new revolt and rage of Antichrist; and, on the other side, hoped to be Bishops, when the world should turn. *Rusticus expectat dum defluat amnis*[5]. They know what followeth. Now, to turn the weapon on their own heads. Because the providence and mercy of our God hath frustrate their hope in their opinion too long, they have thought it best to make open war against God, and all honesty; to send for their friends, and summon their diets in the Low-countries. Thence have proceeded the popish practices: the smoky stirs that were blown in Scotland; the fiery factions inflamed in France; the Pholish[6] treason condemned in England; the popish conspiracy attempted in Ireland: that, as it hath been the old wont, and all the religion of Romish fathers, to maintain, by the sword, that reign of Romulus, first gotten by murder; to set sometime the mother[a] against the son; the son[b] against [a] Irene against Constantine the sixth. the father; the people[c] against the Prince; so they might set realms together by the ears, and arm the subjects against [b] Henry the fourth against Henry the third, Emperors. the Queen; themselves to be maintained in their pride and hypocrisy. When this hath not taken the desired effect, [c] In England, against King John, and Henry the second.

[5] ["Rusticus expectat dum defluat amnis; at ille
    Labitur, et labetur, in omne volubilis ævum."
    (Hor. Lib. i. *Epist.* ii. 42—3.)]

[6] [Polish; Cardinal Pole's. Vid. Schelhornii *Amœnitates Hist. Eccles.* Tom. i. pp. 11—276. Francof. 1737. *Works* of Bp. Pilkington, p. 497. *Early Writings* of Bp. Hooper, pp. 37, 38. edd. Parker Soc.]

[CALFHILL.]

(God giving wonderful and glad success to the noble furtherer of His word and glory,) they have thought it most gainful for them to come in with a new battle; a battle of books: whereof some already be come into our sight; and they say that more do lie in ambush. Thanks be to God, they shed no blood; though they breathe nothing else but sedition and lies. If it have pleased God, at any time, to raise more notable instruments in His Church, as Luther, Zwinglius, and Calvin were; as Knokes, Latymer, and Cranmer have been; to beat down the walls of the malignant Church; and most of them, with their blood, to bear witness to the truth: then are they condemned of the antichristians; and, with all words of beastliness and reproach, slandered. But now they have uttered themselves so far; their malice and impudence is so apparent; that their tongue indeed is no slander at all. They were wont to say, that a man should not belie the Devil.

<small>Folio 6, b.</small> What shame is it then for M. Martiall to belie the Saints? as, that the Reformation at Berna should be under Zwinglius; where he never preached, or had aught to do: the alteration of the state in Helvetia should be in the time of Luther and his abettors; whereas it chanced almost two hundred years before they were born, *sub Bonifacio octavo:* that knowledge of the Gospel in England began in Latimer and Cranmer's days; whereas, in King Henry the third his reign, an. 1374, not only Wickleife and many in his time, but also the King himself, began as good matter of Reformation: (as the Chronicles report.) But they will still be like themselves.

<small>Fol. 7, b.</small> And now M. Martiall brags of his master's arms and recognizance in his forehead. What it is that his forehead hath more than unshamefacedness, I see not: what his tongue hath, we may all be witnesses; the forward and faithful profession of his master. *Ille homicida erat ab initio, et in veritate non extitit, quia veritas in illo non est*[1]: "He was a man-queller from the beginning, and abode not in the truth, because there is no truth in him." Wherefore, dearly beloved, although this ape come forth with ten Articles, in imitation of ten Commandments; yet, God be thanked, they neither be the Commandments, therefore to be followed; nor Articles of our faith, therefore to be believed. But rather, (as in the process it shall well appear,) every one, (as he construes them,) swerves

---

[1] Joan. viii. [S. John viii. 44.]

from the faith; and therefore, by commandment, we ought to beware of them. Judge you indifferently. I appeal to the conscience of every Christian, whether we, (avoiding the occasion of Idolatry,) tend any whit to Paganism, as the Papists by their devices do: or whether we, (by removing all Images, and consequently the Cross too,) do derogate from Christ and from His passion, as they do; which, having the material Cross, cannot come to the knowledge and faith of The crucified.

I confess that I am more aspre[2] in my writing, than otherwise I would, or modesty requireth: but no such bitterness is tasted in me, as the beastliness of them, (with whom I have to do,) deserveth. Bear with me, therefore, (I beseech you;) bear with a truth, in plain speech uttered. Bayard hath forgot that he is a horse; and therefore, if I make the stumbling jade's sides to bleed, blame me not. Impute not to malice and impatience that which is grounded of hatred to the crime, but love to the persons which be touched. I hope, by this means, that, seeing their own shame, they will come to more honesty; or, hearing their own evil doings, surcease, (at least wise,) their evil speaking. They have nothing so rife in their depraving mouths, wherewithal to burden our ministry in England, as heaping together all base occupations; to Fol. 9, a, b. shew that the craftsmen thereof be our preachers. I wis I might answer, and justify the same, that as great a number of learned as ever were; as ancient in standing and degree as they, supply the greatest rooms, and places of most credit. Wherefore they do us wrong, to match the simplest of our side with the best of theirs. As for their famous writers, Rascall, Dorman, Martiall, and Stapleton; which now, with such confidence, make their challenges; be known unto us what they are. But they which, at home, be no more known than contemned, as soon as ever they taste the good liquor of Lovain, they be great Clerks, Bachelors of divinity, Students of the same; they must be magnified, they must be reverenced, as if Apollo suddenly had cast his cortayne[3] about

---

[2] [Asper, harsh; inclined to asperity.]

[3] [Curtain; from the Latin *Cortina*, the covering of the Tripod, from which the Priestess of Apollo delivered responses.

"Delphica damnatis tacuerunt sortibus antra:
Non Tripodas Cortyna tegit."

(Prudentii *Apotheos*. Opp. p. 289. Lugd. 1553.)]

them. But, to grant that the inferior sort of our Ministers were such indeed as these men of spite imagine; such as came from the shop, from the forge, from the wherry, from the loom; should ye not, (think you,) find more sincerity and learning in them, than in all the rabble of their popish Chaplains, their Mass-mongers, and their Soul-Priests? I lament that there are not so many good preachers as parishes: I am sorry that some, too unskilful, be preferred: but I never saw that simple Reader admitted in our Church, but, in the time of Popery, ye should have found, in every diocese, forty Sir Johns[1], in every respect worse. I could exaggerate their case alike, and prove it better; how bawds, bastards, and beastly abused boys, have been called to be Bishops among them: Sorcerers, Simoniacs, Sodomites, pestilent, perjured, poisoners, have been advanced to be Popes among them. Shall this derogate from their holy see? Yet none of ours, of any calling or name amongst us, can, of envy itself, be burdened with the like. As for the rascal of their Religion, what were they? what are they? Adulterous, blasphemous, covetous, desperate, extreme, foolish, gluttons, harlots, ignorants: and so go through the cross row of letters, and truly end it with *Est Amen*. Therefore, if they urge us any further with imperfection in our state; thereby to bring us into contempt and hatred; we will descend to particularities, and detect their filth to the whole world.

We are not, (dear Christians,) the men that the adversaries of the truth report us: we do not lean to our own wisdoms; we prefer not our sayings before the Decrees of ancient Fathers: but, after the advice of the Fathers themselves, we prefer the Scriptures before men's pleasures. This may we do without offence, (I trust.) The Popes themselves have permitted us this. Eleutherius the Pope, writing to Lucius, King of England[2], said thus unto him: *Petiistis*

---

[1] [Or Mass-Johns; though the latter nickname has frequently been given to Presbyterian teachers. See Bp. Sage's *Presbytery examined:* Works, Vol. i. pp. 360—61. Edinb. 1844. ed. Spottiswoode Soc. Compare Chaucer's *Canterbury Tales*, 14816. Spenser's *Shepheard's Calender:* May; 309. Care's *Weekly Pacquet of Advice from Rome*, Vol. i. p. 126. Lond. 1679. Becon's Displaying of the Popish Mass: *Prayers,* &c. p. 267. Latimer's *Sermons*, p. 317. Camb. 1844. edd. Parker Soc.]

[2] In the ancient Records of London, remaining in the Guildhall. [The entire of the Rescript, ascribed to Pope Eleutherus, or Eleu-

a nobis leges Romanas et Cæsaris vobis transmitti, quibus in regno Britanniæ uti voluistis. Leges Romanas et Cæsaris semper reprobare possumus; legem Dei nequaquam. Suscepistis enim, miseratione divina, in regno Britanniæ, legem et fidem Christi. Habetis penes vos in regno utranque paginam. Ex illis, per Dei gratiam, per consilium regni vestri, sume legem; et per illam, Dei patientia, vestrum rege Britanniæ regnum. Vicarius vero Dei esto in regno illo; &c.: "Ye have required of us to send the Roman and imperial laws unto you, to use the same in your realm of England. We may always reject the laws of Rome, and laws of the Emperor; but so can we not the law of God. For ye have received, through the mercy of God, the law and faith of Christ into your kingdom. You have both the Testaments in your realm. Take out of them, by the grace of God, and advice of your subjects, a law; and by that law, through God's sufferance, rule your realm. But be you God's Vicar in that kingdom;" and so forth. If the Lovanists had but a mangled piece of such a precedent for the Pope, as here is for every Prince, Lord, how they would triumph! They would decipher, and, by rhetoric, resolve every letter of it. But let that pass. It is enough, for this place, to shew the Pope's own Decree; that all men's

therius, may be found in Ussher's *Britann. Eccles. Antiquitates*, Cap. vi.; and it has been translated by Collier and others. There is not any certainty as to the exact date of the alleged conversion of Lucius, the first Christian King of the Britons; but the transactions connected with him have been generally referred to the latter half of the second century. With regard to the Epistle in question, though it has been greatly esteemed by many of our writers, there appears to be very little reason for believing in its genuineness. It was printed in the twelfth year of King Henry VIII.; and was afterwards inserted by Lambard in his work *De priscis Anglorum legibus*, published in 1568. (p. 142. ed. Wheloc. Cantab. 1644.) "As for the manuscript in Guildhall, London, it seems," (says Collier,) "at the most, to be no more than two hundred years old." (*Eccles. Hist.* i. 35. Lond. 1840.) Sir Henry Spelman observes, that the Letter is not to be met with until a thousand years after the death of Eleutherius; and where it was first discovered is altogether uncertain. (*Concill.* Vol. i. Conf. Parsons's *Three Conversions of England*, i. 93. Dodd's *Church History*, by Tierney, iii. 143. Lond. 1840. Soames's *Anglo-Saxon Church*, p. 26. Lond. 1838. Jewel's *Def. of Apol.* pp. 10, 11. *Replie*, p. 142. Ib. 1609. Fox's *Acts and Mon.* i. 118. Lond. 1684. Stillingfleet's *Origines Britann.* p. 58. Ib. 1685.)]

devices, be they never so worthied with the name of Fathers, may justly be repelled; and ought to give place to the law of God. Wherefore, if any, of their own imagination, have brought in any thing to God's service, not altogether consonant to the word; not we, but the word, doth wipe it quite away. For I think it meet, according to the Decretal, taken out of Augustin[1], *consuetudinem laudare, quæ tamen contra fidem catholicam nihil usurpare dinoscitur:* "to praise the custom, which; notwithstanding, is known to usurp nothing against the catholic faith." If this faith be retained, I will not contend with any; but the Fathers I will, with all my heart, reverence. The common-place of our adversaries is, to exhort the Prince and other, to keep the ancient Traditions of our Fathers: and I beseech them, with all my heart, that they will defend and maintain those things which they received according to truth. If tyranny of men hath brought in any thing against the Gospel, let not the name of Fathers, and vain opinion of Antiquity, bereave us of the sacred and everlasting Verity. What greater folly can there be than this; to measure God's matters with the deceitful rule of man's discretion; where the pleasure of God, revealed in His word, should only direct us? They that plead at the bar, in civil causes, will not be ruled over by examples, but by law. Demosthenes said very well: οὐχ᾽ ὡς γέγονε πολλάκις ἀλλῶς προσήκει γίγνεσθαι: "It is not meet that things should be ordered as otherwise they have often been." Much less should God's wisdom be set to school unto man's folly. Wherefore, to conclude; the only sweet water, to quench our thirsts, must be fet from the fountain of God's eternal will. There is the well that springeth up into everlasting life[2]. Beware of the puddle of men's Traditions[3]: it infecteth oft; seld it refresheth. We must not

---

[1] Dist. xi. Cap. Consuetudinem. [These are not the words of S. Augustin; but our author was deceived respecting them by some old edition of the Canon Law. They occur in a Decree attributed to Pope Pius I.; (Vid. Binii *Concilia*, Tom. i. p. 72. Colon. Agripp. 1618.) and likewise in an Epistle of S. Gregory the Great to the Bishops of Numidia. (*Epistt.* Lib. i. Indict. ix. Cap. lxxv.)]

[2] Joan. iv. [S. John iv. 14.]

[3] ["Let us diligently search for the well of life in the books of the New and Old Testament; and not run to the stinking puddles of men's Traditions." (*Homily on the knowledge of holy Scripture.*)]

use the pretext of custom; but enquire for that which is right and good. If any thing be good; if it profit, and edify the Church of Christ, let it be received; yea, though it be strange[4]: if any thing be hurtful, and prejudicial to the true simplicity of the Gospel, let it be abandoned; though fifteen hundreth years' custom have confirmed it. For my part, I crave no further credit, than the christian conscience, grounded on the word of God, shall, of indifferency and good reason, grant me. The Lord direct your hearts in his love and fear: confound Satan with all his wickedness; and give the glory only to Christ. His name be praised, for ever and ever. So be it.

[4] Chrysost. in Gen. Cap. xx. [xxx.] Hom. lvi. ["Nam si quidem bonum et utile fuerit consilium, etiam si non sit consuetudo, fiat: Sin damnosum et perniciosum est... etiam si consuetudo sit, rejiciatur." (S. Chrysost. *Opp.* Lat. Tom. i. col. 439. Basil. 1547.)]

TO THE FIRST ARTICLE.

HAVING to erect the house of God, whereto we ought to be fellow-workers, we are bound especially to see to this: that neither we build on an evil ground, thereby to lose both cost and travail; nor set to sale and commend to other a ruinous thing, or any way infectious, instead of a strong defence, or wholesome place whereupon to rest. The Apostle, commending his doctrine to the Corinthians, saith[1]: *Ut sapiens architectus, fundamentum posui:* "As a skilful masterbuilder, I have laid the foundation:" and "other foundation can no man lay than that which is laid, which is Christ Jesus." Christ hath received of his Father all things: He hath conferred upon us no less. He, by his death, hath made entrance into life for us. He is become our wisdom, our righteousness, our sanctification and redemption. By His name we must only be saved: by His doctrine we must only be directed: upon that rock, that faith of His, we must substantially be grounded. If any man teach other lessons than of that, we must say with Paul[2]: *Si Angelus e cœlo:* "If an Angel from heaven teach otherwise than the Apostles have preached to us, let him be accursed;" and with S. John[3]: *Quod audistis ab initio, id in vobis permaneat:* "Let that abide in you, which you have heard from the beginning: so shall you continue both in the Son and in the Father. And this is the promise that He hath promised us, even eternal life." "If any man do not bring this doctrine with him, do not so much as salute him; neither receive him into your houses:" for he that loveth God, heareth His voice, saith Christ[4]; and they in vain do worship Him, that teach the doctrine and precepts of men[5]. Men have their errors and imperfections; and, though they be the children of God, yet they be not guided by His good Spirit always. Every man, that hath an instrument in his hand, cannot play on the same; nor every man, that hath learned the science, can please the ear; but,

Men, in God His matters, not to be believed, without the word.

---

[1] 1 Corin. iii. [10, 11.]   [2] Gallath. i. [Gal. i. 8.]
[3] 1 Joan. [1 John ii. 24, 25. 2 John 10.]
[4] Joan. xiv. [S. John xiv. 21, 23. x. 27.]
[5] Math. xv. [S. Matth. xv. 9.]

if the strings be out of tune, or frets disordered, there wanteth the harmony that should delight: so, whensoever we swerve, never so little, from the right trade of God's holy word, we are not to be credited, we ought not to please. Wherefore, sith the way is dangerous, our feet slippery, that we fall oft, and are sliding ever, no marvel if the best of us sometime do halt. It falleth oft, that such as preach and profess Christ build sometime on Him evil, unsound, and corrupt doctrine. Not that the word of God is occasion of heresies; but that men lack right understanding and judgment of the same, which cometh only by the Spirit of God. And this it is that S. Paul saith[6]; how some do build upon Christ the foundation gold, silver, and precious stones; but some other timber, and hay, and stubble. Yet must we not take the hope of God's mercy from such evil carpenters as lay so rotten a covering upon so sure a building; whereas otherwise they, offending in trifles, be sound enough in greater matters; and stick to Christ, the only substantial and true foundation. Yet, such their errors and imperfections, being brought to the fire of God's Spirit, and tried by the word, shall be consumed. Augustin therefore, when he would frame a perfect preacher, willeth him to confer the places of Scripture together[7]. He sends him, not to the Doctors' distinctions, nor to the censure of the Church, nor Canons of the Popes, nor Traditions of the Fathers; but only to quiet and content himself with the word of God. Therefore, in the primitive Church, when as yet the New Testament was not written, all things were examined according to the sermons and words of the Apostles. For which cause, S. John writeth[8]: *Qui ex Deo est, nos audit:* "He that is of God, heareth us; and he that heareth us not, is not of God." So far, therefore, as men accord with the holy Scripture, and shape their writings after the pattern that Christ hath left them, I will not only myself esteem them, but wish them to

---

[6] 1 Cor. v. [iii. 11, 12.]

[7] De Doctrin. Christiana, Li. ii. Ca. ix. & sequentibus. [*Opp.* Tom. iii. col. 19.—"Ut ad obscuriores locutiones illustrandas, de manifestioribus sumantur exempla; et quædam certarum sententiarum testimonia dubitationem incertis auferant," &c. Compare the second Part of King Edward the sixth's first Homily.]

[8] 1 Joan. iv. [1 John iv. 6.]

be had in most renown and reverence. Otherwise, absolutely to trust to men, which may be deceived; and gather out of the Fathers' writings whatsoever was witness of their imperfection, is neither point of wisdom nor safety.

In every age, God raised up some worthy instruments in His Church; and yet, in no age, any was so perfect, that a certain truth was to be builded on him. Which thing, by example, as well under the Law, as in the time of Grace, God hath sufficiently, by His work, declared. Among the Jews, who was ever comparable unto Aaron? Who fell so shamefully? He assented, for fear, unto the people's idolatry. Among the Ministers of the Gospel, who had so great and rare gifts as Peter? Who did offend so fleshly? For dread of a girl, he denied his Master. Which thing was not done without the providence of Almighty God; thereby to put men in remembrance of their frailty; and further, to instruct them whence truth in doctrine must only be fetched. Trust not me, saith Augustin[1], "nor credit my writings, as if they were the canonical Scripture; but whatsoever thou findest in the word, although thou didst not believe it before, yet ground thy faith on it now: and whatsoever thou readest of mine, unless thou knowest it certainly to be true, give thou no certain assent to it." And, in another place[2], reproving such as will bring forth cavils out of men's writings, thereby to confirm an error, he saith, that a difference should be made between the assertions and minds of men, were they either Hilary, Cyprian, Agrippin, or any other, and Canon of the Scripture. *Non enim sic leguntur,* he saith, *tanquam ita ex eis testimonium proferatur, ut contra sentire non liceat; sicubi forte aliter sapuerint quam veritas postulat. In eo quippe numero sumus, ut non dedignemur etiam nobis dictum ab Apostolo accipere: Et si quid aliter sapitis, id quoque Deus vobis revelabit:* "For they are not so read, as if a testimony might be brought forth of them,

Aaron.

Peter.

---

[1] Pro loco Li. iii. De Trinita. To. iii. [*De Trin.* Lib. iii. §. 2. *Opp.* Tom. viii. col. 562.—"Noli meis literis quasi Scripturis canonicis inservire: sed in illis, et quod non credebas, cum inveneris, incunctanter crede; in istis autem, quod certum non habebas, nisi certum intellexeris, noli firmiter retinere."]

[2] Epist. xlviii. ad Vincent. de vi coer. Hær. [al. *Ep.* xciii. §. 35. *Opp.* Tom. ii. 186.—"Hoc genus literarum ab auctoritate Canonis distinguendum est."]

which it were not lawful for any man to gainsay; if peradventure they thought otherwise than the truth requireth. For we are in the number of them, that disdain not to take this saying of the Apostle to us : 'If any of you be otherwise minded, God shall reveal the same unto you'." Wherefore, with what judgment the Fathers of the Church ought to be read, Basil[3] setteth forth by a proper similitude : *Juxta totum Apium similitudinem, orationum participes nos fieri convenit. Illæ enim neque ad omnes flores consimiliter accedunt; neque etiam eos ad quos volant totos auferre tentant : sed quantum ipsis, ad mellis opificium, commodum est accipientes, reliquum valere sinunt. Et nos sane, si sapiamus, quantum sincerum est, et veritati cognatum, ab ipsis adepti, quod reliquum est transiliemus:* " We must be partakers of other men's sayings, wholly after manner of the Bees. For they flee not alike unto all flowers ; nor, where they sit, they crop them quite away : but, snatching so much as shall suffice for their honey-making, take their leave of the rest. Even so we, if we be wise, having got of other so much as is sound, and agreeable to truth, will leap over the rest." Which rule if we keep, in reading and alleging the Fathers' words, we shall not swerve from our profession : the Scripture shall have the sovereign place; and yet the Doctors of the Church shall lose no part of their due estimation.

There is not any of them, that the world doth most wonder at, but have had their affections; nor I think that you, (adversaries to us and to the truth,) will, in every respect, admit all that any one of the Fathers wrote. Myself were able, from the very first after the Apostles' time, to run them over all; and, straitly examining their words and assertions, find imperfections in all. But I would be loth, by discrediting of other, to seem that I sought some praise of skill : or else be likened to Cham, Noah's son; that, seeing the nakedness of the Fathers, will, in contempt, utter it[4]. But because, in ceremonies and observances, (wherein they scant agreeing with themselves;

None of the Fathers but have erred.

---

[3] Concio. ad Adolesc. [This is the well-known *Opusculum de legendis Antiquorum libris.* The translation here given is substantially the same as that by Leonardus Aretinus, Cap. vi. Argent. 1507. Conf. Fabricii *Bibl. Græc.* ix. 33. Hamb. 1804. The original may be seen in D. Basilii *Opera Græca*, pp. 226—7. Basil. 1551.]

[4] Gen. xxi. [ix. 22.]

every one discording from other, declined all from simplicity of the Gospel;) we are only burdened with the name of Fathers, give us leave sometime to use a Regestion[1]. Let us have the liberty toward other, which Hierom granteth against himself, saying[2]: *Certe, ubicunque Scripturas non interpretor, et libere de meo sensu loquor, arguat me cui lubet:* " Truly, wheresoever I expound not the Scriptures, but freely speak of mine own sense, let any man that list reprove me." Not that I will give so large reins to the headiness of some, which, either of affection or of singularity, will needs dissent; but that I will not exempt any from their just defence, from trial of the spirits whether they are of God[3]. We must follow the example of them of Berrhea[4]; which trusted not to Paul himself, but searched the Scriptures whether they were so. But whereas this precept is general; all men to judge, all men to try, what doctrine they receive; this judgment and trial, to be had by the word, is somewhat indeed, but yet not all that may be said in the matter. I grant the Scripture to be a good judge indeed; but, unless the Spirit of wisdom and knowledge do lighten our wits and understanding, it shall avail us little or nothing to have at hand the word of God, whereof we know not the sense and meaning. Gold is tried by the touchstone, and metals in the fire; yet only of such as are expert in the faculty: for neither the touchstone, nor yet the fire, can any thing further the ignorant and unskilful. Wherefore, to be meet and convenient men to judge of a truth, when we do read or hear it, by the Holy Ghost we must be directed. In this behalf, although I know that the gifts of God have their degrees, yet dare I say, that none is utterly so void of grace, but hath so much conferred on him, as shall be expedient for his own behoof; unless he be utterly, as a rotten member, cut off from Christ. Vain it were to command a thing that lies not in us; and us to deny the possibility, when we have a promise of a thing that shall be, doth argue our inconstancy and misbelief. Wherefore, sith Christ and

Two judges of controversies, the word and the Spirit.

It is possible to try a truth.

---

[1] [Retort.]

[2] In Apo. pro lib. contra Jovin. To. ii. [... "arguat me quilibet." (*Apol.* ad Pammach. *Epistt.* Par. i. Tract. ii. Ep. viii. sig. g, iii. Lugd. 1508.)]

[3] Joan. iv. [1 S. John iv. 1.]   [4 Acts xvii. 11.]

His Apostles say oftentimes, *Videte, cavete, probate;* which words be spoken in the commanding mode[5], and bid us see, beware, and prove; I must needs conclude, that we shall not be destitute of the Spirit of God, so far as shall be most needful for us, if we do ask the same by faith. And whereas Christ doth affirm that we shall know[6]; and S. John, in his epistle, doth assure us that we do know[7], *Spiritum veritatis, et spiritum erroris,* "the Spirit of verity, and spirit of error," we must acknowledge and confess, that the truth is not hid from us, further than we list to shut it up from ourselves.

But here ariseth a doubtful case. If every man shall have authority to give his verdit upon a controversy, which shall seem and say that he hath the Spirit, no certain thing shall be decreed; every man shall have his own way; no stable opinion and judgment to be rested on. Hereto I answer again, that there be two kinds of examination of doctrine; one private, another public. Private, whereby each man doth settle his own faith, to stay continually upon one doctrine, which he knoweth stedfastly to have proceeded from God. For consciences shall never have any sure port or refuge to run unto, but only God. He, when He is called upon, will hear our prayers: when He is desired, will grant us His Spirit. But He hath prescribed us a way beforehand to attain the same, if we bring under all senses of ours unto His word: *Si Patrem habetis Deum, quomodo non agnoscitis loquelam meam?* "If ye have God to your Father," saith Christ, "how falleth it out that ye do not understand my talk[8]?" *Oves meæ cognoscunt vocem meam, et non sequuntur alienum:* "My sheep," saith He, "know my voice, and follow no stranger[9]." Nor doubt it is, but, by the instinct of the Holy Ghost, we be made His sheep; which will not hearken to errors and heresies, (which are the voices of strangers,) but follow the voice of our Master Christ, which, in the Scripture, is crying to us. If these reasons and allegations may not prevail with some, to drive them to a sure and safe anchor-hold in Christ; let them run, and they list, to the other kind of examination of doctrine; which is the common consent of the Church. For, sith it is to be feared greatly, lest there arise some

Two kinds of examination of doctrine. Private. Public.

---

[5] [Imperative mood.]   [6] [S. John viii. 32.]
[7] 1 Joan. iv. [1 S. John iv. 6.]   [8] Joan. viii. [S. John viii. 42—3.]
[9] [S. John x. 4, 5, 27.]

phrenetic persons, which will brag and boast, as well as the best, that they be Prophets, they be endued with the Spirit of truth, and yet will lead men into all errors, this remedy is very necessary; the faithful to assemble themselves together, and seek an unity of faith and godliness. But when we have run as far as we can, we can go no further than to the wall: we must revolt to the former principles; and try, by the Scriptures, which is the Church. Wherefore, in controversies of our Religion, if men's devices were less esteemed, and the simple order of God's wisdom followed, less danger, fewer quarrels, should arise amongst us; more truth, more sincerity, should be retained of us. And, to this end, I could have wished that you, M. Martiall, should have learned, first, to frame your own conscience according to the word: then have ascribed such authority thereto, that we needed not, forsaking the fountain, to follow the infected streams; nor, having the use of sweet and sufficient corn, feed upon acorns still. But I would that had been the most fault of yours, to have attributed much unto the Fathers; and had not otherwise, of malice, wrested them; and, of mere ignorance, sometime corrupted them. The Scripture, which, in the title of your book, hath the first place, in the rest of the discourse hath very little or no place at all; and, under name of Fathers and Antiquity, fables and follies of new-fangled men are obtruded to us. To come to the instants.

The Scriptures last refuge.

First ye bring forth the significations of "Cross" in Scripture. Ye muster your men, whose aid ye will use in this sorry skirmish. And although they be very few, yet ye number one moe than ye have; and, like a covetous Captain, will needs indent for a dead pay. Ye say that the Scripture hath preferred to your band four soldiers: " the Cross of affliction; the passion of Christ; the Cross that He died on; and the material or mystical sign of the Cross: material, to be erected in the church; mystical, to be made with the finger in some parts of the body." These be not many, ye wot; ye might have kept tale of them: but the first and the second, as the word of God commendeth indeed, and be most necessary for our salvation, so will you not deal withal; they be too cumbersome for your company: the third ye confusely speak of; of which, notwithstanding, small commendation in the Scripture is found: the fourth, which ought to strike the greatest stroke,

Folio 18.

Folio 24,

ANSWER TO THE TREATISE OF THE CROSS. 63

is not extant at all. For neither the material, nor mystical Cross, in that sense that ye take them, to that end that ye apply them, be once mentioned in the word of God. Wherefore, ye might blot out of your book Scripture, and take to yourself some other succours; or fight with a shadow. I needed not to trouble myself about your third Cross, which is the piece of wood whereupon Christ died; both for because we have it not, and also you yourself do not take it incident into your purpose to treat of. Yet, because ye make many glosses thereon, and apply to the sign the virtue proper to the thing itself, it is not amiss to examine your folly.

First ye cite a place of Chrysostom, *ex Demonstratione* Folio 13, a. *ad Gentiles*[1]; and, for three leaves together, (although ye do not tell us so much,) ye write another man's words as your own, to praise your pregnant wit. But ye patch them and piece them ill-favouredly; and, whatsoever seems to make against you, ye leave out fraudulently. This is no plain or honest dealing. Indeed Chrysostom stoppeth many a gap with you. The comfort of your Cross doth most rest in Chrysostom[2]. But Chrysostom was not without his faults. Chrysostom. His golden mouth, wherein he passed other, sometime had leaden words, which yielded to the error and abuse of other. I am not ignorant that, in his days, many evil customs were crept into the Church; which, in his works, he reproveth not. He praiseth such as went to the Sepulchres of Saints[3].

[1] [See the extract in Gother's *Nubes Testium*, pp. 161—3. Lond. 1686.; and in the unacknowledged source of his authorities, Nat. Alexandri *Hist. Eccles.* Tom. v. pp. 638—9.]

[2] [Our author's unguarded language, in this place, may best be accounted for by the fact that, at the period when he wrote, it was immensely difficult to distinguish between the genuine and the spurious writings of the Fathers. On the present occasion, S. Chrysostom has probably been censured in consequence of the fictitious treatises, *In S. Crucem; De adorat. Crucis; De confess. Crucis; In adorationem venerandæ Crucis;* and the sometimes questioned Homily *De Cruce et Latrone*, which appears in the Appendix to the fifth tome of S. Augustin's works, and is numbered the clv. of the *Sermones de Tempore.* (ed. Bened. Antw. 1700.) The passages ordinarily made use of by Romanists may be found in the clviii. and clix. chapters of the sixth volume of the *Doctrinale Antiquitatum Fidei Catholicæ*, by Thomas Netter à Walden, Paris. 1523.]

[3] To. iv. ad Pop. lxvi. [The passage has been quoted by Bellarmin; (*De Sanctt. Beatit.* Lib. i. Cap. xix.) who, however, elsewhere confesses that *only twenty-one* of these Homilies are undoubtedly

He maketh mention of Prayer for the dead[1]. Monkery he commendeth above the moon[2]. In his tract of Penance[3], beside many other absurdities, (when he had rehearsed many ways to obtain remission of sins; as alms, weeping, fasting, and such other;) he maketh no mention at all of faith. In his Commentaries upon Paul, he saith, that Concupiscence, unless it bring forth the externe work, is no sin[4]. Wherefore, if he

authentic. (*Dé Scriptt. Eccles.* p. 100. Romæ, 1613. Conf. Possevini *Appar. Sac.* Tom. i. p. 855. Colon. Agripp. 1608. Crakanthorp, *Contra Archiepisc. Spalatens.* p. 413. Lond. 1625. Stapleton's *Fortresse of the Faith,* p. 279. S. Omers, 1625.)]

[1] In 1 Cor. xvi. Hom. xli. [Hom. xli. in 1 Cor. xv. pp. 592—3. Oxford, 1839. *Library of Fathers,* Vol. v. Vid. S. Augustini *Confess.* p. 165. ed. Oxon. 1838. Ussher's *Answer to a Challenge.* Of Prayer for the dead.]

[2] ["Dico Chrysostomum, ut quædam alia, per excessum ita esse loquutum." (Bellarm. *De Missa,* Lib. ii. Cap. x. col. 1083. Ingolst. 1601.) Vid. Morton's *Catholike Appeale,* pp. 46—51. Lond. 1610.]

[3] [It may be a matter for inquiry whether or not our author here alludes to the second of nine authentic Homilies *de Pœnitentia;* or whether reference be not made to what is the fifty-fifth spurious tract in the eighth volume of the Benedictine edition; the twenty-third false treatise in the ninth volume; or to the *Homilia exhortatoria in Pœnitentiam,* which Savile considered to have been the work, not of S. Chrysostom, "sed alterius, fortasse ex veteribus, mediocriter eruditi." The editor is in possession of a *Sermo de Pœnitentia,* strangely ascribed to S. Chrysostom; twice alleged by Gratian; (*Caus.* xxxiii. *Quæst.* iii. *Dist.* i. Cap. xl. & *Dist.* iii. Cap. viii.) and cited also by Peter Lombard; (*Sententt.* L. iv. D. xvi.) both of whom assign it to "Joannes Os aureum." It was printed, with other treatises, about the year 1480; and is generally annexed to Antoninus's *Instructio simplicium Confessorum,* though not contained in a copy now before the editor, and reputed to be of the first impression, about 1470.]

[4] [An exactly opposite sentiment is attributed to him in the Canon Law:—"voluntas, sine opere, frequenter peccat." (*Decr.* ii. Par. *Caus.* xxxii. *Qu.* v. Cap. x.) See also S. Chrys. Hom. vii. on S. Matth. *Library of Fathers,* xi. 104. Oxf. 1843:—"Think not," &c.; "for, in the purpose of thine heart, thou hast done it all." Compare Homily xv. *on the Statues,* §. 12. Vol. ix. p. 257. Ib. 1842. Vid. etiam *De Pœnit.* Hom. vi. Tom. ii. p. 316. ed. Bened. *De Resur. mort.* §. 2. Tom. ii. p. 425. Tom. i. pp. 249—50. Tom. iv. p. 769. Hom. xvii. *in S. Matth.* Tom. vii. 222, sq. Hom. xviii. 241.—Calfhill's charge against S. Chrysostom seems to have been founded upon an unreasonable interpretation of some words at the commencement of the thirteenth Homily *on the Epistle to the Romans.* (Tom. ix. p. 557.) It must be remembered that the language of the Fathers, upon such a subject, was regulated with more precision after the Pelagian controversy.]

had said so much for the Cross as ye misconstrue, and more than accordeth with the glory of Christ, I might lap it up with other of his errors; and, having the Scripture for me, Chrysostom should be no precedent against me. But I will not go this way to work. I admit his authority: but mark, M. Martiall, what his meaning is. In the place that ye allege for the Cross, he dealt with the Gentiles. The mark that he shot at was to prove to them, *quod Christus Deus esset*, "that Christ was God;" as in the title appeareth. Now, because this punishment, to be hanged on the gallows, was marvellous offensive unto the Heathen; nor they could think Him to be a God that was executed with so vile a death; Chrysostom, therefore, goeth as far in the contrary: proving that that, which was a token of curse, was now become the sign of salvation. And because that they spake so much shame of the Cross; derogating therefore from Him that was crucified; the Christians, to testify by their outward fact their inward profession, would make, in every place, the sign thereof. This was the occasion that the mystical Cross crept into custom. But here is no place to entreat of that; though you, taking still *Non causam pro causa*, that which is impertinent for proof of your matter, confound the same.

Notwithstanding, how things, received to good purpose, (as to the judgment of man seemeth,) may afterward grow to abuse, this sign of the Cross sheweth. That which was, at the first, a testimony of Christianity, came to be made a magical enchantment. That which was a reproof to the enemies of the Cross, became, in the end, a cause of conquest against the Christians. Nor it is to be thought, that wheresoever a sign of a Cross was, were it either in mountain or in valley, in tavern or in chamber, in brute bodies or in reasonable, there was by and by a zeal of true devotion; but as well, or rather, an heathenish observance, a superstition of them that never thought on Christ. We read that the Egyptians' great Idol Serapis had a Cross in his breast; and that sign was one of their holy letters. Whereupon Ruffinus reporteth[5], that many of the learned

Things well received, ill continued.

The sign of the Cross an heathenish observance.

---

[5] Li. ii. Ca. xxix. [*Hist. Eccles.* p. 261. Basil. 1549.] Sozom. Li. vii. Cap. xv. [p. 679. Conf. Socrat. Lib. v. Cap. xvii. p. 372. *Hist. Tripart.* Lib. ix. C. xxix. August. 1472. Niceph. Callist. L. xii. Cap. xxvi. p. 379. Paris. 1562. Casalius, *De veter. Ægypt. Ritib.* p. 49. Romæ, 1644. *De veter. sac. Christ. Rit.* p. 6. Ib. 1645. Andrewes,

[CALFHILL.]

among the Egyptians were the rather contented to embrace
Christianity, because they saw the Cross esteemed, which was
before a great ceremony of theirs. And we may well suppose,
that when they pulled down the Images of Serapis out of
their windows and walls, and placed in their stead the sign of
the Cross, they imitated the fact of the Apostle Paul[1]; who,
of the Athenians' superstition, did take occasion to preach a
truth: so these, to win the Egyptians to the faith, would
retain something of their old observance; but applied to
another meaning than they before did understand. So the
custom of running about the streets with firebrands, in honour
Candlemas-day. of Proserpina, was turned, with Christians, into Candlemas-
day[2]. The sacrifice of Ceres, done in the fields, with howling of
women, and crying of children, was made a general observance
Cross-week. with us, in the Rogation-week[3]. The Images of Mercury[4],
set by the highway sides, were afterward converted to Crosses[5]:
And where there was, in Rome, *Templum Pantheon;* a temple,
wherein all the Gods of the world were honoured; the devout

Pattern, p. 49. Lond. 1650. Tenison, *Of Idolatry*, pp. 123—4. Lond.
1678.]
[1] Act. xvii. [22—3.]
[2] [Calfhill may be traced to Erasmus here.—" Religiosi patres
arbitrabantur magnum esse profectum ... si superstitiosa consuetudo
cursitandi cum facibus, in memoriam raptæ Proserpinæ, verteretur in
religiosum morem, ut populus Christianus, cum accensis cereis, con-
veniret in templum, in honorem Mariæ Virginis." (*Modus orandi
Deum*, sig. e. Basil. 1525. Conf. Bedæ *De Temp. ratione Lib.* Cap. x.
Opp. Tom. ii. p. 65. Colon. Agripp. 1612. Baronii *Martyrol.* die Febr.
2. p. 63. Antv. 1613. Hildebrandi *Rituale Orantium*, p. 133. Helm.
1656. Bochart, *Traitté des Reliques*, p. 5. A Saumur, 1656. Raban.
Maur. *De institut. Cleric.* Lib. ii. Cap. xxxiii. Phorcæ, 1505.)]
[3] [..." Si qui segetem stultissimis ritibus lustrare consueverant,
aut Cererem puerorum ac puellarum cantu delinire, circumferrent per
agros vexillum Crucis, hymnos modulantes in laudem Dei ac Divorum."
(Erasmus, ubi supra.)]
[4] [" Si Pagani Mercurium ... viæ viciniæque præfectum statuebant,
quanto magis a nobis convenit Sanctorum Imagines in viis poni?" ...
"Itaque Crux in via posita," &c. (Molanus, *De Hist. S. Imag.* p. 199.
Lugd. 1619. Cf. Binii *Concilia*, iv. ii. 417. Middleton's *Letter from
Rome*, pp. 180—82. Lond. 1742.)]
[5] Con. Polon. 12. [Card. Hosii *Conf. Cathol. Fid. Christ.* fol. 12,
a. Antverp. 1559.—"Dejectæ sunt Statuæ Mercuriales, quæ viarum
indices fuerant; et earum in locum erectæ sunt Statuæ Christi crucifixi."]

fathers, to take away this idolatry, did consecrate a church in the same place unto All-Hallows[6]: that that should now be converted unto Saints, that before was attributed unto false Gods. And yet, whatsoever pretext of zeal they had, this was no good change, no sound reformation: to take away many false Gods; of true Saints to make many Devils: for so they are, when they be honoured; I mean, by that honour of invocation. So that it is not straightways allowable, whatsoever is brought in, under cloke of good intent; nor whatsoever hath been, upon good occasion, received once, (as this was never,) must necessarily be retained still.

^{Bonifac. IV. All-Hallow-en-day.}

Stephanus the Pope hath this Decree[7]: *Si nonnulli ex prædecessoribus et majoribus nostris fecerunt aliqua, quæ ullo* [al. *illo*] *tempore potuerunt esse sine culpa, et postea vertuntur in errorem et superstitionem; sine tarditate aliqua, et cum magna authoritate, a posteris destruantur:* "If any of our predecessors and elders have done any thing, which at any time could be without offence, and afterward be turned into error and superstition; let them, without any more delay, and with great authority, be destroyed of them that come after." Then, since this crossing hath bred such inconvenience, that, the externe action had still in reverence, the inward faith hath been untaught; and that virtue attributed to the sign, (which only proceedeth from Him which it signified;) the sign itself may well be left, and the signified Christ be preached simply. For, as Augustin saith[8]: *Noli putare te injuriam facere montibus sanctis, quando dixeris, Auxilium meum non in montibus, sed in Domino:* "Think not that thou dost any injury to the holy hills, when thou sayest, My help is not in the hills, but from the Lord;" so there is no wrong done to the Cross of Christ, if I say, not the Cross, but The crucified, is to be trusted to.

---

[6] Sigebertus in Chro. Li. x. [Jac. Ph. Bergomensis, in *Suppl. Chronic.* Lib. x. fol. 218, a. Brixiæ, 1485. Conf. Sigeb. *Chronicon,* ad an. 609. fol. 35, b. Paris. 1513. Freculphi *Chron.* Tom. ii. Lib. v. Cap. xxvi. fol. clx. ed. princ. Colon. 1539. *Mirabilia Romæ:* De S. Maria Rotunda. Middleton's *Letter from Rome,* p. 161.]

[7] Dist. lxiii. Cap. Quia. in paragr. Verum. [Cap. xxviii.]

[8] Lib. de Past. Cap. viii. ["Noli putare injuriam facere te montibus sanctis, quando dixeris, Auxilium meum non a montibus, sed a Domino." (*De Pastòribus liber unus.* Opp. Tom. ix. fol. 231, b. Paris. 1541.) In the Benedictine edition, (v. 158.) this treatise is *De Scripturis Sermo* xlvi.; and elsewhere it is *De Tempore Sermo* clxv.]

Which thing your own author meaneth, in the self-same place which is alleged; although it please you to suppress the words. For, after he had said, *Sparsa est in parietibus domorum, in culminibus, in libris, in civitatibus, in vicis, in locis quæ habitantur, et quæ non habitantur;* which place you cite, to shew what use, what estimation of the Cross was every where; the very next words that follow be these: *Vellem audire a Pagano, unde symbolum tam maledictæ mortis ac supplicii omnibus tam desiderabile, nisi magna Crucifixi virtus:* "I would hear of a Pagan, how it cometh to pass, that the sign of so cursed a death and punishment is so desired of all, if it be not the great power of Him that was crucified." This ye leave out, and yet have recourse again unto the words that follow; whereby ye would prove the sign itself to be a token of much blessing, and "a wall of all kind of security:" for so Chrysostom saith.

If, against my objection, ye do reply and say, that the power of Him which was hanged on the Cross made the Cross itself, and the sign thereof, to be of more virtue: that this was not the mind of the Doctor, the conclusion of his tale convinceth. *Hoc mortem sustulit,* saith he; *hoc inferni æreas portas confregit:* "This took away death; this broke the brazen gates of hell," &c. But did there any material thing? Did the piece of wood; did any sign work this effect? Was death and hell conquered by it? The articles of our faith do teach us otherwise; and the phrase of Scripture is far different. *Ipse salvum faciet populum suum a peccatis suis:* "It is He," saith John; [the Angel;] it is Christ, and not the Cross, "that shall save the people from their offences[1]." *Venit Filius hominis quærere et servare quod perierat:* "The Son of man came to seek and save that which was lost[2]." *Misit Deus Filium suum in mundum, ut servetur mundus per Ipsum:* "God sent His Son into the world, that by Him the world might be saved[3]." "As Moses lifted up the serpent in the wilderness, so must the Son of man be exalted; that all that believe in Him perish not[4]." These titles of honour, this work of mercy; to sanctify us, to purchase deliverance from death and hell; as it is acknowledged of us, so is it attributed,

---

[1] Mat. i. [S. Matth. i. 21. Compare S. John i. 29.]
[2] Mat. xviii. [11.] Luc. xix. [10.]   [3] Joan. iii. [17.]
[4] Ibidem. [S. John iii. 14, 15.]

in God's word, to Christ Himself, and not to His Cross. *Et qui loquitur, loquatur tanquam eloquia Dei:* "If any man speak, let him speak as the words of God[5]." Yet evident it is, that Chrysostom, by a figure of Metonymia, did speak of the Cross that which was properly to be applied to the Passion.

From Chrysostom ye climb up to Martialis, whom ye do make *Sapientum octavum,* one of the seventy-two Disciples. Eusebius saith[6], *Septuaginta Discipulorum catalogum nusquam reperiri;* "that the catalogue, the register of the seventy-two [seventy] Disciples is found in no place." But you place them at your pleasure; you are able to point them out with your finger. Hierom, Gennadius, Isidorus, making books, of purpose, of ecclesiastical writers, never do remember this author of yours; whom you, for the name's sake, do like the better. But if his anciency had been such as you pretend, it had been a great oversight of them to have so forgotten him[7]. But, to his place. "The Cross of our Lord is our invincible armour against Satan; an helmet warding the head; a coat of fence defending the breast; a target beating

_{Folio 15, a. Martialis.}

---

[5] 1 Peter iv. [11.]

[6] Lib. i. Ca. xii. ["Septuaginta vero Discipulorum catalogus nullus uspiam fertur." (*Hist. Ecc.* interp. Muscul.) De Discipulorum numero, vid. Blondelli *De lxx. Discip. Dissert.* ad fin. Gaulmin. edit. Lib. *De vita et morte Mosis,* pp. 488—90. Hamb. 1714.]

[7] [The fictitious Epistles of Martial, Bishop of Limoges, were first heard of in the eleventh century; and, from the year 1521, have been frequently published, and adduced by Romanists. His Life is said to have been composed by his disciple Aurelianus, whom, forsooth, he had raised from the dead; and it is appended to the *Historia Apostolica* of Abdias, fol. 154, sqq. Paris. 1566. Miræus (*Auctar.*) is mistaken in saying that Martial's Epistles were written in Greek; and Vossius (*De Hist. Lat.* ii. xxxviii.) apologizes for his having fallen into the same error. S. Gregory of Tours (*Hist. Gall.* i. xxviii, f. v. ed. princ. Paris. 1512.) makes the earliest mention of Martial's episcopate, as having been about the year 250; and Barthius (*Adversar.* Lib. xlv. pag. 2069.) conjectures that Aurelian of Rheims, who, according to Trithemius, lived A.D. 900, was the author both of the counterfeit Epistles, and of the Life. Conf. Placcii *Theatrum Pseudon.* p. 435. Hamb. 1708. Coci *Censur. quor. Scriptt.* p. 51. Lond. 1614. Fabricii *Bibl. med. &. inf. Latin.* xii. 104. Hamb. 1736. Le Nourry *Apparat.* Dissert. ix. Paris. 1703. Riveti *Crit. Sacr.* Lib. i. Cap. vii. Genev. 1642. Hoornbeekii *Miscellanea Sacra,* Lib. i. pp. 57—9. Ultraj. 1677.]

back the darts of the Devil; a sword not suffering iniquity and ghostly assaults of perverse power to approach unto us[1]." If this may be rightly understood according to the letter, we need not greatly to stand in dread of Satan; he is easily vanquished: we need no further armour than the Cross: let Christ alone; this Mars shall suffice us. God said to Job[2], that Behemoth or Leviathan are of another manner of force: none dare come near them; none can resist them: the sword shall never touch them; the spear yieldeth to them: they esteem iron as a straw, and brass as rotten wood. But rotten wood, a cankered, wormeaten, ill-favoured Cross, may keep us safe enough from the Devil. Then is not the Devil such a bug as we talk of: he is, (belike,) some Robin Goodfellow, that only is meet to make babies afraid. But if that you, in your most ruff, at Winchester, had been no more terrible to the boys, with a rod in your hand, than the parish Priest, with confidence in the Cross, is to the Devil; your scholars should have had as little learning, as you discretion, or the Devil dread. But you are not so to be dallied withal.

Folio 15, b. Damascenus. Damascenus saith further for you[3], "that the Cross is given us as a sign upon our foreheads, like as Circumcision was to the Israelites: by this we christian men differ and

---

[1] [Coccius, in his *Thesaurus Catholicus*, (i. 239. Colon. 1619.) gives the original of this sentence from the Epistle to the people of Bourdeaux:—" Crux enim Domini armatura vestra invicta contra Satanam; galea custodiens caput; lorica protegens pectus; clypeus tela maligni repellens; gladius iniquitatem et angelicas insidias perversæ potestatis sibi propinquare nullo modo sinens."—Bellarmin employs these false Epistles to serve his purposes, "quoniam ab aliquibus recipiuntur:" (*Recognit. Opp.*) and though, "multis de causis," he suspects their authenticity, yet he declares (*De Scriptt. Eccl.*) that they are "pious;" and that "non pauca dogmata" might be proved by them against heretics: in short, he consoles himself with the reflection that, whoever may have been the author, they contain "nihil pro adversariis, sed omnia pro nobis." (*De Christo*, Lib. i. Cap. x.)]

[2] Job xl. [xli. Compare Isaiah xxvii. 1. Luther *on Gal.* iv. 29. fol. 226. Lond. 1577.]

[3] ["Hæc nobis signum data est super frontem, quemadmodum Israeli Circuncisio: per ipsam enim fideles ab infidelibus et distamus et discernimur. Ipsa est scutum, et arma, et tropheum, adversus Diabolum. Ipsa signaculum, ut non tangat nos exterminator." (*De orthodoxa Fide*, iv. xii. fol. 89, b. Paris. 1507. See the editio princeps of the Greek, fol. 108. Veronæ, 1531.)]

are discerned from infidels. This is our shield, our weapon, our banner, and victory against the Devil. This is our mark, that the destroyer touch us not." To speak a little of your author: not utterly to discredit him, but in part to excuse him, for that he was not in all points so sound as otherwise it had been to be wished[4]. Eutropius writeth[5], that he lived in the reign of the Emperor Leo Isauricus, the third of that name. Then was the bloody bickering for Images. Then Satan did bestir himself. Then was it no marvel, if a man, learned and godly otherwise, were carried away with the common error. I am not ignorant that Damascen did greatly contend for Images. But out of the Scriptures he brought no proof at all: only by a miracle he would confirm them. We know what illusions are wrought in that behalf: and therefore, against the word, no authority of man, no miracle, must come in place. Ezechias destroyed the brazen Serpent[6], which had a most strange and wholesome miracle to witness with it; (for all were restored to health by it:) and shall forged lies make learned men and godly Princes forbear so great abuse; maintained by fond opinion, and after no sound precept? But let us weigh his reason. He compareth the Cross on the forehead and Circumcision together. If he had shewed as much commandment for the one as is for the other, I could have liked it well: now that Circumcision was straitly enjoined; and the sign of the Cross never spoken of: Circumcision was a thing done in the flesh; the Cross in the forehead is but a sign in the air: I see not how these things can join together. But if Damascenus, (which I rather think,)

[4] [This seems to have been the decided opinion of 338 Bishops in the Council of Constantinople, held A.D. 754. They thus deal with Damascen:—"Manzuri ignominioso et Saracenico anathema. Iconolatræ et falsigrapho Manzuri anathema. Doctori impietatis, et perverso interpreti divinæ Scripturæ Manzuri anathema." (Apud Sept. Synod. Act. vi. *Concill. Gen.* Tom. iii. P. ii. p. 124. Romæ, 1612.)]

[5] Rerum Ro. Lib. xxi. [The *Breviarium Historiæ Romanæ*, by Eutropius, contains only ten books: but the *Historia Miscella* comprises these books interpolated, and with an addition of four others, by Paullus Diaconus. The books from the sixteenth to the twenty-fourth, inclusive, were annexed by Landulphus Sagax; and bring down the History to the year 806. Vid. *Hist. Rom. Scriptt. Minor.* Notit. Liter. p. xvi. Bipont. 1789.]

[6] 2 Reg. xviii. [2 Kings xviii. 4.]

do take the sign in the forehead for the Passion itself printed in our hearts; then, on the other side, there is as great a square. For Circumcision did only serve for a remembrance; but this Cross is the thing itself to be remembered. Lactantius goeth nearer a truth[1]; and compareth together the blood of the Lamb, (wherewithal the door-posts of the Hebrews were sprinkled,) and the sign of the Cross, that men in the uttermost parts of their bodies bear. But Lactantius saith[2]: *Cruor pecudis tantam in se vim non habuit, ut hominibus saluti esset:* "The blood of a beast had not such power in it as to save men." Therefore, (say I,) the sign of the Cross is neither shield, nor weapon, nor victory of ours. And this is mine answer to Damascenus.

Nor I am herein ashamed of the Cross; but I am ashamed of your too cross and overthwart proofs. Ye grant yourself, that the effects aforesaid are to be ascribed to the death of Christ; but yet you swear, (Mary,) that they are not to be done, without the sign of the Cross. Your argument is this: "As men, notwithstanding the merits of Christ's passion, must receive the Sacraments; so fighters against the assaults of Satan must not only have faith, but also the outward sign of the Cross." O cunning comparison! O worthy argument, that all the world may wonder at! Would a man have thought that an Usher of Winchester could have become so deep a Divine? The Sacraments, (ye say,) must concur with faith: *ergo,* the sign of the Cross with Christ. This is as good a reason as if I should say: Notwithstanding God's power, that giveth the increase, I must eat my meat: *ergo,* notwithstanding my labour, whereby I may sustain myself, I must needs covet my neighbour's goods. The respects be like. In the first proposition, God's power and faith, the necessity of Sacraments and of noriture[3], to be compared together. In the second, Christ's passion, to answer our labour; which both are necessary, and the same sufficient means for us: and the lusting after another man's goods, set

---

[1] Lactantius, De vera Sa. Li. iv. Ca. xxvi. ["Frons enim summum limen est hominis; et lignum sanguine delibutum Crucis significatio est."]

[2] ["Non quia cruor pecudis tantam in se vim gerebat, ut hominibus saluti esset; sed imago fuerat rerum futurarum."]

[3] [nurture.]

against the sign of the Cross; whereof there is nere nother[4] commanded, but forbidden. Ye were taught once, out of the Topics[5], that it is an ill argument *A consequenti*, when, in two propositions, things utterly unlike shall be compared together; and the one, by no mean, can infer the other. Sacraments are commanded by express word of Scripture. Ye should have proved, first, that the sign of the Cross is so. Sacraments have a promise annexed to them. Where is the promise to the sign of the Cross? To pass over the rock that, in the midst of your course, ye run upon; that Sacraments are the cause of grace: whereas, in them, the only promises of God, by Christ, both by word and sign, are exhibited unto us: which promises if we apprehend by faith, then is the grace increased in us; and the gift of God, by faith received, is, by the Sacrament, sealed in us. So much, by the way, to teach you true doctrine.

<small>Sacraments no cause of grace. Folio 17, a.</small>

But, to return to the other purpose. If there be such necessity of the sign of the Cross, to fight against Satan; what a fool was Paul, when he furnished a Christian with his complete armour[6], to forget this chief piece of defence, which is able, (belike,) to do more than all the rest? What a fool was Peter, when he gave advice to resist that adversary[7], that said not as well, *Resistite Crucis signo*, as, otherwise, *fide solida?* He might have willed us to have taken a Cross in our hand; or made such a sign in our forehead, and so resisted him; but he only said, "Resist him by stedfast faith." That faith hath this effect, to withstand temptations, is plainly to be seen by the word of God. That the sign of the Cross can do the like, I utterly deny, till you be at leisure to prove it. But why? Doth not Athanasius say[8]: "The Devils, seeing the Cross, oftentimes tremble, flee

---

[4] [neither nor other: neither one nor the other.]
[5] [of Aristotle.]
[6] Ephes. vi. [11—18.]   [7] 1 Peter v. [9.]
[8] Athanasius, Quæstio. xxxix. as M. Martiall quotes it. [There is so much diversity between the various editions of this farrago, that it does not seem reasonable to reprove Martiall thus. He had probably cited what appears as the conclusion of the answer to Quæst. xxxviii., in the second Benedictine volume, and in the previous impressions at Paris and Cologne; and nearly the same words occur at the end of the reply to the fortieth Question: viz. "cum Crucem vident, sæpe tremunt, horrent, sternuntur, ac fugantur." It is far more important

away, and are miserably tormented?" Correct your book, Sir: ye quote it amiss. Indeed, in his book of Questions, Quæst. 15, he demandeth, why the Ass that Christ rode on should not as much be esteemed as the Cross that He suffered on? Whereto he answereth, that upon the Cross our salvation was wrought, and not on the Ass: wherefore, the Devils, seeing that Cross, are still afraid. But what is this to the sign of the Cross; since we have no more that Cross than we have the Ass? But, if we had it, should we think the Devil would be afraid of it, without any further force or resistance? I will answer again by Athanasius[1]. He asketh a question, how charmers do cast forth Devils out of men? Hereto he answereth, "that where it is written in the Gospel, 'If Satan cast out Satan, his kingdom cannot stand,' thereby it is manifest that the charmer doth not cast out Satan, but Satan of his own accord goeth out, to deceive men: and, to the end they shall not go to Christ, by this means he persuadeth them to go to the sorcerers." On like sort, the Devil may seem to tremble and quake, when he seeth a Cross; but it is for no other purpose but this, that we should leave our confidence in Christ, and only repose it in a piece of wood. Wherefore I suspect, as insufficient, the counsel given to the Religious[2]; that, when wicked spirits should set upon them, then they should arm themselves and their houses with the sign of the Cross. For, to retort the argument on your own head:

to observe, that the *Quæstiones ad Antiochum* are utterly supposititious. Bellarmin (*De Scriptt. Eccl.*) bears witness that "Athanasii esse non possunt:" but, nevertheless, he has arrayed them in defence of the Cross; (*De Imag.* L. ii. C. xxviii.) Images in churches; (*De Notis Eccles.* iv. ix. §. xviii.) and Prayer for the dead. (*De Purg.* Lib. i. Cap. x.) In some copies, at Quæst. lxii., the illegitimate author refers to "μέγας Ἀθανάσιος" himself; and ventures to differ from him. Vid. Sixti Senens. *Biblioth.* iv. 218. Francof. 1575. Edit. Bened. Tom. ii. 252. Raynaudi *Erotemata*, p. 127. Lugd. 1653. Chamieri *Panstrat. Cathol.* Tom. ii. p. 867. Genev. 1626. Gerhardi *Patrologia*, p. 213. Jenæ, 1653. Du Moulin's *Masse in Latin and English*, p. 387. Lond. 1641.]

[1] Quæst. xxxii. [al. cxxiv.]

[2] [In the disputable *Life of S. Anthony*, among the works of S. Athanasius; and contained also in the *Vitæ Patrum*, falsely ascribed to S. Jerom. (fol. xx. Lugd. 1520.)—"Quos cum videritis, tam vos quam domos vestras Crucis armate signaculo; et confestim dissolventur in nihilum: quia metuunt illud trophæum, in quo Salvator aëreas exspolians potestates, eas fecit ostentui."]

though "they fear the banner, in which our Saviour Christ, spoiling the powers of the air, brought them forth in open shew," yet doth it not follow, that the sign of this banner is able to work the like effect. The banner that there was spoken of was the death itself: the banner that we bear is scant a figure or shadow of it.

I know how, in this latter age, much crossing hath been used; and how the example thereof hath come from elder years. But the Fathers in many things have thought better than they have written: many times they have borrowed of the common custom improper phrases, and such as seem to maintain an error, the thing itself being otherwise defined in them. So Augustin useth the name of Satisfaction, because it was a common word; but the heresy of Satisfaction he doth plainly reprove. He useth this proposition, *Omne peccatum est voluntarium*, "Every sin is voluntary," because it was a common phrase; yet he excludeth not the birth-sin, which is of necessity. The like could I speak of other. Wherefore, not so much their saying, as their intent and meaning, is to be considered. In this case, many of the Fathers speak of the Cross in the forehead. The Scripture mentioneth the sign in the forehead. But to what purpose? Shall we think that the breaking of the air with a thumb, or drawing of a thing after such a form, is like to that which the Poets call *Orci galea*, "the helmet of hell;" wherewithal whosoever be covered, they cannot be seen, nor any shall hurt them? Then were the Cross worse than the conjuror's mace: then were the forehead accursed for having it. Wherefore, there was a further meaning in it; which, for your instruction, I will now tell you. The forehead betokeneth shame. Whereupon the proverb, *Perfricuit frontem*, "He hath rubbed his forehead," is spoken of him that is past shame. Wherefore the sign of the death of Christ is willed to be set in the sign of shame; to signify unto us, that of Christ's death we should not, at any time, be ashamed. Nor this is my private exposition. Augustin confirmeth the same[3]: *Quia in fronte erubescitur, Ille qui dixit, Qui Me erubuerit coram hominibus, erubescam eum coram Patre meo qui in cœlis est, ipsam ignominiam quodammodo, et quam Pagani derident,*

[3] Tom. viii. in Psal. cxli. [*Explan. Psalm.* fol. cccxxxvii. Paris. 1529. Cf. *Discipuli, Serm.* xli. ed. princ. Colon. 1474.]

in loco pudoris nostri constituit. Audis hominem insultare impudenti, et dicere, Frontem non habet. Quid est Frontem non habet? Impudens est. Non habeam nudam frontem; tegat eam Crux Domini mei. Which is as much to say as this: "Because in the forehead is that whereby we are ashamed of Him that said, 'He that shall be ashamed of Me before men, I will also be ashamed of him before my Father which is in heaven,' the very ignominy and shame, as it were, which the Pagans do laugh to scorn, He hath appointed in the place of our shame. Ye hear a man lay to an impudent person's charge, that 'he hath no forehead.' What is meant by that? He is impudent. Let me not therefore have a naked forehead; let the Cross of my master Christ cover it."

Thus may ye well understand the Fathers, whensoever they teach you to make a Cross in your forehead; for otherwise, the crossing, without believing, is mere enchanting. I gladly do embrace the testimony of Chrysostom, which you bring forth for yourself, *ex Hom.* lv. *in* xvi. *Mat.*[1]: *Crucem non simpliciter digito in corpore, sed magna profecto fide in mente prius formare oportet:* "Thou must not, with thy finger, simply print the Cross in thy body; but, first of all, with great faith, in thy mind." This is it, M. Martiall, that mars all your market. This if ye grant me, (which is your own allegation,) we two shall soon agree. For if this be the Cross that ye mean of, let it be had, a God's name; let it be honoured. But this is no material nor mystical Cross; for neither of them both can be printed in the heart: therefore it is the faith in Christ's passion, which the finger cannot impress in the forehead, but grace can engraff in the mind of man. *Hæc Crux non terribiles, sed despicabiles hominibus Dæmones effecit:* "This Cross hath made Devils, not terrible, but contemptible unto men." In translating of which few words, ye shew yourself to be very negligent, or very ignorant. For thus ye English them: "This Cross hath made Devils not only terrible, but contemptible to men:" where ye should have said, either, "not only not terrible," or else have put "only" in your purse: for the sense cannot stand with it. Now, where ye gather, (but indirectly,) out of Chrysostom's words, that two things be requisite: first, printing the merits of Christ's passion in the mind; after-

---

[1] [Homily liv. See *Library of the Fathers*, Vol. xv. pp. 736—7. Oxford, 1844.]

Marginal notes:
Chrysostom. He doth translate *simpliciter in corpore,* "only in the forehead."

Folio 18, b.

M. Martiall a fine translator.

ward, the signing of the Cross in the body; I briefly answer: *Frustra fit per plura, quod fieri potest per pauciora:* "In vain it is to do by the moe that may be done by the fewer." There is nothing in the world that the Cross can do, but faith can do without the Cross. Leave we, therefore, that which may tend to superstition, and is uncommanded; and betake ourselves to that which is of force enough, and is the foundation of our faith. Here would I stay, with you, from recital of more out of Chrysostom, but that I thought good to warn you, that figures of Hyperbole[2] and Metonymia be often in the Fathers' writings. When they praise a thing, they ascribe more unto it than they mean; and, many times, under the name of one thing, applied fitly to our capacities, they understand another. I remember that Chrysostom hath these words[3]: *Non solum Crucifixum, sed etiam pro Ipso occisorum favillas Dæmones contremiscunt:* "Not only the Devils tremble at Christ crucified, but also they quake at the very ashes of them that were slain for Him." Here is as much attributed to ashes, as was before to the Cross; and think ye, therefore, that Satan would be afraid to tempt you, if ye had a few ashes of dead bones in your bosom? Peradventure some of you may be so sotted in folly, that ye would gather them up devoutly, and keep them as reliques holily. Such I refer to the place of Chrysostom, *in Opere imperfect. Hom.* xliv. *in cap. Mat.* xxiii.[4]; whereupon I shall have occasion hereafter to entreat, when I come to speak of the like absurdity, the little pieces of the Cross kept.

Another note to be observed, in reading of the Fathers.

Now let us hear what ye find in other. Origen ye bring, in his exposition of the Epistle to the Romans, Lib. vi.[5] And

Folio 19, b. Origen.

[2] ["Meminisse oportet, quod et alibi sæpe monuimus, non esse concionatorum verba semper eo rigore accipienda, quo primum ad aures auditorum perveniunt: multa enim declamatores per Hyperbolem crebro enunciant... Hoc interdum Chrysostomo contigit." (Sixt. Senens. *Biblioth. Sanct.* Lib. vi. Annot. clii. p. 533.)]

[3] Tom. iv. de laud. Pauli Hom. iv. [Vol. ii. pag. 493. ed. Ben. vel apud Bedæ *Opp.* Tom. vi. col. 836. Colon. Agripp. 1612. See Jewel's *Replie unto M. Harding's Answer,* p. 371. Lond. 1609.]

[4] [Vid. Sixti Senensis *Bibl. Sanct.* Lib. vi. Annot. cii. p. 510.]

[5] ["Tanta vis est Crucis, ut si ante oculos ponatur, et in mente fideliter retineatur, ita ut in ipsam mortem Christi intentis oculis mentis aspiciatur, nulla concupiscentia, nulla libido, nulla superare possit invidia." (Hom. vi. cit. Coccio, *Thesaur. Cath.* i. 234. Conf. Bucchingeri *Hist. Eccles.* p. 136. Lovan. 1560.)]

although this Father maketh most against you, as afterward shall appear; yet, to the end that such young scholars as you may learn with what judgment ye ought to read the old writers, I think it expedient somewhat to speak of him. In sundry points his doctrine is sound; specially, concerning the Trinity, the two natures in Christ, the Baptism of infants, original sin, and use of Images. But things have passed under his name, where are intermeddled many fond opinions; which both were condemned in his own time, and are not now to be credited of us[1]: as, that, before the creation of the world, there was another world[2]: that the Devils in hell shall, at the last, be saved[3]. And if ye scan his other writings, there will appear either great inconstancy, or very small perfection. In the article of Justification[4], he swerveth from himself; and, in some points, from all other too. The Spirit he taketh, not for the motion of the Holy Ghost, but for the allegorical interpretation[5]. Peter he supposeth to excel the rest, because it was said to him, in the plural number: "Whatsoever thou loosest in earth shall be loosed in the heavens;" whereas to other it is spoken, in the singular number: "It shall be loosed in heaven[6]." These and such other toys are not only in him; but also in other of his time and age: wherefore they ought to be read, as witnesses of things done, not as precedents of faith and doctrine. Yet, unless you, M. Martiall, will set Origen to school again, and teach him what to say, you cannot construe any lesson of his, to pick out a proof of any other Cross than the mind conceiveth, not the hand maketh. For though ye bring a piece of a sentence, wherein the praise of the Cross is put; *Tanta vis est Crucis*, "So great is the

Cœlis et cœlo.

---

[1] [See Stephen Jerom's *Life and Death of Origen*, prefixed to his *Repentance*, Lond. 1619. Cf. Sculteti *Medull. Theolog. Patrum*, p. 134. Francof. 1634. Carionis *Chronicon*, iii. 303. Genevæ, 1625. Huetii *Origeniana*, Lib. iii. Cap. i. et Append. pp. 272-8. Rothom. 1668.]

[2] [Huet. *Origen.* 163.]

[3] [*Origenian*. L. ii. Qu. xi. — "Quanquam etiam diversum ex Origenis scriptis supra protulimus." (*Centur. Magdeb.* iii. x. c. 264.)]

[4] [Huetii *ad Orig. Comment. Observatt.* p. 46. Faber on *Justif.* p. 117. Lond. 1837.]

[5] [Vid. Lib. iv. περὶ ἀρχῶν, Cap. ii. 2 Cor. iii. 6. Boys's *Exposition;* Autumne Part, p. 8. Lond. 1612. S. Aug. *De spiritu et litera*, Cap. v. sig. C c ii. Wittenb. 1519.]

[6] [*Comment.* i. 336-7. ed. Huet.]

power of the Cross," (quoth he;) yet, if ye remembered the very next words that go before, ye should plainly see of what Cross he meant. Discoursing upon these words of the Apostle, "Let not sin reign in your mortal body," he asketh a question, how it is possible to avoid it? He answereth: *Si faciamus illud, quod idem Apostolus dicit: Mortificate membra vestra quæ sunt super terram; et si semper mortem Christi in corpore nostro circumferamus: certum namque est, quia ubi mors Christi circumfertur, non potest regnare peccatum:* "If we do that," saith he, "which the same Apostle willeth us, 'Mortify your members which are upon the earth;' and if we carry about always in our bodies the death of Christ: for it is certain that where the death of Christ is carried about, there can no sin reign." And immediately he inferreth your words: *Est enim tanta vis Crucis Christi:* "For the power of the Cross of Christ is so great." Whereby it is evident that he speaketh of the death of Christ; and that is the Cross that he commendeth. That Cross have you nothing to do withal. But if the picture of a Cross looked on be able to daunt, (as you devise,) concupiscence and sensuality, how hath it fallen out that your spiritual fathers, all to becrossed about their beds, have had their familiars between the sheets? How have your Nuns, (that chaste generation,) with their beads in their hands, been blessed with great bellies? I will no more offend chaste ears.

But Origen's Cross, that is to say, the death of Christ, both may and must be set before our eyes, and faithfully kept in the chest of our hearts, though no visible sign be made thereof; which neither hand can truly counterfeit, nor man's folly ought falsely to forge. Origen therefore, in the behalf of Christians of his time, saith[7]: *Celsus et aras, et Simulachra, et delubra nos ait defugere quominus fundentur, quandoquidem invisibilis nostræ hujus et inexplicabilis communionis fidem et charitatis factionem esse existimat: cum nihil interea videat, nobis quidem, pro aris et delubris, justorum esse mentem; a qua haud dubie emittuntur suavissimi incensi odores: vota, inquam, et preces ex conscientia puriore;* &c. Because his sentence is long in the Latin, I will word for word rehearse it in English: "Celsus doth say that we avoid the making of altars, and Images, and oratories, because he thinketh that

Origen overthroweth Imagery.

[7] Contra Celsum, Libr. viii. [p. 389. Cantab. 1658.]

the faith of our invisible and inexplicable communion and charity is nothing else but a faction: whereas, in the mean while, he seeth not, that instead of altars and oratories, with us the minds of the faithful are; from which, no doubt, most sweet savours of incense are cast out: prayers, I mean, and supplications from a pure conscience. Whereof S. John, in his Revelation[1], speaketh on this sort: 'The prayers of the Saints are incense;' and the Psalmist[2]: 'Let my prayer, O Lord, be in thy sight as incense.' Furthermore, we have images and worthy offerings unto God, not such as be made by unclean workmen, but framed and fashioned by God's word in us: whereby such virtues may rest in us, which shall imitate and resemble The first-begotten of all creatures[3]; in whom examples are, as well of justice, continence, and valiantness, as otherwise of wisdom, godliness, and all virtues. Therefore such images are in all, as have by the word of God gotten them this temperance, this righteousness, this fortitude, this wisdom and piety, with all the frame of other virtues, in which I think it meet the honour be given unto Him, which is the pattern of all images, The image of God invisible;" and so forth. Whereby it appeareth, (as in plain words he speaketh after,) that all images should be such as God Himself commanded; such as should be within man, and not without man; such as consisted in the knowledge of Him, after whose image man himself was made.

No Images in Origen's time but spiritual. Also his testimony serveth for this; that in his time there were no material Images in temples. There was no Rood, no Cross, no likeness of any thing, save only spiritual, of grace and virtues. Consider, I beseech you, how in his fourth book against Celsus[4], he commendeth the Jews: *Nimirum apud quos, præter Eum qui cunctis præsidet rebus, pro Deo nihil unquam sit habitum: nec quisquam, sive Imaginum fictor, sive Statuarum fabricator, in eorum republica fuerit; ut quos procul lex ipsa abigeret, ut ne qua hiis esset fabricandorum Simulachrorum occasio; quæ stultos quosdam mortalium a Deo revelleret, et ad contemplanda terrena animi oculos retorqueret.* That is to say: "Among whom nothing was ever accompted God, beside Him which ruleth all: nor in their commonwealth

---

[1] Apocal. viii. [4. v. 8.]   [2] Psalm. cxli. [2.]
[3] [Col. i. 15. The Heir of the whole creation.]
[4] [See before, Preface, p. 44.]

any carver of Idols, or Image-maker was; as whom the law itself drove away from them, to the intent they should have no occasion to make any Images; which might pluck certain foolish persons from God, and turn the eyes of their souls to the contemplation of earthly things." So much for Origen. And if ye read his book thorough, ye shall see it proved in plain words a frentike[5] part to worship Images; a madness to say that any knowledge of God can be gotten by them. Only this sufficeth here, that your allegation maketh not to your purpose; and your author alleged maketh most against you. Then what should ye talk that, in the primitive Church, Crosses were set up in every place; that every church and chapel had the sign of the Cross erected in it; that Sacraments could not be made without it; that men devoutly kept pieces of it, &c.: whereof Origen, two hundred and eighty[6] year after Christ, knew nothing; but rather, by the law, condemned such observances? Where now is the counsel that you have learned of your elders? Where is the advertisement of grave Fathers? Where is the medicine that you call sovereign, taken from the best physicians of the Church? I will not compare you to a tapster, a tinker, an ostler; but to a lewd apothecary, that understandeth not his bill, but giveth *quid pro quo;* or else to cook ruffian, that mars good meat in the dressing.

Folio 9, a.

But, to proceed, and give somewhat a further taste of your unsavoury sops. Ye bring forth Cassiodore's authority[7]; which may be answered in a word, that he meaneth nothing less than you do imagine. For what though "the signs of the heavenly Prince be printed upon the faithful, as the image of the Emperor is in his coin, whereby the Devil is expulsed from them," &c.: what though "the Cross be the invincible defence of the humble, the overthrow of the proud, the victory of Christ, the

Cassiodor. Folio 19, b.

---

[5] [phrenetic, frantic.]
[6] [Possibly a mistake for 230; as Origen died A.D. 254.]
[7] [" Sicut nummus Imperatoris portat imaginem, ita et fidelibus signa cœlestis Principis imprimuntur. Hoc munimine Diabolus multiformis expellitur... Crux enim est humilium invicta tuitio, superborum dejectio, victoria Christi, perditio Diaboli, infernorum destructio, cœlestium confirmatio, mors infidelium, justorum vita." (*Comment. in Psal.* iv.—Coccius, i. 242, Waldensis *Sacram.* fol. cccxxviii. Paris. 1523. Cf. Fabricii *Biblioth. Latin.* Tom. ii. p. 169. Venet. 1728.)]

[CALFHILL.]

undoing of the Devil, the destruction of hell, the confirmation of heavenly things, the death of infidels, the life of the just;" is a Rood, or a Crucifix, or wagging of a finger, able to shew whose men we are, as the print in the money doth shew whose the coin is? Wheresoever that image and superscription is stamped, there is it certain who hath a right to the coin[1]: but whosoever have the sign or stamp of a Cross upon them shew not thereby whose servants they are. Your Popes and your Prelates have Crosses before them, Crosses hanging upon them, Crosses in their crowns, Crosses in their garments; and yet I fear me lest ye will not affirm them to be the best servants of Christ. You know sometime there be coins of counterfeits. I know the most crossers are not the best Christians. The sign of God printed in the faithful is the belief in Christ, and grace to do thereafter. The Cross that is their refuge, their succour and defence, is the death of Christ, and merits of His passion.

The sign of God in the faithful.

But see what peevishness is in Papists. Wheresoever they read of fire in the Scripture, thence they kindle Purgatory. Wheresoever they hear a body mentioned, there do they tear it to Transubstantiation. Wheresoever they see this word "Cross" come in place, they lift it up to the Rood-loft, or at the least to the forehead. Methinks, M. Martiall, that you might have remembered your first division, where ye made mention of four significations of the Cross, and so applied, (as the troth is,) the sayings of your authors unto the second. But your wisdom foresaw this objection of mine, and therefore ye grant that "nothing can avail or profit man, unless he hath a stedfast faith in Christ, and faithful belief in the merits of His passion." But "Mary," say you, (Mary is much beholding to you; indeed she stands next to the Cross[2]:) "as not every simple, bare, and naked faith, but such as worketh by charity, conquereth the world; so not every faith worketh to man the foresaid effects, but faith assisted by the sign of the holy Cross." Then, by your reason, the sign of the Cross is as necessary to concur with our belief as charity to be with faith: But faith without charity is a Devil's faith: Therefore belief without a sign of the Cross is also devilish. I am sure that no man endued with common sense, howsoever he be affected in cases of religion, but will condemn

Peevishness of Popery.

Fol. 20, a, b.

---

[1] [S. Matth. xxii. 20, 21.]   [2] [S. John xix. 25.]

herein the lack of discretion in you. For tell me, I pray you, what Scripture, what Father, what reason ever taught you to compare the sign of the Cross with charity, with hope, with fasting, and with prayer? None of these but we have an hundreth places in the word of God to commend and command them: but as for the sign of the Cross, what mention is there, much less commendation?

Forsooth ye bring authorities and experiments: authorities of Lactantius and Augustin; experiments of Julian. As for Lactantius, he tieth two points together; the name of Christ, and sign of His passion[3]. The power of the name we read of: " Save me, O God, by thy name[4]." "The name of the Lord is a strong tower: the righteous runneth unto it, and is exalted[5]." And, " Our help is in the name of the Lord[6]." And in the New Testament: " Blessed is he that cometh in the name of the Lord[7]." " In my name," (saith Christ,) " they shall cast out Devils[8]." And the effect thereof was proved in the seventy Disciples, which returned home with joy, and said, " Devils are subject unto us in thy name[9]." " Whatsoever in my name you shall ask my Father you shall obtain[10]." "Whosoever shall call upon the name of the Lord shall be saved[11]." Examples also of Peter: " In the name of Jesus Christ of Nazareth, rise up and walk[12]." Also, " His name hath made this man sound, whom ye see and know, through faith in His name[13]." And, " There is no other name under heaven whereby we may be saved[14]." In all these places there is no sign of the Cross spoken of; yet all these prove a true effect. Wherefore the name of Christ alone would have done as much as the name and the sign together. Nor we must impute the virtue to the sign; though, contrary to the use and example of Scripture, it pleased some men to add it.

Folio 21, a.

Lactantius.

[3] [" Sectatores Ejus eosdem Spiritus inquinatos de hominibus et nomine Magistri sui, et signo passionis excludunt." (*De vera Sapientia*, Lib. iv. Cap. xxvii.)]
[4] Psal. liv. [1.]
[5] Prover. xviii. [10].
[6] Psal. cxxiii. [cxxiv. 8.]
[7] Matth. xxiii. [39.]
[8] Marc. xvi. [17.]
[9] Luc. x. [17.]
[10] Joan. xiv. [S. John xiv. 13, 14. xvi. 23.]
[11] Act. ii. [21.]
[12] Act. iii. [6.]
[13] [Acts iii. 16.]
[14] Act. iv. [12.]

Augustin.

The like may be said of Austin's place: for where he speaketh of the articles of our faith, called in Latin *Symbolum*[1]; which he willed before to be written in the heart, laid up in store in the book of memory; he concluded, that a way to withstand the enemy was *cum Symboli Sacramento*, "with the Sacrament of faith," (which you interpret "a stedfast faith,") *et Crucis vexillo*, "and ensign of the Cross." What meaneth he by that metaphor? What is that ensign of the Cross? The banner that is carried about the churchyard in procession? No: but that which in the self-same sentence before he called *Canticum salutis*, joining it with *Symboli remedio, contra antiqui Serpentis venenum:* "the song of salvation, joined with the remedy of the twelve articles of our faith, against the poison of the old Serpent." Therefore straight after, when he had rehearsed the two chief engines wherewithal our enemy doth afflict us, *voluptatem et timorem,* "pleasure and dread," he doth not bid us to make the sign of a Cross in our forehead, nor run to succour of so weak a shield; but to fence ourselves *timore Domini casto, et fide orationis:* "with the chaste fear of God, and faith of prayer."

Ye see by this time that your authorities make nothing for you. The wrong understanding of the name "Cross" doth make your arguments run of uncertain feet, and halt downright. The jointly concurring of faith and fruits, I know to be necessary; the word of God doth teach me: but the necessary concurrence of the sign of the Cross with faith, is more than you can learn, either of God's word, or else good Father; and therefore more than we ought to believe, unless we wilfully believe a lie. Christ was sufficient schoolmaster to us. He left no precept of His Cross amongst us: only He willed every man to take up his own Cross[2]. The Apostles that gloried in the Cross[3], that is to say, the death of Christ; that lived under the Cross, that is to say, were subject to afflictions, carrying about with them the death of

---

[1] De Symb. ad Cathe. i. [The Sermon here cited is the first of three spurious addresses to Catechumens. The Benedictine editors allow that the author was "much inferior in learning and genius" to S. Augustin. *Opp.* Tom. vi. 406. Antw. 1701.]
[2] Mat. xvi. [24.] Mark viii. [34.] Luc. ix. [23.]
[3] [Gal. vi. 14.]

Christ in their mortal bodies[4]; that did many miracles by Him that hanged on the Cross; never used, (as we read,) the sign of the Cross, nor gave any counsel or commandment for it. Shall Christ our High Priest, "touched with the feeling of our infirmities[5]," be insufficient furnisher of us, and foolish men arm us at all points? Shall the Apostles forget so necessary a piece of defence, and the Pope remember it?

I think indeed that the Cross-quarrellers took all their precedent of Julian the Apostata[6]; that whereas they meant to have as little religion, they would have as light a rescue, as he had. But before I come to recital of his story, let me cite your comparison. It is not odious, but too ridiculous: the bare sign of the Cross ye prefer before naked, sole, and only faith. The sign of the Cross of itself what is it? A beating of the air; a throwing of a stone against the wind; in effect, nothing. But faith, make it as naked and bare as you can, yet is it a quality of the mind, which at the least wise to the world commends us. For let it be as the Schoolmen term it, *fides informis,* "an unshapen faith;" or as Paul calleth it, *fides ficta,* "a feigned faith[7];" or the worst that ye can make it, *Dæmonum fides,* "the Devils' faith[8];" yet doth it teach us somewhat: it taketh away the excuse of ignorance, as Paul to the Romans witnesseth[9]; and forceth a sin upon us, as Christ Himself affirmeth[10]: "If I had not come and spoken to them, they should have no sin." Your naked Cross, as it cannot stand by itself, so in itself it containeth nothing, unless perhaps some worms and spiders be crept into a corner of it. All must rest in the conceit of man and his imagination. I might say with Thomas Aquinas[11]: *Quod fides informis et formata fides est idem habitus; quia ad naturam fidei nihil attinet sive charitas adsit, sive non adsit. Nam hoc per accidens fit;*

Papists take precedent of Julian the Apostata.

Folio 21, a.

---

[4] 2 Cor. iv. [10.]   [5] Hebr. iv. [15.]
[6] [Vid. Pierre de Croix, *Du signe de la Croix,* p. 94. A Arras, 1604.]
[7] 1 Tim. i. [5.]   [8] [S. James ii. 19.]
[9] [Rom. i. 20.]   [10] Joan. xv. [22.]
[11] [Vid. *Summ.* 2. 2. Q. iv. 4 ad 1^m, 3^m, 4^m. *Script. sup. tert. Sententt.* foll. 409, b, 410. Paris. 1574. Conf. Bulli *Harmon. Apostol.* Dissert. post. Cap. ii. p. 37. Lond. 1703. Bellarm. *De Justif.* Lib. i. C. xv. Willet's *Synopsis Papismi,* 979.]

as he saith. Whose words in English be these: "Faith unshaped and shaped faith is all one constant quality; because it skilleth not for the nature of faith whether charity be there or no. For that is an accidental thing." Now, if this were true, a naked faith were far better than a naked Cross; because there should be no difference between a naked faith and a faith clad as well as can be: but if I should stand in defence of this, I should be as foully deceived as your Saint was. I will reason with you out of the Master of the Sentence[1]. Let faith be taken, *sive pro eo quo creditur, sive pro eo quod creditur,* "either for that whereby we believe, or else for that which is believed;" certain it is that the simplest of them both is better than a sign, though it be of the Cross. For be it the latter faith, *quam Dæmones et falsi Christiani habent,* as he saith; "which the Devils and false Christians have:" yet, by the same, *possunt credere Deum, et credere Deo*[2]: "they can believe that there is a God; they can give credit unto His words." But a bare Cross cannot do this. Take me a man that never heard of Christ, and bring him to a Spaniard, to behold all his Crosses at the Mary Mass; and he shall be as learned, when he cometh away, as the Ape is devout when he hath eaten the Host[3]. But if a man neither did, nor could ever hear at all, this naked faith were able to teach him, without any further information, that a God there is; which the very Gentiles did understand. Again, to compare a gift of God, which is in the mind, to the work of man made with the hand, is *canibus catulos conjungere, matribus hœdos*[4]: "to join the whelps and hounds, the kids and goats together."

<small>Julian's example. Folio 21, b.</small>

Now to your Julian. Ye say, that when he had consulted

[1] [Pet. Lombardi] Lib. iii. Sent. Dist. xxiii. Cap. Unicum. [foll. 258, b, 259. Paris. 1553.]

[2] ["Aliud enim est credere Illi; aliud credere Illum; aliud credere in Illum. Credere Illi, est credere vera esse quæ loquitur: Credere Illum, credere quia Ipse est Deus: Credere in Illum, diligere Illum." (*Serm. suppos.* clxxxi. *de Tempore,* inter S. Augustini *Opera,* Tom. x. fol. 215. Paris. 1541.)]

[3] [With regard to the miraculous respect, said to have been rendered on various occasions to the Host, by Beasts, Birds, and Insects, see the Jesuit Bridoul's *School of the Eucharist;* with a Preface by Clagett. Lond. 1687.]

[4] [Virg. *Eclog.* i. 23.]

with sorcerers, and they had made the Devils solemnly to appear[5], "he was stricken in a fear, and forced to make the sign of the Cross in his forehead. Then the Devils looking back, and seeing the figure of the Lord's banner, and remembering their fall and overthrow, suddenly vanished out of sight." Thus much, or so much as this, ye cite out of Theodoret and Gregory Nazianzen. For the truth of the history I contend not with you: but what I judge of the experiment I will tell you. First of all, that wicked, reprobate, and godless persons can use the sign of the Cross as well as other: which proposition shall quite confute all your ninth article. For if such as Julian can cross themselves, and notwithstanding have never a whit the more faith, (as yourself confess;) then how falls it out "that the Cross driveth out heresies;" fol. 94, b: "that the sign of the Cross converteth obstinate sinners;" fol. 114, 115: "that the sign of the Cross maketh wicked men to think upon God;" "that the Cross is comfortable in desperation;" fol. 116.? Secondly, this I note; how sore the Devil was hurt by the Cross; when, it notwithstanding, he retained the possession of whole Julian both in body and soul. Thirdly, that the Devil doth feign himself to be afraid of that, which, with all his heart, he would have men to use. For this is a general rule; that the Devil is a liar, and always will seem to be as he is not. If there were no other matter in the world against you, this only were sufficient to discredit you. For what better reason is there that crossing ought not to be used at all, than that the Devil did seem to dread it. If that indeed he had been afraid of it, he would have doubled a point with you, and not have played so open play. He runs from the steeple to dwell in the people. He counterfeits a flight from the Holy Water bucket, and nestles himself in the bosom of the Priest. He seemeth to give

Fol. 22, a.

Contradictions in Martiall.

[5] [The extract seems to have been taken from the Latin version of Theodoret, in the *Historia Tripartita* by Cassiodorus, Lib. vi. Cap. i.— "Quibus solemniter apparentibus, terrore compellitur Julianus in fronte sua Crucis formare signaculum. Tunc Dæmones, trophæi Dominici figuram respicientes, et suæ recordati devictionis, repente disparuerunt." Conf. Theod. *Hist. Eccles.* Lib. iii. Cap. iii. ed. Basil. 1549. D. Gregorii Nazianz. *Adv. Julian. Orat.* iii. Opp. Tom. i. p. 206. Paris. 1583. Freculphi *Chronic.* Tom. ii. Lib. iv. C. ix. Colon. 1539. *Chron.* Abbat. Ursperg. pag. xc. Argent. 1540. Nicephori Lib. x. Cap. iii. Hickes's *Jovian*, C. vi. p. 144. Lond. 1683.]

place to the charmer's enchantment, and yet that sacrifice doth please him exceedingly. Ye confess that Julian had no hope in Christ, no love to God, no faith; and will ye not confess that he was thereby a desperate person, and a limb of the Devil? The Devil then should have done him wrong, if he had put him in any further danger.

But one thing I marvel at; how you, M. Martiall, a Bachelor of law, sometime Usher of Winchester, now Student in divinity, making a book, intitled to the Queen, perused by the learned, privileged by the King, allowed by Cunner[1], should fall into manifest contradictions, and scape uncontrolled. I see it is true, *quod mendacem memorem esse oportet:* "a liar had need have a good remembrance." Ye said in the leaf before, "The sign of the Cross must concur with faith, and faith with the sign of the Cross:" now ye allow the bare sign of the Cross, without any faith, to have the force and power aforesaid. If I thought ye were ignorant of Satan's practices, I would shew you some of them, to make you more circumspect. But you have been brought up in his school a good while; and therefore I think ye practise after him, endeavouring yourself of set purpose to deceive: for which, like a spider, ye spin a subtile web. You suck out of the Fathers the worst joyce[2] that you can, that you may turn the same into your own filthy and infected nature. Gregory did well, in abhorring the name of Universal Bishop[3]: but Gregory's authority is not taken in that. Gregory said well, when he told us the tale of Speciosus, a Deacon, that would rather forsake his benefice than his wife[4]: but the precedent of that persuadeth you not. Only when Gregory disgraceth himself with old wives' tales, and trifling customs of his corrupted time, then is he meat for your saucy mouths.

A Jew, saith Gregory, "without trust, confidence, or faith

---

[1] [That is, as the editor believes, (for he has not seen the work;) that it had received the Imprimatur of the Censor Cunerus Petri de Browershaven, the first Bishop of Leuwarden in Friesland.]

[2] [juice.]

[3] [*Epistt.* Lib. iv. Capp. lxxvi, lxxviii, lxxx, lxxxii, lxxxiii. Lib. vi. C. cxciv. Opp. Tom. ii. Antverp. 1572.]

[4] [*Epistt.* L. iii. Cap. xxxiv. fol. 193. Cf. Gratiani *Decret.* Dist. xxxii. C. ii. & Caus. xxvii. Quæst. ii. Cap. xx.]

in Christ's passion, was preserved from spirits by the sign of the Cross[5]." I rehearse not the circumstance of the tale, because I have told you more than is true already[6]. For if he had no faith in Christ, the Scripture is plain that there could no spirit be worse than himself. Impossible it is to please God without faith[7]: and shall God, by the Cross, preserve them that please Him not? Who seeth not what a fable this is, or rather a blasphemy, if it be weighed aright? But Gregory hath it; a Doctor of the Church. So hath he more untruths than this. As that, for confirmation of Sacrifice for the dead, he bringeth forth a vision, a dream, or a dotage[8]; such a one as I am ashamed to father upon him, or any one of the faithful; yet proof good enough for such a matter of naught. His tale is this. A certain Priest, that used the baths, went on a day into them; and found a young man, (whom he knew not,) very obsequious and serviceable unto him: he pulled off his shoes, he took his garments, he did whatsoever might be comfortable for him. When this he had often done, one day the Priest going thitherward thought thus with himself: I ought not to seem unthankful unto him, which hath so devoutly been accustomed to serve me whensoever I wash me; but needs I must carry him somewhat for a reward. Then took he with him the tops of two loaves which had been offered at service. And as soon as ever he came unto the

---

[5] [" Quamvis fidem Crucis minime haberet, signo tamen se Crucis munire curavit." (*Dial.* Lib. iii. C. vii. fol. xxvi. Paris. 1513.)]

[6] [Any person would be likely to tell "more than is true," who should absolutely, and without remorse, ascribe these controverted Dialogues to S. Gregory the Great. The learned Robert Cooke has sufficiently examined their style and contents; (*Censura,* pp. 209—12.) and though there is a great deal of difficulty connected with them, they are, for the most part, unhesitatingly recognised only by Romanists, and by those who wish to traduce the early writers of the Church. Many excellent critics have assigned the "salubrious narrations," (as Photius calls them, *Cod.* cclii.) to Pope Gregory II., who lived in the eighth century, and certainly was surnamed *Dialogus.* Vid. Comber's *Roman Forgeries,* Part iii. Cent. v. pp. 126, 193. Lond. 1695. Riveti *Crit. Sacr.* Lib. iv. Cap. xxix. Baronii *Martyrol.* die Decemb. 23.]

[7] Heb. xi. [6.]

[8] Lib. Dial. iv. Cap. lv. [fol. lviii.]

place, he found his man; he used his service as he was wont in all points. Thus when he had washed, and put on his clothes, as he was going out he offered, (as a blessing,) unto the man that had been so diligent about him, that which he brought with him; requiring him courteously to accept that which he offered him in the way of charity. But he, mourning and afflicted, answered, Father, what meanest thou to give me these? This bread is holy; this can I not eat. For I, whom thou seest, sometime was lord of this place; but for my sins now, after my death, am deputed hither. But if thou wilt do any thing for me, offer this bread unto Almighty God for me, to be a mediator for my sins: and then know that God hath heard thy prayer, when thou shalt come hither to bathe thee and find me not. So the next week after the Priest continued in mourning for him; every day did offer the Host for him; and afterward, when he came to the bath, he found him not. Hereupon Father Gregory concludeth: *Qua ex re quantum prosit animabus immolatio sacræ oblationis ostenditur; quando hanc et ipsi mortuorum spiritus a viventibus petunt, et signa indicant quibus per eam absoluti videantur.* In English this: "By which thing it is shewed how much the Sacrifice of the holy oblation profiteth the souls; when the spirits of the dead require this of the living, and shew signs whereby they may appear to be delivered by it." And so far Gregory.

But is it not a pitiful case, that of so weak a ground so wicked a doctrine should be builded, contrary to the manifest word of God? In the eighteenth of Deuteronomy: "Seek not to learn a truth of the dead." And in the eighth of the Prophet Esay: "Should not a people inquire at their God? Shall they depart from the living to the dead?" Howsoever the state of men is after this life, no doctrine should be gathered of the talking of spirits. And furthermore, that dead men do serve in the baths upon the earth; be loosed out of the popish Purgatory, which they affirm to be *subtus terram,* "under the earth," to become as it were barbers' apprentices upon the earth, may well be a legend for Plato his Purgatory, joined with the tale of Danaus' daughters, who pour in water into a bottomless tub. Wherefore, M. Martiall, doubt ye not this; but the wicked spirits, which saw *vas vacuum sed signatum,* "an empty vessel, but signed with the

Cross," were bold notwithstanding, *ad evitandum vacuum,* to enter into him.

As for the words of Lactantius[1], which you bring forth; that when they do sacrifice to their Idols, if there stand any man by that hath his forehead signed," (for that which you add, " with the Cross," is more than ye find in the text;) " then they offer up no sacrifice, neither their wizard is able to give answer," must rather be understood of the faithful christened, than of any that were crossed: for by the signed forehead they signified Baptism, and the faith of Christ which they professed. Otherwise, if it be as you say, "that spirits cannot abide the sign of the Cross, nor continue in place where any man is that hath the sign of the Cross," the best counsel that I can give men is, to be marked, to burn their flesh with an hot iron, and make a durable Cross in their foreheads; whereby they may be free, as long as they live, from fearing of spirits, without any more ado. But I fear me lest this be no sufficient defence. For Serapis and his Priests were all to[2] becrossed; and yet the Devils danced among them. The Pope hath his Crosses, yea double and treble; yet is not the Devil afraid to come at him. Silvester the second, as Platina reporteth[3], was a practiser of naughty arts; and therein addict himself altogether unto the common enemy of mankind. And indeed first he gat the archbishoprick of Reme, and afterward of Ravenna, by simony. Last of all, by the Devil's forwarding help, he gat also the occupying of the Pope's see: howbeit, under this condition; that when he departed this life, he should be all wholly the

Folio 23.

Folio 23.

---

[1] Lib. iv. Ca. xxvii. De vera Sap. ["Nam cum Diis suis immolant, si assistat aliquis signatum frontem gerens, sacra nullo modo litant; Nec responsa potest consultus reddere Vates."]

[2] [altogether: in which sense the phrase is used in Judges ix. 53: " and all to brake his skull :"—but in many Bibles, (for instance Bagster's,) "break" has been wrongly substituted for " brake."]

[3] [*Vitæ Pontiff.* fol. lxxiv. Venet. 1518. In Carranza's *Summa Conciliorum,* p. 569. Salmant. 1551, we read of this Pope: " Is magus fuisse fertur :" but the word " *magus*" has been corruptly altered into "*magnus*" in the following editions: Antverp. 1569.; Paris. 1624.; Rothom. 1655.; Paris. 1677. The Vatican Expurgatory *Index,* in its review of Zuinger's *Theatrum vitæ humanæ,* directs that the term "magus," which had been therein applied to Silvester, should be erased. (p. 720. Romæ, 1607. : p. 592. Bergom. 1608.)]

Devil's, by whose false deceits he obtained so high dignity. Whereupon, as the same Platina, the Pope's own Secretary, doth write; when Silvester was not circumspect enough, in being ware of the Devil's baits, he was killed, all to pulled, of the promoter of his, the Devil: yea, when he was a massing in the church. A strange case, M. Martiall, that so many Crosses as were in the church, so many Crosses as were in the Mass, could not save the supreme Head of the Church from tearing in pieces by wicked spirits; yea, when he was at his holy Mass! Wherefore the Cross, in your fourth signification, is not "the heavenly note and immortal sign." It hath not that effect, "by continual meditation of heavenly things and the life to come, to make men heavenly and immortal."

Folio 23.

Still you do reason *A non causa pro causa;* attributing that unto the outward sign, which is indeed the virtue of Christ, and belief in His passion. Ye say that the sign of the Cross is spoken of by God Himself in His Prophet Esay: but it shall appear, by the very Scriptures that you allege, how ignorantly and how falsely you cite your authorities. God, by the mouth of His servant[1], witnessed how He would bring to pass that the Church, which had continued barren a long while, should now be fruitful; and have such store of children that she should wonder at her own increase, saying: *Quis genuit mihi istos; quum ego sim sterilis et solitaria, relegata et vaga? Quis ergo educavit istos? En ego sola relicta sum; isti ergo undenam sunt?* "Who hath begotten me these; seeing I am barren and desolate, a banished person, and a wanderer to and fro? And who hath nourished them? Behold, I was left alone; and whence are these?" God, to answer this case, and to shew that there should be a spiritual brood, begotten through grace of adoption, not by the common course of nature, but by the secret working of His Spirit, said: *Tollam ad Gentes manum meam, et ad populos signum meum erigam:* "I will lift up my hand to the Gentiles, and set up my standard unto the people:" meaning, that not only the Jews, but also the Gentiles, should be brought to Christ; which, agreeing in unity of one faith together, should be gathered as brethren into one mother's lap.

Folio 23, b.

---

[1] Esay xlix. [21, 22. Cf. Zacagnii *Collect. Mon.* i. 309. Romæ, 1698.]

Now, I beseech you, turn over your histories, consult with your elders, and see what it was that brought the Gentiles to Christianity, the idolatrous nations to true Religion. If it were the sign of the Cross, after your fourth signification, "made of some earthly matter to be set up in churches, or made with man's hand in the air, in form and likeness of the other," then is it somewhat that you have said. But if it were the preaching of the word, (as most certain it is,) which did so work in the hearts of men that, refusing their errors, they became to be faithful; then you are a falsifier of the word, M. Martiall. Learn you of me, that preaching is that hand of God, that standard of His, whereby that merciful effect is wrought, as well in us as in all other, to be brought to the truth from blindness and ignorance. And if ye think scorn to learn of me, learn of God Himself, who in the text before saith, that His mouth is a sharp sweard[2], and that preaching is a chosen shaft, had in the quiver of the Almighty. For the word in operation is as forcible as a sweard[2]: it moveth, it ravisheth, it reneweth men: it pierceth to the heart, it searcheth the secret places: it entereth through, as S. Paul saith[3], "even unto the dividing asunder of the soul and of the spirits, and of the joints and of the marrow, and is a discerner of the thoughts and the intents of the heart. Neither is there any creature which is not manifest in His sight; but all things are naked and open unto His eyes with whom we have to do." This two-edged sweard[2], which God hath put in the mouth of man, doth try the force of things set against it. It cutteth the corrupt affections from the heart: it openeth the festered sores, the pestilent imposthumes of our ill desires: it overthroweth the kingdom of Satan: it slays his host, sin, death and hell. And as an arrow, which is past the bow of a cunning archer, cannot be stayed by hand, before it have his lighting-place; so doth the word hold still his constant course: it maketh way wheresoever it goeth: it falleth as He willeth, which is the only director of it; but fall where it will, it falleth with effect; nor any man can withstand the blow that it giveth.

If you can justly ascribe any such piece of operation to the Cross, in your fourth signification, then will I gladly give

Folio 24, a.

[2] [sword.]   [3] Heb. iv. [12, 13.]

place unto you. But whereas it is certain that no work of man can alter the heart, or once regenerate it to true piety, the standard that Esay the Prophet speaketh of maketh nothing for your purpose. But S. Hierom, ye say, taketh your part; for upon that place he noteth[1]: "Undoubtedly there is meant the banner or sign of the Cross." Indeed S. Hierom hath these words: *Haud dubium quin vexillum Crucis; ut impleatur illud quod scriptum est: Laudibus Ejus plena est terra.* Which is as much to say as this: "No doubt but it shall be the ensign of the Cross; that it may be fulfilled which is written, 'The earth is full of His praises.'" Here Hierom doth explicate himself, what he doth mean by the ensign of the Cross: the setting forth of the praise of God; which is not by setting of a Cross on the altar, but by preaching the crucified Christ unto people. The place of Jeremy the fourth maketh no more for the Cross than it doth for the Candlesticks. For when the Prophet had spoken to the inhabitants of Juda and Jerusalem, to be circumcised to the Lord, and cut off the foreskins of their infected hearts; *ne egrederetur tanquam ignis furor Ejus, et accenderetur, et nemo extingueret:* "Lest His wrath should go forth as fire, and should be kindled, and no man quench it;" he cometh further to declare the obstinacy of men's hearts, that by no means can be brought to goodness, but seek by all means to avoid the reward and plague of wickedness. Wherefore, by an irony, he saith unto them: "Blow the trumpet in the land: cry, and gather together, and say, Assemble yourselves, and let us go into strong cities. Set up the standard in Sion[2]," &c. As if that he had said, I know what you will do: when the wrath of God shall fall upon you, when your enemies shall oppress you, you will not consider the cause thereof; but you will run to your strong holds, you will arm yourselves, and stand at your defence: you will set up your standard in Sion, and think that you shall be safe there. But it will not be so, saith the Lord: *Quoniam Ego malum accersam ab aquilone:* "Because I will bring a plague from the north."

And truly there is no cause why Hierom in this place should run to his allegory, whereas there is so plain and

---

[1] [*Super Esaiam*, Lib. xiii. sig. N v. Venet. 1497.]
[2] Jeremy iv. [4—6.]

sound a sense in the letter. But if his allegory should take place, let all go together, and it maketh against you. For his words be these[3]: *Ingrediamur civitates munitas. Hæreticorum bella consurgunt: Christi monumenta* [al. *munimenta*] *nos teneant. Levate signum Crucis* [*in specula; id est,*] *in sublimitate ecclesiæ:* "Let us enter into the walled cities. The battles of the heretics do arise: let the munitions of Christ hold us. Lift up the sign of the Cross in the height of the church." Let me now ask you this question; whether we must run against heretics with a Cross in our hand? as I remember a Priest of your faculty beat all his parish with the Cross-staff. If this artillery beat not down heresies, think that S. Hierom meant another thing; that is to say, the sign of the Cross in the top of the church, the preaching of the word in the Prelates of the Church.

Now, as for the sign of the Son of man[4], "which shall, before the judgment, appear in heaven," forsooth there is no certain proof that it shall be a Cross[5]. For Chrysostom, in his second exposition upon the twenty-fourth chapter of Matthew, saith[6]: *Quidam putant Crucem Christi ostenden-*

---

[3] [*Super Hieremiam*, Liber i. sig. T v. ed. sup. cit.]
[4] Matth. xxiv. [30.]
[5] [Waldensis (*Sacram.* Tit. xx. Cap. clviii.) attempts to evince from Isaiah lxv. 22,—"as the days of a tree are the days of my people," that the fragments of the Cross are to be collected together with the Elect; preparatively to its appearance in heaven, according to an opinion very generally held by the Fathers. See S. Chrysostom's fifty-fourth and seventy-sixth Homilies on S. Matthew. S. Cyril, *Catech.* xiii. & xv. pp. 323, 383. Paris. 1609. Bellarm. *De Imaginibus*, Lib. ii. Cap. xxviii. *Rhem. Test.* p. 69. 1582. Pierre do Croix, *Discours du signe de la Croix*, p. 288. A Arras, 1604. Leigh's *Annot.* p. 65. Lond. 1650.; and compare the last three lines of the sixth book of the *Sibylline Oracles*, thus translated by Castalio:

"O Lignum felix, in quo Deus Ipse pependit.
Nec te terra capit; sed cœli tecta videbis,
Cum renovata Dei facies ignita micabit."]

[6] Hom. xlix. [*Op. imperf. in S. Matth.* inter D. Chrysost. Opp. Tom. ii. col. 964. Paris. 1570.—The "Opus imperfectum" was interdicted by the *Index Romanus* of Pope Paul IV., in the year 1559: but the prohibitory sentence was withdrawn by Pius IV., in 1564; and by Clement VIII., in 1596. Baronius is indignant at the idea, that S. Chrysostom should be ascribed "ab incerto auctore, sed certo hæretico, hæreticorumque deterrimo, compositas Homilias illas purulentas,

dam esse in cœlo. Verius autem est, ipsum Christum : in corpore suo habentem testimonia passionis ; id est, vulnera lanceæ et clavorum ; ut impleatur illud quod dictum est, Et videbunt in Quem pupugerunt : "Some," (saith Chrysostom,) "think that the Cross of Christ shall be shewed in heaven. But it is truer that Christ Himself shall appear; having in His body the testimonies of His passion ; that is to say, the wounds of the spear and nails; that it may be fulfilled which was said, 'And they shall see Him whom they pierced.'" Nor only content with his own censure, he bringeth after a proof of Scripture, that the words cannot be spoken of the Cross, but of the body of Christ Himself; because the rest of the Evangelists, writing of the same matter, do only say, *Videbunt Filium hominis venientem ;* "They shall see the Son of man coming." Whereupon he concludeth, that all the Evangelists do shew, *signum Christi esse ipsum corpus Christi ; qui in signo corporis sui cognoscendus est a quibus crucifixus est :* "That the sign of Christ is the body of Christ Himself; who in the sign of His body shall be known of them of whom He was crucified." So that ye challenge more a great deal than we need to grant you.

But you shall see how courteously I will deal with you. Admit that the sign of the Son of man is the Cross indeed. What have ye gained now? First, it shall be no material Cross made with man's hand, nor yet a sign printed in his forehead. Therefore ye must run to a fifth signification of "Cross" in Scripture ; for this cannot serve for the fourth.

hæresum scatentes vermibus," &c. (Ad an. 407. p. 264. Tom. v. Antv. 1658.) Bellarmin thinks it credible that the author was a Catholic, but that his work was depraved by the Arians ; (*De Scriptt. Eccl.* p. 100. Conf. Franci *Disquisit. de Papistarum Indicibus,* pp. 102—104. Lips. 1684. Wharton's *Enthusiasm of the Church of Rome,* p. 117. Lond. 1688.) and it has been supposed by Montfaucon that he could not have lived before the sixth or seventh age. (In *Diat.* Op. præfix. Cf. Thilo, *Cod. Apocr. N. Test.* Tom. i. pp. xciv, xcv. Lips. 1832. Vid. Ittig. *De Biblioth. Patt.* Præf. pp. cxviii—cxx. Lips. 1707. Dallæum, *De vero usu Patrum,* p. 56. Genev. 1656. Usser. *De Scriptur. et Sac. vernac.* p. 262. Lond. 1690. Crakanthorp. *Defens. Eccl. Anglic.* p. 556, Lond. 1625. Morton's *Catholike Appeale,* pp. 313—14. Lond. 1610. Natal. Alexand. *Hist. Eccles.* Tom. iv. pp. 161—63. Paris. 1699. James's *Treatise of the corruption of Fathers,* &c. Part ii. pp. 33—39. Lond, 1611.)]

The places that ye cite out of the ninth of Ezechiel, and seventh of the Revelation, where many be sealed into God's servants, (out of which order I fear me lest a number of my Cross-masters may cry with the Friar, *Nos sumus exempti:* "We are exempt[1];") I marvel that you can without blushing utter. But if ye have any shame in you, I will make you to blush. Think you that the sign of GOD in the foreheads was the sign of a Cross drawn with a finger? Is the Spirit of life, and lively faith, (which only express the true print of God,) inspired as soon as a Cross is figured? Is the sign of a Cross sufficient to discern the good from the bad; the faithful from the infidels? Yet such must the sign of the Cross be, if it be the same that either Ezechiel or Saint John speaketh of. Consider this, ye gross Papist; that he that marked the foreheads in Ezechiel was neither Carver, Crosser, nor Conjurer. He was clothed in linen, and had an inkhorn by his side. He bare the type of a Scribe and a Priest. The mark that he gave them was the letter *Thau*[2]; (of which I speak more in the next article:) signifying the law, direction, or rule; to note that the Minister of God's word must print the seal: he must engrave in the very heart the law of God, and rule of faith; and then be they safe and sure from all evil. The blood of the lamb in the old Law was not cast behind the door, but sprinkled upon the door-posts: the mark of God is not set in the back, but in the forehead of all the faithful; that, as things most manifest be said to be written in a man's forehead, and the forehead is the place of shame, so should the servants of the living God, lightened with His word and Holy Spirit, never dissemble it, or be ashamed of it.

The letter Thau.

Again, the persons sealed, as well in Ezechiel as in the

---

[1] [The disturbance of episcopal jurisdiction by the privileges granted to the monastic Orders, and the laxity of life among the "exempt," were facts acknowledged by the Council of Trent. (*Sess.* xxiv. Cap. xi. Conf. De Habermann ab Unsleben, *Dissert. de Pont. Rom. potest.* Sect. iii. pp. 104—7. Gottingæ, 1754.) Launoi imagines a case of an Abbot or a Monk saying, with confidence, to a Bishop of Paris: "Tu potestatem in me nullam habes... Ego exemptus sum: vade vias tuas, et sis anathema maranatha." (*Assert. Inquis. in Chart. Imm. B. Germ.* p. 72. Lut. Paris. 1658.)]

[2] [Bp. Hooper's *Discourse concerning Lent*, pp. 256-7. Lond. 1695. Conr. Bruni *De Cæremon.* Lib. iii. Cap. v. pag. 76. Mogunt. 1548.]

[CALFHILL.] 7

Revelation, do shew that they had a surer mark than a sorry sign of the Cross can be. For in Ezechiel we read: "Pass thorough the city of Hierusalem, and set a mark upon the foreheads of them that mourn and cry for all the abominations that be done in the midst thereof." And in the seventh of the Revelation: "Till we have sealed the servants of our God in their foreheads." Therefore, such as lament and be sorry for abominable wickedness; such as be indeed the servants of God, they be sealed: but all men indifferently have the sign of the Cross; many moe than be grieved with the sight of sin, or do continue in the fear of God: therefore the seal, that in these places is spoken of, is not the sign of the Cross. Julian was crossed; Pope Silvester was crossed; and yet, as it is proved afore, neither of them both did mourn for their sins, or served God. See ye not then how fondly ye pretend Scripture for your Cross? There be only five places brought, and every one of them doth make against you. Wherefore, since these be the only ground of the two kinds of Crosses, whereupon in this treatise ye mind to discourse, and these make nothing for you; what shall we think, not of your slender building, but ill-favoured botching, whose foundation already is shaken unto naught?

_{Folio 24, a.}

Ye please yourself well, and think ye have shewed a great piece of wit, when ye call your adversaries, (me and such other,) "enemies of the Cross." But I think there is no man so mad to believe you, unless ye could tell what the Cross meaneth. Ye say, "that ye attribute nothing to the sign of the Cross, without special relation to the merits of Christ's passion." Then why did ye bring in the example of Julian[1], and the Jew? Why afterward allege ye, "that man, using only the sign of the Cross, putteth away all the craft and subtilty of the Devil?" Ye forget yourself; ye should have one to wring you by the ear. But I will bear with your weakness: although, to confirm your better advisement, ye close up your tale in the first article with as vain a supposal as, in your dreaming devising, ye conceived afore; "that, as God giveth victory in battle, health in sickness, &c., but by the help of men, as external means; so Christ worketh all the effects that shall be, but by

_{Folio 24.}
_{Folio 24.}
_{Folio 92, a.}

---

[1] [Conf. Durant. *Rationale*: De invent. S. Crucis; Lib. vii. fol. clxxx. Nuremb. 1481.]

the holy sign of His Cross." If I might crave so much of your Mastership, I would be a suitor, once to have you prove that which so often you confidently affirm. I acknowledge you not for any such Pythagoras, that it shall suffice me for mine own discharge to say, αὐτὸς ἔφα, M. Martiall hath said the word: but I rather think you to be some scholar of Anaxagoras, which have learned to make *quidlibet ex quolibet;* an apple of an oyster. Pardon me, therefore, if I trust you no further than I have trial of you.

TO THE SECOND ARTICLE.

A FOOL on a time came to a Philosopher, and asked him, What is honesty? Whereto he would make him no answer; for, said he, thou demandest me a question of that that thou hast nothing to do withal. And sith your wisdom, in the second article, doth prove nothing else but that which ye profess ye will have nothing to do withal, it may seem folly in me to make you any answer to it. In the next side of the leaf before, these words ye have: "There be two kinds of signs of the Cross: the one made of some earthly matter, to be set up in churches, and left in the sight of the people; the other expressed or made with man's hand, in the air, in form and likeness of the other, and imprinted in men's foreheads, breasts, and other parts of the body, and used as further occasion requireth. Of which two signs in this treatise I mind to discourse." Now, if either of these signs was prefigured in the law of nature, foreshewed by the signs of Moses' Law, denounced by the Prophets, or shewed from heaven in the time of grace, then think that you have said something, and I have done you wrong in reproving of you. But the passion of Christ and manner of His death was only prefigured. What is this to the sign? And if it were so, (which you shall never prove,) that the sign itself, the God of the Rood-loft, the Cross of the altar were prefigured, what is that to your purpose? What a consecution is this, M. Martiall: "The Crucifix is prefigured in Moses, in the Prophets, and in the time of Christ: therefore no remedy but a Crucifix must be had in the church, borne in procession, and crept unto on Good-Friday?" Then, let me reason with you. The treason of Judas was foretold by prophecy; Psal. cviii. *Fiant dies ejus pauci, et episcopatum ejus accipiat alter:* "Let his days be short," (saith David,) "and let another occupy his room[1]:" which to be understood of Judas, the Acts of the Apostles prove[2]. And in the time of grace there was no less foreshewed, when Christ said, *Unus ex*

---

[1] [Psalm cix. 8.]   [2] [Acts i. 20.]

vobis Diabolus est: "One of you is a Devil[3]:" *Ergo*, we must reverence the treason of Judas; yea, some sign thereof we must have amongst us. The manner of his death was also prefigured, as Augustin affirmeth[4]; how his belly should burst, and he desperately die: therefore let us have one holyday of betraying, another of bursting. For if prefiguring in law of nature, denouncing by the Prophets, foreshewing from heaven in time of grace, be able to enforce the necessary use and estimation of any thing; then why should not this, and many other plagues of God, be honoured as well as the sign of the Cross? Wherefore I will briefly run over your authors, and note by the way sometime how fondly ye apply them. When men from a certain revealed truth will run to their own fantasies and devices, no marvel if sometime they overshoot themselves: and when they leave the histories of the Scripture, and seek for allegories more than need, they breed oftentimes obscurity, and bring men in doubt further than before. Yet I deny not, but, as Augustin saith[5], there may be a spiritual understanding beside a sense literal. Otherwise the Apostle did not well in figuring the two Testaments by the two Children, one of the bond-woman, another of the free[6]; nor we could admit his exposition of Moses' rock to be Christ Himself[7]. But in this case, where every man is led by his own sense, his exposition is most to be allowed, who speaketh most according to piety.

Damascen doth resemble the tree of life in Paradise to the Cross[8]: and as in one sense I condemn it not, so in an-

Folio 25. Damascen.

---

[3] Joan. vi. [70.]

[4] In Psal. cviii. [Conf. Paulini Aquileiensis *Lib. de salutar. Docum.* Cap. lvi. inter S. August. *Opp.* vl. 685. ed. Ben.]

[5] De Civitate Dei, Libro xiii. Cap. xxi. ["Quasi propterea non potuerit esse Paradisus corporalis, quia potest etiam spiritalis intelligi: tanquam ideo non fuerint duæ mulieres, Agar et Sara, et ex illis duo filii Abrahæ, unus de ancilla, alius de libera, quia duo Testamenta in eis figurata dicit Apostolus: aut ideo de nulla petra, Moyse percutiente, aqua defluxerit, quia potest illic, figurata significatione, etiam Christus intelligi; eodem Apostolo dicente, Petra autem erat Christus."]

[6] Galat. iv. [22—24.]

[7] 1 Cori. x. [4.]

[8] ["Hanc pretiosam Crucem prefiguravit vitæ lignum, quod in Paradiso plantatum est a Deo: nam posteaquam per lignum mors, oportebat per lignum donari vitam et resurrectionem." (*De orth. Fid.* iv. xii. 90.)]

other I like it not; for I see that you be deceived by it. He, (shewing how Christ, as a good physician, did cure by contraries,) made, as it were, our life to spring out of His death; and therefore compared the tree of life to the passion. But the words that are inferred savour not of the Scripture; for ye say: "Seeing death came in by the tree, it was convenient that life and resurrection should be given again by a tree." Paul speaketh otherwise[1]: *Per unum hominem intravit mors, et per hominem resurrectio:* "By one man sin entered in, and by one man resurrection:" not by one tree; though one death upon a tree was a mean thereof. Augustin, in divers places, maketh the tree of life to be the wisdom of God: as in his second book *De Gen. contra Manich. Cap.* ix.[2]; and in his thirteenth book *De Civitate Dei, Ca.* xxi.[3] Likewise, as often he doth resemble it to Christ Himself: as in his first book and fifteenth chapter *Contra adversarios Legis et Proph.*[4], speaking of Paradise, where Christ and the thief should meet, saith: *Esse ibi cum Christo, est ibi esse cum vitæ ligno:* "To be there with Christ, is to be there with the tree of life." And whereas Cassiodore, upon the first Psalm, doth refer the tree planted by the river side unto the Cross that bare Christ; how much better Augustin, on the same place, expounds it of Christ Himself: *Qui, de aquis decurrentibus, id est, populis peccatoribus, trahit eos in radice* [al. *radices*] *disciplinæ suæ:* "Which, of the running waters, that is to say, the sinful people, draweth men unto Him in the root of His discipline." For whereas Christ is the Wisdom of the Father, this exposition is consonant unto Scripture, which of that Wisdom saith, *Lignum vitæ est amplectentibus eam:* "She is the tree of life to them that lay hold on her[5]." But if the wood of the Cross be worthily called "the tree of life, because our Lord Christ, who is our life, was hanged there;" why should not the Ass be the beast of life, because our

Folio 25, b.

[1] 1 Cor. xv. [21.]
[2] [*Opp.* Tom. i. 498. ed. Ben.—"Lignum autem vitæ, plantatum in medio Paradisi, Sapientiam illam significat."]
[3] ["Lignum vitæ, ipsam bonorum omnium matrem Sapientiam."]
[4] [*Opp.* viii. 398.—"Esse autem ibi cum Christo, hoc est esse cum vitæ ligno. Ipse est quippe Sapientia, de qua, ut superius commemoravi, scriptum est, Lignum vitæ est amplectentibus eam."]
[5] [Prov. iii. 18.]

Lord Christ, who is our life, did ride upon her? Ye will say, peradventure, that the Ass was no instrument for His death: but for His kingdom she was; and why not the instrument of His kingdom, as well as of His priesthood, be honoured of us? I say it to this end; that if ye think the Fathers of the Church, speaking of the Cross, to be understood so grossly as ye take them, many fond absurdities shall arise thereof. They meant of the death of Christ that which you attribute to the material Cross. They, by a figure, did ascribe to the sign that which is proper to the signified thing. I omit some authorities that you do allege; because they neither do make for you, nor against me.

Cyrillus saith[6]: "The holy Cross brought us up to heaven; and that the Cross is that ark of Noah, by which we are saved from the flood of the water of sin overflowing us," &c. I think there is none so senseless as yourself but construes his words otherwise than you. Too easy, God wot, is that way to heaven, whereto we may be carried a pickback on[7] a Rood. Too soon shall we fall from state of our felicity, if a rotten piece of wood or cankered metal must support us in it. Too dreadful shall this drowning in our sins be, if no better ark than of a Cross material shall preserve us from it. Let the Doctors dally in figures as they fancy; let us not depart from the verity of the word. If they speak one thing, and mean another, let us take their meaning, and let their words alone. Great difference there is, when a doctrine is plainly taught, and when they descant upon a text. Wherefore, the standard of Abraham, according to Ambrose; the wood of the sacrifice, according to Cyril; the blessing of Jacob, according to Damascen; the rod of Aaron, according to Origen; by which all, (is said,) the Cross was prefigured, I wittingly omit. For what if a thousand things else were, (as men imagined,) figures of a Cross; (in which case a man's invention might have scope enough, and find in the Scripture many moe such figures than they have spoken of;) shall this bring such authority to the Cross, (which is the thing that you do shoot at,) that the sign of the Cross shall be in all places set up and honoured?

Folio 26, a.
Folio 26, b.
Folio 27, a.

[6] [*Catech.* xiii. p. 303. Paris. 1609. "Ubique per lignum salus. Noë tempore per ligneam arcam vitæ fuit conservatio."—Cf. Deylingii *Observatt. sacr.* iv. 140. Lips. 1757.]

[7] [on the back of.]

Folio 28.

The lifting up of Moses' hands, Exodi xvii., somewhat will I speak of; thereby to declare that such young men as you, speaking much of the Cross, know not at all the sign of the Cross. That the lifting up of Moses' hand did signify prayer, is evident by consent of all men. Chrysostom *De orando ad Deum, lib.* i. saith[1]: *Quomodo Moses Israeliticum populum in bellis servavit? An non arma quidem cum exercitu discipulo tradidit; ipse vero deprecationem opposuit hostium multitudini? Nos interim docens, preces justorum plus valere quam arma, quam equitatum,* &c. In English thus: "How did Moses preserve the people of Israel in the wars? Did he not deliver unto his scholar his armour and host; but he himself set his earnest prayer against the multitude of his enemies? Thereby teaching us, that the prayer of the righteous is more available than arms or horsemen." And in his Sermon of Moses[2]: *Desinit Israel vincere, Mose desistente in prece; ut dum diversa populis exhiberentur, orationis potentia nobis monstraretur:* "Israel leaves overcoming," (quoth he,) "when Moses left his praying; that when divers effects were shewed unto the people, the power of prayer might be shewed unto us." And truly, if we mark the place itself, much better doctrine may be pyked of[3] it, than to prefigurate I wot not what manner of Cross unto us. The lifting up of Moses' hands, with the rod therein, is nothing else but prayer that proceeds of faith, according unto God's word. So David saith[4]: "Let the lifting up of my hands be as an evening sacrifice." The heavy hands, whereof the story speaketh, do signify the sluggishness and fainting of our flesh in all virtuous and honest exercise. But, as Moses fainting had a stone put under him, so we must have Christ, that spiritual stone, to support our weakness: as Aaron and Hur stayed

---

[1] [The words have been derived not from the first, but from the second dubious treatise Περὶ προσευχῆς, according to the earliest Latin version by Erasmus; (sig. C vi. Basil. 1525.) who considered the Oration to be "non Chrysostomi, sed eruditi cujuspiam."]

[2] [This must mean the spurious Homily on the seventeenth chapter of Exodus, beginning "Stabat Moyses," and enumerated by Sixtus of Siena and Possevinus among those which are "perperam D. Chrysostomo inscripta."]

[3] [picked off.]   [4] Psal. cxl. [cxli. 2.]

up Moses' hands, so the Ministers of the word must confirm the hearts of them that make their prayers with the merciful promises of Almighty God.

But Augustin saith, " that beside all this, the figure of the Cross was foreshewed there." That am I well contented to admit: but your Englishing of the text I will not admit. For whereas the Latin hath *manibus in Crucis figuram extensis*, you to expound it thus, " his hands held up across," is too absurd and foolish. For to stretch out his hands in form of a Cross, and to hold his hands across, is two things. The stretching forth is at the arms' end, as Christ's was on the Cross, with the whole distance of body betwixt them: the holding of the hands across is with one over the other. Wherefore, by your reason, Moses made a Cross, but it was a Saint Andrew's Cross[5]: or, if you will have the figure of the church Cross represented here, then Moses put one of his hands under his other elbow; which the text beareth not. But, O blindness of Popery, that neither understand the Father's writing, nor can give a reason of your own ceremonies! Moses, stretching out his hands, made a figure of the Cross: but your learning cannot reach to know what the old figure of the Cross was. It is like to the Greek Y: which our countryman and late Cardinal M. Poole understood well enough; and therefore, in his new gallery at Lambheth, in the glass windows, he drew this figure Y, in token of the Cross, as is yet to be seen. But what is this figure like to the Rood or Crucifix? What have ye gained by this allegation, but utterly bewrayed your ignorance? And certainly, if God's word would suffer us, (which indeed is against it,) to have and occupy the sign of a Cross, yet the form that we use is against all precedent of Scripture and antiquity. Which, when I come anon to the exposition of the letter *Thau*, shall appear more plainly.

But your fresh argument, inferred of the place afore, moveth me to laughter with an indignation. For it savours nothing of the school, save that it hath *Ergo* before the

^{Objection.}

^{Folio 28, b.}

---

[5] [Vid. S. Just. Mart. *Opp.* pp. 317—18. Lut. Paris. 1615. Conf. Lactant. vel Cecil. *De mort. Pers.* Cap. xliv. p. 267. et Cuperi *Not.* p. 238. Ultraj. 1692. Dallæum, *De relig. Cult. object.* p. 798. Genev. 1664.]

conclusion; which every alewife can do as well as you. It hath neither mode nor figure, wit nor common sense. For this is your reason: "The Devil is discomfited by the Cross of our Lord, which was prefigured by the hands of Moses: But by Moses' hands the sign of the Cross was prefigured: *Ergo*, by the sign of the Cross Devils are overcomed." I need not to shew the error of your argument; for it is too manifest, and hath nothing else but error in it. If thus ye had said: "Devils are discomfited by that which Moses' hands prefigured: But Moses' hands prefigured the sign of the Cross: *Ergo*, by the sign of the Cross Devils are discomfited;" I would have better allowed your argument, and denied your "minor," which is the second proposition: for Moses' hands prefigured not the sign of the Cross, but the Cross itself, which is the death of Christ. Look on the words of your author. But one fault is too familiar with you; that whatsoever is spoken of effect of the passion, you do attribute to the instrument and sign. So the wood of Marah[1] prefigured the glory and grace of the Cross; not of the sign, but of the thing itself: for the bitterness of death is not taken away by a material Cross, or sign in the forehead; but death by death is swallowed[2].

Hitherto of your Cross figures under the Law. Now that the same was denounced by the Prophets, ye run to the places of Ezechiel and Jeremy; which although I have answered at the full in the latter end of the first article, yet somewhat must I add for your further learning. The letter ת *Thau* to be a kind of Cross, (as you out of Tertullian allege,) I grant[3]: but how it can be applied to the sign of our Cross, I see not. For the figure which you make, somewhat like unto our common Cross, is the Greek Tαῦ, or the Latin T[4]: but the Prophets spake Hebrew; and the Hebrew character is a very pair of

---

[1] [Exod. xv. 23—25.]

[2] 1 Cor. xv. [54.]

[3] ["Et ut ad nostra veniamus, antiquis Hebræorum literis, quibus usque hodie utuntur Samaritani, extrema Thau litera Crucis habet similitudinem, quæ in Christianorum frontibus pingitur, et frequenti manus inscriptione signatur." (S. Hieron. *Comment. in Ezech.* ix. Opp. Tom. v. pag. 404. Basil. 1565. Cf. Origen. in eund. loc.)]

[4] [Tertull. *Advers. Marcion.* Lib. iii. Cap. xxii.—"Ipsa est enim litera Græcorum Tau, nostra autem T, species Crucis."]

gallows ת[5]. Your Cross is *Figura duarum linearum in se invicem ductarum; nimirum unius perpendicularis, sub altera diametrali:* "The proportion of two lines drawn together; one directly downward, and another cross overthwart." Whereof if ye will have any figure of old time before you[6], go to the Egyptians' Idol Serapis, which had it just pictured in his breast, as Suidas and Orus Apollo testify. But that the Latin T, or Greek *Tau*, and Hebrew *Thau*, be all alike, none will say but such a great Clerk as you. For indeed, as the Hebrew letter is different in fashion from the Greek, so in signification they were quite contrary. The Hebrews by their ת *Thau* did figure death; the Greeks by their Ταῦ did signify life. Therefore Isidorus[7] writeth, that in old time, when they would note in their registers such as were slain in the wars, they would mark them with the letter Θ, as thrust thorough with a dart, or else of Θάνατος, which is death: but when they would note any one alive, they would put their letter Ταῦ, this cross mark T upon him. Also Asconius Pedianus saith, that when a jury gave up their verdict of guilty or not guilty, such as were condemned to death were

[5] [This argument is rendered nugatory by the fact, that the modern Hebrew letters were not in use until after the time of Ezekiel and the Babylonish Captivity. The Prophet could have referred only to the Samaritan *Thau*, which was not an oblong cruciform character, but appears decussated on coins and medals. The Latin Vulgate and the English Douay version in this case differ from the Septuagint; and Aquila, (or Theodotion, according to S. Jerom,) was the first who changed the interpretation of the text. Vid. Casauboni *Exercit. ad Annales Baronii*, xvi. lxxviii. 620—21. Lond. 1614. Jos. Scaligeri *Animadvers. in Chronol. Euseb.* p. 117. Lugd. Bat. 1658. Leigh's *Critica Sacra*, Suppl. p. 24. Lond. 1662. Sixt. Senens. *Biblioth.* Lib. ii. p. 125. Molani *Hist. Imagg.* iv. 482. Lugd. 1619. *Douay Bible*, Annot. p. 658. Rouen, 1635. Conf. Waltoni *Prolegom.* iii. *Considerator considered,* Chap. xiii. Lond. 1659.—" In nummis Samaritanis, qui in Museis occurrunt, Ταῦ forma Crucis exaratum, ut nos in Tabula expressimus, frequentissime visitur: in quos si incidisset Scaliger, Origenis et Hieronymi testimonio refragatus non esset.", (De Montfaucon, *Palæograph. Græc.* Lib. ii. Cap. iii. p. 133. Cf. p. 122. Paris. 1708.)]

[6] ["Denique si in literis figuram Crucis nancisci cuperemus, ad Æthiopicas, quarum Thau Crux est, confugiendum esset; aut ad Ægyptias Hieroglyphicas, unde tot Cruces inventæ in Serapidis fano." (Steph. Morini *Exercitt. de Lingua primæva*, p. 257. Ultraj. 1694.)]

[7] [*Origin.* Lib. i. C. xxiii. Opp. p. 10. Paris. 1601.]

marked with Θ[1]; but such as were quit were marked with the T[2]. Wherefore there is no reason why your Rood or Crucifix can by any mean be applied to the mark which Ezechiel speaketh of. First, because none have the Prophet's mark but such as be godly, and lament wickedness: but many of the Devil's children, grinagods and such other, be crossed, and cursed too. Then also the proportion is so far different, that there is no likeness betwixt them. But, for the likeness of the effect, they may be well compared together[3]. For as they only were saved which were so signed with the letter ת Thau, so none be saved now, nor yet ever were, but such as have the print of Christ's Cross within them, merits of His passion, and faith in His blood.

Well doth Hierom[4] shew the causes why the sign ת Thau should be made in the foreheads of the elect: first, *ut perfectam in viris gementibus et dolentibus scientiam demonstraret; quia extrema apud Hebræos est viginti et duarum litterarum:* that is to say, "To shew a perfect knowledge in them that mourn and be sorry; because it is the last letter of twenty-two among the Hebritians." That as that letter doth end the alphabet, so when Christ died on the Cross, (which that letter signified,) all things were ended necessary for our salvation; according to the word *Consummatum est:* "It is finished[5]:" the work of our salvation was then fully wrought[6]. Again, saith Hierom, because this letter is the first in the word which signifieth Law among the Hebrews, *Illi hoc ac-*

---

[1] [... "nigrum vitio præfigere Theta." (Pers. iv. 13.)]
[2] [Cf. Paull. Diacon. *De notis Literar.* Godwyn's *Rom. Antiq.* p. 247. Lond. 1658.]
[3] [Hooker, Vol. ii. p. 324. Oxford, 1841.]
[4] In Ezech. Cap. ix. [Lib. iii. sig. EE viii. Venet. 1497.—" Tau, quæ extrema est apud Hebræos viginti et duarum literarum; ut perfectam in viris gementibus et dolentibus scientiam demonstraret: sive, ut Hebræi autumant, quia Lex apud eos appellatur Thora, quæ hac, in principio nominis sui, litera scribitur."]
[5] Joan. xix. [30.]
[6] ["But this reward (saith Ezekiel) is for those, whose foreheads are marked with *Tau;* which (as *Omega* in Greeke) is the last letter in the Hebrew Alphabet, and the marke of *Consummatum est* among them: They onely shall escape the wrath to come. And this crowne is laid up for them, not of whom it may be said, *Currebatis bene,* Ye did runne well; but for those that can say (with Saint Paul) *Cursum*

cepere signaculum, qui Legis præcepta compleverant: "They received this mark, which had fulfilled the precepts of the Law." So that the fashion of the letter is not so much as the mystery [7]; which accordeth well to that which I said before: yet neither the fashion nor the mystery maketh aught for your purpose, M. Martiall. Now I marvel what toy came into your idle head, when, for a proof of the undoubted sign of the Cross, ye bring forth the words of the Psal.[8]: "O Lord, the light of Thy countenance is sealed on us." Do ye think that the light of God's countenance is a piece of wood in the Rood-loft, or a Crucifix on the altar? Or else, do ye think that the light of God's countenance can be fixed with a finger in the fleshy forehead? If none of these be true, what shall I say to you? You have made a whip; yourself shall be beaten with it. Hierom's words be these: *Præcipitur sex viris, ut præter eos qui possunt dicere, Signatum est super nos lumen vultus Tui Domine, cunctos interficiant:* "Commandment is given to the six men, (of whom Ezechiel speaketh,) that they kill all but them that can say, 'O Lord, the light of Thy countenance is sealed on us.'" The light of God's countenance is His favour toward us. Then is it signed in us, when the sense thereof doth come unto us, and breed a confidence and sure hope within us. If the light of God's countenance be the selfsame with the letter ת *Thau,* and the letter *Thau* no other but the sign of the Cross; then whosoever have the sign of the Cross have hope, have confidence, have faith in God. But this is utterly false, as experience itself doth teach us. Therefore the letter *Thau,* though in a mystery it betokened the death of Christ, yet hath it no relation to the sign of the Cross.

consummavi, I have finished my course well." (Bp. Andrewes, *Sermons,* p. 307. Lond. 1635.)—

> Pendemus a Te,
> Credimus in Te,
> Tendimus ad Te,
> Non nisi per Te,
> Optime Christe.]

[7] ["Plurima qui breviter vis discere, disce ubi sola
    Littera Tau magnum complectitur Alphabetum.
   Crux Tau Christum, A et Ω, principium et finem."
        (Cornelius Curtius, *De Clavis Dominicis,* p. 125. Antv. 1670.)]

[8] [Psal. iv. 6. Lat.]

For answer to the other places of Esay and Jeremy, I refer you to that which I said before. Now, to come to the time of grace, I had need to beware of you. Ye come in with that, which ye have good testimony to be true indeed; that a Cross, in the fourth signification, such a Cross as ye speak of, was shewed from heaven to Constantine the Great, with these Angel's words: *In hoc vince,* "In this overcome[1]."

"Nor the good Emperor saw this only, but, as Eusebius writeth, was commanded to make a sign of it, carried it in his standard, and afterward did cause his men in their armour to grave it[2]." But whatsoever it hath pleased God, for His glory's sake at any time to do, must not be drawn for example unto us. Privileges extend no further than to the persons comprised in them. Signs and miracles were shewed to some, which neither be granted to other, nor ought to be asked of all. Moses had a sign to confirm him in his enterprise against Pharao: but Josue had not so. He only had a bare commandment, when he entered upon the land of Chanaan. Gideon was confirmed by miracle to fight against the Madianites: so neither Jephte nor Sampson were. Paul was by a sign from heaven called: so was not Peter, nor any of his successors after. Wherefore, if thus it pleased God to enbolden the heart of Constantine to fight against Maxentius the tyrant, that He would shew him such a sign from heaven; not to confirm his faith, which by the word was to be established, but to put him in assurance of a thing beside the word, that is to say, victory against his enemies[3]; what prece-

---

[1] [Conf. Fabricii *Biblioth. Græc.* Vol. vi. pp. 700—718. Hamb. 1798. Gothofredi *Dissert. in Philostorg.* pp. 16—20. Genev. 1643. Le Nourry *Diss. in lib. De mort. Persec.* pp. 184—190. Paris. 1710. Newman's *Essay on Miracles,* pp. cxxxiii.—cxliii. Oxford, 1842.]

[2] ["Constantinus vidit in nocte apertis oculis igneam Crucem ad Orientem, et audivit Angelum Dei dicentem sibi: *Constantine! in hoc signo vinces.* Et quamvis adhuc esset maximus persecutor Christianorum, tamen, divino edoctus miraculo, signum Crucis vexillis, clypeis, et armis suis et suorum imposuit." (Hermanni Gygantis *Flores Temporum,* p. 46. Lugd. Bat. 1743.)]

[3] ["Magis id quidem ad spem victoriæ in prælio, quod instabat, per fidem potentiæ Christi confirmandam pertinebat, quam ad spem salutis æternæ, quæ majori in periculo versabatur, per eundem Christum consequendæ." (Card. Polus, *De Baptismo Constantini;* ad calc. *Lib. de Concilio,* fol. 62, b. Romæ, 1562.)]

dent is this to prejudice my cause? He newly was converted to the faith: he was weak therein; and therefore he doubted of such success in his affairs as, for His Church cause, God appointed to grant him. For which cause an extraordinary mean was used: and God applied Himself to the capacity of them that He dealt withal; giving such a token to them as might well assure them of conquest in His name. *In hoc signo vince*, said God: "In this sign," that is to say, in His name, whom this figure representeth, " overthrow thine enemies."

It was not the sign that gave the victory: Constantine never thought it. He taught his people otherwise to say; as it appeareth in the solemn prayer which he willed them, with lifting up of eyes and hearts to heaven, daily to make. For as soon as ever he had vanquished the tyrant, he returned unto Rome, and first of all, *Victoriæ Authori gratiarum actionem persolvit*[4], "he gave his thanks to the Author of victory:" then afterward he set up His Cross in the marketplace, to the end it might there remain a testimony of the power of God; that whosoever did behold the same might by and by conceive of Whose Religion this Emperor was, and in Whose name he overcame his foes. Which visible sign, at the first gathering of the Church together, newly come from the Gentiles, (among whom the Cross, and therefore Christ crucified, was utterly contemned,) was thought very necessary; that by this outward mean he might draw them by a little and a little to think better of Christ, and so to serve Him. But what is this to the Cross in churches? Yea, what is it at all to us? God spake this to Constantine. He did well to follow Him. God hath not spoken thus to us. Wherefore should we imitate it? Shall we that have had the Gospel preached so long amongst us, we and our forefathers, stand in need of such extraordinary aids as they that never knew God, nor heard of Him? Whatsoever our need is, through our own default, surely we ought not to have them: God is not pleased with them. For, as Chrysostom[5] said, concerning the like superstitions as you do now maintain, (carrying about of S. John Gospels, keep-

---

[4] Eusebius, De vita Const. Lib. i. [p. 168. Muscul. interp. 1549.]
[5] In xxiii. Matth. Hom. xliv. [Hom. xliii. *Op. imperf.* col. 920. Vide supra, pp. 95, 6.]

ing little pieces of the Cross of Christ, and esteeming of such other reliques,) I may as justly say to you; that it is a madness to seek after such things as heretofore have been, and an impiety now to use them. Chrysostom maketh this objection to himself: Did not the handkercher of Peter, and shadow of his body passing by, preserve them that were sick? Thereto he replies himself, and saith, *Etiam antequam Dei notitia in hominibus esset, ratio erat ut per sanctitatem hominum Dei potentia cognosceretur: nunc autem insania est:* "Yea, before the knowledge of God was in men, it was reason that the power of God should be known by the holiness of men: but now it is madness." Even so say I to you; that although in the time of Constantinus the sign of the Cross, as he did use it, was not only tolerable, but also necessary, so now it is not only superfluous, but, (in respect of our abuse,) impious.

Folio 32.

Thus much for Constantine's apparition. But whereas ye apply his example unto us, saying, "that as he, so long as he served God, and honoured His Cross, ever had good success; so even had we in all conflicts, as long as we served God truly, and contemned not His Cross;" I say that your comparison is not pleadable: each part containeth some piece of untruth. Like a hasty hound, ye run at riot; and in making of likenesses ye be too licentious. Constantine was commanded to have the sign of the Cross. No marvel then, so long as he obeyed, if he also prevailed. But still ye put *Non causam pro causa.* Ye impute his victories as well to the honouring of the Cross, as to the service of God: whereas, of honour done to the Cross no word was before spoken. He carried it; he reverently spake of it; thereby to testify his faith in Christ: but he crouched not to it; he put off no cap to it.

Now for our victories, which, (you say,) we achieved, "as long as we served God truly, and with horrible blasphemies contemned not His Cross." Alas! ye take the matter all amiss. For as long as we so esteemed the material Cross, (as you think good we should,) so long we committed most horrible blasphemies, and served not God at all. Notwithstanding, we had successes granted us; such as, in matters that concern this life, be not denied to the very infidels: for, as Augustin saith, *Qui dat felicitatem in regno cœlorum non nisi solis piis, regnum hoc terrenum et piis et impiis confert; sicut Ei placet, cui nihil injuste placet*[1] : "He, that giveth blessedness in the kingdom of heaven not but to the godly, confers this earthly reign both upon the godly and upon the godless; even as pleaseth Him, to whom nothing is unjustly pleasing." He that gave empire and rule unto the Hebrews, that worshipped but one God, gave dominion and kingdom also to the Persians, that worshipped moe Gods. He, that gave increase of corn and grain to the worshippers of Him, gave plenty also to the honourers of the Idol Ceres[2]. He, that prospered Marius, avaunced Cæsar. He, that furthered Nero, did good to August. On the other side, He, that gave empire unto Vespasian, brought in Domitian. He, that maintained Constantine, did suffer Julian. So that, on both sides, good success in this world is granted; and we cannot gather a liking or misliking of God by it[3]. Yet, if a man should call you to accompt, and judge according to Chronicles' record, you should be condemned in your opinion. For when the Cross was most magnified, we had cross luck among. How came it to pass that the proverb hath been, *Bustum Anglorum Gallia, Gallorum Italia:* "France hath been the burial of Englishmen, and Italy of the Frenchmen?" How prospered, I pray you, the Catholics in the north, when every Priest and Parish-clerk came out with a Cross; every poor Soldier that followed the camp was all to becrossed; and the only cause of their insurrection was altogether masking and crossing? I could rehearse times more than one, when our countrymen have had small cause of triumph, and yet the Cross was esteemed too. When the Normans did invade the land, not all the Bishops and Pope-holy Clergy, with all their Crosses, could once withstand them. When civil discords arose within the realm, on both sides were Crosses, and both sides went to wrack.

Nor you have cause to condemn this age, as cast out of favour with Almighty God, if good success in external things be sign of favour. If plagues of God had been Note.

---

[1] De Civit. Dei, Li. v. [Cap. xxi. Cf. S. Matth. v. 45.]
[2] [Acts xiv. 17.]
[3] [Eccles. ix. 1. Cf. Downame's *Christian Warfare*, p. 96. Lond. 1634. S. Bernardi *Serm.* i. *in Septuag.* Opp. fol. 23, a. Lugd. 1530.]

[CALFHILL.]

frequent among us, and all things had gone backward with us, (as, thanks be to God, they have not;) if God and man, both earth and air, had fought against us, (as we by proof do see they have not;) yet could I with better cause have imputed it to your wilfulness and tyranny, (ye Papists,) which brought men continually to the cross of fire, than to the foregoing of a Cross in the coat. For why should not both heaven and earth cry vengeance on us; since the earth is imbrued with the bloodshed of Saints murthered by you, and air is infected with breath of you living? But God hath hitherto, for His children's cause, deferred the punishment due for your mischiefs. Look for it one day, when neither Cross nor Mass shall deliver you. But why do you falsely abase the goodness of our God toward us? Why do you spitefully impair the glory of our Queen, and her prosperous reign? What honour she gat at Leith, without effusion of blood, how can you be so impudent as to dissemble? What quiet peace, what godly friendship, is between the realms of England and Scotland purchased now; now that your Religion is in both places abolished: whereas, in the time of Popery, there was never but hatred and mortal war. All the world doth see, and justly may say, that, in the time of the Gospel, God hath more abundantly blessed us than ever He did since the land was inhabited. And of the doings at Newhaven, what an honourable peace ensued, (contrary to the wish and will of the enemies of God and of their country, the Papists,) we do now feel, thanks be to God; and you cannot deny. But in the Catholic time, (as you call it,) what success had you; when Calleis and Guines, so hardly won, so long kept, with such glory and gain to the English name defended, was easily in one three days with shame lost? More will I not rehearse of our desperate losses in that tyrannous interreign.

Folio 33, a.

I return to your visions. Julian, (as you cite out of Sozomenus[1],) "had a shower of rain that overtook him; and every drop that fell, either upon his coat, or any other that accompanied him, made a sign of the Cross." Again[2];

[1] [*Eccles. Hist.* Lib. v. Cap. i.—The circumstance is spoken of by Bp. Jewel; (*Replie,* p. 371. Lond. 1609.) who, by referring to "Li. v. Cap. 1:," shows that he quoted from the *Tripartite History.*]

[2] [Lib. v. Cap. xxii. Adonis *Chron.* pp. 149—50. Paris. 1561.]

"When the said Julian counselled the Jews to repair the temple of Jerusalem, destroyed by the Romans, God, to make them desist from that wicked purpose of theirs, caused the ground, where they had digged a great trench for the foundation, to be filled with earth rising out of a valley. And when, this notwithstanding, they continued their work, God raised a great tempest of wind, and scattered all the lime and sand which they had gathered; and caused a great earthquake, and killed all that were not baptized; and sent a great fire out of the foundation, and burned many of the labourers. And when all this nothing discouraged them, a bright glittering sign of the healthful Cross appeared in the element; and the Jews' apparel was filled with the sign of the Cross[3]." The application of these two histories, (which, for this purpose I set out at large, that they may the better be considered,) will make you glad to scrape them out of your book. For ye fare as a fool that walks in a net; or as the children, whose head being hid, they think their bodies cannot be seen. Although ye cast some shadows over you, and think that your head is hid in an hole, yet your ears be so long that they do bewray you[4].

When thus ye have heaped up as many mystical figures of the Cross as you and your learned Counsel can, ye gather a fine conclusion of them: "that God willeth all His highly to esteem the thing which those figures signified; and to believe, that as those figures wrought temporal benefits to the Israelites, so the truth, (that is, the Cross itself,) shall work unto His elect and chosen children, believing in His Son Jesus Christ, and having His sign printed in our foreheads, the like benefits, effects and virtues, spiritually, and much more greater." First, who told you that the truth of those figures was the Cross itself; unless, by a figure, ye take the Cross for The crucified? Then, that those figures wrought temporal benefits, how can you prove? Sure, if they were causes of any good that came, they were *Causæ stolidæ*, as Tully calleth them, mean and instrumental causes; as the axe is cause of the wood cleaving, and not efficient.

Folio 34.

---

[3] [Conf. Ditmari *Chronic.* L. ii. p. 24. ed. princ. Francof. 1580. Trithemii *Annall. Hirsaug.* i. 101. ii. 580. exc. typ. Monast. S. Galli, 1690.]

[4] [De Asini umbra, vid. Erasmi *Adagia*, fol. xlvi. Argent. 1510.]

8—2

Thirdly, if ye would have concluded well, *Distinguenda fuissent ambigua;* those words, that diversely may be taken, should have been severed into their divers significations; that we might have known how to have understood your Mastership. When ye join the truth and the Cross together, what Cross can I tell you speak of? If it be, according to your promise afore, the Cross in the fourth signification, (for thereof ye said you would only entreat;) then is not your Cross the truth itself, but a figure still. Whereas ye couple the belief in Christ, and His sign printed in our foreheads together, what sign is that? The Cross with a finger? If ye mean it so, ye make an unmeet comparison; the one being necessary, the other idle and unlawful too. This am I sure your meaning is, by covert speech to deceive the simple, and cause them to derive the glory from the truth, and transfer it to the figure; to have in reverence your idle sign, and let the thing signified be forgotten.

As for the figures of the old Law, mark what Tertullian[1] saith; and thereby shall you learn a better meaning of them than your mean skill considereth: for thus he saith: *Sacramentum mortis figurari in prædicatione oportebat: quanto incredibile, tanto magis scandalo futurum, si nude prædicaretur; quantoque magnificum, tanto magis adumbrandum,* [al. *obumbrandum,*] *ut difficultas intellectus gratiam Dei quæreret:* "It behoved the Sacrament of the death of Christ to be figured in preaching: for how much more it is incredible, so much more offensive should it be, if nakedly it had been preached; and by how much it was more glorious, so much the more it was to be shadowed, that the hardness of understanding might seek for the grace of God." So far Tertullian. But how little grace of God you have, in sticking still to the easy letter, and never seeking the glory of the death, is too well seen by your doings. The sign of the Cross was shewed to Constantine. He was not yet become a Christian. It was expedient to have a miracle. We do profess great skill and knowledge; and shall we not believe without a sign? That which was once done, shall it be asked ever? That which was commanded to one alone, shall it be drawn a precedent for all? "The sign of the Cross was shewed to Constantine in his great anxiety," (ye say,) "to

---

[1] Adversus Marcio. Li. iii. [Cap. xviii.]

instruct us, that in all anxiety of mind, and pensiveness of heart, the Cross of Christ shall be our comfort." So far I grant. "And the sign," (you say,) "to be a mean to overthrow our enemies." Where find ye that? God hath moe means of comfort than one. He delivereth His that are in danger by divers ways.

We read[2], that when Alexander the Great, for denial of tribute to be paid unto him, was utterly in mind to destroy Hierusalem; and was marching thither with an huge army, which no power of theirs was able to resist; Iaddus, which was the chief Bishop then, put all his pontifical attire upon him, and caused the rest of his Clergy to do the like, and went forth to meet the tyrant so. Alexander no sooner saw him, but he lighted from his horse, fell flat on the ground before him. The lusty roisters that were about him, marvelling at this so sudden change, from wrath to worshipping, from force of arms to submission and prayer, specially to a Priest, whereas the Prince vainly supposed himself to be a god; and where he minded before in heat of his displeasure utterly to have destroyed them, now to become, contrary to his nature, an humble suppliant to them; Alexander made answer thus: "When I lodged in Dio, a city of Macedon, such a personage as this, of like stature, like apparel in all points, appeared to me, and willed me to set upon Asia; promising that he would guide me in the voyage, and in the enterprise always assist me. Wherefore I cannot but greatly be moved at the sight of him, to whom I owe my duty and service." Thus God delivered His people then. Thus God appeared to Alexander the Great, in a Priest's attire. Now, if it be lawful to use your order, and of every particular and private case to gather a general and like rule; I may as well conclude, that the vision of Alexander instructeth us, in all our troubles and distresses to have the sign of a Priest in his masking garments, as the vision of Constantine to have the sign of a Cross. For God used the one mean as well as the other; and no more commandment is of the one, than of the other.

Gregory[3] reporteth a notable history, how God sometime

[2] Josephus, Li. xi. Ca. viii. [*Antiqq. Jud.* pp. 327—28. Basil. 1524.]

[3] Dialog. Li. iii. Cap. i. [foll. xxiii, b, xxiv. Paris. 1513.]

delivered a sort of poor prisoners out of the hands of barbarous aliens; not by the sign of a Cross, nor yet by secret vision, as before, but by a stranger fact of His providence. When the Vandals had spoiled Italy, and carried from thence many captives into Africk with them, Paulinus, a godly man, and Bishop in those parts[1], gave the poor souls whatsoever he had for their relief. And when he could extend his charity no further, but all was gone, a widow on a day came to him, lamenting her estate, that her son was carried away prisoner, and by the King's son-in-law: wherefore she besought him to give her somewhat for his ransom, if haply his lord and taker would accept it. But the good man, devising with himself what he might give for her comfort, found nothing but his own person; and therefore he said: "Goodwife, I have nothing for thee, save only myself: take me: say I am thy servant; and give me up for a bondman in thy son's stead." The woman, hearing this of so great a personage, thought rather that he mocked her, than pitied her: but he persuaded her to do after his advice. Forward they went; the widow as the mistress, the Bishop as the bondman. To Africk they came: they met with the King's son-in-law. The widow makes her humble suit, to have her son restored to her: but he doth not only refuse to assent, but disdain to hear such a caitiff as she was. At length she besought him so much to tender her, as to accept for her son's exchange a servant that she had brought him, presenting the Bishop. When the gentleman had beheld his sweet face and fatherly countenance, he asked him of what occupation he was. "No occupation," quoth he; "but I can keep your garden well." Whereupon he was well contented to accept the servant; and the only son was given up unto the mother. Thus was the pitiful widow gladded. The reverend Father became a gardener.

Now when the King's son-in-law should use to resort into his garden, he questioned often with him; and finding him very prudent in his answers, forsook the company of others his familiars, and rather chose to talk with his gardener. Paulinus, then, accustomed every day to bring salads to his lord's table; and having his dinner with him, go to his work again. When thus he had continued a certain season,

[1] [scil. of Nola, in Campania.]

it fell out on a day, that as his master was in secret talk with him, he said on this sort: "See what ye do: make good provision how the kingdom of the Vandals may be disposed and governed; for the King, (sooner than ye are ware, and very shortly,) shall die." When this he heard, because he was beloved of the King more than the rest, he concealed it not, but uttered all that he understood by his gardener, whom he reputed to be very wise. When the King heard it, he answered: "I would fain see the man that you talk of." Then said his son-in-law, Paulinus' master: "He useth to prepare me salads for my dinner; and to the end ye may know him, I will take order that he shall bring them unto the table where your Highness shall sit." And even so he did: whom as soon as ever the King had espied, he began to tremble; and calling aside his son-in-law, revealed his secret unto him, saying: "True it is that thou hast heard. For this night, in my dream, I saw certain judges sitting in the place of judgment against me; among whom this man was also one: and they awarded the scourge from me, which I sometime took in hand against other. But ask what he is; for I think him not to be any common person, as he seemeth, but rather a man of great worthiness and estimation." Then secretly the King's son-in-law did call Paulinus to him, and enquired earnestly what he was. To whom the good man answered: "I am thy servant, whom thou didst take a substitute for the widow's son." But when more instantly he lay upon him to utter, not who he now was, but what condition and estate he was of in his own country; at length, with much ado, he confessed that he was a Bishop. When his master and lord heard it, he was stricken in a great fear; and "ask," (quoth he,) "whatsoever thou wilt, that thou mayest return into thine own country bountifully rewarded of me." To whom Paulinus answered: "One benefit there is, whereby thou mayest most gratify me; if thou release all the prisoners of my city." Which thing was accomplished; and the captives, sought throughout all the country, were sent home again, and ships full of grain with them.

Thus God, for delivery of His servants, used the ministry of a captive Bishop: and shall we gather of this, that in like extremities we must have a Bishop to become a gardener, and with salads in his hand wait at his master's table? Yet as good reason for this, as for the use of the Cross, grounded on Constantine's apparition. A wise man, of this and such-like examples, would have gathered another manner of rule general; and said, that by this we learn how God never forsaketh His, but by secret means, unknown to the world, worketh their comfort and delivery. The Cross was commanded to Constantine, to be set up, and used in his wars. "Therefore," (say you,) "His pleasure is, at this present day, to have the sign of the Cross made, and set up in open places, used in wars," &c. How prove ye this, M. Martiall? Forsooth ye say: *Quia Jesus Christus heri, et hodie, et usque in sæcula:* "Because Jesus Christ is yesterday, to-day, and He for ever[1]." By the same reason I prove, that we need not, at this day, the sign of the Cross; for Christ is able otherwise to defend us. His power is not abated. He is the same that He was before; and a thousand ways He hath beside to help us. But I gladly conclude with you, that the sign was shewed from heaven at Hierusalem, to declare that the faith and doctrine of the Christians was both preached by men, and shewed from heaven; and that it consisteth not in the persuasible words of human wisdom, but in the shewing of the Spirit and power[2].

The drops of rain, that fell upon Julian, made a print of the Cross in his garment, and the rest's. "Therefore," (say you,) "it is necessary for every man to be signed and marked with the Cross." But the Cross noted them to be persecutors: *Ergo*, it is necessary for us to be noted as persecutors. Ye see how your own examples kill you. There is nothing that ye bring but maketh against you. Indeed Sozomenus writeth[3], that some did interpret the Crosses on that sort: *Christianorum doctrinam esse cœlestem; et oportere omnes Cruce signari:* "That the doctrine of Christians was heavenly; and that all men ought to be signed with the Cross." But God forbid we should have such occasion to be so marked: for none were marked, but such as had reneged their faith. So that the Cross doth not always portend goodness; nor is the sign peculiar unto Christians. If the sign had been of such force as ye make it, Julian the Apostata would not have gone forward with his attempted

---

[1] [Heb. xiii. 8.]   [2] [1 Cor. ii. 4.]
[3] Ecclesi. Hist. Lib. v. Cap. i.

mischief. But forward he went, though the Cross continued on his coat still. Wherefore the Cross is no proof of virtue.

The same may be confirmed by the story that followeth. For the glittering sign of the Cross in the element, the crossing of the Jews' coats when they would have re-edified their Hierusalem, was but a token of God's wrath and vengeance: and although it was *signum salutaris Crucis*, "the sign of the healthful Cross;" yet was it not healthful to them that ware it; but rather a testimony of God's just judgment against them. Wherefore, as God miraculously did work, and used this sign to contrary effects; sometime for comfort, sometime to despair; sometime for the godly, sometime to the wicked; so must we not, contrary to reason, gather an universal only of the one side; and, contrary to His will, abuse it at our pleasure. If it had been always granted to the godly, and to none but them: if it had been always a sign of succour, and not of destruction; your argument then should have had some appearance of troth or likelihood. Now, by your own examples, where the wicked only be signed with the Cross; where the Cross doth work nothing but confusion; the groundwork of your cause is miserably shaken, and you be turned over in your own trip. Of all your examples ye infer your own fancy; what you do think God's meaning was, to shew such signs of the Cross, both under the Law, and in the time of grace: but of your meaning ye bring no proof at all, either out of Scripture, or Doctors that ye brag of. Only for us, your idle supposal, (as you think,) may serve. Lovain hath licentiate you, to make what lies ye lust.

The substantial ground that I spake of before, whereupon we ought to build our Religion, is the word of God: without the which no fact of man, no particular example, can prove any thing. Then, if ye would have the sign of the Cross received into God's service, ye should as well prove God's will therein, and bring His direct authority to us. It sufficeth not to say, "This was once so;" but rather to shew, "This was well so:" nor any one example can bind us now, without express commandment in God's book for it, extending to us, and during for ever. But you deal with God's book as Epiphanius[4]

---

[4] Contra Hær. Lib. i. To. ii. ["Adaptare enitentes ea, quæ recte dicta sunt, his quæ male ab ipsis excogitata sunt." (*Hæres*. xxxi. Opp. p. 59. Cornar. interp. Basil. 1578.)]

reporteth of heretics: *Qui multos decipiunt per male compositam Dominicorum verborum adaptatorum sapientiam:* "Which deceive many by the wisdom of the Lord's words ill-favouredly applied." As if a man should take an Image of some notable personage, lively set forth and adorned with pearl and stone; and afterward should deface the counterfeit of a man in it, and make a dog or a fox of it. Then if he should remove the jewels and garnishing of the one to the picture of the other, and say to them that look upon it: "This is the picture of such a man or such;" and for proof thereof would bring the pearl and stone so cunningly couched; would ye not think him to be a crafty fellow, and yet believe him never a whit the sooner? Even so fare you: for, instead of the text, ye bring forth a contrary misshapen gloss; and then ye apparel it with a few pearls of Scripture, applied as well as a precious diamond to the picture of a grinning-dog. And yet a dog is but a dog, although he had a Bishop's best mitre on his head: no more are you but lewd liars, for all the patch of truth sewed on your cloke of fables. Blear not therefore the people's eyes: deceive not yourselves: learn the true service of God out of His word, and go no further.

The Cross of Christ is necessary for us: His death and passion is only our joy and comfort; our life and our redemption: but the material or mystical sign thereof is more than needeth; too dangerous to be used. We have the word, the ordinary mean, to lead us into all truth: we must not, beside the word, seek signs and tokens. We have the bodies: what grope we after shadows? Ceremonies were given unto the Jews to be a mound, (as it were,) between the Gentiles and them; to sever the people of God from other, not only by inward things, but also by outward; that the people of God should be within that enclosure, the other without: and these outward rites and observances were an assurance unto the Jews, that they were lawful heirs of the promise, and not the Gentiles. But Christ came into the world, to gather one Church of both peoples[1]; and therefore pulled down the wall that was between them: *Decreta ceremonialia:* "The decrees of ceremonies." Christ followed herein the policy of Princes, which, if they will gather into society of one kingdom, as it were, divers peoples, they will take away the

The end of Ceremonies.

[1] [Ephes. ii. 14, 15.]

things that made the difference before; diversities of coins and laws. So Christ, minding to make one people of the Jews and Gentiles, utterly did abolish all legal ceremonies. And Paul compareth them to a hand-writing, whereby we be bound to God; that we cannot stand in argument against Him, and deny our debt. But by Christ this debt is so remitted, that the obligation is cancelled, the hand-writing is put out, as the Apostle saith[2]. Now when the instruments are cut in pieces, the obligations cancelled, the debtor is set free; which we have purchased by Christ's death. Wherefore we read, that the veil of the temple tare; to the end the people might understand thereby, that their sins were remitted, and they discharged from burden of the Law.

But when the wicked and faithless nation continued, after Christ's death, to exercise in the temple ceremonies, which had their end before; and would thrust them unto men as parcel of Religion, and worshipping of God; Christ, using the ministry of the Romans, so destroyed the temple, that for these fifteen hundreth years they have had no place, no respite to repair it. And when they did attempt the matter, they were, (as you alleged,) by divers means destroyed and disappointed; namely, by the dreadful apparition of a Cross. Whereof ye might have gathered, that God so misliked the superstitious ceremonies of the temple, that He would not suffer the stones of it to stand. The like plague shall ensue to all, that, having light, will follow darkness; that, being free, will bring a slavery upon them; that, being delivered by Christ from these outward things, and having Christ, yet will be wedded to these outward things, as if that God were pleased with them. Wherefore remember Saul[3]: let no disguised cloke of a good intent cover an ill act, contrary to the word. Nadab and Abiu brought in strange fire[4], not commanded of the Lord. The fire of the Lord therefore consumed them. Uzah, when the oxen did shake the ark[5], of a good intent did put his hand unto it; and was stricken dead for his offence. *Melior est obedientia quam victimæ*, said Samuel: "Better is obedience than sacrifice." Better is a naked service, with

---

[2] Coloss. ii. [14.]
[3] [1 Sam. xv. 21, 22.]
[4] Levit. x. [1, 2.]
[5] 2 Sam. vi. [6, 7.]

the word, than a gorgeous solemnity, not commanded by the word. *Quicquid Ego præcipio vobis, hoc tantum facite:* "Whatsoever I do command you," (saith the Lord[1],) "do that, and that only:" *Non addes quicquam, nec minues:* "Thou shalt not add any thing to it, nor take away any thing from it."

When Christ shall appear in brightness of His glory: when He shall sit as a just Judge, at His second coming, to ask a straight [strait] accompt of all your life, faith, and Religion; what can ye answer? what will ye say unto Him? "We have garnished Thy temple with gold and silver: we have set up candles upon Thine altars: we have sainsed Thy Saints: we have erected, esteemed, honoured Thy Cross." What shall He then reply to this? The word of His Prophet Esay: *Quis requisivit ista de manibus vestris?* "Who did require these things at your hands[2]?" My temple ought your own hearts to be; as I Myself pronounced[3], and My Apostle Paul bare witness with Me[4]. This should have been adorned with chastity, simplicity, fear of My name, love of My mercies, innocency of life, integrity of faith. Such resting place, and such ornaments thereof, have I required; but you have them rejected. No altar of squared stone have I appointed: Myself on the altar of the Cross abolished it. I only ought to be the altar now, whereupon your sacrifice of praise and thanksgiving should be laid; and light of your good works shining to the world be set upon. But Me and My death ye have adnihilated, to magnify your own imaginations. My Saints should have been patterns of holy life and true faith unto you; not have usurped My room and office to become mediators, and be called upon. The sweet perfume of prayer should have arisen from the saynsure[5] of your heart to Me; and no flinging of coals about the church to other. But you have sticked only to the Jewish and hypocritical observance: the truth exhibited in time of grace ye have not received. The memory of My death, by preaching of the word, and due administration of

---

[1] Deut. xii. [32.]
[2] Esay i. [12.]
[3] Levit. xxvi. [11, 12.] Esay lii. [6.]
[4] 1 Cor. vi. [19.] 2 Cor. vi. [16.]
[5] [censer.]

Sacraments in the church, should have been continued according to My will: the members of My body, the lively counterfeits of Mine own Person, the poor, the naked, the comfortless Christians, should have been relieved, clothed, encouraged[6]. But by your Imagery you have excluded My word: by your Roods, Crosses, and Crucifixes, utterly, (as much as in you lieth,) defaced the glory of My death. Depart ye therefore away from Me, ye workers of iniquity. Let now the god that you have served save you. Enter into everlasting fire, prepared for the Devil and for you his angels.

This when God shall lay unto your charge, this fine[7] shall follow of it: and when, in the terrible conflict with Satan, ye shall call your consciences to accompt; and see those idle toys that you have trusted to to be void of comfort; what shall ye then do but be driven to despair, and say to the mountains: "Fall down upon us[8]." Wherefore, if yet there be any place of repentance left for you[9]; if malice and obstinacy have not utterly secluded God's grace from you; take up by times: seek Christ in His word: forsake your will-worshippings: set not your follies in the service of God against the wisdom of the Almighty revealed in His word. You think your hold is good: God knows it abides no stress. Ye say ye seek the Shepherd: I prove ye find the fox.

[6] [Templa, Deum, Viduas, reparando, colendo, cibando, Martha, Maria, pius Samaritanus eris.]
[7] [end, or penalty.]   [8] [Rev. vi. 16.]
[9] Luke xxii. [xiii. 3.]

TO THE THIRD ARTICLE.

<small>Folio 36, b.</small>

<small>Folio 38, b.</small>

<small>Abdias.</small>

For declaration and proof of your third article; which is, "that every church, chapel, and oratory, erected to the honour and service of God, should have the sign of the Cross;" ye bring four reasons: whereof the two first be too unreasonable, grounded upon foolish fables; the third is insufficient to confirm a doctrine; the fourth is a custom of error not consonant to truth. For the first ye allege one of Abdias' tales; whom you affirm "to have seen Christ in the flesh: to have followed Simon and Jude into Persia; and to have been made Bishop of Babylon by the Apostles." To speak somewhat of your famous Father[1]: that he saw Christ in the flesh, what marvel was it, if he were one of the seventy-two Disciples, as you and Lazius, (that found the lying legend, in his preface upon Abdias[2],) witness? Concerning his anciety, no marvel if ye cite him: for if ye make accompt of his years, by probable conjecture out of his book, ye shall find him almost as old as Mathusale. He lived long after S. John's time; for he citeth authorities out of his Gospel divers: and, speaking of a miracle done at S. John his tomb, how manna sprang

---

[1] [The ten books of the *Historia Certaminis Apostolici* were first published in the year 1551; and were alleged with confidence by many Romanists, until effrontery could persist no longer. Pope Paul IV. condemned them in his *Index*, in 1559: but, strange to say, they were released from censure by the Tridentine Catalogue of 1564, and by Pope Clement VIII. in 1596; in consequence, as Molanus states, of "former ecclesiastical zeal having become seasoned with discretion." (*Hist. S. Imagg.* Lib. ii. Cap. xxviii.) Oudin has placed the Pseudo-Abdias in the beginning of the tenth century; (*Comment.* ii. 418.) and henceforth, it may be safely asserted, with Thilo, "hujus quidem libri auctoritate nemo permovebitur." (*Codex Apocr. Nov. Test.* Tom. i. p. 673. Lips. 1832. Conf. Jewel's *Replie*, Art. i. p. 7. *Conference betwene Rainoldes and Hart*, p. 505. Lond. 1584. Coci *Censur.* pp. 42—47. Blondell. *De Joanna Papissa*, p. 118. Amstel. 1657. Voss. *De Histor. Græc.* L. ii. C. ix. p. 118. Amst. 1697. Grabii *Spicileg.* i. 314. Oxon. 1714. Fabricii *Cod. Apoc. N. T.* Tom. ii. 388—742. Hamb. 1703.)]

[2] [pag. vii.—Abdias does not say of himself that he was one of the seventy Disciples; nor is the statement made by the Pseudo-Dorotheus, Nicephorus, and others. Vid. nomenclatur. apud Wicclii *Hagiolog.* fol. clxxiii. Mogunt. 1541.]

out of it, he saith[3]: *Quam usque hodie gignit locus iste:* that
is to say: "Which manna this place bringeth forth to this
day." Then, if it were so strange a matter as he would have
it seem, many years were run between the death of the
Apostle, and writing of his book. But John himself was an
hundreth year old, lacking two, when he died. For, as your
Abdias saith[4]: *Cum esset annorum nonaginta septem,* &c.:
"When he was fourscore and seventeen year old," Christ
appeared to him; and so forth. And Abdias, if he were one
of the seventy-two Disciples, was called to his ministry the
self-same year that John was to his Apostleship: so that, by
all likelihood, he was then as old as John, and living long
after John. How old was he, say you?

But a man of those years, being broken so much in
travail as he was, to do as he did, was a miracle of itself.
For, if ye credit his own writings, he was at Saint Andrew's
death in Achaia. For in his life[5] he saith: *Diutissime
Dominum clarificans, et gaudens, nobis flentibus reddidit
spiritum:* "He, long glorifying the Lord, and rejoicing,
while we were weeping, gave up the ghost." Whereupon
the marginal note hath: *Ex hoc apparet, Abdiam, hujus
historiæ authorem, passioni interfuisse:* "It appeareth by
this, that Abdias, the author of this history, was present
at the passion." Likewise he was with Thomas in India,
where he was a witness of all his doings. For, speaking of a
miracle shewed in prison, he saith[6]: *Servi Dei dormire non
poterant, quos sic Christus excitabat, neque patiebatur nos
somno dimergi:* "The servants of God could not sleep, whom
Christ had raised so, nor suffered us to be drowned in sleep."
Then, if the nominative [accusative] case plural, "us," includeth
him that told the tale, Abdias then was also there. Beside this,
he was at the death of Saint John in Ephesus; for he saith[7]:
*Gaudebamus quod tantam cernebamus gratiam: dolebamus
quod tanti viri aspectu et præsentiæ specie defraudabamur:*
"We rejoiced for that we saw so great grace: we sorrowed
that we were bereaved of the sight and presence of so great
a personage." And there is noted in the margent: *Et hoc
argumentum est, Abdiam interfuisse morti Johannis:* "And

---

[3] Li. v. in fine. [fol. 70, b. Paris. 1566.] [4] [fol. 68, a.]
[5] Lib. iii. circa finem. [fol. 44, b.]
[6] Lib. ix. [fol. 116, b.]   [7] Lib. v. [fol. 70, b.]

this is a proof, that Abdias was at the death of John." Notwithstanding all this, he went out of Jewry, with Simon and Jude, into Persia. There, (as he witnesseth of himself[1],) he was present at all their doings, and was made Bishop of Babylon by them. For thus he writeth: *Ordinavere autem Apostoli in civitate Babylonis Episcopum, nomine Abdiam, qui cum ipsis venerat a Judæa:* "The Apostles appointed Bishop, in the city of Babylon, one whose name was Abdias, which came from Jewry with them."

Now, I beseech you, how is it possible, that he which immediately came out of Jewry, and had his charge in Babylon, should be at one time, (as it were,) in so divers, and so far distant parts of the world: in Achaia, in India, in Ephesus, in Persia; and, if we give credit to historiographers, also in Scythia? For, as touching Andrew, at whose martyrdom he affirms he was, Eusebius[2] out of Origen, and Sophronius[3], as we read in Ptolome, and Nicephorus[4] do all witness, that he went into the coast of Scythia, far distant from Grecia. And as for his death, Sabellicus[5] doth say, that he suffered in Scythia. Then either was your author a liar, or a lewd Bishop; to forsake his charge, and be such a land-leaper. But a liar he was: for, comparing the times of the Apostles' deaths, and distance of places where they were resident, it is impossible his sayings to be true.

Furthermore, that the antiquity of this Abdias should be such as ye talk of, is more than a miracle to me; since neither Irene, nor Eusebius, nor Hierom, nor any one of the received Fathers, (being nearest to the same time, and writing of the same matter,) do once mention him: yea, to say the truth, both Scripture and Fathers be direct against him. For where he maketh S. John to say[6]: *Virtutum opes habere non posse,*

---

[1] Lib. vi. [fol. 83, a.]   [2] Lib. iii. Cap. i.

[3] [If he were the author of the Life of S. Andrew, which is among the interpolations in S. Jerom's *Catalogue of Ecclesiastical Writers.* Erasmus suspected that the additions were made "ab alio quopiam studioso." (S. Hier. *Opp.* Tom. i. p. 306. Basil. 1565.) Conf. Ern. Sal. Cypriani *Dissertat. de Hieron. Catal.* pp. 7, 8. Francof. & Lips. 1722. Mabillonii *Vetera Analecta,* pp. 196, 197. Paris. 1723.]

[4] Lib. ii. Ca. xxxix. & Li. iii. Ca. i.

[5] Ennead. vii. Lib. iv. [Tom. ii. p. 224. Basil. 1538.]

[6] Lib. v. [fol. 63, a, b.]

qui voluerit divitias habere terrenas: "That he cannot have the substance of virtues, that will have the substance of the earth;" it accordeth not with the doctrine of Christ: for we read in His word of many that were rich, and yet were virtuous notwithstanding. That John should allow the fact of Drusiana[7], which, being a married wife, withdrew herself from her husband's company without his consent, is contrary to the rule of Christ[8], and His Apostle Paul[9]. That he doth attribute to the same Apostle, the prescription of thirty days for sufficient repentance[10], is otherwise than Christ hath taught us: for He will have us to forgive *septuagies septies*, "seventy times seven times[11]." That S. John should use so fond miracles, as to make whole again broken jewels[12]; to turn trees and stones into gold[13]; hath no appearance of truth in it. That in his life-time a church was builded at Ephesus, dedicated to him, and called by his name[14], may be proved false by a thousand testimonies. For beside that it was derogation to God's honour, it was contrary to the use of the primitive Church. And all men agree that, until the reign of Constantinus, there were no chapels or oratories erected in honour of any Saint.

Augustin plainly affirmeth, that in the Church of Christ Martyrs have the highest room. *Nec tamen nos*, (sayeth he[15],) *eisdem Martyribus templa, sacerdotia, sacra, et sacrificia constituimus; quoniam non ipsi, sed Deus eorum, nobis est Deus:* "Yet we build not up temples, appoint officers, service, and sacrifice for the said Martyrs; because not they, but their God, is our God." Again, in another place[16], somewhat more plainly: *Nonne, si templum alicui sancto Angelo excellentissimo de lignis et lapidibus faceremus, anathematizaremur a veritate Christi, et ab Ecclesia Dei; quoniam creaturæ exhiberemus eam servi-*

---

[7] [L. v. 54, a.]
[8] Matth. xix. [6.]
[9] 1 Cor. vii. [10.] Coloss. iii. [18.]
[10] [Lib. v. fol. 65, a.]
[11] Matth. xviii. [22.]
[12] [L. v. 61, b.]
[13] [fol. 62, a.]
[14] [v. 68, a.]
[15] De Civi. Dei, Lib. viii. Cap. xxvii.
[16] Contra Max. Arr. Episc. Lib. i. [This was the old name of what is now termed the *Collatio cum Maximino*. The quotation may be seen in *Opp*. Tom. viii. col. 467. ed. Ben. Antw.]

tutem, quæ uni tantum debetur Deo? *Si ergo sacrilegi essemus, faciendo templum cuicumque creaturæ, quomodo non est Deus verus, cui non templum facimus, sed nos ipsi templum sumus?* "If we should make a temple of wood and stone for any holy Angel, yea though he were the most excellent of all, should we not be accursed from the truth of Christ, and from the Church of God; because we exhibited that service to a creature, which is due to God alone? Therefore, if we should offend in sacrilege, by building a church to any creature, how can it be but He is the true God, to whom we make no temple, but ourselves are temples?" By which places we prove, that in his time there was no church or chapel builded for any Saint; that it was reputed a cursed thing, contrary to truth and the Church of God; that they commit sacrilege, which do build any: finally, that churches and oratories are not erected for God Himself, but to the use of man. Wherefore, in the tale of Saint John his church, your Doctor doted.

Now what say you to this, that Chrysostom affirmeth[1]? *Petri quidem, et Pauli, et Joannis, et Thomæ manifesta sunt sepulchra: aliorum vero, cum tanti sint, minime cognitum est ubi sunt:* "The sepulchres of Peter and Paul, John and Thomas, be well known: but of the rest, as great as they were, it is not known where they were." But your Abdias setteth forth the matter plainly, where every one of them was laid into the ground: wherefore ye must either condemn Chrysostom or him. And yet in these the Doctors agree not. For, to go no further than to S. John, of whom I spake last, Abdias saith that he died not, but was put quick in his grave, and there he commanded mould to be cast upon him[2]. *Omnes benedicens ac valefaciens, deposuit se viventem in sepulchro suo, et jussit se operire:* "Blessing them all, and taking his leave of them, he laid himself down quick in his grave, and bade them cover him." But Hierom saith[3]: *Sexagesimo octavo post passionem Domini anno, mortuus Ephesi, juxta eandem urbem sepultus est:* "The

---

[1] To. iv. in Cap. ad Heb. xi. in Ho. xxvi. [*Opp.* Lat. Tom. iv. col. 1820. Basil. 1547.]

[2] Lib. v. in fine. [fol. 70, b.]

[3] In Catal. Scrip. Eccle. [apud Fabricii *Biblioth. Eccles.* p. 57. Hamburgi, 1718.]

threescore and eight year after the passion of our Lord, he died at Ephesus, and was buried hard by the said city." What shall we now think of your Abdias? whom you know to have been one of the seventy-two Disciples; but Eusebius saith[4], that no such matter is known: whom you affirm, out of his own books, to have been made Bishop of Babylon; but I have proved, out of the same, that he could not be in so many places and so far distant: whom you do think to be worthy credit; but evident it is, that he speaketh naught but repugnancy to the Scriptures, and more than any Father beside himself alloweth.

For further proof whereof, examine your dedication, of which ye make so great accompt; and it shall be no "levity," (as you would have it appear,) if a man, stayed by the grace of God, refuse to lean to so weak a staff. A church is consecrated, or made an holy place, not by super- *The true manner of dedication.* stitious words of magical enchantment; not by making of signs and characters in stones; but by the will of God, and the godly use. His will is set forth in His word unto us, wherein He hath commanded His people to assemble themselves together; and hath annexed a promise to it, that He will be there in the midst of them. The use that maketh a place holy is, to have the word purely set forth in it; the Sacraments duly to be received; and prayers humbly to be made therein. Take away the commandment; take away the right use; the place remaineth profane still: yea, though a thousand Angels should be said to cross it. Shall we think that any place, any creature of God, is of itself unclean? Shall we think that Devils lie in stone walls, that, once besprinkled with a little Holy Water, will be packing straight? When God had made all the creatures of His, *vidit quod essent omnia valde bona:* "He saw that all things were very good[5]." And Augustin, in his Confessions[6]: *Singula bona sunt, et omnia valde bona, quæ Tu fecisti:* "Every thing by itself, and all things are exceeding good," (he saith,) "which Thou hast made, O Lord." And as for the place, it is prepared for men, and not for God. For "God dwelleth not in temples made with hand[7]:" but, as the Martyr saith, in Pru-

---

[4] [*H. E.*] Lib. i. Ca. xii.   [5] Genesis i. [31.]
[6] Lib. vii. Ca. xii. [pp. 116-17. Oxon. 1838.]
[7] Act. xvii. [24.]

dentius[1]: *Ædem Sibi Ipse mente in hominis condidit, vivam, serenam*, &c.: " He made a temple to Himself within the mind of man, living and clear." Then is not any earthly place holy of itself; but inasmuch as holy things are done therein, it is called holy. S. Paul, speaking of meats, saith, that they are sanctified *per verbum Dei, et orationem:* " by the word of God, and prayer[2]:" but that a sanctification should come to a creature by making of the sign of a Cross, is more than Abdias himself, or you, can, out of Scripture or good authority, avouch. Salomon made a temple to the Lord : and no Angel of God came down to hallow it; nor any Priest was called to conjure Spirits out of it. Hallowed it was, when according to God's will and ordinance it was used. Constantine built divers churches; and yet this example he never followed : nor, although he had the Cross in admiration, as which was from heaven revealed to him, yet did he ever bring the Cross into the church.

Wherefore, your Bartholomeus' dedication I have in as good credit as the rest of the tales that Abdias tells concerning S. Bartholomew. For this he affirmeth; that the Devil, giving marks of him to his friends, said among the rest[3]: *Viginti sex anni sunt, ex quo nunquam sordidantur vestimenta ejus; similiter et sandalia ejus per viginti quinque annos nunquam veterascunt :* " Now are there twenty-six years since that his garments never filed[4]; nor his shoes for these twenty-five years ever waxed old." We read that the like miracle was shewed to the children of Israel[5], when as they were in wilderness, and had no ordinary mean to come by necessaries. But that S. Bartholomew, a King his nephew, a trim fellow, with precious stones in every corner of his coat; in such credit with a Prince, as he was with Polymius; in such a populous country as India was; (which things all Abdias doth write of him;) should have his garments kept from wearing, was more than needed, more than with reason may be believed. Again, Abdias witnesseth, that S. Bartho-

---

[1] Lib. Peristephanon. [*Opera*, foll. 153-4. Antverp. 1540.]
[2] 1 Timo. iv. [5.]
[3] In Vita Barth. Lib. viii. [fol. 96, b.]
[4] [were defiled.—" Sacrilege is to *file* holy þing." (Wicliffe's *Apol.* p. 22. Lond. 1842. ed. Camden Soc.)]
[5] [Deut. viii. 4.]

lomew came in to the King Polymius when the doors were shut; which never was heard tell of but only of Christ[6]: and now, by his doctrine, we may fall a reasoning of the dimensions of S. Bartholomew's body. Then, in the same legend, he reporteth also, that Mary, the mother of Christ, did make a vow of chastity: with many other points, most strange, and dissonant from all godly learning. But see how these lying losels[7] do detect themselves. Abdias saith[8], that Astyages, brother to Polymius, caused S. Bartholomew *fustibus cædi, cæsumque decollari:* " to be all to bebatted, and afterward to be beheaded:" but he shews not where, save only in some piece of India. Nicephorus, another of your authors, saith[9]: *Hierapoli in Crucem actum:* "that he was hanged at Hierapolis." But he that makes *Supplementum Chronicorum* writeth[10]: *In Albana, Majoris Armeniæ urbe, primo cæsum, dein excoriatum:* " that in Albana, a city of Greater Armenia, first he was slain, and afterward was flayed." So, by this means, the poor Saint should first be beheaded, I wot not where in India; then, afterward, lose his life on the gallows at Hierapolis; and, last of all, have his skin pulled over his ears in Armenia[11], a good while after that his head was gone. It is a sport, and yet a spite, to see how men of your profession, (Master Martiall,) that vaunt yourselves to be friends to the Cross of Christ, can do nothing almost but lie. Wherefore, these things condemning utterly your author's credit, I need not to wade no further in confutation of his church-hallowing. It confuteth itself, with shame enough to you. Only I marvel, that as " the Angel[12]," (as you say,) "engraved with his finger in the square stones the sign of the Cross; and further, from God commanded them to make such a sign in their foreheads;"

Folio 38, a.

[6] [S. John xx. 19, 26.]   [7] [knaves, cheats.]
[8] Lib. viii. circa finem. [fol. 102, a.]
[9] [Lib. ii. Cap. xxxix. Nicephorus, however, adds that S. Bartholomew escaped from death at Hierapolis, in Phrygia; and that, " aliquanto post tempore, Urbanopoli, provinciæ Ciliciæ, in Crucem rursus actus, ad unice desideratum Christum migravit."]
[10] Lib. viii. anno a Christo 80. [Jac. Phil. Bergomensis *Supplem. Chronic.* fol. 153. Brixiæ, 1485.]
[11] [Cave maintains that Albanople, in Armenia the Great, was "the same no doubt which Nicephorus calls Urbanople, a city of Cilicia." (*Antiqq. Apostol.* p. 562. Lond. 1742.)]
[12] [Abdias, foll. 100-1.]

commanded not as well, (which had been more to purpose,) to make the like signs in other stones, in dedication of other churches. I would wish, in the next print it might be put in; that your popish church-hallowing, (whereof I will speak anon,) might seem to have some precedent for it.

But, for S. Bartholomew, I have said enough. And the same answer may suffice for S. Philip; as his example is out of the said Abdias brought. For, as S. Hierom saith[1]; (touching the name of Zachary, of whom mention is made Matth. xxiii.; that some would have him to have been the eleventh of the Prophets, but some other to have been the father of S. John Baptist:) *Hoc, quia de Scripturis non habet authoritatem, eadem facilitate contemnitur, qua probatur:* "This, because it hath not authority of the Scripture, is as easily contemned as proved;" so may I say for the words which ye father upon S. Philip: "In the place where Mars seemeth to stand fast, set up the Cross of my Lord Jesus Christ, and adore the same[2]:" because it is contrary to the Scripture, and is but the report of a lying legend, I may, with good cause, reject the authority. For neither was the change allowable, to destroy one Idol, to make another; (as in the first article I proved:) nor to adore it, was in any wise tolerable; as afterward more at large appeareth. Wherefore, your reason being, (as it is,) absurd and foolish, we be not driven to any such shift as ye talk of, to say that faith should be fixed in a wall. We know no such melody to move, as you say, hard stones; or make brazen pillars to understand: though your magical minstrelsy hath been such, that rotten stocks have spoke at your pleasure; spoken good reason, (as you have esteemed it.) Remember ye not the Rood of Winchester, that cunningly decised a controversy between the Monks and married Priests; pronouncing in Latin: (for he was better taught than his masters the Monks:) *Non bene sentiunt qui favent Presbyteris:* "They think not well that favour the Priests?" Who was that Orpheus, that wrought that understanding there? Dunstan, or the Devil, or both? It hath been always a popish practice, to make Roods and Images to roll their eyes, to sweat, and to speak; (whereof infinite examples might be brought:) but that of men, professing the Gospel; of Protestants, (as ye call

---

[1] Super xxiii. Matth. [*Opp.* Tom. ix. p. 70. Basil. 1565.]
[2] [Abdias, fol. 122, b.]

them,) there hath been any such delusion, is not in any writing of any age to be found. Wherefore ye do us wrong, in burdening us with such untruths; unless, by remembrance of your own follies, ye will force us, (as it were,) to open and disclose your shame.

But let me come to your Councils. The first ye fetch from the record of Ivo[3] and Gratian[4], alleging a Synod kept at Orleance in France. Ye do right well to cite your authors; otherwise I might have suspected the authority: for, in all the Canons of the Council itself, we read not the words that make for your purpose[5]. But you do wisely, not to pass the compass of your own profession; and therefore say no more than the popish Decrees do teach you. But, if a man may be so bold in your own faculty to oppose you; how do the words of this your Council prove, that every church must have the sign of the Cross? "Forsooth," (say you,) "because it is decreed, that no man build a church, before the Bishop of that diocese come, and set up a Cross." By the same reason, the ring of the church-door is a piece of God's service too. For, as the fixing of a Cross, the pitching of a stake, (as it were,) in the ground, doth shew that the Bishop hath limited out the compass of the church; so the other is a proof of Induction of the Priest. Yet, as this sign of possession taken is no part of duty within the church discharged; so the other sign of authority to build given is no part of service within the building to be done. And this is the point, which in this article ye go about to prove; "that every church and chapel" must have a Cross erected in it, to the honour and service of Almighty God. But this Cross serveth another turn; to a civil Policy, and no point of Religion: for, lest that men should presume to build churches without authority ecclesiastical, it was decreed, that the Bishop of the diocese should view the place; appoint where the body of the church should

Folio 4

---

[3] [*Decret.* iii. Par. Cap. viii. fol. 84, a. Lovan. 1561.]

[4] ["Nemo ecclesiam ædificet, antequam Episcopus civitatis veniat, et ibidem Crucem figat." (*De Consec.* Dist. i. Cap. ix.)]

[5] [They are in reality the words of the sixty-seventh Novel of the Emperor Justinian; which has, of course, been cited by Cornelius à Rynthelen. (*Jurista Romano-Cathol.* pp. 224, 259. Colon. Agripp. 1618. Conf. *Rhythm. de S. Annone*, cura Mart. Opitii, pag. 50. Dantisci, 1639.)]

be; and leave his mark behind him : which mark might as well have been his Crosier as his Cross; but that the one was less chargeable than the other. If ye credit not me, turn over your Decree. There shall ye find, that order is taken for things necessary before the church be builded: but we do inquire what is necessary service in a church hallowed. Wherefore, I see not how that Council Provincial, *triginta trium Episcoporum*, "of three and thirty Bishops," as the book doth tell us[1], can make any thing for you. But if there were most plain determination for the Cross, in that or any other such-like Council; I am no more bound to the authority thereof, than you will be to the English Synods, held in King Edward's days, and in the Queen's Majesty's reign that now is. Yet, the duty of a subject, (if ye were honest,) might drive you to this; whereas there is no cause, that might enforce my consent to the other.

Now for your second at Towres, whose Canon is this: *Ut corpus Domini in Altari, non in Armario*[2], *sed sub Crucis titulo, componatur:* which you do English after this sort: "That the body of our Lord, consecrated upon the Altar, be not reposed and set in the Revestry, but under the Rood." Where we may learn two school points of you. First, that *Armarium* is Latin for a Revestry[3]: then, that *Titulus Crucis* is Latin for a Rood. But if your scholars have been taught heretofore to translate no better, a rod had been more meet for the Usher: for *Armarium* may well be taken for a library, for a closet, or Almerie[4]; but no more for the Revestry than for the belfry. Yet will I not greatly in that word contend with you. Be it that their foolish meaning was for a Revestry; yet doubtless they were not so mad as to put *Titulus Crucis* for a Rood. *Titulus Crucis* is "the title of the Cross:" and I marvel

---

[1] [Vid. Binii *Concilia*, Tom. ii. P. i. p. 548. Colon. Agr. 1618.]

[2] [Instead of "non in armario," (Crabbe's reading,) we now generally find "non in imaginario ordine," in the third Canon of this Synod of Tours. Binius (ii. ii. 231.) tells us, that the remodelled injunction signifies, that the Host should be placed, not among the sacred Images, but immediately under the Cross which was upon the middle of the Altar.]

[3] [or Vestry.]

[4] [Almonry. In old Records the words "Almonarium," "Almorietum," and "Almeriola" occur; and mean a repository for provisions for the poor.]

that you would not rather expound it for a Pix, than a Rood; being driven by this to carry God's body sacred from the Altar into the Rood-loft. We have not heard afore this time, that the Sacrament was reverently kept under the Rood; that, the Altar refused, the Rood-loft should be reverenced.

Now as concerning the sixth General Council, kept at Constantinople in Trullo ; " whereby," (ye say,) " it may be gathered, that the sign of the Cross was kept and had in churches ;" I pray you allege the Canon of that Council, out of which ye gather it[5]. I am not ignorant that, in the Pope's law, it is cited so[6]: but I am not yet persuaded that it is so. Belike the patchers of those ragged reliques mistook the name of the sixth for the seventh. For, as it is certain that, in the sixth Council of Constantinople, there was a long discourse *contra Monothelitas*, " against them which affirmed there was but one will in Christ;" so, in all the Actions that are come abroad to the sight of the world, there is not so much as mention of the Cross. It is an easy matter to say : " Such a Council defined so the case ;" and bring no proof at all, nor so much as a word, to rule the case over. This is too slight dealing, in so great a cause, as you will have the Cross to be. But, on the other side, as you have brought but the bare name of three Councils for you, whereof there is none that confirmeth your error ;

[5] [Martiall must have alluded to the eighty-second Canon of the Quinisext Council, which allowed Pictures of the Saviour to supplant typical representations of Him by a Lamb. This Trullan Synod was held in the year 692; and though its Decrees were recognized by the second Council of Nice, they are now received only by the Eastern Church. Pighius wrote a tract to prove that the Acts both of the sixth and seventh Council were forged: (*Controv. præcip.* foll. 271-292. Paris. 1542.) but, whatever may be the fate of other Ordinances, Bellarmin will not permit the Canon, above referred to, to escape; for he declares that "iste Canon semper receptus fuit ab Ecclesia." (*De Imagin.* Lib. ii. Cap. xii.) Vid. Bevereg. *Pandectt.* i. 252. Binii *Concill.* iii. i. 224. Lupi *Synod. Decr.* ii. 1041. Lovan. 1665. Comber's *Discourse of the second Nicene Council*, p. 56. Lond. 1688. Jenkins's *Histor. Exam. of Gen. Counc.* p. 14. Ib. 1688. Crakanthorp. *Defens. Eccles. Anglic.* p. 382. Lond. 1625. Coci *Censur.* p. 231. Du Moulin, *Nouveauté du Papisme*, p. 907. A Genève, 1633.]

[6] [Ant. Augustini *De emendat. Gratiani, Dial.* xv. Lib. i. pp. 125-6. Paris. 1607.]

so, if I bring three Councils indeed, as famous as they, which
in plain words, by public and free assent, shall overthrow it,
will ye be then content to give over? Howsoever your frowardness in this behalf shall lead you; yet, that other may
understand, how men of sounder judgment have assembled
themselves also together, and alway resisted the heresy of
Imagery, I will only rehearse three other to you.

Constantine the fifth, son to Leo, surnamed Isauricus,
(otherwise, by a nickname of Iconolatræ, called Iconomachus;
of Image-worshippers an Image-enemy;) in the year of our
Lord 746[1], called a Council at his princely palace of Constantinople; where Eutropius[2] reporteth, that the Bishop of
Ephesus, the Bishop of Perga, the Bishop of Constantinople,
with other moe to the number of three hundred and thirty-
eight Prelates were; as appeareth by the subscriptions: (or, as
Sigebertus[3] reporteth, three hundred and thirty.) There they
sat, deliberating upon the matter, from the tenth of February
till the eighth of August. In the end they concluded, as
touching the Image of Christ, thus: *Si quis divinam Dei
Verbi secundum incarnationem figuram*, &c. The Acts of
which Council I will therefore insert at more large into my
writing[4]; because they contain very learned reasons against
the Picture of Christ to be made, or Image of any other in
place of God's service used.

Sanctorum Patrum[5] *et Universalium Synodorum puram,
et inviolatam, et a Deo traditam fidem nostram et con-
fessionem observantes, dicimus: Non debere quenquam
divisionem aut confusionem, ultra verum sensum et volun-
tatem inexprimibilem, et incognoscibilem illam unionem duarum, secundum Hypostasim unam, naturarum, comminisci.
Quænam est hæc insana opinio pictorum; ut, lucri turpis et
miseri causa, ea, quæ effici nequeant, studeant conficere: ut*

---

[1] [754. Sigebertus says 755.]
[2] Eutropius, Rer. Rom. Lib. xxii. [See before, page 71, n. 5.]
[3] Sigebertus in Chro. [fol. 54, a. Paris. 1513.]
[4] [They are extant among the Acts of the second Council of Nice:
and Calfhill quotes from what is styled by Sirmondus the "vulgata
editio," and what Labbé, Daillé, and others have erroneously supposed
to be the old Latin translation; whereas it is merely the version
made by Gybertus Longolius, in the year 1540.]
[5] [*Concill. General.* Tom. iii. P. ii. p. 97. Romæ, 1612.]

et ea, quæ ore et corde sunt tantummodo confessa, impiis manibus figurare intendant? Arbitratus autem sic est, ipsam Imaginem Christum vocando. Est autem Christus hoc nomine Deus et homo. Sequitur, ut Imago Dei sit et hominis. Et consequens est, ut, aut juxta opinionem vanitatis suæ, Deitatem, quæ circumscriptione creatæ carnis circumscribi non potest, circumscripserit; aut inconfusam illam unitionem, impietatis confusione, confuderit; et geminas blasphemias in Deitatem, et per descriptionem et confusionem, intulerit. Iisdem ergo blasphemiis earum adorator involvitur: et væ illud utriusque præmium; quod scilicet et cum Ario, Dioscoro, Eutyche, et Acephalorum hæresi erraverint. Damnati autem a cordatis viris in eo, quod incomprehensibilem et incircumscriptibilem divinam Christi naturam ipsi depingere studuerunt, ad aliam aliquam prava inventione apologiam confugiunt; quod solius carnis quam vidimus et palpavimus, et cum qua versati sumus, illius inquam Imaginem exhibemus: quod sane impium est, et Nestoriana diabolica inventio. Considerandum est et hoc: quod si, juxta orthodoxos Patres, simul caro, simul Dei Verbi caro, nunquam partitionis notitiam suscepisset, sed totaliter tota natura divina assumpta, et totaliter et perfecte Deitate arrepta fuisset; quomodo in duas diducetur, et ab impiis illis, qui istud facere conantur, privatim separabitur? Consimiliter vero et de sacra Ejus anima se habet. Postquam enim assumpsisset Deitas Filii in propria Hypostasi carnis naturam, inter Deitatem et carnis crassitudinem anima mediam se interposuit: et quemadmodum simul caro, simul Verbi Dei caro; sic simul anima, simul Verbi Dei anima. Et ambabus simul conspectis, videlicet anima et corpore, inseparabilis ab ipsis Deitas extitit; et in ipsa etiam disjunctione animæ a corpore, in voluntaria passione. Ubi enim anima Christi, illic etiam Deitas: et ubi corpus Christi, et illic quoque Deitas consistit. Siquidem igitur in passione inseparabilis ab iis mansit Deitas, quomodo insani isti, et quavis imprudentia irrationaliores, carnem Deitate conjunctam, et deificatam, dividunt; et hanc, ut nudi hominis Imaginem, pingere conantur? Et ex hoc in aliud impietatis barathrum labuntur. Nam, carnem a Deitate separantes, et per se subsistentem eam inducentes; aliamque personam in carne constituentes, quam in Imagine represen-

tari dicunt; quartam personam Trinitati adjiciunt, et divinam assertionem prædicant impiam. Itaque fiet illis, qui Christum depingere nituntur, ut aut Deitatem circumscriptibilem, et cum carne confusam dicant: aut corpus Christi expers Deitatis, et divisum; præterea personam per se subsistentem in carne asserant; et ita Nestorianæ Deo repugnanti hæresi similes existunt. In talem igitur blasphemiam et impietatem cadentes, pudore suffundantur; aversentur seipsos; et talia facere desinant: nec hii solum qui faciunt, verum etiam qui falso nomine factam, et dictam ab ipsis Christi Imaginem venerantur. Absit a nobis ex æquo et Nestorii divisio, et Arii, Dioscori, Eutychis et Severi confusio; male sibi ipsa repugnantia, et quæ utraque ex æquo impietatem procurant.

Which words in English be these:

"We, following therein the pure and inviolable faith, delivered from God, received of holy Fathers and General Councils, do say: That no man ought to imagine a division or confusion, contrary to the true sense and will not able to be expressed; and the same union, being above reach of knowledge, of two natures agreeable to one Person. For what a mad opinion is this of painters; who, for filthy lucre's sake, endeavour to make those things that cannot be made; and go about with their wicked hands to express counterfeits of those things, which are only with heart and mouth acknowledged? Undoubtedly such was the judgment of him, that called the Image itself Christ. But Christ is by this name both God and man. It followeth then, that it is the Image of God and man. And that also followeth, that either, according to their vain opinion, he hath circumscribed the Deity; (shut up the Godhead within a compass;) the which cannot be circumscribed, (or limited his room,) as is the nature created: or that he hath confounded, by confusion most wicked, that uniting and knitting together of the two natures, which are inconfusible; (and in themselves distinct:) and so, by his description and confusion, hath committed against the Godhead a double blasphemy. Such therefore as worship them are enwrapped in the same blasphemies, and the curse is reward to either of them; in that they have erred with Arrius, Dioscorus, and Eutyches, and such also as are infected with the heresy of the Acephali. Notwithstanding, they, being condemned of men of understanding, in that they have attempted to paint the divine nature of Christ, which is not only not to be measured and bounded in, but also not to be comprehended, (or by wit comprised,) do flee through their ungracious invention to some other defence; that we do set forth alone the Image of that nature only, of that, (I say,) which we have seen, handled, and been conversant with: and that is very wicked, and a devilish device of Nestorius. This also is further to be considered: that if so be, according to the mind of the right believing Fathers, that flesh, which is not only flesh, but the flesh of the Son of God, did never learn the way to be divided, but the whole nature of the Divinity received, and perfect Deity thereunto was taken; how shall it of these wicked ones, which endeavour this thing, be divided into two; and each by itself be separated? Like is the state and condition of His sacred soul. For after such time as the Godhead of the Son had assumpted in proper Person the nature of flesh, the soul placed herself a mean between the Deity and the grossness of the flesh: and as that flesh was not only mere flesh, but also the flesh of God the Word; even so the soul, not only an human soul, but also the soul of God the Word. And both together being seen, (that is to say, the soul and the body,) the Godhead remained as inseparable from them; yea, and that even in the separation itself of the soul from the body, in that passion, which willingly He suffered. For wheresoever the soul of Christ is, there is also the Godhead: and where the body of Christ is, there is also the Godhead. If that therefore the Godhead could not be separate from these in the passion, how do these madmen, (as rash, and altogether unreasonable,) make a division of flesh, joined with the Divinity, and deified; and attempt to paint the same as the Image of a natural man only, and no more? And, forth of this, they slip into another bottomless pit of impiety. For, in that they do separate the human nature from the Divinity, and do bring in the same subsisting by itself; and thereby do make another person in the flesh, the which they say to be represented in the Image; they do join a fourth person to the Trinity, and give sentence that the word of God is wicked. Therefore, it must needs follow of them which attempt to paint Christ, that either they must say, that the Godhead is circumscriptible; (such as may be contained within a certain compass;) and so confounded with the flesh: or else affirm, that the body of Christ is void of the Godhead, and divided, and moreover a person by itself subsisting in the flesh; and so join with the heresy of Nestorius, impugning God's truth. Forasmuch then as they fall into such blasphemy and impiety, let them be ashamed; let them abhor themselves; let them cease to practise such things: neither they only which do make them, but those likewise which do worship that which they make, and untruly name the Image of Christ. Let therefore be far from us, (as reason requireth,) as well the division of Nestorius, as also the confusion of Arius, Dioscorus, Eutyches, and Severus; wickedly disagreeing one with another, and on either side causing an impiety."

And a little after the said Council hath:

Imaginum falsi nominis prava appellatio neque ex Christi, neque Apostolorum, neque Patrum traditione cœpit; neque precationem sacram ullam, qua sanctificari possit, habet: sed manet communis [et] inhonorata, quemadmodum ab artifice pictore absoluta est. Quod si autem quidam ex eo errore existentes dixerint, recte ac pie a nobis dictum esse, in subversione Imaginis Christi a nobis facta, propter indisseparatam et inconfusam essentiam duarum naturarum in una Hypostasi convenientium: tamen iterum dubitare oportet, propter Imagines ter inculpatæ et supergloriosæ Dominæ Deiparæ, Prophetarum, Apostolorum, et Martyrum, cum sint meri nudique homines; neque ex duabus naturis, divina scilicet et humana, in una Hypostasi consistant, quemadmodum in solius Christi Imaginibus fieri renuntiavimus. Dubitare autem oportet, propter Imagines ter inculpatæ et supergloriosæ Deiparæ Dominæ, Prophetarum, Apostolorum, et Martyrum, cum fuerint nudi homines, et non ex duabus naturis constituti, quidnam conveniens aut commodum ad has dicere potuerint, subverso priore argumento. Profecto nihil est quod hic habe[n]t. Sed quid dicimus de subversione? Quandoquidem Catholica nostra Ecclesia, media existens inter Judaismum et Gentilitatem, neutram illis consuetam sacrificationem accepit; verum novam pietatis et mysticæ constitutionis a Deo datæ formam et viam ingreditur. Nam cruenta Judæorum sacrificia et holocaustomata non admittit; et Gentilitatis in sacrificando omnem Idololatriam et Statuarum copiam aversatur. Hæc caput et inventrix abhominabilis istius artis fuit. Nam cum spem Resurrectionis non haberet, dignum sibi ludicrum excogitavit; ut per eum lusum absentes tanquam adhuc præsentes exhiberet. Siquidem igitur nihil novi sapit hæc res, profecto, tanquam alienum dæmoniacorum hominum inventum, ab Ecclesia Christi longissime abjiciatur. Cessent itaque ora omnium, quæ loquuntur impia et contumeliosa contra hanc nostram Deo gratam sententiam et Decretum. Sancti enim qui Deo placuerunt, et qui ab Eo dignitate sanctitatis honorati sunt, etiamsi hinc transmigraverint, non tamen eos odiosa mortua ars unquam faciet redivivos: sed quicunque, ex Gentilium errore, illis Statuas aut Imagines erigere fuerit conatus, blasphemus judicabitur. Quomodo autem et valde laudatam Dei Matrem, quam obumbravit plenitudo Deitatis, per quam nobis eluxit lumen quod adiri nequit; Matrem, inquam, ipsis cœlis altiorem, sanctiorem Cherubin, vulgaris Gentilium ars pingere audet? Rursus, quomodo eos qui cum Christo regnaturi sunt, et in sedibus cum Eo sedebunt judicaturi orbem terrarum, conformes Ejus gloriæ, quibus non erat dignus mundus, ut divina miracula asserunt; quomodo, inquam, eos non timent per artem Gentium exhibere? Profecto non fas est Christianis, qui spem Resurrectionis habent, Dæmonum culturæ consuetudinibus uti. Et eos, qui in tanta et tali gloria resplendebunt, non decebat ignominiosa et mortua materia ignominia afficere. Nos autem ab alienis nostræ fidei demonst[r]ationes non recipimus; et in Dæmonibus testimonia non requirimus. Ad hæc, exquisita et exputata nostra sententia, tum ex Scriptura divinitus afflata, tum ex Patrum electorum testimoniis efficacibus, convenientibus nobis, et asscrentibus piam nostram intentionem, exhibebimus nostram definitionem; quibus non contradixerit is, qui conatur hæc in dubium vocare: qui vero ignorat, discat is, et erudiatur, quod scilicet a Deo sunt. Principio verbum divinæ vocis, sic dicentis, præmittimus: Deus est Spiritus: Quicunque Deum adoraverit, in spiritu et veritate adoret. Et iterum: Deum nemo vidit unquam: neque vocem Ejus audivistis, neque formam Ejus vidistis. Beati sunt qui non viderunt, et crediderunt. Et, in Veteri Testamento, ait ad Moysen et populum: Non facies tibi Idolum; neque omnem

*similitudinem, quæcunque sunt in cœlo supra; et in terra
infra. Quam ob causam in monte, in medio ignis, vocem
verborum vos audivistis; similitudinem autem non vidistis,
sed tantummodo vocem. Et, Mutaverunt gloriam immortalis Dei, per Imaginem, non solum ad mortalis hominis
similitudinem effictam; et venerati sunt et coluerunt ea quæ
condita sunt, supra Eum qui condidit. Et rursum: Si
enim cognovimus Christum secundum carnem, jam non
cognoscimus. Per fidem enim ambulamus, non per speciem.
Et hoc, quod ab Apostolo aperte dictum est: Igitur fides ex
auditu; auditus autem per verbum Dei. Si enim cognovimus Christum secundum carnem, jam non cognoscimus.
Per fidem enim ambulamus, non per speciem. Eadem
etiam et Apostolorum discipuli et successores, divini Patres
nostri tradunt. Epiphanius enim Cyprius, inter antesignanos præclarus, sic inquit: Attendite vobis, ut servetis
traditiones quas accepistis. Ne declinetis, neque ad dexteram, neque ad sinistram. Quibus infert hæc: Estote
memores, dilecti filii, ne in ecclesiam Imagines inferatis;
neque in Sanctorum cœmiteriis eas statuatis: sed perpetuo
circumferte Deum in cordibus vestris. Quinetiam neque in
domo communi tolerentur. Non enim fas est, Christianum
per oculos suspensum teneri, sed per occupationem mentis.
Idem, in aliis quoque Sermonibus suis, de Imaginum subversione multa dixit; quæ studiosi quærentes facile invenient.
Similiter et Gregorius Theologus in Versibus suis dicit:
Flagitium est, fidem habere in coloribus, et non in corde.
Ea enim, quæ in coloribus existit, faciliter eluitur; quæ vero
in profundo mentis, illa mihi amica. Joannes autem Chrysostomus sic docet: Nos, per scripta, Sanctorum fruimur
præsentia; non sane corporum ipsorum, sed animarum Imagines habentes. Nam quæ ab ipsis dicta sunt animarum
illorum Imagines sunt. Maxima vero ad recti investigationem, inquit Magnus Basilius, meditatio Scripturarum,
divino afflatu nobis datarum. In his enim et rerum argumenta inveniuntur; et vitæ beatorum virorum perscriptæ,
veluti Imagines quædam animatæ, secundum Deum politica
imitatione operum exhibentur. Et Alexandriæ lumen Athanasius dixit: Quomodo non miseratione prosequendi sunt,
qui creaturas adorant: quod illi qui vident non videntibus
cultum exhibent; et audientes non audientes orant, precan-*

turque? *Creatura enim a creatura nunquam servabitur:
Similiter Amphilochius, Iconii Episcopus, sic inquit: Non
enim nobis Sanctorum corporales vultus in tabulis coloribus
effigiare curæ est, quoniam his opus non habemus; sed politiæ
illorum virtutum memores esse debemus. Consentanea his
etiam Theodorus,* [al.] *Theodotus,] Ancyræ Episcopus, sic
docet: Sanctorum formas et species ex materialibus coloribus formari, minime decorum putamus: horum autem
virtutes, quæ per scripta traditæ sunt, veluti vivas quasdam
Imagines, reficere subinde oportet. Ex his enim ad similium
imitationem et zelum pervenire possumus. Dicant enim
nobis, qui illas erigunt Statuas, quænam utilitas ex illis ad
se redit. An quod qualiscumque recordatio eos habet ex
tali speciali contemplatione? Sed manifestum est, quod
vana sit ejusmodi cogitatio, et diabolicæ deceptionis inventum. Similiter et Eusebius Pamphili, ad Constantiam
Augustam, petentem Christi Imaginem ad se ab illo mitti,
talia dicit: Quoniam autem de Christi Imagine ad me scripsisti, ut tibi mitterem; velim mihi significes quamnam
putes Christi Imaginem: utrum illam veram et incommutabilem, natura Illius characteres ferentem; aut hanc quam
propter nos assumpsit, servilem formam pro nobis induens.
Sed sane de divina forma non arbitror etiam ipse ego te
esse solicitam; cum fueris ab Illo edocta, neminem Patrem
cognovisse, præter Filium; neque Ipsum Filium condigne
quempiam cognovisse, nisi qui Illum genuit Pater. Et post
alia: Sed omnino servi requiris Imaginem formæ, et carnem
quam propter nos induit: sed et hanc gloria Deitatis suæ
commixtam esse didicimus, et passam, mortuamque. Et
post pauca: Quis igitur gloriæ ejuscemodi et dignitatis
splendores lucentes et fulgurantes, effigiare mortuis et inanimatis coloribus, et umbratili pictura posset? cum neque
divini Illius Discipuli in monte Illum contemplari quiverint: qui, cadentes in faciem suam, non posse se ejuscemodi spectaculum inspicere confessi sunt. Igitur si carnis
illius figura tantam ab inhabitante in ea Divinitate accepit
potentiam, quid oportet dicere tunc, cum mortalitatem exuit;
et, corruptionem abluens, formam servi in Domini et Dei
gloriam transtulit: post mortis scilicet victoriam; post ascensum in cœlos; post cum Patre, regio in throno, a dexteris
confessum;* [consessum;] *post requiem in ineffabilibus et inno-*

[CALFHILL.]

minandis sinibus Patris: in quam ascendentem et desidentem cœlestes potestates, illi benedicti, [al. *Illi benedictis*] *vocibus acclamabant, dicentes: Principes, tollite portas vestras: aperiamini portæ cœlestes: introivit Rex gloriæ? Hæc igitur ex multis pauca Scripturæ Patrumque testimonia, in hac definitione nostra, parcentes sane copiæ, ne in longum res protraheretur, collocavimus. Reliquis enim, quæ infinita sunt, volentes supersedimus, ut qui velint ipsi requirant. Ex his igitur a Deo inspiratis Scripturis, et beatorum Patrum sententiis stabiliti, et super petram cultus divini in spiritu pedes confirmantes, in nomine sanctæ et supersubstantialis vivificantis Trinitatis, unanimes, et ejusdem sententiæ, nos, qui Sacerdotii dignitate succincti sumus, simul existentes, una voce definimus: Omnem Imaginem, ex quacunque materia improba pictorum arte factam, ab ecclesia Christianorum rejiciendam, veluti alienam et abominabilem. Nemo hominum, qualiscunque tandem fuerit, tale institutum, et impium et impurum, posthac sectetur. Qui vero ab hoc die Imaginem ausus fuerit sibi parare, aut adorare; aut in ecclesia, aut in privata domo constituere, aut clam habere; si Episcopus fuerit, aut Diaconus, deponitor: si vero solitarius, aut laicus, anathemate percellitor, imperialibusque Constitutionibus subjicitor; ut qui divinis decretis impugnet, et dogmata non observet.*

The English of which words is this:

"The wicked calling of Images by a false name neither had his beginning by tradition from Christ, nor of His Apostles, or yet the ancient Fathers; neither had it any holy prayer, wherethrough to be sanctified: but it remaineth profane, even as it is wrought and finished of the painter. But if certain, (delivered of that error,) affirm, that we have godlily and uprightly said, in throwing down the Image of Christ, because of the inseparable and inconfusible substance of two natures joined in one Person; yet, notwithstanding, some occasion of doubt remaineth in them, as touching the Images of the Virgin most glorious and undefiled, the Mother of God, of the Prophets, Apostles, and Martyrs, seeing that they be only men, and no more; neither do consist of two natures, that is to say, the divine and human joined in one Person, as before we have signified to be in Christ, and the contrary thereof practised in His Images: there groweth indeed some matter of doubt, as touching the Images of the most glorious and undefiled Mother of God, of the Prophets, Apostles, and Martyrs, seeing that they were only men, and not framed of two natures, what they be able to say to any purpose with reason unto these. The former argument overthrown, certainly they have nothing at all in this case to say. But what say we to overthrowing Images? Forasmuch as our Catholic Church, being a mean between the Judaism and Gentility, hath received neither of the manner of sacrifices accustomed to them; but hath entered into a new way and order of godliness, and mystical constitution given and delivered of God: for it doth in no wise admit the bloody sacrifice and burnt-offerings of the Jews; and it doth utterly abhor, not only all Idolatry in sacrificing, but also multitude of Images of Gentility: (for this was the head and first most abominable deviser of this art; which, (having no hope of Resurrection,) invented a toy, worthy itself; whereby always the absent might be shewed as present:) therefore, since this practice smelleth not of any novelty, doubtless let it be removed most far off from the Church of Christ, as a strange and foreign device of men possessed with the Devil. Let the tongues then of all such surcease, which spew forth wicked and blasphemous things, to the derogation of this our judgment and Decree, most acceptable to God. As for the holy men who pleased God, and which were honoured by Him with the dignity of holiness; although that they be departed hence, yet that dead and hateful practice shall never make them again alive. But whosoever, (poisoned with the error of the Heathen,) shall attempt to set up Images to them, he shall be adjudged as one that hath committed blasphemy. And how dare the rascal occupation of Gentiles presume to paint that most praiseworthy Mother of God, whom the fulness of the Godhead hath overshadowed; through whom hath shone upon us that light, which cannot be come unto; that Mother, (I say,) higher than the heavens, holier than the Cherubins? Again, why fear they not, (I say,) according to the art of Ethnicks to counterfeit them, which shall reign with Christ, and shall sit on seats with Him to judge the world, conformed unto Him in glory; of whom the world was unworthy, as the godly miracles affirm? Verily it is not lawful for Christians, (which believe the Resurrection,) to use the order of worshipping of Devils. Neither yet doth it beseem, by vile and dead kind of matter to reproach them, the which shall shine in so great and passing glory. As for us, we use not to receive of strangers demonstrations of our faith; neither yet in Devils to require testimony. Furthermore, (our sentence searched and discussed, both out of the Scripture inspired from above, and out of the effectual testimonies of piked [picked] Fathers, agreeing with us, and affirming our good intent,) we will exhibit in this case our resolute determination; which he shall not be able to gainsay, which laboureth to call these things in question. As for him that is ignorant, let him learn and be instructed, that these things are taken out of the word of God. First, we place before the rest this sentence of God's voice, saying: 'God is a Spirit: whosoever will worship God, in spirit and truth let him worship.' And again: 'No man at any time saw God.' 'Neither have ye heard His voice, or seen His shape.' 'Blessed are those which have not seen, and yet believed.' And, in the Old Testament, He said to Moses and the people: 'Thou shalt not make to thyself any graven Image; neither the likeness of any thing in heaven above, or in the earth beneath. For the which cause, you heard the voice of His words in the mountain, in the midst of fire; but His shape ye saw not, but only heard His voice.' And: 'They have changed the glory of the immortal God, by an Image framed after the shape of a mortal man; and they have honoured and worshipped the things which are created, above Him which hath created.' And again: 'For if we have known Christ according to the flesh, now we know Him not.' 'For we walk by faith, and not by the outward appearance.' And this also, which is most plainly spoken of the Apostle: 'Therefore faith cometh of hearing; but hearing cometh by the word of God.' 'For if we have known Christ according to the flesh, now we know Him not.' 'For we walk by faith, and not by outward appearance.' The very self-same things our godly Fathers, (the scholars and successors of the Apostles,) do teach us. For Epiphanius of Cyprus, (most famous amongst the foremost,) thus saith: 'Take heed unto yourselves, that ye keep the traditions which ye have received: see ye lean not, neither to the right hand, nor to the left.' Unto which he addeth these words: 'Remember, dear children, that ye bring no Images into the church; neither place them in the sleeping places of the Saints: but see that continually ye carry about in your heart the Lord. Neither yet let them be suffered in a common house. For it is not lawful for a Christian to be holden in suspense by his eyes, but by the contemplation of his mind.' The same Father also, in many other of his Sermons, hath declared many things touching the overthrow of Images; which the studious seeking for shall easily find. Likewise also Gregory the Divine saith in his Verses: 'It is a thing most abominable, to believe in colours, and not in heart: for that which is in colours is easily washed away; but such things as are in the depth of the mind, those like I well.' John Chrysostom also teacheth thus: 'We, through writing, enjoy the presence of the Saints; although that we have not the Images of their bodies, but of their souls. For those things which are spoken by them are Images of their souls.' Basilius also the Great saith, 'that the chiefest thing, serving to the outfinding of truth, is the meditation of the Scriptures, given unto us by divine inspiration. For in these not only arguments of things are found; but also the written lives of holy men are printed unto us, as certain lively Images; and that through the politic imitation of their works, according to God.' Also Athanasius, the light of Alexandria, said: 'How are they not to be lamented which worship creatures: that those that see yield service to those which are blind; those that hear do pray and beseech those which are altogether deaf? For the creature shall never be saved of a creature.' Likewise Amphilochius, Bishop of Iconium, thus saith: 'We accompt it a matter of no estimation, to counterfeit in tables with colours the bodily countenances of the Saints; because that of these we have no need: but we ought rather to be mindful of the policy of their virtues.' Agreeable also hereunto doth Theodorus[1], Bishop of Ancyra, teach in these words: 'We judge it nothing seemly at all, to make the forms and shapes of holy men with material colours: but it is requisite, that we often repair and make fresh their virtues; which by writings are delivered unto us, even as though it were certain lively Images. For by these we may come to the zealous following

[1] [Gennadius (*De Vir. illust.* Cap. lv.) calls him Theodorus; but generally he is named Theodotus.]

of the like. Let those tell us, which set up the same Images, what profit they have by them: whether they have any kind of remembrance, by such special kind of beholding them. But it is most apparent, that every such thought is vain, and an invention of devilish deceit.' Likewise also Eusebius Pamphili signified after this sort to Constantia the Empress, craving of him to send the Image of Christ unto her : 'Forasmuch as ye have written to me of the Image of Christ, that I should send it unto you; I would you should shew me what thing you think the Image of Christ to be : whether that same true and unchangeable creature, bearing the marks of the Deity; or that which He assumpted for our sakes, taking on Him the shape of a servant. But as touching the Picture of the Deity, I judge ye be not very careful; inasmuch as ye have been taught of Him that none hath known the Father, but the Son; and that none hath worthily known the Son, but the Father which begat Him.' And after other things : 'But ye altogether desire the Image of the servant's shape, and of the flesh which He took on Him for our sake : but we have learned that this is coupled with the glory of the Godhead, and that the same suffered and died.' And a little after : 'Who can therefore counterfeit by dead and insensible colours, by vain shadowing painter's art, the bright and shining glistering of such His glory? whereas His holy Disciples were not able to behold the same in the mountain : who, therefore, falling on their faces, acknowledged they were not able to behold such a sight. If therefore the shape of flesh received such power of the Godhead, dwelling within the same; what shall we then say, when as it hath now put off mortality, washing away corruption; and hath changed the shape of a servant into the glory of the Lord and God? What shall we say now, after His victory over death ; after His ascending into heaven; after His sitting in the kingly throne on the right hand of His Father; after rest in the not utterable secrets of the Father; into the which He ascending and sitting, the heavenly powers, those blessed ones, with voices together do cry : Ye Princes, lift up your gates; ye heavenly gates, be ye opened ; and the King of glory shall enter in?' These few testimonies therefore of Scriptures and Fathers, out of many, we have placed here in this our determination : avoiding indeed multitude, lest the matter should be too prolix;' and abstaining of purpose from the residue, (which be infinite,) that those which lust may themselves seek them. Being therefore throughly persuaded by these Scriptures, (inspired from God,) and by the judgments of the blessed Fathers; (staying our feet upon the rock of the worship of God in spirit :) we, which are girded with the dignity of the Priesthood, being of one mind and judgment, assembled together in one place, do with one voice determine, in the name of the holy, supersubstantial, and quickening Trinity : That every Image, made by painter's wicked art of any kind of matter, is to be removed forth of the church of Christians, as that which is strange and abominable. Let no man from this time forward, (of what state soever he be,) follow any such kind of wicked and unclean custom. Whosoever therefore, from this day forward, shall presume to prepare for himself any Image, or to worship it; either to set it in a church, or in any private house, or else to keep it secretly; if he be a Bishop or a Deacon, let him be deposed : but if he be a private person, or of the lay fee, let him be accursed, and subject to the imperial Decrees; as one which withstandeth the commandments of God, and keepeth not His doctrine."

Whereupon the Council's determination, so far as concerneth this case, ensueth thus :

Si quis non confessus fuerit Dominum nostrum Jesum Christum, post assumptionem animatæ, rationalis, et intellectualis carnis, simul sedere cum Deo et Patre; atque ita quoque rursus venturum, cum paterna majestate, judicaturum vivos et mortuos; non amplius quidem carnem, neque incorporeum lumen, ut videatur ab iis a quibus compunctus est; et maneat Deus, extra crassitudinem carnis; anathema.

Si quis divinam Dei Verbi, secundum incarnationem, figuram materialibus coloribus studuerit effigiare; et non ex toto corde, oculis intellectualibus, Ipsum sedentem a dextris Patris, super solis splendorem lucentem, in throno gloriæ, adorare; anathema.

Si quis incircumscripti[bi]lem Verbi Dei essentiam, et Hypostasin, propterea quod incarnatus est, naturalibus coloribus in Imaginibus, ad formam hominis, depinxerit; et qui non theologice sensit, eam post carnem non minus incircumscriptibilem remansisse; anathema.

Si quis indivisam Dei Verbi naturæ et carnis secundum Hypostasin unitionem; videlicet ex utrisque unam, inconfusam, et impartibilem perfectionem factam, in Imagine depingere conatur; vocatque eum [eam] Christum; (Christus enim nomine uno et Deum et hominem significat:) et ex ea re confusionem duarum naturarum monstrose asserit; anathema.

Si quis carnem Hypostasi Verbi Dei unitam diviserit; et, in nuda excogitatione mentis eam habens, ex eo conatus fuerit illam in Imagine depingere; anathema.

Si quis unicum Christum in duas hypostases diviserit; ab una parte Dei Filium, et ab altera parte Mariæ filium collocans; neque continuam unitionem factam confitens; et ob id in Imagine, tanquam per se subsistentem, Mariæ filium depinxerit; anathema.

Si quis ex unitione ad divinum Verbum deificatam carnem in Imagine pinxerit; veluti dividens eam ex assumpta et deificata Deitate; et indeificatam ex hoc eam conficiens; anathema.

Si quis in forma Dei existentem Deum Verbum, servi formam in propria Hypostasi assumentem, et per omnia nobis similem factum, sine peccato, conatus fuerit materialibus coloribus figurare, veluti si nudus homo fuisset; et hoc modo ab inseparabili et incommutabili Deitate sejungere; veluti quaternitatem inducturus in sanctam et vivificantem Trinitatem; anathema.

"If any person shall not acknowledge our Lord Jesus Christ, after the taking of living, reasonable, and understanding flesh, to sit together with God and His Father; and that He shall so return again, with the majesty of His Father, to judge both quick and dead; not any more flesh, and yet notwithstanding having a body, that He may be seen of those of whom He was pricked; and that He doth remain God, without the grossness of flesh; let him be holden accursed.

"If any person shall attempt to counterfeit the divine figure of God the Word, as He became man, with material colours; and doth not worship with all his heart, with eyes of understanding, Him, sitting on the right hand of His Father, glistering above the brightness of the sun, in the throne of His glory; let him be holden as accursed.

"If any person do paint the incircumscriptible nature and substance of God the Word, and His Person, with natural

Incircumscriptible is that which cannot be

colours in Images, after the fashion of a man, because that He took flesh; and doth not also think, after the doctrine of true divinity, the same divine nature, after the assumpting of flesh, to remain notwithstanding incircumscriptible; let him be holden as accursed. *[sidenote: measured, or compassed within any certain bounds.]*

"If any person do enterprise to paint and set forth, in an Image, the indivisible uniting in one Person of the natures of God the Word and flesh; that is to say, the perfection made of both twain, which neither is to be confounded of either, nor one from the other to be severed; and doth call the same Christ; (for Christ in one name doth signify both God and man:) and by that means most monstrously doth affirm the confusion of the two natures; let him be holden as accursed.

"If any person shall divide the human nature, united to the Person of God the Word; and, having it only in the imagination of his mind, shall therefore attempt to paint the same in an Image; let him be holden as accursed.

"If any person shall divide Christ, being but one, into two persons; placing on the one side the Son of God, and on the other side the son of Mary; neither doth confess the continual union that is made; and by that reason doth paint in an Image the son of Mary, as subsisting by himself; let him be accursed.

"If any person shall paint in an Image the human nature, being deified by the uniting thereof to God the Word; separating the same as it were from the Godhead assumpted and deified; making the same as though it were not deified; let him be holden as accursed.

"If any person shall presume to counterfeit in material colours God the Word, being in the shape of God, and taking on Him in His proper Person the form of a servant, and by all things made like unto us, (yet without sin,) as though that He were but only bare natural man; and by this means to divide Him from the inseparable and unchangeable Godhead; as though he would bring in a quaternity into the holy and quickening Trinity; let him be holden as accursed."

And so far the Council of Constantinople, concerning this case: whose authority if you admit not, yet let their reasons take place, or be answered : let the word of God, which they faithfully alleged; the testimony of Fathers, which they roundly brought out, take away this wicked and abominable worshipping of God with an Image. Let not the natures of Christ be confounded. Let not the one from the other be severed. Christ on the Cross was both God and man: that on our Cross is but an Image only of a man. Christ on the Cross was the Son of God: that on our Cross is but the Image of the son of Mary. Christ hath an inseparable and unchangeable Godhead : that on our Cross maketh two persons of one ; four persons in Trinity. Therefore accursed be that Cross to the Devil. And thus much for the first Council.

Now about the same time[1], when the controversy was hot in Greece, they began also to stir in Spain: and there, at a city called now Granata[2], was a Council held of nineteen Bishops, and six and thirty Elders. The chief among them was Fœlix, Bishop of Aquitane. When they maturely had weighed the matter, with one assent they agreed on this point[3] : *Placuit, Picturas in ecclesia esse non debere; ne quod colitur aut adoratur in parietibus depingatur.* Which words in English are these : " Our pleasure is, that there should be no Pictures in the church; that the thing be not

Concilium Elibertinum. [Eliberitanum.]

---

[1] [There is an extraordinary anachronism apparent here: for the Synod of Elvira was held about the year 305; and is not, even by Baluze, put later than 324. (See Cardinal De Aguirre's *Notitia Conciliorum Hispaniæ*, p. 36. Salmant. 1686.) In order to account for so great an error, it may be suspected, that our author looked hastily into Carranza's *Summa*: (p. 64. Salm. 1551.) where he might have found his marginal words, " Concilium Elibertinum ;" and the observation, " Hæc omnium fere consensu dicitur Granata ;" together with the remark, that the Synod had been holden " circa Nicæni Concilii tempora :" which last statement he may have construed into an allusion to the *second*, instead of to the *first* Council of Nicæa. The editor of Latimer's *Sermons*, in 1758, has endeavoured to propagate the same confusion : for he declares, that the first General Council " instituted the veneration due to the Virgin Mary, the holy Cross, and to the Images or representations of Christ, His Apostles, and of other departed Saints."! (Vol. i. p. 237. Comp. p. 443.)]

[2] [Granada has absorbed the ancient Elvira : but, strictly speaking, it is not true that Elvira is now called Granada.]

[3] Can. xxxvi. [Ivonis *Decretum*, iii. 40. Gonzalez *Collect. Can. Eccl. Hisp.* col. 287. Matriti, 1808. Routh *Reliquiæ Sacræ*, iv. 51. Oxon. 1818.]

painted on the walls which is served or worshipped." The like also is repeated after, Can. 41. But "these," (ye say,) "were condemned by the seventh General Council kept at Nice, where three hundreth and fifty Bishops, (men of great virtue, profound knowledge, and deep sight in divinity,) were." But that was also condemned after, by another Council, assembled at Frankford in the year of our Lord 794 : where all the learned of Charles his dominions, of France, Italy, and Germany were present: whither Adrian the Pope sent also his embassadors, Theophylact and Stephan : where Charles himself was in proper person, upon occasion of the said Council of Nice, which the Pope had sent him to be approved. But he doth call it *stolidam et arrogantem Synodum*, " a doltish and a proud Synod ;" and the Decree there made, touching the adoration of Images, (which you, M. Martiall, do teach so stoutly,) *impudentissimam traditionem*, " a most impudent and shameless tradition." I refer you to the four books of Carolus [4] ; in which at large is set forth, not only the vanity of those reverend Asses, which went about to establish Images, but also the effect of the Council of Frankford not utterly abolishing, (which was their imperfection,) but plainly condemning the adoration and worship of them. But in this case, where Council is against Council, and necessary it is, that one of them be deceived, which must we trust to ? I know that the latter age hath received the worse, the seventh of Nice. But we must not follow the authority of men, were they never so many ; but the direction of God His Spirit, and truth revealed in His holy word. What moved the faithful to refuse the second of Ephesus [5], and willingly embrace the Council of Chalcedon, but that, examining their Decrees by Scripture, they found Eutyches' heresy confirmed in the one, which the other con-

---

[4] [Published by Joannes Tilius, at Paris, in 1549; and reprinted by Goldastus, in his valuable collection of the *Imperialia Decreta de cultu Imaginum*, Francof. 1608. The Caroline Capitular was composed about the year 790; and the perusal of it is forbidden by the Tridentine *Index*, p. 40. Antverp. 1570. A full examination of the disputes concerning it is contained in Dorschei et Grambsii *Collat. ad Concil. Francofurd*. pp. 40—93. Argentor. 1649. Cf. Mabillonii *Præf. in iv. sæc. Bened*. §. 20. Præfatt. p. 183. Rotom. 1732.]

[5] [Σύνοδος λῃστρική.]

demned? So, when the manifest word of God shall try where the Spirit of God doth rest, there must the credit, and there only, be given.

And to the end that all readers hereof may understand and see what vanity there was in the Prelates of Nicene Council; what more than vanity is in the magnifiers of so mad a company; I will set forth the allegations of the Image-worshippers, and the confutation which the servants of God made: that every man thereby may judge so, as the Spirit of God shall lead him, and as himself shall see good cause. First of all, their general position was[1]; that the Images of Christ, the Virgin Mary, and other Saints, were sacred and holy; therefore to be worshipped. Hereto the Synod answered; that the antecedent, the former proposition, was false: inasmuch as they are neither holy in respect of the matter whereof they be made, nor of the colours that be laid upon them; nor yet for any imposition of hands, nor by any canonical consecration: therefore they be not at all holy; much less therefore to be worshipped. The noble John, the legate of the Easterlings, brought forth another reason: God made man after His own image and likeness: therefore Images are to be worshipped. Hereto the Catholics justly replied; that he made a false argument, *Ab ignoratione Elenchi:* by applying that to Image-worshipping, which made nothing at all to purpose. For both out of Ambrose and Augustin they proved, that man is called the image of God, not for his external shape, which Images well enough may represent; but for the inward man, the mind, the reason, the understanding, and virtues consonant to the will of God. For Ambrose saith[2]: *Quod secundum imaginem est, non est in corpore, nec in materia, sed in anima rationabili:* "That which is according to the image of God, is not in the body, nor in the matter, but in the reasonable soul." Likewise Augustin[3]: *Accedit utcunque anima humana interior, homo recreatus ad imaginem Dei, qui creatus est ad imaginem Dei:* "The inward soul of man, the new-born man, which is made after the image of God, cometh after a

---

[1] Car. Mag. Li, i. Cap. xx. & To. ii. Con. Concil. Nice. II.
[2] In Psal. cxviii. Ser. x. [*Opp.* Tom. ii. 958. Lut. Paris. 1661.]
[3] In Psal. xcix. [fol. ccxxix. Paris. 1529.]

sort near unto God His image." But that wheresoever a similitude and likeness is spoken of, there is also an image to be meant, Augustin disproveth[4]: *Ubi similitudo, non continuo imago, non continuo æqualitas*, &c.: "Where a similitude or likeness is, not by and by an image, not by and by equality." So that the folly of him was great, to abuse the Scripture to so impertinent a purpose.

But the Nice masters proceed and say; that as Abraham worshipped the sons of Heth[5], and Moses Jethro, the Priest of Madian[6]; so must Images be worshipped of men. Hereto the Council, (as Charles the President thereof affirmeth,) answered[7]: *Dementissimum est, et ab omni ratione seclusum, hoc, ad astruendam Imaginum adorationem, in exemplum trahere; quod Abraham populum terræ, et Moses Jethro, Sacerdotem Madian, leguntur adorasse:* "It is a thing of most madness, and utterly severed from all reason, to bring for example, to confirmation of Image-worshipping, that Abraham is read to have worshipped the people of the earth, and Moses Jethro, the Priest of Madian." The Saints of God, in token of their obedience and humility, sometime have bowed themselves; have shewed some piece of courtesy to such as pleased them, and had authority in the earth: but what is this for the honour done to a dead stock? Why is this example made to be general, extending to all, both quick and dead, both good and bad: whereas the Saints themselves sometime abhorred this worship to be given them; sometime refused to give it unto other? *Imagines vero, nusquam, nec tenuiter, quidem adorare conati sunt:* "But as for Images, they never attempted in any place, or in any so slender wise, to worship them." Let them learn of Augustin[8], that Abraham and Moses, doing as they did, were examples of humility, not patterns of impiety. Let them learn, that there is no less diversity between the worshipping of an Image, and worshipping of a man, than is between a living man, and a man painted upon the wall. Let them learn how love, reverence, and charity towards men, is in the Scripture commanded oft; the bowing, the kneeling, the service to an Image, is in every place forbidden and accursed.

[4] Octog. trium Quæst. Ca. lxxiv. [*Opp.* T. vi. col. 47.]
[5] Gen. xxiii. [7, 12.]   [6] Exod. xviii. [7.]   [7] Lib. i. Cap. ix.
[8] De Doctri. Christ. Li. i. Cap. i. [Prolog. *Opp.* Tom. iii.]

The Papists' figure, to make the Scripture serve their purpose.

But a familiar figure the Papists have, to make the Scripture to serve their fancies; *Acyrologiam*, which you may call "Abusion," "improper speeches." As, wheresoever in the Hebrew text they read any word that betokeneth bowing, saluting, blessing, they do full wisely turn it "worshipping." And is this honest and upright dealing? Yet how they dally on this sort, both with the world and with the word of God, the next allegation of theirs declareth[1]: *Jacob, suscipiens a filiis suis vestem talarem Joseph, osculatus est eam, et cum lachrymis imposuit oculis suis. Ergo,* &c. Which words in English, according to their translation, be these: "Jacob, receiving of his sons Joseph his long garment, he kissed it, and with tears laid it upon his eyes: and therefore Images are to be worshipped." And is not this a reason[2], that might have been fette[3] out of a Christmas pie? Will any man hereafter find fault with Papists depraving of the Scripture, since they take them leave to make what Scripture they list? Where find they this text in all the Bible; that Jacob kissed his son's garment, and laid it upon his eyes? The place is the thirty-seventh of Genesis; where only we read, that the sons of Jacob brought unto their father Joseph his party-coloured coat, and said: "This have we found: see now whether it be thy son's coat or no. Then he knew it, and said, It is my son's coat. A wicked beast hath devoured him. Joseph is surely torn in pieces. And Jacob rent his clothes, and put sackcloth about his loins, and sorrowed for his son a long season." Where is the kissing of the coat, and laying it on his eyes? But if kissing had been there, what is that to worshipping? But to kiss and to worship is all one with them. They worship where they kiss: let them kiss where they worship not.

Another worthy Father of that sacred assembly, because he would have a fresh device, coined out of hand another piece of Scripture, saying[4]: *Jacob summitatem virgæ Joseph adoravit:* "Jacob worshipped the top of Joseph's rod:" Therefore we may worship the Picture of Christ. Let me ask of his fatherhood, where he findeth the

---

[1] Carol. Mag. De Ima. Li. i. Ca. xii.
[2] [Does the author play upon the words *raison* and *raisin*?]
[3] [fetched.]
[4] Car. Mag. De Imag. Li. i. Ca. xiii.

place? Let him put on his spectacles, and pore on his Portasse⁵. If this be lawful, that every noddy that cometh to a Synod may chop and change the word of God as he will; what need we to care for Moses' writing, or Esdras' restoring, or Septuagint's translating, or the Apostles' handling of the Scripture? The great virtue and profound knowledge of those synodical men may serve and suffice us. And, to prosecute the cause of Jacob, another riseth up, and puts in his verdict, saying⁶: *Benedixit Jacob Pharaonem, sed non ut Deum benedixit: adoramus nos Imaginem, sed non ut Deum adoramus:* "Jacob blessed Pharao, but he blessed him not as God: we worship an Image, but we worship it not as God." This man had wit without all reason. He compared the blessing that the holy Patriarch gave unto the King; the bounden man to the well deserver; the subject to the superior; unto the worship of a senseless Image, that standeth in the wall, and doth no more good.

But another brought in a sounder proof; and framed his argument after this sort⁷: *Propitiatorium, et duos Cherubin aureos, et arcam testamenti, jussu Dei Moses fecit. Ergo, licet facere et adorare Imagines:* "Moses, by the commandment of God, made the Propitiatory, and the two golden Cherubins, and the ark of witness. Therefore it is lawful to make and worship Images." This fellow began in good divinity, but ended in foolish sophistry: for in the Conclusion he put more than was in the Premisses. Moses made this and that: therefore we may both make and worship. Where doth he read that they were worshipped? Yea, how can those examples be applied unto Images, since they be set in the face of the people, only to this end, to be gazed on; but the ark of witness, with the furniture thereof, was in the oracle of the house, in the most holy place, covered⁸, that it might not be seen without. Again, the Cherubins were but a peculiar ordinance of God⁹; and therefore could not prejudice an universal law. But, to proceed: It is written in the Law¹⁰, (say they¹¹:) *Ecce vocavi ex nomine Beseleel, filii [filium] Ur, filii Hor, de tribu Juda;*

---

⁵ [See page 16, note 2.]
⁶ Car. Mag. Li. i. Cap. xiv
⁸ Num. iv. [5.]
¹⁰ Exod. xxxi. [2-5.]

⁷ Cap. xv.
⁹ 2 Par. [Chron.] v. [7, 8.]
¹¹ Car. Mag. Lib. i. Ca. xvi.

et replevi eum spiritu sapientiæ, et intelligentiæ, ad perficiendum opus ex auro et argento. Ergo, licet adorare Imagines: " I have called by name Bezaliell, the son of Uri, the son of Hur, of the tribe of Juda ; whom I have filled with the spirit of God, in wisdom, and in understanding, and in knowledge, and in all workmanship, to find out curious works to make in gold and silver. Therefore it is lawful to worship Images." A reason, as if it had been of your making, M. Martiall, *Ab ignoratione Elenchi.* Therefore the Synod answered; that it was not only an extreme folly, but a mere madness, to apply the figures of the old Law, which only were made as God devised, and had a secret meaning in them, to the Images of our time; which every carver, goldsmith, and painter make, as their fancy leadeth them, to an ill example, and to no good use in the world. But what should I stand in exaggerating of their folly? I will truly report the reasons of the one part; and abridge what I can the answers of the other.

Iconolatræ.   *Sicut Israeliticus populus Serpentis ænei inspectione servatus est; sic nos, Sanctorum effigies inspicientes, salvabimur*[1] *:* " As the people of Israel was preserved by the looking on the brazen Serpent, so we shall be saved by looking on the Images of Saints;" quoth the Image-worshippers.

THE ANSWER.

Iconomachi.   They that repose their hope in Images are condemned by the Apostle; (quoth the Fathers of Frankford Council:) *Spes quæ videtur non est spes :* " That hope which is seen is no hope[2]." Furthermore, the brazen Serpent was not commanded to be worshipped: therefore the worshipping of an Image is falsely inferred of it. Thirdly, the brazen Serpent was commanded of God: but no piece of Scripture doth bear with Images.

THE REASON.

Iconolatræ.   *Si, secundum Mosis traditionem, præcipitur populo, purpura hyacinthina in fimbriis, in extremis vestimentis poni, ad memoriam et custodiam Præceptorum ; multo magis nobis est, per adsimulatam Picturam sanctorum virorum, videre exitum conversationis eorum, et eorum imitari fidem, secundum Apostolicam traditionem*[3]. Which, word for word

---

[1] Car. Mag. Lib. i. Ca. xviii.
[2] Rom. viii. [24.]   [3] Car. Mag. Lib. i. Ca. xvii.

in English, is thus: "If, according to Moses' tradition, a purple violet be commanded to the people, to be put in their purfles[4], and skirts of their garments, for a memory and keeping of the Commandments; much more must we, by the counterfeit Picture of holy men, see the end of their conversation, and imitate their faith, according to the tradition Apostolic."

THE ANSWER.

Each part of this argument consists of untruths. First, Iconomachi. by corrupting the Scripture, in calling it a purple violet; whereas purple is one colour, and violet another. Then, by comparing things unlike together; wearing of a garment, and worshipping of an Image. Thirdly, in alleging a most untruth of all; that the conversation of holy men is seen in an Image. For faith, hope, and charity, (which be the chief virtues of Saints,) are things invisible: but Images and Pictures are visible. As for imitation, what it ought to be, the Apostle sheweth us, saying[5]: *Imitatores mei estote, sicut filii charissimi:* "Be ye followers of me, as most dear children:" and, in another place[6]: *Imitatores mei estote, sicut et ego Christi:* "Be ye followers of me, even as I am of Christ." Whereby it appeareth, that the tradition of the Apostles is, to behold the godly conversation of the Saints, not in Pictures, but in virtues: to imitate their faith, not in feigned Imagery, but in sincere good works.

THE REASON.

Jesus Nave duodecim lapides statuit, in Dei memoriam. Iconolatræ. *Ergo, licet adorare Statuas*[7]: "Josue did set up twelve stones, for a remembrance of God. Therefore it is lawful to worship stocks and stones."

THE ANSWER.

Josue meant nothing less than to teach the Israelites to Iconomachi. worship stones: but to put them in mind, that they were the stones of the river, that was dried for them.

THE REASON.

Nathan adoravit Davidem. Ergo, nos Imagines[8]: Iconolatræ. "Nathan did worship David. Therefore we may Images."

[4] [Embroidered borders, or trimmings: from the French *pour filles.*]
[5] 1 Cor. iv. [14-16.]   [6] 1 Cor. xi. [1.]
[7] Car. Mag. Lib. i. Ca. xxi.   [8] Car. Mag. Lib. i. Ca. xxii.

[CALFHILL.]

THE ANSWER.

Iconomachi. Nathan did not worship David, set forth in colours, or painted on a wall; but a living creature, set in the throne of justice, supplying the room of God. Wherefore there is no comparison betwixt them.

THE REASON.

Iconolatræ. *Signatum est super nos lumen vultus Tui Domine. Item, Vultum Tuum requiram. Ergo, Imagines sunt adorandæ*[1]: "'Thy countenance, O Lord, is signed upon us[2].' And, 'Thy countenance I will seek after[3].' Therefore Images are to be worshipped."

THE ANSWER.

Iconomachi. If these words of David did any thing appertain to Images, we might justly enquire what countenance they have, and how this countenance may be signed in us. The countenance of God is Christ His Son; to the knowledge of whom we must aspire by Scripture, and not by Picture. Wherefore, sith the countenance of God cannot be seen in material Images, which have no eyes; it is too fond to apply it to Images. In the same Psalm[4] the Prophet hath: "He that desireth life, and will see good days," what shall he do? Pore upon Pictures? seek after Images? No. *Declinet a malo, et faciat bonum:* "Let him refrain from evil, and do the thing that is good."

THE REASON.

Iconolatræ. *Vultum tuum deprecabuntur omnes divites plebis. Ergo, Imagines sunt adorandæ*[5]: "'All the rich of the people shall make their homage before thy face[6].' Therefore Images are to be worshipped."

THE ANSWER.

Iconomachi. Homage is done before the face of such as can both hear, and have understanding. Since neither of these is in an Image, it cannot be that by the face of God is meant an Image.

---

[1] Car. Mag. Lib. i. Ca. xxiii.
[2] Psal. iv. [6.]   [3] [Psalm xxvii. 8.]
[4] [Psalm xxxiv. 12-14. xxxvii. 27. 1 Pet. iii. 10, 11.]
[5] Car. Mag. Lib. i. Ca. xxiv.   [6] Psal. xliv. [xlv. 12.]

THE REASON.

Dilexi decorem domus Tuæ. Sed Imagines pertinent ad Iconolatræ. *decorem templorum. Ergo, Imagines sunt diligendæ*[7]: "'I have loved,' (saith David[8],) 'the beauty of Thy house.' But Images pertain to the beauty of churches. Therefore Images are to be loved."

THE ANSWER.

The house of God is not the material church, of lime Iconomachi. and stone; but the congregation of faithful people, in whose hearts He dwelleth: nor the beauty hereof consisteth in outward garnishing, but spiritual virtues; not in Imagery, but in piety. They which renounced the world, and withdrew themselves from the sight of evil, had no Images to deck their houses. They dwelt in simple and vile cottages; and yet they loved the beauty of God's house. Wherefore the beauty thereof doth not consist in Images.

THE REASON.

Sicut audivimus, ita vidimus. Ergo, Imagines sunt ado- Iconolatræ. *randæ*[9]: "'As we have heard, so have we seen;' (saith David.[10]) Therefore Images are to be worshipped."

THE ANSWER.

The promises of God to them that fear Him, to be their Iconomachi. refuge, help, and deliverance, were the things that they had heard foretold by the Prophets, and seen in themselves. And if they had not felt a stronger effect of God's power than a sorry Picture could have brought unto them, they should have continued all the days of their life, in body, slaves; in soul, ignorant.

THE REASON.

Damnantur inimici, qui malignantur in Sanctis Dei. Iconolatræ. *Ergo, Imagines contemnentes damnantur*[11]: "Those enemies, that do work evil to the Saints of God, are condemned[12]. Therefore such as despise Images are condemned."

THE ANSWER.

To omit the phrase of *malignantur*, for *malum inferunt;* Iconomachi.

---

[7] Car. Mag. Lib. i. Ca. xxviii. [8] Psal. xxvi. [8.]
[9] Car. Mag. Lib. i. Ca. xxx. [10] Psal. xlviii. [8.]
[11] Car. Mag. Lib. ii. Cap. i. [12] Psal. lxxiv. [3.]

what a gross ignorance was this, to put the Saints of God for the Sanctuary itself? Wherefore the Synod answered: The Psalm entreateth of such as had spoiled the temple of Hierusalem; had taken away the furniture thereof, which God had commanded. What is that to Images? He neither speaketh of the Saints of God; nor Images are the Saints of God.

THE REASON.

Iconolatræ. *In civitate Tua, imagines ipsorum ad nihilum rediges. Ergo, Imagines sunt adorandæ*[1]*:* "'Thou shalt bring their images in Thy city to naught[2].' Therefore Images are to be worshipped."

THE ANSWER.

Iconomachi. The city of God sometime is taken for the soul of man, inhabited of God: sometime for His congregation upon earth. Sometime also for the heavenly Hierusalem; as in this place[3]: that as they have defiled the image of God upon earth; so their own images shall not appear in heaven, but be reserved in everlasting pain.

THE REASON.

Iconolatræ. *Scriptum est: Exaltate Dominum Deum nostrum, et adorate scabellum pedum Ejus; quoniam sanctus est. Ergo, Imagines sunt adorandæ*[4]*:* "It is written: 'Exalt the Lord our God, and fall down before His footstool; for He is holy[5].' Therefore we must fall down to Images."

THE ANSWER.

Iconomachi. It is no proof that Images should be worshipped, because it is written, that we should fall down before the footstool of God. For we must not esteem His footstool according to the use of men; nor deem that God is circumscript with quantity, or needeth a thing to bear up His feet withal. We must not think that any thing is to be worshipped but only God; the same God that telleth what His footstool is, saying: *Cœlum*

---

[1] Car. Mag. Lib. ii. Ca. iii.   [2] Psal. lxxii. [lxxiii. 20.]
[3] Augustinus, Tom. viii. in Psal. lxxii. ["Nonne digni sunt hæc pati: ut Deus in civitate Sua imaginem eorum ad nihilum redigat; quia et ipsi, in civitate sua terrena, imaginem Dei ad nihilum redegerunt?" (*In Psalm.* fol. clxiii, b. Paris. 1529.)]
[4] Car. Mag. Lib. ii. Ca. v.   [5] Psal. xcix. [5.]

Mihi sedes, terra autem scabellum: "Heaven is My seat, and the earth My footstool[6]." But shall we worship the earth, which is the creature of God? No, but as Ambrose saith[7]; by the earth is the flesh of Christ signified, which He took from the earth. It is therefore lewdly applied to Images, which appertaineth to the mystical service of our Lord Christ.

THE REASON.

Scriptum est: Adorate in monte sancto Ejus. Ergo Imagines adorandæ[8]: "It is written: 'Worship Him in His holy hill[9].' Therefore Images are to be worshipped." *Iconolatræ.*

THE ANSWER.

The Prophet saith not, The hill is to be worshipped; but, God to be worshipped in His holy hill. And if he had said, Worship the hill; yet wise men would have construed it for God, and not for Images. For the Church itself, the congregation of faithful people, is that hill of His, that Sion wherein He dwelleth. Then in that hill we must not superstitiously worship Images; but Christ Himself, the Captain of that hill: who, to purchase that hill unto Him, vouchsafed not only to take our shape, but in our shape to suffer death. *Iconomachi.*

THE REASON.

Scribitur in Canticis: Ostende Mihi faciem tuam. Ergo Imagines ostendendæ[10]: "It is written in the Canticles[11]: 'Shew Me thy face.' Therefore Images are to be shewed." *Iconolatræ.*

THE ANSWER.

The Church it is, whom Christ there speaketh to: whom sometime He calleth a dove; sometime His fair one; sometime His love. The Church, (that is to say,) His elect and chosen, He willeth there to rise, that is to say, believe; to hasten to Him, to fructify in good works; to come, that is to say, receive an everlasting reward. The face of this Church is *Iconomachi.*

---

[6] Psal. [Isaiah] lxvi. [1.] Act. vii. [49.]

[7] [*De Spiritu Sancto*, Lib. iii. C. xii. Opp. Tom. iv. 264. —"Sed nec terra adoranda nobis, quia creatura est Dei. Videamus tamen ne terram illam dicat adorandam Propheta, quam Dominus Jesus in carnis assumptione suscepit."]

[8] Car. Mag. Lib. ii. Ca. vi. [9] Psal. xcviii. [xcix. 9.]
[10] Car. Mag. Lib. ii. Ca. x. [11] [ii. 14.]

not corporal, but spiritual: not by proportion of Imagery, but by properties of virtue to be discerned. Then is it an impudent application of the face of this Church to Images; unless whatsoever is there spoken mystically must be taken carnally.

THE REASON.

Iconolatræ. *Erit altare in medio Ægypti. Ergo, Imagines in medio templi*[1]: "'There shall be an altar,' (saith the Prophet[2],) 'in the midst of Egypt.' Therefore Images in the midst of the church."

THE ANSWER.

Iconomachi. This prophecy was performed in Christ: who, in the midst of Egypt, that is to say, the world, hath erected His altar, His faith and belief; by which we may make our prayers to Him. *Stolidum est ergo*, say they; "It is a doltish part" to apply it to Images.

THE REASON.

Iconolatræ. *Nemo accendit lucernam, et ponit eam sub modio. Ergo, Imagines habendæ sunt, et colendæ luminibus*[3]: "'No man lighteth a candle, and putteth it under a bushel[4].' Therefore Images must be had, and worshipped with candles."

THE ANSWER.

Iconomachi. *O res inconsequens, et risu digna!* "O matter impertinent, and worthy to be laughed at!"

THE REASON.

Iconolatræ. *Ecce virgo concipiet, et pariet filium. Hanc autem prophetiam in Imagine nos videntes, videlicet virginem ferentem in ulnis quem genuit; quomodo sustinebimus non adorare et osculari*[5]*?* "'Behold,' (saith the Prophet[6],) 'a virgin shall conceive, and bring forth a son.' And whereas we behold this prophecy in a Picture, seeing a virgin carrying her son in her arms; how can we forbear but worship it and kiss it?"

THE ANSWER.

Iconomachi. The performance of this prophecy must not be seen in uncertain Images of man's hand, but fastly be fixed in the

---

[1] Car. Mag. Li. ii. Ca. xi.
[3] Car. Mag. Li. ii. Ca. xii.
[5] Car. Mag. Li. iv. Ca. xxi.
[2] Esay xix. [19.]
[4] Matth. v. [15.]
[6] Esay vii. [14.]

heart of man. Nor the mysteries thereof to be sought in Pictures, but in holy Scriptures. And as for worshipping or kissing a senseless thing, who will presume so to do? (say they.) *Quis tale facinus perpetrare audebit?* "Who shall dare commit such an heinous fact?":

THE REASON.

Imaginis honor in primam formam transit. Ergo, Iconolatræ. *Imagines honorandæ*[7]: "The honour done to an Image passeth into the first shape after which it was made. Therefore Images are to be honoured."

THE ANSWER.

A strange case, never heard tell of before; never to be Iconomachi. proved hereafter. Christ said not, That which you have done to Images, you have done to Me; but, "Whatsoever you have done to one of these little ones, ye have done to Me[8]." Nor thus He said, He that receiveth an Image, receiveth Me; but, "He that receiveth you," (Mine Apostles,) "receiveth Me[9]." Nor Christ His Apostle said, Let us love Images; but, "Love one another[10]." Wherefore, it is a vain dream, contrary to all Scripture and reason too, that honour done to a senseless thing shall pass to him, that neither peradventure hath the like shape, nor ever is present with it. But if it were possible, (as they falsely affirm,) that honour and reverence done to an Image redoundeth to the glory of the first sampler; how can we imagine that Saints are so ambitious, that they will have such honour done to them? If in the flesh they did abhor it, in the spirit shall they accept it?

THE REASON.

Suscipio et amplector honorabiliter sanctas et venerandas Iconolatræ. *Imagines, secundum servitium adorationis, quod consubstantiali et vivificatrici Trinitati emitto: et qui sic non sentiunt, neque glorificant, a sancta, Catholica, et Apostolica Ecclesia segrego; et anathemati submitto; et parti, qui abnegaverunt incarnatam et salvabilem dispensationem Christi, veri Dei nostri, emitto*[11]: "I do receive," (quoth Constantinus, Bishop of Constance in Cyprus,) "and honour-

---

[7] Car. Mag. Lib. iii. Ca. xvi.   [8] Matth. xxv. [40.]
[9] Matth. x. [40.]   [10] 1 Joan. iii. [11, 23. iv. 7, 11.]
[11] Car. Mag. Lib. iii. Ca. xvii.

ably embrace, the holy and reverend Images, according to that service of adoration and worship which I give to the Trinity, of one substance together, of one quickening power: and those that think not so, nor glorify them so, I separate from the holy, Catholic, and Apostolic Church. I pronounce them accursed, as such as take part with them that denied the incarnate and salvable dispensation of Christ our true God."

THE ANSWER.

Iconomachi. O horrible blasphemy! What man in his right wits would ever say such a thing, or consent to the saying; that a vile Image or a blind Picture should be honoured as the eternal and almighty Trinity? That an earthly creature should have the service that is only due to the heavenly Creator? Who could abide him, *Nauseantem potius quam loquentem:* "Spewing rather than speaking?" What honest ears would not rather detest than delight in the hearing of him? It only sufficed his fatherhood to affirm the damnable and shameless heresy. It only sufficeth to rehearse his absurdities, to make all Christians mislike with him and maintainers of such lies and devilish devices. For, suppose that it were good to have Images, and to honour them; shall it therefore be made equivalent with a matter of our faith, without the which we cannot be saved? Shall we be accursed for that, which Scripture never taught us; but is direct contrary against the Scripture? *Dominum Deum tuum adorabis, et Illi soli servies:* "Thou shalt honour the Lord thy God, and Him only shalt thou serve[1]."

THE REASON.

Iconolatræ. *Qui Deum timet, honorat omnino, adorat, et veneratur, sicut Filium Dei, Christum Deum nostrum, et signum Crucis Ejus, et figuram Sanctorum Ejus*[2]*:* "He that feareth God, doth honour, worship, and reverence the sign of the Cross of Christ, and figure of His Saints, no otherwise than the Son of God, even Christ our God."

THE ANSWER.

Iconomachi. This is a different phrase, a contrary opinion to all the Scripture. The holy men of God did ever teach the fear of

---

[1] Deut. vi. [13. S. Matth. iv. 10.]   [2] Car. Mag. Lib. iii. Ca. xxviii.

God; and never taught the service of an Image. David[3] saith not, He that feareth God, worshippeth Images; but, "He that feareth God, greatly delighteth in His commandments." So that the fear of God consisteth not in worshipping of Images, but in observance of the law of God. And if none fear God, but the same worship Images, what is become of the Saints aforetime, which never had them?

THE REASON.

Imago Imperatoris est adoranda. Ergo, etiam Christi et Sanctorum[4]*:* "The Image of the Emperor is to be worshipped. Therefore the Image of Christ and His Saints." Iconolatræ.

THE ANSWER.

By that which is of itself unlawful, they go about to confirm a thing more unlawful. For it is not to be proved, that the Image of man is to be worshipped: yet, if that were granted, great odds there is in the comparison. The Emperor is local; and, being in one place, cannot be in another: but God is every where. And to comprise Him within the compass of a stone wall, or a little table, which is all in all; and whole every where: whom the earth containeth not, nor heavens comprehend; is too profane a case, cousin to infidelity. Iconomachi.

THE REASON.

Qui adorat Imaginem, et dicit, Hoc est Christus, non peccat. Ergo, Imagines adorandæ[5]*:* "He that worshippeth an Image, and saith, This is Christ, sinneth not. Therefore Images are to be worshipped." Iconolatræ.

THE ANSWER.

He that maketh a lie, sinneth. But he that affirmeth so vile a thing as an Image is to be Christ Himself, maketh an impudent lie. Therefore he that so sayeth, sinneth. Iconomachi.

THE REASON.

Imagines sacris vasis, Cruci Dominicæ, et libris Scripturæ divinæ æquiparantur. Ergo, adorandæ[6]*:* "Images Iconolatræ.

---

[3] Psal. cxi. [cxii. 1.]   [4] Car. Mag. Lib. iii. Cap. xv.
[5] Car. Mag. Lib. iv. Cap. i.
[6] Car. Mag. Li. ii. Cap. xxix. Cap. xxviii. & Cap. xxx.

are comparable with the holy vessels, with the Cross of Christ, and books of holy Scripture. Therefore to be worshipped."

THE ANSWER.

Iconomachi. A sort of lewd comparisons. For, as for holy vessels, they were commanded: so are not Images. And yet not the vessels commanded to be worshipped. Therefore, to gather a worshipping of Images by them, is folly. Then also, the Cross hath wrought miraculous and merciful effects to our salvation: so can Images do none. And yet, by the way, they plainly declare[1]: *Per Crucem non lignum illud significari, sed totum opus Christi, et afflictiones piorum:* "That by the Cross there is not signified the piece of wood, but the whole work of Christ, and afflictions of the godly." The Scripture also, (by the inspiration of the Holy Ghost,) was delivered to men, and bringeth a most certain commodity with it. Images, as they sprong from error of Gentility, so have they no profit, but perverting in them.

THE REASON.

Iconolatræ. *Jacob erexit lapidem in titulum. Ergo, Imagines adorandæ*[2]: "'Jacob took a stone, and set it up as a pillar[3].' Therefore Images are to be worshipped."

THE ANSWER.

Iconomachi. Although this be a lubberly reason; (to use the term of Charles the Great, who plainly called it *Rem non mediocris socordiæ;*) yet somewhat will I say according to mine author, to shew the difference between Jacob's fact and their affection.

One thing it is, the holy Patriarchs by some notable mark to foreshew things that were to come; and another, to have an idle workman to make an Image in remembrance of things past. One thing it is, to be inspired with the Holy Ghost; and a far other, to have the art of carving or graving. One thing it is, to trust to God's working; and another, to put an occupation in practice. One thing it is, that Jacob set up a pillar; another, that a workman shall set up an Image.

---

[1] Car. Mag. Li. ii. Cap. xxviii.
[2] Car. Mag. Li. i. Cap. x. [3] Gen. xxxi. [45.]

THE REASON.

Jesus ad Abgarum Imaginem Suam misit. Ergo, Ima- Iconolatræ.
gines adorandæ[4]: "Jesus sent His Image unto Abgar. Therefore Images are to be worshipped."

THE ANSWER.

It is no Gospel, that Jesus sent His Picture unto Abgar. Iconomachi. And Gelasius himself, sometime Pope of Rome[5], numbereth both the Epistle that Christ is said to have sent unto him, and also the report of the Picture[6], *inter Apocrypha;* among the writings not received to be read publicly in the church, nor serving to prove any point of Religion. Wherefore the reason is insufficient.

THE REASON.

Images did miracles[7]; and are comparable to the hem of Iconolatræ. Christ's garment, by the touching whereof the woman was healed of her issue of blood. Therefore to be worshipped.

THE ANSWER.

That Images did any miracles, is a very lie. Yet, if Iconomachi. miracles they had done, it is not enough to prove them to be worshipped.

THE REASON.

That they did miracles, is proved by examples[8]. The Iconolatræ. Image of Polemon preserved one from the act of adultery. The dream of an Archdeacon, whom an Angel in his sleep commanded to worship an Image. A Monk lighted a candle before the Image of our Lady; and five or six months after he found it burning.

---

[4] Car. Mag. Li. iv. Cap. x.

[5] [In the Synod which consisted of seventy Bishops; A.D. 496. Vid. Gratiani *Decretum*, Dist. xv. C. *Sancta Romana Ecclesia*.]

[6] [This is a mistake: for the story of the Image is of a later date; and is brought forward, as genuine evidence, in the fifth Act of the second Council of Nicæa. Gretser informs us truly, that "Gelasius nunquam Imaginem ipsam apocryphis deputavit; quidquid tandem sit de Epistolis. Et Concilium II. Nicænum non Epistolis, sed Imagine Edessena nititur." (*De Imagg. non manufact.* Opp. Tom. xv. p. 192. Ratisb. 1741.)]

[7] Car. Mag. Lib. iii. Ca. xxv.

[8] Car. Mag. Lib. iii. Ca. xxi. & Cap. xxvi. et Li. iv. Ca. xii.

THE ANSWER.

Iconomachi. For the first, there is no reason to induce us, that the tale is true. Yet, if it were true, there is no less difference between the miracles of Christ and miracles of Polemon, than is between the Person of Christ and person of Polemon. For the second, it is an unwise and unwonted thing, to confirm by a dream a doubtful case. Whether he dreamed it or devised it, there is no proof at all, no witnesses of the matter. And yet, if he so dreamed indeed, our doubt by good reason may be no less. But it is well enough; a drunken device to be confirmed with a drowsy dream. As for the third, the circumstance of the fact itself, the person, the place, the time considered, we may justly derogate all credit from it. For neither we are assured of the honesty of him that told the tale; nor it is reported where, or when, or after what sort it was done. Wherefore it sounds so like a lie, that a true man ought not to believe it. Yet, if it were a most certain truth, that a candle burned five or six months together, we ought not to ground thereof an adoration of a thing unreasonable. Balaam's Ass opened his mouth to reprove his master[1]; preserved the children of God from cursing. Shall then the tongue of the Ass, or his tail be honoured?

Thus have ye heard how the Nice Council confirmed as they could, by Scripture and by miracles, not only the having, but worshipping of Images. Ye have heard in it how the learned Fathers, assembled at Frankford, answered their idle and impudent allegations. But lest I should seem to suppress any thing, that in appearance maketh for our adversary, I will shew what Fathers and Doctors of the Church Hireneis [Irene's] chaplains brought forth for them.

Iconolatræ. First of all, Augustin; who saith: *Quid est imago Dei, nisi vultus Dei, in quo signatus est populus Dei?* "What is the image of God, but the countenance of God, in which the people of God is sealed?" Therefore Images are to be worshipped.

THE ANSWER.

Iconomachi. The image of God is Christ His Son, according to Paul: *Qui est imago Dei invisibilis:* "Which is The image of the

---

[1] Num. xxii. [28. 2 Pet. ii. 16.]

invisible God?." And to apply that to a stock or a stone, which is peculiar unto Christ, is horrible. Nor Augustin's meaning was so[3]: but, as it is evident by his own words, he, speaking of Christ, whom he calleth the image and countenance of the Father, saith, that in Him we be sealed, *Qui dedit pignus Spiritus in cordibus nostris:* "Which gave the pledge of His Spirit in our hearts[4];" whereby we are sealed into the right of His children, against the day of redemption[5].

Then brought they forth an authority out of Gregorius Nyssenus[6]. To which the Synod answered, that inasmuch as his life and doctrine was unknown to them[7], they could not admit his testimony, for approving of a thing in controversy.

They alleged also Cyril[8] upon John[9]: but corrupting his sentence, depraving his sense; that, as the words were brought unto them, it was as hard to pick out construction, as to find a pin's head in a cart-load of hay.

Likewise they dealt with Chrysostom[10]; alleging that he should say: *Vidi Angelum in Imagine:* "I saw an Angel in an Image." Whereto was answered, that it was nothing likely; because Angels are invisible.

Nor otherwise with Ambrose[11]: *Nam et ipsius sententiam ordine, sensu, verbisque turbarunt:* "For they troubled his sentence, both in the order, the sense, and the

[2] [Col. i. 15.]
[3] Car. Mag. Lib. ii. Ca. xvi.   [4] [2 Cor. i. 22.]
[5] [Ephes. iv. 30.]   [6] Car. Mag. Lib. ii. Ca. xvii.
[7] [As this plea can hardly be esteemed sufficient, it is right to observe that, in the fourth Act of the second Council of Nicæa, a passage was cited from S. Gregory's Oration *De Deitate Filii et Spiritus, et in Abraham;* in which he relates, that he was much affected by beholding a Picture of the offering up of Isaac. (*Opp.* Tom. ii. p. 908, Paris. 1615.)]
[8] Car. Mag. Li. ii. Cap. xx.
[9] [Or rather upon S. Matthew; as Pope Adrian testifies in his Epistle to Constantine and Irene, *Act.* ii.]
[10] Car. Mag. Li. iii. Cap. xx. [Sept. Syn. *Act.* iv.—The words were quoted from the dubious Homily, *Unum et eundem esse Legislatorem utriusque Testamenti;* and, at all events, only stated, that the writer was pleased with a representation of the Angel destroying the Assyrians.]
[11] Car. Mag. Li. ii. Cap. xv. [Pope Adrian's Letter, in the second Act, notifies that the extract was derived from one of the books "ad Gratianum Imperatorem."]

words." Nor this is my private opinion. The whole Council affirmed it so; and the Acts are evident to prove no less.

As for the example that they brought of Silvester[1], how he presented the Images of the Apostles to Constantinus; it maketh nothing for them. He shewed him, peradventure, Pictures to look upon; no Images to adore.

But I must not forget how they brought an example of a certain Abbot[2]; which made an oath to the Devil, that he would not worship the Picture of Christ, or of His mother: but afterward he brake his oath; saying, that it was better for him to haunt all the brothel-houses in the city, than to abstain from worshipping of Images. I need not to rehearse the Council's answer to it. There is no such babe, but seeth their beastliness. Only their greatest reason, that doth remain, is this.

THE REASON.

Iconolatræ. Epiphanius, discoursing upon all the sects of heretics, doth not accompt them for any that worship Images. Therefore it is no heresy to worship Images[3].

---

[1] Car. Mag. Li. ii. Cap. xiii. [A more decisive answer might have been elicited from the fact, that the *Acts of Pope Silvester*, from which the narrative was taken, and which are the main foundation for the fables respecting the Leprosy, Baptism, and Donation of Constantine, are an extravagant fiction. (See Crakanthorp's *Defence of Constantine*, pp. 206—232. Lond. 1621.) If it be argued, that their genuineness seems to be established by the Gelasian Decree, at the end of the fifth century; we may reply, in the first place, that Archidiaconus, Cardinal Cusanus, and the Gregorian Glossators concur in bearing witness, that the sentence in question, and a great many others, "absunt a plerisque vetustis Gratiani codicibus:" and secondly, even if the legitimacy of the paragraph be admitted, it only affirms, that the Acts were "read by many Catholics in the city of Rome;"—a declaration which need not be much more than equivalent to the assertion, (if it were true,) that many Protestants study the Golden Legend.]

[2] Car. Mag. Li. iii. Cap. xxxi. [The tale is recorded in the fourth and fifth Acts of the Deutero-Nicene Council; and is said to be adduced from the *Limonarium* of Sophronius of Jerusalem. The *Limonarium*, or *Pratum spirituale*, is not, however, the work of Sophronius, but of Joannes Moschus, who lived in the year 630; and of the author of the performance Baronius has been forced to ask: "Cum hæc compingat ea narratione mendacia, quæ fides in reliquis?" (*Annall.* Tom. v. ad an. 407. p. 270. Antv. 1658.)]

[3] Car. Mag. Li. iv. Cap. xxv.

THE ANSWER.

Epiphanius, discoursing upon all the sects of heretics, doth not accompt them for any that condemn Images. Therefore it is no heresy to condemn Images. But that the same Epiphanius did not only mislike with worshipping of Images, but also with the having of them[4], shall appear hereafter.

It sufficeth now that I have set forth to you the best part of the Acts of the noble Council. Ye see the learned reasons that they made: the deep and profound judgments: the pith, the strength, the marrowbones of their matter; wherewith they did so begrease themselves, that now they shine so glorious in your eyes. If men had devised matter to mock them withal, I suppose they could not have found any so absurd as they brought with them. Yet these be they that represented the state of the universal Church. These be they that could not err. These be they that you only depend on. These be the three hundreth and fifty Bishops, that condemned the three hundreth and eight and thirty that were before assembled at Constantinople. These be the judges that gave sentence against the Council gathered in Spain. These be the worthy pillars that bare up the Cross and Images. And if a man considered by what spirit they were led when they came to Nice, he needed not to marvel at the strange and horrible success of their doings. For who then bare the sway? Who did assemble them, but that Athalia, that Jesabel Irene; which was so bewitched with superstition, that, all order, all honesty, all law of nature broken, she cared not what she did, so she might have her Mawmots[5]? She burned her father's bones. She murthered her own son. She perverted by violence all order of lawful counsel, that she might go a whoring with her Idols still. When Constantine the fifth, father to her husband Leo, (by marriage of whom she

---

[4] [Erasmi *Stultitiæ Laus*, p. 116. Basil. 1676.]

[5] [The term "Mawmots" or "Mammets" signifies Puppets; (See before, p. 31.) and "Mawmetry" means the worship of Images. The names have doubtless been corrupted from "Mahomet" and "Mahometry." See Selden, quoted by Dr Wordsworth; *Eccles. Biog.* Vol. i. p. 368. Hincmar of Rheims, speaking of the Council of Frankfort, uses the apposite expressions, "*Puparum* cultum;" (*Cont. Hinc. Laudun. Episc.* Cap. xx.) and, in Becon's works, we read of "Mahound-like Mawmets." (*Prayers*, &c., p. 233. ed. Parker Soc.)]

most unworthy came to her estate,) had lien dead and buried a good while in his grave, she digged him up: she shewed her cruelty on his carcase: she cast his bones into the fire; and caused his ashes to be thrown into the sea. This did the good daughter, the defender of Images, because her father, when as yet he lived, had broken them in pieces; affirming simplicity, rather than sumptuousness, to be most fitting for the church of Christ. Thus raged she during the nonage of Constantine her son; and made the palace of Constantinople a sink of sectaries, a follower of deformed Rome. But when the Emperor himself, (her son,) grew to discretion, he trod in his father's and grandfather's steps; and did so much mislike with his mother's Mawmetry[1], that he began to bridle her insolent affection: he took the sword out of her mad hands; and threw down the monuments of superstition, which she, (with such diligence and cost,) had erected. Whereupon the malice of her wicked breast was so incensed, that she spared not to set on fire her own house; to conspire the death of her own child; only to maintain her Images in the church. Therefore she not only forgat her duty to her Prince, her love to her son, but she joined with a sort of cut-throats: she utterly cast off the nature and condition of a woman: she became more savage than a wild beast. For beside that she craftily betrayed the Emperor, she traitorously bereaved him of his inheritance the crown: she most unwomanly scratched out the eyes of the same her own son: she most abominably cast him into prison: most detestably at length she murthered him. Thus was the living for the dead; the Prince for a Puppet; the natural child destroyed, for the naked unnatural use of Imagery.

And to declare the wrath of God, justly deserved for this execrable fact, Eutropius reporteth thus[2]: *Obtenebratus est sol per dies septemdecim, et non dedit radios suos: ita ut errarent naves maris; omnesque dicerent, quod propter excæcationem Imperatoris, sol obcæcatus radios suos retraxerit:* "The sun was darkened for seventeen days, and gave not forth his light: so that the ships of the sea wandered; and all men affirmed, that for the putting out of the Emperor's eyes, the sun, being blinded, withdrew his beams." The cause of which

---

[1] [See the preceding note.]
[2] [See page 71, note 5.]

terrible and strange effect, the only practiser of all the foresaid outrages, was only that Irene, that President of Nicene Council: for that only cause, for which she gathered that conspiracy together. And when she saw, that without extortion and violence, she was not able to compass her wicked enterprise, she fell to tyranny: she stopped the mouths of her adversary part; and either banished them out of the way, or kept them in such hold, that they should not hurt her. And was not this a goodly Council then: the cause so unlawful; the caller so horrible; the parties so beastly; the order so unconscionable? Brag as ye please of your Nice Council; undoubtedly they gave unwise counsel. Nor it rested in them to bind or loose in heaven what they would. They did not answer the points of their commission: therefore they had not the effect of power. Which thing considered, I trust you will detest their impiety; who, for a Picture, have defaced Scripture; who, for a fancy of their own brain, have fallen into a phrensy of too much superstition: apparelling their Idols with garments of God's service; and cloking their Idolatry with a face of true worshipping. Folio 41, b.

Now that I have battered about your ears this your "Ajax' shield," which ye thought to use as a special defence; "the name of Councils, General and Provincial;" of which some do make nothing for you, the rest ought not to have authority with any; let me now, I say, descend unto your Doctors. Ambrose[3] affirmeth, "that a church cannot stand without a Cross:" and thereupon ye infer, "that a Cross must needs be in the church." I grant ye, Master Martiall: and yet have ye gained nothing. For though he spake of the sign of a Cross, yet it rests to be proved that he meant of your Cross. He maketh many mysteries of the Cross: as the hoised sail, the earing[4] plough, the blowing Ambrose.
Folio 42, a.

---

[3] Serm. lvi. [This is the second Sermon *De Cruce Domini*, and the fifty-second of the *Sermones de Tempore*, inter Opp. S. Ambr. Vol. ii. Tom. v. 71—2. Lut. Paris. 1661. It is the identical Discourse *De Cruce*, which Gennadius (*De Vir. illust.* Cap. xl.) ascribes to Maximus Taurinensis, who was really the parent of it. Coccius has divided one authority into two, by citing extracts from the same Homily, under the names of both Fathers. (*Thesaur. Cath.* i. 240—41. Conf. Latini Latinii *Biblioth. Sacr. et Profan.* pp. 137, 164. Romæ, 1677.)]

[4] [tilling.—Gen. xlv. 6. Exod. xxxiv. 21.]

[CALFHILL.] 12

winds from each quarter of the earth, the lifted up hands of the faithful people: and every one of these, according to Ambrose his allegation, is a very Cross. Then may ye have any one of these, and have a Cross: yea, impossible it is almost to do any thing, but that ye shall have the sign of a Cross[1]. *Aves quando volant ad œthera, formam Crucis assumunt. Homo natans per aquas, vel orans, forma Crucis vehitur. Navis per maria antenna Cruci assimilata sufflatur:* as Hierom saith[2]: "When the birds fly into the air, they take the form of a Cross. A man when he swimmeth in the water, or prayeth, is carried after the manner of a Cross. The ship in the sea is blown forward, with the sail-yard hanging Crosswise at the mast." Also Arnobius[3], answering the Heathen, that in despite laid unto the Christians' charge, that they honoured Crosses, said plainly: *Cruces nec colimus, nec optamus:* "Crosses we neither worship, nor wish for." But, on the contrary side, he proved that they had as many Crosses as the Christians. For their banners and ensigns, what were they but gilded and adorned Crosses? Their spoils of enemies, carried on the spear's point, the noble signs of their valiant victory, represented not only the fashion of a Cross, but also the Image of a man nailed on it. So that the sign of a Cross is naturally seen in the ship sailing, the plough earing, the man praying. And among the rest, I think, (as you say,) that there is no church can stand with-

[1] [Conf. S. Just. Mart. *Apol.* Opp. p. 90. Lut. Paris. 1615.]
[2] Hiero. in xv. Marci. [With regard to these Commentaries on S. Mark, we learn from Sixtus Senensis, that "*magis abhorrent a stylo Hieronymi quam ignis ab aqua. Hos esse hominis, qui non multum Latine, minus etiam Græce et Hebraice noverit, argumento sunt orationis barbaries, et inepta peregrinarum vocum interpretatio.*" He adds that, in the exposition of the *fifteenth* Chapter, some mutilated verses, concerning the figure of the Cross, are inserted; having been borrowed from Sedulius, who lived several years subsequently to S. Jerom. (*Biblioth. Sanct.* Lib. iv. p. 266. Cf. *Index Theol. et Scriptur.* ab Angelo Roccha a Camerino, p. 106. Romæ, 1594.)]
[3] Libro viii. [There are only seven books by Arnobius, *Adversus Gentes;* and the memorable words here referred to are to be found in the treatise by Minucius Felix, *De Idolorum vanitate:* p. 89. Oxon. 1678. This Dialogue is named *Octavius:* but, in the old editions of S. Jerom's work *De Viris illustribus,* as well as in his Epistle to Magnus, it is incorrectly styled *Octavus;* and, for a considerable time, it passed for an eighth book by Arnobius.]

out it. For unless ye have the cross beams and the cross pillars, with one piece of timber shut into another, (which is the very sign of a Cross,) I cannot tell how the building can abide. But what is this to your Rood and Crucifix, or to a sign drawn with a finger? If a Cross be so necessary, then look on the roofs and walls of your houses; and there shall ye find as substantial a Cross as in the Rood-loft or upon the Altar. If the sign of a Cross must needs be worshipped, (as you in every place do teach,) then, by Ambrose his reason, we are as well bound to adore and worship the sail of the ship, the plough of the field, the winds of the air, and the arms of a man. For in the same place alleged by you, where the Cross is extolled, these signs are mentioned: *Hoc Dominico signo scinditur mare, terra colitur, cœlum regitur, homines conservantur:* "By this sign of our Lord the sea is cut, the land is ploughed, the sky is ruled, and men be preserved." Yea, the very effects that you do attribute to the church Cross, S. Ambrose ascribeth to the mast of a ship: and yet no man did ever crouch unto it, unless it were to keep him from the weather.

Wherefore your ignorance or unfaithfulness is too apparent, in that ye father the words of Ambrose: "If a church lack a Cross, by and by the Devil doth disquiet it, and the wind doth squat it:" (for his words be these:) *Cum a nautis scinditur mare, prius ab ipsis arbor erigitur, velum distenditur; ut, Cruce Domini facta, aquarum fluenta rumpantur: et, hoc Dominico securi signo, portum salutis petunt; periculum mortis evadunt. Figura enim Sacramenti quædam est velum suspensum in arbore; quasi Christus sit exaltatus in Cruce: atque ideo, confidentia de mysterio veniente, homines ventorum procellas negligunt; peregrinationis vota suscipiunt. Sicut autem ecclesia sine Cruce stare non potest; ita et sine arbore navis infirma est. Statim enim [et hanc] Diabolus inquietat; et illam ventus allidit. At ubi signum Crucis erigitur, statim et Diaboli iniquitas repellitur; et ventorum procella sopitur.* The English is this: "When the sea is furrowed of the mariners, first they hoise up the mast, and spread abroad the sail; that, the Lord His Cross being made, the waves of the water may be broken: and they, (secure with the sign of our Lord,) reach unto the haven of health; and scape the danger of

Folio 42.

death. For the sail, hanging upon the mast, is a certain figure of an holy sign; as if that Christ were exalted on the Cross: and therefore, through confidence of the mystery, cunning men do not care for the storms of winds; they undertake their appointed pilgrimage. And as a church cannot stand without a Cross; so is a ship weak without a mast. For straight the Devil doth disquiet it, and the wind squat it. But where the sign of the Cross is hoised up, the iniquity of the Devil is driven back; and tempest of wind is calmed." Whereupon, I beseech you, doth he infer, "the Devil doth disquiet, and wind squat it?" Not upon the mention of a ship without a mast? Whereupon did he talk? Of the church Cross, or the ship Cross? If the mast of the ship did no more preserve and save the vessel, than the Crucifix on the Altar, or Cross in the Rood-loft can do the church; neither should the ship be preserved in the water, nor the church at any time be consumed with the fire. We needed not to fear, (if your opinion were true,) the burning any more of Paul's. Make a Cross on the steeple, and so it shall be safe. But within these few years it had a Cross, and reliques in the bowl, to boot: yet they prevailed not; yea, the Cross itself was fired first. Wherefore, S. Ambrose his rule, (as you most fondly do take him,) holdeth not. If ye say, that his rule doth hold notwithstanding, because Paul's was burned in the time of schism: I answer, that in your most catholic time, the like plague happened, twice within the compass of fifty years; and therefore S. Ambrose was not so foolish to mean as you imagine.

Lactantius. As for Lactantius, (whose verses ye bring to confirm the use of a Rood in the church;) I might say with Hierom[1]: *Utinam tam nostra potuisset confirmare,* [al. *affirmare,*] *quam facile aliena destruxit:* "I would to God he had been able as well to have confirmed our doctrine and Religion, as he did easily overthrow the contrary." For many errors and heresies he had; among the which I might reckon this: *Flecte genu, lignumque Crucis venerabile adora:* "Bow down thy knee, and do honour to the worshipful wood of the Cross." For upon the word of the Prophet Hieremy, *Lignum de saltu præcidit:* "He hath cut a tree

[1] Ep. ad Paulinum. [*Æpistt.* Par. iii. Tract. ix. Ep. xxxviii. sig. 000. Lugd. 1508.]

out of the forest;" S. Hierom[2] taketh occasion to speak of the Gentiles' Idols, adorned with gold and silver, of whom it is said[3]: "A mouth they have, and speak not: ears they have, and hear not." And lest it might be thought, that the making and honouring of such appertained peculiarly unto the Heathen, he said: *Qui quidem error ad nos usque transivit*: "Which error indeed hath come over unto our age." And then inferreth this: *Quicquid de Idolis diximus, ad omnia dogmata quæ sunt contraria veritati referri potest. Et ipsi enim ingentia pollicentur; et Simulachrum vani cultus de suo corde confingunt. Imperitorum obstringunt aciem; et a suis inventoribus sublimantur. In quibus nulla est utilitas; et quorum cultura proprie Gentium est, et eorum qui ignorant Deum.* Which words are in English these: "Whatsoever we have spoken of Idols may be referred unto all doctrines contrary to the truth. For they also do promise great things; and devise an Image of vain worship, out of their own heart. They blind the eye of the ignorant; and by the inventors of them are set aloft. In which there is no profit; and the worshipping of which is an heathenish observance, and a manner of such as know not God."

Wherefore the words alleged by you, (as out of Lactantius,) sufficed to discredit him; because he will have a piece of wood to be worshipped: omitting all his other errors; and that Gelasius the Pope, in consideration of many his imperfections, reckoneth his books *inter Apocrypha;* such as may be read, and no doctrine be grounded on. But I will answer to you otherwise: disprove it, if you can. I verily suppose, that those verses were never written by Lactantius[4]. The causes

[2] In Hieremiam x. [sig. V v, vi. Venet. 1497.]
[3] Psal. cxiii. [cxv. 5, 6.]
[4] [Calfhill's supposition is altogether true: for Possevinus *(Appar. Sac.* ii. 4.) acknowledges that the Poem, *De Passione Domini,* "nullibi inter antiquos Lactantii codices inventus est." Bellarmin *(De Scriptt. Eccl.)* stamps it as "ambiguous:" but, with questionable honesty, he has, at least four times, employed it as an indubitable testimony: *(Apol. pro Respons. ad lib. Jacobi Regis,* Cap. viii. p. 126. an. 1610. *De Imaginibus,* Lib. ii. Cap. xii. & Cap. xxviii. *De notis Ecclesiæ,* L. iv. C. ix. §. xviii. Conf. Dorschei *Hodeget. Cathol. Anti-Kirch. Prælim.* p. 89. Argentor. 1641. Zornii *Opusc. Sacr.* i. 52. Altonav. 1743.) Pelliccia, too, has called it "antiquissimum monumentum Imaginis Christi, Cruci affixi." *(De Christ. Eccles. Polit.,* cura Ritteri. Tom. i. p. 335. Colon. ad Rhen. 1829. Cf. Bartholini *De Cruce Hypomnem.* p. 104. Amstel. 1670.)]

that induce me to this are these: S. Hierom[1], making mention
of all his writings, (yea, of many moe than are come unto our
hands,) maketh no mention of this. Again, churches in his
time were scarcely builded: for he lived in the reign of
Dioclesian, by whom he was called into Nicomedia, as Hierom writeth. Afterward, when he was very old, he was
schoolmaster to Crispus, Constantinus' son, and taught him in
France. Now, in the reign of Dioclesian, the poor Christians
had in no country any place at all, whither they might
quietly resort, and "stand still a while, looking on the Rood,
with his arms stretched, hands nailed, feet fastened." They
had neither leisure nor liberty, to be at such idle cost. They
contented themselves with poor cabins, whereto they secretly
resorted; and yet, notwithstanding, had them pulled on their
heads. Eusebius, writing of the persecution under Dioclesian, saith[2]: *Oratoria a culmine ad pavimentum usque,
una cum ipsis fundamentis dejici; divinasque et sacras
Scripturas in medio foro igni tradi, ipsis oculis vidimus:*
"We saw with our eyes, that the oratories," (he calleth them
not temples, for so they were not;) "were utterly thrown down,
from the top to the ground; yea, with the very foundations
of them: and that the sacred and holy Scriptures, in the midst
of the market-place, were committed to the fire." Then was it
no time for them to make Images of Christ; whose faith,
(without peril,) they could not profess: nor solemnly to set
up Roods, where privately they had no place thereto. And
this was in the most flourishing time of Lactantius. Yea,
afterward, in the beginning of Constantinus' reign, Maximinus
gave licence first, that Christians might build *Dominica
oratoria*[3]: "The Lord's places of prayer." And the first
temple that Constantinus built was at Hierusalem, the thirtieth
year of his reign[4]. Wherefore, methinketh, impossible it is,
that Lactantius should write: *Quisquis ades, mediique subis
in limina templi;* with the rest of the verses rehearsed by
you.

Then how different the doctrine is, both from that which
himself teacheth, and generally was received in his days,

---

[1] In Catalogo. [*Lib. de Vir. illust.* Cap. lxxx.]
[2] Lib. viii. Ca. ii. [*Eccles. Hist.* ed. Lat.]
[3] Eus. Lib. ix. Cap. x. [p. 143. Basil. 1549.]
[4] Sozom. Li. ii. Cap. xxvi. [p. 579.]

that lewd verse (*Flecte genu, lignumque Crucis venerabile adora,*) sheweth: for in his books he plainly affirmeth, that no man ought to worship any thing on the earth[5]. And further he saith, that whosoever will retain the nature and condition of a man, must seek God aloft: in heaven, not in earth; in heart, not in workmanship of hand[6]. His argument is this[7]: *Si Religio ex divinis rebus est, divini autem nihil est nisi in cœlestibus rebus; carent ergo Religione Simulachra: quia nihil potest esse cœleste in ea re, quæ fit ex terra:* "If Religion consist of holy things, and there be nothing holy but in heavenly things; then Images are void of Religion: because in that thing, which is made of the earth, there can be nothing heavenly." You will grant me now, that a Rood is made of some earthly matter, of stone, or timber. Then doth Lactantius repute it unholy, and to have no Religion at all in it. And will he have us to bow the knee to adore and worship an unholy thing, a thing of no Religion?

Eusebius, living in the same age, and somewhat after him, thought it a strange case to see an Image stand in Cæsarea: which Image, notwithstanding, was not yet crept into the church; as in the preface I have approved. Furthermore, Arnobius[8], schoolmaster to Lactantius, hath a number of places to disprove this assertion. For he telleth how the infidels laid to the Christians' charge, that they hid Him whom they honoured, because they had neither temples nor altars. But he sheweth what temples they had erected then: *In nostra ipsorum dedicandum mente; in nostro imo consecrandum pectore:* "To be dedicate to Him in our own mind; consecrate to Him in the bottom of our breast." Whereupon he inferreth: *Quem colimus Deum, nec ostendimus nec videmus: imo ex hoc Deum credimus; quod Eum sentire possumus, videre non possumus:* "The God, that we worship, we neither shew nor see: but rather by this we

Eusebius.

Folio 8. [p. 28.]

Arnobius.

---

[5] Divi. Insti. Li. ii. Ca. i. [*De orig. Error.* ii. i. Vid. sup. pp. 25, 26.]
[6] Cap. ix. [Lib. ii.]   [7] Divi. Inst. Lib. ii. Ca. xix.
[8] Adversus Gentes, Li. viii. [M. Minucius Felix is, as before, the author who should have been mentioned. His *Octavius* is annexed to the work of Arnobius, published by Elmenhorst, Hanov. 1603; and the sentences here alleged are in pages 392, 389, of this edition. The editor's copy once belonged to Primate Ussher.]

believe Him to be God; because we can feel Him, but we cannot see Him." Yea, to go no further than to the Cross itself, to the Rood that ye talk of; Arnobius affirmeth plainly: *Cruces nec colimus, nec optamus. Vos plane, qui ligneos Deos consecratis, Cruces ligneas, ut Deorum vestrorum partes, forsitan adoratis:* "We neither worship, nor wish for Crosses. You, that consecrate wooden Gods, peradventure worship the wooden Crosses as parts of your Gods." Whereby is evident, as well by the undoubted words of Lactantius himself, as otherwise by the testimony of S. Hierom, and witness of Eusebius, and doctrine of Arnobius; first, that the verses should not seem to be his. Then, that by all likelihood there were no churches in Lactantius his time; and therefore no Roods in churches. Thirdly, that no holiness, no Religion is in any earthly matter; and therefore in no Rood. Lastly, that neither Crosses nor Crucifixes were either worshipped, or wished for: but that it was thought a mere Gentility to bow down unto them.

Augustin.

As for S. Augustin, Ser. xix. *de Sanctis*[1], he speaketh nothing else but of the mystery of the Cross, as you yourself allege. *Crucis mysterio basilicæ dedicantur:* "By the mystery of the Cross," (and not "by the sign of the Cross," as

Folio 43.

you do ignorantly translate it[2];) "churches are dedicated." Now you be to learn what is a mystery; learn it of Chrysostom, who saith[3]: *Mysterium appellatur, quoniam non id quod credimus intuemur; sed quod alia videmus, alia credimus:* "It is called a mystery, because we see not that which we believe; but that we see one thing, and believe another." Then is it not the sign, (which you do take for the material thing,) but the mystery, that maketh the dedication: not the thing that we see, but that which we believe: the death of Christ, which in the congregation He will have shewed, until

---

[1] [The ownership of this Sermon cannot, by any means, be vindicated for S. Augustin. It is the third Discourse *De Annuntiatione Dominica:* Opp. Tom. x. foll. 263, b, 264. Paris. 1541.]

[2] [Inaccuracy, and not ignorance, ought to have been censured for this error. The previous sentence commenced with "Hujus Crucis mysterio;" and that intended to be adduced is, "Cum ejusdem Crucis charactere basilicæ dedicantur," &c.]

[3] Chrysostomus in 1. ad Cor. Ca. ii. Ho. vii, b. [*Library of Fathers,* Vol. iv. p. 79. Oxford, 1839.]

His coming[4]. As for the lifting up of a couple of fingers, which you do call a benediction, or the material Cross set up at dedication; they be nothing profitable without the mystery: but with the mystery they be very perilous: nor we do read that ever Augustin, (although he mentioneth the Cross often,) doth ever speak of a man's Image on it, with side wounded, and body blooded. *Crucem nobis in memoriam Suæ passionis reliquit,* he saith: "He hath left us the Cross in remembrance of His passion." But so immediately in the same sentence, upon the same words, he inferreth also: *Crucem reliquit ad sanitatem:* "He hath left us a Cross for our health." But as the sign of the Cross is no ordinary mean, whereby God useth to confer health upon the sick; so hath He not ordained it to remain in the church, for any remembrance of His death and passion. His word He left us, to put us in mind hereof: and to the end our eyes might have somewhat still to feed upon; that Christ might never be forgotten of us; He hath left among us the lively members of His own body; the poor, the naked, the comfortless Christians[5]: who, being always subject to the Cross, might both excite our thankfulness toward Him, and prepare ourselves the better for the Cross. As for the Rood, and Crucifix on the Altar, which have hands nailed, arms stretched out, feet pierced, with a great wound in the side, and a bloody stream issuing out; they may well be compared to the Gentiles' Idols; which have mouths, and speak not; eyes, and see not.

You will answer, (I dare say,) that ye know well enough the Cross is nothing but a piece of metal; and he that hangeth in the Rood-loft is not Christ indeed, but a sign of Him. So did the Heathen know, that all their Idols were silver and gold, the work of men's hands: yet the Holy Ghost did often tell them of it, as if they had forgotten it; because that the livelier the counterfeit is, the greater error is engendered. Some of the Gentiles would excuse their Idolatry by alleging, that they did not honour the matter visible, but the Power invisible; as Augustin, in the person of the Idolater, doth say[6]: *Non hoc visibile colo; sed Numen quod illic invisibiliter habitat:* "I worship not the thing that I see; but

---

[4] 1 Cor. xi. [26.]   [5] [Comp. p. 125.]
[6] In Psa. cxiii. [*Serm.* ii. fol. cclxix. Paris. 1529.]

the Power that I see not, and dwelleth therein." So, among the Christians, some have been so fond, through making of Images, and applying the shape of man or woman to them, that they have thought greater virtue to rest in one than in another; and therefore from one would resort to another. But, by the censure of S. Augustin, the Apostle condemneth them all, saying[1]: *Non quod Idolum sit aliquid; sed quoniam quæ immolant Gentes, Dæmoniis immolant, et non Deo: et nolo vos socios fieri Dæmoniorum:* "Not that the Idol is any thing; but that these things which the Gentiles sacrifice, they sacrifice to Devils, and not unto God: and I would not that ye should have fellowship with the Devils." Therefore, in the Christian, I may justly say, that the opinion itself of holiness in an Image is very devilish.

But you, M. Martiall, have a better evasion. Ye ascribe not so much to the substance itself, and matter of an Image; but, with the Nice Masters, ye use it to this end: "that ye may come to the remembrance and desire of the first sampler and pattern which it resembleth:" and withal you exhibit some courtesy and reverend honour to it, because "honour and reverence, done to an Image, redoundeth to the glory of the first sampler; and he, that adoreth and honoureth an Image, doth adore and honour that which is resembled by the Image." So did the Gentiles cloke their Idolatry; as Augustin plainly reporteth. Yet were they nothing the less Idolaters. For this he saith of them[2]: *Videntur autem sibi purgatioris esse Religionis, qui dicunt: Nec Simulachrum, nec Dæmonium colo; sed per effigiem corporalem ejus rei signum intueor, quam colere debeo:* "They seem to be of more pure Religion, which say: I neither worship the Image, nor the Power thereof; but by the corporal likeness I behold the sign of the thing, which I ought to worship." Yet, notwithstanding, because they called their Idols by the names of Vulcanus and Venus, as we our Images by the name of Christ, and of our Lady; because they did some outward reverence to their Idols, as we unto our Images; both for them and us, as Augustin saith: *Apostoli una sententia pœnam damnationemque testatur:* "One sentence of the Apostle witnesseth our punishment and condemnation." And what sentence is that? *Qui transmutaverunt veritatem*

[1] 1 Cor. x. [19, 20.]   [2] In Psa. cxiii. [ut sup.]

Dei in mendacium; et coluerunt et servierunt creaturæ potius quam Creatori, qui est benedictus Deus in sæcula: "Which turned the truth of God into a lie; and worshipped and served the creature, forsaking the Creator, which is the blessed God for evermore[3]." But how is the truth turned to a lie; and the creature rather served than the Creator? It followeth in the place alleged: *Effigies, a fabro factas, appellando nominibus earum rerum quas fabricavit Deus, transmutant veritatem Dei in mendacium: res autem ipsas pro Diis habendo et venerando, serviunt creaturæ potius quam Creatori:* "By calling the Pictures, made of the workman, by the name of those things which God hath made, they change the truth of God into a lie: and when they repute and worship the things themselves as Gods, they serve the creature rather than the Creator." Wherefore, Augustin noted very well; that Paul (*priore parte sententiæ Simulachra damnavit; posteriori autem interpretationes Simulachrorum:*) "in the first part of his sentence condemned Images; and in the latter the interpretation and meaning of them." So that if your cause be all one with the Gentiles, and excuse one; and yet both of them condemned by the Scripture, and convinced by authority; it followeth, that no Rood nor Crucifix in the church ought to be suffered: for it is Idolatry.

Of the same metal that the Cross is made, we have the candlesticks, we have the censers: yet they, which most do think that God is served with candlesticks and censers, attribute not the honour unto them, that they do to the Cross. What is the cause? S. Augustin declareth: *Illa causa est maxima impietatis insanæ; quod plus valet in affectibus miserorum similis viventi forma, quæ sibi efficit supplicari, quam quod eam manifestum est non esse viventem, ut debeat a vivente contemni. Plus enim valent Simulachra ad curvandam infelicem animam, quod os habent, oculos habent, aures habent, nares habent, manus habent, pedes habent; quam ad corrigendam, quod non loquentur, non videbunt, non audient, non odorabunt, non contrectabunt, non ambulabunt:* "This is the greatest cause," sayeth he, "of this mad impiety; that the lively shape prevaileth more with the affections of miserable men, to cause reverence to be done unto it, than the plain sight, that it is not living, is able to work that it be con-

[3] [Rom. i. 25.]

temned of the living. For Images are more of force to crook an unhappy soul, in that they have mouths, eyes, ears, nostrils, hands and feet; than otherwise to straighten and amend it, in that they shall not speak, they shall not see, they shall not hear, they shall not smell, they shall not handle, they shall not walk."

And so far Augustin. Which words might utterly dehort us from Imagery; and drive both the Rood and the Cross out of the church; if we were not such as the Prophet speaketh of, become in most respect like them[1]. For with open and feeling [seeing] eyes, but with closed and dead minds, we worship neither seeing nor living Images. More could I cite, as well out of him, as out of the rest before alleged, for confirmation of this truth of mine. I could send you to the iv. book of Aug. *De Civit. Dei, Ca.* xxxi.; where he commendeth the opinion of Varro, that affirmed, God might be better served without an Image than with one. I could allege his book *De Hæres. ad Quodvultdeum;* where he mentioneth one Marcellina[2], whose heresy he accompteth to be this; that she honoured the Pictures of Christ and other. I could refer you to his book *De Con. Evan. Li.* i. *Ca.* x.[3]; where he sayeth: *Omnino errare meruerunt, qui Christum non in sanctis codicibus, sed in pictis parietibus quæsierunt:* "They have been worthy to be deceived, that have sought Christ, not in holy books, but in painted walls." These, I say, with divers other, I could bring forth; but that I think that this sufficeth to prove, that the Fathers were not so fondly in this case affected, as you would have it appear to other.

Folio 44. Concerning Paulinus[4], I will not greatly contend with you, but that in his days, which was four hundred and forty-eight[5] year after Christ, there was in some churches the sign of the Cross erected. But, as I said before, it sufficeth not to say: "This was once so;" but proved it must be, that

[1] Psa. cxxxiv. [cxxxv. 18.]

[2] [The partner of Carpocrates; "quæ colebat Imagines Jesu, et Pauli, et Homeri, et Pythagoræ." (S. Aug. *Liber de Hæress.* Cap. vii. fol. 22. ed. Danæo. Genev. 1578.)]

[3] [*Opp.* Tom. iii. P. ii. col. 6. ed. Ben. Antw.]

[4] [Conf. James, *Treatise of Corruption,* Part 4. p. 88. Lond. 1611. Gee's *Answer to the Compiler of Nubes Testium,* p. 81. Lond. 1688. Tertullian, Vol. i. p. 113. Oxford, 1842.]

[5] [Paulinus died A.D. 431.]

"This was well so." Paulinus[6] commendeth the woman that separated herself from her own husband, without consent, under cloke of Religion: and hath the word of God the less force therefore, which saith[7]: "Whom God hath coupled together, let no man put asunder?" Paulinus[8] affirmeth, that the book of the Epistles which the Apostles wrote, laid unto diseases, healeth them: and shall we think that in vain it is, that "the Lord hath created medicines [out] of the earth? He that is wise will not abhor them[9]." He that will follow whatsoever hath been, is a very fool.

I know that Justinian taketh order, (which is yet but politic;) that no man build a church or monastery, but, (as reason is,) by consent of the Bishop: and that the Bishop shall set his mark, which, (by his pleasure,) should be a Cross. But what is this, say I, to the Rood or Crucifix, in places consecrate, where God is served? The same answer, that I made before to the Synod which was kept at Orleance, may serve to this Emperor's Constitution: although it be not prejudicial to truth, if he that lived, by your wise computation[10], a thousand year after Christ; indeed five hundreth and thirty; at the least in time of great ignorance and barbarity; should enact a thing contrary to a truth. Yet, to say the truth, I see no cause why I should not admit his grave authority; since he neither speaketh of Rood, nor Crucifix, nor yet of mystical sign on the forehead; which are the only matters that you take in hand to prove. Loth would we be to cite him for our part, (inasmuch as we depend not upon men's judgments;) unless he spake consonant unto the Scriptures; and brought better reason for other matters with him, than you or any other allege for the Cross. For the truth of an history, we admit him as a witness for us: for establishing of an error, we will not admit him or any other to be a judge against us.

It sufficeth you to use the name of Justinian, how small soever the matter be to purpose: but I will bring you for one two; that, (not in doubtful speech, but in plain terms,

[6] Epi. iii. ad Aprium. [ad Aprum. *Opp.* fol. cli. Paris. 1516.]
[7] Mat. xix. [6.]
[8] Ad Citherium: [Carm. ad Cytherium. fol. ccxx.]
[9] Eccle. xxxviii. [Ecclus xxxviii. 4.]
[10] In Catalogo post Præfationem.

and under grievous pain,) have decreed in all their seigniories and countries a direct contrary order unto yours. Not that there was no Cross then used, (which might well answer Justinian's case;) but that there should not be any. Petrus Crinitus[1], *ex libris Augustalibus*, doth make mention of the law; the same which Valens and Theodosius concluded on[2]. His words be these: *Valens et Theodosius, Imperatores, Præfecto prætorio ad hunc modum scripsere: Cum sit nobis cura diligens in rebus omnibus superni Numinis Religionem tueri; signum Salvatoris Christi nemini quidem concedimus coloribus, lapide, aliave materia fingere, insculpere, aut pingere; sed quocunque loco reperitur, tolli jubemus: gravissima pœna eos mulctando, qui contrarium decretis nostris et imperio quicquam tentaverint:* "Valens and Theodosius, Emperors, wrote on this sort to their Lieutenant: Whereas in all things we have a diligent care to maintain the Religion of God above; we grant liberty to none to counterfeit, engrave, or paint the sign of our Saviour Christ, in colours, stone, or any other matter; but wheresoever any such be found, we command it to be taken away: most grievously punishing such as shall attempt anything contrary to these our decrees and commandment." Here is another manner of order taken, than out of any writing of received author can justly be alleged for your part. So that, with Erasmus[3], I may justly say; "that not so much as man's constitution doth bind, that Images should be in churches."

Ye see, (M. Martiall,) I have not concealed any one of

---

[1] De honesta Disc[iplina,] Lib. ix. Cap. ix. [Crinitus has been obliged to submit to anything but honest discipline, in consequence of his having been so communicative: for, in Cardinal Quiroga's Expurgatory *Index*, it is commanded, that the entire Chapter, with the exception of fifteen lines, should be exterminated. (fol. 183. Madriti, 1584.)]

[2] [This remarkable Constitution of the Emperors Theodosius and Valentinian was promulgated in the year 427. It is contained in Justinian's *Codex*; (Lib. i. Tit. viii.) and is the first among the *Imperialia Decreta* collected by Goldastus. Compare Sutcliffe's *Answer to Parsons*, p. 299. Lond. 1606. Norris's *Antidote*, Part i. p. 293. an. 1622. Becon's *Catech*. &c., p. 71. ed. Parker Soc.]

[3] In Cathech. sua. [*Symboli Catech*. vi. p. 165. Basil. 1533.— "Nam ut Imagines sint in templis, nulla præcipit vel humana constitutio."]

your authorities. I have omitted no piece of proof of yours ; and yet authority, being rightly scanned, doth make so much against you, that your proofs be to no purpose at all. As for the use of that, which you call "the Church," and is indeed the Synagogue of Satan, I need as little to cumber the readers with refuting of, as you do meddle with approving of it. Only this will I say; that, ever since Silvester's time, such filth of Idolatry and superstition hath flowed into the most parts of all Christendom out of the sink of Rome, that he needed indeed as many eyes as Argus, that should have espied any piece of sincerity; until the time that such (as your worship and wisdom, according to your catholic custom, when the scalding spirit of scolding comes upon you, call "heretics and miscreants;") began to reform the decayed state, and bring things to the order of the Church primitive and Apostolic. Wherefore, if ye stick upon a custom, consider your Decree[4]: *Nemo consuetudinem rationi et veritati præponat* : *quia consuetudinem ratio et veritas semper excludit* : " Let no man prefer custom before reason and truth : because reason and truth always excludeth custom." And in the same Distinction[5], out of Augustin is alleged this : *Qui, contempta veritate, præsumit consuetudinem sequi, aut circa fratres invidus est et malignus, quibus veritas revelatur; aut circa Deum ingratus est, inspiratione cujus Ecclesia Ejus instruitur. Nam Dominus in Evangelio* : *Ego sum, inquit, veritas* : *non dixit, Ego sum consuetudo. Itaque, veritate manifestata, cedat consuetudo veritati* : *quia et Petrus, qui circumcidebat, cessit Paulo veritatem prædicanti. Igitur, cum Christus veritas sit, magis veritatem quam consuetudinem sequi debemus* : *quia consuetudinem ratio et veritas semper excludit* : " He that presumeth," (saith Augustin[6],) "to follow custom, the truth contemned, either is envious and hateful against his brethren, to whom the truth is revealed; or unthankful unto God, by whose inspiration His Church is instructed. For our Lord in the Gospel said : 'I am the truth.' He said not : I am custom. Therefore, when the truth is opened, let custom give place to truth : for even Peter, that circumcised, gave place to Paul when he preached a truth. Wherefore,

[4] [Gratiani] Decr. i. Parte. Dist. viii. Parag. Veritate.
[5] Parag. Qui contempta.
[6] De Baptis. parvulorum. [*De Bapt. cont. Donat.* Lib. iii. Capp. v, vi. Opp. Tom. ix. col. 75. ed. Ben. a J. Cler.]

since Christ is the truth, we ought rather to follow truth than custom: because reason and truth always excludeth custom."

Then be not offended, good Sir, I pray you, if, following better reason than you have grace to consider; more truth than is yet revealed to you; we refuse your catholic schism and impiety. Be not spiteful to them that know more than yourself. Be not ingrate to God, that, in these latter days, to knowledge of His word hath sent more abundance of His Holy Spirit. Dwell not upon your custom. Bring truth, and I will thank you. Speak reason, and I will credit you. *Non annorum canities est laudanda, sed morum. Nullus pudor est ad meliora transire*[1]: "Not the ancienty of years, but of manners, is commendable. No shame it is to pass to better."

Folio 64, b.

The tale of the superstitious, (whom you call virtuous lady,) Helena, I shall speak more of in the eight article. Certain it is, that superstitious she was; as is proved afterward in the eight article; who would gad on pilgrimage to visit sepulchres[2], &c. Likewise Constantinus, her son, was not throughly reformed. For, as Theodoret reporteth[3], after he came to Christianity, *fana non subvertit:* "he overthrew not the places of Idol worshippings." Wherefore it is no marvel, if they, building churches, should have some piece of Gentility observed, a Cross or a Rood-loft. Yet, where mention is made that Helena did find the Cross, we find not at all that she worshipped the Cross, but rather the contrary. For Ambrose saith[4]: *Invenit titulum; Regem adoravit: non lignum utique; quia hic Gentilis est error, et vanitas impiorum:* "She found the title; she worshipped the King: not the wood pardie[5]; for this is an error of Gentility, and vanity of the wicked." And where we read[6], that Constantinus the Great, for his miraculous apparition and good success, did greatly esteem the Cross; graved it in his men's armours;

---

[1] Ambros. in Epi. ad Theo. & Valent. [S. Ambrosii *Epist. ad Imp. Valentin.* Epp. ii. xii. Opp. Tom. v. 199. Lut. Paris. 1661.]
[2] In Orat. funebri, de obitu Theodo. [S. Ambr. *Opp.* Tom. v. col. 123. Vol. ii.]
[3] Theodoretus, Lib. v. Ca. xx. [ed. Lat. Camerario interp.]
[4] Ambros. De obitu Theodosii: [ut sup.]
[5] [Verily; *par Dieu:* like the Latin *Hercle.*]
[6] Euse. De vita Const. Lib. iv. [*Eccl. Hist. Auctt.* p. 206.]

and erected it in the market-place; yet we never read that he made a Rood-loft, or placed the Cross upon the Altar. And think ye that Eusebius would have forgotten this, which did remember far smaller matters, if any such thing of a truth had been? Wherefore, whatsoever you deem of other, or whatsoever your own wisdom be, your supposal in this case is neither true, nor likely to be true. Peradventure ye suppose, that your hot interrogations of "Shall we think?," and constant asseverations of "No man of wisdom can think," will make us by and by yield unto a lie. But we are no children: we are not to be feared with rattles. Ye must bring better matter than your own thinking, and sounder proofs than Silvester his writing, or else your Cross shall be little cared for. *Folio 47.*

We know what idle tales and impudent lies of Constantine's Donation, Peter and Paul's apparition, with such other like, are in the Decrees ascribed to Silvester. And thence ye fetch your authority, that "Constantine made a church in honour of S. Paul, and set a Cross of gold upon his cophyne[7], weighing an hundreth and fifty pound weight[8]." O what an oversight was this in Eusebius; that, writing his life, avauncing his acts, suppressed such a notable and famous piece of work[9]! O what a scape was this of Sozomenus; that, making mention of his little chapel[10], forgat the great church! But, as the Prophet saith[11], "An Image is a teacher of lies;" so must your Imagery be defended with lies, or else they will fall to naught. I perceive ye be driven to very narrow shifts, when ye bring the authority of a Bishop of Orleance[12], to avouch the anciency of the sign of a Cross. Sweet *Folio 47.*

[7] [coffin.]
[8] [" Sed et Crucem auream super locum beati Pauli Apostoli posuit, pensantem libras 150." (*Vita* Silvest. Pap. I. apud Binii *Concill.* Tom. i. P. i. p. 215. Colon. Agripp. 1618.) With respect to the imaginary endowment of S. Paul's church, see Geddes, *The grand Forgery display'd*, p. 10. Lond. 1715.]
[9] [Conf. Pet. Molinæi *Iconomachum*, p. 59. Sedani, 1635.]
[10] [*Eccl. Hist.* ii. xxvi.]
[11] Hiere. x. [Jer. x. 8. Habak. ii. 18.]
[12] [The editor conjectures that there is an error here; and that *Arles*, not *Orleans*, was the city which Martiall should have named: for it is certain, from Gratian's Decree, that *Arelatensis* and *Aurelianensis* have been sometimes confounded. In the third Homily, *De Paschate*, ascribed to Cæsarius Arelatensis, we read: "Hæc est illa

flowers be rare where nettles be so made of. But, alas, what hath he, that furthereth your cause? Take away the term of *legitimus*, whereby he calleth it a lawful custom, and I will not contend for any piece of his assertion. I know that it crept not into the Church first in the time of Charles, to have the sign of the Cross used. I know the custom, received in some places, was three hundreth year elder than he; yet not without contradiction at any time. Wherefore, in this and such other cases; where, either against the universal Scripture, a custom general is pretended; or a private custom, without the word, established; let the rule of S. Augustin[1] take place rather: *Omnia talia, quæ neque sanctarum Scripturarum authoritatibus continentur, nec in Conciliis Episcoporum statuta inveniuntur, nec consuetudine universæ Ecclesiæ roborata sunt; sed [pro] diversorum locorum diversis moribus innumerabiliter variantur, ita ut vix aut omnino nunquam inveniri possint causæ, quas in eis instituendis homines secuti sunt; ubi facultas tribuitur, sine ulla dubitatione resecanda existimo:* "All such things, as neither are contained in the authorities of holy Scriptures, nor are found enacted in Councils of the Bishops, nor are confirmed by custom of the universal Church; but, according to the divers orders of divers places, innumerably do vary, so that the causes may scant or not at all be found, whereby men were induced to ordain them; I think that they ought without all controversy be cut away." Then, sith the sign of the Cross of Christ is not commanded in holy Scripture: sith no more Councils have confirmed the use of it, than have condemned it: finally, sith the universal Church never hath received it, but only some private places where the great Antichrist of Rome prevailed: nor they themselves able to allege a just and lawful cause of this their ordinance and will-worship; I conclude and say, that the sign of the Cross out of all churches, chapels, and oratories, out of all places, deputed peculiarly to God His service, ought to be removed.

Crux, quam in postibus regiis, signatam in fronte gestamus; quam justissime in professione receptam Dominus Cardinalis et Imperator *legitimus* impressit." This Homily is likewise inserted among the rhapsodies attributed to Eusebius Emisenus.]

[1] Epist. cxix. [In ed. Bened. *Ep.* lv. Cap. xix. §. 35. *Opp.* ii. 107. Calfhill may possibly have transcribed the passage from the Canon Law, in which the word "pro" is omitted. (*Dist.* xii. C. xii.)]

TO THE FOURTH ARTICLE.

AND whereas ye be now beaten from the walls of your greatest fort, and run into the castle; ye leave off meddling with Rood or Crucifix, and fall to defence of the sign mystical; I must lay some battery to this hold of yours, and I fear me not but I shall fire you out. That ceremonies were of old received in the Church, and among the rest the sign of the Cross drawn with a finger, I deny not, I do confess. When men were newly converted from Paganism, and each man was hot in his profession, the Christian would not only with his heart belief and tongue confession shew what he was; but also, in despite of his Master's enemies, declare by some outward sign, and, by crossing of himself, testify to the world that he was not ashamed of Christ crucified. Hereof have I witness Tertullian, *in Apologetico*[2], and in his book *De Corona Militis*[3]. Whereupon the Fathers, of a zeal and devotion, admitted, (almost in all things,) this sign of the Cross; received it into God His service, as a laudable ceremony; and wished all men to use it. Hieronymus *ad Eustochium*[4], *et Demetriadem*[5]*:* Prudentius *in Hymnis*[6]. Yet can it not be denied, but some were too superstitious in this case; ascribing more to the outward sign, than to the virtue signified: and so they made, of a well meaning custom, a magical enchantment. Nor

[2] [Cap. xvi.]
[3] [Cap. iii.—This treatise was written after he had become a Montanist.]
[4] ["Ad omnem actum, ad omnem incessum, manus pingat Crucem." (*De Virg. servand.* sub fin. *Æpistt.* Par. iii. Tract. iv. Ep. xvi. Lugd. 1508.)]
[5] ["Crebro signaculo Crucis munias frontem tuam; ne exterminator Ægypti in te locum reperiat." (Par. iii. Tract. v. Ep. xvii.) This must not be mistaken for the Pelagian *Epistola ad Demetriadem:* for, in the latter part of it, S. Jerom speaks thus of the previous Epistle to Eustochium: "Ante annos circiter triginta, de Virginitate servanda edidi librum." Cf. Riveti *Crit. Sacr.* iii. xvii. p. 314. iv. xi. 418.]
[6] [Vide Hymnum *ante Somnum:* Hymnum *omni hora:* Hymnum *in honorem Hemetrii et Cheledonii:* Apotheos. *Advers. Judæos;* et Cont. Symmach. Lib. i. *De potentia Crucis.* Opp. foll. 66, 81, 99, 196, 233. Antverp. 1540.]

only the simple did in this case abuse themselves; but such as had more learning than the rest, and ought to have been good schoolmasters to other, taught superstitious and unsound doctrine.

I report me to Ambrose, if he be the author of the funeral Oration for Theodosius; and also to Ephræm[1], *De Pœnit.* Cap. iii.; *et De Armatura Spirituali*, Cap. ii. Which effect if we had not seen by experience in our days follow, we would not for the ceremony contend so much. But whereas we see the people so prone to superstition, that of every ceremony they make a necessity; that they bend not their hearts to the consideration of the heavenly mystery, but defix their eyes, and repose their affiance in the earthly sign; we are forced to refuse the same. For doctrine in this case will not prevail, if the thing that they trusted to be not taken from them. So that the thing which the ancient Fathers, (in a better age, with less abuse,) were contented to admit, must not so straitly be enforced upon us, in a worse time, to maintain a wicked error. For, as Augustin saith[2]: *Non verum est quod dicitur: Semel recte factum nullatenus esse mutandum. Mutata quippe temporis causa, quod recte ante factum fuerat ita mutari vera ratio plerumque flagitat, ut cum ipsi dicant, recte non fieri si mutetur, contra veritas clamet, recte non fieri nisi mutetur: quia utrumque tunc erit rectum, si erit pro temporum varietate diversum. Quod enim in diversitate personarum uno tempore accidere potest, ut huic liceat aliquid impune facere quod illi non liceat; non quod dissimilis sit res, sed is qui facit: ita ab una eademque persona, diversis temporibus, tunc oportet aliquid fieri, tunc non oportet; non quod sui dissimilis sit qui facit, sed quando facit:* "It is not true that is said, 'A thing that was once well done must in no wise be altered.' For when the cause of the time is changed, good reason doth require the well done thing afore so to be changed now, that where they say, it cannot be well if it be changed, the truth on the other side crieth out, that it cannot be well if it be not changed. For that which may chance at one time in diversity of persons, that one may do a thing without offence

---

[1] [In whose case, the editor is obliged to confess with Bellarmin: (*De Scrippt. Eccles.*) "non vacavit mihi legere, nisi Sermones aliquos."]

[2] Ad Marcellinum, Epist. v. [alias cxxxviii. *Opp.* Tom. ii. 311.]

which another may not; not that the matter is of itself unlike, but the party that doth it: so in respect of divers times, of the self-same person now may a thing be done, and now may it not be done; not that he is different from himself that doth it, but the time when he doth it."

Wherefore I like well that counsel of Gregory, which he gave to Augustin the Monk, whom he sent into England to plant a Religion[3]: *Novit fraternitas tua,* (saith he,) *Romanæ Ecclesiæ consuetudinem, in qua se meminit esse nutritam. Sed mihi placet, ut sive in Romana, sive in Gallicorum, sive in qualibet Ecclesia [aliquid] invenisti, quod plus omnipotenti Deo possit placere, sollicite eligas; et in Anglorum Ecclesia, quæ adhuc in fide nova est, et in constitutione præcipua, quæ de multis Ecclesiis colligere poteris, infundas. Non enim pro locis res, sed pro rebus loca amanda sunt. Ex singulis ergo quibuscunque Ecclesiis, quæ pia, quæ religiosa, quæ recta sunt, elige: et hæc, quasi in fasciculum collecta, apud Anglorum mentes in consuetudinem depone:* "Your brotherhood knoweth the custom of the Romish Church, wherein ye remember ye have been brought up. But my pleasure is, that whatsoever ye have found, be it either in the Church of Rome, or French Church, or any other, that more may please almighty God, ye carefully choose the same: and the best constitutions that you can gather out of many Churches, pour into the Church of England, which is as yet raw in the faith. For the customs are not to be embraced for the country sake; but rather the country for the custom sake. Choose ye therefore out of all Churches, whatsoever they are, the things that are godly, religious, and good: and these being gathered into one bundle, repose them as customs in the Englishmen's hearts." So that of the wise it hath been always reputed folly, to stick to prescription of time or place. Only the lawfulness of the use hath brought more or less authority to the thing. Wherefore ye have no advantage of me, in that I granted the use of crossing to be ancient in the Church[4]. For if it had been well in our fore-

---

[3] Dist. xii. Cap. Novit. [Respons. ad Interrog. iii. *Opp.* Tom. ii., fol. 275, b. Antverp. 1572.]

[4] ["Wee confesse that there was a holy and commendable vse of the transeant signe of the Crosse in the primitiue Church: to wit, as

fathers, yet, by Augustin's rule, it might be ill in us; and therefore to be altered. And stiffly to defend one certain custom, without apparent commodity to the Church, is by Pope Gregory himself disproved. Only I am sorry, that imperfections of wise men have given such precedent of error to the wilful. I am loth to say, that the Fathers themselves were not so well affected as they ought. But ye drive me to lay my finger on this sore, and continually to scratch it.

Folio 48.

The tale of Probianus, which ye cite out of Sozomen in the Tripartite History[1], hath small appearance of truth in it. For if he adored not the material Cross, he was the better Christian for that: but if he believed not the death of Christ, then was he not converted unto the faith at all. For without Christ, and the same crucified, our faith is all in vain. Wherefore, when it is said, "that he would not worship the cause of our salvation[2];" either the writer of this history doth ill apply this to the wood material, or you do ill apply it to your purpose. It should seem to be a tale framed out of Constantinus' apparition; when foolish worshippers of the Cross would still have moe miracles to confirm their Idolatry. But, as thieves that have robbed do leave alway some mark behind them, whereby they may be known, either what they were, or which way they be gone; so this author of yours, leaping over the pale, hath left a piece of his cloke behind him, and ye may track him

a badge of Christian profession; to signifie that they were not ashamed of their crucified God, which the heathen and wicked Iewes vsed to cast in their teeth: and so of the permanent Crosse, erected in publike places, to be as it were a trophee and monument of the exaltation of Him that dyed on the Crosse." (Beard's *Retractive from the Romish Religion*, pp. 239—40. Lond. 1616.)]

[1] [Lib. ii. Cap. xix.—"Totius vero salutis causam, id est sacratissimam Crucem, nolebat adorare. Hanc habenti sententiam divina virtus apparens signum monstravit Crucis, quod erat positum in Altario ejus ecclesiæ. Et aperte palam fecit, quia ex quo crucifixus est Christus, omnia, quæ ad utilitatem humani generis facta sunt, quolibet modo præter virtutem adorandæ Crucis gesta non essent, neque ab Angelis sanctis, neque a piis hominibus." Conf. Sozom. *Hist. Eccles.* Lib. ii. Cap. iii.]

[2] [In the original it is related, merely, that Probianus, while a semi-pagan, would not admit that the Cross had been the source of salvation.]

by the foot. For if he meant, (as you devise,) "that, ever since the death of Christ, whatsoever good hath been wrought to mankind, either by good men, or holy Angels, the same hath been wrought by the sign of the Cross;" then Angels by like[3] have bodies to bear it, have hands to make it. But Angels, being ministering Spirits[4], have from the beginning wrought many virtues for man's behoof: have been by God's providence a defence of the faithful, and overthrow of the wicked: yet can they not make any material Cross, such as is set up in churches; nor yet mystical, such as men use to print in their foreheads. Wherefore, either the collector of this tale was a liar, or you a fond applier. Howsoever it falls out in rhyme, yet the reason is good. But rather of the two I would excuse the author, who, by the Cross, meant Christ His passion; and lay you in the fault, which understood him not.

For doubtless if there were such an apparition to Probianus, (as I am not yet persuaded of,) yet that the meaning of it should be such as you say, "to drive him to the worship of a Cross in earth," hath neither Religion nor reason in it. Constantine himself, which was as newly converted to the faith, neither was commanded to do the like, nor ever did it. Cyprian, Augustin, and Chrysostom, entreating all of the passion of Christ, do use the term of the Cross as the Apostle himself doth; 1. ad Cor. i. et ad Gal. v.: *Ut Crux sit prædicatio de Crucifixo:* "That when they name the Cross, by a figure they mean The crucified." Notwithstanding, I grant that in ministration of Sacraments, and sometime otherwise, they seemed all to use a certain sign of Cross; not sign material, but such as men do print in their foreheads. Shall we therefore be restrained to that, whereof there is no precept in Scripture, nor they themselves yield lawful cause[5]? But

Folio 50, b.

---

[3] [belike.]   [4] Heb. vii. [i. 14.]
[5] [The matured judgment of the Church of England, about the matter, is made known in the xxxth Canon of 1603; to which we are referred by our Prayer-book, at the end of the Baptismal Service. Compare Gother's *Discourse of the use of Images,* p. 14. Lond. 1687. Barlow's *Summe of the Conference* at Hampton Court, p. 74. Lond. 1625.]

admit their authority. Think you, they did attribute so
great virtue to the wagging of a finger, that the Holy
Ghost could be called down, and the Devil driven away by
it? Think you, they would have neglected churches; refused Sacraments; doubted of their health; if a Priest had
not broken the air first, and with his holy hand made an
overthwart sign? Learn more good, (ye Puine,) than so
fondly to think, and falsely report of the holy Fathers. Read
their learned writings with riper judgment. Examine duly
the very words which ye do allege as making for you; and
ye shall see, (good young scholar,) that ye have not learned
your lesson well.

Cyprian, ye say, writeth[1]: "Whatsoever the hands be,
which dip those that come to Baptism; whatsoever the
breast is, out of which the holy words do proceed; *Operationis authoritas, in figura Crucis, omnibus Sacramentis
largitur effectum:* 'The authority of operation giveth effect
to all Sacraments, in the figure of the Cross.'" I acknowledge the place. It is in his work *De cardinalibus Operibus Christi: quod inter suspecta et notha est.* But weigh
the reason. First he excludeth, (as touching any merit,)
not only the hand, but the heart of the Priest. He careth
not what he be, so that he do the thing that he cometh for.
The institution of Christ retained, God worketh inwardly
that which no outward fact can give. If the hand be evil,
can the work of the hand be good? In no wise; unless the
work be commanded. Then shew the commandment for the
sign of the Cross, if ye will have Cyprian to mean of it.
Experience in part we have of more witchcraft and sorcery,
wrought by the sign of the Cross, than by any thing in the
world beside. Wherefore it is neither the Priest himself, nor
any thing that he doth, no not the sign of the Cross made,
that giveth effect unto the Sacraments. Cyprian, in plain

---

[1] De cardinalibus Operibus Christi: suspectum opus. [The words
are contained in the tract *De Passione Christi*, which is the ninth of
twelve treatises in a work now well known to have been composed
by Arnoldus Carnotensis, Abbas Bonæ-vallis, about the year 1160. Vid.
James, *Treatise of Corruption*, Part i. pp. 12—16. Lond. 1611. Coci
Censur. pp. 72—75. Lond. 1614. Raynaudi *Erotemata de malis ac
bonis libris*, pp. 135—6. Lugd. 1653. Jamesii *Eclog. Oxonio-Cantab.
Lib.* i. p. 46. & Lib. ii. p. 10. Lond. 1600. Baillet, *Jugemens des Savans*,
Tome i. p. 255. A Paris, 1722.]

words, affirmeth this[2]: *Veniebat Christus ad Baptismum ; non egens lavacro, in quo peccatum non erat; sed ut Sacramento perennis daretur authoritas, et tanti virtutem operis nulla personarum acceptio commendaret : quoniam remissio peccatorum, sive per Baptismum, sive per alia Sacramenta donetur, proprie Spiritus Sancti est, et Ipsi soli hujus efficientiæ privilegium manet. Verborum solemnitas, et sacri invocatio Nominis, et signa institutionibus Apostolicis Sacerdotum ministeriis attributa, visibile celebrant Sacramentum : rem vero ipsam Spiritus Sanctus format et efficit ; et consecrationibus visibilibus invisibiliter manum totius bonitatis Author apponit.* Mark well the words : in English they be these : " Christ came to Baptism ; not wanting a washing, in whom there was no sin ; but to the end that a continual authority might be given to the Sacrament, and no accepting of persons commend the virtue of so great a work. For remission of sins, be it either given by Baptism, or by other Sacraments, properly appertaineth to the Holy Ghost, and the privilege of this effect remaineth unto Him alone. As for the solemnity of words, and calling upon the name of God, and signs attributed to the Apostolical institutions, through the ministry of the Priests, they make a visible Sacrament : but the thing itself the Holy Ghost doth frame and make ; and to the visible consecrations the Author of all goodness invisibly doth put His hand." Here do ye see that the effect is given to the Holy Ghost, and only to the Holy Ghost, which you do attribute either to the Priest, or to the sign of the Cross.

But let me deal with you as you deserve a while. Let me forget that you are a Bachelor of law. Let me forget that you were M. Usher. Let me go to work, as with a scholar of Winchester. C. What is the saying of S. Cyprian, Sirrah ? M. " The authority of operation giveth effect to all Sacraments, in the figure of the Cross." C. What is the principal verb, John ? M. " Giveth." C. What is the nominative case ? M. " Authority." C. Well then, it is authority that giveth effect. But what authority,

---

[2] De Baptismo Christi. [This is the fourth of the same tractates, by "Arnoldus Abbas, Cypriani nomen mentiens." (Thilo, *Cod. Apoc. N. Test.* i. 632. Lips. 1832.) Vid. S. Cypr. *Opp.* p. 662. Venet. 1547; vel Append. ii. in edit. Oxon. p. 30. 1682.]

John? M. "Authority of operation." C. To whom refer you this operation? M. "Forsooth to the Priest, that makes the Cross with his thumb." C. Down with him. Give me the rod here. Have ye forgot that ye learned out of Ambrose[1], *Aliud est elementum, aliud consecratio; aliud opus, aliud operatio:* "The element is one thing, and consecration another; the work is one thing, and operation another?" The work is done by the Priest, but the operation by God. So Ambrose saith also that the consecration is[2]: *Non sanat aqua, nisi Spiritus Sanctus descenderit, et aquam illam consecraverit:* "The water healeth not, unless the Holy Ghost descend, and consecrate that water." And is thy wit so short, that thou rememberest not the text of Cyprian, that I told thee even now? One expoundeth the other. As there he said, The effect of Sacraments properly appertaineth to the Holy Ghost, and that privilege is His alone; so here he saith, The authority of operation giveth effect to Sacraments. Well; go forward. *In figura Crucis:* English me that, John. M. "In the figure of the Cross." C. What is that? M. "Forsooth, the red mark that I see in my master's Mass-book[3]." C. Down again. Is your wit so good? Must ye be beaten twice for one sentence? Construe it. M. *Autoritas operationis,* "The authority of operation," *largitur effectum,* "giveth effect," *omnibus Sacramentis,* "to all Sacraments," *in figura Crucis,* "in the figure of the Cross." C. Why, young man, do ye bring in the sign of the Cross there?

Shall I take you in hand again? The Cross must

---

[1] De Sacram. Lib. i. Ca. v. [*Opp.* iv. 355. Conf. Gratiani *Decret.* De Consec. Dist. iv. Cap. ix.—The genuineness of the six books on the Sacraments cannot be easily maintained. Vid. Card. Bonæ *Rerum Liturg.* Lib. i. Cap. vii. p. 41. Romæ, 1671. Zaccariæ *Biblioth. Ritual.* Tom. ii. p. 18. Romæ, 1778. Morton's *Catholike Appeale,* p. 96. Lond. 1610. Riveti *Crit. Sacr.* Lib. iii. Cap. xviii. Du Pin's *Eccles. Hist.* Vol. i. p. 284. Dubl. 1723. Dallæi *De Cultt. Latinor. relig.* Lib. ix. Cap. xiii. p. 1231. Genevæ, 1671.]

[2] Ibidem.

[3] [The Canon of the Mass commences with the letter T; ("Te igitur," &c.;) which used often to be illuminated, and made to serve for a representation of the Cross. Now there is commonly a print of the Crucifixion in this part of the Roman Missal. Compare a marginal note by Pamelius, in Tom. ii. *Opp.* D. Gregorii Magni, fol. 368, b. Antverp. 1572. Molanus, *De Hist. S. Imagg.* Lib. iv. Cap. vi. p. 484.]

go before in procession. I tell you, construe it by the points as the words do lie. M. *Operationis authoritas,* "The authority of operation," *in figura Crucis,* "in the figure of the Cross," *largitur effectum,* "giveth effect," &c. C. That is another matter. Well now: The authority of operation, (that is to say, the power of the Holy Ghost,) in the figure of the Cross, giveth effect to Sacraments. But is the power of the Holy Ghost in the red mark of your master's Mass-book? No, but it is in the figure of the Cross: that which the Cross figureth; even Christ Himself. So ye have learned a true doctrine now; "That the power of the Holy Ghost, in Christ, giveth effect to Sacraments." Bear it away, lest ye bear me a blow. But now I remember myself; you shall not tarry long for it. *Hem tibi.* Do ye use to make a down point before ye come to the end of a sentence? Do you not see a comma, a conjunction copulative, and a chief piece of the matter follow; and will you falsely leave it out all? Take the book in your hand, and read. M. *Autoritas operationis, in figura Crucis, omnibus Sacramentis largitur effectum: et cuncta peragit Nomen, quod omnibus nominibus eminet, a Sacramentorum Vicariis invocatum:* "The authority of operation, in the figure of the Cross, giveth effect to all Sacraments: and The name above all names, being called upon of the Deputies of the Sacraments, goeth through withal." C. If ye had remembered yourself, (Sir boy,) and taken this latter clause with you, you would not have attributed operation to the Priest, nor effect of Sacraments to the sign of the Cross; nor have been laid over the form for it. But ye feel not the stripes: I am very sorry for that: verily, verily, ye have well deserved them. For if S. Cyprian would not ascribe so much virtue to the name of God, that It should be able to do all; (otherwise than called upon, which respecteth the faith of the receiver:) shall we think that he had a sorry breaking of the air, whereby the Cross is made, in such high reverence and admiration?

On a time the same Father was demanded his judgment, whether such as were baptized bedrid were Christians, or no. Whereto he answered[4]: *Æstimamus in nullo*

[4] Cyprianus Magno, Epist. lxiv. [Ad Pamelii num. *Ep.* lxxvi.: in edit. Oxon. *Ep.* lxix. pp. 185—6.]

mutilari et debilitari posse beneficia divina; nec minus aliquid illic posse contingere, ubi plena et tota fide et dantis et sumentis accipitur, quod de divinis muneribus hauritur: " We think that the benefits of God cannot in any thing be mangled and made the weaker; nor any thing less can happen there, where the grace that is drawn from the spring of God's goodness is apprehended with full and perfect faith, as well on the giver's behalf as on the receiver's." If such as were baptized in their beds, having but a little water sprinkled upon them, wanting a great number of ceremonies, which Cyprian thought Apostolic and necessary, were in as good case as the rest; *Quia stant et consummantur omnia,* (as he saith,) *majestate Domini, et fidei veritate:* " Because all things do stand, and be brought to perfection, by the majesty of God, and sincerity of faith;" shall we think that the idle ceremony of a Cross can give effect to Sacraments, and Sacraments be imperfect without a Cross? Your own Doctor doth overthrow you.

Folio 49, b.

But ye cite two authorities of S. Augustin, to confirm your error. For the first, where he saith[1]: "With the mystery of the Cross the ignorant are instructed and taught; the font of regeneration is hallowed," &c.; I answer as I did before, according to the true meaning of the word "mystery;" that the meaning of the Cross which we believe, and see not, (for so Chrysostom saith[2];) and not the visible and material Cross, worketh the effects aforesaid. For you will grant me that the sign of the Cross is but an accessory thing. The substance of the Sacrament may consist without it. Augustin saith not[3]: *Accedat Crucis signatio ad elementum, et fit*

---

[1] ["Hujus Crucis mysterio rudes catechizantur: eodem mysterio fons regenerationis consecratur."—S. Augustin must not be held responsible for the language of the spurious *Sermo xix. de Sanctis,* which is in this place alleged.]

[2] Chrysos. 1 ad Cor. Cap. ii. Hom. vii. [p. 79. Engl. trans. Oxf.]

[3] Aug. in Jo. Tract. xl. et De Catacl. Cap. iii. [The lxxxth tract upon S. John's Gospel should have been referred to: and the Sermon concerning the Deluge is very far from being authentic. According to the Benedictine editors, the style of it is "rudis, ac demissus, minimeque Augustinianus." (Tom. vi. 398.) The phrase "Accedit verbum ad elementum, et fit Sacramentum" was manifestly stolen from the tract just mentioned; in which are also the succeeding words. (*Opp.* iii. ii. 512. ed. Ben. Antw.)]

Sacramentum : "Let the sign of the Cross concur with the element, and it is a Sacrament;" but, Let the word come to the element, and it is a Sacrament. And yet he doth not attribute so much to the element itself, or to the word, as you do to the sign of the Cross. For of Baptism he saith: *Unde ista tanta virtus aquæ, ut corpus tangat, et cor abluat, nisi faciente verbo? Non quia dicitur, sed quia creditur. Nam et in ipso verbo, aliud est sonus transiens, aliud virtus manens :* "Whence cometh this so great virtue of the water, to touch the body, and wash the soul, but by the working of the word? Not because the word is spoken, but because it is believed. For in the word itself, the sound that passeth is one thing, and the virtue remaining another." If only faith bring effect to Sacraments; if the word itself be not available without belief; shall we think that S. Augustin made such accompt of the sign of a Cross? Indeed he made great of the mystery of the Cross, because on it only dependeth faith. But the mystery you have nothing to do withal. For unless it be a material Cross, or a Cross made with a finger in some part of the body, ye profess that in this treatise ye will speak of none. _{Folio 24.}

And now to the second allegation out of Augustin. As the manner of signing with the Cross was in his time usual, so would I wish, for your own sake, that ye could content yourself with his significations; and wade no further in so dangerous a puddle, than he hath dipped his foot before you. Well doth he please himself in a subtile device[4] of his, when he will refer the Apostle's words, Ephe. iii. to the figure of the Cross: meaning by the breadth, that there is spoken of, Charity; by height, Hope; by length, Patience; by depth, Humility. But these make no more for Paul's meaning, than the geometrical proportion that Ambrose, out of the same place, gathereth. Only there is some edification in the words: and though ye apply them to _{Folio 48, b.} your most advantage, yet can ye not infer your purpose of

---

[4] [This device is exhibited, not only in the tract next quoted, but also in the viith Sermon *De verbis Apostoli;* (Opp. x. 62, b. Paris. 1541.) and thence it appears to have descended to the counterfeit *Sermo* clxxxi. *de Tempore,* in the same volume. (fol. 216.) Of these two the latter is entitled *De Symbolo,* in the Benedictine edition; (Tom. vi. 758.) and the former is number clxv. in Tom. v. 554.]

them. For you would have it appear, that no Sacrament were made and perfected rightly, without the sign of the Cross. But Augustin goeth not so far. Only he saith[1]: *Nihil eorum rite perficitur:* "None of them is solemnly done, and according to the received order." For are you, (M. Lawyer,) ignorant of this common position among the Civilians; *Quod recte justitiam causæ, rite solennitatem respicit:* "That this term *recte* hath respect unto the righteousness and truth of the cause; but *rite*," which is the word that Augustin useth, "doth go no farther than to the order and solemnity thereof?" So I grant you well, that in Augustin's time, if there wanted a Cross, there wanted a ceremony; and yet were the Sacraments perfect notwithstanding. In our Church of England, a Cross is commanded to be made in Baptism: yet was it never thought of any wise or godly, that Baptism was insufficient without it. Go to your Canon, where order is taken[2], *Ut omnia Sacramenta Crucis signaculo perficiantur:* "That all Sacraments shall be made perfect with the sign of the Cross." Yet in the Gloss upon the same place, ye shall find, twice in one leaf, these words: *Non removet quin aliter possint sanctificari, et valere ad remissionem: sed refert factum; nec aliter fit solennis Baptismus:* "He doth not take away this, but that otherwise," (that is to say, without the sign of the Cross,) "they may be sanctified, and the thing be available unto remission. But it is requisite that the thing be done;" (that is to say, the sign of the Cross be made:) "nor otherwise it is a solemn Baptism." This is the Pope's Law, and your Gospel. Wherefore I beseech you, (good solemn Sir,) be not so hard master to us, that, for default of solemnity, we shall be defaulked of fruit of Sacraments.

Folio 50, a. As for Chrysostom, (I have answered you oft;) he speaketh of a Cross that you have nothing to do withal. It is too heavy for you to bear. It is not to be seen as yours, but to be felt as ours. Then trouble not yourself more than ye need. We are agreed by this time, Chrysostom, and you, and I, and all, that a Cross we must have. The matter is certain; but the metal we doubt of. I promise

---

[1] Trac. in Joan. cxviii. [ad fin.]
[2] De Consecr. Dist. v. Cap. Nunquid non. [The Gloss, as transcribed, belongs to the preceding Cap. viii. *Dictum est.*]

you, I cannot brook the charming of Simon Magus, nor hammering of Alexander the coppersmith. Wherefore ye must bring better proofs than these, or else ye shall be sure to fail of your purpose. If ye will have any game at all, run in better order; lest all that behold you cry, *Extra oleas:* "Ye range beyond the bounds." Ye have filled your cheeks with a great deal of vain wind: and when ye have gaped as wide as ye can, what bring ye forth? A vision of Probianus; a proper lie. And what conclude ye of it? "That inasmuch as neither Angels, nor men, have ever done any thing for the weal of man, without the sign of the Cross; therefore no Sacraments can be made without it." But Angels, say I, have no hands to make such Crosses as we do, nor such as you do treat of. Therefore instruct your Angel better, whensoever ye will call him to speak on your side.

As for your other authors, what shall I say to? Ye misconstrue Cyprian. Ye understand not Augustin. Chrysostom maketh nothing for you. Therefore awake out of your dream at last, and good-morrow, M. Martiall. Ye noted out of Cyprian, [Folio 50, b.] that because he hath *Operationis autoritas*, "the authority of operation;" "thereupon is grounded an authority and commission from God, to make and minister His Sacraments." But this was in your dream. For whosoever hath the use of eyes or his right wits, will see and consider, that there is meant, no Priest gesturing, but Holy Ghost working. Ye noted out of Augustin, that in his time "churches, fonts, and altars were hallowed; children confirmed," &c. But if ye go to hallowing and confirming of our days, and compare it with that which was used then; ye shall see no more likeness than is between chalk and cheese. We read[3] how Constantinus, that lived in the same age with Augustin, about forty year before him, hallowed his church at Hierusalem. He called together the Fathers that were assembled at Tyrus: he courteously entertained them: he royally feasted them: he charitably did deal unto the poor: he liberally did endue the church. What did the Bishops on the other side? They prayed and preached. Some read their lessons of divinity: some did reveal their secret contemplations: other some did make their learned Sermons: and the rest did occupy themselves in prayer for

[3] Euseb. Li. iv. de vita Constantini, [Capp. xliii—xlv.] & Athanas. in Apol. ii. [*Apol. cont. Arian.* Opp. i. i. 201. Paris. 1698.]

the peace of the Church, and preservation of the Emperor. And although this order seemeth to have sprung *a Judæorum encœniis,* " of the Jews' observance in their dedication ;" without commandment of God to us, and therefore a will-worship ; yet read we not of any magical enchantment, or any such popish pageant, as *Episcoporum Pontificale* teacheth.

In Augustin his time, they needed no more for hallowing of a church but a Sermon and prayers; in which, peradventure, (that I may feed your humour,) they made the sign of a Cross with their finger. But since his time, and ever since Popery hath had the upper hand, a great number of things else have been exacted by law[1], and thought more necessary than any of the other two. As an Holy Water sprinkle, a bucket, salt, water, wine, ashes, mortar, tyleshardes[2], bones, baggage, frankincense, oil, cream, searcloth, clouts, twenty-four crosses, twenty-four candles. These tools to work withal being in a readiness, the Bishop comes; (for none can do the feat but he:) and first he conjures water and salt ; *Ut sit omnibus sumentibus salus mentis et corporis : et quicquid ex eo tactum vel respersum fuerit, careat omni immunditia, omnique impugnatione spiritualis nequitiæ*[3]*:* "That to all the receivers it may become health of mind and body : and that whatsoever be touched or sprinkled therewith may lack all uncleanness, and all assault of spiritual wickedness." That Devils, diseases, corruptions of airs, infections of bodies, and whatsoever may be prejudicial to health and welfare, may quite be voided, wheresoever any drop of this water falleth. A sovereign medicine, not only sufficient to discredit physic, but also to decay Priests' occupation. Wherein I marvel at their discretions, right provident otherwise for the purse ; that, by avauncing one thing of less importance, they would derogate authority from the moe helps to hell ; so many wholesome suffrages, so many Saints' intercessions, so many meritorious and devout Masses : that I speak nothing of the blood of Christ ; which, among the rabble of Romish heretics, is a thing of a thousand least accompted of.

But what shall I stand in searching their absurdities,

Consecration of churches by popish order.

---

[1] In Pontificali; de consecratione ecclesiarum. [fol. lxxxix. Lugd. 1511.: p. 209. Antverp. 1663.]

[2] [tilesherds.]

[3] [*De benedictione primarii lapidis;* ad init.]

in whose life and doctrine there is nothing else but devilish and absurd? Thus, when the sorcerer hath made his first charm, he goeth thrice about the church, casting of Holy Water on the stone walls. First low, then high, then highest of all; and at every time knocketh at the church-door with a Cross in his hand, saying: *Tollite portas Principes vestras:* which words, (as they translate them,) be: "Ye Princes, lift up your gates:" whereas David saith[4]: *Tollite portæ capita vestra:* "Ye gates, lift up your heads." But a small matter to falsify the Prophet, whom they never truly understood yet. As for this text, is a shipman's hose with them. Sometime they apply it to Christ, going down to hell: sometime to Magistrates, to make a way open to Christ: sometime also to Salomon's temple.

Well, when thus in a mockery M. Bishop hath knocked twice, and twice gone solemnly about the church, with as much devotion as a horse; at the third time, the great door openeth: for he shut in one before, of purpose to open it when his quew[5] came. Then setteth he up a Cross in the midst of the church, and maketh another charm: saying, that the piece of wood, (which he calleth the Cross of Christ,) may be a stay and defence for all suppliants there; that that piece of wood may triumph there and for evermore. Then must the ashes be thrown into the church; (O horrible witchcraft!) and the Bishop must write with his Crosier his a, b, c, in Greek, upon the ground. After this, a confection is made of salt, wine, and ashes: such a drug, as I would wish no worse for my lord's own holiness, whensoever his queysie[6] stomach doth loathe better nurture of the word of God; for doubtless it is restority to such. See what he saith to it: *Ut vinum, cum aqua et cinere mixtum, armatum cœlestis defensione virtutis,* &c.: "That wine, mixed with water and ashes, may be armed with defence of heavenly virtue." Then oil and cream is put into the Holy Water. Sure that is a purgative, and a strong one belike: for the marble stones be anointed with it; and a verse of the Psalm sung: "The Lord hath anointed thee with the oil of gladness above thy fellows[7]." O stony hearts! to apply the words which the Spirit of God properly spake of Salomon, and, under Salomon's person, of

[4] Psal. xxiii. [xxiv. 7, 9.]
[5] [Or cue; humour.]
[6] [queasy, squeamish.]
[7] Psalm xlv. [7.]

[CALFHILL.]

Christ, to a greasy stone, that every man doth tread on, every dog bewrays.

Then doth the quire sing: *Erexit Jacob lapidem:* "Jacob reared up a stone[1];" whereof they know not the signification. Also they bleat out with wide throats: *Ibi est Benjamin adolescentulus, in mentis excessu:* "There is little Benjamin, out of his wits;" as they translate it. And think ye that they were well in their wits, which, for *Dominator eorum*, would put *in mentis excessu?* whereas they should have said: There is little Benjamin, their Governor[2]; to say: There is young Benjamin, ravished of his wits? But this is Scripture of church-hallowing. This is the purpose. These be the texts. The prayers are the same that Salomon used, when he was commanded to make the temple: save that they will have a crop of *Colocyntida*, to mar a whole pot full of pottage[3]. For they add unto these invocation of Saints, derogation to God, and abuse of His creatures. When this is done, the rotten bones and reliques are hallowed, with like ceremonies and solemnities as they had before. And then they put on their masking coats; and come, like blind fools, with candles in their hands at noon-days, and so proceed to the holy Mass; with renting of throats, and tearing of notes, chanting of Priests, howling of Clerks, flinging of coals, and piping of organs. Thus they continue a long while in mirth and jollity: many mad parts be played. But when the Vice[4] is come from the Altar, and the people shall have no more sport, they conclude their service with a true sentence: *Terribilis est locus iste:* "This place is terrible." And have they not fair fished, think you, to make such ado to bring in the Devil? O blind beasts! O senseless hypocrites! whom God hath given over unto themselves; that they shall not see their own folly, and yet bewray their shame to all the world beside. And is not this your church-hallowing, that ye talk of? This is it that your Church hath ordained.

Now that ye may prove, in particularity, that which generally ye did avouch before; ("the sign of the Cross to be used in all Sacraments;") ye come to an enumeration of them all. And I dare say ye be glad to catch such occasion

---

[1] Genes. xxviii. [18.]
[2] Psalm lxvii. [lxviii. 27.]
[3] [2 Kings iv. 39, 40.]
[4] [A Jester in a Play.]

to treat of the seven Sacraments: yet doubt I not, but before I have done with you, I shall make ye contented to cut off five of them. First, as touching the use of Baptism, ye begin with Dionysius; to whom ye give the surname of Areopagita, and honourable title of "Saint Paul's scholar." Eusebius[5] indeed maketh mention of such a one; and saith that he was the first Bishop of Athens: and this he speaketh of the report of another Dionysius of Alexandria[6]. But as for any writing of his, he hath no word at all: and doubtless, if it had been true, which you affirm, he would not have suppressed it. S. Hierom[7] maketh mention of two of that name. One that was at Corinth, in the reign of Marcus Antoninus Verus, and Lucius Commodus. Another, that was scholar sometime to Origen; and Bishop afterward of Alexandria, in the reign of Galienus. But not a word yet among all their writings, (which he most diligently doth rehearse;) either of the Heavenly or Ecclesiastical Hierarchy; out of which ye cite all your authorities. Wherefore it is a bastard book[8], unjustly fathered upon S. Paul his Dionyse; whereas the style itself, and matter there entreated of, do argue that it is of no such antiquity.

Dionysius Areopagita. Folio 52, b.

For, to go no further than to those words that you do allege of his; "how the Bishop assigneth some man to be Godfather to him that is to be baptized;" here is a plain lie: for

Folio 52.

[5] Euseb. Eccl. Hist. Li. iii. Ca. iv. & Lib. iv. Cap. xxi.

[6] [Corinth.—Conf. Usserii *Vet. Epistt. Hibernic. Syllog.* pp. 59, 67. Dublin. 1632.]

[7] In Catal. Script. Eccles. [Capp. xxvii, lxix.]

[8] [It can scarcely be necessary to enlarge upon this point, after the almost infinite discussion which it has undergone. The author of the *Hierarchia* cannot have lived antecedently to the fourth century; and Daillé and many others have wished to reduce him to the sixth age. Morinus has shown that these books were never produced until the year 532; and that they then emanated from the Severian heretics. Very few will be affected by Bellarmin's statement, "quod alicubi latuerint" until the days of S. Gregory the Great. (*De Scrippt. Eccl.* ad an. 71.) Conf. Pearsonii *Vindic. Ignat.* Par. i. Cap. x. Dallæum, *De libris suppos. Dion. Areop. & Ignat. Ant.* Genevæ, 1666. Le Nourry, *Apparat. Dissert.* x. Paris. 1703. Perkinsii *Præpar. ad Demonst. Problem.* pp. 8—10. Cantab. 1604. *Problême proposé aux Sçavans;* par le Pere Honoré de Ste Marie: A Paris, 1708. Jac. Sirmondi *Dissertat.* & Launoii *Varia de duobus Dionysiis Opuscula:* Paris. 1660. Ant. Reiseri *Launoii Anti-Bellarmin.* pp. 765—777. Amstel. 1685. Stillingfleet's *Answer to Cressy,* p. 132. Lond. 1675.]

14—2

the use of Godfathers was not invented forty year after. It is evident by consent of all men; yea, the Decree itself beareth witness with me, that Hyginus was first founder of Godfathers[1]: and, among all the received writers of that age, ye shall not lightly read of any gossipping. But suppose it be true, that our records have, that Hyginus hatched this egg; he lived at the least an hundreth and forty year after Christ. And how can S. Paul his scholar, whose life yourself can stretch no longer than to the ninety-sixth year after Christ, speak of that which he never thought on; which was so long devised after?

In the names of the authors alleged by Martiall.

But to the matter. I know right well, that within two hundred year after Christ, there were crept into the Church many idle ceremonies; and the simplicity of Christ His ordinance refused. Each man, as he had either credit or authority, presumed of himself to add somewhat to Christ's institution: and the flesh, delighting in her own devices[2], delivered the same with as strait a charge as if that Christ Himself had taken order for it. Notwithstanding, if aught beside the authority of Scripture were so ancient indeed, (as I last spake of;) and admitted at any time into God His service; yet were we no more bound to observe the same, than the Fathers themselves have yielded to it. For if they have repelled the traditions of their elders, and after established some other of their own; their example proveth no use Apostolic or necessity to have been in the one; and their precedent authorizeth, that we may as lawfully disannul the other. Enforce not therefore a doctrine of a custom. Traditions always have varied: and many such as Cyprian, Tertullian, Augustin, with other, have thought to

Traditions no ground of doctrine.

Traditions vary.

---

[1] De Cons. Dist. iv. Cap. In Catechismo. Platina in vita Hygini. [Neither the Decree nor Platina bears witness to any such thing. The decision merely was, that, in case of necessity,—"si necessitas cogit,"— *the same* person, or *one* person, might appear as Sponsor both at Baptism and Confirmation. Platina testifies that this Pope desired, "*unum saltem* Patrimum, unamve Matrimam Baptismo interesse." The argument is entirely invalidated by the fact, that the Ordinance, which the Canon Law attributes to Pope Hyginus, in truth proceeded from Theodore, Archbishop of Canterbury, about the year 680.—Vid. Theodori *Pœnitentiale,* Cap. iv. p. 5; itemque not. Jac. Petit, p. 95. Tom. i. Lut. Paris. 1677.]

[2] [Page 23, line 14: p. 47, l. 26.]

be necessary for salvation, the Church of Rome itself hath not thought expedient to be used for instruction. Christ gave commandment, Baptism to be ministered in the name of the Father, and of the Son, and of the Holy Ghost[3]. The Apostles continued in the same order[4]. Ceremonies, or circumstances, we read of no more in Scripture: save only the water[5]; without all conjuration, consecration, or insufflation; the persons baptized; the preaching of God His promises, and faith in Christ, and prayer of the faithful. Now, come ye down to Tertullian's time; and ye shall find many strange inventions[6]. Three dippings in the water: tasting of milk and honey: abstaining from all other washing for a sevennight after. In Hierom's time, there was no honey used[7]; but, in lieu thereof, wine and milk were given[8]. In Cyprian's time, there was consecration of water; and such estimation of oil, that no man was thought to be a Christian, that was baptized without it[9]. In Augustin's time, the witnesses made answer, in the infant's behalf, to the Articles of the faith demanded of them[10]: and yet the infant himself was suffered immediately to be partaker of the Supper of the Lord[11]; and the same thought as requisite as was his Baptism. Notwithstanding, the latter age, (yea, the Church of Rome, which you call "Catholic,") hath taken most of all these away.

Then what do ye windless[12] fetch about to prove, folio 53, but that the sign of the Cross hath been used in Baptism, and therefore now to be had in reverence? By the same reason, honey, milk and wine shall be restored in Baptism, and every infant receive the Communion. For greater authority you have not for the Cross, than I for these. Indeed Rabanus Maurus[13], a Bishop of Mentz, living in the most corrupt age

---

[3] Matth. xxviii. [19.]   [4] Actes x. [47—8.]
[5] Luc. iii. [16.]   [6] Lib. de Coro. Mil. [Cap. iii.]
[7] [How then are we to understand "Deinde egressos lactis et *mellis* prægustare concordiam?" (*Æpistt.* Par. i. Tract. ii. Ep. xii. Cont. Lucifer. sig. h iv. Lugd. 1508.)]
[8] Lib. xv. Com. in Esaiam. [*Super Esai.* lv. 1.]
[9] Epist. lxxii. [*Ep.* lxx. in edd. Pamel. & Oxon.]
[10] Epi. ad Bonifacium. [xcviii. al. xxiii.]
[11] De Pec. mer. & remis. Cap. xx. [Lib. i. C. xx. §. 27. *Opp.* Tom. x. ed. Ben.]
[12] [out of breath.]
[13] De inst. Cler. Cap. xxvii. [sigg. d ij, iii. Phorcæ, 1505.]

of the Church, in the same place that you have quoted, doth not only make mention of the Cross sign, but, refusing the traditions of the learned Fathers, (of which I spake even now,) bringeth in his own; as salt, spittle, tapers, and such other like. Salt was by the Law commanded to the Jews: and if it had been Christ His pleasure, that His Ministers should have had respect unto the Jewish ceremonies, then either Christ would have commanded it, or the Apostles would have used it. But neither of these is true. Therefore it is a vain device. The spittle, whereby they defile and infect the child, is taken out of the miracle *Joannis nono*[1]. But the Apostles saw that done: and yet none of them all daubed his spittle upon the ears and nostrils of them whom they baptized. Christ His spittle, there is none but would wish, both for himself and for his: but the spittle, sometime of a pestilent infected Priest; most times of a stinking drunkard; always of a sinner; I know not who would be so fain of. God keep my friend's child from it.

As for burning of tapers at noon-day, is mere foolish, and taken out of the fond Gentility. In the old time, the Christians, in their assemblies, used burning candles at time of God's service: but in the night time, because they durst not resort together in the day time; and it had been uncomfortable and discommodious to sit in the dark. Whereupon S. Hierom answereth[2]: *Cereos non clara luce accendimus, sicuti frustra calumniaris; sed ut noctis tenebras hoc solatio temperemus; et vigilemus ad lumen, ne cæci tecum dormiamus in tenebris:* "We light no tapers in the broad day, as thou dost vainly slander us; but that, by this comfort, we may temper the darkness of the night; and may watch at the light, lest with thee we sleep in the dark." Thus doth S. Hierom say for his tapers. Let them answer to him, (as doubtless they shall to God,) that otherwise do use them. Thus have I shewed, how simply Christ did set forth His holy Sacrament; how diversely men have swerved from His order, and therefore in ceremonies ought not to prejudice us. But your Church Cacolique, not content with the ordinance of Christ and His Apostles; not sticking to the ceremonies of the

---

[1] John ix. [6.]
[2] Adversus Vigilant. [*Æpistt.* Par. i. Tract. ii. Ep. x. sig. h. Lugd. 1508.]

received Fathers; have chosen rather, of their own fantastical and idle brain, to use crossing and conjuring, begreasing and bespewing of the poor infants. Therefore I like not the generation: their order I detest.

And now to Confirmation; which you affirm to be no new device, "as new bold Biblers babble;" but I shall prove to be no Sacrament, as young lewd liars lay for themselves. And first, where ye snatch a piece of Augustin[3], wherein he calleth the Chrism a Sacrament, I answer; that he attributeth no more thereto, than otherwise to prayer, and to the word of God. Yea, the Master of the Sentences[4] himself teacheth you, that many things improperly be called Sacraments, which must not in reasoning be numbered among the Sacraments of Christ His Church. But if on this sort every sign visible, and the same holy, be a Sacrament with you; then shall every Image in the church be a Sacrament. For they be signs, and you say they be holy. As for the example of Christ, who embraced little children in His arms[5], and, laying His hands upon their heads, blessed them, I answer; that as every fact of Christ doth not serve for our imitation, but instruction; so must we not make a Sacrament of each of them. For so the breathing upon His Apostles[6], whereby He gave them the Holy Ghost, should be a Sacrament. Only this sign may be a precedent for us, that children appertain to the kingdom of God; that they ought not be denied the sign, which are partakers of the grace; and therefore should be baptized. Then afterward, if ye will have them confirmed, I allow it well; retaining that order, which in the primitive Church was, and in the English Church is, used: that children, after certain years, be presented to the Bishop; and, rendering an accompt of that faith of theirs, (which by their sureties in Baptism they professed,) have hands laid on them; which is nothing else but prayer made for them. *Quid enim est aliud*, (saith S. Augustin[7],) *manuum impositio, quam oratio super hominem?*

<sub>Confirmation.
Folio 54.</sub>

[3] [*Cont. lit. Petil.* Lib. ii. Cap. civ. Opp. Tom. ix. 199. ed. Ben. Ant.]
[4] [*Sententt.* Lib. iv. Dist. i. Compare the Homily *Of Common-Prayer and Sacraments.*]
[5] Mark x. [16.]   [6] John xx. [22.]
[7] De Bap. cont. Don. Lib. iii. Cap. xvi. [*Opp.* T. ix. 79. ed. Ben.]

"For what is laying on of hands else, but prayer over a man?"

One thing will I ask of these apish imitators. If they will ground upon Christ His doing their Confirmation, how dare they presume to do more than Christ did? Whence have they their oil? Who gave them authority to exhibit what sign of the Holy Ghost they would? What promise have they of grace annexed unto their Sacrament, unless they have shut the Holy Ghost in their grease-pot? They apply, I know, whatsoever is spoken of the grace of God's Spirit to this: but ineptly[1]. For Christ saith simply[2], that God will give His good Spirit to them that ask it: and to the faithful, that He will not leave them fatherless[3]; but send the Spirit of truth unto them, and Himself dwell with them. But they do restrain this unto their ceremonies: that whosoever is not anointed of them, is not accepted of God; no, nor he is a perfect Christian. For this they write[4]: *Omnes fideles, per manus impositionem Episcoporum, Spiritum Sanctum post Baptismum accipere debent, ut pleni Christiani inveniantur:* "All faithful must receive the Holy Ghost after Baptism, by the imposition of the Bishop's hands, that they may be found full Christians." And in the next Decree: *Spiritus Sanctus, qui in fonte plenitudinem tribuit ad innocentiam, in Confirmatione augmentum præstat ad gratiam:* "The Holy Ghost, that in Baptism hath given fulness to innocency, in Confirmation performeth increase to grace." But let them shew me what warrant of God His word they have for this; what promise of God is sealed in us by this their new-found Sacrament. Is Christianity now to be fet out of Popery? Is the truth of God, contained in the Scriptures, insufficient to inform us? Is there no full Christian, unless he be anointed? Alas, where are so many Apostles, so many Martyrs become, that never were anointed? Is Baptism insufficient without Confirmation? Is Baptism available, as the Decree hath, only for them that should die straight; and Confirmation for them that should live longer? Doth Baptism only regenerate us to life, but Confirmation furnish us unto the fight? What is it then that Paul hath: "We are buried with Christ by Baptism into His death; that

---

[1] [foolishly.]   [2] Luc. xi. [13.]
[3] Joh. xiv. [18.]   [4] De Conse. Dist. v. Ca. i.

like as Christ was raised up from the dead by the glory of the Father, so we also should walk in newness of life[5]?" This partaking of death and life with Christ is nothing else but the mortifying of our own flesh, the quickening of the spirit, in that the old man is crucified, and we may walk in newness of life.

But, by this their device, they take away half the effect of Baptism; rejecting therein the commandment of God, to establish their own tradition[6]. Wherefore I will reason with you as Christ did with the Pharisees[7]. Is the Confirmation, (which you call a Sacrament,) ordained to be so from heaven, or of men? If it be of men, it is no Sacrament. If it be of God, then shew the word. Ye have the example of the Apostles in the cha. viii. and xix. of the Acts: but no example sufficeth for a Sacrament. The Apostles themselves usurped not so much. But see how well ye follow the example. "When the Apostles, which were at Hierusalem, heard say that Samaria had received the word of God, they sent unto them Peter and John: which, when they were come down, prayed for them, that they might receive the Holy Ghost. For as yet He was come down on none of them; but they were baptized only, in the name of the Lord Jesus. Then laid they their hands on them, and they received the Holy Ghost[8]." Now, are ye ignorant what here is meant by the Holy Ghost? I will tell you. The gift to speak in divers languages; to work miracles; and other particular graces of the Holy Spirit. And although they had received the common grace of adoption and regeneration through Baptism; yet had they not these other qualities, which in the beginning of the Church were granted, and now be denied. So that laying on of hands served to good use then, when it pleased God at instance of the Apostles' prayers to confer the visible graces of His Spirit: but now that there is no such ministry in the Church; now that miracles be ceased; to what end should we have this imposition of hands; the sign without the thing? If a man should now-a-days prostrate himself upon the bodies of the dead, because Helias and Paul used this ceremony in raising of their dead, should he not be thought preposterously to do? So that it might

Folio 54, a.

[5] Rom. vi. [4.] [6] Mar. vii. [9.]
[7] Mat. xxi. [25.] [8] Actes viii. [14—17.]

well be a kind of Sacrament in the Apostles' time; but, the cause ceasing, what should the sign continue?

Yet ye content not yourselves with the Apostles' order: ye will, (as I said before,) have somewhat of your own. For neither Peter nor John anointed the Samaritans; but you do besmear whomsoever you lay hands on. Ye call it *Chrisma salutis:* "The Chrism of salvation." But whosoever seeketh salvation in the Chrismatory, shall be sure to lose it in Christ. Oil for the belly, and the belly for oil; but the Lord shall destroy both the one and the other. Good Lord! what beast but a Papist, what Papist but a Devil, durst presume to say, that salvation should be fet out of an oil-box? The Apostle calleth us from impotent and beggarly things[1]: and if we be dead with Christ, he saith, we must not be burdened with traditions[2]. Wherefore ye take the matter all amiss; that, by the doings of S. Peter and S. John in Samaria, or else by the fact of S. Paul at Ephesus[3], do ground your Sacrament of Confirmation. One reason ye have heard: because the ceremony of laying on of hands served for particular graces, which were but temporal; and therefore now, the thing abolished, the sign should not remain. Another I will bring you. The Apostles laid their hands, but only upon certain persons, even such as the gifts aforesaid were bestowed on. Confirmation is extended unto all: gracious and graceless; come who will, none is denied it. Who gave you authority? Where is your commission to bestow that indifferently upon all persons, which the Apostles gave but unto few? Indeed, if it be so necessary to salvation, as ye make it, I cannot greatly blame you. But then, on the other side, blame you I must, that you are so negligent in bestowing it. For this is your doctrine: that without Confirmation there can be no perfect Christian. And I beseech you, how many be suffered to die unconfirmed? Unless the Bishop chance to pass by, which is once peradventure in seven year; all they that depart in the mean season are Jews, belike, or in state of damnation. And can your charities suffer, without remorse of conscience, so many semi-christians to pass you? Thus every way you confute yourselves. For if your Sacrament

---

[1] Gala. iv. [9.]   [2] Colos. ii. [8.]
[3] Act. xix. [6.]

ANSWER TO THE TREATISE OF THE CROSS. 219

of Confirmation be, as you say, "such an ointment, with Folio 55, a.
whose most holy perfection, the gift and grace of Baptism is
made perfect:" if it be an ointment, "altogether holy and
divine, the perfection itself and sanctification, the beginning,
the substance, the perfecting virtue of all holiness given us
from heaven;" then are you wicked persons, that take no
order that the moe may have it. But if there be no such
virtue in it, then do ye lie the more.

Again, yet further to note your absurdity. Your Decree, 3.
in case of Confirmation, is this[4]: *Manus quoque impositionis
Sacramentum magna veneratione tenendum est; quod ab
aliis perfici non potuit [potest] nisi a Summis Sacerdotibus:
nec tempore Apostolorum, ab aliis quam ab ipsis Apostolis
legitur aut scitur peractum esse: nec ab aliis quam qui
eorum tenent locum, cuiquam [unquam] perfici potest, aut
fieri debet. Nam si aliter præsumptum fuerit, irritum
habeatur et vacuum:* "The Sacrament of laying on of
hands must be held with great worship; which cannot be
made of any, but only of the High Priests: nor it is read or
known, that in the Apostles' time it was ministered by any,
but only by themselves: nor it can or ought to be done of
any, save only such as supply their rooms. For if it be
presumed to be otherwise, let it be void and of no effect."
But how came the Bishops by this prerogative? How chance
that every Priest may minister Baptism, and the Supper of
the Lord; but only Bishops may confirm? Only the
Apostles did in their time minister these Sacraments: and
therefore, by that reason, only Bishops should have that office
now. But are only Bishops the Apostles' successors? When Papists con-
ye inhibit any of the lay fee to take the Host in his hand, themselves.
this cause ye allege; that it was delivered only to the
Apostles. In this case, ye admit every poor Priest a successor unto them. But why not in the other? Because if
any be less successors to the Apostles than other, they be
your Bishops. But, to make a device of your own brain,
although in matters of Religion it be not sufferable; yet, to
make a lie of the Holy Ghost, to falsify the Scripture, is Papists belie
more intolerable. And is it not a strange case, that the holy the Scripture.
Father writing the law; Gratian collecting it; so many
seraphical Doctors commenting of it; so long use in all

[4] De Consecr. Dist. v. Cap. Manus quoque.

realms confirming it; it should there be written, and suffered to remain, that in the Apostles' time it was never read or known, that imposition of hands was done by any, but by the Apostles themselves?

Why, what did Ananias? He laid his hands upon Saul; whereby he received his sight, and was endued with the Holy Ghost[1]. What Bishop was he? No Bishop, forsooth. But a Monk, by all likelihood. For, by the Canon Law[2], they be always the Apostles' vicegerents. See you not, by this time, your own shame? Shall this, notwithstanding, your Confirmation be still a Sacrament; having nothing else but man's devices, and a sort of impudent lies to support it? If it had been a truth, that only the Apostles had laid on hands: if it were a good order, that only Bishops should do the like; how falleth it out that the Popes themselves have dispensed with the matter? Gregory writeth thus[3]: *Ubi Episcopi desunt, ut Presbyteri etiam in frontibus baptizatos Chrismate tangere debeant, concedimus:* "Where Bishops want, we grant that Priests also may anoint in the foreheads such as be baptized." How is this presumption avoided? How doth the Sacrament now stand in force? But who will seek for any reason, constancy, or truth in Popery? The example of Christ is pretended. Yet Christ never bad it: nor the fact of Christ can be drawn to imitation; nor theirselves will stick unto it. Christ never used oil: they make it necessary. Christ promised indifferently to all the faithful His Holy Spirit: they do restrain it to their own ceremonies. Christ, for our behoof, instituted Baptism; that we might die to sin, and live to righteousness: they by Confirmation have cut away half the effect thereof. The Apostles withdraw us from the elements of this world: they will have us seek our salvation in an oilbox. The Apostles used imposition of hands; which had effect when miracles were in place: they will have the same order, although they cannot have the same end. The Apostles laid hands, but only upon some, which had the gift of the Holy Ghost withal: they, without respect or differences,

Monks Apostles' vicegerents.

---

[1] Acte. ix. [17.]

[2] In Glosa preced. Dist. ["Alibi Monachi dicuntur tenere locum XII. Apostolorum: alibi Sacerdotes."]

[3] Decr. Parte i. Dist. xcv. Ca. Pervenit.

of persons, confirm every body. Therefore it is but a mere tradition; and the same neither christian nor Apostolic. In the order of it, they be contrary to themselves. They will have it necessary to salvation: and yet they let many die without it. They say, that only Bishops are the Apostles' successors: and yet in other cases they grant, that every Priest is a successor too. They affirm, that the Apostles gave them only their precedent: and yet Ananias, that was no Apostle, is proved to have done the same. They teach, that a Bishop must only minister it: and yet they dispense for a Priest to do it. And may not we Biblers be bold to call you babblers?

If only these heresies, lies, absurdities, were in your proofs of Confirmation, they only were sufficient to confirm you fools. But see a fouler matter, of all christian ears to be abhorred. While ye go about to avaunce your invention, ye deface the ordinance of almighty God, and overthrow the groundwork of our salvation. Confirmation a Sacrament? Yea, a Sacrament worthier than Baptism. For the Master of the Sentence sayeth[4]: *Sacramentum Confirmationis dicitur esse majus Baptismo*: "The Sacrament of Confirmation is said to be greater than the Sacrament of Baptism." And afterward the cause is added: *Quia a dignioribus datur, et in digniore parte corporis*: "Because it is given of worthier persons, and in the worthier part of the body." For only Bishops, (as is said,) confirm; but every Priest may minister Baptism. And in Baptism, oil is laid upon the head; but in Confirmation, upon the forehead. Where, first, is to be noted, that ye stick in one mire still; ascribing more to the oil your invention, than to the water, which is God's element. It sufficeth us to have, as Christ and His Apostles had, fair water in our Baptism: your oil is better for a salad than a Sacrament. Then also by the way ye fall into another heresy. For when ye decree the bishopping of children to be greater Sacrament than Baptism is, because every Priest may christen, but only Bishops may confirm; shew ye not therein yourselves to be very Donatists[5]; esteeming the dignity of the Sacraments of the worthiness of the Minister? Yet not only the Master of the Sentence, but also the Decree confirmeth that doctrine. Melchiades, an

Papists attribute more to oil in Baptism than to water.

Papists are Donatists.

[4] Lib. iv. Dist. vii. Cap. ii.
[5] [Oliver Ormerod's *Picture of a Papist*, p. 49. Lond. 1606.]

author of yours, and a Pope, saith[1]: *Sacramentum manus impositionis, sicut nisi a majoribus perfici non potest, ita et majori veneratione venerandum est et tenendum:* "The Sacrament of laying on of hands, as it cannot be made but only of the greater, so is it to be worshipped with greater reverence, and so to be defended."

<small>Definition of popish bishopping.</small> But, O God, what a strange Religion is this! A drop of grease, infected and filed with the stinking breath of a sorcerous Priest, enchanted and conjured with a few fumbled words, to be compared to Christ's holy Sacrament; preferred to the water sanctified by the word of God. But this is your manner, to deprave the Scriptures in every point; corrupt the Sacraments with your own leaven; and let nothing that good is stand in due force, for your spiritual policies and fresh inventions. Give over therefore at length the breast of fornication: leave sucking of the dregs of superstition and Popery: whereto I persuade myself, that rather fond nurses have inured you, than conscience or reason persuaded you. For, Scriptures have ye none, but the same condemn you: nor godly Fathers any, but the same be against you. For proof whereof, as I have hitherto discoursed of your Scriptures for Confirmation, and uttered your doctrines, disagreeing from the same; so now will I come to judgment of your Doctors.

For Confirmation to be a Sacrament, ye bring Denise and Fabianus: of which the one I have already sufficiently disproved; the other was but a Pope, and never received author[2]. But I will set against them Tertullian and Augustin: two for two; substantial and honest, for suspected and infamous. Tertullian[3], speaking of the Sa-

---

[1] De Con. Dist. v. Cap. De his vero. [The preceding words from Peter Lombard, and the extract from Gratian, in this place, are derived only from one of the feigned Epistles of the early Popes; of which Bellarmin, with interesting cautiousness, declares: "nec indubitatas esse affirmare audeam." (*De Rom. Pont.* Lib. ii. Cap. xiv. Vid. Blondelli *Pseudo-Isidor. & Turrian. vapulantes*, p. 429. Genev. 1628.)]

[2] [As the putative evidence of an ancient Roman Prelate cannot be so easily disposed of, it is right to remark, that Martiall must have quoted the second spurious Epistle of Pope Fabian. The Rhemists likewise have alleged it, for the same purpose. (*New Test.* p. 313 Rhemes, 1582. Conf. Blondell. ut sup. p. 294.)]

[3] Adversus Marcionem, libro iv. [Cap. xxxiv.]

craments of the primitive Church, reckoneth no more but Baptism and the Supper of the Lord, saying: *Quomodo tu nuptias dirimis; nec conjungens marem et fœminam, nec alibi conjunctos ad Sacramentum Baptismatis et Eucharistiæ admittens?* &c.: "How dost thou break marriage; neither coupling the man and the woman together, nor, being coupled otherwise, admitting them to the Sacrament of Baptism and thanksgiving?" Likewise, in his book *De Corona Militis*[4], entreating purposely of the order of the Church, beginneth with Baptism, and sheweth what ceremonies were observed therein: and then he proceedeth to the Supper of the Lord; and, (for Sacraments,) no further. Augustin also most plainly saith[5]: *Dominus signis nos non oneravit; sed quædam pauca pro multis, eademque factu facillima, et intellectu augustissima, et observatione castissima, Ipse Dominus et Apostolica tradidit disciplina: sicuti est Baptismi Sacramentum, et celebratio corporis et sanguinis Domini.* Which words in English be these: "Our Lord hath not burdened us with signs; but Christ Himself and the discipline of the Apostles hath delivered us, in the stead of many, a very few; and the same most easy to be done, most royal to be understood, most pure to be observed: as are the Sacrament of Baptism, and celebration of the body and blood of the Lord." The like whereof, and in effect the same, he hath, *Ad Januarium*, Ep. cxviii.[6]

This is the doctrine of the true Church. This only ancient; and whatsoever is against it, new. What it pleased men to use in the ceremony of Confirmation maketh very smally to purpose: and the thing itself being so shamefully abused as it hath been, the sign of the Cross to have been used therein is a good matter against you. But sorry I am, and ashamed of you, that still ye bewray your ignorance and folly. Needs will ye have seven Sacraments; and yet in your discourse ye confound them: alleging that, for proof of Confirmation, which the authors only did mean of Baptism. Thus do ye fall into the old absurdity: that, as before, wheresoever ye read this word "Cross," ye would lift it to

---

[4] Cap. iii.
[5] De Doctrin. Christiana, Lib. iii. Cap. ix. [*Opp.* Tom. iii. col. 37, ed. Bened. Ant.]
[6] [al. liv. *Opp.* ii. 93.]

the Rood-loft, or to the forehead; so now, wheresoever ye hear mention of oil, ye make it only to serve for bishopping. Learn, (M. Martiall,) to understand your author, before ye presume to become a writer. Denise, Tertullian, Augustin, and Cyprian, in the places that ye bring of Christians' anointing, spake, (as it is evident,) but only of baptizing them. For in their days, (as is before approved,) oil was received to the element of water.

<small>Denise.
Folio 55, b.</small>

And specially the words of Denise do confute you: for he joineth together the Christening, the Chrisom[1], the Chrism, and the Communion; which all in one Sacrament of Baptism did concur. Then what is this to your purpose, that Tertullian hath[2]: *Caro signatur, ut anima muniatur:* "The flesh is signed, that the soul may be defended?" Was there never any signing of the flesh, but in Confirmation? Yourself, I dare say, will not admit it. But if ye were so fond as to affirm it, yet Tertullian himself disproveth you. For the very next words that follow be these: *Caro manuum impositione adumbratur:* "The flesh is overshadowed by imposition of hands." And whereas divers things be spoken of, Confirmation, (if in any place,) must be understood in the latter clause; and there is no word of the sign of the Cross. Wherefore, how doth it appear by these your proofs, "that the holy Fathers used also the sign of the Cross in this your holy Sacrament?" Augustin[3], (if you had ever read him,) should not have been alleged of you. For in all the chapter he treateth, how the Jews were brought to Hierusalem by those means, as are figures unto us; mentioning especially Baptism, represented in the water of Jordan, and the Supper of the Lord, by slaying of the lamb, whose blood was sprinkled on the door-posts: upon which words he immediately inferreth: *Passionis et Crucis signo,* &c.: "Thou must be marked in thy forehead with the sign of the passion and Cross of Christ, as it were in a post." What is this to Confirmation? As much as a text out of Bevys of Hampton.

<small>Tertullian.</small>

And as for Cyprian, although the words, alleged by you, be the very worst in all his works; (which argueth very small

---

[1] [A white garment, put upon a child at the time of its Baptism. See Keeling's *Liturgiæ Britannicæ*, p. 251. Lond. 1842.]

[2] [*De Resurrect. carnis,* Cap. viii.]

[3] Augus. Lib. de catech. rudib. Ca. xx. [*Opp.* vi. 208.]

discretion in your choice:) yet are they quite from the purpose too. I omit how Cyprian, without a commandment, made in God His service anointing necessary : condemning therein all that before him had been baptized, and had not any oil poured upon them. Forsooth, by his reason, not heretics only, returning to the Church, should be partakers of his heretical re-baptization; but the Baptism of Christ, of the Apostles, of all them that we read of in the Scripture, should be insufficient. For neither will he have the element of water to be sufficient to baptize withal, unless it be consecrate; (*Oportet mundari et sanctificari aquam prius a Sacerdote*[4] *:* "The water must be cleansed and sanctified first of the Priest:") nor yet this consecrated water to serve, unless we have a little oil to boot. *Ungi quoque necesse est eum,* &c. : "It is necessary," (saith he,) "that whosoever is baptized, be anointed : that, the ointment being once received, he may be the anointed of God, and have in him the grace of Christ." Yet we never read that the Apostles used any words of consecration; that they thought themselves in that case to be Priests, whom the New Testament calleth Ministers of the word; or that they could repute, contrary to the express word, any creature unclean. *Omnia munda mundis :* "All things are clean to the clean[5]."

Christ, by His word and institution of Baptism, sanctified all water, used according unto His will. No man ought to add to His ordinance any thing. No Priest by conjuring can bring such holiness and perfection unto it, that in his respect, as Cyprian would have it, it shall be more available for remission of sins. Wherefore S. Cyprian was too far wide herein; and applied unjustly unto the Priest the word, (*Aspergam super vos aquam mundam:* " I will sprinkle clean water on you[6];") which God peculiarly promiseth of Himself. Then also to enforce a necessity of oil, that Baptism cannot consist without it; whereas Christ did not appoint it, nor Apostle use it; passed his commission : *Ut ne quid gravius.* But to attribute more unto the oil, (man's own invention,) than to Baptism itself, the ordinance of Christ, I must needs say was proud and blasphemous. Yet Cyprian so did; for he said, that unless they were on his wise anointed, they could not be true Christians.

[4] De Hæret. bapt. Ep. lxxii. [al. lxx. p. 190. edit. Fell.]
[5] Ad Tit. Ca. i. [15.] & Ro. xiv. [14.]
[6] Ezech. xxxvi. [25.]

To have The anointed of the Father, Jesus Christ, within them, was not enough, unless a little oil had also besmeared them. A pitiful case, that so good a Father, so faithful a Martyr, should have so foul a blot to blemish his authority[1]. But, (as I said,) we must not gather out of the Fathers' writings whatsoever was witness of their imperfection. Yet do I marvel most, what mad conceit ye had, to bring this place for the use of the Cross in bishopping of children. Only S. Cyprian, in all that Epistle and divers other, goeth about to prove, that heretics should be baptized. And this is far from Confirmation: full little doth it confirm your Cross.

Against the assertion of seven-fold grace. Folio 57, a.

Now, to speak a word of your "seven-fold grace," which you say is conferred at bishopping; I beseech you shew me the ground of your device[2]. I know that you delight in the odd number, as all enchanters have done of old: and therefore seven Sacraments; seven kinds of graces of the Holy Ghost. But wherefore seven? Because Esay[3] numbereth but seven: and this is the reason of all the Papists that ever wrote. But I might bid them tell them, as Tom Fool did his geese. Esay numbereth but six, and the seventh is their own. Therefore

Papists falsifiers of Scripture.

still I prove, that Papists are falsifiers of the word of God. And yet if the Prophet had rehearsed seven, (as it is of every man to be seen he did not;) to gather out of that a seven-fold kind of grace, were too absurd; inasmuch as other places attribute of divers effects[4] divers other titles to the Holy Ghost: nor the faithful are only partakers of those that Esay doth speak of, which are, Wisdom, Understanding Counsel, Strength, Knowledge, and Fear of God; but also of other, as Chastity, Sobriety, Truth, Holiness, which in like

---

[1] [See Donne's *Sermons*, Vol. i. p. 329. Lond. 1640.]

[2] [Rev. i. 4. iii. 1. iv. 5. Zech. iv. 2, 10. 1 Cor. xii. 4.—The hymn "Veni, Creator Spiritus," introduced twice into our Prayer-book, at the last review, commences thus:
"Come, Holy Ghost, our souls inspire,
And lighten with celestial fire.
Thou the anointing Spirit art,
Who dost Thy *seven-fold gifts* impart."]

[3] Chapt. xi. [2. See Prynne's *Briefe Survay and Censure of M. Cozens his couzening Devotions*, pp. 59, 68. Lond. 1628.]

[4] [" There be nine of them set downe; nine manifestations of the Spirit: (1 Cor. xii.) some of them nine: there be nine more set down nine fruits of the Spirit: (Gal. v.) some of them nine: some gift I will give." (Bp. Andrewes; *Sermons*, p. 607. Lond. 1635.)]

manner do flow from the same spring. Then also, to thrust the power of God's Spirit into such a corner, that it shall have but seven holes to start to, is too strait a compass, and cannot contain Him. But this I may excuse you, as the painter did himself; who, being reproved that he had left out a Commandment, whereas he was bidden to write them all in a table, answered: There is more than ye will keep. So you, in rehearsal of your seven-fold grace, speak of six more than you are partaker of.

Wherefore, to make my Apostrophe to the readers; (as you do:) seeing Dionysius is justly disproved to be of no such authority and antiquity as the Papists pretend: seeing S. Augustin is depraved of them; S. Cyprian alleged, where he defendeth an heresy; the example of Christ and His Apostles most falsely drawn to proof of Confirmation; I trust you will more esteem, and better regard, the authority of ancient Fathers indeed, whose plain assertions I have brought to the contrary; you will more reverence the word of God, the bread of life, by them abused to most impiety, than the stinking leaven of these lying hypocrites: who speak of Scripture, but esteem it not; who lay the Fathers for them, but understand them not; who pretend antiquity, but are carried about with every wind and puff of new doctrine: being, as S. Cyprian saith[5], beginners of schisms, authors of dissension, destroyers of faith, betrayers of the Church, and Antichrists indeed: who, going about to deface the Catholic Religion, commanded by Christ, taught by the Apostles, continued in the Church by the Holy Ghost; have defaced, (as it were,) the truth of Christ's ordinance, to place their own dreams and devices: as it appeareth by the number of their Sacraments; by declining in all points from the order of Christ and His Apostles; by oil, cream, salt, spittle, candles, and such-like, added unto Baptism; by preferring bishopping of children afore it; by making oil, of their own addition, of more effect and virtue than the element of water, sanctified by the word of God: finally, ascribing perfection of Christianity, which consisteth in the spirit, to the outward work of conjuring and crossing.

Now, M. Martiall, to come to your Holy Orders; which,

[5] Epistola ad Novatianos. [Not S. Cyprian, but some unknown writer, was the author of the *Epistola ad Novatianum hæreticum.*]

among your Sacraments, ye put in the third place. I marvel that ye are so barren in the ground, which of itself is so fruitful, that whereas ye number but seven Sacraments, this one hath begotten by spiritual generation six moe. For the Master of the Sentence[1], (whom ye and all your faction do follow,) maketh seven degrees of Orders. *Et hii Ordines Sacramenta dicuntur*[2]: "And these Orders," (saith he,) "be called Sacraments." He saith not, that they do all concur to make a Sacrament. So, by this means, we have now thirteen Sacraments: a plentiful increase. And to set forth the more the dignity of their calling, in every one of these Holy Orders they have Christ Himself a companion with them. But whereas Sacraments must have a promise annexed to them, a promise immediately from God; if any of these Orders, or they altogether should make a Sacrament, some piece of Scripture should be brought for proof of it. Neither Angels nor men can make a Sacrament. Therefore they lie, when they do call their Orders Sacraments; inasmuch as they which are called among them *Ordines minores*, " the inferior Orders," by their own confession were never known in the primitive Church, but long devised after. Hosius himself[3]; out of whom you took your authorities, as well of Augustin, as of Leo, to prove your Orders a Sacrament; confesseth in the same place, that of old time, *Ordines ii minores inter Sacros non numerabantur*: "These inferior Orders were not reckoned among the Holy ones." But now they be Holy all, and Sacraments all. If I should rehearse the idle ceremonies that are observed in every one of them; the Jewish disagreements of the Doctors themselves, when each man hath a sere[4] assertion of his own, defended with tooth and nail; the clouted[5] Religion of old patches of Judaism, Paganism, and Christianity together, whereby they commend this their Sacrament to the world; I should cumber the readers too long with unfruitful matters, and busy myself more a great deal than needed, to confute that, which you, M. Martiall, (such is your modesty,) are ashamed to allege.

[1] Lib. iv. Dist. xxiv. Cap. i. [fol. 345. Paris. 1553.]   [2] [fol. 349.]
[3] In Confess. Polonica, Cap. li. [fol. 138, a. Antverp. 1559.]
[4] [Dry, withered: or, more probably, *late* as to its origin; in the sense of "'Οψιμαθία," "*sera* eruditio."]
[5] [Josh. ix. 5.]

The Ministry of the word, commended unto us by Christ Himself, I can well admit to be a Sacrament; and therefore allow, in a right sense, the title that Augustin doth give unto it. For therein is a ceremony, that is taken out of the word of God; and a sign of spiritual grace conferred, as Paul doth witness[6]: yet am I not contrary to myself herein, who before affirmed, that there were only two Sacraments of the Church; Baptism, and the Lord's Supper. For when in general we treat of Sacraments, we truly say that there are but two; because there are no more ordinary, and appertaining to all the faithful. But ordering of Ministers is a special thing; contracted to a few, belonging only to a peculiar function: so may it well be called a Sacrament, and yet be denied to be a Sacrament of the Church. But where I attribute to christian Ministry so much as I spake of, there is no cause of pride for popish Priests. For they swerve so far from Christ's institution, that they serve not at all for any godly purpose. Christ did ordain His Apostles to preach; and to that end He breathed on them[7], shewing, by that sign, the power and virtue of the Holy Ghost, wherewithal He endued them: but the Romish apes only retain the sign, the thing itself being farthest from them; and as for the end which Christ respected, they have least regard of. For they have taught their Priests, that it is least part of their duty to preach; most to do sacrifice, and say Mass. And this doth the words of their institution prove; and a great proctor of theirs, Hosius[8], affirm. For where, in the verse of incantation, they have, *Potestatem illis dari placabiles offerendi Deo hostias:* " That power is given them to offer acceptable sacrifice unto God;" this do they restrain only to the Mass. And Hosius doth wrestle marvellously about the word; driving [deriving] it still from the Greek λειτουργεῖν, which he will have to signify sacrifice. So in the end, to raise their own gain, they derogate all from Christ His death and His passion.

We know that Christ did offer Himself sufficiently; and made a perfect satisfaction for our sins. We know that He needeth not any Priest's help, to be as acceptable to His Father, for his service sake, as Christ for that one and only Sacrifice of His body was. Christ gave command-

[6] 1 Tim. iv. [14.]   [7] Joh. xx. [22.]
[8] De Sacramento Ordinis. [fol. 145, a.]

ment to be faithful Ministers, not bloody conjurors. Christ gave an injunction to feed the flock, not to offer sacrifice. Christ hath promised His Holy Ghost, not to purge and take away sins, but to maintain the Church, and keep it in good order. And as for the argument, that the most learned Papists do build upon the Greek word, may easily be answered. For Chrysostom, when he had considered how Paul had written[1], that he was a Minister of Jesus Christ, consecrating the Gospel; (for so S. Augustin turneth it:) that there might be an acceptable oblation and sacrifice of the Gentiles, saith; that the Apostle there did make full mention of all the sacrifice that he could make; using both the terms of λειτουργία and ἱερουργία, whereupon the Papists will ground their idolatrous Mass. This is my sacrifice, to preach the Gospel, saith he: my sword is the Gospel; my sacrifice is the Gentiles. And now would I fain see what these enchanters can say; bragging themselves therefore to be Priests, because they can juggle so finely, that things shall pass out of their nature by them.

The Priesthood and sacrifice that the Apostles had, was to convert the simple souls, to daunt the cruel courages of men, to make an offering of them unto the Lord; not through gross miracle, or by bloody knife, but by the spiritual armour of the power of God; whereby counsels are overthrown, and every high thing that avaunceth itself against God is vanquished[2]. And whosoever will be successors unto the Apostles, must use this Ministry, this trade of doctrine: which if they continue in, being lawfully called thereunto by God, and have gifts competent to approve their calling unto the world; they need not to care for the sign of the Cross to be imprinted in them, the virtue whereof never departeth from them. Certain it is, that neither Scripture, nor any learned Father, commendeth any blessing, but of prayer, to us. And how your wisdom doth esteem the wagging of a Bishop's fingers, I greatly force not. I looked rather, that ye should have commended the oil for anointing, which the greasy merchants will have in every mess. For the *character indelebilis*, "the mark unremoveable," is thereby given. Yet there is a way to have it out well enough; to rub them well-favouredly with salt and ashes: or, if that will not serve, with a little soap.

---

[1] Rom. xv. [16.]   [2] 2 Cor. x. [4, 5.]

But ye had very little to say in the matter; and therefore, as soon as you had alleged your Doctor Denise, (whose authority notwithstanding we may justly deny;) "ye plucked down your sail, and cast your anchor there." Very wisely done of you. For perilous it is, to carry too high a sail upon a rotten mast.

Now, for a proof that the sign of the Cross should be used also in the Supper of the Lord; (which you blasphemously do call the Mass, which is nothing else but the sacrifice of the Devil;) ye bring the places of the xxvi. chap. of Matthew, and xiv. of Mark, where ye do find this word, *Benedixit*; that is to say, "He blessed." And that this blessing should be but a certain gesture of the hand, ye cite Albertus Magnus[3]; and compare the places of Scripture together, where it may appear that the self-same thing is meant. I am glad ye admit the conference of places. I perceive you will play small play, rather than sit out, when Albertus Magnus is worthied of authority. But how well you and he do understand the Scriptures, shall, by God's grace, appear anon. The words of Matthew be these[4]: λαβὼν ὁ Ἰησοῦς τὸν ἄρτον, καὶ εὐχαριστήσας, ἔκλασεν: which words, (if ye understand any Greek,) be these: "Jesus taking the bread, and giving thanks, brake it." Likewise in Mark[5]: λαβὼν ὁ Ἰησοῦς ἄρτον, εὐλογήσας, ἔκλασε: "Jesus taking the bread, when He had given thanks, He brake it." In the first place, it is evident that the word of your old translation, *Benedixit*, cannot be taken for the sign with a finger, because of the proper word of giving thanks, which cannot be applied to an extern gesture. Then also the word of Mark, if ye observe the etymology of it, must signify the same. For what is ἐν, and what is λογεῖν; what is *bene*, and what is *dicere?* The words are compounded of "well" and "speak." So that to bless is, to speak well, and not to cross well. When ye were last at Mass, and heard the Priest sing aloud, *Gratias agamus*, ye might have learned what it is *benedicere*. For it was at the first received in the Church, that when they came unto the mysteries of the Lord's Supper, they should bless, that is to say, should be thankful for them.

[3] [Lib. *de myster. Missæ.* Conf. Coccii *Thesaur. Cathol.* ii. 630.]
[4] Mat. xxvi. [26.]   [5] Mark xiv. [22.]

Which thing is proved right well by Chrysostom[1]: who, upon these words, *Calix benedictionis cui benedicimus, nonne communicatio sanguinis Christi est?* "The cup of blessing which we bless, is it not the partaking of the blood of Christ?" 1 Corin. x.; because blessing is twice spoken of, saith: *Cum benedictionem dico, eucharistiam dico: et, dicendo eucharistiam, omnem benignitatis Dei thesaurum aperio, et magna illa munera commemoro: etenim cum calice inenarrabilia Dei beneficia, et quæcunque consecuti sumus addimus. Ita ad Eum accedimus; cum Eo communicamus; gratias agentes, quod humanum genus errore liberavit; quod cum spem nullam haberemus, et impii essemus, fratres et consortes Suos ascripsit. Hiis et cæteris hujusmodi gratiarum actionibus accedimus.* Which words of the Doctor may be translated thus: "When I speak of blessing, I speak of thanksgiving: and, speaking of thanksgiving, I open all the treasure of the goodness of God, and rehearse those great gifts of His: for with the cup we add the unspeakable benefits of God, and whatsoever we have obtained. So we come unto Him; we communicate with Him; thanking Him, that He hath delivered mankind from error; that when we had no hope, and were wicked persons, He admitted us brothers and companions to Himself. With these, and such other renderings of thanks, we come unto Him."

Here ye see what Chrysostom took blessing to be. Set Chrysostom against your Albert. But let us see further conference of the Scriptures. Not only Christ, in His last Supper, used this form of blessing, (which you do make chief point of consecration;) but also in other of His miracles doing, whereof we read in every one of the Evangelists. As where Matthew[2], Mark[3], and Luke[4], speaking of the five thousand, beside women and children, fed with five loaves and two fishes, report, that Christ used such order, as the word importeth to be blessing; εὐλόγησεν. S. John[5], entreating of the same matter, expoundeth what is meant by blessing: for he saith; καὶ εὐχαριστήσας, διέδωκε: "And giving thanks, He

---

[1] Chrysost. in Epi. ad Co. 1. Cap. x. Hom. xxiv. [*Library of Fathers*, Vol. iv. p. 326. Oxford, 1839.]
[2] Mat. xiv. [19.]
[3] Mar. vi. [41.]
[4] Luc. ix. [16.]
[5] Joh. vi. [11.]

delivered." Likewise, where mention is made of the seven loaves[6], Christ blessed also; but the Evangelists set it out by the word of thanksgiving: καὶ εὐχαριστήσας, ἔκλασε: "And when He had given thanks, He brake." So that most evidently appeareth, by the word of God, to all reasonable creatures, that it is all one thing, to bless, and to give thanks. Yea, where yourself allege the word of *Benedixit*, in the xxiv. ch. of Luke; that Christ, lifting up His hands, blessed His Apostles; ye shall also find, the next sentence save one after, the same word applied unto the Apostles themselves; that they also did bless, and bless God. For the text hath: *Erant assidui in templo, laudantes et benedicentes Deum:* "They were continually in the temple, praising and blessing God[7]." Think you that this blessing was with a certain sign of the hand? Is this the meaning of the word of God, where still we be warned to bless the Lord? If this be absurd, (as I am sure ye will grant;) then grant, that blessing is another manner of matter than crossing.

Wherefore, since I have proved by nature of the words themselves, by consent of all the Evangelists, by testimony of the Apostle Paul, by judgment of Chrysostom, that blessing is thanksgiving; I may justly conclude your assertion to be vain and frivolous, that Christ used crossing in ministering of His Supper. What rite or ceremony was received after, diversely, according to the disposition of divers times and persons, is not material. For I have sufficiently proved afore, that it is not enough to say, This was once so; but it must be proved, that It was well so. For I well allow the proceeding of Cyprian against Stephen the heretic[8], which urged, (as you do,) traditions to be kept. But what said he to it? *Unde est ista traditio? Utrum de Dominica et Evangelica authoritate descendens; an de Apostolorum mandatis atque Epistolis veniens?* "Whence is this tradition of theirs?" (saith he.) "Doth it descend from the authority of Christ and His Gospel; or from the writings and commandments of His Apostles?" As for that which is written by Christ, he proved necessary to be observed: likewise whatsoever is contained in the Acts of the

---

[6] Mat. xv. [36.] Mar. viii. [6.]
[7] Luc. xxiv. [53.]
[8] Cyprianus Pompeio frat. Ep. lxxiv. [p. 211. ed. Oxon.]

Apostles, or other of their writings: but otherwise, he would not be bound to admit any thing. And therefore ye may prate as long as ye lust, what men in this time and that time received; and, without better proof, bind us no whit to observance of it.

Thus have you made a fair muster, M. Martiall, with signs and proffers, and proved nothing. While ye travail to bring the Cross to seven Sacraments, you have discoursed on four, and confounded them all. And as for the three, which you have put in the rearward, ye use only this reason: "All Sacraments of the Church," (as Augustin saith,) "are made with the sign of the Cross: But Matrimony, Penance, and Extreme Unction are Sacraments of the Church: Therefore the sign of the Cross is used in them." For answer whereof, neither is the first Proposition, (as you understand it,) to be admitted; nor the second in any wise is true. Therefore the Conclusion doth follow but ill-favouredly. First, ye are abused in your own conceit, in esteeming the sign of the Cross to be a thing of such necessity, as that the Sacraments may not be made without it; whereas it is but an accessory thing, devised by man, whereof in Scripture we have no precedent. And Augustin[1] would not say, (as you fondly do,) that simply Sacraments are made with the sign of the Cross; but mentioning that, as a piece of a ceremony more than needed, brought in withal the necessary point, (that you leave out,) the calling upon the name of Christ. For Sacraments consist of the sign, and thing signified; of the word, and the ceremony. And in Baptism, the water and sprinkling thereof, in the name of the Father, the Son, and the Holy Ghost, upon the party that is to be christened, is the whole sign and ceremony to be done. But remission of sins, participation of life, fellowship with Christ and with His members, also the gifts of the Holy Ghost, which are by grace conferred, be the signified thing, the promise of mercy so sealed in us. Here is no word of the sign of the Cross, and yet is the Sacrament made perfect thus. Nor in Christ's institution we hear any mention of such a ceremony; nor that Christ in His own Baptism, nor the Apostles in theirs, were blessed with a finger. Wherefore the Major is falsely set. But the Minor is farther out of square.

[1] Ser. clxxxi. de Tempore. [See before, p. 205.]

For before Gregory's time, although every man granted Matrimony to be an holy ordinance of God, yet who ever affirmed it to be a Sacrament? Forsooth, (say you,) Ambrose, Augustin, and Leo. So the same Ambrose[2] calleth the words and works of Christ, whereby He shewed His Divinity, hidden otherwise in God, a Sacrament. And Augustin hath nothing more familiar in him than *Sacramenta Scripturarum,* " the Sacraments of the Scriptures ;" whereby he understandeth the dark speeches and spiritual meanings of the Holy Ghost. So that, if ye take a Sacrament for that whereby any thing is signified unto us, then Matrimony, I grant, may be a Sacrament. But see what absurdity ensues thereon. As many Parables as we have in Scripture, so many Sacraments. The grain of mustard seed, the goodwife's leaven, the door of the house, the shepherd, the giant, the thief, (for by all these the kingdom of God and Christ are signified ;) must be Sacraments. So the washing of hands, the shaking of dust from the Apostles' feet, and every act of Christ, may be a Sacrament. Then we shall not keep us within the number of seven, (which you appoint ;) but, ere we have done, we shall have seven score, yea, seven hundred Sacraments. But if ye take a Sacrament for such a sign as God hath ordained for us; to confirm our faith, and seal the promise of His grace within us ; then are you too far wide. For proof of Baptism we have : " Whosoever believeth, and is baptized, shall be saved[3]." For the Supper of the Lord we have : " Take, eat ; this is My body." " Drink ye all of this : this is My blood, which is shed for many for the remission of sins[4]." And have we the like for Matrimony ? Then take a wife, and thou shalt be saved. Then take a wife, and thy sins be forgiven thee. This is your doctrine, (M. Martiall ;) this is your Lovain learning.

But ye say for yourself, that S. Paul called it a Sacrament[5]. Ye forget yourself : he neither used the term, nor

---

[2] In Ep. ad Tim. 1. Ca. iii. [S. Ambrosii *Opp.* iii. 579.—This Commentary was not written by S. Ambrose ; but probably by Hilarius Diaconus : though even that is uncertain. Conf. Oudin. i. 481. Schoenemann, *Biblioth. Patrum Latin.* i. 307. Lips. 1792.]
[3] [S. Mark xvi. 16.]   [4] Mat. xxvi. [26—28.]
[5] Ephe. v. [32.—Compare Gregory Martin's *Discoverie of manifold Corruptions,* p. 245. Rhemes, 1582. Fulke, *New Test.* p. 619 : *Defense,*

applied it to that purpose. To admit that it were so, as your ignorant and gross translator hath; (whereof I will speak more anon;) yet your discretion and skill might have considered the correction that follows, when the Apostle saith plainly, that he speaketh not of the man and woman, but of Christ and His Church: so that the Sacrament is referred to them, and not to Matrimony. But the ignorance of the Greek word hath only bred this error; where for a Mystery it is translated a Sacrament. I marvel greatly that the name of Sacrament should be so seriously urged in this place, being otherwise in all places of the Scripture beside neglected. For your said old translator hath, in the same Epistle to the Ephesians, and i. cha.: *Ut notum faceret nobis Sacramentum voluntatis Suæ*: "That He might notify to us the Sacrament of His will[1];" (for 'the mystery of His will.') By the same reason now, the Scripture itself, whereby God's will is revealed to us, shall be a Sacrament. And in the Epistle to Timothy[2], your old translator hath: *Magnum est pietatis Sacramentum, quod manifestatum est in carne:* " Great is the Sacrament of godliness;" (for 'great is the mystery of godliness;') " which is, God is manifested in the flesh." By which reason, the incarnation of Christ should be also a Sacrament. Nor there shall be any end of Sacraments, if, wheresoever we read of mystery, we shall understand the Sacraments of the Church.

Folio 67, a.

Martiall's reason.

Your wisdom supposeth, that because a mystery and a Sacrament do not so far differ, but that that which is called a mystery may also be a Sacrament, therefore your ground is good enough, that Matrimony is a Sacrament. This do ye prove by a sad tale of old mother Maukin, that " thought her Saint Edmund to be no minstrel because he was a Minister; whereas in these latter days a minstrel," (as you say,) "may be a Minister, and serve both turns for a need." But if mother Maukin[3] had been such a daukin[3], as to think every Minister to be a minstrel,

---

164. Lond. 1617. Cartwright's *Confutat.* p. 496. 1618. Ward's *Errata*, p. 87. Dubl. 1841. Moquot, *L'Examen et Censure des Bibles*, Tome ii. Art. xxxiv. p. 385. A Poictiers, 1617.]

[1] Ad Eph. i. [9.]   [2] 1 Timo. iii. [16.]

[3] [*Maukin* or *Malkin* signifies a slattern; and *Daukin* or *Dawkin* has a similar meaning.]

as you do every mystery to be a Sacrament; then Martiall and Maukin, a dolt with a daukin, might marry together; and the Vicar of Saint Fool's[4] be both minstrel and Minister, *simul et semel*, to solemnize your Sacrament. But we must not dally with the signification of the word with you; but we must consider what is the definition, and what is required in a Sacrament; and then we shall find nothing lack in Matrimony, that is or ought to be in any other Sacrament. "It is," (you say,) "a visible sign of invisible grace." But what is that grace? Salvation, justifying, or sanctification, conferred upon them that are partakers of it? If it be so, some thing it is that ye say. But it is not so. For he that is married is not in that respect more the child of God, than if he were unmarried. He that is married hath no peculiar promise, that for his marriage sake his sins are remitted him. And yet these things are requisite in a Sacrament; that, by the visible sign, some such promise as this may be sealed in us. I will bring against you, for this point, no other divinity but your own. The Master of the Sentence sayeth[5]: *Sacramenta non tantum significandi gratia instituta sunt, sed etiam sanctificandi. Quæ enim significandi gratia tantum instituta sunt, solum signa sunt, et non Sacramenta; sicut fuerunt sacrificia carnalia, et observantiæ ceremoniales veteris Legis,* &c.: "Sacraments are not only ordained to signify, but also to sanctify. For those that are only appointed to signify, are only signs, and no Sacraments; like as the carnal sacrifices, and ceremonial observances of the old Law were." So that he, which otherwise defendeth as many heresies as you[6], overthrows your reason; which do make Matrimony to be a Sacrament, because it is a sign of invisible grace. For so were all the sacrifices; so were all the ceremonies of the old Law. And indeed he confesseth, that they and such like are called Sacraments, *licet minus proprie,* "though not so properly." And so do I grant you, that it may be called a Sacrament, and yet not such as we here speak of.

Folio 67, b.

[4] [Vid. Maitland's *Dark Ages,* p. 156. Lond. 1844. Gregory's *Episcopus puerorum,* p. 119. Lond. 1663.]
[5] Lib. iv. Dist. i. Cap. i.
[6] ["He found not so much as a word touching seven Sacraments before Peter Lumbard." (Bp. Carleton's *Life of Bernard Gilpin,* p. 5. Lond. 1629. Compare Stillingfleet's *Council of Trent examin'd and disprov'd by Catholick Tradition,* p. 74. Lond. 1688.)]

Absurdities in popish doctrine, concerning the Sacrament of Matrimony.

But mark how great and how many absurdities follow of your doctrine. First, where ye make Wedlock a Sacrament, ye go against yourselves; and destroy the holy number of seven, making eight Sacraments at the least. For Wedlock out of Wedlock hath engendered another, and begotten two Sacraments. This is not my device. I read it in your Decrees. For, in the treatise of Matrimony and the act thereof, it is written[1]: *Duo sunt Sacramenta: unum Dei et animæ: aliud Christi et Ecclesiæ. Dei et animæ, in sponsis: Christi et Ecclesiæ, inter virum et uxorem:* "There are two Sacraments: one of God and the soul: another of Christ and the Church. The Sacrament of God and the soul is in the parties espoused: the Sacrament of Christ and the Church is between the man and the wife." So that the very talk of Matrimony hath gotten young ones. And by this we may see the foolish end of wavering heads, tossed with doubtful floods of opinions. Sometime ye will have but seven Sacraments, and always this is a defended principle: yet in your books sometime ye make eight; sometime as many as a man will imagine.

Another absurdity.

Furthermore, whereas ye make a Sacrament of Wedlock, how falleth it out, that afterward ye condemn it as a piece of uncleanness? Ye say, when a man will marry, then he goeth to the world. Ye write that Marriage is a carnal thing. Ye maintain in your laws, that in Matrimony are profane lusts, defiling concupiscence: that a man in that state cannot please God; cannot be heard of God. And yet still, ye will have it a Sacrament. Innocentius Pope, in his Decree, saith[2]: *Neque eos ad sacra officia fas sit admitti, qui exercent etiam cum uxore carnale consortium; quia scriptum est: Sancti estote, quoniam Ego sanctus sum; dicit Dominus Deus vester:* "Nor let it be lawful for them to be admitted to holy rooms, which use carnal company with their wife; because it is written: 'Be ye holy, for I am holy; saith the Lord God[3].'" Where, first, (I beseech you,) mark, how the lawful use of Matrimony is called carnal company: then also how despitefully the place of Scripture,

---

[1] Decr. ii. Parte. Caus. xxvii. Que. ii. in Glo. [Cap. *Cum societas.* fol. cccxli, b. Paris. 1518.]

[2] Decr. prima parte. Dist. lxxxii. Cap. Proposuisti.

[3] Lev. xx. [7, 26. & xi. 44, 45.]

"Be ye holy, for I am holy," is applied against Matrimony. The words were spoken by God unto the Hebrews, when He forbad them that they should not offer up their sons to Moloch; that they should not follow the sorcerers and the witches: and in the latter end of the chapter it is repeated again; where incest with mother, sister, or such-like, is condemned. Wherefore, by wresting this to lawful Marriage, what did they but condemn the married of ungodliness? Yet God commanded the Priests of the old Law to be holy; whom, notwithstanding, He never did restrain from Marriage.

But Innocentius goeth forward in his Decree, and saith: *Multo magis igitur Sacerdotes, quibus et sacrificandi et orandi juge officium est, semper debebunt ab hujusmodi consortio abstinere. Quia si contaminatus fuerit carnali concupiscentia, quo merito se posse exaudiri credit; cum dictum sit: Omnia munda mundis; coinquinatis autem et infidelibus nihil est mundum, sed coinquinata est eorum mens et conscientia?* &c.: "Therefore much more Priests, which have a continual office to sacrifice and pray, ought always to abstain from such company. For if he be defiled with carnal concupiscence, by what merit of his, thinks he, that he can be heard; whereas it is said: 'All things are clean to the clean; but to them that are defiled, and to the unfaithful, nothing is clean, but their mind and conscience is defiled[4]?'" And can there be any thing spoken or devised more contumelious against the state of Matrimony, than that such as are married are thereby defiled with carnal lusts, and their prayers cannot be heard? What shall the honest couples throughout all Christendom think of this; that when, in the fear of God, they use the ordinance that God hath willed them, that day they need not to make their prayers; for the Pope saith they shall not be heard? Wherefore all men, by this man's holy order, must either utterly refuse prayer[5], or refuse to give due benevolence to their wives[6]: which both are shameful inconveniences. I omit that, in the same Decree, he applies to the married this sentence of Paul: *Qui in carne sunt, Deo placere non possunt:* "They that are in the flesh cannot please God[7]." Then woe be to the married: they are out of God's favour, and therefore condemned. I omit that Siricius

[4] [Tit. i. 15.]   [5] Luc. xviii. [1.] Colo. iv. [2.]
[6] 1 Cor. vii. [3.]   [7] [Rom. viii. 8.]

calleth the use of Matrimony *obscœnas cupiditates,* "filthy lusts[1]." I omit that another, Innocent by name, (but nocent, and noisome indeed ;) saith[2], that to marry a wife is, *cubilibus et immunditiis deservire,* "to serve wantonness and uncleanness." Thus do they deface the ordinance of God, to commend their own unchaste and filthy state. Yet will they have Matrimony to be a Sacrament. A sorry Sacrament; that, by your law, is nothing else but carnal company, carnal concupiscence, uncleanness, wantonness, filthy lusts, severing us from God's people, making our prayers not to be heard.

How say you, (M. Martiall,) are you yet ashamed of your profession? Will you stand to this still, that Matrimony is a Sacrament? Then let me proceed a little further with you. Wherefore do you exclude your Priests from Marriage? Why are ye so injurious unto them, that they shall not partake the holy Sacrament? Shall they alone be graceless, where so great grace, as you say, is given? Or else are your Sacraments so singular and self-will, that they cannot in one subject agree together? But ye do not exclude them from the Sacrament, (you say;) but only from the carnal knowledge. But the carnal knowledge, (say I,) by your own authority, is a chief part of the Sacrament; and therefore ye exclude them from the Sacrament itself. For these be the words of your Canon Law[3]: *Cum societas Nuptiarum ita a principio sit instituta, ut, præter commixtionem sexuum, non habeant in se Nuptiæ conjunctionis Christi et Ecclesiæ Sacramentum:* "Whereas the fellowship and society of Marriage is so ordained from the beginning, that, beside the commixtion of sexes, Marriage hath no Sacrament of the conjunction of Christ and His Church together," &c. Whereby it appeareth, that the carnal knowledge between man and woman, (which you forbid your Priests, though not absolutely, yet only so as they might lawfully use it;) is that Sacrament of yours. Therefore ye do wrong to your shorn and anointed, to forbid them Marriage, your new-made Sacrament, if for no other respect but this, *Ut sacris vestris operentur.* But ye have a remedy for it, damnable and devilish. I will not speak it for shame. God make you honest.

The third absurdity for the Sacrament of Matrimony.

---

[1] Dist. lxxxii. Ca. Quia ali[quanti.]
[2] Dist. xxviii. Cap. Decernimus.
[3] Decr. ii. Parte. Causa xxvii. Quæst. ii. [Cap. xvii.]

Again yet, where ye touch that Matrimony is a Sacrament; yea, the company itself of man and wife together in the act of Matrimony to be a Sacrament; and every Sacrament, (you say,) conferreth grace; how doth this hold together, that in the act of Matrimony, in the company of man and wife together, ye deny the presence of the Holy Ghost? For your law affirmeth it to be sin, though a sin venial[4]. Shall it now be a Sacrament, and anon no Sacrament? Shall all Sacraments confer grace; and this be a Sacrament, and confer none? Shall it be holy, and yet profane; a Sacrament, and yet a sin? *The fourth absurdity for the Sacrament of Matrimony.*

Last of all, to prove that, in all your devices of error and hypocrisy, ye seek for nothing else but to colour and cloke abominations; consider what an heap of mischiefs is covered with this face of holiness. When ye have determined that Matrimony is a Sacrament, ye take the knowledge of causes matrimonial unto yourselves: for spiritual cases must not be handled of profane judges. Then have ye made such horrible laws to confirm your tyranny, that they are not only impious to God, but injurious to man. As, that young folk, wilfully contracting themselves without their parents' consent, may marry well enough: that there shall be no Marriage within the seventh degree: that he, that divorceth an adulterous person, may not marry another: that Gossips, (as we call them,) may not be man and wife together: that from three weeks before Lent, till the octaves of Easter; from Advent to Twelfthtide; and for three weeks before Midsummer; there shall be no marrying at all, without a dispensation. No marvel then if ye have made a Sacrament of Matrimony, since that is the milch cow that yieldeth so large a meal of spiritual extortion. *The fifth absurdity for the Sacrament of Matrimony.*

Now, to come to Penance, which ye make a Sacrament as well as Matrimony. Ye call it "a bath of tears, a despoiling of the old life, the second board after shipwreck." These titles argue not that it is a Sacrament; nor I contend who giveth it these titles: certain I am, that some of them be blasphemous and abominable. For, to go no further than to this, "that it is called the second table after shipwreck," *Quia si quis innocentiæ vestem in Baptismo* *Penance. Folio 68, a.*

[4] Dec. i. Parte. Dist. xiii. Cap. Item advers. in Glo. [fol. xii. Paris. 1518.]

[CALFHILL.] 16

perceptam peccando corruperit, per Pœnitentiæ remedium reparare potest: "Because," (saith the author[1], whose name I suppress as well as you;) "if any have marred his garment of innocency, which in Baptism he gat, by the remedy of Penance he may repair it." This is as much to say, as if the effect of Baptism were taken away by sin: whereas we be bound to call our Baptism to remembrance whensoever we sin; that, by the promise exhibited in Baptism, the sinful soul may be refreshed, and Penance out of it gathered. Therefore, as the Gospel itself doth say, John preached the Baptism of Penance to remission of sins[2]; so the Fathers of the Church do call Baptism sometime the Sacrament of Penance[3]. But to your reason, whereby ye prove Penance to be a Sacrament. "It is a visible sign of invisible grace," (ye say;) "and the visible sign is the external act of the Priest, absolving the penitent." By this reason ye prove better Absolution to be a Sacrament than Penance: and so shall our Sacraments multiply still. I beseech you, what hath Penance to do with the Priest's Absolution? Can there be no remission of sins, unless the Priest assoyle[4] me? I will prove that manifestly false, and by your own law. For Confession goeth before Absolution; and yet without Confession there may be good remission. So, by this reason, we stand not in need of the visible element: the invisible grace is granted without it. For, according unto your Canon[5]: *Voluntas remuneratur, non opus:* "The will is rewarded, and not the work." Then is it a lie which you affirm, "that sins are remitted by mean of the external work."

I know that you be more conversant in the Pope's Decrees than in Austin's works: therefore I will shew you what Gratian gathereth out of them[6]. The sorrow of my heart, though I speak never a word, nor Priest lay hand upon my head, purchaseth me pardon. *Id quod probatur autoritate illa prophetica*[7]: *In quacunque hora peccator fuerit conversus et ingemuerit: non enim dicitur, ore confessus fuerit, sed tantum conversus fuerit et ingemuerit;*

---

[1] [Pet. Lombardi] Lib. iv. Sent. Dist. xiv. Ca. i. [fol. 317, b.]
[2] Mar. i. [4.]   [3] Dec. Caus. xv. Quæst. i. [Cap. iii.].
[4] [absolve.]   [5] De Pœn. Dist. i. Ca. Si cui. [xxx.]
[6] De Pœn. Dist. i. Ca. Facilius. [xxxii.]
[7] [Ezek. xviii. 27, 28.]

vita vivet, et non morietur: "Which thing is proved," (saith he,) "by the authority of the Prophet, saying: 'In what hour soever a sinner shall be turned and lament:' for he saith not, when he shall be confessed, but when he shall be converted and lament; then shall he live, and not die." Likewise after [8]: *Evidentissime apparet, quod sola cordis contritione, sine confessione oris, peccatum remittatur:* [*remittitur:*] "It appeareth most evidently, that by the only contrition of heart, without confession of mouth, sin is remitted." And yet again[9]: *Confessio quæ soli Deo fit, quod est justorum, purgat peccata:* "The confession which is made to God alone, (which is the part of the righteous,) purgeth the offences." By which places all, it is plainly to be seen; first, that your Eareshrift[10], (one part of your Penance,) is to no purpose: then that Absolution, which is your external work, your Sacrament, (as you call it,) is no mean of remission. Furthermore, to rake out this kennel of Popery; Penance is a Sacrament, (ye say.) Every Sacrament a visible sign. The visible sign herein is the external act of the Priest: the invisible grace is the remission of sins to the penitent. So the sign and Sacrament is in the Priest; but the grace in the people. But how is this grace conferred? Forsooth, by the Priest, the ghostly father. And on whose head soever the Priest layeth his hands under Confession, hath he remission? Yea, forsooth: *Quia Sacramenta novæ Legis efficiunt quod figurant*[11]: "Because the Sacraments of the new Law do bring to pass that which they figure." Then every murderer, thief, adulterer, though he never repent, hath clear remission, for he hath the Sacrament. O shameless impudency!

But if it were so, (which is great impiety,) that by the external act remission were obtained, yet I see not how that should be a Sacrament. "For the matter of this Sacrament," (say you,) "is the external act of the penitent, containing these three points; Contrition, Confession, and Satisfaction[12]." Among all these, where is the visible element? *Ubi est illa corporalis species, quæ fructum habet spiritualem?* as Augustin

Folio 69, a.

---

[8] Ca. Qui natus. [xxxvi.]   [9] Ca. Quidam Deo. [xc.]
[10] [Auricular Confession.]   [11] Lib. iv. Sent. Dist. i. Cap. i. & iii.
[12] ["Judas had all the three parts of popish Repentance, Confession, Contrition, and Satisfaction; yet not saving Repentance." (Hill's *Olive-branch of Peace, budding in a Sermon;* p. 9. Lond. 1648.)]

saith[1]: "Where is that bodily shape, which hath the spiritual fruit?" Hath Contrition, Confession, or Satisfaction a body? Be these subject to the eye, as bread, wine, and water are? Be they not virtues proceeding from the mind, or things uttered by the mouth: and will you make them to be things sensible, as boys and girls brought out in a pageant? Wherefore your Sacrament is cut off by the waist. Make as good shift with the words as you can, your visible and bodily sign is gone. And I marvel how ye dare so precisely speak of your Sacrament of Penance, affirming the external act to be the visible sign of release of sin the invisible grace: whereas your Master of the Sentence is put to his shifts in this case[2]; and, putting two opinions, determineth upon none. Whether the outward act should be the Sacrament; or else the outward and inward together. As for the outward, which you do rest upon, he feareth to grant, lest this inconvenience ensue: *Non omne Sacramentum Evangelicum efficere quod figurat:* "That all the Sacraments of the Gospel have not the effect of that which they figure." But who is so bold as blind bayard[3]? Hitherto have I spoken not so much as I might, to derogation of your Devil's doctrine, but so much as your ignorance and oversight doth cause me of conscience to put you in mind of. For the rest ye refer me to the book of the seven Sacraments, set forth by the late King of famous memory, Henry the eighth[4]. And because this is but a popish device, (whosoever defend it,) I refer you to the same book, to know what ye ought to think of the Pope.

margin: Unity in Papists' doctrine.
margin: Folio 69, b.
margin: Extreme Unction. Folio 70, a.

Now as for Extreme Unction, which you say was provided of God's mercy and goodness, that in the last and perilous extremity we should not be destitute of aid and comfort. Indeed God never forsaketh His. He hath left His promises to heal the mind's infirmities, and use of physic for diseases of the body. But that oil can enter into the soul, or is so sovereign a medicine for the flesh, resteth to be proved. "The Apostles anointed with oil many sick folks,

---

[1] Ser. de Bap. Infan.
[2] Lib. iv. Sent. Dis. xxii. Ca. ii.
[3] [A bay horse.]
[4] [The *Assertio septem Sacramentorum*, against M. Luther, was translated into English, and published by authority, Lond. 1687. The first Irish edition was that of Dublin, 1766.]

and they were healed[5]:" the Priests anoint every sick body, and none of them is the better. The Apostles were commanded to cast out Devils, to cure diseases, to cleanse the lepers, and to raise the dead: the Priests never had any such commission. The Apostles signified by their anointing the virtue and power of the Holy Ghost, by which the cure was wrought: the Priests with their oil mock the Holy Ghost, and make the body but greasier for the grave. If every example that we read in Scripture shall be followed of us; if every thing that was a sign to other shall be a Sacrament to us; then dust and spittle shall be a Sacrament to heal sore eyes: then the pool of Siloah[6] shall be a Sacrament to wash away the filth: then lying on the dead[7] shall be a Sacrament to raise them up to life. Wherefore, though anointing were in the primitive Church used, and the same was a sign of grace conferred, yet cannot this precedent extend to us, because the commandment concerneth us not, and also the effect and end thereof is ceased.

Ye have a common proverb in your law: *Accessorium sequi naturam principalis:* "That the accessory thing doth follow the nature of the principal." Wherefore, since the principal is gone, the working of miracles and healing of the sick, what shall we do with the accessory, the sign thereof, and outward anointing? Ye urge vehemently the institution of God by His Apostle S. James: but the Apostle meant not preposterously[8] to draw to imitation that which was temporal, and only touched the present state. When the doctrine of Christ was raw in the people's mouths, and a new Church began to be gathered, miracles were necessary; many gifts were granted; and, amongst the rest, the power of healing: the Ministers whereof used their oil, not as a cause of health, but as a sign that the virtue proceeded from above, and they were but instruments of the same. Now, since the gift of healing is gone, (as I am sure ye will confess;) to what purpose is it to use the oil? If ye will therein be the Apostles' successors; if ye will follow Saint James his counsel; save the sick and[9] you can: shew the grace of your grease.

<small>Anointing was a sign of healing.</small>

<small>Anointing no cause of health.</small>

<small>Anointing must cease, because the gift of healing ceaseth.</small>

[5] Mark vi. [13.]   [6] Joan. ix. [7.]   [7] Act. xx. [10.]
[8] [inverting the order of things: putting the future instead of the present time.]
[9] [an', if.]

The greasy merchants, that take this cure now-a-days in hand, be no more exhibiters of the grace then granted, than the Player on the stage is a King indeed, when he cometh disguised in a golden coat. Christ dispensed many things by His Apostles, the effect whereof He denieth unto us. And anointing better might be used of such as have the power of healing, Surgeons or Physicians, than of such as have no skill, but only in murdering and in killing.

Contradiction in Papists' doctrine.

Here I rehearse not the contradiction that in your idle Decrees I find, and is only sufficient to disprove your assertion: for whilst each man goeth about to establish his own device, and each man is contrary to another[1], ye shew therein that ye be liars all. You say, that Priests only

Folio 70, a, b.

must be the Ministers of this Sacrament: "Priests must be called for, Priests must anoint." But Innocentius, a Father of your Church, hath long ago decreed the contrary. For Sigebertus, in his Chronicle[2], affirmeth that he made an Act, *Oleo ad usus infirmorum ab Episcopo consecrato licere uti, non solum Presbyteris, sed omnibus etiam Christianis, in suam suorumque necessitatem ungendo:* "That it should be lawful, not only for the Priests, but also for all Christians, to use the oil consecrated of the Bishop for the behoof of the sick; anointing therewith, according to the necessity of themselves and their friends." But ye allege Saint James for you[3]: "Is there any sick among you, let him bring in the Priests of the Church;" (for so ye translate it:) "and let them pray over him, anointing him with oil, in the name of our Lord." Ye abhor the name of the Lord; (for, by Storie's position, that is the mark of an heretic[4]:) and yet all Prophets and Apostles use it. Then it followeth: "The prayer of faith shall save the sick; and if he be in sins, they shall be forgiven him."

How the Papists in all points swerve from S. James his order.

Now if a man should grant, (which I have proved to be most untrue,) that the anointing here spoken of agreed to

---

[1] [Cf. Dallæum, *De Extrema Unctione*, Lib. i. Cap. ii. Genev. 1659.]

[2] Anno Domini 404. [*Chron.* fol. 5, a. Paris. 1513. Vid. Pithœi *Cod. Canon. vet.* p. 336. Lut. Paris. 1609. Clagett's *Discourse concerning Extreme Unction*, Part ii. Sect. iii. Lond. 1687.]

[3] James v. [14, 15.]

[4] [Comp. Fox's *Acts and Mon.* Vol. iii. pp. 460, 470. Lond. 1684. *Exam.* of Philpot, pp. 9, 47. ed. Parker Soc.]

this age; yet had ye furthered your cause nothing, inasmuch as so shamefully ye do decline from the Apostle's order. Saint James will have all to be anointed, if they be sick: you only anoint in case of mortality and danger of death, when one foot is in the grave already. If oil be your Sacrament, and the promise of grace be annexed to it, to heal both bodily and ghostly, (as you say;) then what hard hearts have you, that suffer so many to languish in extremity, that come not by your wills before the last gasp? S. James will have the sick to be anointed of many: you will admit but one alone, with his head in his sleeve, muffled as an ape, with a bell before him, as a bat-fowler for an owl. S. James will have the Elders to be called to this office, which were not only of the Ministry, but also of the lay fee: you will have a rabble of shorn Priests, and none but them. S. James is content with simple oil: you will have none but such as a Bishop hallowed; with many a stinking breath warmed; with many a sorcerous word enchanted; with many a beck, many a knee to the ground idoled. S. James will have unction, (the sign of God's Spirit,) and prayer of the faithful to concur together; noting that it is not the oil that healeth, but good men's prayers are always available: you most blasphemously do ascribe remission of sins unto your oil-box.

The absurdities. 1. 2. 3. 4. 5.

Now brag of your unction: go sell your kitchen-stuff. Try it, and ye lose it. It is too stale to make a Sacrament. It stinketh, I tell you. For whereas in a Sacrament two things be required: first, that it be a ceremony instituted of God; then, that it have a promise of grace in it: in the first we respect that the ceremony be delivered unto us; in the second that the promise also concern us. And forasmuch as neither the ceremony was commanded us, nor the promise apperteineth to us; both being temporal, and long ago surceased; I may well conclude, that Extreme Unction is no Sacrament. Whatsoever in the Council of Florence[5], or in the late

---

[5] [The mention of this Council, with reference to the Romanistic Sacraments, proceeded from a misconception of no slight moment. It is to be remembered, however, that the error is one into which the author has fallen in company with many of our best writers; for example, Stillingfleet (*The Council of Trent examin'd and disprov'd*, pp. 93, 109. Lond. 1688.) and Hooker. (vi. vi. 11. Vol. iii. p. 93. Oxf.

Synod of Trent, hath been decreed to the contrary, shall not prejudice my truth. For I, having reason and Scripture for me, with the learned and sound determinations of moe Fathers of the Church than these, will not be prescribed by conventicles and conspiracies. You pretend authority: we bring the Scripture. You call us heretics: we prove you no less. And which shall take place: God's word, or men's wills; a talk, or a proof? If all the fat bulls of Basan did draw together, and the Devil their carter did drive them to Trent, there to feed and stand fast for their provender, shall the Lord's sheep therefore be starved? shall His work be neglected? If ten thousand of your affinity, bewitched with the sorcery of Romish Circe, should hold a Council, and call all men to the trough of your own draff[1], should not I acknowledge and confess with Gryllus, in whom, (bearing the figure of a reasonable creature,) enchantment could take no place, that reason and Religion should be preferred to the belly? What reason is in this; their sentence to hold, who be the parties accused, and yet judges of the cause? What Religion is in this; that, for filthy lucre, man's idle ordinance shall displace the commandment of almighty God? Wheresoever I see this shame and disorder, (as in all your popish Councils it is,) I appeal from them; I say with Paul: *Mihi pro minimo est ut a vobis judicer:* "I pass very little to be judged of you[2]."

As for the place of Hilarius against Auxentius the Arrian[3],

1841.) Bellarmin's words are these: "*Porro Græcos agnoscere pro vero Sacramento Extremam unctionem, patet primo ex Concilio Florentino, ubi sine ulla contradictione receperunt instructionem Armenorum, ubi inter alia Sacramenta numeratur Extrema unctio.*" (*De Extr. Unct.* Cap. iv. col. 1647. Ingolst. 1601. Cf. *Catech. Concil. Trid.* pp. 226, 273, 333. Lovan. 1567.) This statement exhibits consummate carelessness, if nothing worse: for it is manifest beyond contradiction, that the Instruction given to the Armenians, and prescribing to them the seven Sacraments, owes its origin not to the Council of Florence, but to the schismatical Pope, Eugenius IV. The *Instructio Armeniorum* is dated x. Calend. Decemb. 1439, exactly *four months after the departure of the Greeks from Florence;* an event which took place on the 20th and 21st of July, in the same year. Vid. Coci *Censuram,* pag. 232. Cosin's *Schol. Hist. of Canon of Scripture,* §. clviii. Lond. 1672. *History of Transub.* pp. 157—9. Ib. 1676. Dallæum, ut sup. ii. xxi. p. 148.]

[1] [Food for swine.]   [2] 1 Cor. iv. [3.]
[3] [S. Hilarii *Opp.* 1269. ed. Bened. Paris. 1693.]

how fitly it may be applied unto you, (and not to us, whom you would seem to touch,) all they that have eyes do see. For you can say nothing but "These new Ministers are heretics; they are Calvinists, and therefore Devils." Proof bring ye none, but the same is reproved. I trust therefore ye have credit according. But to you I say: Ye be fallen with Auxentius: ye do participate with Arrius' heresy. Who is the Devil's Angel then? Who is to be avoided? Nor I am contented only to say it, (as you do;) though in this respect my word were as well to be accepted as yours, but I prove it too. For when ye make an Image of God the Word, *Creaturam facitis Eum, qui omnia creavit;* as Epiphanius sayeth[4]: "Ye make a creature of Him that created all things." Wherefore, if ye would assent to the Decrees of the first Nicene Council, and go no further, these words needed not betwixt you and me. But when ye take away the name of Nicene, and put Florence or Trent in place thereof, ye are as true a man as he that stale a goose, and sticked down a feather. For all Councils are not alike. Nor all they that brag of the Holy Ghost, are by and by inspired with His grace. For Hilarius, your own author, (whom to no purpose ye brought forth last;) hath, to good purpose, this[5]: *Multi sunt, qui, simulantes fidem, non subditi sunt fidei, sibique fidem ipsi potius constituunt quam accipiunt: sensu humanæ inanitatis inflati, dum quæ volunt sapiunt, et nolunt sapere quæ vera sunt: cum sapientiæ hæc veritas sit, ea interdum sapere quæ nolis. Sequitur vero hanc voluntatis sapientiam sermo stultitiæ: quia necesse est, quod stulte sapitur, stulte et prædicetur:* "Many there are," (saith he,) "which, feigning a faith, are not subject to faith, and rather do appoint themselves a faith than receive it: puffed up with the sense of man's vanity, while they understand those things that they lust, but will not understand those things that be true: whereas the truth of wisdom is, sometime to understand those things that thou wouldest not. But the talk of folly cometh after this will-wisdom: for necessary it is, that foolishly it be uttered, that foolishly is understood."

Fol. 71, 72.

Fol. 72, b.

---

[4] Lib. ii. Tom. ii. Hær. xcvi. [Hær. lxix.—The *Panarium* was written against *eighty* heresies.]

[5] Hilarius, Li. viii. de Trinit. [*Opp.* 947.]

TO THE FIFTH ARTICLE.

ALTHOUGH ye bend yourself in all this article, and stretch every vein of your feeble skill, to prove a matter, which, although it be in part untrue, yet, being granted, did not hurt my cause; ("That the Apostles and Fathers of the primitive Church blessed themselves with the sign of the Cross, and counselled all christian men to do the same; and that in those days the Cross was set up in every place convenient for it:") yet, because ye still appear in your likeness, and it is so requisite ye be known to the world, a clouter of a patch of troth upon a whole cloke of lies; I will not disdain to make an easy proof of your three tagless points: for any greater stress they will not abide. And first of all, the term of blessing is ill applied to signing in the forehead. For what it is to bless, I declared in the article before: to speak well, profess well, live well. This is εὐλογεῖν: this is *benedicere;* which you do use alway to translate "bless." S. Augustin hath[1]: *Benedicam Dominum in omni tempore: semper laus Ejus in ore meo. Quod est in omni tempore, hoc est semper. Et quod est benedicam, hoc est laus Ejus in ore meo:* "I will bless the Lord in all time: always His praise shall be in my mouth. And that which He sayeth, in all time, is ever. And that which He sayeth, I will bless, is, His praise in my mouth." Likewise Chrysostom[2]: *Quando Dominus benedicitur, et aguntur Illi gratiæ ab hominibus, tunc uberior ab Illo solet benedictio dari, propter quos Ipse benedicitur. Nam qui benedixerit, debitorem Illum facit majoris benedictionis:* "When God is blessed, and thanks be given of men unto Him, then more plenteous blessing is wont to be given of Him, for their sakes by whom He is blessed. For he that blesseth maketh Him debtor of a greater blessing." Where ye see plainly what the nature of the word is, and in what sense it hath been taken of old. But if you have learned of your old

---

[1] August. in Psa. xxxii. [xxxiii. al. xxxiv.]
[2] Chrysos. in Gen. Ca. ix. Hom. xxix. [*Opp.* Lat. Tom. i. coll. 238—9. Basil. 1547.]

mother Maukin, (of whom ye spake before,) another sense; if you have borrowed of foolish custom a new-found signification of the word, to note a signing of a Cross in the forehead; ye do very ill apply it to the Apostles' time, and primitive Church: where we never read, *Benedicebant se signo Crucis, sed signabant se :* "That they blessed themselves, but marked themselves with the sign of the Cross:" yet that the Apostles did ever practise any such thing, is not to be found in any approved writer.

Your authorities ye fetch out of Abdias. Such lips, such lettuce[3]. Him have I proved in the third article to be a very liar, a vain foundation to build a truth upon. Wherefore, as loth to be tedious, (as you,) I will travail no further in confuting of these two or three leaves together, which are wholly gathered out of his legends. If any think any piece of more credit to be given to him, let him resort to that which I sayed before, or read his tales. I wish no better confuter than himself. As for Clement, whom, (you say,) S. Peter appointed to be his successor, I would fain have you to reconcile your authors before I do fully believe it[4]. For Irenæus[5] reckoneth Linus first after Peter; then Anacletus; and Clement to be the third. Eusebius[6] affirmeth the same: adding further, that after Linus had occupied the see twelve year together, then he resigned his bishoprick to Anacletus, the second year of Titus. Epiphanius[7], although he vary in the name, yet in the order he doth agree, saying: *Episcoporum in Roma successio hanc consequentiam habuit: Petrus et Paulus, Linus, Cletus, Clemens:* "The succession of Bishops in Rome had this orderly sequel: Peter and Paul, Linus, Cletus, Clemens." And whereas in the same place report is made, that both Linus and Cletus enjoyed the room twelve year apiece, I marvel that Clement, according to Peter's will, did not immediately succeed, but tarried for it twenty-four year. A great modesty of the man, or much immodesty of the makers. But, to come to the purpose; that,

<small>Fol. 73, 74, 75.</small>

<small>Clement. Folio 75.</small>

---

[3] ['Similes habent labra lactucas:'—"notissimum dicterium, de asino carduos comedente." (Erasmi *Adagia*, fol. 1. Argent. 1510.)]

[4] [Vid. Pearsonii *Opera posthuma*: ed. Dodwell. Lond. 1688.]

[5] Contra Hæres. Li. iii. Ca. iii. [p. 159. Paris. 1575.]

[6] Eus. Li. iii. Cap. xiii. [*Hist. Eccles.*].

[7] Epiph. Lib. i. To. ii. Hæ. xxvii. [p. 35. Cornar. interp. Basil. 1578.]

which ye cite of his authority, hath no credible author to support it. Indeed I find in his Recognitions[1] a notable place or two for the material Cross; which I think convenient to speak of more hereafter in the tenth article.

Folio 75, 76. The tales of S. Anthony, S. Martin, Donatus, Bishop of Euoria[2], and Paula, the noblewoman of Rome, I pass over with silence; because if they did sign themselves, (as you say,) they be no precedents to enforce an imitation: and yet a man may doubt, whether such things were done as are reported, or no. Erasmus his judgment is, that S. Hierom wrote the life of Paul the Heremite only for his exercise[3]. And in the same *Fol. 76.* place that ye bring for your proof; "where S. Anthony armed his forehead with the impression of the healthful sign, and by and by the monster, running swiftly over the field, vanished out of sight;" we read these words[4]: *Hæc utrum Diabolus ad terrendum eum simulaverit; an, (ut solet,) eremus, monstruosorum animalium ferax, istam quoque gignat bestiam, incertum habemus:* "Whether the Devil did counterfeit these things to fear him; or else, whether the wilderness, being very fruitful of monstrous beasts, do bring forth also this beast, I know not." So that we may doubt of the truth of the history. And most likely it is, (as S. Hierom himself saith;) that the Devil, feeling the Heremite's affection, would make the sign of the Cross, wherein he delighted, to be, (as ever since it hath been,) a cause of further sickness, a stone of offence, a stumbling-block to fall at. Therefore he ministered an occasion, whereby he might run to this sorry succour; and feigned himself to be afraid of it, that men might put more affiance in it. Wherefore we ought to doubt the worst, lest these external means do make our enemy have more advantage of us, and our inward faith to be the less.

Not whatsoever hath been may now be done. Notwithstanding, if in the doings of elder age there were no such offence, yet, considering how things in time have grown to abuse and superstition, such as have been tolerably

---

[1] [See before, pages 20, 21.]

[2] [Evoria, in Epirus. Vid. Sozom. *Hist. Eccl.* Lib. vii. Cap. xxv.]

[3] ["Videtur et hoc Hieronymus exercitandi ingenii gratia lusisse." (*Opp.* S. Hieron. Tom. i. p. 237. Basil. 1565.)]

[4] Hieron. in Vita Pauli Eremitæ. [Inter *Vitas Patrum*, S. Hier adscript. fol. xv, b. Lugd. 1520: vel in edit. Rosweyd. p. 18. Antverp. 1615.]

received must now of right and conscience be condemned. Remember the Decree of Stephen[5], whereof I spake before; that if any of the predecessors have done any thing which at any time could stand without offence, and afterward is turned to error and superstition, it ought immediately to be removed. And I see not but Christians may better forsake it than keep it.

I am glad that ye esteem so much S. Hierom's report of Paula. I trust ye will not reject him when in a greater matter he shall be alleged. Epiphanius, a Bishop of Cyprus, who lived about the year of our Lord three hundred and ninety, writing to John, the Patriarch of Hierusalem, hath these words[6]: *Quod audivi quosdam murmurare contra me, quia quando simul pergebamus ad sanctum locum qui vocatur Bethel, ut ibi collectam tecum ex more ecclesiastico facerem; et venissem ad villam quæ dicitur Anablatha; vidissemque ibi præteriens lucernam ardentem, et interrogassem quis locus esset, didicissemque esse ecclesiam, et intrassem ut orarem; inveni ibi velum pendens in foribus ejusdem ecclesiæ, tinctum atque depictum, et habens Imaginem quasi Christi, vel Sancti cujusdam: non enim satis memini cujus Imago fuerit. Cum ergo hoc vidissem, in ecclesia Christi, contra authoritatem Scripturarum, hominis pendere Imaginem, scidi illud; et magis dedi consilium custodibus ejusdem loci, ut pauperem mortuum eo obvolverent et efferrent.* Which words, right worthy to be considered, are in English these: "In that I heard certain did grudge against me, for that, when we went together to the holy place which is called Bethel, to make a gathering there with thee, according to the manner of the Church; and came to a village called Anablatha; and, as I passed, saw a candle burning, and asked what place it was; and when I had learned that it was a church, and had entered in to make my prayers, I found there a vail hanging in the church-porch, becoloured and painted, and having the Image as it were of Christ, or of some Saint, upon it: for I do not well remember whose Image it was. Therefore when I had seen this, that in the church of Christ, contrary to the authority of the Scriptures, there hanged the Image of a man, I cut it; and gave counsel rather

Epiphanius an enemy to all Images.

---

[5] Dist. lxiii. [Cap. xxviii. *Decret.* Par. i. Vid. p. 67.]
[6] [See before, page 42.]

to the churchwardens, to wrap some poor dead man in it, and bury him." So far Epiphanius. And a little after he requesteth the Bishop of Hierusalem to give commandment: *In ecclesia Christi, ejusmodi vela, quæ contra Religionem nostram veniunt, non appendi. Decet enim honestatem tuam hanc magis habere solicitudinem; ut scrupulositatem tollat, quæ indigna est Ecclesia Christi, et populis qui tibi crediti sunt:* "That in the church of Christ there should be no such clothes hanged, which come against our Religion. For it becometh your honesty," (saith he,) "rather to have this care; to take away the scrupulosity which is unworthy of the Church of Christ, and people which are committed to your charge." Whereby we see that certain Images of Christ and other were in those days crept into the church; but the faithfuller Bishops did straight remove them. We see also that in S. Hierom's time, (to approve that which in the Epistle I said before;) the use of Images was not publicly received in churches, but judged disagreeant unto the Scriptures. For otherwise, (to use your own reason;) S. Hierom would not have winked at his fault, nor translated the Epistle without correction, if he had thought that his doing had been ill, or his words untrue.

The church Cross condemned by Epiphanius.

But what could ye have more evident against your Cross, than that which Epiphanius most freely said? First, that it is against the authority of the Scripture, to have the Image of a man hang in the church of Christ. Then, that he desired that such painted clothes should not be hanged up, because he thought them against our Religion. Last of all, that he deemed the use of such to be but a scrupulosity, unworthy of Christ's Church, unworthy of Christians[1]. We teach no more than Epiphanius did; yet you condemn us as heretics. Was Epiphanius ever accompted such? Would Saint Hierom have turned his Epistle out of the Greek into Latin, if it had contained any unsound doctrine? Would he have given such a testimony of him, (as we read he did,) if he might have been stained with any point of heresy? Writing to Pammachius, against John of Hierusalem, he saith[2]:

[1] [For the substance of these remarks, and for several authorities adduced by Calfhill, see Bp. Ridley's *Treatise concerning Images*.]

[2] Hieronymus ad Pammachium. [*Epistt.* Par. i. Tract. iii. Ep. xx. sig. m iii. Lugd. 1508.]

Habes Papam Epiphanium, qui te aperte missis [al. *multis*] *literis hæreticum vocat. Certe nec ætate, nec scientia, nec vitæ merito, nec totius orbis testimonio, major illo es... Eo* [al. *Et*] *tempore quo totum Orientem, (excepto Papa Athanasio atque Paulino,) Arrianorum et Eunomianorum hæresis possidebat;* [al. *possideat;*] *quando tu* [al. *in*] *Occidentalibus, et in medio* [al. *Judeæ*] *exilio Confessoribus non communicabas; ille vel Presbyter monasterii ab Eutitio audiebatur, vel postea Episcopus Cypri a Valente non tangebatur. Tantæ enim venerationis semper fuit, ut regnantes hæretici ignominiam suam putarent, si talem virum persequerentur:* "Thou hast," (quoth he,) "the Pope Epiphanius;" (where is to be noted, that the Pope in old time did signify but a Father; and the name was given not only to them of Rome[3], but also to them of Cyprus and Alexandria:) "who, in his letters to thee, calleth thee heretic. Truly neither in age, nor knowledge, nor worthiness of life, thou art greater than he. At such time as the heresy of the Arrians and Eunomians possessed all the East, (except Father Athanasius and Paulinus;) when thou diddest not communicate with them of the West, and such as confessed the truth in midst of their exile; he, being but a poor Minister of a religious house, was heard of Eutitius, and being afterward Bishop of Cyprus, was not touched of Valens. For always he was of such worship and reverence, that when the heretics reigned, they thought it a shame for them, if they should persecute such a man as he."

Here have ye the testimony of S. Hierom for Epiphanius. Ye have heard what his opinion was. I would fain know what your judgment is of it. S. Hierom praised Paula: so did he Epiphanius. S. Hierom wrote the life of Paula: so did he discourse upon Epiphanius, and translated his doings. Then set the fact of Paula against the fact of Epiphanius, and see which is to be preferred. She made the sign of a Cross in

---

[3] [The name of "Pope" was not restricted to the Bishop of Rome until a Decree for its appropriation was issued by Gregory VII., in the year 1076. Vid. Morton's *Grand Imposture of the (now) Church of Rome*, p. 249. Lond. 1628. Usser. *De Christianar. Ecclesiar. success. et statu*, Cap. v. p. 64. Lond. 1687. Casauboni *Exercit.* xv. *ad Annall. Baronii*, p. 422. Lond. 1614. Laud's *Conference* with Fisher, p. 181. Ib. 1639. Binii *Concilia*, iii. ii. 297, 398. Erasmi *Stultitiæ Laus*, p. 182. Basil. 1676.]

her forehead: he would have no sign in the church remaining. She prostrate herself before the Image on the Cross: he cut in pieces the cloth that had the Image on it. She, without reason, not according to skill, gave example of a thing: he, by Religion and Scripture, condemned it. She was a woman, but he a man. She unlearned, but he learned. She lived after, in a corrupter age: he went before, nearer the sincerity of the Apostles' times. Then if ye urge the one, I will burden you with the other. Yet admit, with Epiphanius, no Cross, no Crucifix, no Image in the church; and I will not *Folio 78, 79.* stick with a mystical sign of the Cross with Paula. Ye reckon up a sort that used of devotion to make in their foreheads this Cross sign: ye make no mention of them that used it not; in zeal as good as they, and in number moe. Wherefore, as Dionysius answered, when it was laid unto him how many had escaped the peril of the sea, by Neptune's aid, whose garments and monuments were hanged up to be seen; "Yea," (quoth he,) "but there are no monuments of them that perished:" even so say I; though you keep a calendar of the crossers, yet where is the register of them that crossed not[1]? If I should in number contend with you, I well near might be equal; but if antiquity should be respected, you should be far inferior. For as for Abdias' fables, all wise and honest esteem as much as the famous pamphlets that come from Lovain.

But I will not use so slender a defence. I will not, (as you do,) cumber the readers with more idle talk than needful proof. For if in any thing, sure in Religion, this sentence taketh place: *Non vivendum exemplis, sed legibus*: "We must not live by examples, but by laws." Yet here ye triumph marvellously; God wot, before the victory, before any blow given. For when ye have rehearsed the names of certain which in their days did use this ceremony, ye *Folio 80, a.* vehemently say: "Shall we so far discredit and disauthorize these grave, virtuous, and learned men, as though they knew not the Scriptures, and true interpretation of the same; as though they knew not light from darkness, verity from heresy, true Religion from vain superstition? Alas, God forbid." Alas, good man, how fell you out with yourself?

[1] [Cf. Gul. Reginaldi *Calvino-Turcismum*, p. 94. Colon. Agripp. 1603.]

Who hath chafed your charity? Be men discredited that be not in every point followed? Hath your wisdom forgotten that the selfsame Fathers, which twice or thrice ye rehearse by tale, both did and taught more oft and more earnestly other things than that, wherein yourself refuse to follow them? I will take pains for your pleasure to run them over again, in such order as ye put them, that ye shall not say but I deal faithfully with you.

Tertullian is put in the first rank. He saith[2]: "Whensoever we go forth and move forward, whensoever we come in or go out, whensoever we put on our apparel and draw on our shoes, when we wash, when we sit down at the table, when we have light brought in, when we go to our chambers and sit down, whatsoever we have to do, we make the sign of the Cross in our foreheads." The very next sentence, (save one,) before, these words he hath also: *Die Dominico jejunium nefas ducimus, vel de geniculis adorare. Eadem immunitate a die Paschæ in Pentecostem usque gaudemus:* "We think it a wickedness to fast upon the Sunday[3], or to serve God on our knees[4]. And the same immunity we enjoy from Easter-day to Whitsuntide." And before that: *Oblationes pro natalitiis annua die facimus:* "We make every year an offering for our birthday[5];" we keep the wakes. And now, M. Martiall, how chance that ye kneel at your Mass on Sunday? Why do you not offer up a cake on Monday? Tertullian thought the one a wickedness; the other he commanded as a necessary service. Dare ye so discredit and disauthorize Tertullian? Alas, God forbid. Ye will rather never serve God at all; never fast, never kneel; but drink and be merry, and pipe up John taberer[6], "To-morrow shall be my father's wake." These toys and such other, as he borrowed of Montane, (notwithstanding afterward condemned by Council;) so you of conscience and tender heart will follow, thinking therein you are a good Catholic.

Tertullian. Folio 79, b.

Tertullian's traditions.

[2] De Corona Militis. [Cap. iii. Compare Du Moulin's *Treatise of Traditions*, pp. 159—161. Dubl. 1750.]
[3] [Conf. Gratiani *Decret.* De Cons. Dist. iii. Capp. xiii, xiv, xv.]
[4] [See the xxth Canon of the first Nicene Council.]
[5] [By these "birthdays" are to be understood the days upon which the memory of Martyrs was annually celebrated.]
[6] [A player on the Tabour or Tambourine. Compare the use of the word "tabering," in Nahum ii. 7.]

[CALFHILL.]

258 THE FIFTH ARTICLE.

Ephræm.

The next in your array is holy Ephræm[1]. He saith[2]: "Let us paint in our gates, and print in our foreheads, faces, breasts, and all parts of our body, the lively sign." In the same book also, *De Pœnitentia*[3], four times together he calleth Christ *Legislatorem*, "a law-maker." And is this catholic? Where have ye read the like? He prayeth also to the Virgin Mary, saying[4]: *Sub alis tuis custodi me:* "Keep me under thy wings." What word or sense of Scripture for this? David, in four or five places, doth attribute the same to God; Psalm xvi, xxxv, lvi, lx, lxii; [xvii, xxxvi, lvii, lxi, lxiii;] but to none other: and the whole course of Scripture is indeed against it. Yet here ye will follow him. Then what say you to this? Divers times he feigned himself to be mad, for fear lest they should lay a bishoprick upon him. Will ye follow him in this? I doubt your modesty.

Folio 78.
Chrysostom.

Chrysostom, (you say,) doth counsel us, "with great study and earnest zeal, to set in our foreheads and minds the Cross[5]." So doth he every man to have the Bible in his house[6]. How like ye that? Every man and woman, as well and rather the lay fee than the Clergy, to be conversant in Scripture[7]. Admit ye that? That wheresoever the Bible lieth, the Devil can have no power there[7]. Believe ye that? That Monks had their minds void of all affections, and their bodies like

---

[1] [S. Ephræm of Edessa lived about the year 370. Th. Bartholinus has therefore wrongly placed him in the third century. (*De Morbis Biblicis*, p. 124. Francof. 1672.)]

[2] ["Pingamus in januis, atque in frontibus nostris, et in ore, et in pectore, atque in membris omnibus vivificum signum." (Lib. *de Pœnit.* C. iii. cit. Bellarm. *De Imaginibus*, L. ii. Cap. xxix. & Card. Hosio, *Opp.* fol. 7, a. Antverp. 1566.)]

[3] De compunctione cordis, Lib. i. Ca. v. [This tract should not be confounded with the treatise *De Pœnitentia.* Conf. Trithem. *De Scriptt. Eccl.* lxxviii.]

[4] De laudibus Mariæ. [In edit. Voss. Tom. iii.—The genuineness of many of these Sermons has been questioned. Vid. Riveti *Crit. Sacr.* iii. xxi. 339. Crakanthorp styles the author "Impostorem, non Patrem." (*Cont. Archiep. Spalatens.* p. 413.)]

[5] ["In fronte quoque, ac mente, magno studio Crucem inseramus." (*Hom.* lv. *in S. Matth.* apud Coccium, i. 236.)]

[6] Hom. ix. in Epis. ad Coloss. [*Library of Fathers*, Vol. xiv. p. 287. Oxf. 1843.]

[7] De Lazar. Conc. iii. & iv. [*Opp.* Lat. Tom. ii. Paris. 1570.]

Adam's before the fall[8]; (wherein is denied original sin.) Confess ye that? If in these points ye think it no shame to swerve from Chrysostom, think it no discredit to refuse the other.

S. Hierom "counsels us to make the sign of the Cross[9]." *Folio 78. Hieron.* So doth he also to trust to the merits of the Priest; or else to think there is no due Sacrament[10]. He saith that our souls, as long as they are young, are without sin[11]; and that to marry twice is as ill almost as to play the harlot[12]. If in these cases ye think he had the true interpretation of the Scripture, I marvel not if ye trust him in the other. But if in these he was deceived, why do ye so earnestly urge him in the other?

Saint Augustin "commandeth us to make the sign of the *Folio 78. August.* Cross[13]." So doth he also that Infants should receive the Communion[14]. If ye discredit him in this, who thought it as necessary for them to take the Lord's Supper as to be christened, will ye think it so great a matter, in such a trifle as the other is; which, without any word, without any binding us to it, he only spake of; a little to dissent?

Cyrillus ye name, but cite no authority. When we come *Folio 79, b.* to his place, in the latter end of the ninth article, you shall hear more news of him.

Prudentius he saith[15], "that when we go to sleep, we *Prudentius.* must in our foreheads make the sign of the Cross." But, in the same book[16] also he saith, that it was the woman that subdued the Serpent; transferring the glory from Christ unto Mary. And as he doth infer a reason for the Cross, because *Folio 79.* "a mind earnestly fixed on that sign cannot be inconstant and waver;" so doth he for the dignity of Christ's mother, saying: "The Virgin, that deserved to bring forth God, bringeth

---

[8] In Cap. Mat. xxi. Hom. lxix. [Tom. ii. col. 498.]

[9] [*Epist. ad Demetriad.*: vel potius in *Expos.* suppositit. *Psal.* lviii.]

[10] In iii. Sopho. [sig. q viii. Venet. 1497.]

[11] [viz. *actual* sin: as he had previously declared, "quod nullus in die quo nascitur pravum aliquid committere potest."] In Ezech. Ca. xvi. [sig. GG. eod. vol.]

[12] Contra Jovin. [*Æpp.* Par. i. Tract. ii. Epist. v. Lugd. 1508.]

[13] [*In S. Joan. Tractat.* cxviii.]

[14] De Pecc. mer. & remiss. Libr. i. Cap. xx. [*Opp.* Tom. x.]

[15] [*Cathem.* Hymn. ante somnum. *Opp.* fol. 66. Antverp. 1540.]

[16] Cathemeriνῶν, Hymno ante cibum. [*Opp.* fol. 48, b.]

all poison and ill power unto naught." And the doctrine of the one is as true as the other.

Wherefore, since it is not to be denied, but that every one of the Fathers of the Church, (whom I, notwithstanding, with all my heart do reverence;) have had their errors and imperfections; (though not in like degree all:) ye do us wrong to say we discredit them, if we do not clearly in all things follow them. They themselves refused that honour and authority. They must be trusted, but yet as men. As long as they bring their warrant for them, God forbid, indeed, but we should admit them. If we established our traditions, and destroyed theirs; if we devised a worship of our own, and despised theirs, we were to be blamed: but when, in respect of God's commandment, (which no man ought, on peril of his life, transgress;) we reject a custom and device of man, we are not to be burdened with pride or singularity. Yourselves think it lawful to alter and innovate, at your own pleasures, all traditions and ceremonies of elder time: as, taking away milk and honey from Christenings, contrary to Tertullian; and denying infants the Supper of the Lord, contrary to Augustin; with an hundred moe that I could rehearse. And wherewithal do you supply them? With your own fancies, your own follies. Yet you neither discredit nor disauthorize the Fathers. We, if we stand not to every iote, that any one of the Fathers heretofore hath written[1], and hath pleased the Pope of his power absolute to admit, are compted heretics, schismatics, such as have separated ourselves from the Church.

Folio 80.

Folio 81.

Apology of the Church of England.

Indeed we profess a separation from you, as our Apology doth witness[2], and shew good reason why. Therein your fineness doth call us patchers. I wis all the pack of you hath not cloth in your shops to make the like. But, separating ourselves from you, the enemies of God and of His truth, we join, (as we ought,) with the Church of

---

[1] [There is here a manifest allusion to a Gloss in the Canon Law; *Dist.* ix. Cap. *Noli meis:*—"Scripta sanctorum Patrum .. hodie jubentur omnia teneri usque ad ultimum iota."]

[2] ["We have indeed departed, not as heretics ever have done, from the Church of Christ; but, as good men ought to do, from the contagion of wicked men and hypocrites." (Bp. Jewel's *Apol.* Chap. iv. §. 18. p. 65. Lond. 1685.)]

Christ. For what is the unity that you appoint us? The humble obedience of the Church of Rome, whom you will have to be the Mother Church; whom you do call the bosom and the lap, that all men ought to run unto, which will be numbered among God's children. You with this unity content yourselves; seeking rather yourselves over Christ, than Christ over the flock to reign: compassing rather how yourselves may daintily live in this world, than how the members of the Church may be brought to Heaven. But we must appoint such kind of unity, as must not depend upon one particular or private Church; be it either of Antioch, or of Hierusalem, or of Rome itself; but upon the Catholic and universal Church, which was not only before Rome in antiquity, but shall continue when Rome is gone. This must we search out of the Scriptures. *Unum corpus multi sumus in Christo*, saith the Apostle[3]: "We, being many, are one body in Christ." Christ is the head, and we be the members. How do the members and the head agree? With one flesh, one blood, one spirit, and one life. As Christ is in the Father, and the Father in Christ, so we all by Christ are one in God. If one Spirit rule us, we must all think one thing. If we be all one body, we must not hate our own flesh. As brotherly love and charity is necessary for us, to declare by the same that we be Christ's disciples: as peace and quietness among us all is a thing most expedient, as a band to knit us in the unity of the Spirit; so they, which are thus united unto Christ, must not only be quickened with the same Spirit, but be comforted and maintained with the same faith and hope.

margin: Unity of Papists.

margin: Unity of Christians.

Wherefore, if you will have us to continue the unity of your Church with you, then make it first a Catholic Church; and of a sink of Idolatry, a follower and furtherer of true Religion. It is not by and by the unity of the Church, which comes under colour and name of it. Hierom, a Doctor of the Church, writeth[4]: *Sub Rege Constantio, Eusebio et Hippatio Consulibus, nomine unitatis et fidei, infidelitas*

---

[3] Rom. xii. [5.]

[4] Contra Luciferianos. [The reading is strangely different in the editor's earliest edition:—" Sub Rege Constantino, Eusebio et Hippatio; cognomine unitatis et fidei, infidelitas *non* agnoscebatur." (*Æpistt.* Par. i. Tractat. ii. Ep. xii. lit. L. Lugd. 1508.)]

scripta est: "In the time of Constance the King, Eusebius and Hippatius being Consuls, under the name of unity and faith, infidelity was written." And such an unity do you deliver us, (not you alone, I mean, but all the rabble of popish heretics with you;) as consisteth of Idolatry, false worshippings, simony, with a corrupt body, and a counterfeit head, even Antichrist himself. You say that the unity of the Church doth hang upon observance of ceremonies, old rites and customs: we say that it standeth upon Faith and Spirit. Which are the truer in this behalf? S. Paul biddeth us to be careful to keep the unity of the Spirit, till we meet together in the unity of Faith[1]. Augustin, entreating of the Sabbath fast, saith[2]: *Interminabilis est ista contentio; generans lites, nunquam* [al. *non*] *finiens quæstiones:* "This contention is endless; still engendering strife, never ceasing from doubts."

And what, I beseech you, do you that brag of your unity? Dissent from all antiquity, not agree with yourselves, contend about trifles, damn the true faith, derogate all from Christ's death and His passion, and giving it to your own free will and works. The works that you command be your own devices. The works that God commands, you have nothing to do withal. Break God's commandment, and it is no matter. Break yours, we die for it. It is a wonder how bold you will be to pronounce heretics, to serve your turn. Victor, Bishop of Rome, would excommunicate and condemn of heresy all the Churches of Asia[3], because they did keep their Easter *Quartadecima luna primi mensis,* when the Jews' sweet bread is eaten, and not at the time that he kept it at Rome. A sore point, I promise you. But you condemn us of heresy for preaching of the Gospel, against the traditions and precepts of men. If they, from whose ordinances we do depart, had either thought their traditions necessary, or shewed Scripture whereupon they grounded them, we would not presume to withstand their authority, or gainsay their good reason. But when they deliver them as things indifferent, and plainly profess that they have no word of the Lord for them; a hope of commodity may cause us to retain them, but an apparent mischief must drive us to refuse them. Ter-

---

[1] Ephesi. iv. [3, 13.]
[2] Epist. lxxxvi. [al. xxxvi. Cap. ix. *Opp.* ii. 58. ed. Ben. Ant.]
[3] Euseb. Ecclesiast. Hist. Lib. v. [Cap. xxiv. ed. Vales.]

tullian himself, when he had rehearsed a great sort of traditions, among which this was the last that we now do speak of, (the manner of signing with the Cross in the forehead,) immediately inferreth[4]: *Harum et aliarum ejusmodi disciplinarum si legem expostules Scripturarum, nullam reperies:* [al. *invenies:*] "If thou require a law of Scripture for these and such-like orders of discipline, thou shalt find none."

Wherefore, since they build not upon the Scripture, they do not expound upon the word. When these toys be taught, we cannot, (as you say,) "discredit and disauthorize them, as though they knew not the Scriptures, and true interpretation of the law." When you do make a lie of your own, do I discredit your knowledge in the law? A lawyer may sometime be a liar, as you prove unto us, and yet not the law to wit. When the Fathers bring an invention of their own, do I otherwise deny them the right sense of Scripture? The Fathers may have sometime their fancies, and yet beside the word. Then, if their fancies be misliked, is their exposition of the word condemned, whereas they meddle not with the word? Apelles' shoemaker was worthily checked, when he would be busy above the knee[5]; but that did not let but he might have judgment good enough of the shoe. Yet, in a shoe made on another's last, the best shoemaker, for all his skill, may chance be deceived. Indeed, good cause we have only to depend upon the word of God, and not be ruled over by time or custom; because, in matters of our Religion, as Christ hath taken perfect order therein, so hath He commanded us to go no further, but Him obey. Socrates was wont to say[6]: *Unumquemque deum sic coli oportere, quomodo seipsum* [*se ipse*] *colendum esse præcepisset:* [*præceperit:*] "That every god was so to be served, as he himself had commanded to be served." And this was the cause why the Romans would never receive the God of the Hebrews. For, grounding upon this foresaid principle, they saw it necessary, that either all their Idols should be excluded, and only the true God entertained, or He only not admitted, the rest be honoured. For

Folio. 79, b.

---

[4] Tertullian. De Corona Militis. [Cap. iv.]

[5] [See the origin of the proverb, "Ne sutor ultra crepidam," explained in Erasmi *Apophthegmata*, Lib. vi. fol. 282, b. Paris. 1532.]

[6] August. De consen. Evan. Li. i. Cap. xviii. [*Opp.* iii. ii. 8. Cf. p. 34.]

by the word of God they found that they could not agree together; and contrary to His word they would not seek to serve Him.

If they had this affect, as Augustin declareth, gathered by moral reason, and by no further insight of faith; shall we, that profess more knowledge and perfection, be foolisher than they, hearing continually Christ and His Apostles inveighing against will-worshippers? Therefore, I say, we ask for the word: you answer us by will. We call for Scripture: you reach us custom. Martial[1], a merry man, a poet of your name, a man of more learning and wit than you, had sometime to do with such a lawyer as you. For a neighbour of his had stolen three goats. The matter was called into the court: the party should come to prove the indictment. He gat him a counsellor to declare the case. When the judge was ready to hear it, his counsellor fell a discoursing of the fight at Cannas, the battle with Mithridates, the wrongs and injuries sustained by the Africans. Thus, when he had filled their ears a great while with din, thumping on the bar, and squeaking in his small pipes; Martial, tendering his own cause more than the babbling of his vain advocate, at length pulled him by the sleeve, and said: "And please your worship, I gave ye my fee to talk of three goats." And thus had I need to put you in remembrance. For where ye appointed to speak of God's service, ye tell us a tale of this man and that man; what he did, and they did: and yet not a word what God hath commanded.

Fol. 82.

Martiall corrupteth Tertullian.

Ye call us curious, when we require Scripture. We can get at your hands nothing else but custom. And, speaking of custom, according to your custom ye make a lie, and falsify Tertullian. For these are your words: "We say with Tertullian, that custom, increaser, confirmer, and observer of faith, taught this use of the Cross," &c. As if the increase, confirmation, and observing of faith proceeded of custom. His words are otherwise. For, speaking of his traditions, he saith: *Si legem expostules Scripturarum, nullam reperies. Traditio tibi prætendetur auctrix, consuetudo confirmatrix, et fides observatrix;* "If thou demand a law of Scripture for these, thou shalt find none. Tradition shall be pretended to thee as increaser, custom confirmer, and faith observer of them."

[1] Epig. Lib. vi. [19.]

Where you may see, that custom is not made increaser and confirmer of faith, but faith observer of custom. Notwithstanding, I must still bear with you: for ye be driven to narrow shifts, and fain would ye say something. But it is a foul shift to make a lie. This custom, ye prove, came of tradition. "For," (as Tertullian saith[2],) "how can a thing be used, if it were not first delivered?" To grant it a tradition, I will not stick with you. But Tertullian will have the same to be builded upon reason, or else he refuseth it. He maketh the antithesis, not between written and unwritten, but between written and reasonable. And so he thinketh a tradition not written to be admitted, so it be reasonable. Therefore he saith: *Rationem traditioni, consuetudini, fidei patrocinaturam perspicies:* "Ye shall see that reason will defend tradition, custom, and faith." And afterward: *Non differt scriptura an ratione consistat, quando et legem ratio commendet:* "It is no matter whether custom consist of writing or of reason, inasmuch as reason also commendeth law." So that reasonable must be the tradition. And how shall this reasonable be defined? Tertullian himself doth tell you; limiting how a man may make a custom, if he conceive and decree *duntaxat quod Deo congruat, quod disciplinæ conducat, quod saluti proficiat:* "Only that is agreeable to God, furthering unto discipline, and profitable to salvation." If the tradition of the Cross sign may be proved to be such, I will yield unto you with all my heart.

Consider the reasons and the examples that the Doctor useth. First, of the Lord's authority, who said: *Cur non et a vobis ipsis quod justum est judicatis? Ut non de judicio tantum, sed de omni sententia rerum examinandarum:* "'Why do you not of yourselves judge that that is righteous[3]?' That it be not only understood of judgment, but of every sentence of things to be examined." And it followeth: *Dicit et Apostolus, Si quid ignoratis, Deus vobis revelabit. Solitus et ipse consilium subministrare, cum præceptum Domini non habebat, et quædam edicere a semetipso; sed et ipse Spiritum Dei habens, deductorem omnis veritatis. Itaque consilium et edictum ejus divini jam præcepti instar*

Martiall is still by his own authors overthrown.

[2] ["Quomodo enim usurpari quid potest, si traditum prius non est?"] Tertullian. De Corona Militis. [Cap. iii.]

[3] [S. Luke xii. 57.]

obtinuit, de rationis divinæ patrocinio. Hanc nunc expostula; salvo traditionis respectu, quocunque traditore censetur: nec authorem respicias, sed authoritatem, &c.: "And the Apostle saith, 'If ye be ignorant of anything, God shall reveal it to you[1].' He himself, when he had not a commandment from the Lord, was wont to give counsel, and prescribe some things of himself[2]; but as one that had the Spirit of God, director of all truth. Wherefore, his counsel and edict hath now obtained to be, (as it were,) the commandment of God, through supportation and defence of the reason divine. This reason inquire for; saving the respect of tradition, whosoever be the deliverer thereof: nor respect the author, but the authority."

So far Tertullian. And in his words many notable points are to be observed. First, that in all judgments and examinations of things, we must follow that that is right and good. Then, that no man presume to ordain anything in the Church, unless he have the Spirit of God to guide him. Thirdly, that S. Paul's tradition should not have stood in force, unless it had been consonant unto the Scripture. Fourthly, that in all customs, we must have an eye unto God's law, seek what accordeth to it; having no respect to the custom-maker, but Scripture-confirmer. Thus ye might have learned how to judge of traditions. Tertullian might have taught you. But as soon as ever you had made a lie of him, there ye left him.

In a custom-maker, the Spirit of God in custom, commodity and agreeableness to Scripture, must be considered.

Folio 82, a. Basil.

To Basil, who saith[3], "If we reject and cast away customs, which are not written, as things of no great value or price, we shall condemn, before we be ware, those things which in the Gospel are accompted necessary to salvation;"

---

[1] [Phil. iii. 15.]   [2] [1 Cor. vii. 12, 25, 40.]

[3] ["Nam si consuetudines, quæ scripto proditæ non sunt, tanquam haud multum habentes momenti, conemur rejicere, imprudentes et ea damnabimus quæ in Evangelio necessaria ad salutem habentur." (*De Spiritu Sancto*, Cap. xxvii. p. 104. edit. princ. Erasm. interp. Basil. 1532.) Erasmus, who first translated this work, informs us, in his dedicatory Epistle to Joannes Dantiscus, that when he had accomplished half of his task, without weariness, he perceived that the style of the treatise became greatly changed; and hence he was led to suspect, "studiosum quempiam, quo volumen redderet auctius, multa intertexuisse, vel ex aliis autoribus decerpta emblemata, vel ex sese reperta."]

I answer, that of traditions there be three kinds. Some *Three kinds of traditions.* that necessarily are inferred of the Scripture. Such were 1. the Apostle's traditions: as, that a woman in the congregation should not be bare-headed; that in the congregation she should keep silence: that the poor should labour with their own hands, and get their living. Which all, and such other, although they were not expressly in the word, yet consequently they followed of the word. And therefore Paul did not obtrude them of his authority, but by the Scripture prove them. These, and the like, I confess to be necessary, and of all Christians to be retained. Prove ye the Cross sign to be one of these, and I will recant. But there 2. have been other things delivered to the Church, direct contrary to the word: as, Latin service, worshipping of Images, vowing of chastity, communicating under one kind, and an infinite number of popish prescriptions. These ought not in any wise to be received; but, (what pretext of antiquity or authority soever they have,) be utterly refused.

The third kind of traditions is of such as be indifferent; 3. neither utterly repugnant to the word of God, nor necessarily inferred of it. Herein we must follow the order of *In traditions indifferent, what to be observed.* the Church; and yet not absolutely, but with a limitation. First we must see, that those observances be not set forth as a piece of God's service, wherein some special point of holiness or Religion shall consist. For they may be kept for order, for policy, for profit of the Church: but otherwise the Scripture itself hath God's store, and plenty of things, expedient for His honour and service, our comfort and salvation. *Felix Ecclesia*, (sayeth Tertullian [4],) *cui totam doctrinam Apostoli cum sanguine* [*suo*] *profuderunt:* "Happy is the Church, to whom the Apostles poured out the whole doctrine, together with their blood." There is no insufficiency, no imperfection. Therefore we must especially beware, that in our traditions, indifferent of themselves, we repose no holiness or devotion. Then also, that we think them not to be of such necessity, that at no time they may be removed. The Church must still retain her right to be judge and determiner of such traditions: either to bear with them,

---

[4] Tertul. De præscrip. adver. Hæreti. [Cap. xxxvi.—Tertullian was speaking of the Church of Rome, when he exclaimed, "Ista quam felix Ecclesia"! &c.]

or else abolish them, as best may serve for edification. Last of all, this must not be forgotten; that the people of God sometime be oppressed with traditions and ceremonies; and, for outward solemnities, the inward true service of God is neglected. As in the popish Church, on a high day, there are so many gaudes[1], that there is no place for a preacher. Wherefore, the superfluities, the long train of ceremonies, must be cut off; lest they do hinder the course of godliness, and by gay shew engender a confidence to be put in them. S. Augustin, in his time, complained that the Church was too full of presumptions. And of them, that have been added since, a man may make many large volumes.

<small>The Church had too many ceremonies in Augustin's time.</small>

Wherefore, these provisos had, the order of the Church, (I mean not Rome, for that is no member of it;) may be kept in traditions which are indifferent. But in this number you cannot justly comprise the Cross. And although of some Fathers it hath been accompted such, yet must ye remember, (as I said before,) that they did not alway build gold and silver, but sometime hay and stubble, upon Christ. Nor every thing, that is pretended to be the Fathers' writings, must by and by be thought to be theirs. Many bastard babes have been put in the cradle; either when there was no lawful child, or the same overlaid and stifled by the nurse. As, for example, Athanasius, (whom you cite for proof that the Cross was used in his time;) hath many things that be none of his. Evagrius, in the Ecclesiastical History[2], doth plainly say, that many works of Apollinarius were ascribed unto him. And as for the book, which you allege, *Quæstionum ad Antiochium*, [*Antiochum*,] is evident to be another's; for Athanasius himself is cited in it[3]. The words are these: *Et hæc quidem multum valens in divina Scriptura magnus Athanasius:* "And these things did great Athanasius, a mighty one in the Scripture of God." Would Athanasius have reported this of himself? Wherefore, in that ye bring prescription of time and writings of the Fathers for you, ye do both reason upon an uncertain principle, and fail in your proof. For the principle, I say, and I doubt

<small>Fol. 84, a.
Athanasius.

Evagrius.</small>

[1] [Ostentatious rites.]
[2] Li. iii. Cap. xxxi. [p. 766. ed. Lat. Basil. 1549.]
[3] Quæst. xxiii. [Vide supra, pp. 73—4; et Bellarm. *De Scriptt. Eccles.* p. 65. Romæ, 1613.]

not but ye will subscribe unto me; that whatsoever hath been delivered, and otherwise esteemed Apostolic, is not to be followed and thought inviolable.

To begin with that, which bred in the Church a miserable schism for many years together, the Easter fast[4]: was it always, and in every place, uniformly observed? Nothing less. All the Asians dissented from the Romans; and each of them said they had a tradition, yea, from the Apostles. The Asians would have Easter-day to be the fourteenth of the month Nisan, howsoever it fell; were it either the first, second, third, fourth, fifth, or sixth fery[5]. The Romans would have it only on that day which is called *Dominicus,* " the Sabbath." The Asians were the stronger part. They had Philip the Apostle, and his daughters; John the Evangelist, and Polycarpus, his scholar, for them. The Romans had the whole succession of Bishops, from Peter forward. Which of these parts will you approve? Ye are a Romanist, and therefore ye will hold with Anicetus rather; following the custom that is of him received. But now ye must not condemn the other, lest ye be guilty of the same crime that Irenæus did reprove in Victor. For he held it tyranny, to throw the thunderbolt of excommunication, for a little storm that rose of ceremony. Notwithstanding, they squared still. For when Polycarpus came to Rome, Anicetus being Bishop there, many quarrels there were betwixt them, well afterward composed; but of this point they could not agree. *Neque enim Anicetus Polycarpo persuadere* [*suadere*] *poterat, ne servaret quæ cum Joanne Discipulo Domini nostri, ac reliquis Apostolis, quibuscum fuerat conversatus, semper servaverat. Nec Polycarpus Aniceto suasit ut servaret; qui sibi Presbyterorum, quibus successerat, consuetudinem servandam esse dicebat. Et cum ista sic haberent, communionem inter se habuerunt:* "For Anicetus could not," (as Eusebius saith[6],) " win Polycarpus, that he should not keep those things which, (with John the Disciple of our Lord, and the rest of the Apostles, with whom he was conversant,) hitherto he had

Easter fast. Read Eusebius in the Eccle. His. the v. book, the xxiv. xxv. and xxvi. cha.

---

[4] [Vid. Ussher's *Religion of the ancient Irish and British,* Chap. ix. p. 92. Lond. 1631. Beaven's *Account of S. Irenæus,* pp. 44—53. Lond. 1841.]

[5] [Holy-day.]

[6] [*Hist. Eccles.* v. xxvi. 83. interp. Muscul.]

kept. Nor Polycarpus could persuade Anicetus to yield unto them; who said that the custom of the Elders, whom he had succeeded, was to be kept of him. And whereas things stood on this sort, yet had they a communion betwixt them."

For diversity in traditions and ceremonies, men not to be condemned.

A worthy example for this our age; wherein such Victorines as you, (M. Martiall,) will by and by condemn of schism and heresy whosoever in traditions do not agree with you. These holy Fathers dissented in opinion of the mean actions: yet in the end they joined; and by the way friendly communicated. We, because we do not in opinion agree; because we go not against our conscience and the word of God, are accompted heretics. "But after the way, (which you call heresy,) we worship the God of our fathers; believing all things which are written in the Law and Prophets[1]." If so great offence hang upon transgressing of Tradition, we shall condemn all faithful before us, all congregations, and Rome itself. For it was

Polycarpus. Traditions, how they vary.

a tradition, in Polycarpus' time, to keep Easter-day sometime on one day, sometime on another. And Irenæus reporteth of him: *Hic docuit semper quæ ab Apostolis didicerat; quæ et Ecclesiæ tradidit, et sola sunt vera*[2]: "He taught always those things that he learned of the Apostles; and those he delivered unto the Church, and they only be true." Yet you observe the Easter on one day ever; the Sunday, (as you call it.) It was a tradition, in Tertullian's time[3], to give milk and honey to Infants at their Christening; and this he held Apostolic: yet you keep it not. It was a tradition, in Augustin's time[4], that men should not fast from Easter to Whitsuntide: yet you decree the contrary. It was a tradition, in Cyprian's time[5], (which Augustin also confirmeth;) that the Supper of the Lord should be ministered to Infants; and this was thought necessary to salvation: yet you decline from this. It was a tradition, in Epiphanius' time[6], that for six days before Easter men should eat nothing but bread and drink with a little salt: yet you observe not this. It was a tradition, in Basil's time[7], (which also Tertullian doth record;) that

---

[1] Act. xxiv. [14.]   [2] Irenæus, Contra Hær. Li. iii. Cap. iii.
[3] Tertul. De Corona Militis. [Cap. iii.]
[4] Augustinus Casulano. [Epist. xxxvi.]
[5] Cyprian. De lapsis. [*Opp.* p. 132. ed. Oxon.]
[6] Epiphanius, Adversus Arrium. [*Hæres.* lxix.]
[7] Basilius, De Spir. Sanct. [Cap. xxvii. p. 107.]

no man should serve God with bowing of the knee on the Sabbath-day, nor yet all the time from Easter to Whitsuntide: yet you mislike with this. Wherefore, sith traditions, honoured with the name of the Apostles, accompted of the Fathers and Doctors necessary, do notwithstanding so often vary, and you yourselves in no wise admit them; what reason is it, that we should be condemned for refusal of the like; which, with less reason, more inconvenience, it pleaseth yourselves to confirm and stablish?

I have hitherto had in hand your two first points; and stretching them a little, they be broken both. For neither have you proved sufficiently, that they of the primitive Church used the sign of the Cross themselves, and counselled other to do the like; nor, if it had been proved, it were sufficient to drive me to assent. Now to the third, "that the said Cross was erected in every place;" although in the third article I have in part declared the contrary, yet to your further proof I must answer something. And so, first, to your Martialis[8], (though he were last found; after fourteen hundreth years' sleep and odd, suddenly astarted;) I say, King Arthur was a noble King: he had twelve Knights of the round table; and whether Launcelot du Lake were one of them, I do not well remember: but he was a Martial man too: he was a doughty Knight: he did many worthy feats, as it followeth in the text. Are ye not ashamed to vouch him to be one of the seventy and two Disciples, whom neither they of the Apostles' time, nor they that succeeded after, ever mentioned or knew? Shall he now by miracle be raked out of a dunghill, where he hath lien a stinking fourteen hundreth years? Shall we now disprove Eusebius, and all other writers, to make your matter good? Yet, to say the truth, his words, without wringing or wresting at all, be taken of soberer wits than your own to import much less than you do talk of. For we may have the Cross in a sign, (according to the words of Christ in His last Supper, "Do this, as oft as ye do it, in remembrance of Me;") though we have not the sign of the Cross. Therefore you be forsworn once; for ye said: "In good faith it could not be so."

Martialis.

Fol. 83, b.

Seek for this about the beginning of the first article.

Folio 83, b.

But what shall I seek for any truth of you, who, shaving your crown, have shaken all honesty and faith from you?

[8] [Vid. ante, p. 69.]

Folio 84, b.
Athanasius.

You wish with a sigh, (alack, good heart!) "that the readers should see, how, in the time of Athanasius, christian men made Crosses, like unto the Cross of Christ, and adored the same." I should here pass the bounds of modesty, and justly offend the good reader's ears, if I should answer according to your professed impudency, and shameless deserving. Thought you that your writing should never come to scanning? Was it not enough for you to belie them that be most unlike you, the Ministers of the Church of Christ now living; but that you would still falsify the Scriptures, and make lies of the Fathers? Remember your writings: your words are

Folio 84, a.

these: "Now that it stayed not here, but was set up and had in reverence in other places, and other ages, it appeareth by Athanasius: who, asking the question, Why all faithful christian men make Crosses like unto the Cross of Christ, and make nothing like to the spear, reed, or sponge, being holy as the Cross; answereth and sayeth: *Crucis certe figuram, ex duobus lignis componentes, adoramus,* &c.: 'We certes, making the figure of the Cross of two pieces of wood, adore and worship it.'"

These are your words: yours I may call them, for they be furthest off from Athanasius' meaning. And in the margent the place is quoted; *Quæst.* xxxix. *ad Anti.* Here

Martiall maketh three lies of Athanasius together.

be three lies together. First, by suppressing a piece of Athanasius: saying of the spear, reed, and sponge, that they are "holy as the Cross;" where the author hath, that they are "as holy as the Cross." Then remember this "as." Also, by corrupting of the text, putting in the words of "adore and worship," which are not in the book. Last of all, referring us to the thirty-ninth Question, whereas there are not so many in all. Indeed, *Quæstione* xvi., these are his words[1]: *Quare credentes omnes ad Crucis Imaginem Cruces facimus; lanceæ vero sanctæ, aut arundinis, aut spongiæ figuras nullas conficimus: cum tamen hæc tam sint sancta, quam ipsa Crux? Responsio. Figuram quidem Crucis, ex duobus lignis compingentes, conficimus; ut si quis infidelium id in nobis reprehendat, quod veneremur lignum, possimus duobus inter se disjunctis lignis, et Crucis dirempta forma, ea tanquam inutilia ligna reputare; et infideli persuadere, quod non colamus lignum, sed quod' Crucis typum venere-*

---

[1] Quæst. xvi. ad Antio. [Vide supra, pp. 73—4.]

mur: in lancea vero, aut spongia, vel arundine, nec facere hoc, nec ostendere possimus. Which in English are these: "Why do all believers make Crosses after the Image of the Cross; but make no figures or likenesses of the spear, the reed, or the sponge: whereas, notwithstanding, these are as holy as the Cross itself? The answer. We make indeed the figure of the Cross, by putting of two sticks together; that if any of the infidels reprove that in us, that we worship wood, we may, by separating two pieces of wood, and taking away the form of a Cross, accompt them as unprofitable sticks; and persuade the infidel, that we worship not wood, but the thing represented by the Cross: which in the spear, sponge, or reed, we neither can do nor shew."

Here, first, it is evident, that the reed or spear is as holy as the Cross, and therefore as well to be worshipped as the Cross, although the word of comparison you would fain suppress. Then, that there is not any word or half word for worshipping: yea, the whole sequel of the matter doth convince the contrary. Yet your honesty is such, as to put in of your own, (under name of Athanasius,) "adore and worship." By the Pope's own law[2], (for being such a falsary,) ye should have your crown pared, and be made an abbey-lubber as long as ye live. And may not I use the words of your zealous spirit, and say: "Ah! see, good readers, what a sot we have to do withal?" Because ye read, (or hear say at the least,) that a Cross was made, therefore ye conclude it was set in the Rood-loft: for "no man," (say you,) "maketh him a velvet coat to lay it up in his press, or his friend's picture to be put in the coal-house." But doth any wise man, when he hath a new garment, proclaim it in the market-place? or hang the counterfeit of his friend upon a pole to be seen? By your own slender reason, as ye judge of the one, so imagine of the other.

Folio 84, b.

Now, to come to the Ecclesiastical History, where mention is made of the Idol Serapis[3]; I would the readers

[2] Dist. 1. Ca. Si Episcopus. ["Si Episcopus, Presbyter, aut Diaconus capitale crimen commiserit, aut chartam falsaverit, aut falsum testimonium dixerit; ab officii honore depositus, in Monasterium retrudatur: et ibi, quamdiu vixerit, laicam tantummodo communionem accipiat."]

[3] [Cf. Mariana, *De rebus Hispaniæ*, Tom. i. Lib. iv. p. 159. Moguntiæ. 1605.]

[CALFHILL.]

Roods, Crosses, Images, counterfeits of Serapis.

should well consider it. For Roods, Crosses, and Images, have been nothing else but counterfeits of Serapis. The Priests of Egypt, the votaries of those days, (for Ruffinus[1] calleth them ἀγνεύοντας; such as had made themselves, (and God will,) chaste;) set me up in their temple a monstrous Idol, reaching from one side of the wall to the other. To purchase more credit to it, they had made a little window eastward, where the morning Sun might glimmer in, and, taking the just height of their Idol, should shine no lower nor higher than they would; but that, when their god was shrined, might be full in his face, and upon his lips. And so by this means a miracle was wrought: the Sun with a kiss bade him welcome to church. Again, where the nature of the loadstone is to draw iron to it, they made, (as curiously as workmanship could devise,) the Image of the Sun in iron: that whereas the Sun was in the vawte[2], and the Image directly underneath it, the Image sometime might rise and hang in the air. But lest the ponderosity of the metal might come to his course again, they conveyed it away, and said: "The Sun hath now taken his leave of Serapis, and gone to his business." These and such other inventions they had to deceive the people. Such hayes[3] they pitched to purchase their profit. But these were but gross, in respect of the fineness of our Parish-Priests and popish Chaplains[4]. For they have made Roods with rolling eyes and sweating brows, with speaking mouth and walking feet. I report me to the Rood of Grace, the Rood of Winchester, the very Cross of Ludlow, and Jack Knacker of Witney. Nor marvel if the Cross be so deep in your books, that can stand a high-lone, and walk on the Altar; that can run in the night-time from S. John's chapel into our Lady's, and will not for jealousy abide from her.

But I would the world should understand, that as the Egyptians and Christians, Serapis and the Cross sign, in name do differ; so the Priests of them both be of one

---

[1] Ruffinus, Ecclesias. Hi. Lib. ii. Cap. xxiii. [Inter *Eccl. Hist. Auctt.* p. 259.]

[2] [vault.]

[3] [Nets for catching rabbits.]

[4] [See Marchetti's *Official Memoirs;* translated by the Rev. B. Rayment. Lond. 1801.]

Religion, like conversation. Tyrannus, a Chantry-Priest[5], serving at Saturnus' altar, had a way to creep into his god's belly; (for he was hollow, as most part of our Images are, meet for to make swine's troughs:) and whensoever any gentlewoman's devotion served her to come to make her orisons, if the Priest liked her person, answer was made from within, that she must abide there all that night, in privy contemplations. The silly husband was glad that he had any thing to do his god a pleasure; and therefore would deck her and trim her up in her holy-day array: and to church she goeth, with penny in her purse, and taper in her hand, to offer for her sins. The Priest, before all the people, shuts the church-door; he leaves the woman within, and home he goeth. But afterward, by a privy vault underneath the ground, he conveys himself into the body of the Image: and while the lamps be burning, and she praying, he roareth somewhat out of his trunk; partly to fear her, partly also to make her well apaid, that she should be worthied to have a god to talk to her. But when he had wrought whatsoever he thought good, either to astony her, or entice her to folly, then suddenly, by a vice, all the candles go out; he playeth the Priest, &c. Thus, in conclusion, many honest men's wives, many worshipful and honourable, under colour of holiness, and by mere hypocrisy, were instruments many years to satisfy the pleasure of the filthy Priest. At length, a discreeter matron than the rest, abhorring the vice, and observing the manner of it, knew the Priest's voice, and detected it to her husband. Hereupon the Priest was apprehended; the Idol ransacked; the starting holes espied; the crimes confessed; the hypocrisy abhorred.

And, would to God, that the like wickedness, and far more horrible, daily committed by the unchaste generation of sole-lived Priests, might cause alike all countries and nations to detest your shame. Ye blame lawful marriage: ye think it a life dissolute, and satisfying of the lusts of the flesh. But how live ye? how live ye? With viler shifts than Saturnus' Priest. Adultery no fault. For the most part ye practise it all. It is worse, it is worse. I appeal to your conscience, (M. Martiall,) whether ye know it to be so, or no? Myself will not speak what I do know. But accursed be he, that taught

[5] Ruffinus, Eccl. Hist. Lib. ii. Cap. xxv. [p. 260. ed. Basil. 1549.]

the boys of Winchester to know that, which M. Hide, (ye remember,) so severely punished. Ye lay unto our charge pride, carnal lusts, sensuality, much babble of the Lord, no good works in Christ, in talk much vehemency, in deed no charity: and of late there hath stepped up a famous Clerk, who, sifting a private fault in one only person that professeth the truth, and exaggerating the same, concludeth with doting Demipho: *Unum nôsti, omnes noveris:* "Know one, and know all." And may I not answer as unto Davus, *Ad pistrinum vel capistrum Dave?* But if I should unrip, (as, if ye leave not your slanders, I will do by God's grace, if life and leisure serve me;) the lives of your popish Doctors, and your own selves; O Lord, what perjury, what impiety, what incontinency, what sodomitry, would burst out together! But here I stay, and will return to Serapis.

Schoolmaster of Winchester.

LewesEuank. [Lewis Evans.]

Folio 85, a.

I told you before, that if ye would have any precedent of the Cross sign, ye must go to the Egyptians' Idol Serapis. The Christians, therefore, thinking that a mean to bring them sooner unto the faith, pulled down the scutcheons of the Idol, and in every place set up the Cross[1]: not to have them fall from one Idolatry to another, (which is by worship of it;) but that it might be an introduction unto further knowledge, and procuring of a credit unto our Religion. For the Cross being one of their letters, which they called ἱερατικαὶ, "priestly and holy letters[2]," made them, for affection to their own tradition, think the better of ours. For the author saith: *Qui tunc, admiratione rerum gestarum, convertebantur ad fidem, dicebant, ita sibi ab antiquis traditum; quod hæc, quæ nunc coluntur, tamdiu starent, quamdiu viderent signum istud venisse in quo esset vita. Unde accidit, ut magis ii, [hi,] qui erant ex Sacerdotibus vel Ministris templorum, ad fidem converterentur, quam illi, quos errorum pro vestigiæ [præstigiæ] et deceptionum machinæ delectabant:* "They which, by wondering at things that were done, were converted to the faith, said, that it was told them of old, that these things, which now are worshipped, should stand so long as they should see that that sign was come, in which there was life. Whereof

[1] Ruffinus, Ecclesia. His. Lib. ii. Ca. xxix. [p. 261.]
[2] [See Wall's *Ancient Orthography of the Jews*, Part i. Chap. ii. p. 45. Lond. 1835.]

it came to pass, that rather they, which were of the Priests and Ministers of the church, were converted to the faith, than such as took a pleasure in sorceries of error, and trains of deceit." So that it was better than a preaching unto them, because they had such a prejudice thereof. Now if the case were, that Heathen should be converted to the faith, and they beforehand had the Cross in reverence, I would in this respect admit it. But among Christians, where The crucified is daily preached, and ought to be known without such external mean, great folly it is to have it.

Hitherto of the doings in Alexandria. Now, to come to Constantinople: as touching Chrysostom, I have said enough in the first article. Only therefore will I add this, which may be a bone for you to pick on; that whereas he speaketh[3] of houses, markets, wildernesses, highways, sea, ships, garments, parlours, walls, windows, armour, and such other things, where the Cross should be, only he saith not, that the Cross was in the church. Reckoning up so many, would he have forgotten the chief, if any such order had been received then? It is not credible. Augustin, (if ye were not too wilfully set,) should not be urged of you[4]. For he meaneth nothing less than either the material or your mystical Cross. He plainly speaketh of the passion of Christ: and incident into that is the form thereof, which was His suffering upon the Cross: *Crux Christi,* (saith he,) *feriæ sunt, et nundinæ spirituales:* "The Cross of Christ is our holy feast, and spiritual fair." Do ye keep the feast unto the piece of wood? Do ye buy anything of the external sign? If ye do not, ye mistake S. Augustin. For immediately upon the foresaid words he inferreth those that you allege: "Before the Cross was a name of condemnation; now it is made a matter of honour: before it stood in damnation of a curse; now it is set up in occasion of salvation." Where I grant, indeed, that he maketh a difference between the Cross in the old Law, and Cross in the new Law: but what is meant by that Cross? The material thing? That is but as you guess; for I am sure of the contrary. The Scripture saith not, *Maledictum lignum,* "Cursed is the tree;" but, *Maledictus omnis qui pendet*

Folio 85, a.

---

[3] Chrysostom. Demonst. contra Gentiles. [Supra, p. 63.]
[4] August. De Cruce et Latrone. [Vid. ante, pag. 63. not. 2.]

in ligno, "Cursed is every one that hangeth on the tree[1]." Wherefore your collection is vain, "that as then the material Cross was a name of ignominy, so now the material Cross is a thing of honour." Did the ignominy consist in the wood then? No, but in the person. For if ye were hanged, M. Martiall, (to use a familiar example,) the shame were not in the gallows, but in yourself, man. Then the honour is not in the material Cross, but Him that died on it. And that the words, (*Nunc erecta est,* "is now at this present set up,") cannot be racked to a metaphorical sense is very strange to me: for if it be true, that *Christus idem heri et hodie,* that "Christ is the same both to-day and yesterday[2];" and that He is the Lamb, *Qui occisus est ab origine mundi,* "which was slain from the beginning of the world[3];" methinketh it is no absurdity to say, that now at this present, in the time of grace, Christ daily suffereth; His passion is set out as a spectacle unto us[4].

Folio 86. Constantine.

And now, to conclude with Constantine the Great; whose fact is such a defence unto you, that ye think yourself full armed with it: but without any school-play, with a downright blow, ye may be touched on the bare. For although Constantinus, (not fully yet instructed in the faith,) "sometime defended his face with the sign of salvation; sometime shewed forth the victorious banner; sometime erected it in a painted table; sometime did hang it up before the courtgate;" yet we never read, that of so many churches as, (you say,) he builded, he brought the sign of the Cross into any of them[5]. Then did he not repose any holiness therein, nor his doings otherwise are to be drawn to example;

---

[1] Deut. xxi. [23.] Gal. iii. [13.]   [2] Heb. xiii. [8.]
[3] Apo. [Rev.] xiii. [8.]   [4] [Galat. iii. 1.]
[5] [Bellarmin (*De Imagin.* L. ii. C. ix.) informs us that "Eusebius, lib. 3. & 4. de vita Constantini, dicit, in templis a Constantino exstructis in Palæstina, fuisse maximam copiam Imaginum aurearum et argentearum." Unfortunately for the Cardinal's veracity, Eusebius merely records the number "ἀναθημάτων χρυσοῦ καὶ ἀργύρου." (Lib. iii. Cap. xl.) It is to be hoped, nevertheless, that Bellarmin's offence may be palliated by the fact, that he may possibly have adopted, through negligence, the shameless corruption of the passage in the Latin version by Joannes Portesius, who has transformed "*Donaria*" into "*Imagines.*" (p. 681. edit. Basil. 1559. Conf. Dallæum, *De Imagg.* Lib. iii. pp. 255—6. Lugd. Bat. 1642.)]

unless ye have need to return with him from paganism to the faith, and have as large commission as he. Wherefore, sith your ignorance understandeth not the Fathers' writings; sith your impudency falsely corrupteth them; sith presumptions have always cumbered the Church of God; and traditions in every age with every sere[6] Bishop varied; we are not to be thought otherwise than followers of the Apostles, although we decline from some thing that men have called, and in their conceits reputed, Apostolic. Flatter not yourself, as if any were so mad, having common sense, to be persuaded with your glorious words, which in every leaf have so good trial of your shameless lies. Learn what the Church is; then talk thereof. Be a member of the Church, and I will make more accompt of you. Be no preacher to other of their soul health, unless ye take better order for your own.

[6] [late.—" O *seri* studiorum."—See note 4, p. 228.]

TO THE SIXTH ARTICLE.

Martiall.
Fol. 88.

"That divers holy men and women got little pieces of the holy Cross, and enclosed them in gold or silver; and either left them in churches to be worshipped, or hanged them about their necks, thereby to be the better warded." To which assertion, considering what in the articles afore hath been said and proved, a short answer may serve. For inasmuch as all your reasons be grounded on a false principle, (authority of men, which in God's matters can take no place;) ye spend in this article a great many moe words than all the matter in your book is worth. Tertullian himself[1], speaking of a tradition more reasonable than this, pretendeth not authority, but saith that he will prove, *Hoc exigere veritatem: cui nemo præscribere potest; non spatium temporum, non patrocinia personarum, non privilegium* [al. *privilegia*] *regionum. Ex hiis enim fere consuetudo, initium ab aliqua ignorantia vel simplicitate sortita, in usum per successionem corroboratur, et ita adversus veritatem vindicatur. Sed Dominus noster Christus Veritatem Se, non consuetudinem cognominavit. Si semper Christus, et prior omnibus, æque veritas sempiterna et antiqua res:* "That the truth requireth this: against the which no person, no space of time, no mastership of men, no privilege of countries, can prescribe. For most commonly by the mean of these, custom, (that began of some ignorance or simplicity,) is by succession confirmed into an use, and so exception taken against the truth. But Christ our Lord called Himself the Truth[2], and not the custom. If Christ be always, and before all, the truth itself is as well eternal, and of most ancienty[3]." Let them consider and mark well this, who accompt it new, that in itself is old. No novelty, but verity, confoundeth heresy. Whatsoever is against the

---

[1] Tertullian. De Virginibus velandis. [ad init.]
[2] [S. John xiv. 6.]
[3] [" Ἐμοὶ δὲ ἀρχεῖά ἐστιν Ἰησοῦς Χριστός." (S. Ignatii *Ep. ad Philadel*. §. viii.)]

truth, the same is heresy: yea, the old custom itself, as saith Tertullian.

Wherefore ye should not presume so much upon the credit of Helena, Paulinus, Gregory, that whatsoever they did should be a sufficient precedent for us to do the like. The Fathers of the Old and the New Testament are not to be drawn for example always. For then why not David defend an adulterer, and a lecherous captain willing to despatch his trusty soldier? Why were it any fault to abjure the faith, or otherwise dissemble with God, if the like fact in Peter[4] might be followed? Augustin very wisely saith[5]: *Non debemus imitari semper aut probare quicquid probati homines egerunt; sed judicium Scripturarum adhibere, an illæ probent ea facta:* "We must not always imitate or allow whatsoever allowed persons have done; but lay the judgment of Scriptures to it, whether they allow the doing of it." If then I drove you unto this issue, that ye should prove by the word of God the alleged examples good, ye had need to require a longer term, and yet in the end you would make a non-suit. For ye shall not find in all the Scripture any piece of word, or example of any, that can by force be wrested to the reservation of little scraps of wood, or reposing any hope or affiance in them. Too vain and heathenish is that observance: too foul and horrible is that Idolatry.

Yet will I not deface those forenamed persons, upon whose authority ye ground yourself; nor say that otherwise they were ungodly, though in this point no godliness appeared. Paul writeth of the Jews in his time thus: *Testimonium illis perhibeo, quod studium Dei habent, sed non secundum scientiam:* "I bear them record, that they have the zeal of God, but not according to knowledge[6]." And I doubt not but these whom you have named had a zeal

---

[4] [Gal. ii. 11—13.]

[5] ["Non itaque debemus quidquid in Scripturis etiam Dei testimonio laudatos homines fecisse legerimus, consentiendo approbare, sed considerando discernere; adhibentes judicium non sane nostræ auctoritatis, sed Scripturarum divinarum atque sanctarum:" &c.] Aug. Contra ii. Ep. Gauden. Lib. ii. [*Contra Gaudent.* Lib. i. Cap. xxxi Opp. Tom. ix.]

[6] Rom. x. [2.]

of their own; thought to serve God: yet, serving their fancy first, they did offend against the majesty of God, and were occasion of fall to many that came after. The holy Chronicles[1] report of Jehosaphat, that "he walked in the first ways of his father David, and sought not Baalim; but sought the Lord God of his father, and walked in His commandments, and not after the trade of Israel." The like testimony also is given him in the xx. ch.: Jehosaphat "walked in the way of Asa his father, and departed not therefrom; doing that which was right in the sight of the Lord. Notwithstanding, the high places were not taken away." Beside this, he made affinity with Ahab, "and loved them that hated the Lord[2]." Did any man therefore, for those imperfections, condemn Jehosaphat as a wicked Prince? Or will any man excuse him for the same? On like sort, I will not utterly disprove your authors. I think not the contrary, but that they were God's children; although in this matter, for which their authority is pretended, there is none with safe conscience that can like with them. Gideon, among the Judges of Israel, was the least stained; yet, through devotion, (as he esteemed it,) he grievously sinned against the Lord[3]. For when, as a mighty champion, he returned home from conquest of Midiam, the soldiers laden with golden prey, he required their ear-rings to be given to him. Which amounting to a great sum, he made an Ephod of it; he deputed it to holy uses; and served in the tabernacle. By which means it came to pass, that all Israel went a whoring after it, and it was the destruction of Gideon and his house.

So that we see by David, by Peter, by Jehosaphat, by Gideon, that men, of singular graces otherwise, sometime do fall into great absurdities, and are not to be drawn to imitation. Which thing I speak unto this end; that you shall not say I condemn your Fathers as Infidels and Idolaters, although unadvisedly they gave too just occasion of such offence to other. Yet were it no deadly sin, if I called Nicephorus and Gregory fabulous; Paulinus and Helena superstitious: which as I have already in part proved, so were it easy to be confirmed. But I had rather as men excuse them, than as Gods follow them. The Pharisees did wear

---

[1] 2 Par. xvii. [3, 4.]
[2] 2 Paral. [Chron.] xix. [2.]   [3] Jud. viii. [24—27.]

their phylacteries, their scrolls of parchment, upon their long robes, wherein the Commandments of God were written. A juster pretence had they to continue that ceremony, (the word of God commanding them that the Law should never depart from their eyes[4];) than ever any had for pieces of the Cross. Notwithstanding, Christ reproved their hypocrisy, and pronounced upon them the heavy woe[5]. Shall not this be done unto all them, that for a vain glory devise a will-worship; and ascribe their defence to a rotten stick, that only dependeth on the providence of God? If ye think the comparisons are not like; the writing of the Commandments on the coat, and enclosing a piece of the Cross in gold; then read what Hierom sayeth. Lay down affection; and, to condemn your error, speak out your conscience. His words are these[6]: *Non intelligentibus Phariscæis quod hæc in corde portanda sunt, non in corpore: alioquin et armaria et arcæ habent libros, et notitiam Dei non habent. Hoc apud nos superstitiosæ mulierculæ in parvulis Evangeliis, et in Crucis ligno, et istiusmodi rebus, quæ habent quidem zelum Dei, sed non juxta scientiam, usque hodie factitant; culicem liquantes, et camelum glutientes:* "Where the Pharisees understood not," (saith S. Hierom,) "that the Commandments are to be carried in the heart, and not in the body: for otherwise studies and chests have books, and have not the knowledge of God. This do superstitious women to this day with us, in little Gospels, and pieces of the Cross, and such other things; which have the zeal of God, but not according to knowledge; straining a gnat, and swallowing a camel."

Here doth S. Hierom compare together the broad phylacteries, and little pieces of the Cross. He calleth them the Pharisees' hypocrisy, and these to be women's superstitious folly. He granteth them both a zeal of God, but neither according to knowledge. And so little did he esteem the Reliques of the Cross; so fond a thing he thought it to be enclosed, carried or worshipped of any; that he would not attribute the folly unto men, which ought of congruence have

---

[4] [Exod. xiii. 16. Deut. vi. 8.]
[5] Mat. xxv. [xxiii. 13—29.] Luke xi. [42—44.]
[6] Hieron. in xxiii. Mat. [*Opp.* Tom. iv. col. 109. ed. Bened. Paris. 1706.]

more discretion, but *superstitiosis mulierculis*, to such as your old mother Maukins are. And sith you urge authority so much, who is more to be credited? Helena, a silly woman, or Hierom, a learned man? Nicephorus, a suspect writer, or Hierom, a received Doctor of the Church? Paulinus, a Bishop, or Hierom, (as you say,) a Cardinal? Gregory, a Pope, or Hierom, a Saint canonized? They carried, they sent, they reverenced, little pieces of the Cross. But he condemns it, as more than a womanish superstition, as straining of a gnat, and swallowing of a camel.

And whereas ye cite Chrysostom[1]; that such as could get any piece of the Cross "enclosed the same in gold, as well men as women, and made it meet for their necks;" it is not to be thought, that this he spake as a praise of the parties, but a practice of the time. For Hierom and he lived both in one age, and then were men too much addicted to such idle toys. If ye ask me then, why Chrysostom did not in the same place disprove the fact; I answer, that he had to do with the Heathen, which caught occasion of every man's private doing to bring the Religion of Christ in obloquy. Therefore it was no wisdom for Chrysostom, to have revealed the shame of Christians; which might have hindered his cause very much, and discouraged the other from coming to the faith. Myself, if I should convert an Infidel, would not uncover the shame of Papists, but hide it what I could: assured of this, that there is no Turk nor Sarazin in the world, that will forsake his own Idolatry, to fall into a worse of Popery. So that it was not without good consideration, that Chrysostom so cleanly did excuse the fact, which he liked not, that he might not offend them whom he sought to win. Think you that a Jew can be brought from confidence in his Τετραγράμματον, the name of God written in four letters[2], if he chance to see a sorry piece of wood had in like reverence? They were wont to enclose that in gold: even so do you pieces of the Cross. They thought themselves safe from all perils by it: even so do you by this. And is there any hope, that the Jews can think well of that Religion, which condemneth their superstition about the name of God, (had in such reverence

---

[1] Chrysostom. in Dem. ad Gentiles.
[2] [:יהוה]

among them, that they dare not presume with tongue to utter it;) and useth a worse about a piece of wood? May we not suspect, that there is some piece of truth more than we are ware of; some piece of secret operation, (as Serenus Salmonicus[3] doth write[4],) in the word of *Abracadabra*[5], to heal one of the fever; if a splinter of a rotten post, against all kind of mischief, sufficiently may defend us? I marvel not now, that your Soul-Priest in the Tower was found with Hosts hanging about his neck in a silken purse, if a piece of wood have such power to save us. I doubt not but shortly you will also bring in *aurea Alexandri numismata*, "the golden coins of Alexander," of which Chrysostom speaketh[6], to tie to your feet; and S. John's Gospels, to hang about your necks.

These superstitions, these witchcrafts and sorceries, were used in Chrysostom's time, and are not yet forsaken of some. But what Chrysostom thought of them[7], and of such Reliques as you do talk of, appeareth in his second exposition upon Matthew; where he expostulateth with the Priests for their phylacteries and Gospels, saying[8]: *Dic Sacerdos insipiens, nonne quotidie Evangelium in ecclesia legitur, et auditur ab hominibus? Cui ergo in auribus posita Evangelia nihil prosunt, quomodo eum poterunt circa collum suspensa salvare? Deinde, ubi est virtus Evangelii? in figuris literarum, aut in intellectu sensuum? Si in figuris, bene circa collum suspendis: si in intellectu, ergo melius in corde posita prosunt, quam circa collum suspensa:* "Tell me, thou foolish Priest, is not the Gospel daily read and heard of men in the church? Therefore, who hath no profit by hearing of

---

[3] [Or Sammonicus. Vid. Königii *Biblioth. vetus et nova*, p. 719. Altdorf. 1678.]

[4] [See the extract, and figure of the amulet, as given by Baronius; ad an. 120. §. xvii.]

[5] [Conf. Irenæum, *Advers. Hæres.* Lib. i. Cap. xxiii.]

[6] Ad pop. Antio. Ho. xxi. [*Hom.* xix. §. 15. Cf. *Hom.* xliii. in 1 *Cor.* sub fin.; & *in S. Matth. Hom.* lxxii. S. Isidor. Pelusiot. *Epist.* cl. Lib. ii. p. 178. Heidelb. 1605. Suiceri *Thesaur.* in verb. Εὐαγγέλιον. i. 1227. Amstel. 1728.]

[7] [Bingham's *Antiq.* Book xvi. Ch. v. §. vi.]

[8] Chrysostomus, in caput Mat. xxiii. Hom. xliii. [*Opp.* Lat. Tom. ii. col. 920. Paris. 1570. Vide supra, pp. 95—6. Bp. Jewel's *Works*, Part i. p. 327; ed. Parker Soc.]

the Gospel, how can it save him by hanging it about his neck? Furthermore, wherein consisteth the virtue of the Gospel? in the proportion of the letters, or understanding of the sense? If in the letters, well dost thou hang them about thy neck; but if in the understanding, then would it profit more, reposed in thy heart, than hanged about thy neck."

Thus much Chrysostom. And lest peradventure ye should think, that this only superstition were reproved of him, he proceedeth further, and toucheth matter that doth more nearly concern our case. *Alii, qui sanctiores se ostendere volunt hominibus, partem fimbriæ aut capillorum Suorum alligant et suspendunt. O impietas! Majorem sanctitatem in Suis vestimentis volunt ostendere, quam in corpore Christi: ut qui, corpus Ejus manducans, sanatus non fuerit, fimbriæ Ejus sanctitate salvetur; ut, desperans de misericordia Dei, confidat in veste hominis.* In English: "Some other, which will shew themselves holier unto men, do bind together and hang up a piece of the hem of Christ's garment, or His heare[1]. O wickedness! They will shew more holiness in the garments, than in the body of Christ: that he, which is not healed by eating of His body, shall be saved by the holiness of His garment hem; that he, that despaireth of the mercy of God, shall put his confidence in the garment of a man." And think ye not, that the coat of Christ, which touched His blessed body; that the heare[1] of Christ, which grew upon His holy head, is of as great virtue as a piece of the Cross whereupon He died? Then if Chrysostom compted it impiety, to have such estimation of the coat or heare[1] of our Saviour Christ, shall we think that a piece of wood was in such price with him? Would he enclose the Cross in gold, or counsel other to do the same, which held it wickedness so to esteem a parcel of His body? Christ hath left us His body indeed, for a memory of Him, for a comfort of us to be received: and shall we seek for external means, which neither have part of promise, nor be devoid of peril? We read in the Gospel[2], that after Christ was crucified, Joseph required the body, and interred it: the Marys were beholders of His passion and burial: there was no sparing of

---

[1] [hair.]
[2] Mat. xxvii. [57—61.] Luk. xxiii. [50—56.]

cost for ointment: yet none of them all cared for the Cross. If it had been such a jewel as you do make it, they would have brought it, stolen it, or spoken at the least wise of it. Many other things, of less importance, (than this is, by your supposal,) be mentioned in the Scripture, as necessary or expedient. Only, (more than that Simon of Cyrene carried it,) we read nothing of the Cross that He died on.

I remember that it is a great argument of yours, how God will not suffer His Church to err. I remember ye alleged in the article before, *Quod in hanc Apostoli plenissime contulerunt omnia quæ sunt veritatis:* "That the Apostles most plentifully conferred on the Church all things appertaining unto the truth;" as Irenæus doth truly say[3]. How chanceth it then, that this truth of the Cross, for four hundreth years together, was hidden from them? From the death of Christ till the time of Helena[4], no man or woman ever talked of it. When she came, she found it, two hundreth years after it was utterly consumed. I think that such idle Chaplains, such morrow-mass Priests as you, so slenderly furnished out of the storehouse of faith to feed the people, would be glad to deal more of your popish plenty, if this at the first were gently accepted. We should have extolled S. Leonard's bowl, S. Cornely's horn, S. George's colt, S. Anthony's pig, S. Francis' cowl, S. Parson's breech, with a thousand Reliques of superstition as well as this. For miracles have been done by these, (or else you lie;) nor authority of men doth want to these. Longolius[5], a learned man, and Charles the V.[6], a noble Emperor, requested to be buried in a Friar's cowl, and so they were. Therefore the Friar's cowl must be honoured. Ye

Folio 87, b.

---

[3] Lib. iii. Ca. iv. Contr. Hær. ["Tantæ igitur ostensiones cum sint hæc, non oportet adhuc quærere apud alios veritatem, quam facile est ab Ecclesia sumere; cum Apostoli, quasi in depositorio dives, plenissime in ea contulerint omnia quæ sint veritatis."]

[4] [Bartholinus, *De Cruce*, p. 23. Amstel. 1670. Patrick's *Devotions of the Roman Church*, pp. 343—348. Lond. 1696. Comber's *Roman Forgeries*, p. 155. Lond. 1689. Chamieri *Panstrat. Cathol.* ii. 872. Genev. 1626. Newman's *Essay on Miracles;* prefixed to Fleury's *Eccles. Hist.* Vol. i.; pp. cxliii.—clxx. Oxford, 1842.]

[5] [Vid. Hanmer's *Great bragge and challenge of M. Champion confuted*, fol. 6, b. Lond. 1581.]

[6] [Cf. Strada, *De Bello Belgic.* Lib. i. Dec. i. Gul. Zenocarus, *De Rep. et Vita Car. Max.* iv. 221. v. 292. Antverp. 1596.]

remember what the host in Chaucer said to Sir Thopas for his lewd rhyme[1]. The same do I say to you, (because I have to do with your Canterbury tales,) for your fair reasons.

One thing remaineth, which I do you wrong if I omit; the singular virtue that is not only in every portion of the holy Cross, but also in every sign thereof; inasmuch as "it only driveth away all subtilty and crafts of evil Spirits; destroyeth witchcraft; doth as much as the presence of Christ in earth; proceedeth with like efficacy as the first sampler." Strange effects, I promise you. But, first, I marvel why you are offended with us for preaching only faith justifieth, since you do teach us that the only sign of the Cross can do as much as it. If only wood, if only making an overthwart sign, disappoint the might of adversary Powers; he is but a fool that will be troubled with Sprites; he is but a beast that will fear the Devil. *Signo Crucis tantum utens homo, omnes horum fallacias pellit:* "Man, using only the sign of the Cross, putteth away all their subtilty and craft." If a piece of wood, that worms do breed in; that never God nor good man commended otherwise than wood, have such "spiritual water flowing thereinto, which is known to be salvation of faithful souls;" shall we be condemned for attributing the like effect to spiritual and lively faith; which the word of God so oft, so earnestly, with such promise of grace, such assurance of safety, commendeth to us? If the sign of a Cross, drawn with a finger, "do the same that the presence of Christ did in earth," (as is by you alleged;) O men unmerciful, that suffer so many halt, so many lame, so many blind, so many sore, to live in misery, and miscarry with us. Christ cured the like: He by His presence brought health and comfort to all diseased. Why do not you, (my Cross Masters,) the like? If these allegations be true, (as confidently they be printed of you,) why cease your miracles? Confirm us in your foolish faith. When we see the effects, we shall consider of the cause.

Thus have I shewed you, that in cases of Religion, (as this is one,) no men's authority should prescribe unto us; no time, no custom prejudice a truth. Examples be dangerous to be followed; both because they be sometime but personal,

---

[1] [Tyrwhitt's Chaucer, Vol. ii. p. 239. Lond. 1775.]

and are not always of God's good guiding Spirit: which, if it be true in them, of whose faith and holiness we have in the Scripture honourable commendation; we may the more mistrust of other, whose lives and virtues we can by no means be so well assured of. As for authorities, (though Scripture itself doth suffice the faithful, and such as delight not to be contentious;) yet, that men of good judgment utterly abhorred, as heathenish, devilish, and idolatrous, this keeping, enclosing, honouring of a piece of wood, or any such earthly matter, I have brought you Hierom and Chrysostom; whose plain words condemn the superstition of you, and all other that you do talk of. Last of all, I have touched the gross absurdities that consequently do follow of your doctrine; which, (though I have not thoroughly unripped, your beastliness and vanity being so loathsome to me; yet) have I touched sufficiently to drive you, (if any grace be in you,) to consider your duty better; to write with more reason, or be still with less shame. Is this the profession of your Priesthood; is this the commission that men of your coat have; to preach the fables of old Gentility, and stir up the kennel of stinking superstition, which every old wife is aweary of, every child doth scorn at? Learn Christianity of Christ Himself; true order of preaching of the Apostles. Seek not so much what men have done, but how well they have done.

It is written to the Hebrews[2], that "God of old time spake at sundry times, and in divers manners, to our fathers by the Prophets; but in these last days hath spoken unto us by His dear Son." Whereby what other thing is to be meant, but that God hereafter will not use the mouth of many, nor heap us prophecy upon prophecy, revelation upon revelation; but that He did so fully instruct us by His Son, that the very last and everlasting testimony of truth must be had of Him? He gave Him, therefore, a singular prerogative, to be our Prophet, our Master, and our Guide: commanding Him only, no Church, no Council, no man to be heard. The Church, (I trust,) will take no more upon them than the Apostles did. What the Synagogue of Antichrist doth, I care not: what the true Christians ought to do, I prove. Christ sent forth His Apostles into the world, and gave them commission to teach and preach, not whatso-

[2] Hebr. i. [1, 2.]

ever they could invent, but what He had first commanded them[1]. And nothing could be more plainly said, than that which He speaketh in another place: "Be not ye called Rabbi," as masters or rulers over your brothers' faith: for one is your Doctor and your Teacher, Christ[2]. Then, if nothing can be allowed in matters of faith and salvation but that which is grounded on Christ and the Gospel, all doctrines of men, all Crosses, all Crucifixes, Rood-lofts and all, which have no colour of Scripture to defend them, but be most injurious and contrary to the same, must clean be abolished and put out of the Church. If Christ did call them hypocrites, and honourers of Him in vain, which teach the doctrines that proceed of man[3]; surely you Papists, (for fouler name of heresy can I give you none[4];) which bring us men's authorities, without the warrant of God's holy word; that bind us to believe things most contrary to it, are neither shepherds nor sheep of the fold; but, for all your fleece, be ravening wolves.

This doth Ignatius on this wise confirm[5]: *Omnis igitur qui dixerit præter ea [illa] quæ tradita sunt, tametsi fide dignus sit, tametsi jejunet, tametsi virginitatem servet, tametsi signa faciat, tametsi prophetet, lupus tibi appareat in grege ovium:* " Whosoever speaketh anything more than is written, although

---

[1] [S. Matth. xxviii. 20.]
[2] Math. xxiii. [8.]
[3] Math. xv. [7—9.]
[4] [Baronius, on the contrary, maintains that they could not be adorned with any "more sublime title of glory." (*Martyrol.* die 16 Octob. Conf. Leslæum, *De rebus gestis Scotorum;* Paræmes. p. 23. Romæ, 1578. Bellarm. *De notis Ecclesiæ,* Cap. iv. Crakanthorp's *Vigilius dormitans,* p. 188. Lond. 1631. Rhem. *Annot.* on Acts xi. 26. Schelhornii *Amœn. Hist. Eccles.* Tom. i. p. 968. Francof. 1737. Kellison's *Survey of the new Religion,* p. 95. Douay, 1603. Morton's *Catholike Appeale for Protestants,* p. 678. Lond. 1610. Challoner's *Authority of the Catholic Church,* p. 95. Dubl. 1829. Dodd's *Church Hist. of England,* by Tierney, Vol. i. pp. 311, 450. Lond. 1839. Du Moulin's *Anatomy of the Mass,* p. 87. Dubl. 1750. Lynde's *Case for the Spectacles,* p. 150. Lond. 1638.)]
[5] In Episto. ad Hieronim. [*Heronem.*—This Epistle is certainly not authentic, though it has been patronised by an assailant of *Ancient Christianity.* (i. 119.) Calfhill has used the old Latin version, published by Jacques Le Fevre, Argentor. 1527. Vid. cl. Usserii edit. p. 164. Oxon. 1644.]

he be worthy credit, although he fast, although he keep his virginity, although he do miracles, although he prophesy; yet let him seem to thee a wolf in the flock of sheep." This hath been always the opinion of the godly. This all the Doctors have taught and written. Only you, (good Sir,) and certain of your factious fellowship, will be wiser than Christ; bolder than the Apostles; better learned than the Doctors; and give us out new lessons that Scripture never thought of.

I will not tarry here in rehearsal of your errors in other points, which hasten to the end of my reproof of this. Only you, (good readers,) I shall exhort, and, for the mercies of Christ, beseech you, that, as ye tender your own health, and wish to be gathered into the fold of life, ye will hearken to the voice of your Shepherd Christ, and come at no stranger's call. Give credit to no man in matters of your faith, further than he brings his warrant with him. Believe no report, for it is a liar. Beware of the wolvish generation, which now being hungry kept, and feeding upon carrion, breathe out nothing else but horrible blasphemies and stinking lies. They prate of good life: themselves most licentious. They burden men with breach of laws: themselves most rebellious and dissolute. They go about to discredit us as teachers of carnal liberty: themselves imbrued with all kind of filth and abomination. As for all their doctrine and Religion, I may say unto them, as Christ did to the Pharisees: *Populus iste labiis Me honorat, cor autem eorum longe est a Me:* "This people honour Me with their lips, but their hearts are far off from Me[6]." Their eyes, their hands, their head, their feet they frame in such wise as shall tend to some piece of observance of the law. Their winking, their nodding, their moving, their crossing, is all God's service, as they do tell us. But where is the heart? Where is the mind, and inward purity that God requireth? When they hear, "Thou shalt not kill;" "Thou shalt not steal;" "Thou shalt not commit adultery;" the purest of them all, what do they? Peradventure, not draw the sword to slay any man; not lay their hands on other men's goods; not depart their bodies with harlots, (which yet is a marvellous rare bird to be hatched in the nest of Popery;) but they

[6] [S. Matth. xv. 8.]

compass mischief and destruction in their hearts: they burn in desire: they fret and consume away for envy. So, that which is the chief of the law is least among them. That which seemeth gay to the outward shew is only retained and kept.

And, for conclusion, beside that they expel faith, which is the goodness of all works, they set up works of their own making, to destroy the works of God, and be holier than they. First, with their chastity, they destroy the chastity that God ordained, and only requireth. With their obedience, they take away the order that God in this world hath set, and exacteth none other. With their poverty, they pervert humility and the true poverty of the spirit, which Christ taught only, which is only not to love the worldly goods. With their fast, filling their unsatiable paunches, they forget the fast which God commandeth, a perpetual soberness, to tame the flesh. With their pattering of prayers, they have put away the prayer that God hath taught us; which is either thanks for benefits received, or desiring help, with trust to be relieved. Their Crosses have displaced Christ. Their Pictures have defaced Scripture. Their Laymen's books[1] have abolished the Law. Their holiness is to forbid that which God ordained to be received with thanksgiving: as meat and matrimony. Their own works they maintain: they let God's decay. Break theirs, and they persecute to the death: break God's, and they either look through their fingers, or else give a flap with a fox-tail, for a little money. Then is it easy to be espied what they are. Let them disguise themselves never so closely, yet, by this examining of their natures and properties, they will bewray themselves. Chrysostom, commenting upon the seventh of Matthew, saith: *Si quis lupum cooperiat pelle ovina, quomodo cognoscet eum, nisi aut per vocem, aut per actum? Ovis inclinata deorsum balat. Lupus in aëra convertit caput suum contra cœlum, et sic ululat. Qui ergo secundum Deum vocem humilitatis et confessionis emittit, ovis est. Qui vero adversus veritatem turpiter blasphemiis ululat contra Deum, lupus est.* Which is thus in English: "If any man," (saith he,) "cover a wolf with a sheep's skin, how shall he know him, but by his voice or by his doing? The sheep bows

[1] [See Preface, p. 21.]

down the head to the ground, and bleats. The wolf lifts up his nose into the air, and barks. Therefore whosoever, according to God's word, speaketh with the voice of humbleness and confession, he is a sheep. But he that, contrary to the truth, blatters out blasphemies against God, is a very wolf." That the Papists are such, as it doth sufficiently appear already, so shall it abundantly, (ere I have done,) be proved. Therefore I say, Beware of Papists.

TO THE SEVENTH ARTICLE.

ALTHOUGH we ought not, in discussing of a truth ruled over by the word, greatly contend what rites and ceremonies have of presumption or toleration been brought into the Church; yet, that you may see before your eyes what ill of such precedents hath issued; how one inch granted to superstition, a whole ell hath followed; consider a while your Litanies and Processions. "The singing and saying of Litany," (you say,) "is commonly called Procession:" but Litanies were received long before Processions did come in place. For Litanies, what are they but humble prayers and supplications unto God, to procure His favour, and turn away His wrath? These have been received in the Church of old, and, according to occasion, diversly used.

Folio 93, b.

We read that when Constantinus the Emperor had purchased peace unto the Church of God, about a three hundreth and thirty year after Christ, then publicly the Christians repaired together. Then were there in the congregations, (as Eusebius reporteth[1],) *Orationes, Psalmodiæ, sacrorum operationes, mysteriorum participationes, gratiarum actiones:* " Prayers, singing of Psalms, business about holy things, participation of mysteries, and giving of thanks." And, (that which is worthy to be remembered,) he writeth of the good Emperor on this sort[2]: *Cantare primus incepit, una oravit, Conciones stans reverenter audiit: adeo ut rogatus ut consideret, responderit, Fas non esse dogmata de Deo remisse ac segniter audire:* "Himself began first to sing, prayed with the rest, and reverently heard the Sermons, standing on his feet; so far forth, that when he was required to set him down, he answered, 'That it was not lawful to hear the precepts of God with slackness and with sloth.'" Hilarius also, three hundred and seventy year after Christ, writeth of the order of the Church in his time thus[3]: *Audiat orantis*

A notable example of a Prince.

---

[1] Euseb. Eccle. Hist. Lib. x. Cap. iii.
[2] De vita Const. Li. iv.
[3] Hilarius, in expos. Psal. lxv. [*Opp.* col. 174. ed. Ben.]

populi consistens quis extra ecclesiam vocem; spectet celebres hymnorum sonitus; et inter divinorum quoque Sacramentorum officia responsionem devotæ confessionis [*accipiat:*] "A man that standeth without the church may hear the voice of the people praying; may behold the solemn sound of hymns; and, as the Sacraments are a ministering, the answer of a devout confession." Likewise Ambrose[4]: *Præcepit Apostolus fieri obsecrationes, postulationes, gratiarum actiones, pro omnibus hominibus,* &c.: "The Apostle commandeth," 1 Timoth. ii., "supplications, prayers, intercessions, and giving of thanks to be made for all men." "Which rule and law," saith Ambrose, "all Priests and faithful people do so uniformly observe, that there is no part of the world wherein such prayers are not frequent." So that it is evident that Litanies were then in use, although we read not of any Processions till the time of Agapetus, Pope[5]; who, (as Platina reporteth[6],) did first ordain them, anno five hundred and thirty-three; although we read the like of Leo the Third, about eight hundred and ten year after Christ. Surely, whensoever Processions began, they were taken of Gentility.

We read oft in Livy, that the Romans, in all their distresses, would run to every sere Idol that they had; would go their circuits from this place to that place, and think they did acceptable service unto God. We read in Arnobius[7] thus much of their folly: *Nudi cruda hyeme discurrunt: alii incedunt pileati: scuta vetera circumferunt, pelles cædunt, mendicantes vicatim Deos ducunt. Quædam fana semel anno adire permittunt: quædam in totum nefas visere est: quædam viro non licet: nonnulla absque fœminis sacra sunt: etiam servo quibusdam ceremoniis interesse piaculare flagitium est,* &c.: "They gad about naked in the raw

[4] Ambros. De voc. Gentium, Cap. iv. [Lib. i.—The two books, *De vocatione Gentium*, are unquestionably spurious.]

[5] Polidor. De inven. Li. v. Cap. x. [Polydorus Vergilius, *De rerum inventoribus*, Lib. vi. Cap. xi. p. 416. Basil. 1550.]

[6] [Platina, in his Life of Pope Agapetus I., does not speak of the institution of Processions: but he elsewhere (in *Vit.* Leonis I.) states, that Litanies or Supplications were first introduced by Mamercus, Bishop of Vienne. The appointment of the observance of the Rogation-days, at Rome, he attributes to Pope Leo III.]

[7] Arnobius, Contra Gent. Lib. viii. [Minucius Felix, *De Idolor. vanitate*, p. 73. Oxon. 1678. Vid. ante, pp. 178, 183.]

winter: other have their caps on: they carry about with them old targets; they beat their skins; they lead their Gods a begging round about the streets. They suffer some chapels to be gone to once a year: some must not be seen at all: some a man must not come unto: some other are holy enough without women; and for a servant to be at some of them, is a heinous offence."

So much Arnobius, concerning the Romans. And think you not that our Processions, with banners displayed and Idols in arms, be lively described here? Certainly, amongst the christened, I never read that any used Processions, before the Montanists and the Arrians. Tertullian[1] maketh mention of the one, and Eusebius[2] of the other. Meet it is, therefore, that Papists, participating with their errors, should also take part of their idle ceremonies. Concerning Litanies, (as of latter years they have been ordained,) you must understand, that some be called *minores*, "the less;" some *majores*, "the greater." The less were instituted by Mamertus, [Mamercus,] Bishop of Vienna, [Vienne,] in the year of our Lord four hundred and sixty-nine, [four hundred and sixty-eight,] as Sigebertus[3], or four hundred and eighty-eight, as Polychronicon[4] reporteth. The order of them was but a solemn assembly of people unto prayer, at such time as we call the Rogation-week. The cause was, *Pro terræ motu, pro tempestatibus, et bestiarum incursionibus, quæ tum temporis populum contriverunt:* "For earthquakes, and tempests, and invasions of wild beasts, which then did greatly destroy

---

[1] Tertullian. Li. ii. ad Uxorem. [Cap. iv.—Calfhill was mistaken in supposing that Tertullian was a Montanist when he composed the books *Ad Uxorem:* and it is very probable that he was deceived by the Centuriators, with regard to the Montanistic origin of Processions. (Vid. *Cent.* iii. Cap. x. col. 241. Basil. 1559.) The word "procedendum," which Tertullian uses, can assuredly not refer to any *public* display in those days of persecution, but merely to *private* attendance upon religious ordinances.]

[2] Euseb. Eccle. Hist. Libro vi. Cap. viii. [Through inadvertence, *Eusebius* has been quoted instead of *Socrates*.]

[3] [*Chron.* fol. 18. Paris. 1513.]

[4] [By Ranulphus, or Radulphus Higdenus; who has been accused of excessive plagiarism. It is said that Rogerus Cestriensis was the original writer; and that "Ralph stole his pretended work from Roger." (Bp. Nicolson's *Engl. Histor. Library*, p. 52. Lond. 1776.)]

the people." The greater Litany was devised by Gregory the Pope[5], anno five hundred and ninety-two; when, as the occasion being like as before, the superstition began to be more. For by reason of a great pestilence following of a flood, the Bishop, by ceremonies, thought to appease the wrath of God; and therefore made *septiformem Litaniam*, "a sevensort Litany." One of the Clergy, another of the Monks: one of men, another of their wives: one of maidens, another of widows: the last, of poor and children together. These people, so distinct into seven orders, should come from seven several places, and then it was thought they should be heard the sooner. But in their Procession, fourscore persons were stricken with the plague[6], to shew how well God was pleased with them.

Notwithstanding, how things, of a good devotion instituted, in time do grow to great abuse, these Litanies, that you talk of, do prove. For what the order and solemnity of them was, we read in the Council of Mentz, celebrated eight hundreth and thirteen year after Christ. The words of their Decree be these[7]: *Placuit nobis, ut Litania major observanda sit a cunctis Christianis diebus tribus*[8] *: et sicut sancti Patres nostri instituerunt; non equitando, nec pretiosis vestibus induti, sed discalceati, cinere et cilicio induti, nisi infirmitas impedierit:* " Our will is, that the greater Litany be observed of all Christians three days: and as our holy Fathers have ordained it; not riding, nor having precious garments on them, but bare-footed, in sackcloth and ashes, unless infirmity do let." So far the Council. Contrary to which, the popish

Papists degenerate from all good order.

---

[5] Gregorius, Indic. vi. Cap. ii. [*Epistt*. Lib. xi. Ep. ii. Conf. Pet. de Natalibus *Catalog. Sanctt.* L. iv. fol. cii. Lugd. 1508. Durant. *Rationale;* Lib. vi. fol. clx. Nuremberg. 1481.—Both S. Gregory I. and Walafridus Strabo have given the name of "Litania major" to the Rogations which the former instituted at Rome. It would seem, however, that the Litanies of Mamercus have been incorrectly styled the "less." See Bingham's *Antiq.* B. xiii. C. i. §. xi.; and compare Hildebrand's *Rituale Orantium,* pp. 128—131. Helm. 1656.]

[6] Sigebertus, in annum 591. [fol. 33.]

[7] Concilium Moguntiacum. [Cap. xxxiii. Binii *Concilia,* Tom. iii. P. i. Sect. ii. p. 201. The Decree is extant also in pag. 20 of the *Gesta Concilii Mogunciaci,* first published Basil. 1532.]

[8] [Cf. Caroli Magni et Ludov. Pii *Capitula,* ab Ansegiso Abbate et Bened. Levita collect. Lib. v. fol. 105, a. Paris. 1603.]

Procession is never solemn, but when all the copes do come abroad, and every wife is ready to scratch another by the face, for going next the Cross. And as the devotion of men is less, so are the words of invocation used among the Papists worse: which I shall have occasion anon to speak of, when I come to the Litany that Augustin the Monk used, at entering into our land. With you, M. Martiall, I will proceed in order.

Fol. 93, b.

The Arrians, as you cite out of Sozomenus, being set beside their churches at Constantinople, had secret conventicles, whither they resorted: much like to men of your occupation in England, which have their Mass in corners. They divided themselves into companies, and sung psalms and hymns, made in rhyme after their own guise; with additions for proof and defence of their own doctrine, as popish Portusses and hypocritical Hymnals have; such as you in Oxford were delighted to sing about the Christmas fire. "Which thing," (say you,) "the good Bishop and vigilant Pastor Chrysostom espying; lest some of the Catholics, allured with the pleasant casure[1] of the metre, and sweet sound of their rhyme, should go to their assemblies; devised also certain hymns in metre, and made them sing them in the same tune that the Arrians did: whereby it came to pass, that the Catholics far passed them in number, and in solemnity of Procession. For, (saith Sozomenus:) *Argentea Crucis signa una cum cereis accensis præcedebant eos:* 'Before the Catholics went two silver Crosses, with tapers or torches burning.'" Thus far you, Sir. And, doubtless, herein you have shewed a great piece of skill. You have noted in the margent, (because we shall not forget it,) how Crosses and tapers were carried in Procession. And is not the Cross much beholden to you, that now make it a candlestick; that now will compare it to a link, or a staff-torch, or to the pole that carrieth the cresset[2]? And may not your Lovanists greatly joy in you that can devise? May not we also greatly joy in them that can oversee, and suffer such a proof to go to print?

Give me leave a little to examine your history. First of all, that which is the chief circumstance ye utterly omit: that the Arrians' assemblies were in the night. Where-

---

[1] [cadence.]
[2] [A light set upon a beacon.]

upon Sozomenus saith[3]: *Noctu congregati, et in cœtus divisi:* "That in the night-time they were gathered together, and divided themselves into companies." And Socrates saith[4]: *Et hoc maxima noctis parte faciebant:* "And this they did most part of the night." Again, where ye say, that the Catholics had two silver Crosses, it is more than ye found in the text; and peradventure less: for *argentea Crucis signa* may be as well many silver signs of the Cross, as one. But what were those silver Crosses? Such as ye would make the ignorant believe? Such as you do use to carry in Procession? If other be so mad to credit you, yet we do know too much to be abused by you. Socrates writeth of the matter thus[5]: *Joannes, veritus ne hujusmodi cantionibus simpliciorum quisquam ab Ecclesia avelleretur, opposuit illis quosdam e suo populo; qui et ipsi nocturnis hymnis dediti, et illorum studium hebetarent, et suos in fide confirmarent. Videbatur quidem utile fore hoc Joannis propositum, verum cum perturbatione est et periculis terminatum. Cum enim homousiani hymni in nocturnis illis hymnodiis illustriores redderentur; (excogitaverat enim argenteas Cruces, quibus erant impositæ cereæ faces accensæ, ad quam rem Eudoxia Imperatrix sumptus suppeditaverat:) Arriani numero multi;* and so forth. Which words are in English these: "John," (Bishop of Constantinople,) "fearing lest by these songs of the Arrians any one of the simple might be pulled from the Church, set certain of his own people against them: which being also given to sing the night hymns, might both hinder the purpose of the adversary, and confirm in faith the minds of the Catholics. This intent of John seemed to be profitable, but it ended with trouble and perils. For when the songs of the Catholics in their night tunes were made more notable; (for he had devised certain cross pieces of silver, whereupon were put burning tapers of wax, whereof Eudoxia the Empress did bear the charge:) the Arrians endeavoured to revenge themselves."

Here it is evident wherefore these Crosses, (that you do talk of,) were had: that inasmuch as their assemblies were in the night, when lights were necessary; and those lights of

The Crosses of Constantinople.

[3] Lib. viii. Cap. viii. [*Hist. Eccl.*]
[4] Lib. vi. Cap. viii.
[5] Socrates, Ecclesia. Hist. Lib. vi. Cap. viii. [Musculo interp.]

theirs could not be carried on a straight piece, they would have a piece to go cross overthwart, to set many candles on : which being made of silver, the lights glimmering thereupon made a beautiful and goodly shew. This is the history. This was the Cross; these were the tapers of Chrysostom's time. But what is this to popish Procession? As much as if I said, My Lord Mayor hath a perch to set on his perchers[1], when his gesse[2] be at supper: therefore the Priest, when he is at his prayers, must have a Crucifix to go before him. The barber in his shop hath a laten[3] plate to set on his candles, to shave men thereat: therefore the Priest, when he goeth his stations about the churchyard, must have a silver Cross carried before him, and a couple of boys with tapers in their hands, to light him at noon-days. I remember of old that on Tenebre-Wednesday[4], or one of the solemn days before Easter, ye were wont to have a right counterfeit in the church of Constantinople's Cross; save that the one was of silver, the other of wood. And this was Judas' Cross, whereupon was set a great sort of candles, which at service-time were put out in order. But this I think is not the Cross that ye speak of. For you will have a silver Cross, (or copper at the leastwise,) after the pattern of Chrysostom's Catholics. But then you must stick it full of candles too, or else you be not like nother.

And have you not great cause, M. Martiall, upon this example to infer these words of triumph and victory: "Lo, good readers, Chrysostom, an ancient Father, and one of the most famous Doctors of the Greek Church, and renowned for virtue and learning throughout the world, had the sign of the Cross, and tapers with light, carried in his church of Constantinople, before his people in Procession?" And was it indeed a Cross, M. Martiall? In which signification of yours; the first, second, third, or fourth? Doubtless you were much over-seen, that did not make the fifth signification of "Cross" to be the cross staff that carried the candles. And was this Cross carried in

---

[1] [The editor imagines that the meaning of this phrase is, that my Lord Mayor hath a chandelier for his large wax candles.]

[2] [guests.]   [3] [latten, iron tinned over.]

[4] [Wednesday in Passion-week: so called from the Romish Service *Tenebræ*.]

the church? I had thought it had been in the streets. For the Arrians could not come into the church; and yet they met with them, with flinging of stones, and cracking of pates. "The Arrians had no Cross;" (you say.) Why then they went darkling, or were content with a lantern. Lo, good readers, hath not M. Martiall said much to the matter? First, that in Constantinople there should be carried two silver Crosses. And that is a lie. For there is no number mentioned. Then, that they should be carried in Procession. And that is a lie. For it was only *in processu*, in their marching forward. Thirdly, that they were carried in the church. And that is a lie. For it was in the streets. Fourthly, that they were carried, as ours are, in the day-time. And that is a lie. For it was in the night-season. What? four lies together, in so small room? Too much, of conscience. But mark the conclusion. " Forsooth, we gather out of Sozomenus, by the godly Father Chrysostom's fact, that we must carry a candlestick instead of a Cross in Procession." A proper collection: and yet very true. For the Crosses of Constantinople, to prove a doctrine of the church Cross, is as good as the cressets on midsummer-night, to prove the censers at high Mass in Paul's. *[sidenote: Martiall in one story maketh four lies, and yet the matter maketh nothing for him.]* *[sidenote: Martiall's conclusion out of Sozomenus.]*

And thus much for the Cross. Now to the candles. If they were of old used in the service of the Church, no marvel at all, since their meetings were in the nighttime, where to be darkling it was uncomfortable. We read in Eusebius[5], that in the reign of Antoninus Verus, in France, in Lyons and Vienna, [Vienne,] the Christians were forbidden to have any houses to dwell in, to enter with other folk into the baths, to walk abroad in the streets, or to be seen in any place. By reason whereof, they were compelled to get them caves, and there under the ground to hide them. But when, for their comfort in Christ, they would resort together, they did it in the night-time, for fear of suspicion: and thereof many slanders did rise upon them, for treasons, conspiracies, whoredoms, and murder. Yet candles they had, and necessary they were. Likewise we read, that when Justina the Empress, favouring the Arrians, had granted them the use of the church in Milan, Ambrose withstood it; and kept it day and night, with watch and *[sidenote: The use of tapers.]*

---

[5] Eusebius, Eccl. Hist. Lib. v. Cap. i.

ward[1]. Then Litanies were sung, and then were tapers used. But when persecutions ceased, and men might freely serve God abroad: when rewards were given to the servers of Him, and service appointed in the day-time; that candles should be used, they had no ground of reason. I see not whence you may have a precedent of your burning tapers at noon-day, so well as from the sacrifices of Saturnus[2]. *Aras Saturnias non mactando viros, sed accensis luminibus excolebant:* "They decked and furnished the altars of Saturn, not with the blood of men, but with burning of candles." And we never read that any returned from Gentility, but retained somewhat of their old observances.

If ye urge the old custom, that so many hundreth years ago tapers were used in God's service, I will reply with reproof of that custom by a General Council. For in the Synod held in Spain, called *Concilium Elibertinum*[3], it was straitly enjoined, that none should light candles in the day-time. Lactantius, inveighing against the heathenish or popish superstition, (*conveniunt enim in uno tertio,* "for" Papists and Pagans "agree in a third;" that is to say, lighting of candles unto their Gods:) saith[4]: *Accendunt lumina velut in tenebris agenti Deo. Sed si cœleste lumen, quod dicimus Solem, contemplari velint, jam sentiant quod non indigeat lucernis eorum Deus, qui in usum hominis tam candidam lucem dedit. Et tamen quum in tam parvo circulo, qui propter longinquitatem non amplius quam humani capitis videtur habere mensuram, tantum sit fulgoris, ut eum mortalium luminum acies non queat contueri; et si paulisper intenderis, hebetatos oculos caligo ac tenebræ consequantur; quid tandem luminis, quid*

---

[1] Augustinus, Li. Confes. ix. Cap. vii. [p. 155. Oxon. 1838.]

[2] ["Aras Saturnias non mactando viros, sed accensis luminibus excolentes."] Macrob. Saturn. Li. i. Cap. vii. [p. 241. ed. Zeun. Lipsiæ, 1774. Gronovius reads "viro," from a MS.]

[3] Cap. xxxiv. [Çonzalez, *Col. Can. Eccles. Hisp.* 287. Matriti, 1808. —The Synod of Elvira should not have been designated as "General." (See before, p. 154.) An elaborate apology for its decisions was composed by Don Fernando de Mendoza; which was published, with additional notes by others, and with the commentary of Emman. Gondisal. Tellez, Lugduni, 1665.]

[4] Lactantius, De vero Cultu Dei, Li. vi. Cap. ii. [Vol. ii. p. 5. Bipont. 1786. Compare Meagher's *Popish Mass,* p. 154. Limerick, 1771.]

claritatis apud Deum, penes quem nulla nox est, esse arbitremur: qui hanc ipsam lucem sic moderatus est, ut neque nimio fulgore, neque calore vehementi, noceret animantibus; tantumque istarum rerum dedit ei, quantum aut mortalia corpora pati possunt, aut frugum maturitas postularet? Which is to say in English: "They light candles unto God, as if He were in the dark. But if they will behold the heavenly light, (that we call the Sun,) they may understand that their God lacketh no lights, that for the use of man hath given so clear a light. And yet, whereas in so small a circle, which by reason of the distance seemeth no bigger than a man's head, there is so great a glistering, that the engine of man's eye is not able to look directly on it; and if for a while ye fix your sight thereon, dimness and darkness do follow your dased[5] eyes; what light, what clearness may we think to be with God[6], with whom there is no night at all: who hath so ordered this light of his, that neither by too much shining beams, nor over parching heat, he should hurt the cattle; and yet of both hath departed[7] so much as either the bodies of man may bear, or riping of the fruits require?" Wherefore he concludeth: *Num igitur mentis suæ compos putandus est, qui Authori et Datori luminis candelarum ac cerearum* [al. *aut cereorum*] *lumen offert pro munere?* "Is he to be thought to be in his right wits, that to the Author and Giver of light offers up the light of candles and tapers for a gift?"

And can there any thing more plainly be said, to condemn the use of burning tapers on the Lord's table? "God hath required another light of us," (saith Lactantius;) "and the same not dim and smoky, but clear and bright, proceeding from the mind, which for that cause is called φῶς," as much to say as 'light:' "which doubtless is impossible for any to set forth, but him that knoweth God." Then, if we set up in the day-time a candle for ourselves, we be blind fools: if for the use and service of God, we be blasphemous. *Terrenum enim facimus Eum, et in tenebris agentem:* "For we make Him earthly, and shut Him up," (as it were,) "in a dark prison." *Itaque istiusmodi cultores, quia cœleste nihil sapiunt, etiam Religiones quibus deserviunt ad terram revo-*

<small>There must be no tapers on the Lord's table.</small>

---

[5] [dazzled.]   [6] [S. James i. 17.]
[7] [separated.]

cant. *In ea enim lumine opus est, quia ratio ejus et natura tenebrosa est:* "Therefore such worshippers, because no heavenly thing savours with them, call down their Religions, which they observe and keep, unto the earth; wherein we stand in need of light, because the respect and nature of it is cloudy altogether and full of darkness."

Thus much have I said to your first proof of Cross and tapers at time of Litany. Now, where you find yourself aggrieved, that we have not likewise your ceremonies in ure[1], saying, "Our heretics now-a-days will have no Cross at the singing of their Lord's Prayer, because neither their Lord nor they can abide the sight of the Cross;" truly, I had thought that we had had all one Lord before; that we had all depended upon Christ, and justly might have been called Christians: now that ye refuse Him in the plain field, what shall I call you but Antichrists and Apostatæ? For evident it is who is our Lord, by the Prayer that we use, and Christ hath commanded us: you, by condemning the Prayer, also deny the Lord. For what mean you by this: "Heretics at their Lord's Prayer?" Have we any other Lord's Prayer than that which is written in the vi. of Matthew, and xi. of Luke? If this ye acknowledge, ye might as well have said, "at the Lord's Prayer," or, "at our Lord's Prayer," as, "at their Lord's Prayer:" but if ye have such a sect of yourselves, that do mislike with the Lord's Prayer, I would be gladly taken as an heretic of such; and all your Religion I hold accursed. "They cannot be heretics," say you, "that can abide the sight of the Cross." And will you abide by that? Ye have proved by this time Luther no heretic: for always he is pictured full devoutly kneeling before the Cross; and truly no Papist had the sign of the Cross in more reverence than he. Wherefore you must restrain your position, or lessen much the number of your heretics.

Justinian's laws, though in civil cases I do gladly admit, and in some matters of correction I like very well; (*Ut quod pæderastis virilia confestim exsecari voluit:*) yet in Religion we are not bound to this order. I know that in his time many superstitions were come in place[2]: and

---

[1] [use: from *usura*.]

[2] [The object of Justinian, in requiring the formality of a public Procession, at the time of the consecration of a church, was simply

since he lived in the same age with Agapetus the Pope, first founder of Processions, no marvel if he followed some piece of his fancy. Mamertes and Gregory, that first devised Litanies, although they make mention of divers orders and solemnities that were used in them, (namely of the use of the Bishop's Pall[3];) yet speak they no word that the Cross should go before them. Wherefore I greatly force not, whether the order of Crosses in Litanies were used somewhat before his time, or first by himself devised; since we have example of so many faithful, that prayed without it; and promise that our prayer shall be heard, though we want it. Myself will not discredit the Emperor, which being, as Suidas saith, ἀναλφάβητος, "utterly unlearned," deserved well of learning. But what he was, both for his laws and execution of justice and Religion, read Alciate[4] and Evagrius[5].

The tale and titles of Augustin the Monk, (who commonly is called the Apostle of England,) I have not in such credit and estimation, that I think us, (as you say,) next unto God most beholden to him for our faith and Religion. For ever since the time of Eleutherius of Rome, and Lucius of England[6], Christianity hath been received, and never failed among us. Indeed some parts of the realm, which now are accompted chief, and then lay most open to the spoil of enemies, were blinded with paganish superstition, and the faithful Christians fled into the mountains. The Saxons, for the part that they possessed, were most idolater. The Britons remained Christians; insomuch that when Augustin came among them, he found seven bishopricks and an archbishoprick, beside divers

Augustin the Monk, commonly called the Apostle of England.

---

to suppress conventicles. He declares, that many persons had previously pretended to erect oratories; but that they yielded to their morbid fancies, and became the founders "non orthodoxarum ecclesiarum, sed illicitarum speluncarum." (Vid. *Constit. nov.* lxvii. p. 121. & *Const.* cxxiii. p. 212. Greg. Haloandro interp. ed. princ. Noremb. 1531.) The marginal notes in the editor's copy are attributed to Melancthon.]

[3] [Vid. Spelmanni *Glossar.* in verb. Butler's *Lives of the Saints*, i. 760. Dubl. 1833.]

[4] Alciat. Li. iv. Disp. Cap. vii. [*Opp.* T. iv. col. 200. Francofurti, 1617.]

[5] Evagrius, Libro iv. Ca. xxx. et xxxii.

[6] [See before, pp. 52—3.]

and sundry Monasteries: which all had faithful and learned Prelates, keeping their flocks in most godly order. Nor utterly was the faith extinguished where Augustin landed. For Ethelbert, the King of Kent, (as Polydor[1] writeth,) was meetly well instructed by a godly wife[2], that came out of France, and a christian Bishop[3] that attended on her. But Augustin, when he came, in place of Idolatry planted superstition: and where Religion was sincerely taught, he laboured what he could, of a certain ambitious proud heart, to pervert it. For, finding in the city of Bangor[4] a notable sort of Monks, (not idle bellies, as of late years they have been, but learned, and living of the sweat of their brows[5];) insomuch that, being divided into seven parts, there were no less than three hundreth of a company; this Romish Prelate required subjection of them; and further would have enjoined them to become servitors, in preaching of the Gospel to their mortal enemies, the Saxons. Which conditions when they refused, Ethelbert the King, partly in Austin's quarrel, partly of an old grudge of his own, stirred up the rest of the Saxon Kings to make war upon them. So they came to Chester, wherein the religious people had assembled themselves; and when the city was taken, there were twelve hundreth of the good men most cruelly slain[6]. And whereas their rage was not so quieted, but needs they would come to destroy Bangor; the Britons' confederates, assembling them-

[1] [Polydorus Vergilius, in *Anglic. Hist.*]
[2] [Bertha.]
[3] [Luidhard.]
[4] [Vid. Broughton's *Memorial of Great Britain*, Chap. iv. p. 39. 1650.]
[5] [Bp. Lloyd's *Historical Account*, p. 158. Lond. 1684.]
[6] [Bede completely exonerates Augustin from participation in this crime: for he states that it was perpetrated, "ipso jam multo ante tempore ad cœlestia regna sublato." (*H. Ecc. Angl.* Lib. ii. ad fin. Cap. ii.) It is true that these words are wanted in King Alfred's Saxon version; and this fact has induced Abp. Parker, Bp. Godwin, Cave, and a multitude of others, to consider them an interpolation. Mr Stevenson, however, after Whelock, informs us, that "the MSS. universally exhibit this passage." (Not. in loc. p. 103. edit. Lond 1838. Compare Pantin's *Observations on Dr Arnold's "Christian duty of granting the Roman Catholic claims,"* p. 85. Lutterworth 1829.)]

selves, withstood them, and slew ten thousand and threescore of them. *Hactenus Galfridus*[7].

Which great murder cannot be imputed to any thing so much as to the ambition of the Monk. And although Beda[8] reciteth the history somewhat otherwise, yet his witness proveth that Augustin was much to blame, which would so seriously contend about trifles. For what were the matters that he exacted? *Primo, ut eodem quo Romana Ecclesia tempore festum Paschatis celebrarent: secundo, communibus ritibus et cœremoniis cum Romanis in Baptismi ministerio uterentur: tertio, ut, communicata opera, et communibus laboribus, genti Angliæ Evangelium prædicarent.* That is to say: "First, that they should celebrate the Easter feast at the same time that the Church of Rome did. Secondarily, that they should use, in ministration of Baptism, the self-same ceremonies with the Romans. Thirdly, that they should communicate their travails, that jointly they should take pains together, in preaching of the Gospel to the English nation." These conditions, because they were not received, the people, (as he saith,) were plagued.

But in this behalf, the wonderful judgment of almighty God is worthy to be considered, that exerciseth His people with plagues among: and although of His mercy sometime He grant them *Alcyonia tempora*, "some little breathing whiles;" yet tempests do arise anon, and the Cross accompanieth true Christianity. Which, in this age of the Church, wherein Gregory, (by surname the Great,) and Augustin, of whom we last have spoken, lived, may well be seen. For, after the flourishing time of Constantinus, wherein most liberty was granted Christians; after the learned age of Augustin and Ambrose, when all good knowledge was at the ripest; suddenly ensued a strange and lamentable alteration: when, for light, darkness; for God's service, ceremonies; for learning, ignorance and barbarity succeeded. That if ye pass six hundreth year after Christ, ye shall see nothing but cloud of ceremonies, darkening the Sun of eternal truth; and a sort of willworships, defacing the true honour of the almighty God.

[7] [In *Historia Britonum*.—Stillingfleet does not commend the prudence of those who "swallow Geoffrey of Monmouth whole, without chewing." (*Antiquities*, p. 78. Lond. 1685.)]

[8] Hist. gent. Ang. Lib. ii. Cap. ii.

And then might you seek all Christendom, and scarcely find a learned Father, excepting Gregory and Fulgentius. These two were the best, and almost the only to be accompted of: and yet these, (God wot,) shewed in what time they lived; when every man delighted to have a God's service of his own making. And then was our hap to receive this Pope's Apostle from Rome, *Crucem pro vexillo ferens argenteam:* "carrying a silver Cross for his banner," and the Image of Christ painted in a table.

<small>Folio 96, a.</small>

<small>How far we differ from Augustin the Monk, as well in ceremonies as in time.</small>

Where, by the way, ye may observe, that ceremonies, the elder they are, do grow the more. For, whereas Augustin brought in but a bare Cross, we have received not only a Cross, but also a Crucifix graved thereon: and whereas he carried a Picture but painted on a table, we have the same carved and embossed. Augustin, coming unto them that never had heard of Christ, politicly devised somewhat, wherewithal first he might feed their eyes, that afterward, lending him their ears, he might instruct their hearts. Wherefore, if this fact of his might be excused by the state and condition of the country; yet cannot we, in our Cross-carrying, have the like pretence, and therefore ought not to use the like example. Notwithstanding, his Litany was good; and I marvel that the Romish Church is not at this day contented with the like. He came not in with *Ora pro nobis:* he made no intercession to Saints for us; but only sung this sweet Litany: *Deprecamur Te Domine, in omni misericordia Tua, ut auferatur furor et ira Tua a civitate ista; quia peccavimus:* "In all Thy mercy, we beseech Thee, O Lord, that Thy indignation and fury may be taken away from this city; because we have sinned." Which Litany of his, if it be compared with ours, the selfsame thing shall be seen in both. But the popish Litany, as it is different from this, so is it idolatrous. Virgin Mary, pray for us: Peter, pray for us: Paul, pray for us; and so forth to Abbots, Monks, Hermits, Nuns, Friars, and all to pray for us. I may say to you, as Tertullian, by an irony said to the Gentiles[1]: *Vos religiosi salutem quæritis ubi non est: petitis a quibus dari non potest: præterito Eo in cujus est potestate. Insuper eos (Christianos) debellatis, qui eam sciunt petere, qui etiam possunt impetrare dum sciunt petere. Nos enim, pro salute Imperatorum, Deum vocamus æternum*

---

[1] Tertullianus, in Apologetico, Ca. iii. [Capp. xxix, xxx.]

Deum verum, et Deum vivum, quem et ipsi Imperatores propitium [al. *proprium*] *sibi præter cæteros malunt:* "You devout persons," (said Tertullian,) " seek for salvation where it is not to be found. Ye ask it of them that cannot give it: omitting Him in whose hands it is. Nor content with this, ye beat down those Christians, which know to ask health, which also be able to obtain it, because they know how to ask it. For we, for the Emperors' good state and preservation, do pray to the eternal God, the true God, and living God, whom the Emperors themselves had rather than all other to be merciful unto them."

This, (I say,) do we for all magistrates and rulers; for all things necessary for this life of ours. Nor we think it necessary to observe any other form and ceremony in our praying, than the same Tertullian setteth forth of Christians in his time, without any Cross at all: *Ad cœlum,* (saith he,) *suspicientes Christiani, manibus expansis, quia innocuis; capite nudo, quia non erubescimus; denique sine monitore, quia de pectore oramus; precantes sumus omnes semper*[2] *pro omnibus Imperatoribus, vitam illis prolixam, imperium securum, domum tutam, exercitus fortes, senatum fidelem, populum probum, orbem quietum, et quæcunque hominis et Cæsaris vota sunt. Hæc ab alio orare non possum quam a quo scio me consecuturum: quoniam et Ipse est qui solus præstat, et ego sum cui impetrare debetur: famulus Ejus, qui Eum solum* [al. *solus*] *observo; qui Ei offero opimam et majorem hostiam, quam Ipse mandavit; orationem de carne pudica, de anima innocenti, de Spiritu Sancto profectam:* " We Christians, looking up to heaven, with hands stretched out, because they are harmless; bare-headed, because we are not ashamed; without any prompter, because we pray from the heart; always do make our supplications for all Princes and rulers: beseeching God to send them a long life, a quiet reign, an household in safety, and valiant soldiers, counsellors faithful, and people virtuous, a merry world, and whatsoever themselves wish for beside. These things I cannot pray for of any but of whom I know I shall obtain, because He it is that only performeth; and I am he that must obtain: His servant, which honour and esteem Him only;

[2] [al... "*sine monitore, quia de pectore; oramus pro omnibus Imperatoribus,*" &c.]

which offer unto Him a fat and full sacrifice, which He hath commanded me; a prayer that proceedeth from a sober and chaste flesh, an innocent soul, and from the Holy Ghost."

In which words Tertullian declareth the order of God's service in his time; which consisted not in outward shews, but inward verity: nor in their distresses they called upon any, (as you do in your Litanies,) save only upon Him, that only can and will reward His. Wherefore, your Litanies of late devised be most unlawful; and, notwithstanding your Crosses, you be most superstitious. *Superstitiosi enim [autem] vocantur,* (as Lactantius saith[1],) *non qui filios suos superstites optant; (omnes enim optamus:) sed aut hii qui superstitem memoriam defunctorum colunt; aut qui, parentibus suis superstitibus,* [al. *superstites,*] *colebant* [al. *celebrant*] *Imagines eorum domi, tanquam Deos Penates. Nam qui novos sibi ritus assumebant, ut in Deorum vicem mortuos honorarent, quos ex hominibus in cœlum receptos putabant, hos superstitiosos vocabant:* "For they are called superstitious, not that desire their children to be long lived; (for so we do all:) but either such as have the memory of the dead fresh with them, and esteem the same; or such as, having their parents alive, did worship their Images at home, as their household Gods. For they that took new fashions unto them, to honour the dead instead of the Gods; which men they supposed to have been received out of earth into heaven; them did they call superstitious." And forasmuch as you, (M. Martiall, and your fellows,) be such which so diligently retain the memory of the dead; which call upon the dead, and make your prayers to them; Lactantius saith you be not religious, but superstitious.

Papists superstitious; and why.

Folio 97, a

As for the ensign of our Master Christ, "which," (you say,) "we labour to have out of the field;" because we know the fight of our adversary is uncessant, without any truce or intermission, until this soul of ours do unbody, we carry this ensign always with us; we never suffer it to depart from the walls of our heart; but, sleeping and waking, eating and drinking, at church and at home, we have it always afore us. And this is indeed the Cross of Christ; not carried on a staff, not set upon an Altar, but fixed in our hearts, with a joyful remembrance of His merits for us. *Hoc enim vexillo,*

[1] Lactantius, Divin. Inst. Li. iv. Ca. xxviii.

antiquus hostis, non Imaginibus, victus est: hiis armis, non colorum fucis, Diabolus expugnatus est: per hanc, non per Picturas, inferni claustra destituta sunt: per hanc, non per illas, humanum genus redemptium est. In Cruce namque, non in Imaginibus, pretium mundi pependit. Illa ad servile supplicium, non quædam Imago, ministra extitit. Hoc est nostri Regis insigne, non quædam Pictura, quod nostri exercitus indesinenter aspiciunt legiones. Hoc est signum nostri Imperatoris, non compaginatio colorum, quod ad prælium nostri [nostræ] sequuntur cohortes: "For by this ensign," saith Charles the Great[2], "not by Images, our ancient enemy is overcome. By this artillery, not by any counterfeits of colours, the Devil is vanquished. By this, and not by Pictures, the dungeons of hell are emptied. By this, and not by them, mankind is all redeemed. For the price of the world hanged on a Cross, and not in Images. The Cross, and not an Image, was the matter of a servile punishment. This, and not a Picture, is the ensign of our King, which the bands of our army continually do look on. This, and not a tempering of certain colours, is the sign and banner of our Emperor and Captain, which our hosts of men do follow to the wars." By which relation of contraries, it appeareth plainly, what the Cross is that we ought to reverence, and what Christ's banner that we ought to display. Not the Image, the sign and Picture, but the memorial of His death and passion. Wherefore he concludeth: *Non quædam materialis Imago, sed Dominicæ Crucis mysterium vexillum est, quod in campo duelli, ut fortius confligamus, sequi debemus:* "It is not any material Image, but the mystery of the Cross of Christ," (tho death itself,) "which is our ensign, that in the field of our conflict we ought to follow, to the end we may more manfully fight." And thus you see, that all authority and reason condemns you. There is nothing in God's service that you mislike in us, but rather ought to be reputed praise.

The Reliques of Anastasius, brought in with Procession, (which ye also do bring to prove the use of a Cross,) shew that you stand in great need of good proofs, when you can be contented with so slender aids. I need no more to answer, but that a superstitious instrument was meetest to serve a super-

The materia no ensign of Christ.

The true ensign of Christ.

Folio 97, b. For Reliques.

---

[2] Car. Mag. De Imag. Lib. ii. Cap. xxviii. [p. 280. ed. Goldast.]

stitious effect. We read in the Old Testament[1], that whosoever touched the dead corpse of any man, and purged not himself, defiled the tabernacle of the Lord, and should be cut off from Israel. And shall, in the New Testament, the rotten bones of a dead carcase make men the holier? If all the Scripture be read over, and writings of the Fathers, for three hundred year after Christ, we shall find no commandment or example in the world of Reliques kept, or bones translated. We read of Moses, the servant of the Lord, that "he died in the land of Moab;" and the Angel of the Lord "buried him in a valley: but no man knoweth of his sepulchre unto this day[2]." Which thing was of purpose, by the providence of God, appointed so, that the Jews might have no occasion thereby to commit Idolatry. But if the translating of dead bones had made either for the glory of God, or commodity of man, the Reliques of such a one as Moses was should not have been hidden. For doubtless of all Prophets he was the greatest, by the testimony of God Himself: who called him "faithful in all His house[3];" to whom He spake mouth to mouth, and by vision, and not in dark words: yet was not his body shrined, nor his bones carried in Procession, nor any chapel erected for him. Indeed the Devil did attempt no less than to make it a matter of superstition; (for we read[4] that there was a strife betwixt him and Michael about Moses' body:) but the Angel of the Lord withstood it. And although, peradventure, by some instruction ye shall hap upon the story of Joseph, who required his brothers to carry his bones into the land of Canaan[5]; yet doth it not make for your Reliques nother. For who kneeled ever to Joseph's tomb? Who brought it ever into the sanctuary? Who lighted ever any candle to it? Only to assure them of his faith in God's promises, and to confirm them that the land of promise they should enjoy, he willed them, as a witness, to take his body with them.

Joseph's body.

Next unto Moses, among the Prophets, were Samuel and Elias. "Samuel died," (as the Scripture saith,) "and all Israel assembled, and mourned for him, and buried him in his own house[6]:" more we have not. Elias was rapt

---

[1] Num. xix. [13.] [2] Josue xxxiv. [Deut. xxxiv. 5, 6.]
[3] Num. xii. [7, 8. Heb. iii. 2, 5.] [4] Ep. Jude, [9.]
[5] [Gen. l. 24, 25.] [6] 1 Samu. xxv. [1.]

in a fiery chariot[7]: his body was translated, not into the church, but into heaven; both to testify the reward of immortality prepared for the faithful, and to cut away occasion of men's Idolatry. Furthermore, "Elisha died, and they buried him. And certain bands of the Moabites came into the land that year. And as they were burying a man, behold they saw the soldiers: therefore they cast the man into the sepulchre of Elisha: and when the man was down, and touched the bones of Elisha, he revived, and stood upon his feet[8]." Yet, after so great a miracle, his bones were not translated: there was no pilgrimage appointed to him; there was no chapel erected for him. "While he lived," (sayeth Jesus the son of Syrach[9],) "he was not moved for any Prince, neither could anything bring him into subjection: nothing could overcome; and after his death his body prophesied: he did wonders in his life, and in death were his works marvellous. Yet, for all this, the people repented not." So that this miracle, confirming the doctrine and calling of Elisha, served as a preaching of penance to them, and not to enforce a worshipping of the body. For which cause it is plainly said, his body prophesied. When zealous and good Josias had taken the bones of the false Prophets out of their graves, and burned them upon the altar, seeing the sepulchre of the man of God, he said: "Let him alone; let none remove his bones[10]." Great cause in appearance, why they should have been removed thence, where so many wicked had lien buried: but suffered they were, and honoured they were not. In the New Testament, what shall we think the cause that so little mention is made either of the burial, or else assumption of the Virgin Mary, whose undefiled body was the worthy temple of the Holy Ghost, but that the wisdom of God foresaw what mischief and Idolatry would soon have risen of it? Of John Baptist we read, that after he was slain, "his disciples came, and took up his body, and buried it[11]." Likewise of Stephen, when he was stoned, that "certain men that feared God carried him among them to be buried, and made great lamentation for him[12]:" but of their bones reserving, or bodies translating, not a word at all. Doubtless,

[7] 2 Reg. ii. [2 Kings, ii. 11.]   [8] 2 Reg. xiii. [20, 21.]
[9] Ecclesi. xlviii. [12—15.]   [10] 2 Reg. xxiii. [18.]
[11] Mat. xiv. [12.]   [12] Act. viii. [2.]

if such Reliques had been thought profitable to the Church of Christ, there should not have been such silence of them. Notwithstanding afterward, upon abundance of zeal, not only the memories of the faithful Martyrs, but also some parcels of their mangled bodies, began to be kept; to little use of them, and ill example to their posterity. Wherefore, methink, they made a right good excuse, that, denying the body of Polycarpus to them that sued for it, said: *Ne, Christo relicto, hunc colere inciperent*[1]: It should not be delivered; "lest, Christ forsaken, they should begin to serve him." None of the Saints, but have left behind them a better memorial than a scull or a carcase, in writing or in doing. Let their writings then be perused of us; the virtuous conversation of their life be followed; and they, (no doubt,) will be best contented. Erasmus, entreating of such superstitions as you do most embrace, said very wisely to the soldier of Christ[2]: *Veneraris Divos; gaudes eorum Reliquias contingere: sed contemnis quod illi reliquerunt optimum, puta vitæ puræ exempla. Nullus cultus gratior Mariæ, quam si Mariæ humilitatem imiteris. Nulla Religio Sanctis acceptior, magisque propria, quam si virtutem illorum exprimere labores. Vis tibi demereri Petrum et Paulum? Alterius fidem, alterius imitare charitatem; et plus feceris, quam si decies Romam cursitaris.* That is to say: "Thou worshippest the Saints; thou art glad to touch their Reliques: but the best thing that they have left behind them, which is, the examples of a pure life, thou contemnest. No service more acceptable unto Mary, than if thou imitate the lowliness of Mary. No Religion more welcome and more proper unto Saints, than if thou study to express their virtue. Wilt thou procure the favour of Peter and of Paul? Follow and resemble the faith of the one, and charity of the other; and thou shalt do more than if thou shouldest gad ten times to Rome." So much as touching Anastasius' Reliques.

Now that I have proved the Cross of Chrysostom to

---

[1] Euse. Eccle. His. Li. iv. Cap. xvi. [p. 57. ed. Lat.]
[2] In Enchir. Can. v. [*Enchiridion Militis Christiani*, Canon v. foll. 56—7. Argentinæ, 1521.—This work has been sufficiently expurgated by the various Indexes: and it is strange that it should have been ascribed to Luther, instead of to Erasmus, in Smedley's *History of the Reformed Religion in France*, Vol. i. p. 18. Lond. 1832.]

make nothing for you; the laws of Justinian not to prescribe me; the example of Augustin the Monk not to bind me; the translating of Reliques not to be esteemed of me; it remaineth, that your proofs for having of a Cross at singing or saying Litany are insufficient. I have shewed you, by the way, whose device were Litanies; whence came Processions; how far we swerve, both in the one and in the other, from those will-worshippers that first invented them. I have declared no less the fond abuse of tapers, and shameful superstition of Reliques in the Church, both by God's word, and testimony of good men condemned. Wherefore let us, forsaking vanities of men's devices, seek God, and service of Him in Scripture. Let us walk before Him in innocency of life. Let us be followers of Saints, as they were of Christ. Let us in humbleness of our heart make our prayers unto Him, although we have no Cross in Procession before us. But for avoiding of the Cross, (the plague of God due for our deserts,) let us often use our godly Litany; and let us instantly always say: "From the tyranny of the Bishop of Rome, and all his detestable enormities[3]; from all false doctrine and heresy, from hardness of heart, from contempt of Thy word and commandment; good Lord deliver us."

[3] [These words were contained in the first and second Books of King Edward VI., 1549, and 1552; but were omitted from the Litany, when revised upon the accession of Queen Elizabeth, in 1559.]

TO THE EIGHTH ARTICLE.

THAT MANY STRANGE AND WONDERFUL MIRACLES WERE WROUGHT BY THE SIGN OF THE CROSS.

IF signs and miracles, which, in these latter days, have been ofter wrought by power of the Devil than by Spirit of God, should be brought to confirm a doctrine in the Church; no vain Idolatry of the Gentiles, no wicked worshippings among the Christians, but by the same reason shall be authorized. When Accius Navius, the great wizard, had dehorted Tarquin the old from invocating anything, until he had been stalled[1] by him, and received at his hands certain observances; the King, scorning his occupation[2], willed him to ask counsel of his birds, whether it might come to pass, that he had conceived, or no. When answer was made that it might, he delivered him a whetstone, and commanded him to cut it with a razor in two: which thing he did; and thereupon the sorcerer's Image was erected. When the Veii were overthrown, and their city taken, a soldier was sent to fetch away Juno Moneta from them[3]: and when in sport he asked her whether she would go to Rome, the Image answered that she would. When the mother of the Gods, (according to Sibylla's oracle,) was brought from Pessinuns[4]; [Pessinus;] and the ship, being set on the sands in Tyber, could by no force or policy be moved; Claudia, (which otherwise was of suspected fame,) besought the Goddess, that if she thought her to be a maid, she would suffer the ship to be drawn to the shore by her girdle: and so it was. When Rome was afflicted with a mortal plague, and everywhere some died of the pestilence; Æsculapius, conveyed from Epidauro, purged the air, and conferred them health[5]. When Appius Claudius[6], (contrary to divine responsal,) would have

---

[1] [installed.]   [2] Livius, Deca. i. Lib. i. [xxxvi.]
[3] Livius, Dec. i. Lib. v. [xxii. Cf. Val. Max. L. i. C. viii. 3.]
[4] Decadis iii. Lib. ix. [L. xxix. ad fin. Ovid. iv. *Fast.* 152, sq.]
[5] [Liv. Lib. x. Cap. xlvii. ad calc. L. xi. *Epit.* Conf. S. Aug. *De Civ. Dei*, x. xvi.]
[6] Decad. i. Li. ix. [xxix. Valer. Max. Lib. i. Cap. i.]

transferred the sacrifices of Hercules to common servants, he had by miracle his eyes put out for it. When Pyrrhus had spoiled the Revestry[7] of Proserpina, and taken away all the treasure that he found; soon after he was drowned[8], and nothing saved but only the good lady's money.

Infinite such examples I could allege, whereby the Heathen were blinded in Gentility[9], as you be now in Popery. But shall we gather of those, that witches and wizards must be consulted with? that Juno Berecynthia, Æsculapius, Hercules, and Proserpina, must have sacrifice and service done them? If this ye admit not, I will as little grant the sign of the Cross to be admitted, for any miracle that hath been wrought by it. Jupiter and Diana, with the whole rabble of ethnic Idols, did heal many of their diseases, and strangely delivered them: whereof S. Cyprian doth make a feate[10] discourse. You will grant, (I dare say,) that this was done by power of the Devil. And can the Devil then do such deeds? Can he heal? can he restore? He can, when God's pleasure is: and he doth among them that are subject to his tyranny; that will walk in a popish blindness: before whose eyes he casteth such a mist, that they think themselves in the meanwhile to be worshippers of God, and to be aided of Him. For the Devil himself hath so ill a name, that if he were never so dear to men, yet they would not profess him openly, nor call upon him by express words. Wherefore, he doth so daze[11] the minds of them that he hath gotten under his rule, that they think with themselves they serve no man less than the Devil; when he indeed pulls them clean away from the worshipping of God, and salvation that is in Him, to make them partakers of his unhappy state and condemnation.

Miracles are wrought by the Devil; and how.

Therefore these wicked Spirits[12] do lurk in Shrines, in

[7] [or Revestiary; Vestry.]
[8] [Liv. L. xxix. C. xviii. Justin. Histor. Lib. xxiii. C. iii. Plutarch. in Vit. Pyrrhi.]
[9] [Conf. Lactant. Lib. ii. De orig. Error. C. vii, xvi.]
[10] [skilful, ingenious.]   [11] [dazzle.]
[12] [" Hi ergo Spiritus sub Statuis atque Imaginibus consecratis delitescunt. Hi afflatu suo Vatum pectora inspirant, extorum fibras animant, avium volatus gubernant, sortes regunt, oracula efficiunt, falsa veris semper involvunt. Nam et falluntur, et fallunt; vitam turbant, somnos inquietant. Irrepentes etiam in corporibus occulte mentes terrent, membra distorquent, valetudinem frangunt, morbos

Roods, in Crosses, in Images: and first of all pervert the Priests, which are easiest to be caught with bait of a little gain. Then work they miracles. They appear to men in divers shapes; disquiet them when they are awake; trouble them in their sleeps; distort their members; take away their health; afflict them with diseases[1]; only to bring them to some Idolatry. Thus when they have obtained their purpose, that a lewd affiance is reposed where it should not; they enter, (as it were,) into a new league, and trouble them no more. What do the simple people then? Verily suppose that the Image, the Cross, the thing that they have kneeled and offered unto, (the very Devil indeed,) hath restored them health; whereas he did nothing but leave off to molest them. *Hæc est enim,* (as S. Cyprian saith,) *ipsorum medela, cum cessat ipsorum injuria :* "This is the help and cure that the Devils give, when they leave off their wrong and injury."

Nor truly we cannot justly allege, that such things were done among the Gentiles only, nor yet only among the Jews, (as we do read it was[2];) but among the Christians it both hath been and shall be so. S. Paul hath a notable place in his second Epistle to the Thessalonians, the second chap. "The wicked man," (saith the Apostle,) "shall be revealed: whose coming is by the working of Satan, with all power and signs and lying wonders; and in all deceivableness of unrighteousness among them that perish[3]." Whereby it is evident, that signs and wonders shall be wrought in the time of Antichrist, that shall be able "to seduce, (if it be possible,) the very elect[4]." Have we not warning in the Gospel, that some shall come to Christ after such a sort in the latter day, saying: *Domine, Domine, nonne per nomen Tuum prophetavimus; et per nomen Tuum Dæmonia ejecimus; et per nomen Tuum multas virtutes præstitimus?* "Lord, lacessunt, ut ad cultum sui cogant; ut nidore altarium, et rogis pecorum saginati, remissis quæ constrinxerant, curasse videantur. Hæc est de illis medela, cum illorum cessat injuria." (S. Cyprianus, *De Idolor. vanitate.* Opp. p. 14. ed. Oxon.)]

[1] [Vid. Pinamont. *Exorcista rite edoctus*, Lucæ, 1690.; et omnino Hieron. Mengi *Flagellum Dæmonum,* ac *Fustis Dæmonum*, Venet. 1683.]
[2] Deu. xiii. [1—5.]
[3] 2 Thes. ii. [8—10.]
[4] [S. Mark xiii. 22.]

Lord, have we not by Thy name prophesied; and by Thy name cast out Devils; and by Thy name done many great works?" To whom God shall answer notwithstanding: *Nescio vos:* "I know you not[5]." So that it is not a sufficient proof to make the thing good, to say, that miracles were wrought by it. God doth abhor adultery: yet by the act of it sometime doth He suffer a miracle to be done, in the conception, the generation, the bringing of the child into life. God is offended with theft: yet doth He suffer stolen bread to feed us; which is only the power of His miraculous and secret working. Now if ye gather, that the use of the Cross is commendable, because of miracles done by it; by the same reason the adulterer and thief may defend and maintain their unlawful doings, because as great and greater miracles are wrought by them.

Notwithstanding, I know, some miracles are better than other some; and great difference there is betwixt them. Christ and His Apostles wrought miracles: so did Simon Magus and other sorcerers. But as God's glory was furthered by them, so private gain was sought for in these. As for the heavenly doctrine of Christ, a confirmation was fet from miracles; so is there no devilish superstition, but the same hath had strange wonders for it. Wherefore S. Augustin hath a goodly rule[6]: *Si Angeli sacrificia sibi petant fieri, et adhibuerint signa; ac e diverso alii testentur uni Deo sacrificandum, neque ulla miracula fecerint; iis utique, non illis, credere oportet.:* "If Angels require sacrifice to be done unto them, and work signs withal; and contrariwise some other testify, that sacrifice must only be made to God, and yet do no miracles; we must believe these, and not them." And in another place, concerning the Manichees, he saith[7]: *Signa ut vobis credatur nulla facitis: quamvis si ea faceretis, vobis credendum non esset:* "Ye work no miracles," (saith Augustin to the Manichees;) "whereby ye may induce us to believe you: though, if ye did work such, we ought not therefore to credit you." And so say I to you, (M. Martiall.) You say the Cross is able

---

[5] Matth. vii. [22, 23.]
[6] Augustinus, De Civitat. Dei, Li. x. Cap. xvi.
[7] Contra Faustum. [Lib. xiii. Cap. v.—"Miracula non facitis: quæ si faceretis, etiam ipsa in vobis caveremus."]

to do this and that: we see it not: no miracles ye work: and yet if ye did so strange things as ye talk of, we were not bound to believe your doctrine. For miracles alone are not sufficient to confirm and stablish us in a right faith. First of all, by the line of Scripture, we must examine the doctrine that is taught us: then, if it do agree to that, we must believe it; yea, though we have no miracle at all. But if miracles do come beside, then are the believers more established; and such as yet do not believe[1] be made the more attent to hear, and have a way made for them to come to the faith. Wherefore, in some condition, they be like to Sacraments. For both are added as assurances to promises, as seals to writings. And as Sacraments do bring no comfort, unless they be received by faith; so miracles do not avail, except we have first a regard to doctrine. In this diversity, to make no difference, is oversight; to commend the worse, and omit the better, is falsehood.

Miracles alone no proof of doctrine.

Miracles in some part like to Sacraments.

Folio 99, a.

You are, (you say,) "in a great perplexity where ye shall begin; as he that sitteth at a table furnished with many delicate dishes, whereof he shall first taste." And I marvel that you, so fine a feeder, will fall to your crambe[2]. Ye are "come to a garden, set round about with fresh fragrant flowers:" and yet ye gather but an handful of nettles for us to smell unto. Christ, by the touch of His hand, spittle of His mouth, by a plaster of dirt, (as you call it,) healed the sick, opened the ears of the deaf, restored the eyes of the blind. And why should not the dirt of the street be as well honoured as the Cross of the Altar; since the Scripture doth commend the dirt, but maketh no mention at all of the Cross; since better proof we have of miracle wrought by the one, than ever can be made for the other? If any external means, whereby strange wonders have come to pass, be to be had in admiration; why not such as Christ and His Apostles used, and the Scripture mentioneth, rather than the idle device of man, whereof there is no lawful precedent? Again, if your assertion were true, ("that miracles were wrought by the sign of the Cross;") yet were they not only by the sign of the Cross: and there-

Three reasons why miracles should not make for the Cross.

---

[1] [1 Cor. xiv. 22.]

[2] [Cabbage. "Δὶς κράμβη θάνατος." "Occidit miseros crambe repetita magistros."]

fore the Cross only, (according to your treatise,) should not without the rest be magnified. Last of all, if it were true, (as ye shall never prove,) that such things, (as you allege,) were done sometime by the sign of the Cross; yet this can be no reason why the Cross should now be had in estimation; unless ye will have all means and instruments of wonders heretofore wrought, as the hem of Christ's garment[3], the spittle and the clay[4], the shadow of Peter[5], and napkin of Paul[6], to be likewise honoured and esteemed of us.

But let me come to rehearsal of your miracles. Among them this is the first: and because I will have your truth in allegations appear, I will put it down as you have written it, word for word in order. "At what time the virtuous lady Helena, willed, as the story mentioneth, by revelation from God, to seek the Cross of Christ in Hierusalem, found, after long digging in the mount of Calvary[7], three Crosses, so confuse, that neither by the title that Pilate set up in Hebrew, Greek, and Latin, neither by any other means, they could discern which was the Cross that bare our Saviour Christ; a noblewoman of the city, consumed and spent with long sickness, did lie at death's door," &c. Ye note for your credit, in the margent, the place whence ye have the story: and that you affirm to be out of Eusebius his Ecclesiastical History, the tenth book, the seventh and eighth chapters. But this is a shameful lie: for Eusebius hath no such word. And this is a better proof of the vanity of your history; that where Eusebius, in his third book, *De vita Constantini*, maketh mention of Helena, and the place itself of Christ's sepulchre, which by the Emperor's commandment was cleansed, yet he speaketh not a word of this miraculous invention of the Cross[8].

_{Martiall.}

_{Euseb. Li. x. Cap. vii. & viii. Eccl. Histo.}

_{Martiall belieth Eusebius.}

[3] [S. Matth. ix. 20. xiv. 36.]   [4] [S. John ix. 6.]
[5] [Acts v. 15.]   [6] [Acts xix. 12.]
[7] [In the sixty-fourth Legend of the *Lombardic History*, we read that the Cross was discovered, first by Seth, the son of Adam; next by Solomon, on mount Lebanon; thirdly, by the Queen of Sheba, in Solomon's temple; fourthly, by the Jews, in the pool of Bethesda; and lastly by Helena, on mount Calvary. The authority alleged, with regard to Seth, is the apocryphal *Gospel of Nicodemus*.]
[8] [Conf. Theod. Bolmanni *Tumbam Servatoris*, p. 20. Helm. 1703.— Baronius (ad an. 326. §. xlii.) and Bellarmin (*De Imaginibus*, ii. xxvii. 1015.) assert that Eusebius, in his Chronicle, has borne witness of the invention of the Cross. They are, however, greatly astray: for there

[CALFHILL.]

Yet he lived at the same time, and was more likely to know a truth than other. Ye be to blame, therefore, to belie Eusebius. Indeed Ruffinus, in his first book and seventh chapter, hath the like that ye talk of. But what may be judged of the story shall afterward appear.

And first for the virtue of lady Helena, (though I would be glad to speak as much good of my countrywoman[1] as I can;) yet she was a concubine, (by your leave,) to Constance[2]; as it appeareth in *Catalogo Cæsarum*, Cap. i., which is inserted into the Ecclesiastical History[3]. Likewise S. Ambrose calleth her *Stabulariam*[4], "a woman brought up in an hostrie[5]." And as for her superstition, (which in part I have touched before,) it is too evident. But whatsoever she was, let us go to her fact. If she found the Cross, a time was when she found it; and the same must be after her conversion, when Silvester was Bishop of Rome: for otherwise she could not be so virtuous and religious, (as ye talk of.) And Nicephorus affirmeth[6], that by Silvester she was converted to the faith. For which cause the author, (whose credit in this tale ye follow,) doth write the invention of the Cross to have been in the reign of Constantinus the Great. But what saith your Pope-holy law to this? Read your Decree[7]. *Eusebius Papa.*

is not any such testimony in the original Greek; but it appears only in the falsified Latin version. See Du Moulin's *Masse in Latin and English*, pp. 392—3. Lond. 1641. Comber's *Roman Forgeries*, p. 155. Lond. 1689.]

[1] [Vid. Usserii *Britann. Eccles. Antiqq.* Cap. viii. p. 94, sqq. Lond. 1687.]

[2] [Eusebii *Chron.* pp. 48, 180. Amstel. 1658. Orosii *Histor.* Lib. vii. Cap. xxv. fol. cccxvi. Colon. 1561.—Selden confutes the supposition by an extract from Josephus Ægyptius. See a note upon the *Historia Sacra* of Severus Sulpitius; Lib. ii. Cap. xlix. p. 371. Amst. 1665.]

[3] [At the end of the Latin version of Theodoret, by Joachimus Camerarius, who was the author of this *Catalogus*.]

[4] Ambros. De obitu Theodosii. [*Opp.* Tom. v. 123. Lut. Paris. 1661.]

[5] [Hosterie, or Hostelrie, an Inn.]

[6] Nicephorus, Li. vii. Ca. xl. [Cap. xxxvi.]

[7] In Decre. De Consec. Di. iii. Cap. Crucis. [xix. This Chapter consists of an extract from the third spurious Epistle of Pope Eusebius, presently referred to again. Vid. Blondelli *Pseudo-Isidor. et Turrian. vapulantes*, pp. 420—22.]

Crucis Domini nostri Jesu Christi, quæ nuper, nobis gubernacula sanctæ Romanæ Ecclesiæ tenentibus, quinto nonas Maii inventa est: " Eusebius the Pope. The Cross of our Lord Jesus Christ, which of late was found the third day of May, while I had the governance of the holy Church of Rome;" and so forth. Whereby it is evident, that your law saith how the Cross was found in Eusebius' time : your author saith it was in Silvester's time. And yet many years were run betwixt: yea, the whole reign of Melchiades the Pope, beside many odd years of their own continuance in the Romish see. Wherefore, you must either say, that your popish law doth teach you lies; or else that your author in this behalf is a liar. It is always to be observed, how uncertain tales be delivered of Papists as truths unto us.

<small>The Papists agree not for the invention of the Cross.</small>

Marianus saith[8], that the Cross was found in the reign of Constance, father to Constantinus.

Ruffinus saith[9], that in Silvester's time it was found out; which, by Hierom's computation, must needs be a good while after the fifth year of Constantinus' reign : for only in the fifth year of Constantinus Silvester began his popedom. And therefore Sigebertus saith[10], that he cannot see how this gear may stand together.

In the first tome of Councils, we have three Epistles of Eusebius, Pope of Rome; whereof the last is *Ad Thuscos et Campanos;* where order is taken, that the invention of the Cross, found in his time, should be kept holy-day[11]. Then "God

---

[8] [Ad an. Chr. 306. col. 304. Basil. 1559.—De Mariani Scoti *Chronic.* Vid. Sigeb. ad an. 1082.]

[9] [*Hist. Eccles.* Lib. i. Cap. viii.]

[10] Lib. viii. Chro. [The *Chronicon* of Sigebertus is not divided into Books; and, as it commences at the year 381, it cannot contain such a statement at all. It would appear that the author has confounded Sigebertus with Jac. Phil. Forestus, Bergomensis; in whose *Supplementum Chronicarum* we find the following words : "Quæ res quomodo stare possit ignoro." (Lib. viii. fol. 179. Brixiæ, 1485.) In Genebrard's *Chronographia* we read : " Nam quod Lib. i. Conc. in Epist. Eusebii, tribuit ejus institutionem Eusebio Papæ, constare non potest." (Lib. iii. ad an. 320. Paris. 1600. Conf. Naucleri *Chronog.* Vol. ii. Gen. xi. pp. 499, 505. Colon. 1579. Martini Poloni *Chron.* pag. 187. Antverp. 1574. Bedæ *Serm.* Opp. Tom. vii. 356—7. Colon. Agr: 1612. Pet. de Natalibus *Catal. Sanctor.* Lib. iv. fol. ciii. Lugd. 1508.)]

[11] [Binii *Concilia*, i. i. 207.—Bellarmin readily admits that the au-

inspired" not "the heart of Helena to seek the Cross." It was found to her hand: yea, long before she was converted to the faith.

Again, if it were admitted that Helena did find it; (being driven thereunto by womanish curiosity, or a foolish zeal[1]:) yet, in the rest of the tale, I see no constant truth. For you say "that she found, after long digging in the mount of Calvary, three Crosses, so confuse, that neither by the title that Pilate set up in Hebrew, Greek, and Latin, neither by any other means, they could discern which was the Cross that bare our Saviour Christ." But Saint Ambrose hath the quite contrary; for, entreating of the same matter, he saith[2]: *Tria patibula confusa reperit; quæ ruina contexerat, inimicus absconderat. Sed non potuit obliterari Christi triumphus. Incerto hæret ut mulier: sed certam indaginem Spiritus Sanctus inspirat, eo quod duo latrones cum Domino crucifixi fuerint. Quærit ergo medium lignum. Sed poterat fieri, ut patibula inter se ruina confunderet, casus mutaret et inverteret. Redit ad Evangelii lectionem: invenit quia in medio patibulo prælatus titulus erat, Jesus Nazarenus, Rex Judæorum. Hinc collecta est series veritatis. Titulo Crux patuit salutaris.* The English whereof is this: "She found three trees of execution confounded together; which the ruin and fall had covered, the enemy had hidden away. But the triumph of Christ could not so be blemished, and quite forgotten. As a woman, she did stick in doubt: but the Holy Ghost inspired a sure way of trial, inasmuch as two thieves were crucified with our Lord. Wherefore she seeketh the tree that was in the midst. But it might be, that, in the

---

thenticity of this Epistle is "non certum." (*De Confirmat.* Lib. ii. Cap. vii. 414.) Surius and Binius, in their notes upon it, have determined that the part which relates to the discovery of the Cross is undoubtedly surreptitious. Mr Taylor, however, has cited this counterfeit document without any hesitation. (*Ancient Christianity*, Vol. ii. p. 298. Lond. 1842.) It is remarkable that Pope Gelasius, in the year 496, condemned as apocryphal the "Scripta de inventione S. Crucis Dominicæ:" (*Dist.* xv. Cap. iii.) and we may leave it to Baronius to investigate what these writings were. Vid. *Martyrol. Rom.* die Maii 3. p. 186. Antverp. 1613.]

[1] ["Stulta curiositas," vel "ineptus Religionis zelus." (Calvin. *De Reliqq.* p. 276.)]

[2] Ambros. De obitu Theodosii. [ut sup.]

spoil of the place, the gibbets might be confounded: some chance might change them; some occasion displace them. Wherefore she returneth to the reading of the Gospel: she findeth, that, on the middle gallows, this title on the top was set: 'Jesus of Nazareth, King of the Jews.' Hence was the course of truth gathered. The healthful Cross was well known by the title."

So far S. Ambrose. Now see the repugnancies in this proof of yours. Marianus saith that the Cross was found in the reign of Constance. Ruffinus ascribeth it to the time of Constantine. Eusebius doth challenge the glory of the miracle unto his time. Silvester denieth it, and saith that in his time it was first sought and found. The Canon Law doth hold with Eusebius. The Ecclesiastical History taketh part with Silvester. You cite the story, "that by the title which Pilate set up" the Cross by no means could be discerned. And S. Ambrose saith plainly, that by the title[3] the Cross was discerned. Whom shall we credit now? What shall we build upon so uncertain ground? You made a lie of Eusebius Pamphilus, that in his Ecclesiastical History he should report the story that he doth not. Eusebius the Pope and the Canon Law prove that you do lie, referring the invention of the Cross to Silvester's time, who converted Helena; whereas it was found a good many years before, in Eusebius' reign, or else do they lie. Wherefore, sith Eusebius of Cæsarea, that was most likely to know the truth, living in the same age, writing of the same matter, maketh no mention how the Cross should thus miraculously be found; sith your own authors agree not in their tales, but in every circumstance of time, of persons, of manner of the doing, vary; I may justly doubt, whether Helena were inspired of God to seek the Cross, or that by any such strange miracle the Cross was found. "As God worketh nothing in vain," (as you say;) so not every vanity that you devise God worketh, say I.

Nothing else but repugnancy and contradictión in popish doctrine.

From the whole Cross ye descend to every piece thereof: as, "that it should have the like efficacy and force, for that it was once imbrued with the water and blood of our Saviour Christ." But if every piece of wood, that is stoutly

Folio 101.

[3] [.. "etsi vetustate propemodum abolitus." (Polyd. Vergil. *De rer. inventor*. L. v. C. vi. pag. 334. Basil. 1550.)]

affirmed to be a piece of the holy Cross, were once imbrued with the blood of Christ, then Christ in His body had as much blood as any great river hath drops of water. What land in Christendom, what city, what monastery, what private parish, but hath had some piece of it? Helena sent the one part of it to Constantine, her son; (Ruffinus, *Ecclesi. Hist.* Lib. i. Cap. vii. [viii.] Sozomenus, Li. ii. Cap. i.) which was set upon a pillar at Constantinople. The other part she enclosed in a silver coffin; and that she commanded to be kept at Jerusalem. Notwithstanding, a halting wench, that waited sometime on lady Helena, and afterward ran away from her mistress, stale a piece of the said Cross, and brought it to Poytiers in France. Another piece fell down from heaven, and is kept as a Relique in the holy chapel of Paris. Another piece, as much as an Angel could lug on his back, was brought to Rome, and a whole Rood was made thereof. Finally, the Cross hath so replenished all places of the world[1], that if all the pieces were gathered together, no ship, no hulk of greatest burden, were able to bear them. And yet poor Simon of Cyrene carried sometime the whole.

Many lies be made of pieces of the Cross.

If ye go to the constant opinion of men, the Cross is yet remaining, (most of it,) at Jerusalem. Wherefore we must go fight against the Turks, and recover the holy Cross. But, being so mangled as it hath been, what by theft, and what by friendship, impossible it is that anything should remain of it; yea, though it were so big as Noah's ark: unless it be like the monster Hydra, that for every head cut off ariseth seven; for every splinter taken from it, another greater piece, as big as an oak, doth grow. The Ecclesiastical History saith[2]: *Ligni ipsius salutaris partem detulit filio; partem vero thecis argenteis conditam dereliquit in loco:* That Helena "brought one part of the healthful wood unto her son; and the other part she left in the place at Jerusalem, enclosed in a silver coffin." To this accordeth Theodor. *Eccle. Hist.* Li. i. Cap. xviii., and Sozomenus, Li. ii. Cap. i. So that by them it should appear, that whereas she sent but one piece of the Cross to Constantine, which was reserved at Constantinople, *supra columnam porphyream,* "upon a red-marble pillar;" "the greatest part

---

[1] [S. Cyrilli Hier. *Cateches.* pp. 79, 216. Paris. 1609.]
[2] Ruffinus, Li. i. Cap. viii.

thereof," *maxima portio*, as Sozomenus writeth, was left at Hierusalem. But Jacobus Philippus Bergomensis saith[3], that a piece of it was brought to Rome; and the same, (as it should seem,) that the other authors affirm to have been left at Hierusalem. For his words be these: *Crucis ipsius partem detulit; quam quidem et thecis argenteis, atque gemmis pretiosissimis exornari fecit; quamque denique, Romam veniens, secum cum magna veneratione detulit:* " She brought a piece of the Cross," (saith he;) " which she caused to be garnished with silver cover, and precious stones: which also at length, coming unto Rome, she brought with great worship with her." Whereby we are brought in doubt where Helena did bestow the Cross: and what became of any part of it, our Doctors agree not.

Furthermore, as concerning the nails wherewithal Christ was fastened to the Cross, a greater controversy doth arise. Theodoret, *Ec. Hist.* Li. i. Ca. xviii., writeth thus: *Clavorum alios galeæ regiæ inseruit; qui præsidio essent capiti filii sui, et hostium tela repellerent: alios frenis equestribus conjunxit:* " Some of the nails Helena did put in the King's helmet; which might be a defence to her son's head, and repulse the weapons of his enemies: other she put to his horse's bridle." But Sozomenus saith[4]: *Galeam ex illis et frenum equorum fabricasse:* That the Emperor himself " made him an helmet and an horse-bridle of them." So that, first, they agree not in this; whether it should be the mother's device, or the son's. Then also, whether the nails were clenched in the helmet, and joined to the bridle; or else that a whole helmet, and bridle too, were beaten out of them. Ambrose varieth from them both; for he affirmeth[5]: *De uno clavo frenos fieri præcepit. De altera [altero] diadema intexuit. Unum ad decorum, [decorem,] alterum ad devotionem vertit:* " She commanded of one nail a bridle to be made. She wove the other into his coronet. One to the shew, the other she turned to devotion." And as for the third, she kept. Now, to carry a thing in sign of honour, as it were in triumph, is one thing: to make it a special point of defence another. A sallet[6] is one thing, and a cap another: an helmet is one

The nails that Christ was crucified withal.

[3] Lib. ix. [*Supplem. Chronicar.* L. ix. fol. 182. Brixiæ, 1485.]
[4] Lib. ii. Ca. i.   [5] Ambrosius, De obitu Theodosii.
[6] [salade, headpiece.]

thing, and a crown another. To join a nail unto my bridle is one thing: to make a bridle of a nail is another. Beside this, Bergomensis is different from them all. For, in his Chronicle[1], he speaketh of three nails: whereof the first, he saith, *Constantinus ipse in frenum equi sui transtulit, quo in prælio tantummodo utebatur. Alterum vero in galea sua [galeæ suæ cono] collocavit. Et tertium [ut Divus testatur Ambrosius,] in Adriaticum mare, ad comprimendas sævientis maris procellas dejecit :* "Constantine himself transposed into his horse's bridle, which in the wars he only used. Another he placed in his helmet. The third he cast down into the gulf of Adria, to assuage the storms of the raging sea." So that Sozomenus dissenteth from Theodoret: S. Ambrose teacheth a contrary to them both; and Bergomensis agreeth with none of them at all.

The truest opinion is, that there were not past three nails in all[2]. Which three you see how they were bestowed. One was put into an helmet, or into a crown: another was annexed to a bridle, or else a bridle beaten out of it: the third was cast into the bottom of the sea. Notwithstanding, I know not how it cometh to pass, but every one of these is extant to this day: and although the helmet be gone, the bridle consumed, the sea continueth, yet the very selfsame nails be come abroad again, and reserved as Reliques. Yea, more than ever were driven on the Cross; unless they will make of five wounds fifteen. For Calvin, (whom I am not ashamed, for honour's sake, to name, and none of you all is able to disprove;) in his book of Reliques, proveth, of his knowledge, that in Italy, France, and Germany, there be at the least fourteen remaining. And I could easily bring forth the fifteenth, which was here in England in Queen Mary's days, with a taper burning solemnly before it. Thus is the Cross, and every nail thereof, an anvil to strike men's lies upon. This is the constancy in men's doctrine. By this may be gathered, that popish fantasies are as Poets' fables;

---

[1] [loc. sup. cit.]

[2] [The number four is insisted on, and the whole subject fully discussed, by the Augustinian Cornelius Curtius; *De Clavis Dominicis Lib.* Antverp. 1670. Conf. D. Greg. Turon. *De gloria Martyr.* Lib. i. Cap. vi. p. 9. Colon. 1583. Henningii *Archæolog. Passional.* Cap. xx. p. 200. Francof. 1676.]

and as much credit to be given to them otherwise, as to the legends of Lucian.

Ye urge a miracle for every little piece and splinter of the Cross; inasmuch as a church and a religious house was preserved from burning by it. Paulinus doth tell the tale. But if such a thing happily [haply] were done, when miracles did stand in force, and men stood in need of them, yet were they not made to establish a worshipping, or having at all of a Cross with us; but to confirm a faith in the crucified Christ in them; and to teach us, not to do the like, but to believe the like. Many tales have ye heaped up; as, "That a woman should be preserved from rape and witchcraft by the sign of the Cross, and name of Christ. That a woman was brought safe out of the stews by the grace of Christ, and sign of the Cross. That a canker in a woman's breast was healed by the Cross. That a dragon was killed with the Cross. That S. Martin made certain Gentiles stand still, and preserved himself from the fall of a tree, by the sign of the Cross. Finally, that a soldier was killed for forsaking the bearing of the sign of the Cross." The credit of these stories all I remit to the authors. Only I affirm, that they prove not your cause; for it is no good reason: "The sign of the Cross hath done this miracle and this: *Ergo*, the sign of the Cross must be set up and honoured." If ye could avouch that the sign of the Cross were able now to do the like, I would admit your case the rather: though absolutely, (as I said before,) miracles do not enforce a doctrine.

The woman of which Epiphanius[3] reporteth, when she was in the baths, felt one by enchantment touch her, whom she saw not, and made the sign of a Cross: which was no cause of her preservation, but witness of her faith that did preserve her. And this Epiphanius himself testifieth: *Signavit se in nomen Christi, ut quæ Christiana esset:* "She signed herself into the profession and name of Christ, as who was a Christian." And after he saith not that the signing served her; but *per signaculum et fidem:* "By the sign of Christ and by faith" the woman received hope. And faith doubtless, without the sign, had been able to have wrought as much as that; but that it pleased God to shew a miracle, which, (to another end,)

[3] Lib. i. Tom. ii. Hær. xxx. [pp. 42—3. Basil. 1578. Cornario interp.]

He would by some visible sign to be expressed. The end was, to shew the virtue of belief in Christ, and to convert an heathen man, which could not see the secret faith that so prevailed against enchantment, and therefore stood in need of an outward sign. Wherefore Epiphanius, in the same place, concludeth: *Hoc tertium instructionis ad fidem opus Josepho contigit:* "This third work happened unto Joseph, for instruction of his faith." So that when it pleased God to use a miracle for conversion of an Infidel, we must not gather that He hath left an example for us to do the like: yet is not such power ascribed to the sign, as you collect; but, the virtue remained in the name of Christ. Notwithstanding, as oft, in the Scripture, *causa per effecta, fides per opera declaratur,* "the cause is declared by the effects, as the faith by works;" so, many times, and specially for the world's instruction, the inward purity and persuasion is notified to men by the outward fact: which fact needeth not now to be the sign of the Cross; since we live not among Turks and Sarazins, but all men without it know of whom we hold, in whom we do believe. Thus have I answered the place of Epiphanius: and by this you may learn never to allege a place, but to consider better the circumstance of the same. I think a man should have much ado with you, if ye were able at this day to shew the like virtue and effect of a Crucifix, as hath been of old reported. Yet this ought to be approved, afore we do confirm the necessary use thereof.

A Catholic of yours, for all his confidence in the Cross, would be loth to adventure his daughter in a common brothel-house, (as your tale is of the woman of Corinth;) although he had taught her never so much to cross her. Peradventure she might be as good a maid as she that took such pleasure in massing and in crossing, that out of the church she would never come, unless it were to a man's bed. Only I marvel, if the sign of the Cross be so soveraign a medicine to preserve chastity, why so many of your order, that most delight therein, make stews as it were of their own houses; none so great lechers as the superstitious; none more incontinent than popish Priests. And they think they have warrant of your Religion for it. For in that

Foli. 104, a.

Why Papists are more licentious and advouterous[1] than other.

---

[1] [adulterous. See Wicliffe's *Apology*, pp. 76, 78. Lond. 1842. ed. Camden Soc.]

tyrannous interreign of Antichrist, eight year ago, when a Priest of Oxford was accused to Cardinal Poole's commissioners of an horrible offence, not to be named of a Christian, but commonly practised among the Papists; *Nefas est accusare Sacerdotem*, cried out the Datary[2]: "It is a wickedness to accuse a Priest" of such crime or such. But the matter was evident; the parties confessed it. And what was awarded him? Forsooth, to ask his fellow whether he were a thief: to tell a tale in another's ear, which was as good as himself. So that Confession salved that sore straight. About the same time an old fornicator, in Red-cross street, in London, declared the effect of your Religion; which is, to breed a security in sin: for, being taken in adultery by such as are yet alive, and have good cause to remember it, he sped himself as fast as he could to church; would needs have a Mass; and when he had heard it, he came home again. His wife laid the matter bitterly to his charge: his friends most grievously did expostulate with him: and when he had nothing to excuse himself; nothing to lessen the fault withal, he said: "There is none of you all, though you would see me hanged, but knows I believe in the Sacrament of the Altar. Well then, I believe well; I thank God of that." Yet he thought his belief in the Sacrament of the Altar was enough for him, though otherwise he played the varlet egregiously.

You think that a sign of a Cross sufficeth, (as it did for Lucian [Julian] and the Jew;) though no faith in Christ, no goodness do come withal. And this may be supposed to have encouraged your devout fathers to live so licentiously as they have done. Wherein if I had Lewis Evans his vein, I could with truths make those ears to glow, which now do glory in his shameless lies. "The sign of the Cross," (say you,) "maketh that harlots would live chaste." How happens it then, that a friend of yours, (a bastard, or Bishop, or both was, peradventure[3],) which is not, I warrant you, without a Cross or twain, should have from his bedside a privy postern? Not, that when his Bacchus had bathed him, his Venus might warm him? How falleth it out, that a chief maintainer of your faction, that joyeth as much in the Cross

Fol. 116, a.

What chastity in crossing Papists.

---

[2] [An officer attached to the Court of Rome, through whom many Benefices are conferred.]   [3] [Gardiner?]

sign as you, loathed always his lawful diet, and delighted most in stolen venery? What hap was this, that sometime a Warden of your College, that daily devoutly would kneel before the silver Cross, and attempted as earnestly to bring all Christians to the wooden Cross, should keep both the mother and the daughter in Oxford; and after for perjury wear a paper in Windsor[1]? I will no further offend chaste ears, with rehearsing the shame of your unchaste generation. Only will I say, (and if ye further urge me, in particularity will prove;) that, as I am now entreating of miracles, so ever in my time it hath been greatest miracle to see a chaste Votary.

But, to return to your allegations: if ye will have us credit you in your doctrine, then let us see the fruits: let miracles be wrought; let the Cross make you honest; and I will verily affirm it a miracle. If the sign of a Cross do heal diseases, and kill dragons: if it keep us from the fall of trees, and make our enemies stand still before us; then farewell physic: I will occupy no weapons; I will fear no danger; I will conquer where I lust. A vanity it is of you, M. Martiall, to bring for proof of a present use that which was done so long ago. Remember what Father Gregory doth say[2]: *Nolite fratres amare signa, quæ possunt cum reprobis haberi communia: sed charitatis atque pietatis miracula amate; quæ tanto securiora sunt, quanto et occulta; et de quibus apud Dominum eo major fit retributio, quo apud homines minor est gloria:* "Brethren, be not in love with signs, which may be had common with the reprobate: but love ye rather the miracles of charity and true godliness; which, the more secret the more secure: and for the which, the less estimation that there is with men, the greater is the reward with God."

Miracles past no proof of present use.

In the first beginning and gathering of the Church[3],

[1] [See Dr London's picture in Fox. ii. 469. ed. 1684.]
[2] In Evan. Jo. Hom. xxix. [*Opp.* Tom. ii. fol. 131, b. Antverp. 1572.]
[3] [" Sed hæc necessaria in exordio Ecclesiæ fuerunt. Ut enim ad fidem cresceret multitudo credentium, miraculis fuerat nutrienda. Quia et nos, cum arbusta plantamus, tamdiu eis aquam infundimus, quousque ea in terra jam coaluisse videamus; et si semel radicem fixerunt, irrigatio cessabit. Hinc est enim quod Paulus dicit, Linguæ in signum sunt, non fidelibus, sed infidelibus." (S. Greg. Mag. fol. sup. cit.)]

many things were necessary, which now be needless. Miracles were used then, which outwardly be denied now. When we go about to plant a tree, so long we water it, until we see that it hath taken root; but when it is once substantially grounded, and branches spread abroad, we take no more pain to water it: on like sort, as long as the people were altogether faithless, this mean of miracles was of indulgence granted them; but when spiritual instruction had taken better place, the corporal signs surceased straight. Wherefore the Apostle sayeth: *Linguæ in signum sunt, non fidelibus, sed infidelibus:* " Strange tongues are for a sign, not to them that believe, but to them that believe not[4]." And plainly to argue that a thing is good, because a miracle is shewed by it; or else to approve a present use by that which needfully sometime was done; hath too many absurdities and inconveniences to be yielded to. S. Augustin denied that argument of Petilian[5]: he would not admit the doctrine of the Donatists; although they had wrought all wonders in the world. *Non dicat,* sayeth he, *ideo verum est, quia illa et illa mirabilia fecit Donatus, vel Pontius, vel quilibet alius; aut quia homines ad memorias mortuorum nostrorum orant et exaudiuntur; aut quia illa et illa ibi contingunt:* "Let not the adversary say, therefore it is true, because Donate or Pontius, or any other hath done these and these wonderful and strange things; or else because men do make their prayers at the tombs of our dead, and be heard; or because such things and such things do happen there:" for these may be as well *figmenta mendacium hominum, vel portenta fallacium Spirituum:* "the feigned devices of lying men, or strange wonders of deceitful Spirits."

Wherefore, if miracles prove the use of a Cross, why should they not confirm the doctrine of the Donatists? Yea, if miracles may commend a thing, I will not only have the sign of a Cross, but the sign of a Devil. Macrobius, *in his Saturnalibus,* Li. i. Ca. vii., speaking of the sacrifices used in the reign of Tarquin the Proud, sayeth: *Effigies maniæ, suspensæ pro singulorum foribus, periculum, si quod immineret familiis, expiabant:* " The Images of madness,

A similitude.

As well we may have any sign of Idols as the sign of the Cross, if miracles may make it.

[4] 1 Cor. xiv. [22.]
[5] Aug. De uni. Eccle. Cap. xvi. [Cap. xix. *Ep. cont. Donat.* Opp. Tom. ix. 252.]

hanged before every man's door, made clear for all dangers that hanged over the household." Wherefore I will thus reason with you:

Either the miracles that you do speak of were false tales, or else they were truths.

If they were false tales, a true man ought not to allege them, nor a Christian believe them.

Whether it be true or false that M. Martiall reporteth of the Cross, it cannot prove the lawful use thereof.

The Scripture warneth us, that in the latter days there shall be strong Spirits of illusion; so that the elect themselves, (if it be possible,) may be seduced. Wherefore, if the Devil at any time by the Priests, as of old time by the wise men of Egypt, have wrought wonders about Roods and Images; no doubt but, by shewing unwonted things, he goeth about to allure us to things unlawful: and therefore such miracles should not be credited. But, on the other side, if it pleased God to use the sign of a Cross indeed, as a mean to work some miracles in the world; yet is it no sufficient cause to confirm the having, much less the honouring of it now.

To mollify the hearts of visible and mortal men, God used visible and mortal means; not to confirm a reverence to them, but to establish an honour and service to Himself. God spake *Moses' bush.* unto Moses out of a fiery bush[1]. Shall now the fire or the bush be honoured? A good cause is brought why God appeared in a bush, rather than any thing beside: that the people's eyes might teach them that which their hearts and souls ought to believe. For the thorns of the bush did signify the sins for which the Law came. And as the bush pricks not in the root, but is gentle and smooth, though the body and branches be full of thorns; so are not our sins of our first creation, but, by growing in the flesh, we have gathered them unto us. As the bush was not consumed by the fire, but the fire glisteringly did set forth the bush; so were not sins abolished by the Law, but only notified; not taken away, but laid open afore us. For the Law could no more but tell us our disease: only the grace of Christ doth cure us. As God appeared in form of fire, and not in an earthly shape; so must we learn to follow God; to raise our thoughts and desires upward, and not be depressed with downfall cares. As God vouchsafed to appear in a mountain, thereby to put us in mind of His height, far passing Princes

[1] [Exod. iii. 2. Acts vii. 30.]

and all worldly sublimity; so must we consider the worthiness of our calling; and be well assured, that such a hill must be climbed of us, as hath all the earth subject underneath it. Wherefore, as so great miracle was wrought by fire, in a bush, on a mountain, not to enforce an estimation of the means, but only to drive men to the ends aforesaid; so by the Cross miracles have been wrought; not for the wood's sake, not for the metal, but only for confirming of a faith in Christ. This faith then let us retain, and let the Cross alone.

Moses avoided the wrath of God, and escaped death, by cutting off the foreskin with a sharp stone[2]: and this is as much as Saint Martin's sign, whereby he avoided the fall of a tree. Shall now a sort of stones be brought into the church, and honoured of us? Moses did see the Angel of the Lord ready to destroy him, because he, (dwelling in the land of Midian,) neglected the circumcising of his son; and he, that was a messenger of the God of Abraham, had not in his child the sign of the faith of Abraham, wherein the Jews might and did glory. This Circumcision then, whereby such peril miraculously was shunned, was done by a stone; not that an earthly stone should be the more esteemed, but Christ, the Corner-stone, be signified; by whom all sins and transgressions be cut off, and by whom the danger of eternal death only is avoided. The rod of Aaron was often turned into a Serpent[3], often returned into the own nature; which in a figure represented Christ, from life to death, from death arising unto life again: or else that, as the rod, by dividing the Red Sea[4], made a passage open into the land of promise; so Christ, through Baptism into His death, hath prepared the way into life for us. Shall now the rod of Aaron, because it wrought such miracle, be set up in the church? The tree that was cast into the waters of Marah[5] did make them sweet; in token that the bitterness of the Law was taken away by the death of Christ, and now the minds of the faithful people be replenished thorough it with spiritual and abundant pleasure. Shall therefore the sign of that piece of wood now be worthied of honour?

Circumcision.

Aaron's rod.

The wood of Marah.

The Jews were preserved from the Serpents' stings[6] by *The brazen Serpent.*

[2] Exod. iv. [24—26.]   [3] Exod. vii. [9, 10.]
[4] [Exod. xiv. 16.]   [5] Exod. xv. [25.]
[6] Num. xiv. [xxi. 9.]

looking on the brazen Image; representing also the death of Christ, which from infection of damned Spirits saveth His elect. Shall now a piece of brass, or sign of a Serpent, be set up in churches, and reverently adored? The rock, smitten with Moses' hand[1], gushed out of water; and the streams flowed in the parched fields, to satisfy the drought of the thirsty people: whereby is signified Christ to be the stone cut out of the quarry, *sine manibus præcidentium*, "without any workman's hand[2];" which, by the lively liquor of His eternal Testament, quencheth the thirst of incredulity; crying continually: *Si quis sitit, veniat ad Me et bibat:* "If any man thirst, let him come to Me and drink[3]." Shall now, for this respect, the rock or river be exalted, and set in place of God's service? The fleece of Gideon[4] was only moisted with the dew, when all the earth beside was dry: again, it was only dry upon the fleece, when the dew fell upon all the ground: to note the Gentility of all the world destitute of grace; void of that heavenly and spiritual dew; when only the fleece of Israel, the people of the Jews, were comforted with the showers of God's word and promises. Again, that for want of true belief the foresaid people should wither with the drought of infidelity; when the heathen folk should be all to besprinkled with the dew of heaven, as now we are by preaching of the Gospel. But where the threshing-place of the barn, and fleece of Hierobaal[5], were the means whereby the miracle was wrought, shall any of them both be now magnified of us? Sampson, with the jaw-bone of an ass, slew a thousand men[6]; and out of the cheek-tooth thereof the water ran, to assuage his thirst: in signification how Christ, our Advocate and Mediator, hath overthrown the adversary Power; hath by one death destroyed all the enemies of life; and hath refreshed the dry souls of faithful people, which be the members of His body, with the spiritual drink of affiance in Him. Shall we now have jaw-bones and cheek-teeth in the church?

Elias with his cloke divided the water of Jordan[7]: insinuating unto us how Christ, by His incarnation, hath made

---

[1] Nume. xx. [11.]
[2] [Dan. ii. 34, 45.]
[3] Joan. vii. [37.]
[4] Jud. vii. [vi. 36—40.]
[5] [Judges vii. 1.]
[6] Jud. xv. [15, 19.]
[7] 2 Reg. ii. [2 Kings, ii. 8.]

a way to Baptism; that, by faith in Him, we may walk on the dry land of security, dreadless of the waves of sin. Shall therefore a cloke be hanged up, and a candle lighted before it? Naaman the Syrian, by washing himself in Jordan, was cleansed of his leprosy[8]: and shall the sign of Jordan be worshipped of us? The hem of Christ's garment conferred health upon the woman touching it[9]: and shall the sign of this be had in estimation? The shadow of Peter healed also some that passed by[10]: likewise the kerchief and handkerchiefs of Paul cured diseases[11], and drove out evil Spirits. Shall now the sign of a shadow; shall a sorry clout, be so much made of? Therefore, if miracles of old time past, wrought, (as I may grant you, though absolutely I am not bound to believe all that you do bring;) by mean of a Cross, shall be sufficient cause to make the sign thereof, or the selfsame thing, to be erected and honoured; then shall the fiery bush, the mountain of the Lord, the Circumcision of Moses, the rod of Aaron, the wood of Marah, the brazen Serpent, the water of the rock, the fleece of Gideon, the jaw-bone of Sampson, the cloke of Elias, the washing of Naaman, the hem of Christ's coat, the shadow of Peter, the handkerchief of Paul, be set up in the church themselves, or their signs. For by none of these but miracles were done: and as good reason in this respect to set up in the church any one of these, as otherwise the Cross.

As I have shewed you the effect and end of other miracles reported in the Scripture, so when it pleased almighty God to bring moe nations to one faith in Christ, and used the Cross as a mean to work the like by, you must as well understand the meaning, not to bring the wood into an admiration, not to teach us the service of a sign, but to confirm the faith in The crucified, and due obedience to Him that was signified. "A jewel," (you say,) "a precious stone of some strange virtue, if a man have it, must be kept warily, nor the stone be suffered to be broken. And shall we christian men break the Cross of Christ? &c. An herb in the garden, medicinable for this or that disease, must not be rooted out. And shall we root out of our gardens the holy sign of the Cross?" and so forth. Well,

[8] 2 Reg. v. [14.]
[9] Mat. ix. [20—22.]
[10] Act. v. [15.]
[11] Act. xix. [12.]

[CALFHILL.]

M. Martiall, let me ask you this question: If ye have but a glass, and repute it a diamond, doth your estimation bring virtue to the thing? If ye had a good herb, and the same be now withered, will ye make as much of it as if it were in the prime? The Cross that ye make so great accompt of, that ye covet to have set up in churches, hath not the virtue and power that ye talk of: it cannot heal: it cannot preserve: it cannot daunt the affections of the flesh: it cannot drive the wicked Spirits from us. As the mean is gone of the foresaid effects, so are the effects themselves ceased.

Possible it is that, in time past, men did some good by signing them with a Cross: now is it not, according to your position, "medicinable against all conjuration, enchantment, sorcery, and witchcraft;" but rather daily used in all these. Wherefore, your proofs be too weak; your miracles to no purpose; your Doctors much like yourself. "The Heathen, the New-Indians, the Jew, the Apostata," these are desirous of the sign of a Cross; "These signed themselves with a Cross on the forehead: Therefore the sign of the Cross must be used and honoured." As like as if I said: These were idolaters; they knew no true worship; the Devil deluded them; and therefore we must follow them. May I not therefore with juster cause than you complain, and say as you do, *O tempora!* "O miserable days! O times too licentious!" when every Erostratus may become famous by burning of Diana's temple; when every insolent and idle brain, if he can inveigh against the state of his country; defame them that in learning and virtue be far unlike himself; shall presume to write, and be suffered to print, his ignorant allegations and impudent untruths, to deface the Gospel, to set agog seditious and new-fangled heads?

You would have men judge no better of us, but that we go about "to overthrow the Religion of Christ, take away the memory of His passion, and say that there is no Christ at all." This do ye set forth by an example of Andrew Lampugnan, which gat an audacity to slay the Duke of Milan, by striking oft his Image; and by a similitude of a chamber of presence, wherein whoso cometh and pulleth down the cloth of estate, or otherwise breaketh Prince's arms in pieces, he is no loyal and faithful subject. Let the world judge betwixt you and us, who seek less the defacing of Christ and His Gospel; who would more abolish the memory of His death. We by continual preaching of it, or you by often painting of it. We by referring all glory unto God, or you by transferring all praise unto yourselves. We by setting forth our state of salvation so as Christ Himself hath taught us, saying, "Search ye the Scriptures;" or you by following the Devil's doctrine, and perverting the word, affirming, that we daily must gaze upon Pictures[1].

There be other means to remember Christ, (as in the Preface I have at large declared;) than by laying two sticks across, or breaking the air with a thumb on my forehead. Nor they deny Christ which affirm Him to be God, and therefore in heaven seek Him; but such as make an Image of Him, severing thereby His Divinity from humanity, and only as man upon earth honour Him. Wherefore your history is ill applied. Galeatius Maria, (as your own author[2] saith,) being Duke of Milan, was a wicked tyrant, a common ravisher of all honest women, a violent oppressor of all his subjects: therefore God stirred the hearts of some to conspire his death. And for the same cause the word of that arms is, *Vel in Ara*, that God in every place, yea, to the Altar itself, pursueth the revenge upon the ungodly. And therefore the man, which otherwise stood in dread of the Prince, was by another mean heartened. But God stirreth the heart of none to work any vengeance on Christ His Son: therefore the comparison is not like. Again, Lampugnan gat him the lively Image of the Duke: we have the Image I wot nere of whom: sure the Image of Christ it is not; but, in respect of the abuse, a damnable Idol. Then, if the striking at the Image of Christ be sign that Christ Himself is hated, consider with yourself who is more faulty, who is more despitefully set herein; you, or we. We peck at a stone or a piece of wood, which hath no likeness in the world of Christ: you burn and butcher the lively members of Christ's own body, the perfect counterfeits of Him departed hence. We pull down the dumb and the deaf Idols, the instruments of abuse: you murder the Saints; you destroy the Prophets; you spite that any liveth honester than yourselves. Who now, (I beseech you,) be more enemies of Christ? Who be more like to fall into apostasy: the over-

Papists deny Christ.

[1] [Comp. p. 28.]   [2] Paradinus, in Symbolis.

throwers of Idols, or destroyers of Saints; the mislikers of a dead stock or stone, or murtherers of quick and living men?

Folio 109, b. You request me to tell you, "if a man come into a chamber of presence, and pluck down the cloth of estate, and break the Prince's arms in pieces, is it not his intent to have the Prince deposed." Indeed, Sir, if the Prince have set it up, and give commandment that it shall there stand, it is too great an offence to break it. But if the Prince have proclaimed the contrary, that none shall presume to draw his arms, or set up any cloth of estate for him; and yet, notwithstanding, some in despite or mockery shall hang up a beggarly and stinking clout; or, instead of his royal arms, erect some monument of reproof and shame; if I came in place, I would pull it down, and be the faithfuller subject for that. And this is the very state of our cause. Christ and His Apostles, (as I have proved before,) have utterly forbidden Images. There is no Cross that hath any likeness of our Redeemer on it. Christ hath taken order, only by His word to be set forth unto us. Therefore the Cross of wood, stone, or metal, may without offence be removed of us. For it is not the cloth of estate of His; the arms and recognizance of His kingdom. It is a wicked invention of the Papists, a crafty delusion of the Devil, to supplant Christ; to take away the knowledge and true service of Him. Alexander, (as Horace saith[1],)

> Edicto vetuit ne quis se, præter Apellem,
> Pingeret, aut alius Lysippo duceret æra,
> Fortis Alexandri vultum simulantia:

"Gave charge that but Apelles none in colours should him dress,
Or but Lysippus should in brass his countenance express."

Then, if a simple botcher had attempted to draw him, contrary to his commandment, should he not have committed petty treason, trow you? On like sort, Christ hath given out His word, whereby He hath witnessed of Himself[2]. He hath straitly enacted, that whosoever worship Him, in spirit and verity they shall worship[3]: they shall not

---

[1] Episto. Lib. i. [Lib. ii. i. 239—41.]
[2] Joan. iv. [41. v. 31. viii. 14, 18.]
[3] Joan. v. [iv. 24.]

more simply conceive of Him than of the Majesty of a God, the second Person in Trinity, with our flesh carried up into heaven with Him. Now cometh the workman with his tools, and maketh a corporal and lying shape, to bring an outward and earthly worship. Alexander the coppersmith crieth out for his advantage. Simon Magus, the sorcerer, contendeth for his share. S. Paul is against it[4]. S. John condemneth it[5]. What shall we now do? go to the lying Image, and forsake the true; forbid the word, and bring in a Picture; have our hearts here in earth, where our God is in heaven? *Quisquamne tam ineptus est, ut putet aliquid esse in Simulachro Dei; in quo ne hominis quidem quicquam est præter umbram*[6]? "Is any man so foolish as to think, that any piece of God or godliness is in an Image; wherein there is no point incident into a man, beside the shadow?" Shall this be the arms and cognizance of our Master; in nature whereof there is nothing like Him, in use, whereof there is nothing but misliketh Him?

I doubt not but the Cross, if it had any sense or understanding, would bow down itself to the maker of it, and not abide the maker to do honour to it. For had not the maker bestowed some cost and workmanship upon it, it might well enough have been locked in the coffer and laid in the chimney. Then, what preposterous thing is this: they that have sense to set up the senseless; the reasonable creatures to worship the unreasonable; the living to fall down before the dead; the workmanship of God, and children of His kingdom, to adore a corruptible piece of earth? An ill effect of a vile occupation.

O curvæ in terras animæ, et cœlestium inanes! Persius.

"O crooked souls, bent to the earth, and void of heavenly things!"

We rather ought to erect our hearts and eyes thither, where our end is, whither we look to go, than be defixed on that which presently doth cumber us, and long we shall not enjoy. *Humi miseri volutamini,* (as Lactantius doth say[7];) *et pœnitet quadrupedes non esse natos, cum deorsum quæritis*

---

[4] Rom. i. [23.]   [5] Epi. i. Ca. v. [21.]
[6] Lactantius, De falsa Rel. [*De origine Error.*] Lib. ii. Cap. ii.
[7] De fal. Reli. [*De orig. Erroris,*] Lib. ii. Cap. ii.

quod in sublimi quærere debuistis: "Ye wretches tumble upon the earth; and seem to be sorry that ye be not made four-footed beasts, when ye seek below that which ye ought to find above."

For your Crosses and Crucifixes, your Images and inventions, what pretext soever they have to commend them, what colour and cost soever to garnish them, yet are they but earth: from thence they came, and thither they will. What should ye then be subject unto things inferior to yourselves? *Quum vos terræ summittitis, humilioresque facitis, ipsi vos ultro ad inferos mergitis, ad mortemque damnatis; quia nihil terra inferius et humilius, nisi mors et inferi: quæ si effugere velletis, subjectam pedibus vestris terram contemneretis, corporis statu salvo; quod iccirco rectum accepistis, quo oculos atque mentem cum Eo qui fecit conferre possetis. Contemnere autem et calcare terram nihil aliud est quam Simulachra non adorare;* [*quia de terra ficta sunt*[1]*:*] "When you submit and abase yourselves unto the earth, ye throw yourselves voluntarily to hell, and condemn you to death; for nothing is inferior and worse than the earth, but death and hell: which if ye would avoid, ye should contemn the earth that is under your feet, preserving the state and condition of your body; which for this respect ye have received upright, that ye might resemble and compare both eyes and mind with Him that made them. But, to contemn and despise the earth, is nothing else but not to worship Images, which are made of earth." Thus much Lactantius.

Now, if Christ be so slenderly received of us, and all His benefits so lightly passed over, that our memory must be holpen; and, unless we have somewhat subject to our eyes, we shall soon forget Him; we have the poor; we have beside the seals of His mercy, the Sacraments of His grace, which when He delivered He said: *Hoc facite in Mei commemorationem:* "Do this in remembrance of Me[2]." "For as oft as ye eat this bread, and drink this cup," saith the Apostle, "ye shew the Lord's death till He come[3]." Wherefore, let this confirm our memory, that Christ thought needful for us: let us not seek any further aids than Christ, (expert of our infirmities,) hath left us. If Christ and His death be

---

[1] Lactantius, ibidem. [2] [S. Luke xxii. 19.]
[3] 1 Cor. xi. [26.]

duly preached to us, no force if all Crosses be cast into the fire. But if preaching of Christ and hearing of His word do fail us, a sorry Cross can but delight our eyes, and straight corrupt our hearts. The miracles that have been done, although they may in part without any shame be doubted of, without any impudency denied; yet, granted to be true, must not be brought for confirmation of a Cross, lest the like be alleged to make Simon Magus a Saint. Indeed we read, that for the like effects he had an Image in Rome set up to him, with this inscription: *Simoni deo sancto*[4]: "To Simon the holy god." But Christ also speaketh of the like, which in the latter day shall come unto Him, saying: "Lord, have we not cast out Devils in Thy name; and by Thy name done many great works?" To whom notwithstanding Christ shall answer this: "I never knew you: depart ye from Me, ye workers of iniquity[5]." Therefore your miracles, if they be false, be devilish: if they were true, yet now are impertinent. But if we should deny them as untrue, (wherein we might have good authority to support us;) should we therefore, according to your gathering, "deny the omnipotency of God, as though He could not work any such miracles?" Why, we rather do advance it much; acknowledging that God, without such external means, is able to work more effects than these. Only beware you, lest by ascribing too much unto the mean, ye be ignorant of the end, and disgrace the Author.

Fol. 111, a.

We see by experience, that virtues wrought, or so supposed to have been, by the sign of a Cross, hath caused sensing[6], kneeling, offering, and all kind of wicked Idolatry to the Cross. And so, where Christ should have been only praised, a piece of wood is honoured. A good matter it is to receive a benefit, and so acknowledge it. A vile part it is to enjoy the pleasure of one man's travail, and bestow the thanks upon another. Yet so it falleth out among the superstitious. God worketh the miracle: they worship the mean. So did the children of for-

---

[4] Eusebi. Li. ii. Cap. xiii. [S. Justin Martyr, who presented his Apology to Antoninus about the year 140, is the first of the Fathers who mentions this circumstance. Many writers have supposed that the statue had been erected to *Semo Sancus*, a Sabine deity; and authorities on both sides of the question are enumerated by Dr Burton, in the forty-second note upon his *Bampton Lectures*. Oxf. 1829.]

[5] Mat. vii. [22, 23.]   [6] [incensing.]

nication among the Jews of old, whose mother had played the harlot, saying[1]: "I will go after my lovers, that give me my bread and my water, my wool and my flax, mine oil and my drink." "Nor she did know that I, saith the Lord, did give her her corn and oil, multiplied her gold and silver, which they bestowed upon Baal. Therefore will I return, and take away my corn in time thereof, and my wine in the season thereof, and will recover my wool and my flax lent, and discover her lewdness in the sight of her lovers." Whereby we have to understand, that as God is the only worker of all miracles tending to our health and preservation, so doth He accompt it an heinous fault, a spiritual fornication, when the glory thereof is conferred on another. Learn you by this, that the matter of the Cross never had the virtue to work such things as you report; and therefore ought not of any to be worshipped. God by His Prophet, in plain terms, doth call it whoredom, which you for your profit, in speech of hypocrisy, do call devotion. Wherefore, beware of the plague ensuing: derive not the glory from The crucified to the Cross. *Vivum colite, ut vivatis. Moriatur enim necesse est, qui se suamque animam mortuis adjudicavit*[2]*:* "Worship the living God, that you may live. For needs he must die, that hath adjudged himself and his soul unto the dead."

[1] Ose. ii. [5, 8—10.]   [2] Lactan. Li. ii. Cap. ii. [ad fin.]

TO THE NINTH ARTICLE.

WHAT COMMODITY EVERY CHRISTIAN MAN HATH, OR MAY HAVE, BY THE SIGN OF THE CROSS.

As the ground itself, and chief buttress of your cause is taken out of the second of Nice, whose impudent vanities[3] I have sufficiently before declared; so are not you ashamed sometime to allege them with as small trial as they had truth. But as S. Ambrose said of the Council held at Ariminum[4]: *Illud ego Concilium exhorreo*: "That Council I do utterly abhor;" so do I say of this, that with as good cause and with all my heart I refuse their authority, and condemn their doings. A vain allegation it was of Germanus, "that the Images of holy men are a lively description of their stoutness, a representation of holy virtue, a dispensation of grace given them:" a vain application it is of yours, "that even so the Cross and Image of Christ crucified, set before our eyes, is a lively description of His stoutness in bearing the blows of the Jews," and so forth. To speak first of other Images, and so to descend to yours; I beseech you, what stoutness and virtue is described, what holiness and grace is dispensed by them? When the Saints were alive, their virtues could not be discerned with eye: they rested in the mind their proper subject. And shall they now be seen in their dead Images, which have neither mind nor sense to hold them? This is as just as Germain's lips. When I see an Image gorgeously apparelled, with spear, or sword, or book in the hand; another with a box or a babe in her arms; what reason can tell me whether Mars or S. George, Venus or the Virgin the mother of Christ, be there erected? If ye tell me that the superscription discerns them, then if it please the maker to remove the title, that, which before was the Idol Venus, shall now become the blessed Virgin: that, which was Mercury, shall

---

[3] ["Multæ apocryphorum quisquiliæ." (Ant. Pagi *Crit. in Annales Baronii*, Tom. i. p. 45. Colon. Allob. 1705.)]

[4] Li. Ep. v. Epi. xxxi. [*Epistt.* Lib. ii. Ep. xiii. Opp. v. 204.]

anon be Paul: and so, as it pleaseth the workman to name it, it shall be reverenced and esteemed.

But whereas they be called Laymen's books[1], impossible it is without a schoolmaster to read them. But when they be read, what lessons have they? Such as Cherea did learn in Terence; or such as Venus Gnidia did teach in Lucian. For when they behold strange and costly Images, wondrously adored, with coronets on their heads, rings on their fingers, precious stones on their garments; what may they think, but that some stately Princes, with their proud apparel and disguised train, be come in presence? and then they fall down and worship the body, or the garment; the Idol, or the gold; or peradventure both. The body is stiff, for it is a stone: the garments as stiff, for they are of gold. The shape enforceth an honour to the Image: the furniture provoketh a coveting of the goods. So at one time two Idolatries be committed. If your maids do look upon Mary Magdalen, as in the churches she is set forth, with nice apparel and wanton looks; what can they behold in her but the pranks of an harlot? what can they learn of her but lusts of vanity? Doubtless, if Images must be admitted to set forth the Saints, the Saints themselves shall not be honoured, but dishonoured: and we shall espy no example of soberness, of chastity, of contempt of riches, and vanity of the world; but of excess, of wantonness, of pride and covetousness. For if the external decking, the trimming of the Puppets, do lively describe anything; it is not the nature of holy Saints, but childish affection of old doting fools, which must have such babies to play them withal. But that play of folly doth end in earnest of gross Idolatry.

The reason of our time for Images.
And although some affirm, that in these days men be too wise and learned to take any hurt or offence by Images; they know what they are; they gad not into far countries after them; the preachers otherwise inform them: and therefore, (as they suppose,) it is not unlawful or wicked absolutely to have Images in churches; though it may, (for the danger of the simpler sort,) seem to be not altogether expedient. To this I reply, that none in these days in this respect is better instructed in the fear of God than

[1] [Preface, page 21.]

Ezechias was; more zealously affected to the truth than
Josias; more endued with wisdom from above than Salomon. They knew what an Idol or Image was: they were
not likely for their own persons to sustain any harm or
damage by them: they armed other against the danger
of them. Yet would not Ezechias suffer the brazen Serpent,
(the sign of Christ our Saviour,) to stand[2]. Josias, for all his
knowledge, which could not in that case be himself abused,
took away all occasion of ruin from his people, and utterly
removed all Idols[3]. Salomon, for all his wisdom, by suffering
his wanton paramours to bring their Idols into his court and
palace, was by carnal harlots persuaded, and brought at the
last to the committing of spiritual fornication; and of a most
wise and godly Prince became a most foolish and vile
idolater[4]. Then let Ezechias and Josias teach us utterly to
remove all occasion of fall, as well from other as from ourselves: let Salomon also fear us from suffering any such to
stand, lest by transgression our wisdom be folly, and understanding error. "He that loveth danger shall perish therein[5];"
and "Let him that standeth beware he fall not[6]."

I am sure there is no Prince of the world more furnished
with skill than was that Salomon: none have more graces
conferred on them: and yet he was abused by Images; by
Images, that he knew to be but stocks and stones. For
"horrible it is to fall into the hands of the living God[7]:" and
whoso turneth "the glory of the incorruptible God to the
similitude of the Image of a corruptible man:" whoso turneth
"the truth of God into a lie, and worshippeth the creature,
forsaking the Creator[8]: for this cause God giveth them up to
vile affections," to their hearts' lusts, to uncleanness, &c. Then
let all Princes, all wise of the world beware, that they procure
not God's indignation by breaking His precept, so often given,
so straitly enjoined: "Thou shalt make to thyself no likeness of any thing." Suppose they be so strengthened in
faith, so assisted by grace, that, how great soever the danger
be, yet they fall not in it, they keep themselves uncorrupt
from Idolatry; shall that be sufficient excuse for them, if they

---

[2] 2 Re. xviii. [2 Kings xviii. 4.]
[3] 2 Re. xxiii. [14.]
[4] 1 Re. xi. [1—8.]
[5] Eccle. xiii. [Eccl$^{us.}$ iii. 26.]
[6] 1 Cor. x. [12.]
[7] Heb. x. [31.]
[8] Rom. i. [23—26.]

leave occasion of such offence to other? Shall their learning and wisdom be cause of folly and deceit to the simple? Shall they have such regard of their own fancy, which is to no purpose, but only to gaze on; without a commandment, as they themselves confess; that the silly flock shall be scattered thereby; and the more multitude, being simple, perish; for whom Christ paid as dear a ransom[1] as for the greatest, the wisest, the best learned of the earth?

The Scripture is commanded to be known of all men. "Gather," (saith Moses[2],) "the people together, men, women, and children, and the stranger that is within thy gates; that they may hear, and that they may learn, and fear the Lord your God, and keep and observe all the words of His Law." Likewise, in the New Testament[3], the like commandment is given by Christ, to "search the Scriptures." Which words if any man think do appertain only to the Jews of the old time, or to the Clergy now; by the same reason, (as Augustin doth well prove[4],) he may say, that Christians ought not to know Christ, nor be known of Christ. Notwithstanding, the Scriptures, (contrary to God's will,) have been for a policy forbidden to be read, lest the ignorant might fall into error by them. And shall not the Pictures, forbidden and banished out of God's service, breeding a most vile affection of Idolatry, be removed rather out of the temple, as well in respect of the precept as peril? I have shewed what these Images do describe: pride, avarice, wantonness, and nothing else. If a man say, this Saint in his life-time despised his life, to live with God; continued in poverty, to be rich in Christ; rejected the pleasures and lusts of the flesh, to subdue the same to the good guiding Spirit; his Image by and by controls him of a lie. For he seeth a most cheerful and stately look, a gorgeous and rich attire, an embracing in death of that which in life he most abhorred.

Wherefore, as Images generally describe a contrary effect to their first patterns; as alway they work a more wicked end than in Religion is to be admitted; so the Cross itself doth not nor cannot lead us to The crucified; but estrangeth our

---

[1] [Rom. xiv. 15. 1 Cor. viii. 11.]
[2] Deute. xxxi. [12.]   [3] John v. [39.]
[4] De verb. Domini, Ser. xlv. [al. *De Scripturis*, Serm. cxxix. Opp. Tom. v. ed. Ben.]

hearts from God the Creator to a vile creature. And if the commodity of Images in the Church or Crosses had been such, (as you would have it appear;) I marvel that Christ, our schoolmaster, that His Apostles, our teachers, took no order for them. Paul saith not[5], *Quæcunque picta sunt, sed Quæcunque scripta sunt, ad nostram doctrinam scripta sunt,* &c.: "Whatsoever things are painted, but Whatsoever things are written, are written for our instruction." Not that by Images or gazingstocks, but "thorough patience and comfort of the Scriptures, we may have hope." Nor he saith, "All" Picture, but "Scripture, inspired of God, is profitable to teach, to reprove, to instruct; that the man of God may be perfect, furnished to all good works[6]." Then if the Scripture be a commended and commanded way, and the same sufficient to make us perfect in all points, I see not to what use an Image or a Picture is.

God gave the Law to Moses[7], not set forth with colours, but written in two tables. Josue delivered the same unto the people, not in Imagery, but in word[8]; not glorious to the eye, but gladsome to the ear, comfortable to the heart: so that the mean, whereby they would the benefits of God to be kept in remembrance, was not to paint or grave the likeness of them, but by faithful pen report the noble facts, and so print in the heart a thankful memory. David, entreating of the Incarnation and Nativity, Passion and Death, Resurrection and Kingdom of Christ our Saviour, (which are the proper effects which you will have set forth in Imagery;) saith, in the Person of Christ, thus: *In capite libri scriptum est de Me:* "In the beginning of the book it is written of Me[9]." It is not graved in a piece of metal, or painted on a wall. The Evangelist saith[10]: *Sicut scriptum est in libro sermonum Esaiæ:* "As it is written in the book of Esaie's sermons." He spake of sermons, and not of signs; of a book, and not of an Image. The Apostles also, of whom it is written[11]: "Beautiful are the feet of those that bring tidings of peace, and preach health;" which went throwing their seeds with tears, planting the faith of Christ with affliction, and shall

[5] Rom. xv. [4.]   [6] 2 Tim. iii. [16, 17.]
[7] Exo. xx. [Deut. v. 22.]   [8] Josu. xxiii, xxiv.
[9] Psa. xxxix. [xl. 7.]   [10] Luke iii. [4.]
[11] Esa. lii. [7. Rom. x. 15.]

return again having their hand full[1], with plentiful increase, with joy for gain, and success of the Gospel; sent not a Cross, or history of the Passion painted in a table, to cities or to nations; but their Epistles, the certain witnesses of their minds, their writings. Nor Christ, (that we read of,) conferred on them the art of painting, carving, or engraving; whereby they might convert the Heathen to the faith, or leave a remembrance with their disciples after them: *Sed aperuit illis Dominus sensum Scripturarum*: " But the Lord opened the sense of Scripture to them[2]." S. John, banished into the island Patmos, to receive the secret and divine Revelations, heard at the Lord's hands, *Scribe hæc in libro*: " Write these in a book[3];" and not Work them in stone or metal.

Whereby we are given to understand, that the instruction of our faith, the only aid of a godly memory, must be the Scripture. The Cross, with a Picture of a man upon it, with arms stretched, body pierced, and feet nailed, may peradventure put me in mind of a man so executed: but who it was, for what cause it was, to what wholesome end and effect it was, no Picture in the world can tell me[4]. If preaching, inspired by the grace of God, working effectually in the hearts of hearers, be not able to turn and convert the obstinate: if the lawful use of God's holy instrument, piercing the hearts, and striking the conscience, cannot frame aright, and reform to piety; what shall we think of a dumb, senseless, unlawful thing? If I see a felon, a thief, a murtherer hanged before mine eyes, have I not more to consider mine own estate, than if I beheld a wooden Rood or silver Crucifix? Suppose I know that that Picture representeth Christ, am I furthered anything toward my salvation? or are the mercies of Christ more effectual to me, unless I know that even God the Father hath also chosen me in Christ His Son[5], "before the foundations of the world" were laid, that I "should be holy and without blame before Him in love?" Is there any cause to drive me to thankfulness, or otherwise to virtuous conversation, because I see a gallows; which my horse seeth as well as I, and yet is not the holier? Can I glorify God for sending of His Son, unless I know that He did send Him;

---

[1] Psa. cxxv. [cxxvi. 5, 6.]
[2] Luk. xxiv. [45.]
[3] Apoc. i. [Rev. i. 11.]
[4] [Compare p. 37.]
[5] Ephe. i. [4—10.]

and for me He sent Him; whom "He hath predestinate to be adopted through Jesus Christ unto Himself, according to the good pleasure of His will; to the praise of the glory of His grace, wherewith He hath made us accepted in His beloved: by whom we have redemption through His blood, even the forgiveness of sins, according to His rich grace: whereby He hath been abundant toward us in all wisdom and understanding; and hath opened unto us the mystery of His will, according to His good pleasure which He had purposed in Him: that in the dispensation of the fulness of times, He might gather together all things in one, which are in heaven, and which are in earth, even all in Christ?" If these effects be described in a Cross, the duty of thankfulness is taught withal, the form of obedience is set forth unto us. But no Cross can tell me that Christ came once into the world; much less that He was, before He came: that He came to die for us; that He died to rise again; that He rose to purchase a righteousness for us: yet these and some other articles of our faith we must be first instructed in; or else the sight of the Cross doth no more profit me than, (as I said,) my horse. But neither we are willed by any word of God to fetch our knowledge from such unskilful schoolmasters, nor anything is in them whereof they can to our health inform us.

You say, "that the Cross teacheth the proud and contentious man humility: for if any be wise in his own conceit, and condemneth other men's judgments, and craketh[6] to the people, that the doctrine, which he teacheth contrary to all other, is sure, sound, and grounded upon the word of God; that man, I say, looking intentively upon this sign, may learn humility, and say with S. Paul: 'God forbid that I should brag or glory in any thing, but in the Cross of our Lord Jesus Christ[7].'" Indeed, Sir, humility may well one way be learned of a Cross; for when it is stricken, it strikes not again: when it is reviled, it gives no ill language: will it to stand, and it will not stir. But you, that think yourself as wise as any man, and yet are abused in your own conceit, when ye look on your Cross, what are ye advantaged? Do ye learn to glory in nothing else but Christ crucified? Indeed S. Paul, in that Epistle to the Galatians,

Folio 114, b.

---

[6] [craketh, boasteth.]   [7] [Gal. vi. 14.]

condemned the hypocrites and false teachers, which urged the Law, Circumcision, and Ceremonies: against whose heresy he brought his assertion, that only the death of Christ was his joy and felicity; nor any thing he had but that to rejoice in.

<small>Papists, for all their Crosses, have no humility.</small> If you have learned this lesson of the Cross, I am glad thereof. For then ye condemn your merits and satisfactions: then will ye lay away your idle ceremonies and will-worship. But if you retain a confidence in your works; if you ascribe any righteousness unto them; if you think you are able to deserve salvation, or satisfy any way for another's sins; then do ye glory in somewhat else than the Cross of Christ: then is your humility but hypocrisy. When the Papists behold the work of their own hands, the Cross itself, fair mustering in the church; which might peradventure have been a log for the chimney, or else ..., if they had not given that shape unto it, and garnished it as it is, which now by their means is reverently adored, and thought to be of such singular virtue; no other thought can come into their heads, but that they themselves be better than their handy work, the maker more to be esteemed than the metal: and so for humility a pride is engendered, that they be causes of such wonderful effects; and if God be honoured, they must be thanked.

<small>Folio 115, b.</small> As for obstinate sinners, if they have no better helps to regenerate their hearts than the sign of a Cross to feed their eyes, they are like to be as well converted as Julian and the Jew, (of whom ye spake before;) who, notwithstanding that they made a Cross, remained in their paganism accursed still. We read in the Scripture such power attributed to the word; but to the wood never. *Lex Domini immaculata, convertens animas: testimonium Domini fidele, sapientiam præstans parvulis:* "The law of the Lord is perfect, converting the soul: the testimony of the Lord is sure, and giveth wisdom unto the simple. The statutes of the Lord are right, and rejoice the heart: the commandment of the Lord is pure, and giveth light unto the eyes[1]." If any such authority could be brought for the Cross, I could more easily be brought to believe it. Now that ye bring but your own supposal, I might refute it with a bare denial: but I will bring Chry-

---

[1] Psal. xviii. [xix. 7, 8.]

sostom for me[2]. *Animo desperato nihil pejus. Quamvis signa, quamvis miracula videat, in eadem perstat pertinacia.* Which is to say: "Nothing is worse than a desperate mind. Although he see signs, although miracles be wrought, yet he standeth stiffly in the same self-will frowardness." And there also he bringeth the example of Pharao, whom all the wonders and plagues of Egypt could not make relent. Wherefore, if the Cross be brought unto the like, I am sure small comfort will arise thereof: so that not only the authority, but also the example condemns you.

Athanasius, in the place by you alleged[3], how "the wonted affections be taken out of harlots' hearts; murderers keep their weapon no longer; fearful men conceive a courage; barbarous nations lay away their immanity[4];" doth not ascribe these effects to the Cross, but wholly and solely to the faith of Christ. "Then why doth he mention the sign of the Cross," (say you;) "why was he not contented to put faith, and no more?" Not that they should be joined patent together; but that the one might be testified by the other. And the manner of that time was, they being conversant among the Infidels, by this kind of sign to shew their profession. So that, as it is not enough to have a faith secret to ourselves, whereof we dare not make a confession, but that we must so seem unto the world as inwardly we are; that God be not only glorious in Himself, but so acknowledged of the world; therefore the sign of the Cross and faith, the token of profession and profession itself, be put together. And though ye turn over all histories that ever were, ye shall never find that a Cross without faith did further any man: but that faith alone, without any Cross, is right available, the Scripture in every place witnesseth.

Now where ye contend, that a Cross is necessary, "notwithstanding that men may have godly instructions by reading the Scriptures, and hearing good preachers: because every man cannot read Scripture, nor understand it when he readeth it; and every man cannot at all times so conveniently hear

---

[2] Chrysosto. in Cap. Jo. viii. Hom. liv. [Tom. iii. col. 219. Paris. 1570.]

[3] De human. Verbi. [*De incarnat. Verbi Dei*, §. 50. Opp. i. i. 91. Paris. 1698.]

[4] [savageness.]

a good preacher, as he may see the sign of the Cross; and things seen do move more affection than those that be heard or read[1]:" as your answer to this objection against yourself containeth three pretended causes, so will I in order consider of them. First, that all men cannot read Scripture, or understand it when they read it: I beseech you, be Images and Crosses such books as all men can read and understand? Did not I tell you[2] how Stephen Gardiner, a learned man, made a false construction out of such a book, taking the Image of the King for S. George on horseback? The countenance, the proportion, the apparel of them, is as pleaseth the workman to devise: the virtue, the power, and the qualities of them, is as pleaseth the lookers on to imagine. And let them read in Images that lust; let them understand as they may; nothing doubtless is to be read or understood in them, but the lewd lessons of gross Idolatry, penned by the Devil, tending to damnation. And if there were not apparently such peril in them, (the contrary whereof cannot be avoided;) yet were we bound not only to suspect, but also to refuse such schoolmasters as they, being not authorized by God's commission, but, (as I have proved,) always inhibited. If Christ, (as the Gospel telleth us, twice in one place together,) be the only Doctor and Guide of His, Matth. xxiii.: if God hath spoken in these last days by His Son unto us; in whose Person all wonted ways of instruction, all revelations do cease, Hebr. i.; we must now go no further than to His word; we must seek no teacher but His Holy Spirit. *Ipse nos inducet in omnem veritatem:* "That same will induce us into all truth[3]."

And although I know that the gifts of God have their degrees, yet dare I say, that none is utterly so void of grace, but hath, (for understanding,) so much conferred on him, as shall be expedient for his own behoof; unless he be utterly, as a rotten member, cut off from Christ[4]. But if the skill of reading, or gift of understanding be denied unto any, shall he be driven to seek it where it is not? Then shall he find what he would not. If our heavenly Father refuse to teach us, a

Side notes: Images do speak doubtfully. They be read unlawfully. They teach devilishly. There can be no such ignorance as shall drive us to seek a knowledge in an Image.

---

[1] ["Segnius irritant animos demissa per aurem,
    Quam quæ sunt oculis subjecta fidelibus."
                            (Horat. *Ep. ad Pisones*, 180—1.)]
[2] [Pref. p. 36.]   [3] [S. John xvi. 13.]
[4] [Compare page 60.]

vile creature cannot instruct us. If God withdraw His decreed mean, whereby He may win us, an extraordinary matter, a stock or a stone cannot convert us. If God do not suffer us a preaching Parson, the Devil doth send us such dumb Vicars. If man be not worthied to direct us in a truth, an Image or a Cross will pervert us with a lie. *Posuit thesaurum Suum in vasis fictilibus:* " He hath put His treasure in frail vessels;" (saith S. Paul[5], speaking of the work of God's exceeding mercy,) in sending us men of our own nature, by whom His will may be revealed to us. But if your order and assertion did hold, then had He put His treasure in dumb, and dead, and senseless creatures; and should stand to discretion of the carpenter or smith, where He should best confer His grace. A strange case, that where all the works of God be insufficient to teach humility, to persuade patience, to convert from error, and comfort in despair, the vile work of man's wicked hand is able, (as you say,) to procure and compass the same for us. *That which all the creatures of God cannot teach, a Cross can.*

The world itself is a certain spectacle of things invisible; for that the order and frame of it is a glass to behold the secret working and hidden grace of God. The heavenly creatures and spheres above have a greater mark of His Divinity; more evident to the world's eye than either can be unknown or dissembled[6]. Which thing S. Paul declareth to the Romans[7]; saying, that so much was opened unto men as was requisite to be known of God; in that His invisible powers, yea, till ye come to His eterne virtue and Divinity, being understood from the very beginning and creation of the world, be daily seen amongst us. Notwithstanding, such a knowledge as this, being grown and gathered by such circumstances as be common unto all alike, is natural as it were; and only enforceth this, that no excuse, no cloke of ignorance, can be pretended: but, to alter the heart, to make a new mind, to regenerate it to true piety, is the work of another instrument, and effect of another cause. For the principal and chief point, whereupon dependeth our health and salvation, is not only to know God's absolute and universal authority, (whereof both heaven and earth is full, and all the world is witness;) but also to find out His secret counsels, to consider His

[5] [2 Cor. iv. 7.]
[6] [Psal. xix. 1—4.]
[7] Rom. i. [19, 20.]

judgments, to mark the mysteries of our salvation in Christ our Lord, which is hidden from the world.

Then, if the marvellous works of God be not sufficient to direct our ways, considering how frail we are; and if it hap that through them sometime we fall into any deeper consideration of the heavenly nature, straightways we are pulled from the thought thereof to our own lewdness and imaginations, sliding to the dotages and dreams of the flesh; whereby it cometh to pass, that if perhaps any true instinct do sparkle in us, it is out again before we can get any warmth of it; what shall we think of a silly Cross, that sorry worms and canker doth corrupt; that never God nor good man devised? Shall we run to so wicked and unwieldy succour? Shall we seek so blind a guide to bring us out of darkness? God never hath, no not from the beginning, dealt otherwise with His elect, but that He would strengthen and relieve their weakness with a stronger remedy. For He hath used to their instruction the mystery of His word, *illuminantis oculos, et intellectum dantis parvulis :* "that lighteneth the eyes, and giveth understanding unto the meek[1]."

Therefore the goodman and master of the house said in the Gospel: *Negotiemini donec veniam:* [*Negotiamini dum venio :*] " Occupy till I come[2];" when he, intending to go abroad himself, gave each of his servants his portion to bestow. What portion was it? What was the talent? What was the merchandize that they should traffic with? Not, with the merchants of Tyrus[3], to lade their ships with precious wares; nor, with the mariners of Ahasias[4], seek strange countries to get gold: but His word it was that He charged them withal: that was the treasure, that, being well bestowed, should bring infinite pleasures with it. For His word is the lively water[5], whereby the heats of our lusts are quenched; the bread of life[6], to feed our hungry souls; the pleasant wine[7], to cheer and make us merry; the lantern, to guide our steps[8]; the

---

[1] Psal. xviii. [7, 8.]   [2] Luke xix. [13.]
[3] [1 Kings ix. 27, 28.]
[4] [1 Kings xxii. 48, 49. 2 Chron. xx. 35—37.]
[5] Joan. iv. [10, 14.] Apoc. xxii. [1.]
[6] Joan. vi. [35.]
[7] Cantic. viii. [2.]
[8] Psalm cxix. [105.]

sword, that overthroweth the enemies of the truth[9]; the fiery shield, to defend us against our adversaries[10]; the sure rock, whereupon to build[11]; the touchstone, to try out doctrines[12], and what spirits are of God[13]; the key, to open and shut heaven gates[14]; the sweet-tuned instrument, to pass away the tediousness of this our exile; the medicine for all diseases; the joy, the jewel, the only reliques of Christ departed hence: which, if we mind to know His will, as it becometh obedient children; if we do look to be heirs with Him, as all men do make a reckoning of; then must we seek, observe, and have always in reverence. For hence is the perfect knowledge of all truth only to be had; and all other blessedness, in as ample wise as if that Christ were before our eyes, ready to perform and pronounce the things. Wherefore, sith the Scripture is worthied of these titles, and none of them can justly be applied to the Cross: sith the word is the ordinary and only mean that God now useth for instruction of His; the Cross is a schoolmaster of error and impiety. Let no man plead ignorance for his excuse; which may well be increased, but reformed never, by a beggarly book of wood or stone.

As for the other parcel of your answer, that "because all men cannot so conveniently at all times hear a good preacher, as they may see the sign of the Cross, therefore the Cross must be had beside preaching;" I may turn the argument on your own head: that the more general the matter is, and more easily come by, being in itself unlawful, the more seriously it ought to be reproved, the more justly condemned. For whereas Images do but infect the heart, are occasions of fall, and nothing else; it is a perilous matter, the poison to be more general than the medicine, the remedy to be harder than the offence to come by. *Bonum quo communius eo præstantius*, saith Aristotle: "A good thing, the more common it be, the better it is." But a mischief, the more it spreadeth, the more it annoyeth; and of all mischief, an Image most. For Images, Crosses, Crucifixes, are every man's ware: a good preacher is scarcely to be

Folio 117, a.

The more we may see a Cross, the worse.

[9] Sap. xviii. [Wisdom xviii. 16.] Eph. vi. 17.]
[10] Naum ii. [3.]   [11] Math. xvi. [18.]
[12] 1 Cor. x. [15.]   [13] [1 S. John, iv. 1.]
[14] Apoca. xv. [5. iii. 7.]

found in a country. Images continually do preach Idolatry: the preacher cannot always open his mouth against it. Images are likely to seduce a multitude; all men of nature being prone to Idolatry: the preacher is able to persuade but a few; few men inclined to credit sound doctrine. Wherefore, the doctrine of a good preacher, and a gay puppet set up in the church, being direct contrary; the less we may hear the preacher, the more we may see the puppet; the less is our comfort in Christ our Lord, the more do we stand in the Devil's danger.

Lewd affections stirred by Imagery.

As for affections to be stirred by Imagery, I grant they may be some, but not such as they ought. For impossible it is, (as in the Preface is declared;) an Image to come in place of God's service, and not allure to a wicked worship. Experience hath taught us, and examples do prove, that Princes, for their pleasure erecting Images, have bred the vile affection of Idolatry. The Book of Wisdom is most evident therein. Then, if the Picture of a living man, a mortal creature, be of such force to crook the soul; what shall we think of Images of them that are reputed Saints? of the Image of Christ, our God and Saviour? Whose names be written in the book of life[1], they care not for their faces to be painted on a post. They that, alive, abhorred any worship[2], will not, being dead, provoke so great offence. Christ, that, (as God,) will be honoured in truth, must not to the world be set forth with a lie: *nec qui Spiritu cœperunt carne consummandi;* "nor they, that began in the Spirit, must be made perfite in the flesh[3]." The Heathen, that believed not immortality of soul, and were altogether vainglorious and proud, had a pleasure to have their Images set up; and their children rejoiced in their parents' folly: but this must not be taken as precedent for us Christians. For they had no other reward of well deserving: we look for another manner of crown of glory; which is laid up in store for us, against a better day[4]. They had no laws to forbid such counterfeits; yea, the law itself, to excite men to virtue, decreed *Statuas in foro,* "Images in the market-place:" we have law enough from the majesty of God to condemn

---

[1] Luc. x. [20.]   [2] Act. xiv. [14, 15.]
[3] Gala. iii. [3.]
[4] 2 Tim. iv. [8.]   1 Petr. v. [4.]

Images in place of prayer[5]. Wherefore I may say, with the good Fathers of Frankford[6]: *Si homines mortales protervia vanitatis inflati*, &c.: "If mortal men, puffed up with frowardness of their own vanity," proud of worldly pomp, bragging, ambitious, because they could not be in all places, would be magnified in some place; because they looked for no heavenly profit, would therefore have an earthly praise; shall this enforce us to make a Picture of our God, who is in every place, can be contained in no place, whose seat the heavens are, whose footstool is the earth, who is wonderful in all places, can with the eye be discerned in no place? Where His virtue is so great, His glory so excellent, His might so unmeasurable, He is not with colours to be pourtrayed, to be seen in temples made with man's hand, to be honoured or known in a beggarly Picture; but to be set forth in His worthy works, sought for in the heavens, worshipped in heart: the Prophet saying: *Adorate Dominum in atrio sancto Ejus:* " Worship the Lord in His holy sanctuary[7]:" and the Evangelist: *Deus Spiritus est: et qui adorat Deum, in spiritu et veritate oportet adorare:* " God is a Spirit: and they that worship God must worship Him in spirit and in truth[8]."

Thus have I proved, that our affections to God-ward neither ought nor can be stirred up by the vain painter's or carver's craft, howsoever men's fancies are delighted with them. Yet, to consider your own histories: when Alexander the Great was fair and finely painted, Julius Cæsar beholding him was made more ambitious: and he that otherwise could have been contented with his own estate, was through a Picture made a plague of the world. Scipio the African, by looking on his forefathers' monuments, had more occasion of pride than cause of praise given him. Notwithstanding, if in worldly things, for special policy, such order be tolerable; (to keep in memory the noble facts of other:) if affections at home may be stirred with counterfeits of our absent friends; yet, in God's matters, whose presence is at no time denied us, whose Person cannot be truly counterfeited, whose facts are more lively described

In God's matters no Imagery admitted.

[5] Deu. iv, v, vii. 1 Joh. v. [21.]
[6] Car. Mag. Li. iii. Ca. xv. [pp. 376—7. ed. Goldast.]
[7] Psal. xxviii. [xxix. 2.]   [8] Joh. iv. [24.]

in His word than all the workmen of the world can imitate; this point of Devil's rhetoric, this moving of affections, is not to be yielded to. For the minds of the faithful be only stirred up by the Spirit of God, which inwardly worketh in the heart; and outwardly by His word and Sacraments.

No Imagery with preaching: much less without. Wherefore Erasmus would not admit, that a preacher should bring an Image to the pulpit: he would not have such books as those. Yet then I am sure they might be best read; and affections, (if ever,) would most be moved then. His words be these[1]: *Quidam per Imagines movent affectus, aut per ostensas Sanctorum Reliquias; quorum neutrum convenit gravitati loci in quo consistit Ecclesiastes. Neque enim legimus unquam tale quicquam factum, vel a Christo vel ab Apostolis:* "Some," (saith he,) "do move affects by Images, or shewing of Saints' Reliques; whereof neither agreeth to the gravity of the place that a preacher standeth in. For we read not that ever any such thing was done of Christ or His Apostles."

Then, if Religion will admit no precedent, but only of Christ and His Apostles: if Images with tongues, to tell what they are, be not allowable; shall tongueless things, by man's device be erected in every place, to serve God withal? I told you before what Images do teach: what affections they move is evident to all. As Cherea, when he saw painted in a table how Jupiter, in form of an ingot of gold, came through the tiles, and fell into his lady's lap, rejoiced with himself, and said, If the thundering God played such a part, *ego homuncio hoc non facerem?* "should not I, poor wretch, do this?" so, when a gorgeous and golden god shall stand upon the Altar, will not the covetous wish it in his purse? will not he gather, If God delight to be made and adorned with this precious metal, am not I bound to make much of mine? When a man is pourtrayed in the church, hanging on a gibbet, and another fool is crouching to it, the cause not considered, and circumstance unknown; will not the careless and desperate person think with himself, What shame is it for me to hang, since our God was so served? This is the least harm that can come of it. The wicked adoration, the damnable Idolatry, I wittingly omit. In the next article I shall entreat of it.

[1] Li. iii. Eccle. [*Opp.* T. v. col. 987, D. Lugd. Bat. 1704.]

Now, for the calling unto remembrance of that which hath been taught, or occasioning to learn that which is unknown, ye say: "that Images, if for no other cause, yet because they quicken the memory, which in many is fickle; help ignorance, which in some is lurde;" (I know not what ye mean by the term[2]; but so ye have sent it us uncorrected:) "stir up love, which is waxen cold; help hope, which is almost dead; move devotion, which in all men decayeth; revive faith, which in all men faileth; they might right well be suffered among christian men." For proof of which points ye bring two places: one (as) out of Augustin; another out of Cyril. To the place of Augustin I answer, according to the judgment and censure approved by the Parisians, and set before the work that ye cite[3]: *Quod Sermo, De visitatione infirmorum, locutuleii cujusdam est, nec docti nec diserti. Quid habuerunt vel frontis vel mentis, qui talia scripta nobis obtruserunt nomine Augustini?* "That the Sermon entituled, 'Of the visiting of the sick,' is some babbler's doing, that hath neither learning nor eloquence. What shamefacedness or honesty was in them, which have dashed us in the teeth with such writings, in the name of Augustin?"

To Cyrillus I say, that he had to do with Julian the Apostata; to whom it was expedient to excuse the order of Christians in his time; and therefore he said: "The healthful wood doth make us remember," &c. Indeed, in comparison of the Gentiles' Idols, Jupiter and Ganymedes, Daphne and Apollo, of which he there discourseth, the sign of the Cross was to be preferred: and to the enemy we must not exaggerate the fault of our friend, but cover it what we can. So did Cyrillus. But that he was not in the same heresy with you, see what precedents he bringeth against you. In the selfsame book whereas you bring your authority, these words he hath[4]:

Images not to be admitted for help of memory.
Folio 119, b.

A vain fancy fathered upon Augustin.

Folio 120.

[2] [lurid.]

[3] [This was the judgment of Erasmus. The Divines of Louvain (*Cens.* Tom. ix. Opp. S. Aug.) have decided, with respect to this Sermon, that "non est Augustini:" and Bellarmin uses the expressions, "licet falso tribui videatur Augustino." (*De Extrem. Unct.* Cap. iv. col. 1646. Ingolst. 1601.) Vid. Coci *Censur.* p. 181. Lond. 1614. Conference betwene *Rainoldes and Hart*, p. 199. Lond. 1584.]

[4] Cyrillus, Li. vi. Contra Julianum. [p. 193, D. edit. Spanheim. Lipsiæ, 1696.]

Honestus et bonus erat, (sicut ipse dicit,) Numa; et, splendida præditus intelligentia, etiam plurimas Sacerdotum constituit leges. Diligenter ergo inquiramus, quem habuerit ille cultus modum. Scripsit igitur de illo Dionysius Halicarnasseus, qui Romanorum Historiam diligenter composuit, quod templa quidem et delubra extruxerit, Simulachrum autem in illis erat nullum. Nam quia Pythagoræ philosophiam commendabat, cujus et dogmata sequebatur, cognoverat Deum omnino specie et forma tali carere; affirmabatque Illum gaudere mentalibus, et non carnalibus sacrificiis. Iccirco et constructa templa fidei nominabat; qua sola Deus ab hominibus, quantum capaces sunt, videtur: et subditis præcipiebat, ut per fidem jurarent: "Numa," (saith Cyril, in answer unto Julian,) "as the enemy himself affirmeth, was honest and good; and, endued with notable understanding, made many laws for the Priests. Let us inquire therefore diligently, what manner of service he had. Dionyse of Halicarnassus, which wrote well the History of the Romans, reporteth, that he made temples and oratories, but there was no Image in the world in them. For because he commended the wisdom of Pythagoras, whose doctrine also he followed, he knew that God was destitute of such form and shape; and affirmed, that He took pleasure in sacrifices of the mind, and not of the flesh. Therefore, the temples that he builded, he called the temples of faith; by which only God is seen of men, so far as they are able to reach unto His sight: and he commanded his subjects to take their oath by faith."

In which words many things may fruitfully be observed: first, that where Julian laid Numa his Religion to the Christians' charge, Cyril is contented with his authority; but he useth it to the condemnation of heathenish Idolatry: then, that he alloweth no Images to be in churches; bringing a reason as out of nature itself, whereof the Philosophers were not ignorant, that there can be no likeness of God made; and therefore not of Christ, unless we deny Him to be God. So that if a Cross was used in his time, yet was there no Picture of Christ upon it[1].

Cyril alloweth no Images in churches.

[1] [It should not be supposed that respect for the *Cross*, as the symbol of our faith, is calculated necessarily to superinduce Idolatry: but such an admission is not by any means applicable to the veneration of a *Crucifix*, which is an Image of the Saviour, *Cruci affixus*. See a Letter from Cassander to Bp. Cox: *Zurich Letters;* second Series, pp. 43, 44.]

Last of all, that places deputed unto prayer were only called by the name of that, which is the only mean whereby we apprehend the promises of God, and come to true knowledge of Him. If there were nothing else but Numa his judgment, (whom, notwithstanding, in all these points Cyrillus doth allow;) he were only sufficient to condemn your doctrine. For if Christ be God, and God can have no form or shape, what shall we think of the Pictures of Christ in every Rood-loft, and on every Crucifix? Are they not things utterly unlawful, and such as wherein Numa shall condemn you? Peradventure ye set a Picture of Christ, as of only man; but thereby ye run into a damnable heresy: separating His humanity from His Divinity; and making Him inferior unto His Father, as is proved afore. Again, the wisdom of that Roman King condemneth the foolish superstition of Christians, in giving worse names unto their churches than he did to the temples of his Idols. For he called them all the temples of faith; giving thereby the glory unto God: whereas we do call them Saint John's church, S. Peter's church, S. Mary's church, and such other like. *No Image of Christ to be made. No church to be called by the name of a Saint.*

To join issue in the case, whether memory be holpen by Imagery: if ye speak of God's matters, it is an ungodly memory that is holpen by them. *Infelix memoria, quæ, ut Christi memoretur, qui nunquam a pectore justi hominis recedere debet, imaginariæ visionis est indiga*: "An unhappy memory is that," (as Charles the Great affirmeth[2];) "which, to remember Christ, who never ought to depart out of the heart of the just man, standeth in need of a sightful conceit:" nor otherwise can have the presence of Christ within him, unless he have His Image painted on the wall, or expressed in some other matter. This is not only said, but a reason of the same is brought. "For," (sayeth he;) "such a memory as is nourished and kept by Images proceedeth not of hearty love, but necessity of eyesight." And see by this means how little God is beholden to us. We remember Him as we remember the Devil. For when we are not moved of conscience and good-will to think upon Christ, but only as the eye by occasion is led; then is there no love, but a mere necessity, which maketh me remember, so oft as I see it, any thing that I hate most. So *A devilish memory, that must be holpen with a Cross.*

[2] Lib. iv. De Imag. Ca. ii. [p. 466. Francof. 1608.]

that who are these, that must have their memories quickened with a Cross? Such as, if they were blind, belike would not remember; and, being where no Cross is, will forget Christ. And sure like enough. For there are no worse livers in the world than likers of the Cross. Wherefore, sith the mind of man ought so wholly to be defixed on Him after whose image it was first made, that by no creature it ought to be estranged from the truth, which is Christ; *Dementissimum est eam interpositis materialibus Imaginibus, ne Ejus oblivionem patiatur admoneri debere: cum videlicet hoc infirmitatis sit vitium, non libertatis indicium:* "Most madness it is, that our minds by the mean of material Images must be put in remembrance, lest we fall to forget Him: whereas this is the fault of infirmity, no sign of liberty."

The Apostle Paul saith, that our conversation must be in heaven[1], and hope reposed in heavenly things. *Spes enim quæ videtur non est spes:* "That hope which is seen is no hope[2]." God hath made many creatures of His own, whereby His power may be known of us; and they all, notwithstanding, in their degree serve us. Shall we now shape out a new creature, and serve it? So did the Jews; whom the Prophet bitterly reproveth, saying[3]: "To whom will ye liken God, or what similitude will ye set up unto Him? The workman melteth an Image; or the goldsmith beateth it out in gold; or the goldsmith maketh silver plates. Doth not the poor choose out a tree?" and so forth. Whereby we are given to understand, that all Imagery, (so far as concerneth God's service,) is condemned; not only for the use and adoration, but also for the having and erecting of them. For as yet he spake not of the worshipping of Images, but only of worthying them any place among them. "To whom will ye liken God?" (saith he;) as who should say: Paint what ye will, emboss and burnish, yet shall your workmanship have nothing like with God. Therefore, to aspire unto the knowledge of Him, we must not take counsel of our own folly: but follow the wisdom of God herein; and betake us to His word, which is the lively image and perfect counterfeit of Himself. If this suffice not, let us cast our eyes about upon His creatures, and they will tell us of Him: yea, the poor and hungry, that still

---

[1] Philip. iii. [20.]   [2] Rom. viii. [24.]
[3] Esay xl. [18—21.]

be subject unto the Cross, will lead us straighter to Christ than any Cross. If you will seek for any further aid, I may say unto you, as followeth in the Prophet: *An nescitis? An non audistis? An non vobis annunciatum est ab initio? An non edocti estis a fundamentis terræ?* "Know ye nothing? Have ye not heard? Hath it not been told you from the beginning? Have ye not understood by the foundations of the earth?" Mark, (I beseech you,) what schoolmasters Esay doth appoint us. When he had used the general word of "knowing," he inferred two ways that lead us to knowledge. First is the word, which cometh by hearing. The second is the world, which without our workmanship is daily to be seen. If ye find any more, it is more than the Prophet knew of: it is more than the Spirit of God teacheth: it is more than a christian and godly man may use.

Wherefore, seeing nothing is described by the Cross available for us; no piece of cause or effect of Christ's passion is represented in it; yea, the Person of Christ, (as much as in us lieth,) disgraced by it, and the majesty of God dishonoured: seeing by the Scriptures and authority of the godly such mean of remembrance is both insufficient and utterly unlawful; condemning ourselves of too deadly forgetfulness, and contempt of the order that God hath set us: finally, seeing that it is such a sorry school-master as speaketh doubtfully, teacheth devilishly, is seen dangerously; let the sign of the Cross be cast out of the church, and the Cross itself be preached simply: lest, by suffering the sign of the Cross to stand, the Son of God crucified be contemned; and we fall to worshipping of a Cross material, which in the next article shall be proved damnable.

TO THE TENTH ARTICLE.

THE ADORATION AND WORSHIPPING OF THE CROSS TO BE ALLOWED BY OLD AND ANCIENT FATHERS.

ALTHOUGH in the former articles the folly and unfaithfulness thereof is shewed; yet, that the world may understand upon how weak a ground ye stand, how ruinously ye build, I will assay the force, and soon overthrow the foundation of your cause. Most reason it had been, if ye would have proved an adoration and worship of a Cross, (which appertaineth unto God alone; which to no creature can be applied;) ye should have brought some testimony of the Scripture, which in God's matters only and sufficiently doth take an order. But you saw that Scripture is direct against you: therefore you would not allege that should hinder you. The painter, that had drawn a cock ill-favouredly, commanded his boy to keep the quick[1] cocks away: so you, that shamefully would confirm a lie, reject most wickedly the proof of truth. But I will briefly note, (which you utterly omit,) God's plain and evident commandment to the contrary: whereby ye may learn, that if men in terms had overshot themselves, yet you should have a better aim than, by following their guess, rove so far from all godliness.

If you had proceeded orderly and according to the rule of skill, you would have shewed, first, what "adoration[2] and worship" is; and then have approved, (which you never shall,) the lawful application of it unto the Cross. If ye take it as the word in Hebrew signifieth, it is to bow down or prostrate yourself. The Grecians come very near unto the same, and express it by bowing of the knee, or putting off the cap, &c. Nor I doubt but you in this interpretation agree with me. Notwithstanding, that in no sense it can be given unto an Image, or otherwise to a senseless

---

[1] [living.]
[2] [With regard to the derivation of "Adorare," (*Orare ad,*) see Abp. Tenison's *Discourse of Idolatry,* p. 288. Lond. 1678.]

and dead creature, shall appear anon. In Exodus[3], when God had spoken of all similitudes and likenesses of things in heaven or in earth, He added: "Thou shalt not bow down to them, nor serve them." The Greek is the same, which signifieth worship and adoration: καὶ μὴ προσκυνήσεις αὐτοῖς. Also the Prophet, in God's Person, speaketh[4]: "Is there no knowledge nor understanding to say, I have burnt half of it even in the fire, and have baked bread upon the coals thereof: I have roasted flesh, and eaten of it: and shall I make the residue an abomination? shall I bow to the stock of a tree?" And with a great indignation in another place he saith[5]: "They worshipped the work of their own hands; that which their own fingers made. A man bowed himself, and a man humbled himself: therefore spare them not."

Many other places I could heap hereon, which evidently convince all adoration to other than to God to be accursed. Only when you will us, after the example of your master the Devil, to fall down and worship a silver Cross, or a wooden tree, I will answer with Christ: "Avoid, Satan. It is written: 'Thou shalt worship the Lord thy God, and Him only shalt thou serve[6].'" Now worship and service so jointly do concur together, that the one cannot be without the other. If only we must serve God, Him only we must worship. In the Epistle to the Hebrews[7], S. Paul proveth Christ more excellent than the Angels, because they worship Christ, but are not worshipped again. If Angels have not this adoration, shall a vile stock, or a cold, cankered, corrupt piece of metal have it? In the Acts of the Apostles it is written[8] how Cornelius, the Centurion, fell down at Peter's feet and worshipped him: but the Apostle took him up, and reproved him, saying: "Stand up, for I myself am a man." If so great a Saint as Saint Peter was be not to be worshipped, so foul a block as a Rood is much less is to be set by. In the Revelation[9], an Angel from heaven gave a charge on this wise: "Fear God, and give Him the glory; for the hour of His judgment is come: and worship Him." Which worship, that it ought not to be given to another, in the same book good

[3] Exod. xx. [5.]
[4] Esay xliv. [19.]
[5] Esay ii. [8, 9.]
[6] Matth. iv. [10.]
[7] Heb. i. [4—6.]
[8] Act. x. [25, 26.]
[9] Apoc. xiv. [7.]

precedent we find. For when the Evangelistes fell down at the Angel's feet to worship him, he answered[1]: "See thou do it not: I am thy fellow-servant, and one of thy brethren, which have the testimony of Jesus: worship God." Likewise, about the latter end, this witness ye have[2]: "When I had heard and seen," (saith John,) "I fell down to worship before the feet of the Angel. But he said unto me, See thou do it not: for I am thy fellow-servant, and of thy brethren the Prophets, and of them which keep the words of this Book: worship God." If the Angels of heaven refused worship and adoration; alleging withal that they were but servants, and therefore would not derogate from their Master, ascribing to themselves that which is only due unto God; shall we think that an Image, a Picture, or a post, forbidden to be made, accursed to be used, may, as a dumb god, or a dead Devil, lawfully be thus honoured?

I will not cumber you any more with Scriptures; for that I think you are not so far past shame, but that ye acknowledge that they are against you. Let us come to the Doctors. Ye only cite Chrysostom; and so as it pleaseth Friar Perionie of Paris to make him speak: Augustin, in a work that is none of his; (as here a little before I proved:) Athanasius, corrupted; as in the fifth article I shewed: Lactantius, utterly against himself; as shall anon be justified. And as for Paulinus, Damascen, and the Canon cited as out of the sixth Council General, I have heretofore in sundry places answered. Here are but seven authorities in all; if they were admitted, (as they are not,) to be true. But if I should run over all the ancient Fathers that ever wrote, and truly allege them, (as you do not,) they would all confirm you a liar and idolatrer. For proof I will bring you for seven, seventeen; (beside Councils General:) and among them the selfsame authors which you trust unto; that your blind ignorance or wilful obstinacy may the more appear. I will cite them in order as in anciently they stand.

Clement[3], not past eighty years after Christ, in the work that you do ascribe unto him[4], saith, that when Peter

---

[1] Apoc. xix. [10.]   [2] Apoc. xxii. [8, 9.]
[3] Clemens, Recog. ad Jac. frat. Do. Lib. v. [p. 93. ed. princ. Basil. 1526.]
[4] ["Whiche boke of trueth was neuer of hys makynge." (Barnar-

had spoken much against the Egyptians' superstitious Idolatry; which honoured an ox and a goat, a fish and a serpent, with other sluttish and uncleanly things, *Cloacas et crepitum ventris;* and that the hearers began to laugh thereat, he burst out into these words: *Ridetis vos aliorum dedecora, quia longa consuetudine propria non videtis. Nam Ægyptiorum quidem stultitiam merito ridetis; qui muta animalia, ipsi cum sint rationabiles, colunt. Audite tamen quomodo et illi vos irrideant; aiunt enim: Nos viventia colimus animalia, licet moritura; vos vero, quæ nunquam omnino vixere, hæc colitis et adoratis:* "Ye laugh at others' shame, because by long custom ye see not your own. For with good cause ye may scorn the folly of the Egyptians; which, being reasonable creatures themselves, worship dumb beasts. But hear how they do mock you too; for they say: We worship living creatures, although die they shall; but you do worship and adore those things which never lived yet." And think you not, that he well describeth and condemneth your error of the worship to be given to the Cross? Is it not a dead thing; and therefore to be worshipped a great deal more idolatrous than the beasts of Egypt? They of an external worship judged an unlawful act, and Peter doth approve them in it: you will offend as heinously as that, and yet will not be judged unlawfully to do. Again, he plainly proveth in the same place what spirit you have, when you speak for the Cross. For his words be these: *Per alios item Serpens ille proferre verba hujuscemodi solet: Nos, ad honorem invisibilis Dei, Imagines visibiles adoramus: quod certissime falsum est. Si enim vere velitis Dei Imaginem colere, homini benefacientes, veram in eo Dei imaginem coleretis:* "The Devil," (saith he,) "by the mouth of other, is wont to bring forth such words: 'We, to the worship of the invisible God, worship the visible Images:' and this is most certainly false. For if ye will truly worship God's Image, ye should, by being beneficial unto man, worship the true image of God in him." Thus far Clement: where I beseech you mark, that he doth affirm it to proceed of suggestion of the Devil, that men for God's honour will worship

The worship of a Cross worse than the Egyptians' Idols.

A devilish excuse to say, that to the honour of Christ they worship His Cross.

dine Ochine's *Dialoge of the vniuste vsurped Primacie of the Bishop of Rome,* translated by John Ponet, D.D. sig. Q 4. Lond. 1549.) Vide supra, pp. 20—1.]

[CALFHILL.]

24

Images. Also that he sheweth, how and what Images may indeed be worshipped: men, the true images of God, helped.

[Clem. Alex.] Thus much Pope Clement. Now another Clement, of Alexandria[1], which was about two hundred and fifteen year after Christ, for confutation of your beastly error, bringeth the assertion of Heraclitus the Ephesian: *An non prodigiosi sunt, qui lapides adorant?* "Be they not monstrous, that worship stones?" And what your Cross is better, I see not. As it standeth, it corrupteth. When ye honour it, ye most disgrace it. Sense [Cense] it, and ye singe it, or take the beauty from it. Doubtless such Images, beside the use, which is abominable, in their creation are worse than any living creature: and therefore I may doubt, with Clement, *Quomodo quæ sunt insensilia divino sint honore affecta; et errantium utpote miserorum misereri amentiæ:* "How it cometh to pass, that things devoid of sense have divine honour and worship given them; and worthily pity the madness of those miserable wretches, so deceived as they are." For other creatures, be they small, be they great, whatsoever they be, have either all senses, or else some; or, if sense be denied them, yet life is granted them, they increase, they grow: but Images, Crosses, Crucifixes, are altogether idle, void of good effect, utterly unprofitable. They be cast, they be molten, they be cut, they be graved, they be embossed, they be burnished; and, last of all, with nails they be fastened, that with knees they may be honoured. *Adorant autem hii non Deos et Dæmones, mea quidem sententia; sed terram et artem, quod quidem est Imagines:* "But these folk do worship, in my opinion," (saith old Clement,) "not Gods nor Devils; but earth and workmanship, which is the Images." Wherefore he proveth, that such have fetched their Religion from proud Persians, beastly barbarians, superstitious sorcerers; *Ignorantes Deum; hæc autem egena et infirma, ut ait Apostolus, quæ ad usum hominum ministeriumque facta sunt, elementa adorantes:* "Whereas they know not God; but worship these beggarly and weak elements, as the Apostle calleth them, which are made to the use and service of men." And further he proveth out of God's word, Exod. xx., that to make a Cross is a kind

Clement thinketh them mad that worship a Cross.

---

[1] Clemens Alexandr. Oratione ad Gentes. [*Opera* Lat. pp. 19, 23, 22. Basil. 1566. Calfhill adopts the translation by Gentianus Hervetus.]

of craft.: *Nōbis enim est aperte vetitum artem fallacem exercere. Non facies enim, inquit Propheta, cujusvis rei similitudinem,* &c.: " For it is plainly forbidden us to practise this deceitful occupation: inasmuch as the Prophet saith: ' Thou shalt not make the likeness of any thing.'" Here you perceive what this good Father thought; that it was a monstrous matter, a mad part, worse than service of the Devil, to worship stocks or stones, or any such thing as a Cross is.

Irenæus reproveth the heresy of the Gnostici[2], *Qui Imagines quasdam depictas, quasdam autem et de reliqua materia fabricatas habent; dicentes formam Christi factam a Pilato in illo tempore quo fuit Jesus cum hominibus:* "Which had certain Images, some painted, some made of other matter; saying that the form and Picture of Christ was made by Pilate, at what time Jesus was conversant with men." Thus he, that came near unto the Apostles' time, reputed it an heresy to have, to make, to carry about with them the counterfeit of Christ. What would he have done if they had honoured it? Damned them to the Devil. [S. Irenæus.]

Tertullian, not long after, writing against Marcion[3], sheweth that the only cause of forbidding Images and likenesses of things was the adoration and worship of them: *Similitudinem vetans fieri omnium quæ in cœlo, et in terra, et in aquis, ostendit et causas, Idololatriæ scilicet, quæ substantiam cohibent. Subjicit enim, Non adorabitis ea, neque servietis illis:* "God, forbidding the likeness of any thing in heaven, in earth, or in the water to be made, shewed also the causes which do restrain the substance. And those causes are Idolatry; for he inferreth after: ' You shall not worship them, nor serve them.'". Wherefore, (as he truly saith,) to adore and worship the likeness of any thing, (as a Cross is some thing,) is mere Idolatry; against which offence the holy Martyr Cyprian inveighing, see how he describeth it[4]: *Quid ante inepta Simulachra et figmenta terrena captivum corpus incurvas? Rectum te Deus fecit: et cum cætera animalia prona et ad terram situ vergente depressa sint, tibi* [Tertullian.] [To worship the Cross, Idolatry.] [S. Cyprian.]

---

[2] Irenæus, Adversus Hær. Li. i. Ca. xxiv. [ad fin. Cf. pp. 42—3.]
[3] Tertull. Advers. Mar. Lib. ii. [Cap. xxii.]
[4] Cyprian. Ad Demetrium. [*Ad Demetrianum.* Opp. pp. 191—2. edit. Fell.]

sublimis status; et ad cœlum, atque ad Deum tuum [al. *sursum*] *vultus erectus est. Illuc intuere : illuc oculos tuos erige : in supernis Deum quære. Ut carere inferis possis, ad alta et cœlestia suspensum pectus attolle. Quid te in lapsum mortis, cum Serpente quem colis, sternis ?* "What dost thou bow thy captive body before foolish Images and earthly counterfeits? God hath made thee upright: and whereas all other beasts of the earth are depressed in shape, bending down to the ground-ward, thou hast a lofty state; to heaven, and to thy God thy countenance is erected. Then look up thither : thither cast up thine eyes : seek God above. That hell thou mayest lack, lift up thy doubtful heart to high and heavenly things. What dost thou throw thyself, with the Devil whom thou servest, into the pit of death?" So far S. Cyprian : and by him it is plain, that to bow, to kneel, to shew any sign of reverence to an earthly counterfeit, to the work of man's hand, is contrary to nature, against the dignity of our creation, and a wicked worship.

<small>To worship the Cross, contrary to nature.</small>
<small>Origen.</small>

What Origen's opinion was in this behalf, I have proved afore, in the first article ; and thither ye may resort to find it. Only this will I add; that when he had rehearsed the Commandment of God, Exod. xx., he put his own censure and verdict thereunto, saying[1]: *Erat quidem Legis mens ea ; ut singulis in rebus, ut veritas exigebat, hii versarentur : nec præter verum effingerent aliqua, quæ præ se maris vel fœminæ speciem præ se ferrent,* &c.: "The mind of the Law," quoth he, "was this ; that they should in all things so behave themselves as the truth required : nor that they should beside the truth counterfeit any thing, representing the shape of man or woman." Wherefore, the Picture of Christ upon the Cross, by Origen's opinion, is against the Law. Beside this, he telleth you what adoration and what worship is[2]: *Aliud est colere, aliud*

---

[1] Lib. iv. Contra Celsum. [Vid. p. 182. ed. Spencer. Καὶ ἐβούλετό γε ὁ νόμος τῇ περὶ ἑκάστου ἀληθείᾳ ὁμιλοῦντας αὐτοὺς μὴ ἀναπλάσσειν ἕτερα παρὰ τὴν ἀλήθειαν, ψευδόμενα τὸ ἀληθῶς ἀρσενικὸν, ἢ τὸ ὄντως θηλυκόν.]

[2] In Exod. Hom. viii. Cap. xx. [*Opp.* T. ii. p. 158. ed. Bened. Parisiis, 1733. Combefis restored the Greek of this passage, which differs in some respects from the Latin given in the text :—ἄλλο προσκυνεῖν καὶ ἄλλο λατρεύειν. ὁ μὲν γὰρ ἐξ ὅλης ψυχῆς δουλεύων τούτοις οὐ μόνον προσκυνεῖ ἀλλὰ καὶ λατρεύει. ὁ δὲ καθυποκρινόμενος καὶ διὰ τὰ ἔθνη ποιῶν, οὐ λατρεύει μὲν προσκυνεῖ δέ.]

adorare. Potest quis interdum et invitus adorare: sicut nonnulli, Regibus adulantes, cum eos ad hujuscemodi studia deditos viderint, adorare se simulant Idola; cum in corde ipsorum certum sit, quia nihil est Idolum. Colere vero est, toto hiis affectu et studio mancipari. *Utrumque ergo resecat sermo divinus: ut neque affectu colas, neque specie adores:* "To worship is one thing, and to adore another. For a man may sometime against his will adore: as they, that flatter Princes, when they see them addict to such studies, do feign themselves to worship Idols; whereas in their heart they are assured that an Idol is nothing. But to worship is to enter into a certain servitude and bondage with them, and be addict unto them with all affect and zeal. Therefore the word of God cutteth away both: that neither in heart thou worship, nor in appearance adore." Thus much sufficeth for Origen: whereby it is plain that, whatsoever our minds are, our bodies must not bow to any Cross or creature.

Arnobius, discoursing against the Gentiles[3], who served Idols, and did sacrifice unto them, had the same objected him that you do to us. "We worship the Gods," (said they,) "by their Images." And you: "By worshipping the Cross we serve Christ." And may I not answer to you, as he did to them? *Si hoc non sit, coli Se Christus nesciat? nec impartiri [impertiri] a vobis ullum Sibi honorem existimabit? Per tramites ergo quosdam, et per quædam fidei commissa, ut dicitur, vestras sumit atque accipit cultiones: et antequam sentiat, Cui illud debetur obsequium, Simulachro litatis prius; et velut reliquias quasdam aliena ad Illum ex authoritate transmittitis.:* "If you had not this Cross, should Christ be ignorant that He were served of you? will He think there is no honour done Him? Then doth He receive your service and your worshippings by certain trains, by other put in trust:" (Vicars, if ye will, or Commissaries:) "and before He, to whom the obsequy is due, have any feeling of the matter, ye do your sacrifice unto the Image; and send Him but the scraps from another man's board." *Et quid fieri potest injuriosius, contumeliosius, durius, quam Deum alterum scire, et rei alteri supplicare? opem sperare de Numine, et nullius sensus ad effigiem deprecari? Nonne illud est, quæso, quod in vulgaribus proverbiis dicitur, Fabrum cadere* [al. *cædere*] *cum*

[Arnobius:]

---

[3] Arnobius, Contra Gentes, Lib. vi. [p. 195. Lugd. Bat. 1651.]

ferias fullonem? et cum hominis consilium quæras, ab asellis et porculis agendarum rerum sententias postulare? "And what can be devised," (saith he,) "more injurious, slanderous, uncourteous, than to acknowledge one God, and make thy suit to another thing? to hope for help of God, and pour out thy prayers to a senseless Image? Is not this, (as the proverb hath,) 'To have a quarrel to Rowland, and fight with Oliver?' and where thou seekest for advice of men, to ask the sentence first of porklings and of asses?" Again[1]: *Non iste error est? Non, (ut proprie dicatur,) amentia, supplicare tremebundum fabricatæ abs te rei; et cum scias et certus sis tui esse operis, et digitorum artem, pronum in faciem ruere?* &c.: "Is not this an error? Is it not, (to speak properly,) a madness, in trembling-wise to make thy humble suit to a thing that thou madest thyself; and whereas thou dost know and art assured that it is thine own workmanship, the fruit of thine own fingers, to fall grovelling upon thy face before it?" I will no further deal with Arnobius. All his eight [seven] books contain nothing else but confutation of your Image heresy and Cross shame.

[Lactantius.] Lactantius, his scholar, beside many other places to the like effect, whereof in the former treatise I have touched divers, hath also this[2]: *Quæ amentia est, aut ea fingere quæ ipsi postmodum timeant, aut timere quæ finxerint? Non ipsa, (inquiunt,) timemus, sed eos ad quorum imaginem ficta, et quorum nominibus consecrata sunt. Nempe ideo timetis, quod eos esse in cœlo arbitramini: neque enim, si Dii sunt, aliter fieri potest. Cur igitur oculos in cœlum non tollitis; et, advocatis Deorum nominibus, in aperto sacrificia celebratis? Cur ad parietes, et ligna, et lapides potissimum, quam illo spectatis ubi eos esse creditis?* "What madness is this, either to frame those things which they may after fear, or fear those things which they have framed? No, forsooth, (say they,) we fear not that, but them after whose image they be made, and to whose names they be consecrated. Why then ye fear them, because ye suppose them to be in heaven: for if they be Gods, it cannot otherwise be chosen. But why do you not lift up your eyes to heaven; and, calling upon the Gods by name,

---

[1] [Lib. vi. p. 200.]
[2] Lactantius, De fals. Rel. [*De orig. Error.*] Lib. ii. Cap. ii. [ad init.]

do your sacrifices openly? Why do you rather look to the walls, to the stocks and stones, than to that place where you believe they are?" If Lactantius thought it a wickedness in them to turn their eyes unto the earthly creatures beneath, where God was only to be found above, shall your adoration of a Cross stand? shall the worship of a piece of wood or mass of metal be so esteemed? Where is now *Flecte genu, lignumque Crucis venerabile adora*[3]? Did he condemn the Gentiles for turning of their eye to stocks and stones; and shall he charge the Christians to bow the knee to the worshipful Cross? It is too absurd and impious.

Athanasius is so far from adoration and worshipping of the Cross, that in many places he is most earnest to the contrary. In his first Sermons *Contra Idola*[4], he hath nothing more frequent than that such honour to creatures is accursed. But lest you think he spake only against the Gentiles' Idols, and that concerneth not your Images and your Cross, I will come nearer you, and go to the nature of the word general "adoration." He reasoneth with the Arrians, denying Christ to be equal with the Father, after this sort[5]: *Si adoratur ab Angelis, quia gloria sublimior est, par erat ut omnia inferiora superioribus se in adorando inclinarent. Sed id ita non est: creatura siquidem creaturam non adorat: sed quæ servilis sunt conditionis dominos; et quæ creaturæ sunt Deum adorationibus colunt:* "If Christ be adored of the Angels, because He is higher in glory than they, reason it were that all inferior things should bow down themselves in adoration to their superiors. But that is not so. For one creature adoreth not another: but such as are of servile condition adore their lords and masters; and such as be creatures do worship their God by adorations." Afterward he inferreth the examples of Peter and the Angel, which would not that this service should be done unto them. Whereupon he concludeth: *Solius Numinis est adorari*[6]: "It

<small>Athanasius.</small>

---

[3] [See before, pp. 180—3.]
[4] [*Orat. contra Gentes.*]
[5] Contra Arrianos, Ser. iii. [*Orat.* ii. §. 23. p. 491. Opp. Tom. i. ed. Ben.]
[6] [Calfhill seems to have used the Latin version of the works of S. Athanasius, published at Basle, apud Froben. 1564. In Cardinal Zapata's review of this edition, in his Expurgatory *Index*, Hispali,

appertaineth only to the Godhead to be adored." Wherefore, unless ye make your Cross a God, it can have no worship nor adoration. As for the place which out of his Questions ye allege, I say again, ye lie. For it is not *Crucis figuram; ex duobus lignis componentes, adoramus,* as you do cite it; but, *Crucis figuram, ex duobus lignis compingentes, conficimus.* Mark, good readers, what a true man we have to speak for the Cross. Where Athanasius hath: "We frame the figure of the Cross, making it of two sticks;" this man hath: "We, making a figure of the Cross of two pieces of wood, adore it." O blind ignorance, or blinded malice! If the understanding of a word might have deceived one, yet the circumstance of this place[1] is such, that none in the world can make more against adoration of the Cross. For he yieldeth a reason why they make a Cross of two pieces of wood; that if any infidel lay unto their charge, that they worship wood, they may break the form of it, *et infideli persuadere, quod non colamus lignum,* " and persuade the infidel, that we worship not wood." A marvellous matter, that a fugitive of England, and a Divine of Lovain, should be so lewd a falsifier. But I proceed to other.

Epiphanius, (as is before alleged,) would not suffer a vail to hang in the church that had a man's Image on it. Would he suffer a Cross, think you, to be worshipped? He willed the Bishop to command, *ne ejusmodi vela appenderentur*[2], " that such clothes should not be hanged up," *quod contra christianam Religionem veniunt,* " because they come against christian Religion:" and after he calleth it *scrupulositatem indignam Ecclesia Christi,* " a scrupulosity unworthy of the Church of Christ." Shall we think that he could

---

1632, p. 50, we find the following proscription of a reference to the passage in the text: "In Indice dele sequentia—*Adorari solius Dei esse.*" Here there is no slight intimation conveyed of the danger apprehended by Romanists from an honest perusal of the writings of the Fathers: and a simple proof of their having a guilty conscience, with regard to the absolute worship of the Cross, may be derived from a censure passed by the Belgic *Index Expurgatorius* upon the *Christiani Poetæ,* edited by George Fabricius; which is this: "D. col. 4. dele illud, *Crucem ligneam adorare, aperta Idolatria.*" (p. 11. Antverp. 1571.)]

[1] Quæst. xvi. ad Antioch. [Vid. ante, pp. 73—4, 272—3.]
[2] Epiphanius, ad Io. Epis. Hieroso. [Vid. sup. pp. 42, 253—4.]

allow, not a cloth, but a Cross; not a vail, but a Crucifix? And where he could not suffer the sight of the one, would he abide the service of the other? Entreating of a sect of heretics called Collyridians, which did offer to the Virgin Mary, these words he hath[3] : *Prætextu justitiæ semper subiens hominum mentem Diabolus; mortalem naturam in hominum oculis deificans; Statuas, humanas Imagines præ se ferentes, per artium varietatem expressit. Et mortui quidem sunt qui adorantur. Ipsorum vero Imagines, quæ nunquam vixerunt, adorandas introducunt; adulterante mente ab uno et solo Deo: velut commune scortum, ad multam multiplicis coitus absurditatem irritatum; et quod temperantiam legitimi conjugii unius viri detrivit:* "The Devil, entering into the mind of men, always under pretext of justice; advancing in the eyes of men the mortal nature to the degree of God; hath expressed, thorough variety of cunning, Images, representing the counterfeits of men. And they that are worshipped indeed be dead. And the Images, which never lived, they bring in to be worshipped; the mind thereby committing fornication, and estranging itself from the one and only God: as it were an harlot, departing filthily her body unto many; and as one that had worn away the sober use of lawful company with one husband." And afterward: *Non dominabitur nobis antiquus error, ut relinquamus Viventem, et adoremus ea quæ ab Ipso facta sunt. Coluerunt enim et adoraverunt creaturam præter Creatorem, et stulti facti sunt:* "The old error shall not prevail over us, to leave The living, and worship those things which are made of Him. For they have worshipped and adored the creature beside the Creator, and became fools." So he proceedeth with proof, that neither Helias, nor John, nor the Virgin Mary, nor the Angels themselves, are to be adored. *Ergo*, no Cross.

Worship to Images, fornication.

S. Ambrose, speaking how the Cross was found, said this of Helena[4]: *Regem adoravit, non lignum: quia hic Gentilis est error, et vanitas impiorum:* "She worshipped the King, and not the Cross: for that were an error of Gentility, and vanity of the wicked." What plainer words can you desire? Ye cannot say that he spake of the Gentiles' Idols. He spake

[S. Ambrose.]

---

[3] Li. iii. Tom. ii. Hære. lxxix. [p. 344. Jano Cornar. interp.].

[4] Ambros. De obitu Theod. [Antea, pag. 192. Compare Gee's *Answer to the Compiler of the Nubes Testium*, p. 80. Lond. 1688.]

of the Cross, the same that Christ hanged on: and that, he said, was an heathenish error; and to worship was a vanity of wicked men. If the very Cross whereon Christ suffered be not to be adored, will you conclude that a sign thereof should so be reverenced?

Hierom. Hierom hath: *Notanda proprietas, Deos coli, Imaginem adorari: quod utrumque servis Dei non convenit:* "The property of the words is to be marked, that Gods are worshipped, and an Image adored: whereof neither agreeth to the servants of God." Read more of him, *In Jere.* vi. *et* x. *et Dan.* iii. Ye shall plainly see, that neither worship nor adoration ought to be given to so vile a thing as a Cross is.

[S. Augustin.] Augustin agreeth with his fellows, and sayeth[1]: *Non sit nobis Religio humanorum operum cultus. Meliores enim sunt ipsi artifices, qui talia fabricantur; quos tamen colere non debemus:* "Let not us have a Religion in worshipping of man's works. For the workmen themselves that made them be better; whom, notwithstanding, we ought not to worship."

Chrysostom. Nor Chrysostom, in any work that is his, dissenteth from the rest. Upon the iv. of John, and xxxii. Hom.[2], these plain words he hath: *Adorare creaturæ; adorari non creaturæ, sed Domini est:* "To adore and worship belongeth to a creature; but to be adored belongeth to no creature, but only to the Lord."

[S. Cyril Alex.] Cyril, when he would prove the Divinity of Christ, and that He is of the same substance with the Father, drew an argument from adoration of the Angels: and if that any but only God may be adored, then is his reason none. The words be these[3]: *Nemo ignorat, nulli prorsus naturæ præterquam Dei adorationem a Scriptura contribui:* "No man is ignorant, that adoration in the Scripture is attributed to no kind of nature, save only to the nature of God." And thus the elder Fathers.

---

[1] Augustin. De vera Rel. Cap. lv. [§. 108. *Opp.* Tom. i. 587. ed. Ben.]

[2] [*Opp.* Lat. Tom. iii. col. 131. Paris. 1570.]

[3] Cyrill. Thesauri Li. ii. Cap. i. [*Opp.* Basil. 1546. ed. Trapezuntii. T. ii. col. 32, A. The Greek is somewhat different. *Opp.* T. v. p. 71, C. Lutetiæ, 1638.]

Now, to come down to latter years. Grégory the Pope, [Gregory, Pope.] the first that ever maintained Images, is so much against the adoring of them, that in every sentence, where he speaketh of them, he seriously forbiddeth it[4]: *Zelum vos, ne quid manu factum adorari possit, habuisse laudavimus. Et iterum: Ab earum adoratione populum prohibere debuit. Et tertio: Ut populus in Picturæ adoratione minime peccaret.* In English: "We praise it well, that you had a zeal, that nothing made with hand should be adored." And again: "You ought to have forbidden the people from the adoring of them." Thirdly, "That the people should not offend in adoration or worshipping of a Picture." If Pictures generally be thus commended, [condemned?] so much as concerneth adoration, I leave it to your discretion to consider what is to be said of worship to be done to Roods or Crucifixes. Nor here I will omit a proper workman of your own occupation, Johannes Alfonsus de Castro. He, in his book *Adversus Hæreses*, reporteth, that one Claudius, Bishop of Taurino[5], forbad all in his jurisdiction the adoration and worship of our Lord's Cross. He was of Privy Council to Charles the Great: a worthy Prelate for so wise a Prince. What the opinion of Charles the Great was in this behalf, I [Carolus Magnus.] refer you to his four books *De Imaginibus*, of purpose penned against the insolent and doltish conspiracy dissembling at Nice. If ye look for Councils to condemn your error, I send you back to the third article; and there ye shall find sufficient to confute you.

Thus have I slightly passed over, not all that I could recite, but as many as I thought expedient for clear disproof of your ungodly purpose. Ye would have it appear, that all the Fathers were in your fond belief; whereas ye rehearse but a very few, and the same not only corruptly wrested, but maliciously in most parts falsified. I have brought you the simple and plain words of theirs out of their own approved writings, such as, I trust, you will not gainsay. Now let the good readers judge, whether, according to the false exposition of you, or fond meaning of a few, the Cross should be worshipped and adored; or else, according to the sound censure of the moe, of the godly, of

[4] Epist. Li. vii. Indict. ii. Cap. cix. [*Ad Serenum.* Supra, pp. 9, 30.]
[5] [Turin.]

the Scriptures themselves, be cast out of the church, and deputed to the use that it deserveth.

A brief rehearsal of the Doctors' opinion touching the adoration of the Cross.

As for the adoration, S. Peter compared it with the Gentiles' Idolatry; condemned it as unlawful; and yet saw not the hearts of the worshippers. Clement of Alexandria calleth it a monstruous thing, a mad part, worse than the service of the Devil, to worship stocks or stones: yet we must creep to the Cross, you say. Irenæus accompteth it heresy to carry about the true Image of Christ: yet you will have it catholic to adore and worship the false Cross. Tertullian saith that it is Idolatry to adore the likeness of any thing: then is there no great holiness or safety in the Cross. Cyprian affirmeth it to be contrary to nature, against the dignity of our creation, and a wicked worship, to fall down to a creature: and shall we then adore the Cross? Origen will not admit any external sign of honour, (howsoever the mind otherwise be affected,) to be given to the workmanship of man's hand; but saith that it is against the Commandment: and shall we crouch and creep to the Cross? Arnobius[1] scorneth the esteeming of the Cross; and, to the condemnation of Ethnics, saith: *Cruces nec colimus, nec optamus. Vos plane, qui ligneos Deos consecratis, Cruces ligneas, ut Deorum vestrorum partes, forsitan adoratis:* "As for Crosses, we neither worship nor wish for. But you, which consecrate ye wooden Gods, peradventure worship the wooden Crosses as parcels of your Gods." This spake Arnobius in defence of the Christians, and reproof of the Gentiles: and shall we, direct contrary to this, both wish and worship Crosses, worse than the Gentiles, unworthy name of Christians? Lactantius in like sort condemneth the Gentiles for tooting upon Images; and willeth them to look up to heaven: and shall we still be poring on so blind a book as a Cross is? Athanasius would not that the enemy should have such advantage of him as to say, that he or any other Christian worshipped the Cross: we must have it a doctrine, that every man is bound to worship it. Epiphanius tare the vail that had the Picture of Christ upon it: he affirmed the worshipping of the same to be fornication: we must have a post with a mock man upon it, and afterward do honour to it. Ambrose accompted it an error of Gentility, a

---

[1] Lib. viii. [Minucius Felix.—Vid. ante, pp. 178, 183—4.]

vanity of perverse, to adore the Cross: and we must hold
it a good catholic doctrine, because Master Martiall doth teach
it. Hierom, Augustin, Chrysostom, Cyril, Gregory, condemn,
(as is before confirmed,) all adoration done to any creature:
and yet you think the same, by testimonies of the Fathers,
due to the sign of the Cross. If you had considered the
Fathers well, you would not so ill have slandered them.

You think you have a good evasion, when you say, "that
we must attribute unto it not any divine honour, due only to
God; but, as it hath been right well declared before of others,
an inferior kind of reverence." I marvel that you are so
inconstant, M. Martiall. Even now you would needs have
"adoration and worship to the sign of the Cross;" and they
be proper unto God alone: now will ye have an inferior
reverence. And what is that? Forsooth, you cannot tell;
but it hath been declared of other. I know what other in
this behalf have babbled, making their distinction between
λατρεία and δουλεία[2]. They put two horses into one stable,
to eat at one rack, and reach to one manger: yet they be not

[Folio 128, b.]

[2] [The Sicilian Inquisitor Ludovicus a Paramo (*De orig. Off. S.
Inquis.* Lib. ii. p. 345. Matriti, 1598.) relates a circumstance, which
appears decisive with respect to the real doctrine of the Church of
Rome, as to the worship of the Cross.—Joannes Ægidius, a Canon of
Seville, having ventured to maintain that God was to be adored with
Latria, and the Cross to be reverenced only with *Dulia*, was compelled
to retract his opinion publicly, as heretical; and to declare, that the
Cross was to be honoured with the same supreme adoration as that
which is rendered to Christ the Lord. And the reason put forward is
important; viz: because such an idea as his was plainly opposed to
the tenet of the Roman Church, as expressed in her ritual chants, "O
Crux ave, spes unica," and "Crucem Tuam adoramus."—It should be
well known, likewise, that both in the old *Pontificale*, amended by the
command of Pope Innocent VIII., and in the reformed volume, revised
by the authority of Popes Clement VIII., and Urban VIII., this un-
deniable statement has been sanctioned with regard to the Cross:
"DEBETUR EI LATRIA." (*Ord. ad recip. Imperat.* fol. clxxxv. Lugd.
1511.: p. 486. Antverp. 1663.) Cf. Gretseri *Controv. Bellarm. Defens.*
Cap. xiv. Lib. iii. Tom. ii. col. 940. Ingolst. 1609. *Refut. Hasenmilleri*,
p. 105. Ib. 1594. D. Thomæ 3 Part. Qu. 25. Art. 3. et Cajetani *Comm.*
Alex. de Ales *Op. super tert. Sententt.* 144. c. 4. sigg. p 8, 9. Venet.
1475. Bellarm. *De Imagin.* Lib. ii. Cap. xx. Sutcliffe's *Challenge*, pp.
151, 170. *Answere*, p. 15. Lond. 1602. Holcot, *Super lib. Sap.* Lect.
clviii. sig. G iii. Reutling. 1489.]

served alike, because they have a bar betwixt them. I could speak more of the absurdity hereof, but that I must lay my finger on my line, and tread the only steps of you, that full crookedly have gone before me. If you vouchsafe to tell me what that inferior reverence should be, (which now by silence ye utterly suppress;) ye shall then know further of my mind.

Fol. 129. It only remaineth that I answer your paradox, your strange, your incredible proposition, "that there can be no mistrust nor fear of Idolatry in christian men worshipping and adoring the Cross." To come to "worship and adore" again, where the next line before ye would have but an inferior reverence, maketh me think that you be very fickle, and not settled as yet on any certain ground. But worship, a God's name, adore and deify, (say you;) for certain it is there can be no peril of Idolatry. Ye do very wisely to put men in security; for otherwise they would be very loth to venture. Great is the leap, and the water deep. But how shall we pass? Ye have devised a bridge, as it were, of a bulrush.

A strange proof that no man may fear Idolatry in a Papist. Your argument is this: "All that be Christians are baptized. And if they be baptized, then have they received the faith of Christ; and 'believe in one God, Father almighty,' and so forth; and have learned that Commandment of His: 'Thou shalt have no other Gods but Me.' If then by Baptism they have received the faith of Christ; and believe in one God, Father almighty, &c.; and have learned that Commandment of His, that they shall have no other Gods but Him; then believe they in no other god but in Him; then serve they no other god but Him; then make they to themselves no other god but Him: but whensoever they pray, wheresoever they kneel, whatsoever gestures they use, they give all honour and praise to God; they have their hearts and minds fixed upon Him: nor we may judge the contrary, for they are Christians; and so are we also expressly forbid to judge of other men's consciences, or to be curious or suspicious of other men's doings."

To answer with modesty to so impudent an assertion, is hard: reasonably to deal with so unreasonable a creature, is more than covenant. To use many words where a wand is deserved, is more a great deal than needeth for your reason, unless ye were purged first. For doubtless there is some mad humour reigning, that bringeth forth so absurd reasoning. First, ye have proved, that all Protestants be good Christians; for they be baptized, they have received the faith, &c. Then, that yourself are very much to blame, in deeming amiss of them. For inasmuch as they have learned the Commandments, they also of necessity must obey the Commandments. Thirdly, that all subjects in the realm of England, all Christians beside, are in right good case; for they cannot sin. This is your reason, M. Martiall, and not mine. For thus ye say: "They have learned the Commandment to have no other god but Him: then believe they no other god but Him; then serve they no other god but Him." By the same reason I may reply: The man that is baptized hath received the faith; doth know the Commandment, "Thou shalt not steal;" "Thou shalt not commit adultery:" therefore there is none that is baptized that can be a thief or adulterer. The Jews were circumcised; they had the Law; they knew that they ought to have no other Gods but Him: therefore no Jew that ever was idolatrer. But notwithstanding our Christendom and faith received, many be thieves and murtherers: notwithstanding the Law delivered to the Israelites, they worshipped, (some of them,) the brazen Serpent; and the Scripture saith they were idolatrers therein. Therefore, notwithstanding that men outwardly profess one God, yet do they not worship alway one God, nor serve Him on such sort as they are commanded. So that it bideth still, for all your blind reason, that a man may fear Idolatry in such as do pretend a worshipping of God.

The effect of Martiall's argument.

The absurdities thereof.

And we do not offend, in affirming you idolatrers. For although, (as you say,) one kind of Idolatry be best known unto God alone, who searcheth the heart, yet hath He left a way to try it, a judge to discern it. And therefore, indefinitely and absolutely to say, that Idolatry is a sin lurking and lying secret in the heart, is an inconvenience. Remember how Christ, at the first entrance into His school, gave out this lesson[1]: *Quemcunque puduerit Mei coram hominibus, pudebit et Me illius coram Patre Meo et sanctis Angelis:* "Whosoever shall be ashamed of Me before men, I will also be ashamed of him before My Father and His holy Angels." So that God is not herewith contented, if a

Folio 129, b.

---

[1] Luc. vi. [ix. 26.]

<small>A profession of Christ is requisite in a Christian.</small> man inwardly with heart acknowledge Him; but also severely doth exact, that by our outward profession we testify to the world that His disciples we are. For upon none other condition but this He doth admit us into the society and fellowship of His kingdom. Truly doth Paul say[1]: *Corde creditur ad justitiam; ore confessio fit ad salutem:* "With heart we believe to righteousness; with mouth we confess to salvation." Out of which words it is plainly to be gathered, that there is no true faith before God, but the same engendereth a confession before men: that every man, according to his calling and grace given him, do further by all means, as occasion is given him, the glory of his God. Therefore Peter's precept is general[2], to "be ready always to give an answer to every man that asketh a reason of the hope that is in us." This reason ye refuse: ye keep a bird in the bosom, but it bewrays the nest. For impossible it is, that a good conscience in service of his God shall in appearance do one thing, and in effect another. And although the service acceptable unto God consist in "spirit and truth," as Christ Himself pronounceth[3]; yet will He not only be truly served, but also be known that He is so served. For which purpose these extern actions are right necessary, to be witnesses to the world of our affect within us.

Understand ye therefore, that as two kinds of honour be due to God; one spiritual, resting in the heart; another corporal, consisting in outward gesture; so are there also <small>Two kinds of Idolatry.</small> two kinds of Idolatry. The first, when a man by perverse opinion corrupteth the spiritual worshipping of God: the second, when the honour peculiar unto God is transferred to a creature. In both these ye Papists most heinously do offend. For ye think that God, which is a Spirit, is delighted with your masking and extern pomp, wherein consisteth all Romish Religion; and so, by your own text, ye be proved false worshippers. Also, by your knocking and holding up of hands before an Image, ye shew yourselves whose servants you are, abasing your estate, and serving a creature. For the proof whereof, because it more nearly concerneth our question, let us inquire what bond we be entered in with God, to serve Him as we ought. So shall we see, whether any

---

[1] Rom. x. [10.]   [2] 1 Pet. iii. [15.]
[3] Joan. iv. [23, 24.]

outward and bodily fact may well induce us to say or think any man an idolatrer.

The eternal God requireth at our hands, that His name be glorified both in our spirit and in our body, because that both be His. And if the commandment did not extend so far, yet reason doth convince no less. For inasmuch as our bodies also be redeemed with the precious bloodshed of Christ, what a shame is it to have them subject still unto the Devil's service? our souls to be God's, our bodies to be the Devil's? Whereas our bodies ought to be the temples of the Holy Ghost, what absurdity is this, to defile them with sacrilege? Whereas our bodies are fore-appointed to immortality, and partaking of the glory of God, what wickedness is this, to attaint them with Idolatry? Paul, when he doth inveigh against fornication, useth this argument: Whereas our bodies are "the members of Christ," is it meet to "make them the members of an harlot[4]?" And on like sort I may answer you: Whereas our bodies be the members of Christ, shall we cut them off from this body of His? shall we prophanate them with unlawful worshipping? God, when He would express the peculiar note of His faithful servants, saith of them, that they bowed not the knee to Baal, nor with their mouth kissed him[5]. He might as well have said, that they were not polluted with superstition; they did not accompt Baal for a god. But to intimate unto us, that the inward affect in this case sufficeth not, He expresseth by name the outward gesture as altogether impious. Wherefore, howsoever we flatter ourselves with an hidden opinion, (so secret that ourselves feel it not;) yet the evident and apparent work of capping and knocking, bowing and kneeling, may disprove our heart to be well affected; and we by outward adoration try and discern a mere idolatrer. When God by His Prophet would describe His magnificence and honour due to Him, He said[6]: *Vivo Ego, Mihi flectetur omne genu, et omnis lingua jurabit Mihi:* "I live, saith the Lord, every knee shall bow to Me, and every tongue shall swear to Me." Thus the Holy Ghost by bowing of the knee, by profession of the mouth, describeth true worshipping. But you, M.

[4] 1 Cor. vi. [15.]
[5] 1 Reg. x. [1 Kings, xix. 18.] Rom. xi. [4.]
[6] Esay xlv. [23.]

[CALFHILL.]

Martiall, will have neither good nor bad worshipping to be judged by gesture.

A proper shift ye have, when ye adore an Image and creep to the Cross, saying, you know that to be but a piece of metal; you make not your prayers to that, but unto God alone, whom in spirit you worship, though your face peradventure be turned to the Image. The self-same pretext had the Corinthians. For they resorted to the feasts of Idols, not of superstition: they were too well instructed. And Paul in their person bringeth forth an excuse for them: *Scimus quod Idolum nihil est:* " We know that an Idol is nothing[1]:" we know that one God, one Lord and Saviour Jesus Christ, is to be honoured and served of us. But did this satisfy S. Paul? Nay. But he affirmed rather, that their inward persuasion and pretended excuse was nothing; inasmuch as their example moved the weak to commit Idolatry. "For if any man," saith the Apostle, "see thee, which hast knowledge, sit at table in the Idols' temple, shall not the conscience of him that is weak be boldened to eat those things which are sacrificed to Idols?" And on like sort you affirm, that an Image or a Cross is nothing. But when ye give the outward reverence, when ye adore it, will not the simple deem great virtue in it? shall not your knowledge, (whatsoever it is,) be occasion of your brother's fall, for whom Christ died? Wherefore, sith adoration is so offensive, better it were never to see Image while the world standeth, that our brother be not offended. And this is S. Paul's reason, and not mine.

Folio 130, a. As for your subtile and profound argument, drawn out of the bowels of your professed law; whereby ye make a wondrous demonstration, that there can be no due proof of Idolatry, inasmuch as "Confession" thereof is nothing credible; "Probation" cannot be made but by external signs, and they do only enforce a presumption; and as for "Evidence of the fact," it cannot fall into affects of the mind, where the abomination of Idolatry lieth; I answer, that although we be very ingenious to find out excuses for our own offences, yet the evidence of the outward fact maketh sufficient probation of Idolatry, and is too good a witness of misdemeaning mind. For if the heart conceived not, the body would not do: and

[1] 1 Cor. viii. [4—10.]

if the body called the heart unto accompt, I am sure that at least in the Court of Chancery, where conscience is examined, the heart should be first condemned of misgovernment. When Ezechias destroyed the brazen Serpent, the Jews lacked such an advocate as you, that might have called the King into the law, and tried the case of injustice against him, because he was not able to make proof of any crime. For they would not confess their Idolatry: and their kneeling to the Image made, (as you say,) but only a presumption: and no evidence could be fet from the outward fact, because ye suppose there is no Idolatry but secret in the heart. But flatter yourselves, (as you best can,) with your lurking affect and privy devotion; your apparent impiety shall not only to God-ward, but to the world condemn you. If Daniel's companions had feed such a counsellor, such a lawyer as you, they would not have thrown themselves into such extremity; whereas they could not have been convinced of Idolatry for all their kneeling before the Idol, if in heart they retained the honour and service of the living God. But they would not have their bodies defiled with wicked worshippings, nor of one temple make two Lords; the soul to be God's, the body to be Satan's. S. Paul of the outward conversation condemned the Corinthians as idolatrers, 1 Cor. viii. S. Peter also[2], (as is before rehearsed,) laid to his hearers' charge, that they were worse than the Egyptians, because of the external signs. God, when He setteth forth the true service of Himself, maketh often mention of the outward reverence. Therefore, (as you call it,) so is it indeed "a poor judgment" of yours, that because God is worshipped in spirit and in truth, therefore men, falling before a piece of wood, knocking the breast, and holding up the hands, may not in any wise be thought idolatrers. Enrich, (I beseech you,) this poor judgment of yours with better reason, or hold your tongue for shame.

As touching your wisdom and deep discretion, wherein ye will not be so abased "to be more brutish than beasts, more simple than birds, more foolish than daws; but that ye know a dead Image from a live man, a still Picture from a quick creature;" I say, that Scripture sheweth precedents of the contrary in as wise men as you are: and as for your own part, experience doth teach us otherwise. The juggling

Folio 132.

[2] [The Pseudo-Clement: p. 369.]

of Papists with Roods and Images hath sought by all means
to plant an opinion of holiness and divinity to rest in dead
things. And howsoever you believe of them, yet damnable
is the service that you command unto them; and the more
ye know the vile condition and estate of them, the more just
and terrible is your condemnation, in exacting a worship and
adoration of them. Therefore I say with Paul[1]: "Because
ye know God, and glorify Him not as God, neither are thankful; but become vain in your imaginations, and your foolish
heart is full of darkness; when ye profess yourselves to be
wise, ye be very fools."

¶ And thus have I answered your ten articles; using moe
words in disproof of them than the cause requireth, or any
man of indifferency would look for at my hands. Only I
would not be said to conceal any piece of proof that you
bring for maintenance of your error. Wherefore I have
turned over leaf by leaf, as in the margent every where appeareth; perused each line and word that had any reason in
it; annexing a sufficient and the same abundant confutation
of it. Your Conclusion indeed I deal not withal: for it containeth more than was in the Premisses; more than you be
able or go about to prove. It is but an heap of lies and
slanders, which, impudently spoken, may be best answered
with silence. Nor any news it is, the professors of the truth
to be depraved of you. Paul was blasphemed as a teacher
of heresy[2], as whose Religion should be new and strange.
Constantine was accused as an innovator and perverter of
God's order[3], because he furthered and followed Christianity.
The faithful Fathers wanted not their Cross: they were always
reviled with most words of reproach, and deemed of the
world the vilest persons of the earth. But as they did not
contend in scolding, but stood most stiff in heresy-reproving[4];
so sufficeth me to have detected your folly, and disproved
your untruths, that the simple at leastwise be not abused by
you. The cause itself standeth too fast to be battered with
such feeble assault of yours. The honesty of men, whom you
would seem to touch, is not to be impaired with the running

---

[1] Rom. i. [21, 22.]
[2] Act. xviii. [xxiv. 14. xvii. 20. xviii. 13.]
[3] Sozomenus, Li. i. Cap. xviii. [p. 558. ed. Lat.]
[4] Theodor. Li. iii. Cap. v. [p. 471. *Eccl. Hist. Auctt.* Basil. 1549.]

over of a railing mouth. If ye gather hereafter any sounder skill, and riper discretion do come unto you, ye will correct your former follies, and thank me for the ministering occasion of amendment. But if God hath utterly resigned you to yourself; and wilfulness, reigning in your witless head, breed a confidence to put still your more shame in print; myself will contemn so lewd an adversary, and give place to other, that, with more freedom of speech, and less derogation unto their persons, may answer you according to your shameless deserts.

FINIS.

Quæ meliora tuis placitis hoc tempore noram,
Impartire tibi visum est: hiis utere mecum [5].

---

[5] [... " Si quid novisti rectius istis,
Candidus imperti: si non, his utere mecum."
(Horat. *Ep.* i. vi. 67—8.)
"Sin habes aliquid in hoc argumento melius, sequere quod melius est: sed interim huic nostræ promptæ voluntati saltem hoc præmii rependre, ut quod habes melius, velis nobis esse commune."
(Erasmi *Modus orandi,* ad fin. sig. u 2. Basil. 1551.)]

MORTIS ET CRUCIS COLLATIO.

Qui cupis ad Vitam renovari Morte futuram,
  Mortem Christi animo fac meditere tuo.
Mors ea Vita fuit; Vitamque fidelibus omnem
  Præstitit in sola mortuus Ille Cruce.
Non tamen ipsa licet Cruce Mors inflicta ministra,
  Mortis erit celebri dira ministra loco.
Mors peperit victa solidos de Morte triumphos:
  Crux valet ad Vitam materiata nihil.
Mors affert animis onerum solatia pressis:
  Crux dare lenimen lignea nulla potest.
Stigmata Mortis habent animi defixa fideles:
  Stigmata formatæ sunt malefida Crucis.
Mors in honore piis æterno tempore stabit:
  Effigiata piis Crux abolenda venit.
Mortis ut obrepat mala non oblivio nobis,
  Corporeæ remanet mystica Cœna dapis.
Hæc data firmandis quasi tessera mentibus olim;
  Solaque, perpetuo quæ peragatur, erit.
Non sic Ille Crucem Christus præceptor habendam
  Instituit: valeat Crux, ubi Cœna valet.
Sin Crucis ante oculos monumentum velle videmur,
  Subdita sunt Christi vivida membra Cruci.
Vivida si nequeant animos percellere nostros,
  Incutiantne magis mortua signa fidem?
Perfida visibili gens est contenta figura;
  Dum res interea significata perit.
Sic quos debuerat verum vox viva docere,
  Fusilis errorem semper Imago docet.
Quos Deus, in sacræ demissus viscera mentis,
  Non facit officii sic meminisse sui,
Vana creaturæ facies, subjecta protervis
  Luminibus, memores scilicet efficiat.
Nec tamen hic scelerum finis: sceleratior inde
  Cultus ab affectu deteriore venit.

Namque velut Divi, lapides et ligna coluntur,
Artificis postquam forma fit arte Crucis.
Sin ea forma magis pretioso obducta metallo,
Protinus Idolum Crux facit una duplex.
Ergo Crucifixus nobis in honore locetur;
Cruxque sit a nobis materiata procul.

THE SAME IN ENGLISH.

Who dost desire to Life to come by Death to be restor'd,
Record alway in mindful heart the Death of Christ thy Lord.
This Death gave Life; and He that died did on His Cross alone
Bring everlasting Life to those that Him believe upon.
But though by mean of that His Cross this Death was brought
    to pass,
Yet ought not Cross, instead thereof, to hold the sacred place.
A perfect triumph over Death this Death did once achieve:
But the material Cross to Life no help at all doth give.
This Death doth bring a full release unto the grieved mind:
But in the framed Cross of wood no comfort is to find.
The marks of this most wholesome Death the faithful hearts
    do bear:
The mark of formed Cross, God wot, is but untrusty gear.
With godly men this Death for aye in honour shall abide:
Of godly men the shapen Cross is to be laid aside.
Lest this good Death that bringeth Life should slip out of our
    mind,
He of His sacred body hath His Supper left behind.
This as a pledge to strength our souls is pointed to endure;
And this alone ordained is to be in daily ure.
Our Master Christ commanded not the Cross be holden so:
But where this Supper is in place the Cross may be let go.
But of the Cross some monument if we desire to see,
The lively members of our Christ to Cross still subject be.
If lively ones want force enough to move our resty mind,
Alas, in lifeless signs what force of credit shall we find?
The faithful[1] sort content themselves with signs yseen with eye;
Even while the matter signified is wholly lost thereby.

[1] [faithless?]

So them, that should by lively voice have learn'd the truth
    to know,
The forged Image evermore doth into error throw.
Shall they whom God, that doth descend into the godly breast,
Doth not so make to call to mind the duty they profest;
Shall they, forsooth, in heart be brought to hold the same
    aright
By fickle form of creature, subject to erring sight?
Yet is not here the end of ills: for hereof doth ensue
From worse affect false worship done where it was never due.
For after once a form of Cross is made by workman's art,
To stocks and stones, as heavenly Gods, then honour they
    impart.
But if with precious metal it be garnisht to the eye,
A double Idol of one Cross is honour'd by and by.
Let Him therefore that died on Cross devoutly be ador'd;
And let material Cross be far from us that fear the Lord.

FINIS.

Imprinted at London by Henry

Denham, for Lucas Harrison, dwelling in
𝔓𝔞𝔲𝔩𝔢𝔰 𝔠𝔥𝔲𝔯𝔠𝔥𝔶𝔞𝔯𝔡𝔢, 𝔞𝔱 𝔱𝔥𝔢 𝔖𝔦𝔤𝔫𝔢
𝔬𝔣 𝔱𝔥𝔢 𝔠𝔯𝔞𝔫𝔢.

Anno Domini. 1565.
Nouembris. 3.

A TABLE,

BY ORDER OF THE ARTICLES, BRIEFLY CONTAINING THE EFFECT OF THE WHOLE BOOK.

IN THE EPISTLE.

	PAGE
What famous Clerks be now-a-days become writers	2
What is to be thought of Martiall	3
What arguments he useth	4
How he traitorously taketh away the chief part of the Queen's style	5
How she for her clemency is not gracious to Papists	7
How foolishly he flatters her	7
The Queen's private doings no precedent to all	7
Of every fact not to judge an affection	7
How public order hath taken away Roods and Images	8
How Martiall doth lie, in saying that Crosses are not suffered in high-ways	8
How his three grounds of his cause be laid only upon lies	9
How for the doctrine of the Cross we may stand to judgment of the Fathers, though Scripture were not	11

IN THE PREFACE.

The Cross a forged ensign of Christ	12
Satan's sleight to displace God and His word	12
The Devil is the ape of God	12
All Gentility took precedent of God's service	13
Sacraments of the Hebrews counterfeited by the Heathen	13
Minos followed Moses	13
Hills and groves in imitation of the tabernacle	14
Witches and sorcerers instead of Prophets and Priests	14
The Poets' paradise for Christians' heaven	14
Their purgatory for hell	15
Papists herein the Devil's chief ministers	15
For Baptism of infants, Baptism of bells	15
More solemnity in the Devil's service than in Christ's	15
Holy Water devised in despite of Baptism	15
Ordinance of God, and ordinance of the Devil	17
Sole life exacted in the Devil's ministers	18
Adultery with Papists a light trifle	18
The Devil deputeth Saints intercessors	19
As God made man image of Himself, so the Devil devised Images of God	20
God's books burned; Devil's books advanced	20

	PAGE
Macedonius his answer to Theodosius' men of war	22
Images came from Gentility and foolish zeal	23
Images cannot be without abuse	23
How prone we are to superstition	23
How Lactantius affirmeth no Religion to be where an Image is	25
How Images crept into the church	26
To have an Image is a will-worship, and therefore unlawful	26
Proofs that nothing in God's service should be admitted beside the word	27
Images teachers of lies	28
How God's order is broken by Images	28
That Images came from Gentility, is proved	28
That in Eusebius' time, three hundred and twenty-five year after Christ, no Images in churches	29
Serenus, Bishop of Massilia, brake all Images	30
Fruits of Images	30
Places of Scripture condemning Images	31
Papists' devotion like to Michah	31
Image-maintainers like to Jeroboam	32
Erasmus' opinion of Images	34
Images be proved not to teach otherwise than wickedly	35
That memory is holpen by the story, is answered	37
That God can have no Image made of Him	37
That Christ neither can nor ought have an Image made of Him	41
Images not only forbidden to be worshipped, but also to be had	41
Three reasons why Christ can have no Image made of Him	45
The folly to have a Picture of Christ	46
How Images are honoured contrary to the mind of Gregory	47
A note how Martiall's allegations for the Cross are to be known in this treatise	48
The Papists' hope	49
Martiall lies in his preface	50
Comparison between Papists and true Christians	52

IN THE FIRST ARTICLE.

Men in God's matters not to be believed without the word	56
What judges ought to sit in controversies of Religion	60
How Martiall entreateth of that which is not: applying to the sign the virtue proper to the thing itself	63
Chrysostom his praise of the Cross answered	63
Things well received ill continued	65
The sign of the Cross an heathenish observance	65
Chrysostom mangled by Martiall	68
Martialis, a pretended Disciple, answered	69
Damascenus answered	70
Cross sign no weapon to fight against Satan	73

A TABLE. 395

	PAGE
Athanasius answered	73
Necessary notes to be observed in reading of the Fathers	75
Origen answered for his praise of the Cross	77
Cassiodore answered	81
Martiall's fond reason for necessity of a Cross	82
Lactantius and Augustin answered	83
Martiall's comparison examined	85
Julian's example opened, whereby he will prove the Cross to drive away Spirits	86
The like example of a Jew, out of Gregory	88
Silvester the second, for all his Crosses, in the very Mass-time was torn in pieces by Devils	92
Martiall's allegations, whereby he will prove mention to be made of his Cross in Scripture; and how they are answered	92

IN THE SECOND ARTICLE.

Martiall goeth only about to prove a matter that he promised he would not speak of	100
It is declared, that, although the Cross were prefigured by Moses and the Prophets, yet it follows not that we must needs have the sign thereof	100
His allegations for the prefiguring of the Cross, examined	103
Moses' hands lifted like a Cross	104
The letter *Thau*	106
Constantine's apparition answered	110
For good success in the Cross-time	112
Julian's visions discussed	114
Divers means that God hath miraculously used for delivery of His	117
How Papists deal with God's book	121
The end of Ceremonies	122
What Christ in judgment shall require of us	124

IN THE THIRD ARTICLE.

The four reasons why every church and chapel should have the sign of the Cross, answered	126
Abdias proved fabulous	126
The true manner of dedication of churches	131
Bartholomew's dedication	132
Philip's dedication	134
The Councils by Martiall alleged, answered	135
He bringeth the bare name of three Councils, and nothing else	137
Three Councils which are plain against Images	138
The Council of Constantinople, under Leo Isauricus	138
The Council of Granata, called Elibertinum	154
The Council of Frankford	155

The beastly reasons of the second Council of Nice confirming Images, answered	156
The wickedness of Irene, President of that sixth [seventh] Council	175
The Doctors answered, that seem to command the sign of a Cross in churches	177
Ambrose in that case considered	177
How a cross on the steeple saveth the church from burning	180
Lactantius' authority answered	180
Eusebius thought it strange to see an Image stand in the church	183
Arnobius a great enemy to Images	184
Augustin answered	184
What is a mystery	184
Augustin doth answer the same objections which the Papists make in defence of Images	185
His places against Images	188
Paulinus of Nola answered and disproved	188
Justinian's laws weighed	189
Valens and Theodosius enacted that no Cross should be used	190
The custom of Church considered	191
Silvester's lie concerning the church of Constantinus	193
Augustin's rule for custom	194

IN THE FOURTH ARTICLE.

A proof that although the sign of the Cross have been used, yet doth it not follow that it is lawful now	195
The tale of Probianus disproved	198
Cyprian's authority examined	200
Augustin's authority discussed	204
The difference of *rite* and *recte*	206
The Canon Law condemneth Cross-master Martiall	206
Chrysostom answered	206
Constantinus' church-hallowing	207
Popish church-hallowing	208
Dionysius disproved not to be Areopagita	211
Traditions and ceremonies added to Baptism	212
Confirmation proved no Sacrament	215
Papists' blasphemous doctrine touching Confirmation	216
The reasons against popish Confirmation	217
How Papists falsify the Scripture	219
The absurdity of popish doctrine	220
The Fathers' opinion touching the number of Sacraments	222
Cyprian's error	224
The seven-fold grace of Papists	226
Orders proved to be no Sacrament	227
No due proof can be made, that a Cross with a finger was or ought to be made in the Lord's Supper	231
Matrimony proved no Sacrament	235

	PAGE
Martiall's reason to make Matrimony a Sacrament	236
Absurdities in popish doctrine concerning Matrimony	238
Martiall disproved for his Sacrament of Penance	241
Vanity [Unity] of Papists therein	244
Martiall confuted for his Sacrament of Extreme Unction	244
The absurdities in popish doctrine for Extreme Unction	247
That all Councils are not to be credited	248

IN THE FIFTH ARTICLE.

That Martiall understandeth not what "blessing" meaneth, which applieth it to a sign in the forehead	250
Unlawful authorities brought for blessing	251
Epiphanius' authority, which tare the vail	253
What is to be thought of traditions	256
Tertullian's traditions not to be observed	257
Ephræm not alway sound	258
Chrysostom not in all things to be followed	258
Hierom sometime to be reproved	259
Augustin not always to be admitted	259
Prudentius hath his infirmities	259
The unity of Papists and Christians	261
How Martiall doth corrupt Tertullian	264
In custom what to be considered	266
Traditions three-fold	267
Traditions, how they vary	270
What lies Martiall maketh of Athanasius	272
That Roods, Crosses, Images, are counterfeits of Serapis	274
The godliness and good Religion of Papists	275

IN THE SIXTH ARTICLE.

Authorities unlawful alleged by Martiall, for confirming of the Cross-keeping	280
No authority of men to be grounded on in God's matters	282
Hierom against reserving pieces of the Cross	283
Chrysostom's saying for enclosure of the Cross in gold, answered	284
Chrysostom against such superstition	285
Effects of the Cross and pieces thereof considered	288

IN THE SEVENTH ARTICLE.

That Crosses at the first were not used in Litanies	294
Montanists and Arrians authors of Procession	296
Litanies of two sorts, and when devised	296
How Papists degenerate from all good order	297
The Crosses of Constantinople, what they were	299
How Martiall in one story maketh four lies	301
Concerning the use of tapers	301

	PAGE
There must be no tapers on the Lord's table	303
How Martiall proveth Luther no heretic	304
The affairs of Augustin the Monk in England	305
Papists superstitious, and why	310
The true ensign of Christ	311
For Reliques	311

IN THE EIGHTH ARTICLE.

Miracles no proof of doctrine	316
Wrought by the Devil	317
Three reasons why miracles make not for the Cross	320
How Martiall belieth Eusebius	321
How the Papists agree not for invention of the Cross	323
What lies be made of pieces of the Cross	326
Of the nails that Christ was crucified withal	327
The answer to the miracles, that were affirmed to have been done by the Cross	329
How Papistry breedeth security in sin	330
Miracles past no proof of present use	332
That as well we may have the sign of Idols, as the sign of the Cross for any miracle	333
Whether the miracles of the Cross were true or no, they can prove no lawful use thereof	334
The similitude of the cloth of estate	340
For memory holpen with a Cross	342

IN THE NINTH ARTICLE.

Vanities alleged for commodities of the Cross	345
The true effects of Images	346
The reason that Images should not be unlawful though not expedient, answered	346
God's books commanded, forbidden for policy: man's books for policy must needs be maintained	348
Whether Images can teach things necessary to salvation	350
That Crosses teach no humility, no virtue	351
That Images speak doubtfully, teach devilishly, be read unlawfully	354
That there can be no such ignorance, as should drive us to seek knowledge in an Image	354
The titles and commendation of Scripture	356
That for want of preachers we must not seek to Images	357
What lewd affections be stirred by Imagery	358
What affections were stirred in the Heathen by Images	358
No Imagery with preaching, much less without	360
How Images must not be admitted for help of memory	361

	PAGE
How Cyril alloweth no Images in churches	362
A devilish memory, that must be holpen with a Cross	363

IN THE TENTH ARTICLE.

What adoration and worship is	366
That adoration by the Scripture is forbidden to Images	367
Authorities for adoration of the Cross falsely alleged	368
Authorities of the Fathers against the adoration of the Cross	368
A strange proof that no man may fear Idolatry in worshippers of the Cross	382
The absurd argument of Martiall	383
Two kinds of Idolatry	384
That bowing and kneeling to Crosses and Images doth prove Idolatry	385

THE AUTHORS ALLEGED AGAINST BOTH THE HAVING AND WORSHIPPING OF THE CROSS.

Clemens Rom. Epis.
Irenæus.
Clemens Alexandrinus.
Josephus.
Cyprianus.
Tertullianus.
Origenes.
Arnobius.
Lactantius.
Eusebius.
Athanasius.
Epiphanius.
Ambrosius.
Hieronymus.
Augustinus.
Chrysostomus.
Cyrillus.
Prudentius.
Gregorius PP.
Alfonsus de Castro.
Carolus Magnus.
Petrus Crinitus.
Erasmus.
The author of the Turks' History.

COUNCILS.

The Council of Constantinople, under Leo Isauricus.
The Council of Granata.
The Council of Frankford.

INDEX.

AARON, 23, 33, 58, 104, 335.
Abbot (Robert, Bp. of Salisbury,) *Antilogia*, 6.
Abdias, *Historia Apostolica*, 69: when this work was first published, 126: its genuineness and contents discussed, 126—135: its perusal interdicted, and afterward allowed, 126.
Abgarus, fable of the Picture sent to him by our Saviour; and the earliest writer who mentions it, 41: the second Nicene Council relies upon the fiction; and this is confessed by Gretser, 171: mistake in the Caroline Books with regard to Pope Gelasius and the Edessan Image, 171.
Abracadabra, an amulet used by the Basilidian heretics, 285.
Accius Navius, 316.
Ado, *Breviarium Chronicorum*, 114.
Adrian I. (Pope) 173.
"Advouterous," 330.
Ægeria, 14.
Ægidius (Joannes) compelled to assent to the doctrine, that supreme adoration is to be offered to the Cross, 381.
Æsculapius, 20, 316, 317.
Agapetus I. (Pope) said to have introduced Processions, 295, 305.
Aguirre (Cardinal De) *Notitia Concilior. Hispan.*, 154.
Ahijah, 33.
Albertus Magnus, 231.
Alciatus (Andreas) 305.
Alcoran, 44.
Alexander the Great, his interview with Jaddus, 117.
Alexander I. (Pope) spurious Epistle, alleged for the use of Holy Water, 16.
Alexander III. (Pope) affirms that adultery is but a trifling offence, 18.
Alexander (Natalis) 42, 63, 96.
Alfred (King) 306.
Allatius (Leo) *Confutatio fabulæ de Joanna Papissa*, 6.

"All to," 3, 79, 91, 92, 133, 336.
"Almerie," 136.
Ambrosius (S.) how his testimony was adduced at the second Nicene Council, 173: a Sermon *De Cruce*, by S. Maximus Taurinensis, attributed to him, 177: declares that to worship the material Cross would be a heathenish error, and vanity of the wicked, 192, 377: not the author of the Commentary *in Ep. ad Tim.*, 235: the books *De Vocatione Gentium*, bearing his name, fictitious, 295: what he said of the Council of Ariminum, 345.
—— *In Psalmos*, 156.
—— *De Spiritu Sancto*, 165.
—— *Epistt.*, 192, 345.
—— *Oratio funebris de obitu Theodosii*, 192, 196, 322, 324, 327, 377.
—— *De Sacramentis libri sex*, cited, and their genuineness questioned, 202.
Anastasius, 311.
Anaxagoras, 99.
And, an', if, 5, l. 16; 245, 274.
Andrew (S.) 127, 128.
Andrewes (Bp.) 25, 65—6, 226.
Anicetus (Pope) how S. Polycarp and he disagreed, without a breach of communion, 269—70.
Anno (S.) 135.
Anointing, the symbol of the gift of healing, 245. Vid. Unction (Extreme).
Ansegisus (Abbas) 297.
Anthony (S.) his *Life*, 74: what S. Jerom doubted respecting the monster which appeared to him, 252.
Antioch, People of, rescued from imminent danger by a Monk, 22.
Antiochus, 24.
Antoninus, (Archiep. Florent.) 64.
Apelles, 263.
Appius Claudius, 316.
Aquila, 107.
Aquinas (S. Thomas) his language

[CALFHILL.]

26

about faith, 85: defends the ascription of *Latria* to the Cross, 381.
Archidiaconus. Vid. Guido.
Aretinus (Leonardus) 59.
Ariminum (Council of) 10, 345.
Aristotle, 73.
Armarium, what it signifies, 136.
Arnobius, a treatise by Minucius Felix attributed to him, 178, 183, 295, 380.
—— *Adversus Gentes*, 39, 373, 374.
Arnoldus Carnotensis, twelve treatises by him, attributed to S. Cyprian, 200, 201.
Asconius Pedianus, 107.
"Assoyle," 242.
Athanasius (S.) many works of Apollinarius anciently ascribed to him, 268: the *Index Expurgatorius* of Cardinal Zapata condemns a reference to his declaration that "God alone is to be adored," 375—6; the counterfeit *Quæstiones ad Antiochum* falsified by Martiall, 376.
—— *Orat. cont. Gentes*, 21, 46, 375.
—— *Quæstiones ad Antiochum* spurious, 73—4, 268, 272—3, 376.
—— *Life of S. Anthony*, 74.
—— *Apol. contra Arian.*, 207.
—— *De incarnat. Verbi Dei*, 353.
—— *Cont. Arian. Orat.* ii., 375.
Augustin (S., the Monk,) in what state he found the Britons, 305—6: whether chargeable with the massacre of the Monks of Bangor, 306: what his demands were, 307: his Litany; and how far Romanists differ from him, 308.
Augustinus (S.) Decree falsely assigned to him, 54: a Homily, attributed to S. Chrysostom, found among his works, 63, 277: spurious addresses to Catechumens, 84: fictitious *Sermo* clxxxi. *de Tempore*, (vel *De Symbolo*,) 86, 205, 234: counterfeit *Ser.* xix. *de Sanctis*, 184, 204: Sermon *De Cataclysmo* far from being authentic, and condemned by the Benedictine editors, 204: rejection of the Sermon *De visitatione infirmorum* by Erasmus, the Divines of Paris and Louvain, and by Bellarmin, 361.
—— *Contra Maximin. Arian.*, 10, 129.
—— *De Trinitate*, 27, 58.
—— *Quæst. sup. Jos.*, 33.

Augustinus (S.) *De consen. Evangel.*, 34, 188, 263.
—— *De vera Religione*, 41, 378.
—— *De Fide et Symbolo*, 42.
—— *De Civitate Dei*, 43, 101, 102, 113, 129, 188, 316, 319.
—— *In Psalmos*, 43, 75, 101, 156, 164, 185—8, 250.
—— *Epistt.*, 43, 58, 194, 196, 213, 223, 262, 270, 333.
—— *De Doctrina Christ.*, 57, 157, 223.
—— *Sermones de Tempore*, 63, 67, 86, 205, 234.
—— *Confessiones*, 64, 131, 302.
—— *De Pastoribus*, 67.
—— *Sermones de Scripturis*, 67, 348.
—— *De spiritu et litera*, 78.
—— *De Gen. contra Manich.*, 102.
—— *Contra adversarios Legis et Proph.*, 102.
—— *De Quæstionibus octoginta-tribus*, 157.
—— *Liber de Hæresibus*, 188.
—— *De Bapt. contra Donat.*, 191, 215.
—— *In S. Joannem*, 204, 206, 259.
—— *De verbis Apostoli*, 205.
—— *De Peccat. mer. & remiss.*, 213, 259.
—— *Cont. liter. Petil.*, 215.
—— *De catech. rudibus*, 224.
—— *Serm. de Bap. Infan.*, 244.
—— *Contra Gaudent.*, 281.
—— *Contra Faustum*, 319.
Augustinus (Antonius) 137.
Aurelianus Remensis, 69.

Bagster (Samuel) error in his Polyglott Bible, 91.
Baillet (Adrien) *Jugemens des Savans*, 200.
Bale (Bp.) his statement as to the giving of names to Bells, 15.
Baluzius (Stephanus) 16, 154.
Baptism, how sins are remitted therein, 15—16; ceremonies added to it, 212 —14: grace received through it, 217: Romanists take away half its effect, 216—17; and blasphemously teach that Confirmation is a greater Sacrament, 221—2.
—— of Bells, 15, 16, 17.
Barlow (William) 199.
Baronius (Cardinal) 9, 41: rejects an Epistle of S. Epiphanius, 42: his

description of the *Opus imperfectum* ascribed to S. Chrysostom, 95—6: his account of Joannes Moschus, and the *Limonarium*, 174: exhibits the figure of the amulet *Abracadabra*, 285: considers the name " Papists " to be a sublime title of glory, 290: alleges a falsified translation of the Chronicle of Eusebius, 321—2: referred to respecting the *Scripta de inventione S. Crucis Dominicæ*, condemned by the Gelasian Decree, 324.

—— *Martyrologium*, 66, 89, 290, 324.

Barthius (Caspar) his conjecture about the Epistles and Life of Martial, Bp. of Limoges, 69.

Bartholinus (Thomas) *De Cruce Hypomnemata*, 181, 287.

—— *De Morbis Biblicis*, 258.

Bartholomew (S.) tales concerning him told by Abdias, 132—3: the place and manner of his death, 133.

Basilius (S.) *Concio ad Adolesc.*, 59.

—— *De Spiritu Sancto*: first edition of Erasmus's Latin version; and his judgment concerning the work, 266: cited, 270.

Baxter (Richard) 42.

" Beadsman," 6.

Beard (Thomas) his words with regard to the transient sign, and permanent erection, of the Cross, 197—8.

Beaven (James) 269.

Becon (Thomas) 10, 19, 52, 175, 190.

Beda (Ven.) *De Temporum ratione*, 66: *Homiliæ S. Chrysostomi apud eum*, 77: his testimony exonerative of S. Augustin the Monk from the guilt of murder, 306: *Sermo de inventione sanctæ Crucis*, 323.

Bellarmin (Cardinal) denies that Bells are baptized, 15, 16: quotes a spurious Epistle of Pope Alexander I., 16: rejects an Epistle of S. Epiphanius, 42: adduces from S. Chrysostom a Homily which he confesses not to be authentic, 63—4: acknowledges that S. Chrysostom has sometimes spoken hyperbolically, 64: cites the fictitious Epistles of Martial, Bp. of Limoges, 70: condemns, and yet relies on, the *Quæstiones ad Antiochum*, falsely ascribed to S. Athanasius, 74: referred to, 85, 95, 196, 258, 268, 290: his opinion as to the author of the *Opus imperfectum*, 96: statement respecting the eighty-second Canon of the Quinisext Council, 137: dishonesty with regard to a Poem assigned to Lactantius, 181: unsatisfactory account of the writings of the Pseudo-Dionysius the Areopagite, 211: his timidity in speaking of the counterfeit Epistles of the early Popes, 222: misrepresentation as to the memorable *Instructio Armeniorum*, 248: he adopts a glaring corruption of a passage in Eusebius, *De vita Constantini*, 278: alleges a falsified version of the *Chronicle* of Eusebius, 321—2: stamps as ambiguous a feigned Epistle bearing the name of Pope Eusebius, 323 —4: his words with regard to the Sermon *De visitatione infirmorum*, untruly assigned to S. Augustin, 361: defends the ascription of *Latria* to the material Cross, 381.

Bells, Baptism of, 15, 16, 17.

—— duties of, 15.

Benedictus Levita, 297.

Bergomensis (Jac. Phil.) Vid. Forestus.

Bernardus (S.) 113.

Bertha, 306.

Betuleius (Xystus) 13.

Beverege (Bp.) 137.

Bible, mistake in Bagster's Polyglott, 91.

—— Annotations upon the Douay, 107.

Bingham (Joseph) *Antiquities*, 29, 285, 297.

Binius (Severinus) *Concilia*, 54, 66, 136, 137, 193, 255, 297, 323, 324.

" Birthdays " of Martyrs, the days of their martyrdom, 257.

"Bless;" to, misapplication of the word, 231—33, 250.

Blondellus (David) 69, 126, 222, 322.

Bochart (Matthieu) 66.

Bolmann (Theod.) 321.

Bona (Cardinal) 202.

Boys (John) 5, 25, 78.

Bramhall (Primate) See Florence (Council of).

Brevint (Daniel) 19.

Bridoul (Toussain) 86.

Broughton (Richard) 306.

Brunus (Conradus) 97.

26—2

Bucchingerus (Michael) 77.
Bull (Bp.) 85.
Burton (Edward) 343.
Butler (Alban) *Lives of the Saints*, 6, 305.
Butler (Charles) *Book of R. C. Church*, 5—6.

Cæsarius Arelatensis (S.) a Homily, *De Paschate*, attributed both to him and to Eusebius Emisenus, 193—4.
Cajetanus (Thomas de Vio, Cardinalis) 381.
Calvinus (Joannes) *De Reliquiis*, 324, 328.
Camerarius (Joachimus) 22, 322.
Care (Henry) 52.
Cario (Joannes) 78.
Carleton (Bp.) 237.
Caroli Magni et Ludov. Pii *Capitula*, 297.
Carolus Magnus. Vid. Charlemagne.
Carranza (Bartholomæus) his *Summa Conciliorum* vitiated, 91 : possibly misunderstood by Calfhill respecting the Synod of Elvira, 154.
Cartwright (Thomas) 236.
Casalius (Joannes Baptista) 65.
Casaubonus (Isaacus) 107, 255.
Cassander (Georg.) referred to concerning a *Cross* and a *Crucifix*, 362.
Cassian (S.) 30.
Cassiodorus (Mag. Aur.) *Historia Tripartita*, 65, 87, 114, 198.
—— *Comment. in Psal.*, 81, 102.
Castalio (Sebastianus) 95.
Castro (Alphonsus a) reproves S. Epiphanius, 42 : what he states concerning Claudius, Bp. of Turin, 379.
"Casure," 298.
Cave (Guilielmus) 41, 42, 48, 133, 306.
Cecilius (Lucius) 105.
Centuriatores Magdeburgenses, their statement with respect to the first naming of Bells, 15 : quoted about Origen, 78 : they appear to have misled Calfhill concerning the origin of Processions, 296.
Ceremonies, why imposed upon the Jews, 122.
Challoner (Bp.) 290.
Chamierus (Daniel) 74, 287.
Charlemagne (Emperor) forbad that Bells should be baptized, 16 : what he called the second Council of Nicæa, 155 : his account of the true ensign of Christ, 311 : his description of an unhappy memory, 363 : his books *De Imaginibus* again referred to, 379.
Charlemagne (Emperor) *Caroline Books*, when composed, 42 : interdicted by the *Index Tridentinus*, 155 : where their history and subject are discussed, 155: their contents given at considerable length, 156—175.
Charles V. (Emperor) buried in a Friar's cowl, 287.
Chaucer (Geof.) 52, 288.
Chrysostomus (S. Joannes) speaks of the Monk Macedonius, 22 : spurious treatises ascribed to, respecting the Cross, 63 : fictitious Homily *Ad pop. Ant.* adduced as if from, 63—4 : various references to, 64 : uses hyperbolical language, 64, 77 : *Opus imperfectum* attributed to, 77, 95—6, 111, 285 : uncertain treatise *De orando ad Deum*, 104 : counterfeit *Homily on Exod.* xvii., 104 : dubious Homily, *Unum et eundem esse Legislatorem utriusque Testamenti*, vainly alleged at the second Nicene Council, 173.
—— *Demonstratio ad Gentiles*, 63, 65, 277, 284.
—— *In Genesin*, 55, 250.
—— *Sermo de Pœnitentia*, 64.
—— *De Cruce et Latrone*, 63, 277.
—— *Hom. in S. Matth.*, 76, 95, 258, 259, 285.
—— *De laudibus S. Pauli*, 77.
—— *In Ep. ad Hebr.*, 130.
—— *In Epist. ad Cor.*, 184, 204, 232, 285.
—— *Hom. in Ep. ad Coloss.*, 258.
—— *De Lazaro Conciones*, 258.
—— *Ad pop. Antioch. Hom.*, 285.
—— *In S. Joan.*, 353, 378.
Cicero, 14, 25.
Clagett (William) 86, 246.
Claudius Taurinensis, 379.
Clemens Alex. *Strom.*, 13.
—— *Orat. ad Gentes*, 370.
Clemens Rom. (S.) not the author of the *Recognitions*, 20—21; which are mentioned with reference to the material Cross, 252; retorted against

Romanists, 368—70; and wrongly quoted in S. Peter's name, 380, 387.
Clement VIII. (Pope) *Index lib. prohib.*, 95, 126.
—— *Pontificale*, 381.
Clericus (Joannes) 10, 20.
Coccius (Jodocus) *Thesaurus Catholicus*, 70, 77, 81, 177, 231, 258.
Cocus (Robertus) *Censura quorundam scriptorum*, 69, 89, 126, 137, 200, 248, 361.
" *Collectam facere*," " to perform the Collect," or celebrate the holy Communion, 253.
Collier (Jeremy) 53.
Collin (Nicolas) adduces a false Epistle of Pope Alexander I.. in defence of Holy Water, 16.
Collyridians, 377.
Combefis (Franciscus) 372.
Comber (Thomas) 89, 137, 287, 322.
Confirmation, 215—227.
Conradus a Lichtenau, Abbas Urspergensis, *Chronicum*, 87.
Constantine (Emperor) said to have called the Bishop of Rome a God, 5: sign from heaven shown to him, and his consequent respect for the Cross, 110—12; which, however, he did not introduce into churches, 278 : glaring corruption of a passage in a Latin version of Eusebius, *De vita Constantini*, 278.
Constantinople, Quinisext Council held at, anno 692, an account of its Decrees ; and what its eighty-second Canon permitted, 137.
—— Council of, an. 754, anathematized Damascen, 71: its Acts where to be found, 138 : long and important extracts from them, 138—154.
Constantinus Copronymus, what Council he summoned, and when, 46, 138 : how his remains were treated by the Empress Irene, 175—6.
Conzalez (Franciscus Antonius) *Collectio Canonum Ecclesiæ Hispanæ*, 154, 302.
Cornarius (Janus) 42, 121, 251, 329, 377.
Cosin (Bp.) 19, 226, 248.
Crabbe (Petrus) his reading in a remarkable Canon of the second Synod of Tours altered, 136.

Crakanthorp (Richard) 64, 96, 137, 174, 258, 290.
" Craketh," 351.
" Crambe", 320.
Cranmer (Abp.) 47.
Crashawe (William) *Sermon at the Crosse*, 15.
" Cresset", 298.
Crinitus (Petrus) his work *De honesta Disciplina* expurgated, 190.
Croix (Pierre de) 85, 95.
Cross, sign of the, not mentioned in Scripture as part of the Christian's armour, 73: what that Cross is, which is the refuge of the faithful, 82 : verses in Isaiah and Jeremiah explained, 92—4 : what is to be " the sign of the Son of man in heaven," 95—6 : sealing of the servants of God, 97—8 : lifting up of the hands of Moses, 104 —6; the letter *Thau*, 106—9: token of victory shown to Constantine, 110— 12 : transient sign of the Cross usual among Christians in ancient times, 195, seqq. : judgment of the Church of England relative to this sign, 199 : the word "blessing" wrongly applied, 231—33, 250.
—— material, Justinian's mandate with regard to its occasional erection, 135—6, 189, 304—5 : S. Jerom compares the reservation of fragments of it to the use of Pharisaical phylacteries, 283—4 : what kind of Crosses S. Chrysostom introduced at Constantinople, 298—301 : Invention of the Cross by Helena, 287 : Eusebius does not mention it, but his Chronicle has been falsified respecting it, 321—2 : witnesses agree not in their statements concerning it, 322 —5 : how many times the Cross was discovered, according to the Golden Legend, 321 : fragments of the Cross, 325—27: the nails, 327—8: authorities against the adoration of it, 368 —79 : the Belgic *Index* condemns the assertion, that it is manifest Idolatry to adore the Cross, 376 : proof that *Latria*, or the highest degree of worship, is offered to it by Romanists, 381.—See the " Table."
—— " Cross-bitten", 1.

Crucifix (A) to be regarded very differently from a *Cross*, 185, 362.
Cunner; Cunerus Petri de Browershaven, 88.
Cuperus (Gisbertus) 105.
Curtius (Cornelius) *De Clavis Dominicis liber*, 328.
Cusanus (Cardinal) 174.
Cuspinianus (Joannes) 45.
Cyprianus (Ern. Sal.) 128.
Cyprianus (S.) *Ad Cæcil. frat. Epist.*, 27.
—— twelve treatises, by Arnoldus Carnotensis, ascribed to him, 200, 201.
—— *Ep. ad Magnum*, 203.
—— *Epist.* lxx., 213, 225.
—— fictitious *Epistola ad Novatianum hæreticum*, 227.
—— *Epist.* lxxiv., 233.
—— *De lapsis*, 270.
—— *De Idolorum vanitate*, 317—18.
—— *Ad Demetrianum*, 371—2.
Cyrillus Alexand. (S.) in what manner alleged at the second Council of Nicæa, 173: *Contra Julianum*, 361: allows not Images in churches, 362: *Thesaurus*, 378.
Cyrillus Hierosol. (S.) 95, 103, 326.

Dallæus (Joannes) 96, 105, 202, 211, 246, 248, 278: his error as to a Latin version of the Acts of the second Council of Nicæa, 138.
Damascenus (S. Joannes) 22: his remark respecting the testimony of S. Epiphanius, 42: compares the sign of the Cross to Circumcision, 70: anathematized by the Council of Constantinople, an. 754, 71: affirms that the tree of life prefigured the Cross, 101.
Danæus (Lambertus) 188.
"Dased," 303.
Datary (The) 331. Vid. Ormanet (Nicholas).
"Daukin," 236.
"Daze," 317.
"Departed," 303.
Devil (The) imitates the ordinances of God, 12, seqq.
Deylingius (Salom.) 103.
Dionysius Alexandrinus (S.) 211.
Dionysius Areopagita, the writings attributed to him spurious: when the author of the *Hierarchia* lived: at what time, and by whom his books were first produced: Bellarmin's unsatisfactory statement respecting them, 211.
Dionysius of Corinth, 211.
Dionysius Halicar., 13, 362.
Disciples (The seventy) 69, 126.
Discipulus. Vid. Heroldt.
Ditmarus, *Chronicon*, 115.
Dodd (Charles) 53, 290.
Dodwell (Henry) 251.
Domitian, blasphemous title assumed by, 6.
Donatus, Bp. of Evoria, 252.
Donne (John) 226.
"Dor," A, 2.
Dorman (Thomas) 2, 51.
Dorotheus Tyrius (Pseudo-) 126.
Dorscheus (Joannes Georgius) 155, 181.
Δουλεία, whether acknowledged by Romanists to be a sufficient degree of worship for the material Cross, 381.
Downham (George, Bp. of Derry,) *Papa Antichristus*, 6.
Downham (John) *The Christian Warfare*, 113.
"Draff," 248.
Duræus (Joannes) 42.
Durantes (Gulielmus) 98, 297.

"Eareshrift," 243.
"Earing," 177.
Easter Feast, and ante-paschal Fast, 269.
Eckius (Joannes) 21.
Edward VI. (King) called our Josias, 24: remarkable alteration in the Litany after his reign, 315.
Eleutherius (Pope) Rescript attributed to him, 52—3, 305.
Eliberis, sive Illiberis. Vid. Elvira.
Elijah, 312—13, 336.
Elisha, 313.
Elizabeth (Queen) her title of Defender of the faith omitted by Martiall, 5: her clemency abused by Romanists, 6—7: retained a Crucifix in the royal chapel, 7: called Theodosia, 11: remarkable words omitted from our Litany after her accession to the throne, 315.
Elmenhorst (Geverhardus) 183.
Elvira, Synod of, strange mistake concerning it: when it was held; and

INDEX. 407

what it decreed respecting Pictures in a church, 154: its Ordinance with regard to the lighting of tapers in the day-time in cemeteries, 302: what volume contains the most complete annotations upon its Decrees, 302.

Ephesus, second Council of, what called by the Greeks, 155.

Ephræm (S.) when he lived, 258: the authenticity of many Sermons attributed to him questioned; and what the author of them was called by Crakanthorp, 258.

—— *De Pœnitentia*, 196, 258.

—— *De Armatura spirituali*, 196.

—— *De Compunctione cordis*, 258.

—— *De laudibus Mariæ*, 258.

Epiphanius (S.) *Epist. ad Joan. Patriarch. Hierosol.*, 42, 253—4, 376: S. Jerom's approval of this Epistle, and commendation of its author, 254—5.

—— *Panarium*, 43, 121, 249, 251, 270, 329, 377: how the second Synod of Nicæa argued from this book in defence of Image-worship, 174: reply of the Council of Frankfort, 175.

Erasmus (Desider.) *Adagia*, 2, 115, 251.

—— *Symboli Catechesis*, 8, 34, 190.

—— *Modus orandi Deum*, 66, 389.

—— *Stultitiæ Laus*, 175, 255.

—— *Apophthegmata*, 263.

—— *Enchiridion Militis Christiani*, 314.

—— *Ecclesiastes*, 360.

—— his Latin version and opinion of the treatise *on Prayer* ascribed to S. Chrysostom, 104: his judgment with respect to the additions to S. Jerom's *Catalogue of Eccles. Writers*, 128: what he thought of S. Jerom's *Life of S. Paul the Hermit*, 252: his translation of the treatise *De Spiritu Sancto* assigned to S. Basil; and how far he considered the work authentic, 266: his *Enchiridion Mil. Christ.* attributed to Luther, 314: he would not permit an Image to be brought into a pulpit, 360: his censure upon the spurious Sermon *De visitatione infirmorum*, bearing the name of S. Augustin, 361.

Ethelbert (King) 306.

Eudæmon-Joannes (Andreas) 5.

Eudoxia (Empress) 299.

Eugenius IV. (Pope) his *Instructio Armeniorum* wrongly ascribed to the Council of Florence, 248.

Eusebius Emisenus, a Homily attributed to him, and to S. Cæsarius Arelatensis, 193—4.

Eusebius Pamph., shameless corruption in an old Latin version of his work *De vita Constantini*, 278: Baronius and Bellarmin rely on a falsified translation of his *Chronicle*, 321—2: cited with regard to the statue erected to Simon Magus, 343.

—— *Chronicon*, 9, 321, 322.

—— *Præpar. Evang.*, 14.

—— *Hist. Eccles.*, 23, 28, 41, 69, 128, 131, 182, 211, 251, 262, 269, 294, 301, 314, 343.

—— *De vita Constantini*, 111, 192, 207, 294, 321.

Eusebius (Pope) a spurious Epistle, bearing his name, alleged in the Canon Law, 322: referred to by Calfhill, 323: opinion of Bellarmin, Surius, and Binius, with regard to its authenticity, 323—4: quoted by Mr. Taylor, 324.

Eutropius, Landulphus Sagax mistaken for, 71, 138.

Evagrius Epiphaniensis, the first who speaks of the Edessan Image, 41: when he concluded his *Eccles. History*, 41: declares that many works of Apollinarius were ascribed to S. Athanasius, 268: referred to about Justinian, 305.

Evans (Lewis) 276, 331.

"Exempt" (The) 97.

Faber (G. S.) 78.

Fabian (Pope) a spurious Epistle assigned to him alleged, 222.

Fabricius (Georg.) memorable censure passed by the Belgic *Index* upon words in his edition of the *Christiani Poetæ*, 376.

Fabricius (Joannes Albertus) *Bibliotheca Græca*, 59, 110.

—— *Bibliotheca Latina*, 81.

—— *Biblioth. med. et inf. Latin.*, 69.

—— *Codex Apocr. Nov. Test.*, 126.

—— *Bibliotheca Ecclesiastica*, 130.

Fairfax, *Tasso*, 47.
Falsifiers, punishment of clerical, 273.
Fathers, Calfhill will abide by their decision, 11; and declares that he reverenced them with all his heart, 260: what they teach concerning the second Commandment, 42, 43: it should not be our object to seek for proofs of their imperfection, 58, 226: with what judgment we should read their writings, 59: they frequently use phrases which have been misunderstood, 75: they must be trusted, but yet as men, 260: Romish pretence of observing their injunctions "to the utmost jot," 260: when we are unwilling to adopt their fancies, we do not reject their exposition of Scripture, 263: many supposititious works ascribed to them, and under what circumstances, 268: an instance of the way in which Expurgatory Indexes, while apparently abstaining from censuring, effectually condemn their sentiments, 375—6.
"Feate," 317.
Felix Aquitanicus, the leader at the Synod of Elvira, 154.
Fell (Bp.) 27, 225, 371.
"Fery," 269.
"Fette," 158.
Fevre (Jacques le) 290.
"Filed," 132, 222.
Florence, Council of, Decree of Pope Eugenius IV. wrongly attributed to it, by Stillingfleet, Hooker, [Bramhall, v. 211. Oxf. 1845.] and others, 247—8: Bellarmin's argument respecting the *Instructio Armeniorum* refuted, 248.
Forestus, Bergomensis, (Jacobus Philippus) *Supplem. Chronic.*, 67, 133, 327, 328.
—— probably mistaken for Sigebertus, 67, 323: the reason for this supposition, 323.
Foulis (Henry) 6.
Fox (John) 53, 246.
Francus (Daniel) *Disquisitio de Papistarum Indicibus*, 96.
Frankfort, Council of, condemned the second Synod of Nicæa, 155: by whom it was summoned, and when; and concerning the Caroline Books,
155: the contents of these Books, 156—175: an extract from them, 359.
Freculphus Lexoviensis, 67, 87.
"Frentike," 81.
Fulke (William) 19, 235.

Galfridus Monumetensis, 307.
Gardiner (Bp.) his inconsistency, [See Fox, iii. 454. ed. 1684.] 24: deceived by an Image, 36; 354: probably alluded to, 331.
"Gaudes", 268.
Gaulminus (Gilbertus) 69.
Geddes (Michael) *The grand Forgery displayed*, 193.
Gee (Edward) his *Answer* to Gother, 188, 377.
Gelasius I. (Pope) date of the Roman Council under him, which condemned the Itinerary of S. Peter, 21: whether this Synod rejected the fable of the Edessan Image, as well as the supposed Epistle to Abgarus, or not, 171: what is to be thought of the paragraph respecting the Acts of Pope Silvester I., 174: sentence passed upon the works of Lactantius, 181; and upon the *Scripta de inventione S. Crucis Dominicæ*, 324.
Genebrardus (Gilbertus) 323.
Gennadius Massiliensis, 69, 149, 177.
George (S.) 20, 35, 36.
Gerhardus (Joannes) 74.
"Gesse", 300.
Gideon, 336.
Gieseler (J. C. I.) 6.
Gilpin (Bernard) 237.
Gnostics (The) boasted of having an Image of Christ, and were reproved by S. Irenæus, 42—3, 371.
God, the Pope called, 5, 6.
Godwin (Bp.) 306.
Godwyn (Thomas) 108.
Goldastus (Melch. Haim.) *Imperialia Decreta de cultu Imaginum*, 42, 155, 190, 311, 359.
Gother (John) source of the authorities alleged in his *Nubes Testium*, 63: by whom answered, 188, 377: referred to, 199.
Gothofredus (Jacobus) 110.
Grabius (Joannes Ernestus) 21, 126.
Grace, seven-fold, true doctrine respecting, admitted by the Church of

INDEX. 409

England, on the authority of Scripture, 226.
Grambsius (Joannes) 155.
Granada, whether the modern name of Elvira, 154.
Gratianus, *Decretum*, 5, 16, 18, 19, 21, 54, 64, 67, 88, 171, 174, 191, 193, 194, 197, 206, 212, 216, 219, 220, 222, 238, 239, 240, 241, 242, 243, 253, 257, 260 273, 322.
Gratius (Orthuinus) 16.
Gravamina (Centum) not of Lutheran origin, 16.
Gregorius Nazianzenus (S.) 87.
Gregorius Nyssenus (S.) vainly alleged at the second Nicene Council; and insufficient reply in the Caroline Books to his testimony, 173.
Gregorius Turonensis (S.) 69, 328.
Gregory I. (Pope) condemned the worship of Images, 9, 30, 379 : abhorred the name of Universal Bishop, 88 : tells the tale of Speciosus, 88 : his advice to Augustin the Monk, 197 : his *Litania major*, 297.
—— *Epistt.*, 54, 88, 297.
—— *In Evangel. Hom.*, 332.
—— *Dialogi*, their authenticity questioned, 89 : notable story of Paulinus, taken from, 117—19.
Gregory II. (Pope) 89.
Gregory VII. (Pope) what restriction he placed upon the application of the title " Pope", and when, 255.
Gregory XIII. (Pope) 6.
Gregory (John) *Episcopus puerorum in die Innocentium*, 237.
Gretserus (Jacobus) defends a spurious Epistle ascribed to Pope Alexander I., 16 : declares that the second Nicene Council relied on the fable of the Edessan Image, 171 : maintains that *Latria* should be rendered to the Cross, 381.
Gronovius (Jacobus) 302.
Guido Baisius, vel de Bayso, *Archidiaconus* Bononiensis, 174.

Habermann ab Unsleben (G. Jos. Ig. Jo. Nep. De) 97.
Hales (Alexander de) 381.
Haloander (Gregorius) 305.
Hanmer (Meredith) 287.

Harding (Thomas) 2, 49.
Hart (John) his *Conference* with Rainoldes, 126, 361.
" Hayes", 274.
" Heare", 286.
Helena (Empress) S. Ambrose utterly denies that she worshipped the material Cross, 192, 377: she was the wife, and not the concubine, of Constantius, 322 : Calfhill states that S. Ambrose called her *Stabulariam*, (but his word " asserunt" refers to the enemies of Christianity,) 322 : notice of the time when the Cross was found, 287: how many inventions of it, according to the Golden Legend, 321: difference of statements about the matter, 322—25.
Henningius (Joannes) *Archæologia Passionalis*, 328.
Henry VIII. (King) *Assertio septem Sacramentorum*, 244.
Hermannus Gygas, *Flores Temporum*, 110.
Heroldt (Joannes) 75.
Heshusius (Tilemanus) 19.
Heylin (Peter) See Vaughan.
Hickes (Bp.) 87.
Hide (Thomas) 276.
Hieronymus (S.) date of his death, 9 : *Chronicle*, 9 : his translation of an Epistle of S. Epiphanius, 42, 253—4.
—— *Vitæ Patrum* falsely, when all together, (as was formerly the case,) ascribed to him, 74, 252: his statement with regard to the Samaritan *Thau*, 106—7: interpolations in his *Catalogue of Ecclesiastical Writers*, 128: spurious *Commentaries on S. Mark*, 178: his desire respecting Lactantius, 180: what Erasmus thought of his *Life of S. Paul the Hermit*, 252: the character he gives of S. Epiphanius, 255: counterfeit *Exposition of the Psalms*, 259 : he compares together phylacteries and pieces of the Cross, and equally condemns the use of both, 283.
—— *Apol. adv. Rufin.*, 42.
—— *Apol. ad Pammach.*, 60.
—— *De Scriptoribus Eccles.*, 69, 128, 130, 178, 182, 211.
—— *Super Esaiam*, 94, 213.
—— *Super Hieremiam*, 95, 181, 378.

Hieronymus (S.) *Comment. in Ezech.*, 106, 108—9, 259.
—— *Comm. super Amos*, 8.
—— *Super S. Matth.*, 134, 283.
—— *Epist. ad Magnum*, 178.
—— *Ad Eustochium*, 195.
—— *Ad Demetriadem*, 195, 259.
—— *Cont. Lucifer.*, 213, 261.
—— *Adversus Vigilant.*, 214.
—— *Ad Pammachium*, 254.
—— *S. Paulæ Vita*, 255.
—— *In Sophoniam*, 259.
—— *Contra Jovinian.*, 259.
—— *In Daniel.*, 378.
Higdenus (Ranulphus, vel Radulphus) his character as an author, 296.
Hilarius (S.) *Liber contra Auxentium*, 248.
—— *De Trinitate*, 249.
—— *Expositio Psalmorum*, 294.
Hilarius Diaconus, it is not certain that he was the author of a Commentary in *Ep. ad Tim.*, attributed to S. Ambrose, 235.
Hildebrandus (Joachimus) 66, 297.
Hill's *Olive-branch of Peace*, 243.
Hincmar of Rheims, 175.
Holcot (Robertus) referred to as a witness against the decision of Aquinas, with regard to the worship of the material Cross, 381.
Homerus, 13.
Homilies, 54, 57, 215.
Hooker (Richard) referred to, with regard to the sign of the Cross, 108: his mistake respecting the Council of Florence, 247—8.
Hooper, (Bp. of Gloucester and Worcester,) 35, 49.
Hooper, (Bp. of Bath and Wells,) 97.
Hoornbeekius (Joannes) 69.
Horatius, 2, 49, 340, 354, 389.
Hosius (Stanislaus, Cardinalis) his words about the substitution of Crosses for Images of Mercury, 66: what his confession is relative to the inferior Orders, 228: referred to concerning the Mass, 229; and S. Ephræm, 258.
Hospinianus (Rodolphus) 42.
"Hostrie;" 322.
Huetius (Petrus Daniel) 78.
Hyginus (Pope) mistake committed in assigning to him the institution of Sponsors; and what was really the date and origin of his supposed Decree, 212.

Ignatius (S.) *Ep. ad Philadelph.*, 280.
—— the spurious Epistle *Ad Heronem* alleged by Calfhill, and supposed to be genuine by Mr. Taylor also, 290.
Images. See the "Table."
"Immanity," 353.
Index Expurgatorius, 20, 91, 190, 314, 375—6.
Index librorum prohib., 20, 21, 95, 126.
"Ineptly," 216.
Innocent I. (Pope) censured on account of an Epistle alleged as his by Gratian, 238—40: questionable Decree with regard to the use of consecrated oil, 246.
Innocent VIII. (Pope) *Pontificale*, amended by his command, directs that *Latria* should be offered to the Cross, 381.
Irenæus (S.) reproved the Gnostics for having an Image of Christ, 42—3, 371: in what order he makes the early Bishops of Rome to have succeeded S. Peter, 251: why he rebuked Pope Victor, 269: his account of S. Polycarp's doctrine, 270: referred to respecting the Basilidian heretics, 285: cited, 287.
Irene (Empress) her infamous conduct and cruelty, 31, 175—7: convoked the second Council of Nicæa, 175, 177.
Isidorus Hispalensis (S.) 69, 107.
Isidorus Pelusiota (S.) 285.
Ittigius (Thomas) 21, 96.
Ivo, *Decretum*, 135, 154.

Jaddus, his interview with Alexander the Great, 117.
James (Thomas) 96, 188, 200.
Jenkins (Robert) 137.
Jerom (S.) See Hieronymus.
Jerom (Stephen) 78.
Jewel (Bp.) 2, 53, 77, 114, 126, 260, 285.
Jews, their proneness to Idolatry, 23, 24: why Ceremonies were imposed upon them, 122: consequence of the attempt to rebuild their temple, 115, 121, 123.
Joan (Pope) 6.

Joannes Moschus, when he lived, and what the character given of him by Baronius, 174.
John (S.) fables. concerning him, in the work of the Pseudo-Abdias, 126—131.
John XIV. (Pope) said to have first given names to Bells in Baptism, 15.
John XXII. (Pope) notorious and uncensured Gloss upon his Extravagant *Cum inter*, 5—6.
Joseph, the removal of his remains affords no argument for Relics, 312.
Josephus Ægyptius, 322.
Josephus (Flavius) bears witness of the hostility of the Jews to Images, 44: gives an account of the interview of Jaddus with Alexander the Great, 117.
Jude (S.) 128.
Julian the Apostate, affords a precedent to Papists, with regard to the sign of the Cross, 85—88: shower of rain which overtook him, 114, 120: consequence of his attempt to rebuild the temple of Jerusalem, 115, 121, 123.
Justinian (Emperor) his command that churches were not to be built without episcopal licence, and the erection of a Cross, 135—6: no reason for refusing to admit his authority about the matter, 189: his *Codex* referred to, 190: what his object was in requiring a Procession whensoever a church was to be consecrated, 304—5.
Justinus, 317.
Justinus Martyr (S.) *De Monarchia Dei*, 23.
—— *Dialog. cum Tryphone*, 105.
—— *Apolog.* i., referred to respecting the figure of the Cross, 178; and the statue erected to Simon Magus, 343.
Juvenalis, 14.

Keeling (William) 224.
Kellison (Matthew) 290.
Königius (Georg. Matthias) 285.

Labbe (Philippus) his error as to a translation of the Acts of the second Nicene Council, 138.
Lactantius, what S. Jerom desired concerning him, 180: his works reckoned *inter apocrypha* in some copies of the Gelasian Decree, 181: the verses attributed to him, *De Passione Domini*, entirely spurious, 180—184, 375: Bellarmin's disingenuousness respecting them, 181: Lactantius adduced to prove that Papists are superstitious, 310.
—— *De falsa Relig.*, 13.
—— *De origine Erroris*, 25, 26, 40, 183, 317, 341, 342, 344, 374.
—— *De Vita beata*, 26.
—— *De Opificio Dei*, 26.
—— *De vera Sapientia*, 72, 83, 91, 310.
—— *De mortibus Persecutorum*, 105.
—— *De vero Cultu Dei*, 302.
Lambardus (Gulielmus) 53.
Lampugnan (Andrew) 338, 339.
Landulphus Sagax, confounded with Eutropius, 71, 138.
Latimer (Bp.) 9, 47, 52, 154.
Latinius (Latinus) 177.
Λατρεία, proof that this, the highest species of worship, is offered to the material Cross, 381.
Laud (Abp.) 255.
Launoius (Joannes) his satirical language concerning the "exempt," 97: *Varia de duobus Dionysiis Opuscula*, 211.
Law (The) mentions a certain place appointed for God's service, 32: condemns Images, 37—8, 41—2: all the Fathers teach that the second Commandment is moral, not ceremonial, 42, 43.
Law (Canon) referred to respecting the ascription of Divinity to the Pope, 5—6: valued as highly as the Bible by Romanists, 18, 206: what punishment is prescribed therein for Clergymen guilty of falsification, 273: what date it fixes upon for the invention of the Cross, 322—3.—Vid. Gratianus.
Law (Civil) Vid. Justinian, and Theodosius II.
"Laymen's books," 21, 292, 346.
Lazius (Wolfgangus) asserts that Abdias was one of the seventy Disciples, 126.
Legenda Aurea, 174: recounts five inventions of the Cross, 321.
Leigh (Edward) 95, 107.
Lentulus, Epistle of, 46.

Leo Isauricus, 71, 138.
Leo III. (Pope) what Platina has attributed to him, 295.
Leslæus (Episc.) 290.
Leunclavius (Joannes) 45.
Lewis (John) 35.
Litanies, what they are, 294: "greater" and "less," 296—7.
Livius, 14, 295, 316, 317.
Lloyd (Bp.) 306.
Lombardus (Petrus) cites a spurious *Sermo de Pœnitentia*, attributed to S. Chrysostom, 64: referred to about faith, 86: teaches that many things are improperly called Sacraments, 215: declares that Confirmation is a greater Sacrament than Baptism, 221: corrupt source of this statement, 222: he makes thirteen Sacraments out of seven, 228: overthrows Martiall's attempt to prove Matrimony to be a Sacrament, 237: said to have first spoken of the seven Sacraments, 237: referred to, 242, 243, 244.
London (Dr.) condemned for perjury, (See Fox, ii. 469. ed. 1684.) 332.
Longolius (Christophorus) buried in a Friar's cowl, 287.
Longolius (Gybertus) mistake concerning his translation of the Acts of the second Council of Nicæa, 138.
Lucius (King) 52—3, 305.
Ludovici Pii *Capitula*, 297.
Luidhard (Bp.) 306.
Lupus (Christianus) *Synodorum Decreta et Canones*, 137.
"Lurde," 361.
Luther (Martin) 70, 244: how Martiall unconsciously proved that he could not have been an heretic, 304: a work by Erasmus ascribed to him, 314.
Lynde (Sir Humphrey) 290.

Mabillonius (Joannes) 128, 155.
Macedonius, the Monk, appeases the anger of Theodosius, 22.
Macrobius, 302, 333.
Magdeburgenses. Vid. Centuriatores.
Maitland (S. R.) 237.
Mamercus, Bp. of Vienne, what he instituted, 295, 296: whether his Litanies have been correctly styled the "less," 297.

"Mammots," 31: "Mawmots," "Mawmetry," origin of these words, 175.
Manriq (Thomas) *Censura in Glossas Juris Canonici*, 6.
Manuale Sarisbur., 17.
Marcellina, an heretic, worshipped Images, 188.
Marchetti (Gio.) *Official Memoirs*, relative to *the miraculous events which happened at Rome*, in 1796—7, 274.
Maria (Galeatius) 339.
Mariana (Joannes) 273.
Marianus Scotus, *Chron.*, 323.
Marie (Honoré de S.) 211.
Martialis, 264.
Martialis Lemovicensis, his fictitious Epistles, when first heard of, and published, 69: cited by Bellarmin, 70: not one of the seventy Disciples, 69, 271.
Martin (Gregory) 235.
Martin (S.) 252.
Martinus Polonus, *Chronicon*, 6, 323.
Mass-book, "red mark" in, what it signifies, 202.
Matrimony, not a Sacrament, 235—41.
"Maukin," 236.
Maximus Taurinensis (S.) his Sermon *De Cruce* attributed to S. Ambrose, 177.
Mayerus (Wolfg.) *De vulneribus Eccles. Rom.*, 6.
Meagher (Andrew) 302.
Mede (Joseph) 32.
Melancthon (Philip) 305.
Melchiades (Pope) a fictitious Epistle ascribed to him adduced, 222.
Mendham (Joseph) *Memoirs of the Council of Trent*, 16.
—— *Cathalogus librorum hæreticorum*, (Venet. 1554.) 21.
Mendoza (Fernando de) 302.
Mengus (Hieronymus) 318.
Mentz, Council of, an. 813. its Decree respecting the *Litania major*, 297: when its *Gesta* were first published, 297.
Middleton (Conyers) 66, 67.
Milner (John) 21.
Minos, how he imitated Moses, 13—14.
Minucius Felix, his *Octavius* ascribed to Arnobius, 178, 183, 295, 380.
Miracles. See the "Table," 398.

Miræus (Aubertus) his mistake about Martial's Epistles, 69.
Missale Romanum, 17, 202.
Mitford (W.) 13.
Molanus (Joannes) quotes the spurious Epistle of Lentulus, 46: his language about the Image of Mercury and the Cross, 66: referred to about the letter *Thau*, 107; and the release of the Pseudo-Abdias from censure, 126: also, 202.
Monks, called vicegerents of the Apostles, 220.
Montfaucon (Bernardus de) his supposition as to the time when the author of the *Opus imperfectum* lived, 96: his statement respecting the form of the Samaritan *Thau*, 107.
Moquot (Etienne) 236.
Morinus (Joannes) what fact he has proved with regard to the writings ascribed to Dionysius the Areopagite, 211.
Morinus (Stephanus) cited with reference to the letter *Thau*, 107.
Morton (Bp.) 6, 64, 96, 202, 255, 290.
Moses, how the Devil attempted to subvert the credit of his mission, 13—14: what the lifting up of his hands prefigured, 104—6: the reason for the concealment of his sepulchre, 312: why God appeared to him in a bush, 334: his danger from neglect of Circumcision, 335: the rock smitten by him, 336.
Moulin (Pierre du) 74, 137, 193, 257, 290, 322.
Musculus (Wolfgangus) 28, 69, 111, 269, 299.

Naaman, 337.
Nadab and Abihu, 123.
Natalibus (Petrus de) 297, 323.
Natalitia, birthdays, (or days upon which Martyrs suffered, and commenced their new life,) annually observed, 257.
Nauclerus (Joannes) 323.
" Nere nother", *neither nor other;* or, more probably, *never neither*, 73.
Netter a Walden (Thomas) Vid. Waldensis.
Newman (J. H.) 110, 287.
Nicæa, first Council of, 10: instances of it having been strangely confounded with the second Nicene Synod, 154: ordained that upon Sundays Christians should pray standing: (this posture signifying our restitution through Christ; while kneeling upon other days was intended to represent the fall of man.) 257.
Nicæa, second Council of, referred to respecting the Edessan Image, 41: confirmed the worshipping of Images, 48: Decrees of the Council of Constantinople, an. 754, preserved among its Acts, 71, 138: admitted the Decrees of the Trullan Synod, 137: what Charlemagne called it, and its decisions, 155: contents of the Caroline Books in answer to it, 156—175: opinion of A. Pagi with regard to the authorities alleged thereat, 345.
Nicephorus Callistus, 41, 65, 87, 126, 128, 133, 322.
Nicodemus, Gospel of, 321.
Nicolson (Bp.) 296.
" Noriture", 72.
Norris (Silvester) 190.
Nourry (Nicolaus le) 21, 69, 110, 211.
Nowell (Alexander) 2.
Numa Pompilius, 13, 14, 362—3.

Ochine (Bernardine) 368—9.
Opitius (Martinus) 135.
Oracles (Sibylline) 95.
Orders (Holy) 227—231.
Origen, assigns the reason for Image-makers not having been suffered to dwell among the Jews, 44: his fond opinions, 78: overthroweth Imagery, 79—81: year of his death, 81: Life, Death, and *Repentance*, 78.
—— *Contra Celsum*, 44, 79, 80, 372.
—— *In Ep. ad Rom.*, 77, 79.
—— Περὶ ἀρχῶν, 78.
—— *Commentaria*, (ed. Huet.) 78.
—— *In Ezech.*, 106.
—— *In Exod. Hom.*, 372.
Orleans, first Council of, Canon of this Provincial Synod, relative to the consecration of churches, 135—6.
Ormanet (Nicholas, Datary of Pope Julius III.) 331. [Comp. Fox, iii. 639, ed. 1684.]
Ormerod (Oliver) *Picture of a Papist*, 221.

Orosius (Paulus) 322.
Orus Apollo, vel Horapollo, his testimony with regard to the figure on the breast of Serapis, 107.
Oudinus (Casimirus) the date he assigns to the Pseudo-Abdias, 126: referred to, 235.
Ovidius, 14, 25, 316.

Pagi (Antonius) 9: his words concerning the authorities adduced by the second Council of Nicæa, 345.
Pall, 305.
Pamelius (Jacobus) 202, 203.
Pantin (T. P.) Reply to Dr. Arnold, 306.
"Papists", a foul name of heresy, according to Calfhill; but a sublime title of glory, in the opinion of Baronius, 290.
Paradinus (Claudius) *Symbola heroica*, 339.
Paramo (Ludovicus a) a proof, derived from him, that the highest degree of worship is rendered to the material Cross, 381.
"Pardie", 192.
Paris, Synod of, anno 825, 42.
Parker (Abp.) his reason for suspecting that there was a remarkable interpolation in Bede's *Hist. Eccles. gent. Anglorum*, 306.
Parsons, or Persons (Robert) 5, 53.
Patrick (John) 287.
Paul (S.) handkerchiefs brought from him unto the sick, 337.
Paul the Hermit (S.) 252.
Paul IV. (Pope) *Index Romanus*, 95, 126.
Paula (S.) 252, 253, 255—6.
Paulinus Aquileiensis, 101.
Paulinus Nolanus (S.) said to have been the first who brought Imagery into a church, 26, 29: a notable story of, 117-19: year of his death, 188: censured, 189.
Paullus Diaconus, his additions to Eutropius, 71.
—— *De notis Literarum*, 108.
Pearson (Bp.) 211, 251.
Pelagius II. (Pope) Decree of, concerning second Marriage, 18, 19.
Pelliccia, his words about a passage in a Poem falsely ascribed to Lactantius, 181.

"Pelting" 10.
Penance, 241—44.
"Perchers", 300.
Perionius (Joachimus) 368.
Perkinsius (Guilielmus) 211.
Persius, 4, 108, 341.
Petavius (Dionysius) 9.
Peter (S.) his shadow, 337: erroneously mentioned in connexion with the *Itinerarium*, 380, 387.
Petit (Jac.) 212.
Philpot (John) 246.
Photius, 89.
"Pickback on", 103.
Pierce the Ploughman, 47.
Pighius (Albertus) *De Actis vi. et vii. Synodorum*, 137.
Pilkington (Bp.) 24, 49.
Pin (L. E. Du) 42, 202.
Pinamonti (J. P.) *Exorcista rite edoctus*, 318.
Pithœus (Franciscus) *Codex Canonum vetus*, 246.
Pius I. (Pope) 54.
Pius IV. (Pope) 95.
Pius V. (Pope) 6. Vid. Manriq (Thomas).
Placcius (Vincentius) 69.
Platina (B.) his statement with regard to Pope Silvester II., 91—2: his account of the supposed Ordinance of Pope Hyginus respecting Sponsors, 212: inaccurate reference to him, 295: his evidence concerning Litanies and the Rogation-days, 295.
Plato, 25.
Plinius Sec. (C.) 47.
Plutarchus, 14, 317.
Polus (Reginaldus, Cardinalis) his treason, 49: figure Y in the windows at Lambeth, 105: declares what the sign shown to Constantine intimated, 110: trial of a Priest before his Commissioners, 331.
Polycarpus (S.) how he disagreed, but yet maintained communion, with Anicetus, 269—70: testimony of S. Irenæus as to his doctrine, 270: why his remains were not given to those who asked for them, 314.
Ponet (Bp.) 369.
Pontificale Romanum, gives directions for the Baptism of Bells, 15: ordains the hallowing of Images, 47, 48:

[This form, it is declared, "embodies, in the most perfect manner, the doctrine of the" papal " Church concerning them". (Dr. Wiseman's *Letter to Mr. Newman*, p. 31. Lond. 1841.)] Ceremonies prescribed by it for the consecration of churches, 208—10: its assignment of supreme worship to the Cross, 381.
Pope (The) called God, 5: what the name "Pope" signifies, and when it was restricted to the Bishop of Rome, 255.
Popes, spurious Epistles ascribed to the early. Vid. Blondellus (David); Bellarmin (Card.)
Portass, Portess, Portusses, 16, 159, 298.
Portesius (Joannes) shamelessly corrupted a passage in Eusebius, with a view to defend the erection of Images in churches, 278.
Portiforium, 16, 17.
Possevinus (Antonius) remarkable confession in his *Bibliotheca Selecta*, as to the expurgation of MSS., 6.
—— *Apparatus Sacer*, referred to, 64: contains an enumeration of spurious treatises ascribed to S. Chrysostom, 104: the author acknowledges the falsity of a Poem assigned to Lactantius, 181.
" Prises", 47.
Probianus, what was meant by the declaration, that he refused to adore the Cross, 198, 199.
Processions, their institution to whom ascribed, 295, 305: Calfhill probably misled by the Centuriators respecting them, 296: why the Emperor Justinian required that a Procession should take place whensoever a church was to be consecrated, 304—5.
Prosperus (S.) *Chronicon*, 9.
Prudentius, *Cont. Sym.*, 26, 195.
—— *Peristeph.*, 29, 30, 132.
—— *Apotheosis*, 51, 195.
—— *Hymni*, 195, 259.
Prynne (William) 226.
Ptolemy, 128.
Puppets, 32, 346. Vid. Mammots.
" Purfles", 161.
Pyrrhus, 317.
Pythagoras, 99.

" Quew", 209.
" Queysie", 209.
Quiroga (Cardinal) his Expurgatory *Index*, 190.

Rabanus Maurus, *De institutione Clericorum*, 66, 213.
Rainoldes (John) his *Conference* with Hart, 126, 361.
Raisin and *raison*, 158.
Rastall, or Rastell (John) 2, 51.
Rayment (B.) 274.
Raynaudus (Theophilus) *Erotemata de malis ac bonis libris*, 74, 200.
Reginaldus (Gulielmus) 256. [Calfhill is styled by him " *scriptor politus*".]
Reiserus (Antonius) *Launoii Anti-Bellarminus*, 211.
Reiskius (M. Joannes) 46.
Relics, 311—14.
" Revestry", 136, 317.
Rheims. See Testament.
Ridley (Bp.) his *Treatise concerning Images*, 254.
Rituale Romanum, 17.
Rivetus (Andreas) 69, 89, 195, 202, 258.
Roccha a Camerino (Angelus) 178.
Rogations. Vid. Litanies.
Rogerus Cestriensis, 296.
Rome, Council of, under Pope Gelasius I., 21, 171, 174, 181, 324.
—— fifth and sixth Councils of, 48.
" Rood", 35.
Roscoe (William) 6.
Rosweydus (Heribertus) his valuable edition of the *Vitæ Patrum*, 252.
Routh (Martinus Josephus) *Reliquiæ Sacræ*, 154.
Rufinus, his Latin version of the *Recognitions*, 20, 21.
—— *Hist. Eccles.*, 65, 274, 275, 276, 323, 326.
Rynthelen (Cornelius a) 135.

Sabellicus (Marcus Antonius) 128.
Sacerdotale, false Epistle adduced in the, 16: Benediction in, 17.
Sacraments (The seven) 210—248. Vid. Lombardus (Petrus); Florence (Council of).
Sage (Bp.) 52.
Saints, made to succeed to heathen Deities, 19, 20.

"Sallet", 327.
Salmonicus, vel Sammonicus (Serenus) 285.
Samson, 336.
Saul, 123.
Savilius (D. Henricus) 64.
"Saynsure", 124.
Scaliger (Josephus) 9, 107.
Schelhornius (Jo. Georg.) 49, 290.
Schoenemann (Car. Traug. Gott.) 235.
Scultetus (Abrahamus) 78.
Sedulius, some of his verses introduced into a work untruly ascribed to S. Jerom, 178.
Selden (John) *Titles of Honor*, 6, 35 : his explanation of the words " Mammets" and " Mammetry", 175 : he refutes a falsehood about the Empress Helena, 322.
"Sensing", 343.
Serapis, the Egyptian Idol, had a figure of a Cross upon his breast, 65, 107 : Roods, Crosses, and Images, counterfeits of Serapis, 274 : how the Cross recommended. Christianity to the Egyptians, 276—7.
"Sere", 228, 279, 295.
Serpent (The brazen) 9, 335—6.
Shakspeare (W.) 10.
Siberus (Urban. Godofr.) *De Aquæ Benedictæ potu Brutis non denegando*, 17.
Sichardus (Joannes) 20.
Sigebertus Gemblacensis, *Chronicon*, 67, 138, 246, 296, 297, 323.
—— apparently confounded with Bergomensis, 67; and why this seems to be the case, 323.
Silvester I. (Pope) his *Acts* fictitious, 174 : *Vita* quoted, 193.
Silvester II. (Pope) his character and death, 91—2.
Simon (S.) 128.
Simon Magus, statue erected to him as a god, 343 : what ancient writer first mentions this fact; and what is the conjecture of many critics about the matter, 41, 343.
—— *Dissertatio de duobus Dionysiis*, 211.
Siricius (Pope) words attributed to him, 240.
Sirmondus (Jacobus) *Concilia Generalia*, 41, 138.

Sisinnius, 10.
Sixtus Senensis, *Bibliotheca Sancta*, 74 : confesses that S. Chrysostom has sometimes spoken hyperbolically, 77 : enumerates the spurious treatises ascribed to S. Chrysostom, 104 : referred to about the letter *Thau*, 107 : his description of the *Commentaries on S. Mark* falsely attributed to S. Jerom, 178.
Smedley (Edward) error in his *History of the Reformed Religion in France*, 314.
Soames (Henry) 53.
Socrates Scholasticus, 10, 65, 296, 299.
Solomon, 347.
Sophronius, whether the interpolator of S. Jerom's *Catalogue of Eccles. Writers*, 128.
Sophronius Hierosolymitanus, not the author of the *Limonarium*, as was asserted at the second Nicene Council, 174.
Sozomenus (Hermias) 65, 114—15, 120, 182, 193, 198, 252, 299, 326, 327, 388.
Spanhemius (Fridericus) 31, 361.
Spelmannus (Henricus, Eq. Aur.) *Glossarium Archaiol.*, 35, 305.
—— *Concilia*, 53.
Spencerus (Gulielmus) 44, 372.
Spenser (Edmund) 47, 52.
Spondanus (Henricus) 42.
Sponsors, institution of, wrongly attributed to Pope Hyginus, 212.
Squire (John) 6.
"Stalled", 316.
Stapleton (Thomas) 3, 51, 64.
Stephanus V. (Papa) 67, 253.
Stevenson (Josephus) 306.
Stillingfleet (Bp.) 42, 53, 211, 237.
—— his error with regard to the Council of Florence, 247—8 : his opinion of Geoffrey of Monmouth, 307.
Story (Dr.) 246.
Strada (Famianus) 287.
Strype (John) 7.
Suicerus (Joannes Casparus) 285.
Suidas, testifies that Serapis had a figure of the Cross upon his breast, 107 : what he declares respecting Justinian, 305.
Sulpitius (Severus) 322.
Superstitious, who are so, according to Lactantius, 310.

Surius (Laurentius) 324.
Sutcliffe (Matthew) 190, 381.
" Sweard.", 93.

"Taberer", "tabering", 257.
Tapers, 214, 301—304.
Tarquinius Priscus, 316.
Taylor (Isaac) quotes as genuine a spurious Epistle ascribed to S. Ignatius, 290: cites a counterfeit Epistle, bearing the name of Pope Eusebius, and not generally admitted even by Romanists, 324.
Tellez (Emman. Gond.) 302.
" Tenebre-Wednesday", 300.
Tenison (Abp.) 66, 366.
Teraphim, 32.
Tertullianus, *De præscript. Hæret.*, 13, 27, 267.
—— *De exhort. Cast.*, 13.
—— *Apologet.*, 14, 195, 308—10.
—— *Ad Nat.*, 14.
—— *Advers. Marcion.*, 106, 116, 222, 371.
—— *De Corona Militis*, 195, 213, 223, 257, 263, 265, 270.
—— *De Resurrectione carnis*, 224.
—— *De Virginibus velandis*, 280.
—— valuable note on his *Apology* referred to, 188: a Montanist when he wrote the treatise *De Corona*, 195: acknowledges but two Sacraments, 223: not a Montanist when he composed the books *Ad Uxorem;* and how an expression of his, "procedendum", has not any reference to Processions, 296.
Testament, Notes to the Rheims New, 95, 222, 290.
Τετραγράμματον, a Jew will not cease from confidence in, if he see the material Cross similarly reverenced, 284.
Thau, the letter, what it signifies in the book of Ezekiel, 97: the Samaritan *Thau* like a S. Andrew's Cross, 107: S. Jerom's explanation of the reasons why this sign was to be made in the foreheads of the Elect, 108—9: what the Hebrews figured by their *Thau*, 107: remarks by Bp. Andrewes and Cornelius Curtius upon the meaning of the letter, 108—9: in a

mystery it betokened the death of Christ, 109.
Theodore (Abp.) his Decree concerning Sponsors attributed to Pope Hyginus, 212.
Theodoretus, *Eccles. Hist.*, 22, 87, 192, 322, 326, 327, 388.
—— *Historia Religiosa*, 22.
Theodosia, Queen Elizabeth so called, 11.
Theodosius I. (Emperor) pacified by the Monk Macedonius, 22.
Theodosius II. (Emperor) his and Valentinian's Ordinance with respect to engraving or painting the sign of the Cross on the ground, 190.
Theodotion, 107.
Theodotus, vel Theodorus, Ancyranus, 149.
Thilo (Joannes Carolus) 96, 126, 201.
Thomas (S.) 127.
Tierney (M. A.) 53, 290.
Tilius (Joannes) in what year he published the Caroline Books, 155.
Todd (J. H.) his edition of Wicliffe's *Apology* referred to, 36, 132, 330.
"Tooted", "tooting", 47, 380.
Tours, second Synod of, an alteration in one of its Canons noted, 136.
Traditions, of three kinds; Scriptural or Apostolical, Popish, and Ecclesiastical, 267.
Trapezuntius (Georgius) 378.
Trent, Council of, 247—8.
—— *Catech. Conc. Trident.*, 248.
Trithemius (Joannes) *De Scriptoribus Eccles.*, 69, 258.
—— *Annales Hirsaugienses*, 115.
Trullan Synod. Vid. Constantinople.
"Tyleshardes," 208.
Tyrwhitt's Chaucer, 288.

Unction (Extreme) 244—48.
Unity, of Papists, what it is, 261: how they exhibit what they boast of, 262: upon what true Unity depends, 261.
Urban VIII. (Pope) *Pontificale*, 15, 381.
"Ure", 304.
Urspergensis Abbas. Vid. Conradus.
Ussher (Primate) 53, 64, 96, 183, 211, 255, 269, 290, 322.

[CALFHILL.]

27

Uzzah, 123.
Valentinian III. (Emperor) memorable Ordinance made by him and Theodosius II., with regard to engraving or painting the sign of the Cross on the ground, 190.
Valerius Maximus, 14, 316.
Valesius (Henricus) 22, 262.
Vandals, 30, 118.
Vaughan (Mr.) Bp. Gardiner's letters to him, [See Heylin, *Ref. Edw.* VI., p. 56.] 36.
Vergilius (Polydorus) *De rerum inventoribus*, referred to about Processions, 295; and the title on the Cross when found by Helena, 325.
—— *Angl. Hist.*, 306.
"Vice", 210.
Victor I. (Pope) reproved by S. Irenæus, 269.
Virgilius, 86.
Vives (Ludovicus) his Commentary upon S. Augustin's *City of God* corrupted, 20.
Vossius (Gerardus Joannes) corrects his mistake about Martial's Epistles, 69: referred to, 126.
Vossius, seu Volckens (Gerardus) 258.

Walafridus Strabo, 297.
Waldensis (Thomas) condemns S. Epiphanius, 42: referred to, 63, 81:
his strange argument, with respect to the fragments of the Cross, 95.
Wall (Charles William) 276.
Walton (Bp.) 107.
Ward (Thomas) *Errata of the Protestant Bible*, 236.
Water (Holy) 16, 17.
Wharton (Henry) 96.
Whelocus (Abrahamus) 53, 306.
Wicelius (Georgius) *Hagiologium*, 126.
Wicliffe (John) 36, 50, 132, 330.
Willet (Andrew) 24, 85.
Wiseman (Dr.) See *Pontificale*.
Wordsworth (Christopher) quotes a passage from Selden, with reference to the terms "Mammets" and "Mammetry", 175.

Zacagnius (Laurentius Alexander) *Collectanea Monumentorum*, 92.
Zaccaria (Franciscus Antonius) *Bibliotheca Ritualis*, 202.
Zapata (Cardinal) his *Index* condemns a reference to the words of S. Athanasius, which teach that "God alone is to be adored", 375—6.
Zenocarus a Scauwenburgo (Gulielmus) 287.
Zenzelinus, 6.
Zeunius, 302.
Zornius (Petrus) 181.
Zuingerus (Theodorus) his *Theatrum vitæ humanæ* expurgated, 91.

www.ingramcontent.com/pod-product-compliance
Lightning Source LLC
Chambersburg PA
CBHW052129010526
44113CB00034B/1027